CompTIA Security+ Deluxe Study Guide

Exam SY0-201

OBJECTIVE	CHAPTER
Domain 1.0 Systems Security	
1.1 Differentiate among various systems security threats.	2
Privilege escalation; virus; worm; Trojan; spyware; spam; adware; rootkits; botnets; Logic bomb	
1.2 Explain the security risks pertaining to system hardware and peripherals.	3, 9
BIOS; USB devices; cell phones; removable storage; network attached storage	
1.3 Implement OS hardening practices and procedures to achieve workstation and server security.	5
Hotfixes; service packs; patches; patch management; group policies; security templates; configuration baselines	
1.4 Carry out the appropriate procedures to establish application security.	3, 4
ActiveX; Java; scripting; browser; buffer overflows; cookies; SMTP open relays; instant messaging; P2P; input validation; cross-site scripting (XSS)	
1.5 Implement security applications.	2, 3, 4
HIDS; Personal software firewalls; antivirus; anti-spam; popup blockers	
1.6 Explain the purpose and application of virtualization technology.	**1**
Domain 2.0: Network Infrastructure	
2.1 Differentiate between the different ports & protocols, their respective threats and mitigation techniques.	2, 5
Antiquated protocols; TCP/IP hijacking; null sessions; spoofing; man-in-the-middle; replay; DOS; DDOS; domain name kiting; DNS poisoning; ARP poisoning	
2.2 Distinguish between network design elements and components.	**1**
DMZ; VLAN; NAT; network interconnections; NAC; subnetting; telephony	
2.3 Determine the appropriate use of network security tools to facilitate network security.	**3, 4, 5**
NIDS; NIPS; firewalls; proxy servers; honeypot; Internet content filters; protocol analyzers	
2.4 Apply the appropriate network tools to facilitate network security.	3, 4, 5
NIDS; firewalls; proxy servers; Internet content filters; protocol analyzers	

Sybex®
An Imprint of
(W)**WILEY**

OBJECTIVE	CHAPTER

5.4 Explain and implement protocols. — 7

SSL/TLS; S/MIME; PPTP; HTTP vs. HTTPS vs. SHTTP; L2TP; IPSEC; SSH

5.5 Explain core concepts of public key cryptography. — 7

Public Key Infrastructure (PKI); recovery agent; public key; private keys; certificate authority (CA); registration; key escrow; Certificate Revocation List (CRL); trust models

5.6 Implement PKI and certificate management. — 7

Public Key Infrastructure (PKI); recovery agent; public key; private keys; certificate authority (CA); registration; key escrow; Certificate Revocation List (CRL)

Domain 6.0: Organizational Security

6.1 Explain redundancy planning and its components. — 8

Hot site; cold site; warm site; backup generator; single point of failure; RAID; spare parts; redundant servers; redundant ISP; UPS; redundant connections

6.2 Implement disaster recovery procedures. — 8

Planning; disaster recovery exercises; backup techniques and practices – storage; schemes; restoration

6.3 Differentiate between and execute appropriate incident response procedures. — 4

Forensics; chain of custody; first responders; damage and loss control; reporting – disclosure of

6.4 Identify and explain applicable legislation and organizational policies. — 6, 8

Secure disposal of computers; acceptable use policies; password complexity; change management; classification of information; mandatory vacations; Personally Identifiable Information (PII); due care; due diligence; SLA; security-related HR policy; user education and awareness training

6.5 Explain the importance of environmental controls. — 6

Fire suppression; HVAC; shielding

6.6 Explain the concept of and how to reduce the risks of social engineering. — 6, 8

Phishing; hoaxes; shoulder surfing; Dumpster diving; user education and awareness training

NOTE Exam objectives are subject to change at any time without prior notice and at CompTIA's sole discretion. Please visit CompTIA's website (www.comptia.org) for the most current listing of exam objectives. The objectives in bold contain content that has changed since the 2002 edition of the Security+ exam. In addition, CompTIA offers a Bridge exam for those who are required to update their Security+ certification. The Bridge exam is a condensed version of the new exam that covers *only* the new topics.

Sybex®
An Imprint of
WILEY

OBJECTIVE	CHAPTER

Domain 4.0: Assessments & Audits

4.1 Conduct risk assessments and implement risk mitigation.   6

4.2 Carry out vulnerability assessments using common tools.   **2, 4**

   Port scanners; vulnerability scanners; protocol analyzers; OVAL; password crackers; network mappers

4.3 Within the realm of vulnerability assessments, explain the proper use of   **5**
penetration testing versus vulnerability scanning.

4.4 Use monitoring tools on systems and networks and detect security-related   **4, 5**
anomalies.

   Performance monitor; systems monitor; performance baseline; protocol analyzers

4.5 Compare and contrast various types of monitoring methodologies.   **4**

   Behavior-based; signature-based; anomaly-based

4.6 Execute proper logging procedures and evaluate the results   4, 8

   Security application; DNS; system; performance; access; firewall; antivirus

4.7 Conduct periodic audits of system security settings.   5, 8

   User access and rights review; storage and retention policies; group policies

Domain 5.0: Cryptography

5.1 Explain general cryptography concepts.   **5, 7**

   Key management; steganography; symmetric key; Asymmetric key; confidentiality;
   integrity and availability; non-repudiation; comparative strength of algorithms; digital
   signatures; whole disk encryption; Trusted Platform Module (TPM); single vs. dual
   sided certificates; use of proven technologies

5.2 Explain basic hashing concepts and map various algorithms to appropriate   7
applications.

   SHA; MD5; LANMAN; NTLM

5.3 Explain basic encryption concepts and map various algorithms to appropriate   7
applications.

   DES; 3DES; RSA; PGP; elliptic curve; AES; AES256; one time pad; transmission
   encryption (WEP TKIP, etc.)

Sybex®
An Imprint of
WILEY

OBJECTIVE	CHAPTER
2.5 Explain the vulnerabilities and mitigations associated with network devices.	2,3
Privilege escalation; weak passwords; back doors; default accounts; DOS	
2.6 Explain the vulnerabilities and mitigations associated with various transmission media.	3
Vampire taps	
2.7 Explain the vulnerabilities and implement mitigations associated with wireless networking.	4
Data emanation; war driving; SSID broadcast; blue jacking; Bluesnarfing; rogue access points; weak encryption	

Domain 3.0: Access Control

OBJECTIVE	CHAPTER
3.1 Identify and apply industry best practices for access control methods.	6
Implicit deny; least privilege; separation of duties; job rotation	
3.2 Explain common access control methods and differences between each.	8
MAC; DAC; role & rule based access control	
3.3 Organize users and computers into appropriate security groups and roles while distinguishing between appropriate rights and privileges.	9
3.4 Apply appropriate security controls to file and print resources.	9
3.5 Compare and implement logical access control methods.	**9**
ACL; group policies; password policy; domain password policy; user names and passwords; time of day restrictions; account expiration; logical tokens	
3.6 Summarize the various authentication models and the components of each.	8
One, two, and three-factor authentication; single sign-on	
3.7 Deploy various authentication models and identify the components of each.	1, 3, 5
Biometric reader; RADIUS; RAS; LDAP; remote access policies; remote authentication; VPN; Kerberos; CHAP; PAP; Mutual; 802.1x; TACACS	
3.8 Explain the difference between identification and authentication (identity proofing).	**1**
3.9 Explain and apply physical access security methods.	**6**
Physical access logs/lists; hardware locks; physical access control – ID badges; door access systems; man-trap; physical tokens; video surveillance – camera types and positioning	

NOTE Exam objectives are subject to change at any time without prior notice and at CompTIA's sole discretion. Please visit CompTIA's website (www.comptia.org) for the most current listing of exam objectives. The objectives in bold contain content that has changed since the 2002 edition of the Security+ exam. In addition, CompTIA offers a Bridge exam for those who are required to update their Security+ certification. The Bridge exam is a condensed version of the new exam that covers *only* the new topics.

Sybex®
An Imprint of
WILEY

CompTIA Security+™ Deluxe
Study Guide

CompTIA Security+™ Deluxe
Study Guide

Emmett Dulaney

Wiley Publishing, Inc.

Acquisitions Editor: Jeff Kellum
Development Editor: Jennifer Leland
Technical Editors: Michael Gregg and Bill Ferguson
Production Editor: Christine O'Connor
Copy Editor: Judy Flynn
Production Manager: Tim Tate
Vice President and Executive Group Publisher: Richard Swadley
Vice President and Executive Publisher: Joseph B. Wikert
Vice President and Publisher: Neil Edde
Media Project Supervisor: Laura Moss
Associate Producer: Josh Frank
Media Quality Assurance: Shawn Patrick
Book Designer: Judy Fung, Bill Gibson
Compositor: Craig Woods, Happenstance Type-O-Rama
Proofreader: Kathy Pope, Word One
Indexer: Nancy Guenther
Project Coordinator, Cover: Lynsey Stanford

Library of Congress Cataloging-in-Publication Data
Dulaney, Emmett A.
  CompTIA security+ deluxe study guide / Emmett Dulaney. — 1st ed.
    p. cm.
  ISBN 978-0-470-37296-8 (cloth/cd-rom)
  1. Electronic data processing personnel—Certification. 2. Computer security—Examinations—Study guides. 3. Computer networks—Security measures—Examinations—Study guides. I. Title.
  QA76.3.D82279 2009
  005.8—dc22
                                    2008032247

Dear Reader,

Thank you for choosing *CompTIA Security+ Deluxe Study Guide*. This book is part of a family of premium-quality Sybex books, all of which are written by outstanding authors who combine practical experience with a gift for teaching.

Sybex was founded in 1976. More than 30 years later, we're still committed to producing consistently exceptional books. With each of our titles, we're working hard to set a new standard for the industry. From the paper we print on to the authors we work with, our goal is to bring you the best books available.

I hope you see all that reflected in these pages. I'd be very interested to hear your comments and get your feedback on how we're doing. Feel free to let me know what you think about this or any other Sybex book by sending me an email at `nedde@wiley.com`, or if you think you've found a technical error in this book, please visit `http://sybex.custhelp.com`. Customer feedback is critical to our efforts at Sybex.

Best regards,

Neil Edde
Vice President and Publisher
Sybex, an Imprint of Wiley

For Karen, Kristin, Evan, and Spencer

Acknowledgments

This book would not exist were it not for Mike Pastore, the author of the first edition. He took a set of convoluted objectives for a broad exam and wrote the foundation of the study guide you now hold in your hands. This, the fourth edition, is indebted to his hard work and brilliance so early on.

Thanks are also due to Jeff Kellum, one of the best acquisitions editors in the business, and all of those at Wiley Publishing who worked on this title.

About the Author

Emmett Dulaney is a professor at Anderson University and the former director of training for Mercury Technical Solutions. He is a columnist for *CertCities* and the author of over 30 books on certification and cross-platform integration. Emmett can be reached at eadulaney@comcast.net.

Contents at a Glance

Introduction   *xxiii*

Assessment Test   *xxxix*

Chapter 1   General Security Concepts   1

Chapter 2   Identifying Potential Risks   51

Chapter 3   Infrastructure and Connectivity   107

Chapter 4   Monitoring Activity and Intrusion Detection   171

Chapter 5   Implementing and Maintaining a Secure Network   219

Chapter 6   Securing the Network and Environment   261

Chapter 7   Cryptography Basics, Methods, and Standards   311

Chapter 8   Security Policies and Procedures   381

Chapter 9   Security Administration   435

Appendix A   Security Administrator's Troubleshooting Guide   467

Appendix B   Workbook Exercises   505

Appendix C   Security+ Acronym List   539

Appendix D   About the Companion CD   545

Glossary   549

Index   *595*

Contents

Introduction   *xxiii*

Assessment Test   *xxxix*

Chapter   1   General Security Concepts   1

Understanding Information Security   3
  Securing the Physical Environment   4
  Examining Operational Security   5
  Working with Management and Policies   7
Understanding the Goals of Information Security   12
Comprehending the Security Process   13
  Appreciating Antivirus Software   13
  Implementing Access Control   14
  Understanding Authentication   15
Authentication Issues to Consider   21
Distinguishing between Security Topologies   22
  Setting Design Goals   23
  Creating Security Zones   26
  Working with Newer Technologies   29
  Addressing Business Concerns   33
  Dealing with Telephony Issues   38
Summary   39
Exam Essentials   40
Hands-On Labs   43
  Lab 1.1: Update a Linux System   43
  Lab 1.2: Update a Windows-Based System   43
Review Questions   44
Answers to Review Questions   48

Chapter   2   Identifying Potential Risks   51

Calculating Attack Strategies   53
  Understanding Access Attack Types   54
  Recognizing Modification and Repudiation Attacks   55
  Identifying Denial-of-Service and Distributed
    Denial-of-Service Attacks   56
Recognizing Common Attacks   58
  Back Door Attacks   59
  Spoofing Attacks   60
  Man-in-the-Middle Attacks   60
  Replay Attacks   62
  Password-Guessing Attacks   62
  Privilege Escalation   63

Identifying TCP/IP Security Concerns 64
Working with the TCP/IP Suite 65
Understanding Encapsulation 68
Working with Protocols and Services 69
Recognizing TCP/IP Attacks 72
Understanding Software Exploitation 78
Understanding OVAL 81
Surviving Malicious Code 81
Viruses 81
Trojan Horses 88
Logic Bombs 88
Worms 89
Antivirus Software 89
Understanding Social Engineering 91
Introducing Auditing Processes and Files 93
Summary 94
Exam Essentials 95
Hands-On Labs 98
Lab 2.1: Identify Running Processes on a
Windows-Based Machine 98
Lab 2.2: Identify Running Processes on a
Linux-Based Machine 98
Review Questions 100
Answers to Review Questions 104

Chapter   3   Infrastructure and Connectivity   107

Understanding Infrastructure Security 109
Working with Hardware Components 110
Working with Software Components 112
Understanding the Different Network Infrastructure Devices 113
Firewalls 113
Hubs 118
Modems 118
Remote Access Services 119
Routers 120
Switches 122
Telecom/PBX Systems 122
Virtual Private Networks 124
Wireless Access Points 125
Monitoring and Diagnosing Networks 127
Network Monitors 127
Intrusion Detection Systems 128
Securing Workstations and Servers 129
Understanding Mobile Devices 130

Understanding Remote Access 132
  Using Point-to-Point Protocol 132
  Working with Tunneling Protocols 133
  Using 802.1x Wireless Protocols 135
  Working with RADIUS 135
  TACACS/+ 136
Securing Internet Connections 136
  Working with Ports and Sockets 136
  Working with E-Mail 137
  Working with the Web 139
  Working with File Transfer Protocol 144
Understanding Network Protocols 146
The Basics of Cabling, Wires, and Communications 147
  Coax 148
  Unshielded Twisted Pair and Shielded Twisted Pair 150
  Fiber Optic 152
  Infrared 154
  Radio Frequencies 154
  Microwave Systems 154
Employing Removable Storage 156
  CD-R/DVD-R 157
  Diskettes 157
  Flash Cards 158
  Hard Drives 158
  Network Attached Storage 158
  Smart Cards 159
  Tape 159
  Thumb Drives 161
Summary 161
Exam Essentials 162
Hands-On Labs 164
  Lab 3.1: Examine the Windows Routing Table 164
  Lab 3.2: Examine the Linux Routing Table 164
Review Questions 165
Answers to Review Questions 169

Chapter 4   Monitoring Activity and Intrusion Detection 171
Monitoring the Network 173
  Recognizing the Different Types of Network Traffic 174
  Monitoring Network Systems 178
Understanding Intrusion Detection Systems 179
  Working with a Network-Based IDS 184
  Working with a Host-Based IDS 189
  Working with NIPS 190
  Utilizing Honeypots 191
  Understanding Incident Response 192

Working with Wireless Systems   198
    Wireless Transport Layer Security   198
    IEEE 802.11*x* Wireless Protocols   199
    WEP/WAP   200
    Wireless Vulnerabilities to Know   201
Understanding Instant Messaging's Features   202
    Understanding IM Vulnerabilities   203
    Controlling Privacy   204
Working with 8.3 File Naming   204
Understanding Protocol Analyzers   205
Understanding Signal Analysis and Intelligence   205
    Footprinting   206
    Scanning   206
Summary   207
Exam Essentials   208
Hands-On Labs   210
    Lab 4.1: View the Active TCP and UDP Ports   210
    Lab 4.2: Run Windows Network Monitor   210
    Lab 4.3: Install snort in Linux   211
    Lab 4.4: Make File Extensions Visible in Windows XP 211
    Lab 4.5: Monitor Network Traffic in Linux   211
Review Questions   213
Answers to Review Questions   217

Chapter 5   Implementing and Maintaining a Secure Network   219

Overview of Network Security Threats   221
Defining Security Baselines   222
Hardening the OS and NOS   224
    Configuring Network Protocols   225
    Hardening Microsoft Windows Vista   227
    Hardening Microsoft Windows XP   228
    Hardening Windows Server 2003   229
    Hardening Microsoft Windows 2000   230
    Hardening Unix/Linux   231
    Hardening Novell NetWare   232
    Hardening Apple Macintosh   233
    Hardening Filesystems   234
    Updating Your Operating System   237
Hardening Network Devices   238
    Updating Network Devices   238
    Configuring Routers and Firewalls   239
Hardening Applications   240
    Hardening Web Servers   240
    Hardening E-Mail Servers   241
    Hardening FTP Servers   242
    Hardening DNS Servers   243

Hardening NNTP Servers 244
Hardening File and Print Servers and Services 245
Hardening DHCP Services 246
Working with Data Repositories 246
Summary 251
Exam Essentials 252
Hands-On Labs 254
Lab 5.1: Install OpenLDAP on a SuSE Server 254
Lab 5.2: Work with Performance Monitor and Windows 254
Lab 5.3: Work with Unix/Linux Networking 255
Review Questions 256
Answers to Review Questions 260

Chapter 6 Securing the Network and Environment 261

Understanding Physical and Network Security 262
Implementing Access Control 262
Understanding Social Engineering 270
Scanning the Environment 272
Understanding Business Continuity Planning 281
Undertaking Business Impact Analysis 281
Assessing Risk 282
Developing Policies, Standards, and Guidelines 285
Implementing Policies 285
Incorporating Standards 286
Following Guidelines 287
Working with Security Standards and ISO 17799 288
Classifying Information 290
Public Information 290
Private Information 292
Roles in the Security Process 294
Information Access Controls 295
Summary 299
Exam Essentials 301
Hands-On Lab 303
Lab 6.1: Test Social Engineering 303
Review Questions 304
Answers to Review Questions 308

Chapter 7 Cryptography Basics, Methods, and Standards 311

An Overview of Cryptography 313
Understanding Physical Cryptography 314
Understanding Mathematical Cryptography 316
Working with Passwords 318
Understanding Quantum Cryptography 318
Uncovering the Myth of Unbreakable Codes 319

Understanding Cryptographic Algorithms 321
The Science of Hashing 321
Working with Symmetric Algorithms 323
Working with Asymmetric Algorithms 324
Using Cryptographic Systems 326
Confidentiality 326
Integrity 327
Digital Signatures 328
Authentication 329
Nonrepudiation 330
Access Control 330
Using Public Key Infrastructure 331
Using a Certificate Authority 332
Working with Registration Authorities and
Local Registration Authorities 333
Implementing Certificates 335
Understanding Certificate Revocation 336
Implementing Trust Models 337
Preparing for Cryptographic Attacks 341
Understanding Cryptography Standards and Protocols 343
The Origins of Encryption Standards 344
Public-Key Infrastructure X.509/Public-Key
Cryptography Standards 348
X.509 348
SSL and TLS 349
Certificate Management Protocols 351
Secure Multipurpose Internet Mail Extensions 351
Secure Electronic Transaction 351
Secure Shell 352
Pretty Good Privacy 354
HTTP Secure 354
Secure HTTP 355
IP Security 355
Tunneling Protocols 356
Federal Information Processing Standard 357
Common Criteria 357
Wireless Transport Layer Security 357
Wired Equivalent Privacy 357
ISO 17799 358
Understanding Key Management and the Key Life Cycle 358
Comparing Centralized and Decentralized Key Generation 359
Storing and Distributing Keys 361
Using Key Escrow 363
Identifying Key Expiration 363
Revoking Keys 364

Suspending Keys 364

Recovering and Archiving Keys 365

Renewing Keys 366

Destroying Keys 367

Identifying Key Usage 367

Summary 368

Exam Essentials 370

Hands-On Labs 373

Lab 7.1: Hash Rules in Windows Server 2003 373

Lab 7.2: SSL Settings in Windows Server 2003 373

Lab 7.3: Encrypting a File System in Linux 374

Lab 7.4: Look for Errors in IPSec Performance Statistics 374

Review Questions 375

Answers to Review Questions 379

Chapter   8   Security Policies and Procedures   381

Understanding Business Continuity 383

Utilities 384

High Availability 385

Disaster Recovery 391

Reinforcing Vendor Support 404

Service-Level Agreements 404

Code Escrow Agreements 406

Generating Policies and Procedures 406

Human Resource Policies 406

Business Policies 410

Certificate Policies 412

Incident-Response Policies 413

Enforcing Privilege Management 414

User and Group Role Management 415

Privilege Escalation 416

Single Sign-On Initiatives 416

Privilege Decision Making 418

Auditing 418

Access Control 422

Summary 424

Exam Essentials 425

Hands-On Labs 427

Lab 8.1: Use Automated System Recovery in
Windows Server 2003 427

Lab 8.2: Create a Rescue Disk in Linux 427

Lab 8.3: Create a Backup with SuSE Linux 428

Review Questions 429

Answers to Review Questions 433

Chapter   9   Security Administration   **435**

Understanding Security Management   436
    Drafting Best Practices and Documentation   436
Simplifying Security Administration   444
Understanding Security Awareness and Education   446
    Using Communication and Awareness   447
    Providing Education   447
Staying on Top of Security   449
    Websites   451
    Trade Publications   452
Regulating Privacy and Security   454
    The Health Insurance Portability and Accountability Act   454
    The Gramm-Leach-Bliley Act of 1999   454
    The Computer Fraud and Abuse Act   455
    The Family Educational Rights and Privacy Act   455
    The Computer Security Act of 1987   456
    The Cyberspace Electronic Security Act   456
    The Cyber Security Enhancement Act   456
    The Patriot Act   457
    Familiarizing Yourself with International Efforts   457
Summary   457
Exam Essentials   458
Hands-On Labs   459
    Lab 9.1: Configure Windows Automatic Updates   459
    Lab 9.2: Run the Microsoft Baseline Security Analyzer   459
Review Questions   461
Answers to Review Questions   465

Appendix   A   Security Administrator's Troubleshooting Guide   467

Getting Started   469
Access Control Issues   471
Accountability Concerns   471
Auditing   472
Authentication Schemes   473
    Authentication Factors   473
    Mutual Authentication   475
    Authentication Protection   475
Backup Management   476
Baselining Security   476
Certificate Management   477
Communications Security   478
    Dial-Up   480
    Remote Control/Remote Shell   480
    Virtual Private Networks   480
Directory Services Protection   481

Disaster Planning   482
Documenting Your Environment   483
E-Mail Issues   483
File-Sharing Basics   484
Working with IDSs and Honey Pots   485
Incident Handling   486
Internet Common Sense   486
Key Management Conventions   488
Preventing Common Malicious Events   489
    Antivirus Protection   492
    Making Stronger Passwords   493
Managing Personnel   495
Keeping Physical Security Meaningful   495
Securing the Infrastructure   497
Working with Security Zones   499
Social Engineering Risks   500
System Hardening Basics   500
Securing the Wireless Environment   502

Appendix   B   Workbook Exercises   505

Lab B.1: Change to WPA Security in Windows XP   508
Lab B.2: Turn on the Firewall in Windows XP: Method One   509
Lab B.3: Turn on the Firewall in Windows XP: Method Two   510
Lab B.4: Create a Baseline for Internet Access   511
Lab B.5: Turn on a Screensaver Password for Windows XP   512
Lab B.6: Look for Security Events within Windows XP   512
Lab B.7: Identify User Accounts with Administrator Access
   in Windows XP   512
Lab B.8: Turn on a Screensaver Password for openSUSE   513
Lab B.9: Change a Password in Linux   514
Lab B.10: Find SUID and SGID Files in Linux   514
Lab B.11: Change ACLs on All Files in a Linux Directory   515
Lab B.12: Change Permissions on All Files in a
   Linux Directory   515
Lab B.13: Change the Default Permissions for all Newly
   Created Files in Linux   516
Lab B.14: View all Linux Logins   516
Lab B.15: Change the Group Associated with Files   517
Lab B.16: View Failed Login Attempts   518
Lab B.17: Hide a Linux File   518
Lab B.18: Hide and Access a Windows Share   519
Lab B.19: Encrypt a Windows File   519
Lab B.20: Count the Number of Running Linux Processes   520
Lab B.21: Display the Security Tab in Windows XP   520
Lab B.22: View Effective Permissions in Windows XP   521

Lab B.23: Turn the Guest Account Off   521
Lab B.24: View Internet Explorer Security Settings   522
Lab B.25: Change Internet Explorer Pop-up Blocker Settings   522
Lab B.26: Prevent a Folder from Being Shared   523
Lab B.27: Enable openSUSE Firewall   523
Lab B.28: Configure openSUSE Local Security   524
Lab B.29: Set the Defaults for New Users   524
Lab B.30: View Logged Warnings in openSUSE   525
Lab B.31: Configure AppArmor   525
Lab B.32: View AppArmor Reports   526
Lab B.33: Configure openSUSE as a Kerberos Client   526
Lab B.34: Configure openSUSE as an LDAP Client   527
Lab B.35: Turn Off IPv6 in openSUSE   527
Lab B.36: Turn On Folder Encryption with cipher   528
Lab B.37: Change the Minimum Password Age   528
Lab B.38: Compare Your System to a Security Template   529
Lab B.39: Clear Private Data in Internet Explorer   530
Lab B.40: Clear Private Data in Firefox   531
Lab B.41: Configure SELinux in Fedora   531
Lab B.42: Limit Cookies to First Party   531
Lab B.43: Configure the Phishing Filter   532
Lab B.44: Add a Legal Notice   532
Lab B.45: Configure Windows XP Startup   533
Lab B.46: Run a Remote Desktop   534
Lab B.47: Secure the Account Database   535
Lab B.48: Create a Restore Point   536
Lab B.49: Return to a Restore Point   537
Lab B.50: Boot to a Good Configuration   537

Appendix   C   Security+ Acronym List   539

Appendix   D   About the Companion CD   545

What You'll Find on the CD   546
   Sybex Test Engine   546
   PDF of the Book   546
   Adobe Reader   547
   Electronic Flashcards   547
System Requirements   547
Using the CD   547
Troubleshooting   548
   Customer Care   548

Glossary   549

Index   *595*

Introduction

If you're preparing to take the Security+ exam, you'll undoubtedly want to find as much information as you can concerning computer and physical security. The more information you have at your disposal and the more hands-on experience you gain, the better off you'll be when attempting the exam. This study guide was written with that in mind. The goal was to provide enough information to prepare you for the test, but not so much that you'll be overloaded with information that's outside the scope of the exam.

This book presents the material at an intermediate technical level. Experience with and understanding of security concepts, operating systems, and application systems will help you get a full understanding of the challenges you face as a security professional.

I've included review questions at the end of each chapter to give you a taste of what it's like to take the exam. If you're already working in the security field, I recommend that you check out these questions first to gauge your level of expertise. You can then use the book mainly to fill in the gaps in your current knowledge. This study guide will help you round out your knowledge base before tackling the exam.

If you can answer 90 percent or more of the review questions correctly for a given chapter, you can feel safe moving on to the next chapter. If you're unable to answer that many correctly, reread the chapter and try the questions again. Your score should improve.

Don't just study the questions and answers! The questions on the actual exam will be different from the practice questions included in this book and on the CD. The exam is designed to test your knowledge of a concept or objective, so use this book to learn the objectives behind the questions.

Before You Begin

Before you begin studying for the exam, it's imperative that you understand a few things about the Security+ certification. Security+ is a certification for life from CompTIA (an industry association responsible for many entry-level certifications) granted to those who obtain a passing score on a single entry-level exam. In addition to adding Security+ to your resume as a stand-alone certification, you can use it as an elective in many vendor-certification tracks.

When you're studying for any exam, the first step in preparation should always be to find out as much as possible about the test; the more you know up front, the better you can plan your course of study. The current exam, and the one this book is written for, is the 2008 update. While all variables are subject to change, as this book is being written, the exam consists of 100 questions. You have 90 minutes to take the exam, and the passing score is based on a scale from 100 to 900. Both Pearson VUE and Prometric testing centers administer the exam throughout the United States and several other countries.

The exam is multiple choice with short, terse questions followed by four possible answers. Don't expect lengthy scenarios and complex solutions. This is an entry-level exam of knowledge-level topics; you're expected to know a great deal about security topics from an overview perspective rather than implementation. In many books, the glossary is filler added to the back of the text; this book's glossary should be considered necessary reading. You're likely to see a question on the exam about what a Trojan horse is, not how to identify it at the code level. Spend your study time learning the different security solutions and identifying potential security vulnerabilities and where they would be applicable. Don't get bogged down in step-by-step details; those are saved for certification exams beyond the scope of Security+.

You should also know that CompTIA is notorious for including vague questions on all its exams. You might see a question for which two of the possible four answers are correct—but you can only choose one. Use your knowledge, logic, and intuition to choose the best answer, and then move on. Sometimes the questions are worded in ways that would make English majors cringe—a typo here, an incorrect verb there. Don't let this frustrate you; answer the question, and go to the next. Although we haven't intentionally added typos or other grammatical errors, the questions throughout this book make every attempt to re-create the structure and appearance of the real exam questions. CompTIA offers a page on study tips for their exams at `http://certification.comptia.org/resources/test_tips.aspx`, and it is worth skimming.

CompTIA frequently does what is called *item seeding,* which is the practice of including unscored questions on exams. It does that to gather psychometric data, which is then used when developing new versions of the exam. Before you take it, you are told that your exam may include unscored questions. So if you come across a question that does not appear to map to any of the exam objectives—or for that matter, does not appear to belong in the exam—it is likely a seeded question.

As you study, you need to know that the exam you'll take was created at a certain point in time. You won't see a question about the new virus that hit your systems last week, but you'll see questions about concepts that existed when this exam was created. Updating the exam is a difficult process and results in an increment in the exam number.

Why Become Security+ Certified?

There are a number of reasons for obtaining a Security+ certification:

It provides proof of professional achievement.   Specialized certifications are the best way to stand out from the crowd. In this age of technology certifications, you'll find hundreds of thousands of administrators who have successfully completed the Microsoft and Cisco certification tracks. To set yourself apart from the crowd, you need a little bit more. The Security+ exam is part of the CompTIA certification track that includes A+, Network+, and other vendor-neutral certifications such as RFID+, Convergence+, and more. This exam will help you prepare for more advanced certifications because it provides a solid grounding in security concepts and will give you the recognition you deserve.

It increases your marketability.   Almost anyone can bluff their way through an interview. Once you're security certified, you'll have the credentials to prove your competency. And, certifications can't be taken from you when you change jobs—you can take that certification with you to any position you accept.

It provides opportunity for advancement.   Individuals who prove themselves to be competent and dedicated are the ones who will most likely be promoted. Becoming certified is a great way to prove your skill level and show your employer that you're committed to improving your skill set. Look around you at those who are certified: They are probably the people who receive good pay raises and promotions.

It fulfills training requirements.   Many companies have set training requirements for their staff so that they stay up-to-date on the latest technologies. Having a certification program in security provides administrators with another certification path to follow when they have exhausted some of the other industry-standard certifications.

It raises customer confidence.   As companies discover the CompTIA advantage, they will undoubtedly require qualified staff to achieve these certifications. Many companies outsource their work to consulting firms with experience working with security. Firms that have certified staff have a definite advantage over firms that don't.

How to Become a Security+ Certified Professional

As this book goes to press, there are two Security+ exam providers: Prometric and Pearson VUE. The following table contains all the necessary contact information and exam-specific details for registering. Exam pricing might vary by country or by CompTIA membership.

Vendor	Website	Phone Number
Prometric	securereg3.prometric.com	U.S. and Canada: 800-977-3926
Pearson VUE	www.vue.com/comptia	U.S. and Canada: 877-551-PLUS (7587)

When you schedule the exam, you'll receive instructions regarding appointment and cancellation procedures, ID requirements, and information about the testing center location. In addition, you'll receive a registration and payment confirmation letter. Exams can be scheduled up to six weeks out or as late as the next day (or, in some cases, even the same day).

Exam prices and codes may vary based on the country in which the exam is administered. For detailed pricing and exam registration procedures, refer to CompTIA's website at www.comptia.com.

After you've successfully passed your Security+ exam, CompTIA will award you a certification that is good for life. Within four to six weeks of passing the exam, you'll receive your official CompTIA Security+ certificate and ID card. (If you don't receive these within eight weeks of taking the test, contact CompTIA directly using the information found in your registration packet.)

Who Should Buy This Book?

If you want to acquire a solid foundation in computer security and your goal is to prepare for the exam by learning how to develop and improve security, this book is for you. You'll find clear explanations of the concepts you need to grasp and plenty of help to achieve the high level of professional competency you need in order to succeed in your chosen field.

If you want to become certified as a certification holder, this book is definitely what you need. However, if you just want to attempt to pass the exam without really understanding security, this study guide isn't for you. It's written for people who want to acquire hands-on skills and in-depth knowledge of computer security.

If you purchased the deluxe edition of this book, we've included a special appendix, "Security+ Practical Application." It is designed to give those new to the field of security administration a practical look at how many of the exam objectives relate to the real world.

 In addition to reading this book, you might consider downloading and reading the white papers on security that are scattered throughout the Internet.

How to Use This Book and the CD

We've included several testing features in the book and on the CD-ROM. These tools will help you retain vital exam content as well as prepare you to sit for the actual exam:

Before you begin   At the end of this introduction is an assessment test that you can use to check your readiness for the exam. Take this test before you start reading the book; it will help you determine the areas you might need to brush up on. The answers to the assessment test questions appear on a separate page after the last question of the test. Each answer includes an explanation and a note telling you the chapter in which the material appears.

Chapter review questions   To test your knowledge as you progress through the book, there are review questions at the end of each chapter. As you finish each chapter, answer the review questions and then check your answers—the correct answers appear on the page following the last review question. You can go back to reread the section that deals with each question you got wrong to ensure that you answer correctly the next time you're tested on the material.

Electronic flashcards   You'll find flashcard questions on the CD for on-the-go review. These are short questions and answers. You can answer them on your PC or download them onto a Palm device for quick and convenient reviewing.

Sybex Test Engine   The CD also contains the Sybex Test Engine. Using this custom software, you can identify up front the areas in which you are weak and then develop a solid studying strategy using each of these robust testing features. The ReadMe file walks you through the installation process.

In addition to taking the assessment test and the chapter review questions in the test engine, you'll find practice exams, one if you purchased the standard edition, four if you purchased the deluxe edition. Take these practice exams just as if you were taking the actual exam (without any reference material). When you've finished the first exam, move on to the next one to solidify your test-taking skills. If you get more than 90 percent of the answers correct, you're ready to take the certification exam.

Full text of the book in PDF   The CD-ROM contains this book in PDF so you can easily read it on any computer. If you have to travel but still need to study for the exam, and you have a laptop with a CD-ROM drive, you can carry this entire book with you.

 Real World Scenario

What's Included in the Deluxe Edition?

If you purchased the deluxe edition of this Study Guide, you will notice the two additional appendixes: the security administrator's troubleshooting guide and workbook exercises. Together, these two elements add an additional hands-on component to your studies and can be useful resources long after you've passed the exam and earned your Security+ certification.

Not only is there a difference within the spine of the deluxe edition with the inclusion of the additional chapters, but the CD has been enhanced as well. The deluxe edition contains an additional bonus exam to help you gauge your readiness for the real exam at your closest testing center.

Exam Objectives

CompTIA goes to great lengths to ensure that its certification programs accurately reflect the IT industry's best practices. The company does this by establishing cornerstone committees for each of its exam programs. Each committee comprises a small group of IT professionals, training providers, and publishers who are responsible for establishing the exam's baseline competency level and who determine the appropriate target-audience level. Once these factors are determined, CompTIA shares this information with a group of hand-selected Subject Matter Experts (SMEs). These folks are the true brainpower behind the certification program. In the case of this exam, they are IT-seasoned pros from the likes of Microsoft, Sun Microsystems, VeriSign, and RSA Security, to name just a few. They review the committee's findings, refine them, and shape them into the objectives you see before you. CompTIA calls this process a job task analysis (JTA). Finally, CompTIA conducts a survey to ensure that the objectives and weightings truly reflect the job requirements. Only then can the SMEs go to work writing the hundreds of questions needed for the exam. And in many cases, they have to go back to the drawing board for further refinements before the exam is ready to go live in its final state. So, rest assured the content you're about to learn will serve you long after you take the exam.

Exam objectives are subject to change at any time without prior notice and at CompTIA's sole discretion. Visit the certification page of CompTIA's website at www.comptia.org for the most current listing of exam objectives.

CompTIA also publishes relative weightings for each of the exam's objectives. The following table lists the six Security+ objective domains and the extent to which they are represented on the exam. As you use this study guide, you'll find that I have administered just the right dosage of objective knowledge by tailoring coverage to mirror the percentages that CompTIA uses.

As part of the Department of Defense (DoD) Directive 8570.1—which requires certain DoD technicians and managers to get trained and certified in certain areas, including Security+—CompTIA will release a Security+ Bridge exam. The Bridge exam will test on topics that are new since the previous version of the exam. Individuals required to get recertified can take the Bridge exam to meet the recertification policy. It should be noted that CompTIA does not require individuals to get recertified. Refer to the objective tear out card at the beginning of this book. All objectives that are new to the Security (2008 Edition) are in bold. For more information on Directive 8570.1, visit http://certification.comptia.org/resources/US_Gov.aspx.

Domain	% of Exam
1.0 Systems Security	21%
2.0 Network Infrastructure	20%
3.0 Access Control	17%
4.0 Assessments & Audits	15%
5.0 Cryptography	15%
6.0 Organizational Security	12%
Total	100%

1.0 Systems Security

1.1 Differentiate among various systems security threats.

- Privilege escalation
- Virus
- Worm
- Trojan
- Spyware
- Spam
- Adware
- Rootkits
- Botnets
- Logic bomb

1.2 Explain the security risks pertaining to system hardware and peripherals

- BIOS
- USB devices
- Cell phones
- Removable storage
- Network attached storage

1.3 Implement OS hardening practices and procedures to achieve workstation and server security.

- Hot fixes
- Service packs
- Patches
- Patch management
- Group policies
- Security templates
- Configuration baselines

1.4 Carry out the appropriate procedures to establish application security.

- ActiveX
- Java
- Scripting
- Browser
- Buffer overflows
- Cookies

- SMTP open relays
- Instant messaging
- P2P
- Input validation
- Cross-site scripting (XSS)

1.5   Implement security applications.

- HIDS
- Personal software firewalls
- Antivirus
- Anti-spam
- Popup blockers

1.6   Explain the purpose and application of virtualization technology.

2.0 Network Infrastructure

2.1   Differentiate between the different ports & protocols, their respective threats and mitigation techniques.

- Antiquated protocols
- TCP/IP hijacking
- Null sessions
- Spoofing
- Man-in-the-middle
- Replay
- DoS
- DDoS
- Domain Name Kiting
- DNS poisoning
- ARP Poisoning

2.2   Distinguish between network design elements and components.

- DMZ
- VLAN
- NAT
- Network interconnections
- NAC

- Subnetting
- Telephony

2.3 Determine the appropriate use of network security tools to facilitate network security.

- NIDS
- NIPS
- Firewalls
- Proxy servers
- Honeypot
- Internet content filters
- Protocol analyzers

2.4 Apply the appropriate network tools to facilitate network security.

- NIDS
- Firewalls
- Proxy servers
- Internet content filters
- Protocol analyzers

2.5 Explain the vulnerabilities and mitigations associated with network devices.

- Privilege escalation
- Weak passwords
- Back doors
- Default accounts
- DoS

2.6 Explain the vulnerabilities and mitigations associated with various transmission media.

- Vampire taps

2.7 Explain the vulnerabilities and implement mitigations associated with wireless networking.

- Data emanation
- War driving
- SSID broadcast
- Blue jacking
- Bluesnarfing
- Rogue access points
- Weak encryption

3.0 Access Control

3.1 Identify and apply industry best practices for access control methods.

- Implicit deny
- Least privilege
- Separation of duties
- Job rotation

3.2 Explain common access control models and the differences between each.

- MAC
- DAC
- Role & Rule based access control

3.3 Organize users and computers into appropriate security groups and roles while distinguishing between appropriate rights and privileges.

3.4 Apply appropriate security controls to file and print resources.

3.5 Compare and implement logical access control methods.

- ACL
- Group policies
- Password policy
- Domain password policy
- User names and passwords
- Time of day restrictions
- Account expiration
- Logical tokens

3.6 Summarize the various authentication models and identify the components of each.

- One, two and three-factor authentication
- Single sign-on

3.7 Deploy various authentication models and identify the components of each.

- Biometric reader
- RADIUS
- RAS
- LDAP
- Remote access policies
- Remote authentication
- VPN
- Kerberos

- CHAP
- PAP
- Mutual
- 802.1x
- TACACS

3.8 Explain the difference between identification and authentication (identity proofing).

3.9 Explain and apply physical access security methods.

- Physical access logs/lists
- Hardware locks
- Physical access control—ID badges
- Door access systems
- Man-trap
- Physical tokens
- Video surveillance—camera types and positioning

4.0 Assessments & Audits

4.1 Conduct risk assessments and implement risk mitigation.

4.2 Carry out vulnerability assessments using common tools.

- Port scanners
- Vulnerability scanners
- Protocol analyzers
- OVAL
- Password crackers
- Network mappers

4.3 Within the realm of vulnerability assessments, explain the proper use of penetration testing versus vulnerability scanning.

4.4 Use monitoring tools on systems and networks, and detect security-related anomalies.

- Performance monitor
- Systems monitor
- Performance baseline
- Protocol analyzers

4.5 Compare and contrast various types of monitoring methodologies.

- Behavior-based
- Signature-based
- Anomaly-based

4.6   Executer proper logging procedures and evaluate the results.

- Security application
- DNS
- System
- Performance
- Access
- Firewall
- Antivirus

4.7   Conduct periodic audits of system security settings.

- User access and rights review
- Storage and retention policies
- Group policies

5.0 Cryptography

5.1   Explain general cryptography concepts.

- Key management
- Steganography
- Symmetric key
- Asymmetric key
- Confidentiality
- Integrity and availability
- Non-repudiation
- Comparative strength of algorithms
- Digital signatures
- Whole disk encryption
- Trusted Platform Module (TPM)
- Single vs. Dual sided certificates
- Use of proven technologies

5.2   Explain basic hashing concepts and map various algorithms to appropriate applications.

- SHA
- MD5
- LANMAN
- NTLM

5.3   Explain basic encryption concepts and map various algorithms to appropriate applications.

- DES
- 3DES
- RSA
- PGP
- Elliptic curve
- AES
- AES256
- One time pad
- Transmission encryption (WEP TKIP, and so forth)

5.4   Explain and implement protocols.

- SSL/TLS
- S/MIME
- PPTP
- HTTP vs. HTTPS vs. SHTTP
- L2TP
- IPSEC
- SSH

5.5   Explain core concepts of public key cryptography.

- Public Key Infrastructure (PKI)
- Recovery agent
- Public key
- Private keys
- Certificate Authority (CA)
- Registration
- Key escrow
- Certificate Revocation List (CRL)
- Trust models

5.6   Implement PKI and certificate management.

- Public Key Infrastructure (PKI)
- Recovery agent
- Public key
- Private keys

- Certificate Authority (CA)
- Registration
- Key escrow
- Certificate Revocation List (CRL)

6.0 Organizational Security

6.1   Explain redundancy planning and its components.

- Hot site
- Cold site
- Warm site
- Backup generator
- Single point of failure
- RAID
- Spare parts
- Redundant servers
- Redundant ISP
- UPS
- Redundant connections

6.2   Implement disaster recovery procedures.

- Planning
- Disaster exercises
- Backup techniques and practices—storage
- Schemes
- Restoration

6.3   Differentiate between and execute appropriate incident response procedures.

- Forensics
- Chain of custody
- First responders
- Damage and loss control
- Reporting—disclosure of

6.4   Identify and explain applicable legislation and organizational policies.

- Secure disposal of computers
- Acceptable use policies
- Password complexity

- Change management
- Classification of information
- Mandatory vacations
- Personally Identifiable Information (PII)
- Due care
- Due diligence
- Due process
- SLA
- Security-related HR policy
- User education and awareness training

6.5 Explain the importance of environmental controls.

- Fire suppression
- HVAC
- Shielding

6.6 Explain the concept of and how to reduce the risks of social engineering.

- Phishing
- Hoaxes
- Shoulder surfing
- Dumpster diving
- User education and awareness training

Tips for Taking the Security+ Exam

Here are some general tips for taking your exam successfully:

- Bring two forms of ID with you. One must be a photo ID, such as a driver's license. The other can be a major credit card or a passport. Both forms must include a signature.

- Arrive early at the exam center so you can relax and review your study materials, particularly tables and lists of exam-related information. After you are ready to enter the testing room, you will need to leave everything outside; you won't be able to bring any materials into the testing area.

- Read the questions carefully. Don't be tempted to jump to an early conclusion. Make sure you know exactly what each question is asking.

- Don't leave any unanswered questions. Unanswered questions are scored against you.

- There will be questions with multiple correct responses. When there is more than one correct answer, a message at the bottom of the screen will prompt you to either "Choose two" or "Choose all that apply." Be sure to read the messages displayed to know how many correct answers you must choose.

- When answering multiple-choice questions you're not sure about, use a process of elimination to get rid of the obviously incorrect answers first. Doing so will improve your odds if you need to make an educated guess.

- On form-based tests (nonadaptive), because the hard questions will take the most time, save them for last. You can move forward and backward through the exam.

- For the latest pricing on the exams and updates to the registration procedures, visit CompTIA's website at www.comptia.org.

Assessment Test

1. Which type of audit can be used to determine whether accounts have been established properly and verify that privilege creep isn't occurring?
   A. Privilege audit
   B. Usage audit
   C. Escalation audit
   D. Report audit

2. What kind of physical access device restricts access to a small number of individuals at one time?
   A. Checkpoint
   B. Perimeter security
   C. Security zones
   D. Mantrap

3. Which of the following is a set of voluntary standards governing encryption?
   A. PKI
   B. PKCS
   C. ISA
   D. SSL

4. Which protocol is used to create a secure environment in a wireless network?
   A. WAP
   B. WEP
   C. WTLS
   D. WML

5. An Internet server interfaces with TCP/IP at which layer of the DOD model?
   A. Transport layer
   B. Network layer
   C. Process layer
   D. Internet layer

6. You want to establish a network connection between two LANs using the Internet. Which technology would best accomplish that for you?
   A. IPSec
   B. L2TP
   C. PPP
   D. SLIP

7. Which design concept limits access to systems from outside users while protecting users and systems inside the LAN?
    A. DMZ
    B. VLAN
    C. I&A
    D. Router

8. In the key recovery process, which key must be recoverable?
    A. Rollover key
    B. Secret key
    C. Previous key
    D. Escrow key

9. Which kind of attack is designed to overload a particular protocol or service?
    A. Spoofing
    B. Back door
    C. Man in the middle
    D. Flood

10. Which component of an IDS collects data?
    A. Data source
    B. Sensor
    C. Event
    D. Analyzer

11. What is the process of making an operating system secure from attack called?
    A. Hardening
    B. Tuning
    C. Sealing
    D. Locking down

12. The integrity objective addresses which characteristic of information security?
    A. Verification that information is accurate
    B. Verification that ethics are properly maintained
    C. Establishment of clear access control of data
    D. Verification that data is kept private and secure

13. Which mechanism is used by PKI to allow immediate verification of a certificate's validity?
    A. CRL
    B. MD5
    C. SSHA
    D. OCSP

14. Which of the following is the equivalent of a VLAN from a physical security perspective?

    A. Perimeter security

    B. Partitioning

    C. Security zones

    D. Physical barrier

15. A user has just reported that he downloaded a file from a prospective client using IM. The user indicates that the file was called `account.doc`. The system has been behaving unusually since he downloaded the file. What is the most likely event that occurred?

    A. Your user inadvertently downloaded a virus using IM.

    B. Your user may have a defective hard drive.

    C. Your user is hallucinating and should increase his medication.

    D. The system is suffering from power surges.

16. Which mechanism or process is used to enable or disable access to a network resource based on an IP address?

    A. NDS

    B. ACL

    C. Hardening

    D. Port blocking

17. Which of the following would provide additional security to an Internet web server?

    A. Changing the port address to 80.

    B. Changing the port address to 1019.

    C. Adding a firewall to block port 80.

    D. Web servers can't be secured.

18. What type of program exists primarily to propagate and spread itself to other systems?

    A. Virus

    B. Trojan horse

    C. Logic bomb

    D. Worm

19. An individual presents herself at your office claiming to be a service technician. She wants to discuss your current server configuration. This may be an example of what type of attack?

    A. Social engineering

    B. Access control

    C. Perimeter screening

    D. Behavioral engineering

20. Which of the following is a major security problem with FTP servers?

    A. Password files are stored in an unsecure area on disk.

    B. Memory traces can corrupt file access.

    C. User IDs and passwords are unencrypted.

    D. FTP sites are unregistered.

21. Which system would you install to provide active protection and notification of security problems in a network connected to the Internet?

    A. IDS

    B. Network monitoring

    C. Router

    D. VPN

22. The process of verifying the steps taken to maintain the integrity of evidence is called what?

    A. Security investigation

    B. Chain of custody

    C. Three A's of investigation

    D. Security policy

23. What encryption process uses one message to hide another?

    A. Steganography

    B. Hashing

    C. MDA

    D. Cryptointelligence

24. Which policy dictates how computers are used in an organization?

    A. Security policy

    B. User policy

    C. Use policy

    D. Enforcement policy

25. Which algorithm is used to create a temporary secure session for the exchange of key information?

    A. KDC

    B. KEA

    C. SSL

    D. RSA

26. You've been hired as a security consultant for a company that's beginning to implement handheld devices, such as PDAs. You're told that the company must use an asymmetric system. Which security standard would you recommend it implement?

A. ECC

B. PKI

C. SHA

D. MD

27. Which of the following backup methods will generally provide the fastest backup times?

A. Full backup

B. Incremental backup

C. Differential backup

D. Archival backup

28. You want to grant access to network resources based on authenticating an individual's retina during a scan. Which security method uses a physical characteristic as a method of determining identity?

A. Smart card

B. I&A

C. Biometrics

D. CHAP

29. Which access control method is primarily concerned with the role that individuals have in the organization?

A. MAC

B. DAC

C. RBAC

D. STAC

30. The process of investigating a computer system for clues into an event is called what?

A. Computer forensics

B. Virus scanning

C. Security policy

D. Evidence gathering

Answers to Assessment Test

1. **A.** A privilege audit is used to determine that all groups, users, and other accounts have the appropriate privileges assigned according to the policies of an organization. For more information, see Chapter 8.

2. **D.** A mantrap limits access to a small number of individuals. It could be, for example, a small room. Mantraps typically use electronic locks and other methods to control access. For more information, see Chapter 6.

3. **B.** Public-Key Cryptography Standards is a set of voluntary standards for public-key cryptography. This set of standards is coordinated by RSA. For more information, see Chapter 7.

4. **B.** Wired Equivalent Privacy (WEP) is designed to provide security equivalent to that of a wired network. WEP has vulnerabilities and isn't considered highly secure. For additional information, see Chapter 7.

5. **C.** The Process layer interfaces with applications and encapsulates traffic through the Host-to-Host or Transport layer, the Internet layer, and the Network Access layer. For more information, see Chapter 2.

6. **B.** L2TP (Layer 2 Tunneling Protocol) is a tunneling protocol that can be used between LANs. L2TP isn't secure, and you should use IPSec with it to provide data security. For more information, see Chapter 3.

7. **A.** A DMZ (demilitarized zone) is an area in a network that allows restrictive access to untrusted users and isolates the internal network from access by external users and systems. It does so by using routers and firewalls to limit access to sensitive network resources. For more information, see Chapter 1.

8. **C.** A key recovery process must be able to recover a previous key. If the previous key can't be recovered, then all the information for which the key was used will be irrecoverably lost. For more information, see Chapter 7.

9. **D.** A flood attack is designed to overload a protocol or service by repeatedly initiating a request for service. This type of attack usually results in a DoS (denial of service) situation occurring because the protocol freezes or excessive bandwidth is used in the network as a result of the requests. For more information, see Chapter 2.

10. **B.** A sensor collects data from the data source and passes it on to the analyzer. If the analyzer determines that unusual activity has occurred, an alert may be generated. For additional information, see Chapter 4.

11. **A.** *Hardening* is the term used to describe the process of securing a system. This is accomplished in many ways, including disabling unneeded protocols. For additional information on hardening, see Chapter 5.

12. A.   To meet the goal of integrity, you must verify that information being used is accurate and hasn't been tampered with. Integrity is coupled with accountability to ensure that data is accurate and that a final authority exists to verify this, if needed. For more information, see Chapter 1.

13. D.   Online Certificate Status Protocol (OCSP) is the mechanism used to immediately verify whether a certificate is valid. The Certificate Revocation List (CRL) is published on a regular basis, but it isn't current once it's published. For additional information, see Chapter 7.

14. B.   Partitioning is the process of breaking a network into smaller components that can each be individually protected. The concept is the same as building walls in an office building. For additional information, see Chapter 6.

15. A.   IM and other systems allow unsuspecting users to download files that may contain viruses. Due to a weakness in the file extension naming conventions, a file that appears to have one extension may actually have another extension. For example, the file `account.doc.vbs` would appear in many applications as `account.doc`, but it's actually a Visual Basic script and could contain malicious code. For additional information, see Chapter 4.

16. B.   Access control lists (ACLs) are used to allow or deny an IP address access to a network. ACL mechanisms are implemented in many routers, firewalls, and other network devices. For additional information, see Chapter 5.

17. B.   The default port for a web server is port 80. By changing the port to 1019, you force users to specify this port when they are using a browser. This action provides a little additional security for your website. Adding a firewall to block port 80 would secure your website so much that no one would be able to access it. For more information, see Chapter 3.

18. D.   A worm is designed to multiply and propagate. Worms may carry viruses that cause system destruction, but that isn't their primary mission. For more information, see Chapter 2.

19. A.   Social engineering is using human intelligence methods to gain access or information about your organization. For additional information, see Chapter 6.

20. C.   In most environments, FTP sends account and password information unencrypted. This makes these accounts vulnerable to network sniffing. For additional information, see Chapter 5.

21. A.   An intrusion detection system (IDS) provides active monitoring and rule-based responses to unusual activities on a network. A firewall provides passive security by preventing access from unauthorized traffic. If the firewall were compromised, the IDS would notify you based on rules it's designed to implement. For more information, see Chapter 3.

22. B.   The chain of custody ensures that each step taken with evidence is documented and accounted for from the point of collection. Chain of custody is the Who, What, When, Where, and Why of evidence storage. For additional information, see Chapter 8.

23. A.   Steganography is the process of hiding one message in another. Steganography may also be referred to as electronic watermarking. For additional information, see Chapter 7.

24. C.   The use policy is also referred to as the usage policy. It should state acceptable uses of computer and organizational resources by employees. This policy should outline consequences of noncompliance. For additional information, see Chapter 8.

25. B.   The Key Exchange Algorithm (KEA) is used to create a temporary session to exchange key information. This session creates a secret key. When the key has been exchanged, the regular session begins. For more information, see Chapter 7.

26. A.   Elliptic Curve Cryptography (ECC) would probably be your best choice for a PDA. ECC is designed to work with smaller processors. The other systems may be options, but they require more computing power than ECC. For additional information, see Chapter 7.

27. B.   An incremental backup will generally be the fastest of the backup methods because it backs up only the files that have changed since the last incremental or full backup. See Chapter 8 for more information.

28. C.   Biometrics is the authentication process that uses physical characteristics, such as a palm print or retinal pattern, to establish identification. For more information, see Chapter 1.

29. C.   Role-Based Access Control (RBAC) is primarily concerned with providing access to systems that a user needs based on the user's role in the organization. For more information, see Chapter 8.

30. A.   Computer forensics is the process of investigating a computer system to determine the cause of an incident. Part of this process would be gathering evidence. For additional information, see Chapter 8.

Chapter

1

General Security Concepts

THE FOLLOWING COMPTIA SECURITY+ EXAM OBJECTIVES ARE COVERED IN THIS CHAPTER:

✓ **1.6 Explain the purpose and application of virtualization technology.**

✓ **2.2 Distinguish between network design elements and components.**

- DMZ
- VLAN
- NAT
- Network interconnections
- NAC
- Subnetting
- Telephony

✓ **3.7 Deploy various authentication models and identify the components of each.**

- Biometric reader
- Kerberos
- CHAP
- PAP
- Mutual

✓ **3.8 Explain the difference between identification and authentication (identity proofing).**

Security is unlike any other topic in computing. To begin with, the word is so encompassing that it is impossible to know what you mean just by using it. When you talk about security, do you mean physical security of servers and workstations and protecting them from those who might try to steal them or from damage that might occur if the side of the building collapses? Or do you mean the security of data and protecting it from viruses and worms or from hackers and miscreants who have suddenly targeted you and have no other purpose in life than to keep you up at night? Or maybe security to you is the comfort that comes in knowing that you can restore files if a user accidentally deletes them.

The first problem with security is that it is next to impossible for everyone to agree on what it means because it can include all of these items. The next problem with security is that we don't really mean that we want things to be completely secured. If you wanted the customer list file to truly be secure, you would never put it on the server and make it available. It is on the server because you need to access it and so do 30 other people. In this sense, security means that only 30 people can get to it and not anyone outside of the select 30.

The next problem is that while everyone wants security, no one wants to be inconvenienced by it. To use an analogy, few are the travelers who do not feel safer by watching airport personnel frisk and pat down all who head to the terminal—they just don't want it to happen to them. This is true in computing as well; we all want to make sure data is accessed only by those who truly should be working with it, but we don't want to have to enter 12-digit passwords and submit to retinal scans.

As a computer security professional, you have to understand all of these concerns. You have to know that a great deal is expected of you but few users want to be hassled or inconvenienced by the measures you must put in place. You have a primary responsibility to protect and safeguard the information your organization uses. Many times that means educating your users and making certain they understand the "why" behind what is being implemented.

Security is a high-growth area in the computer industry, and it has been for several years now. The need for qualified people is increasing rapidly, as a search of job boards will quickly illustrate. Your pursuit of the Security+ certificate is a good first step in this process. Security+ is not the only security certification on the market, and it is not even the only entry-level certification available to you. It is, however, the only one to truly focus on the topics that most think of when security comes to mind. To pass it, you must have a broad knowledge of all the different types of security mentioned in the first paragraph.

In this chapter, I'll discuss the various aspects of computer security as they relate to your job. I will introduce the basics of computer security and provide several models you can use to understand the risks your organization faces. Not stopping there, I will also present steps you *must* take in order to minimize those risks.

Understanding Information Security

Information security narrows down the definition of *security*. The term *information security* covers a wide array of activities in an organization. It includes not only the products, but also the processes used to prevent unauthorized access to, modification of, and deletion of information. This area also involves protecting resources by preventing them from being disrupted by situations or attacks that may be largely beyond the control of the person responsible for information security.

From the perspective of a computer professional, you're dealing with issues that are much bigger than protecting computer systems from viruses. You're also protecting an organization's most valuable assets from people who are highly motivated to misuse those assets. Fortunately, most of them are outsiders who are trying to break in, but some of these people may already be inside your organization and discontented in their present situation. Not only do you have to keep outsiders out, but you have to be prepared for the accountant who has legitimate access to files and wants to strike out because he did not get as good a performance review as he thought he should.

Needless to say, this job isn't getting any easier. Weaknesses and vulnerabilities in most commercial systems are well known and documented, and more become known each day. Your adversaries can use search engines to find vulnerabilities on virtually any product or operating system. To learn how to exploit the most likely weaknesses that exist in a system, they can buy books on computer hacking, join newsgroups on the Internet, and access websites that offer explicit details. Some are doing it for profit or pleasure, but many are doing it just for the sheer thrill of it. There have been many glamorized characters on television and in movies who break into computer systems and do things they should not. When was the last time you saw a glamorized security administrator on such a show? If you make things look fun and exciting, there is some part of the audience that will attempt it.

Compounding matters, in many situations you'll find yourself constantly dealing with inherent weaknesses in the products you use and depend on. You can't count on the security within an application to be flawless from the moment it is released until the next version comes out three years later. The following sections discuss in detail the aspects you must consider in order to have a reasonable chance of securing your information, networks, and computers. Make sure you understand that I'm always talking about *reasonable*.

One of the first things you must develop as a security administrator is a bit of paranoia. It's important to remember that you're dealing with both system vulnerabilities and human vulnerabilities—although they aren't the same, they both affect the organization significantly. You must assume that you're under attack right now, even as you read this book.

Information security includes a number of topics of primary focus, each addressing different parts of computer security. An effective computer security plan and process must evaluate the risks and create strategies and methods to address them. The following sections focus on three such areas:

- Physical security
- Operational security
- Management and policies

Each of these areas is vital to ensure security in an organization. You can think of information security as a three-legged stool: If any one of the legs of your stool breaks, you'll fall down and hurt yourself. You must look at the overall business and address all the issues that business faces concerning computer security. Figure 1.1 shows how these three components of computer security interact to provide a reasonably secure environment.

FIGURE 1.1   The security triad

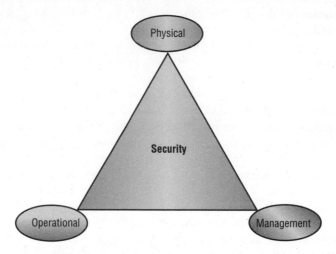

Part of your job is to make recommendations to management about needs and deficiencies; to take action to minimize the risks and exposure of your information and systems; and to establish, enforce, and maintain the security of the systems with which you work. This is not a small task, and you must do each and every one of these tasks well in order to have a reasonable chance of maintaining security in your organization.

Securing the Physical Environment

Physical security, as the name implies, involves protecting your assets and information from physical access by unauthorized persons. In other words, you're trying to protect items that can be seen, touched, and stolen. Threats often present themselves as service technicians, janitors, customers, vendors, or even employees. They can steal your equipment, damage it, or take documents from offices, garbage cans, or filing cabinets. Their motivation may be retribution for some perceived misgiving, a desire to steal your trade secrets to sell to a competitor as an act of vengeance, or just greed. They might steal $1,000 worth of hardware that they can sell to a friend for a fraction of that and have no concept of the value of the data stored on the hardware.

Physical security is relatively easy to accomplish. You can secure facilities by controlling access to the office, shredding unneeded documents, installing security systems, and limiting access to sensitive areas of the business. Most office buildings provide perimeter and corridor security during unoccupied hours, and it isn't difficult to implement commonsense measures during occupied hours as well. Sometimes just having a person present—even if it's a guard who spends most of their time sleeping—can be all the deterrent needed to prevent petty thefts.

Many office complexes also offer roving security patrols, multiple lock access control methods, and electronic or password access. Typically, the facility managers handle these arrangements. They won't generally deal with internal security as it relates to your records, computer systems, and papers; that is your responsibility in most situations.

The first component of physical security involves making a physical location less tempting as a target. If the office or building you're in is open all the time, gaining entry into a business in the building is easy. You must prevent people from seeing your organization as a tempting target. Locking doors and installing surveillance or alarm systems can make a physical location a less desirable target. You can also add controls to elevators, requiring keys or badges in order to reach upper floors. Plenty of wide-open targets are available, involving less risk on the part of the people involved. Try to make your office not worth the trouble.

The second component of physical security involves detecting a *penetration* or theft. You want to know what was broken into, what is missing, and how the loss occurred. Passive videotape systems are one good way to obtain this information. Most retail environments routinely tape key areas of the business to identify how thefts occur and who was involved. These tapes are admissible as evidence in most courts. Law enforcement should be involved as soon as a penetration or theft occurs. More important from a deterrent standpoint, you should make it well known that you'll prosecute anyone caught in the act of theft to the fullest extent of the law. Making the video cameras as conspicuous as possible will deter many would-be criminals.

The third component of physical security involves recovering from a theft or loss of critical information or systems. How will the organization recover from the loss and get on with normal business? If a vandal destroyed your server room with a fire or flood, how long would it take your organization to get back into operation and return to full productivity?

Recovery involves a great deal of planning, thought, and testing. What would happen if the files containing all your bank accounts, purchase orders, and customer information became a pile of ashes in the middle of the smoldering ruins that used to be your office? Ideally, critical copies of records and inventories should be stored off-site in a secure facility.

Examining Operational Security

Operational security focuses on how your organization does that which it does. This includes computers, networks, and communications systems as well as the management of information. Operational security encompasses a large area, and as a security professional, you'll be primarily involved here more than any other area.

Operational security issues include network access control (NAC), authentication, and security topologies after the network installation is complete. Issues include the daily operations of the network, connections to other networks, backup plans, and recovery plans. In short, operational security encompasses everything that isn't related to design or physical security in your network. Instead of focusing on the physical components where the data is stored, such as the server, the focus is now on the topology and connections.

Real World Scenario

Survey Your Physical Environment

As a security administrator, you need to put yourself in the position of an intruder. For this exercise, think of yourself as an outsider who wants to gain access to the company server and damage it. Don't think of trying to steal data but rather of trying to pour water into the server. See if you can answer these questions:

1. How would you gain access to the building? Is a key or code required? Is there any security—a guard, a receptionist, or cameras? Are they highly visible, or does someone have to look to even know they are there?

2. How would you gain access to the floor the server is on? Is the elevator keyed, or can anyone use it? Do the doorways to the stairs only open outward, or can anyone walk up and enter?

3. How would you find the server? Is it sitting in the middle of the office, or is it in a separate room? If the latter, is the door to that room secured? How is it secured—by key, badge, punchpad?

4. After you reach the server, would anyone see what you're doing? Does the server room have glass windows? Is there a camera overlooking the server? Is the server viewable from a distance? Would anyone question why you were there?

5. If you do use cameras for surveillance, where are the tape machines? Are they located near the server so someone can steal the evidence of their crime as well?

If you can easily spot flaws in the security using these questions, then there is a risk that someone could harm your operations.

Finally, try to answer similar questions, but instead of imagining that you're an outsider to the company, use the perspective of someone from accounting who didn't get the promotion they thought they should and now wants to hurt the company. They have already gained access to much of the building—what keeps them from carrying out the crime?

     Some vendors use the acronym NAC to signify network *admission* control rather than the more commonly accepted network *access* control.

The issues you address in an operational capacity can seem overwhelming at first. Many of the areas you'll address are vulnerabilities in the systems you use or weak or inadequate security policies. For example, if you implement a comprehensive password expiration policy, you can require users to change their passwords every 30 or 60 days. If the system doesn't require password rotation, though (it allows the same passwords to be reused), you have a vulnerability that you may not be able to eliminate. A user can go through the motions of changing their password only to reenter the same value and keep it in use.

From an operational perspective, the system described has weak password-protection capabilities. There is nothing you can do, short of installing a higher-security logon process or replacing the operating system. Either solution may not be feasible given the costs, conversion times, and possible unwillingness of an organization—or its partners—to make this switch.

Such dependence on a weak system usually stems from the fact that most companies use software that was developed by third parties in order to save costs or meet compatibility requirements. These packages may require the use of a specific operating system. If that operating system has significant security problems or vulnerabilities, your duties will be mammoth because you'll still be responsible for providing security in that environment. For example, when your secure corporate network is connected to the Internet, it becomes subject to many potential vulnerabilities. You can install hardware and software to improve security, but management may decide these measures cost too much to implement. Again, operationally there may be little you can do.

Much of this book discusses the technologies and tools used to help ensure operational security. Figure 1.2 illustrates the various concerns you face from an operational perspective.

FIGURE 1.2   Operational security issues

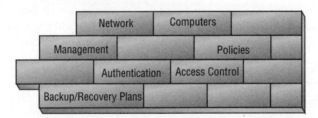

Working with Management and Policies

Management and *policies* provide the guidance, rules, and procedures for implementing a security environment. Policies, to be effective, must have the full and uncompromised support of the organization's management team. Management directions can give security initiatives the teeth they need to be effective. In the absence of support, even the best policies will be doomed to failure.

Information security professionals can recommend policies, but they need the support of management to implement them. There is nothing more ineffective than a self-proclaimed security "czar" who has no support from management. Not only is their tenure often short-lived, but so too is the security of their network.

🌐 Real World Scenario

Survey Your Operational Environment

As a security administrator, you'll need to assess the operational environment of your network by looking for "doors" that an outsider could use to gain access to your data. Securing the network involves far more than simply securing what exists within the four walls of your building. Look for openings that intruders can use to enter your network without walking through the door. Don't think of the safeguards that may currently exist, but rather focus on ways someone not on your network might join it.

See if you can answer these questions:

1. How do users on your network access the Internet? Do any users use dial-up connections within the office? Do they use dial-up access when they take their laptops home with them? Are proxy servers in use? Do you use private or public IP addresses? If you are using private IP addresses, are you using something as simple as Internet Connection Sharing or as complex as Network Address Translation (both perform the same function, but the latter offers more functionality and security)?

2. Are there wireless access points on the network? Can a mobile user with a laptop configure their settings to join the network? What is the range of your access points? Are signals stopped at the perimeter, or can someone sitting in the parking lot access the network?

3. Are dial-in connections allowed? Can users call in from home? Can they call in from hotel rooms? Do you verify the number they are calling from or merely allow anyone in with a correct username/password combination?

4. Do you use Terminal Services? Are thin clients employed/allowed? Are entire sessions on the server run remotely? Is remote administration enabled?

5. Do your users have shares on their laptops that would potentially compromise the laptop's data security?

6. What ports are open on your routers and firewalls (or on a user's personal firewall solution)?

The issues that must be decided at the management and policy level affect the entire company and can greatly impact productivity, morale, and corporate culture. Policies also establish expectations about security-related issues. Security policies should be treated no differently than an organization's vacation, sick leave, or termination policies. Most people can tell you exactly how many days of vacation they get per year; however, many can't tell you what the company's information usage or security policies are. This can be solved by posting such information on an intranet or including it in a manual issued to all employees (with a note in each employee's personnel file indicating that they've received the manual).

A number of key policies are needed to secure a network. The following list identifies some broad areas that require thought and planning:

- Administrative policies
- Disaster recovery plans
- Information policies
- Security policies
- Software design requirements
- Usage policies
- User management policies

Administrative Policies

Administrative policies lay out guidelines and expectations for upgrades, monitoring, back-ups, and audits. System administrators and maintenance staff use these policies to conduct business. The policies should clearly outline how often and when upgrades appear, when and how monitoring occurs, and how logs are reviewed. They should also identify—not by name, but by title—who is responsible for making decisions on these matters and how often decisions should be reviewed. Ideally, the policies should also include information about who wrote them, who signed off on them, and at what date they were mandated.

The policies must be specific enough to help the administrative staff keep focused on the business of running the systems and networks. At the same time, they must be flexible enough to allow for emergencies and unforeseen circumstances. This trade-off is common to most policies, and you always want to be careful to avoid leaving a gap too wide, making the policy virtually ineffective or unenforceable.

Disaster Recovery Plans

Disaster recovery plans (DRPs) are one of the biggest headaches that IT professionals face. The DRP is expensive to develop and to test, and it must be kept current.

Many large companies invest huge amounts of money in DRPs, including backup or hot sites. A *hot site* is a facility designed to provide immediate availability in the event of a system or network failure. These sites are expensive to maintain and sometimes hard to justify. The likelihood that an organization will need a hot site is relatively small, and the site may seem unimportant—right up to the point when you don't have one and you need it.

A good DRP takes into consideration virtually every type of occurrence or failure possible. It may be as simple as a single system failing or as complicated as a large multinational company needing to recover from a cataclysmic event. The key to its success is its completeness. For example, if a company is located in the Midwest region of the United States, plans should be in place to address tornadoes, floods, fires, and every conceivable disaster.

Information Policies

Information policies refer to the various aspects of information security, including access, classifications, marking and storage, and the transmission and destruction of sensitive information. If your company records audio communications, that should be addressed as well.

The development of information policies is critical to security. It is not uncommon for such a policy to include a data classification matrix that defines various classification levels. The levels are usually similar to the following examples:

Public   For all advertisements and information posted on the Web

Internal   For all intranet-type information

Private   Personnel records, client data, and so on

Confidential   Public Key Infrastructure (PKI) information and other items restricted to all but those who must know them

 The terms used for data classification might differ with different organizations—many used *top secret*, *secret*, and *sensitive*, for example—but the most important concept for the organization is that a matrix of levels exist.

As with all other policies, the key is to be as comprehensive as possible. Little should be left to chance or conjecture when you're writing information policies.

Security Policies

Security policies define the configuration of systems and networks, including the installation of software, hardware, and network connections. Security policies also define computer room and data center security as well as how identification and authentication (I&A) occurs. These policies determine how access control, audits, reports, and network connectivity are handled. Encryption and antivirus software are usually covered. Security policies also establish procedures and methods used for password selection, account expiration, failed logon attempts, and related areas.

 Although each security policy is intended for a specific purpose, there may be scope overlap in many of the different policies. It is not uncommon as well to have overlap between information policies and security policies.

Software Design Requirements

Software design requirements outline what the capabilities of the system must be. These requirements are typically part of the initial design and greatly affect the solutions you can use. Many vendors will respond to every bid and assure you that they're secure. You can use the requirements to have vendors explain proposed solutions. A software design policy should be specific about security requirements. If your design doesn't include security as an integral part of the implementation, you can bet that your network has vulnerabilities.

Design requirements should be viewed as a moving target. The requirements that exist today shouldn't be the same in two years when the network environment has been significantly modified.

Usage Policies

Usage policies cover how information and resources are used. You need to explain to users how they can use organizational resources and for what purposes. These policies lay down the law about computer usage. Usage policies include statements about privacy, ownership, and the consequences of improper acts. Your usage policies should clearly explain usage expectations about the Internet, remote access, and e-mail.

They should also address how users should handle incidents—whom they should contact if they suspect something is awry. The policy should spell out the fact that monitoring can take place and that users agree to it. Consequences for account misuse, whether termination or something less severe, should also be stated.

User Management Policies

User management policies identify the various actions that must occur in the normal course of employee activities. These policies must address how new employees are added to the system as well as training, orientation, and equipment installation and configuration.

Employee transfers are a normal occurrence within a company. If an employee transfers to a new job, the privileges and access they had in the old position may be inappropriate for the new position. Establishing new access rights allows the employee to continue working. If you forget to revoke the old privileges, this user may have access to more information than they need. Over time, this can result in a situation called *privilege creep*. The user may acquire administrative privileges to the system by accident.

Terminated employees pose a threat to information security. In some cases, a terminated employee may seek to gain access to customer lists, bank accounts, or other sensitive information. When employees leave the company, it's imperative that their accounts be either disabled or deleted and that their access be turned off. You'd be amazed how often system administrators don't know about personnel changes. Your user management policies should clearly outline who notifies the IT department about employee terminations as well as when and how the notification occurs.

 Real World Scenario

Assemble and Examine Your Procedures

It's surprising how many businesses think they have a policy in place when one can't be produced when needed. See if you can answer these questions:

1. Does your company have administrative policies in place? What are they, and where can they be found? Are they easily accessed by, or provided to, new employees? Does each written policy offer some indication of who to contact if there is a question or a breach?

2. When were the software design requirements last checked and/or updated? Are they routinely given to vendors? Who is responsible for reviewing them?

3. When was the last time the disaster recovery plan was checked? Do all administrators know it? Is it in writing and accessible from a remote location should this site become inaccessible?

4. Are informational policies easy to locate? By whom?

5. Are security policies updated frequently? Are they updated with each software change? Do they incorporate the latest patches?

6. Are usage policies part of the employee handbook? Do users sign off that they have seen the policies and are aware of them? How do users receive updates to the policies and signal that they have them and understand them? How do they know when those updates exist?

7. Can the user management policies be located and adhered to in the event that a situation occurs while the chief administrator is at a conference? Is there an escalation procedure in writing indicating who should be notified and when?

Policies not only need to exist, they also must be readily available so they can be referenced by all relevant parties. If this can't be said of the policies we've discussed, then their value is drastically diminished.

Understanding the Goals of Information Security

Like so many things, the goals of information security are straightforward. They create the framework that is used for developing and maintaining a security plan. They're remarkably easy to express but extremely hard to carry out. These goals are as follows:

Prevention   *Prevention* refers to preventing computer or information violations from occurring; it is much easier to deal with violations before they occur than after. Security breaches are also referred to as *incidents*. When an incident occurs, it may be the result of a breakdown in security procedures.

Incidents come in all shapes and sizes. Simple incidents include things such as losing a password or leaving a terminal logged on overnight. They can also be quite complex and result in the involvement of local or federal law enforcement personnel. If a group of hackers were to attack and deface your website, you would consider this a major incident. Ideally, your security procedures and policies would make you invulnerable to an attack; unfortunately, this isn't usually the case. The better your prevention policies, however, the lower the likelihood of a successful attack occurring.

Detection   *Detection* refers to identifying events when they occur. Detection is difficult in many situations; an attack on your system may occur over a long period before it's successful. Incident detection involves identifying the assets under attack, how the incident occurred, and who carried it out (or is still doing so). The detection process may involve a variety of complicated tools or a simple examination of the system log files. Detection activities should be ongoing and part of your information security policies and procedures.

Response   *Response* refers to developing strategies and techniques to deal with an attack or loss. Developing an appropriate response to an incident involves several factors. If the incident was a probe, the attacker may have done no actual harm but may be gathering intelligence about your network or systems. These types of attacks may be random or targeted, and they usually cause little damage. Occasionally, an attack will be successful. When that happens, it is helpful to have a well-thought-out and tested plan you can use to respond, restore operation, and neutralize the threat. It's always better to have a set of procedures and methods in place to recover from an incident than to try to create those processes on-the-fly.

These goals are an important part of setting benchmarks for an organization. You can't allow these policies or goals to become insignificant. If you do, you and your organization are setting yourselves up for a surprise. Unfortunately, the surprise won't be pleasant, and it may be very costly to deal with.

Comprehending the Security Process

It helps to think of security as a combination of three Ps: *processes*, *procedures*, and *policies*. The security of information involves both human and technical factors. The human factors are addressed by the policies that are enforced in the organization as well as the processes and procedures your organization has in place. The technology components include the tools you install on the systems you work with. There are several parts to this process, and each is described in the following sections.

Appreciating Antivirus Software

Computer *viruses*—applications that carry out malicious actions—are among the most annoying trends happening today. It seems that almost every day someone invents a new virus. Some of these viruses do nothing more than give you a big "gotcha." Others contaminate networks and wreak havoc on computer systems. A virus may act on your data or your operating system, but it's intent on doing harm—and doing so without your consent. Viruses often include replication as a primary objective and try to infect as many machines as they can, as quickly as possible.

The business of providing software to computer users to protect them from viruses has become a huge industry. Several very good and well-established suppliers of antivirus software exist, and new virus-protection methods come on the scene almost as fast as new viruses. Antivirus software scans a computer's memory, disk files, and incoming and outgoing e-mail. The software typically uses a virus definition file that is updated regularly by the manufacturer. If these files are kept up-to-date, the computer system will be relatively secure. Unfortunately, most people don't keep their virus definition files up-to-date. Users will exclaim that a new virus has come out, because they just got it. Upon examination, you'll often discover that their virus definition file is months out-of-date. As you can see, the software part of the system will break down if the definition files aren't updated on a regular basis.

Implementing Access Control

The process of implementing *access control* is critical. Access control defines how users and systems communicate and in what manner. In other words, it limits—or controls—access to system resources, including data, and thus protects information from unauthorized access. Three basic models are used to explain access control.

The Mandatory Access Control Method

The *Mandatory Access Control (MAC)* model is a static model that uses a predefined set of access privileges for files on the system. The system administrators establish these parameters and associate them with an account, files, or resources.

The MAC model can be very restrictive. In a MAC model, administrators establish access. Users can't share resources dynamically unless the static relationship already exists.

The acronym MAC appears in numerous computer-related contexts. One of the most common uses is to represent the Media Access layer in networking. Be careful not to confuse MAC addressing as it relates to network cards with Mandatory Access Control.

MAC uses *labels* to identify the level of sensitivity that applies to objects. When a user attempts to access an object, the label is examined to see if the access should take place or be denied. One key element to remember is that when mandatory control is applied, labels are required and must exist for every object.

The Discretionary Access Control Method

The *Discretionary Access Control (DAC)* model allows the owner of a resource to establish privileges to the information they own. The difference between DAC and MAC is that labels are not mandatory but can be applied as needed.

The DAC model allows a user to share a file or use a file that someone else has shared. It establishes an access control list (ACL) that identifies the users who have authorization to access that information. This allows the owner to grant or revoke access to individuals or groups of individuals based on the situation. This model is dynamic in nature and allows information to be shared easily between users.

The Role-Based Access Control Method

The *Role-Based Access Control (RBAC)* model allows a user to act in a certain predetermined manner based on the role the user holds in the organization. The roles almost always shadow the organizational structure.

Users can be assigned roles systemwide and can then perform certain functions or duties based on the roles they're assigned. An example might be a role called *salesperson*. The user assigned the salesperson role can access only the information established for that role. Users may be able to access this information from any station in the network, based strictly on their role. A sales manager may have a different role that allows access to all of the individual salespersons' information.

The RBAC model is common in network administrative roles.

Understanding Authentication

Authentication proves that a user or system is actually who they say they are. This is one of the most critical parts of a security system. It's part of a process that is also referred to as *identification and authentication (I&A)*. The identification process starts when a user ID or logon name is typed into a sign-on screen. Authentication is accomplished by challenging the claim about who is accessing the resource. Without authentication, anybody can claim to be anybody.

Authentication systems or methods are based on one or more of these three factors:

- Something you know, such as a password or PIN
- Something you have, such as a smart card or an identification device
- Something physically unique to you, such as your fingerprints or retinal pattern

Systems authenticate each other using similar methods. Frequently, systems pass private information between each other to establish identity. Once authentication has occurred, the two systems can communicate in the manner specified in the design.

Several common methods are used for authentication. Each offers something to security and should be considered when you're evaluating authentication schemes or methods.

Biometrics

Biometric readers use physical characteristics to identify the user. Such devices are becoming more common in the business environment. Biometric readers include hand scanners, retinal scanners, and soon, possibly, DNA scanners. To gain access to resources, you must pass a physical screening process. In the case of a hand scanner, the screening may include fingerprints, scars, and markings on your hand. Retinal scanners compare your eye's retinal pattern to a stored retinal pattern to verify your identity. DNA scanners will examine a unique portion of your DNA structure to verify that you are who you say you are.

Certificates

Certificates are another common form of authentication. A server or *certificate authority (CA)* can issue a certificate that will be accepted by the challenging system. Certificates can be either physical access devices, such as smart cards, or electronic certificates that are used as part of the logon process. A *Certificate Practice Statement (CPS)* outlines the rules used for issuing and managing certificates. A *Certificate Revocation List (CRL)* lists the revocations that must be addressed (often due to expiration) in order to stay current.

This chapter provides only an overview of certificates. Certificates, along with Public Key Infrastructure (PKI) and related topics, are discussed in detail in Chapter 7, "Cryptography Basics, Methods, and Standards."

A simple way to think of certificates is to think of hall passes at school. Figure 1.3 illustrates a certificate being handed from the server to the client after authentication has been established. If you have a hall pass, you can wander the halls of your school. If your pass is invalid, the hallway monitor can send you to the principal's office. Similarly, if you have a certificate, then you can prove to the system that you are who you say you are and are authenticated to work with the resources.

FIGURE 1.3   A certificate being issued after identification has been verified

Challenge Handshake Authentication Protocol

Challenge Handshake Authentication Protocol (CHAP) challenges a system to verify identity. CHAP doesn't use a user ID/password mechanism. Instead, the initiator sends a logon request from the client to the server. The server sends a challenge back to the client. The challenge is encrypted and then sent back to the server. The server compares the value from the client and, if the information matches, grants authorization. If the response fails, the session fails, and the request phase starts over. Figure 1.4 illustrates the CHAP procedure. This handshake method involves a number of steps and is usually automatic between systems.

FIGURE 1.4   CHAP authentication

Kerberos

Kerberos is an authentication protocol named after the mythical three-headed dog that stood at the gates of Hades. Originally designed by MIT, Kerberos is becoming very popular as an authentication method. It allows for a single sign-on to a distributed network.

Kerberos authentication uses a *Key Distribution Center (KDC)* to orchestrate the process. The KDC authenticates the *principle* (which can be a user, a program, or a system) and provides it with a ticket. After this ticket is issued, it can be used to authenticate against other principles. This occurs automatically when a request or service is performed by another principle.

Kerberos is quickly becoming a common standard in network environments. Its only significant weakness is that the KDC can be a single point of failure. If the KDC goes down, the authentication process will stop. Figure 1.5 shows the Kerberos authentication process and the ticket being presented to systems that are authorized by the KDC.

Multi-Factor Authentication

When two or more access methods are included as part of the authentication process, you're implementing a *multi-factor* system. A system that uses smart cards and passwords is referred to as a *two-factor authentication* system. Two-factor authentication is shown in Figure 1.6. This example requires both a smart card and a logon password process.

FIGURE 1.5 Kerberos authentication process

1. User requests access to service running on a different server.
2. KDC authenticates user and sends a ticket to be used between the user and the service on the server.
3. User's workstation sends a ticket to the service.

FIGURE 1.6 Two-factor authentication

Both factors must be valid:
•User ID and Password
•Smart Card

Mutual Authentication

Whenever two or more parties authenticate each other, this is known as *mutual authentication*. A client may authenticate to a server, and a server authenticate to a client when there is a need to establish a secure session between the two and employ encryption. Mutual authentication ensures that the client is not unwittingly connecting and giving its credentials to a rogue server; which can then turn around and steal the data from the real server.

Commonly, mutual authentication will be implemented when the data to be sent during the session is of a critical nature—such as financial or medical records.

Password Authentication Protocol

Password Authentication Protocol (PAP) offers no true security, but it's one of the simplest forms of authentication. The username and password values are both sent to the server as clear text and checked for a match. If they match, the user is granted access; if they don't match, the user is denied access. In most modern implementations, PAP is shunned in favor of other, more secure authentication methods.

Security Tokens

Security tokens are similar to certificates. They contain the rights and access privileges of the token bearer as part of the token. Think of a token as a small piece of data that holds a sliver of information about the user.

Many operating systems generate a token that is applied to every action taken on the computer system. If your token doesn't grant you access to certain information, then either that information won't be displayed or your access will be denied. The authentication system creates a token every time a user connects or a session begins. At the completion of a session, the token is destroyed. Figure 1.7 shows the security token process.

FIGURE 1.7   Security token authentication

Smart Cards

A *smart card* is a type of badge or card that gives you access to resources, including buildings, parking lots, and computers. It contains information about your identity and access privileges. Each area or computer has a card scanner or a reader in which you insert your card. Smart Cards often also require the use of a small password called a PIN (personal identification number); which further secures the smart card if lost by the true card holder, so that it cannot be used by someone else to gain access to data and resources.

Figure 1.8 depicts a user inserting a smart card into a reader to verify identity. The reader is connected to the workstation and validates against the security system. This increases the security of the authentication process because you must be in physical possession of the smart card to use the resources. Of course, if the card is lost or stolen, the person who finds the card can access the resources allowed by the smart card.

FIGURE 1.8   The smart card authentication process

Username/Password

A *username* and *password* are unique identifiers for a logon process. When users sit down in front of a computer system, the first thing a security system requires is that they establish who they are. Identification is typically confirmed through a logon process. Most operating systems use a user ID and password to accomplish this. These values can be sent across the connection as plain text or can be encrypted.

The logon process identifies to the operating system, and possibly the network, that you are who you say you are. Figure 1.9 illustrates this logon and password process. Notice that the operating system compares this information to the stored information from the security processor and either accepts or denies the logon attempt. The operating system might establish privileges or permissions based on stored data about that particular ID.

FIGURE 1.9   A logon process occurring on a workstation

Logon or Security Server

Authentication Issues to Consider

You can set up many different parameters and standards to force the people in your organization to conform. In establishing these parameters, it's important that you consider the capabilities of the people who will be working with these policies. If you're working in an environment where people aren't computer savvy, you may spend a lot of time helping them remember and recover passwords. Many organizations have had to reevaluate their security guidelines after they've already invested great time and expense to implement high-security systems.

Setting authentication security, especially in supporting users, can become a high-maintenance activity for network administrators. On one hand, you want people to be able to authenticate themselves easily; on the other hand, you want to establish security that protects your company's resources.

Be wary of popular names or current trends that make certain passwords predictable. For example, during the first release of *Star Wars*, two of the most popular passwords used on college campuses were C3PO and R2D2. This created a security problem for campus computer centers.

Whenever an issue arises between identification and authentication, *identify proofing* is often called upon. As mentioned earlier in this chapter, the identification process starts when a user ID or logon name is typed into a sign-on screen. Authentication is accomplished by challenging the claim about who is accessing the resource.

Identification proofing is invoked when a person claims they are the user, but cannot be authenticated—such as when they lose their password. Since they can't provide the password, they are typically asked to provide another value—such as mother's maiden name—to prove their identity.

Real World Scenario

Multi-Factor Authentication and Security

The owner of your company is becoming increasingly concerned about computer security and the laxness of users. She reports that users are regularly leaving the office at the end of the day without signing out of their accounts. The company is attempting to win a contract that involves working with the government and that will require additional security measures. What would you suggest to the owner?

The best suggestion is to consider implementing a multi-factor authentication system. This system could consist of a smart card and a logon/password process. Most smart card readers can be configured to require that the card remain inserted in the reader while the user is logged on. If the smart card is removed, say at the end of the day, the workstation will automatically log the user out. By requiring a logon/password process, you can still provide security if the smart card is stolen.

This solution provides reasonable security, and it doesn't significantly increase security costs. The government will probably require additional access control, such as perimeter alarms and physical access control to sensitive areas. However, these measures won't force users to log out when they leave their workstations.

An inherent problem with many identify proofing implementations is that they ask questions which someone other than the user could easily guess or learn the value of (what color are your eyes). To increase the difficulty of someone fraudulently proofing, you should only use questions that are more difficult to guess, or implement biometrics such as voice identification. Under no circumstance should the person proofing be allowed access immediately—instead their access information should be sent to their email account of record.

Distinguishing between Security Topologies

The *security topology* of your network defines the network design and implementation from a security perspective. Unlike a network topology, here we're concerned with access methods, security, and technologies used. Security topology covers four primary areas of concern:

- Design goals
- Security zones
- Technologies
- Business requirements

Setting Design Goals

When setting design goals for a security topology, you must deal with issues of confidentiality, integrity, availability, and accountability, all four of which are discussed continually throughout this book as they apply to various topics. Addressing these four issues as an initial part of your network design will help you ensure tighter security. You'll often see confidentiality, integrity, and availability referred to as the *CIA* of network security, but the accountability component is equally important—design goals must identify who is responsible for the various aspects of computer security. The next few sections introduce these four security components.

Confidentiality

Meeting the goal of *confidentiality* is to prevent or minimize unauthorized access to and disclosure of data and information. In many instances, laws and regulations require specific information confidentiality. For example, Social Security records, payroll and employee records, medical records, and corporate information are high-value assets. This information could create liability issues or embarrassment if it fell into the wrong hands. Over the last few years, there have been a number of cases in which bank account and credit card numbers were published on the Internet. The costs of these types of breaches of confidentiality far exceed the actual losses from the misuse of this information.

Confidentiality entails ensuring that data expected to remain private is seen only by those who should see it. Confidentiality is implemented through authentication and access controls.

If you address confidentiality issues early in the design phase, the steps that must be taken to minimize this exposure will become clear.

Integrity

Meeting the goal of *integrity* involves making sure that the data being worked with is the correct data. Information integrity is critical to a secure topology. Organizations work with and make decisions using the data they have available. If this information isn't accurate or is tampered with by an unauthorized person, the consequences can be devastating.

Take the case of a school district that lost all the payroll and employment records for the employees in the district. When the problem was discovered, the school district had no choice but to send out applications and forms to all the employees, asking them how long they had worked in the school district and how much they were paid. Integrity was jeopardized because the data was vulnerable and then lost.

You can think of integrity as the level of confidence you have that the data is what it's supposed to be—untampered with and unchanged. *Authentic, complete,* and *trustworthy* are often used to describe integrity in terms of data.

Availability

To meet the goal of *availability*, you must protect data and prevent its loss. Data that can't be accessed is of little value. If a mishap or attack brings down a key server or database, that information won't be available to the people who need it. This can cause havoc in an organization. Your job is to provide maximum availability to your users while ensuring integrity and confidentiality. The hardest part of this process is determining the balance you must maintain between these three aspects to provide acceptable security for the organization's information and resources.

 Real World Scenario

Compute Availability

Availability is often expressed in terms of *uptime*. High availability strives for 99.9999% uptime over the course of the year (24 hours a day, 7 days a week, 365 days a year). For this exercise, compute how long data wouldn't be available over the course of the year with the following availability percentages. For example, with 98% uptime, there is a 2% downtime of 525,600 minutes in a year. That means the data would be down for 10,512 minutes, or 7⅓ days! Try your math on the following:

1. 99%

2. 99.9%

3. 99.99%

4. 99.999%

5. 99.9999%

The increments may seem small, but over the course of a year, they represent a significant difference in the amount of time data is and isn't available. Answers: (1.) 5,256 minutes, which is over 87 hours and 3.5 days; (2.) 525 minutes, or a little less than 9 hours; (3.) 52.56 minutes; (4.) 5.25 minutes; (5.) About half a minute.

 The key to availability is that the data must be available when it's needed and accessible by those who need it.

Accountability

The final and often overlooked goal of design concerns *accountability*. Many of the resources used by an organization are shared between departments and individuals. If an error or incident occurs, who is responsible for fixing it? Who determines whether information is correct?

It's a good idea to be clear about who owns the data or is responsible for making sure that it's accurate. You should also be able to track and monitor data changes to detect and repair the data in the event of loss or damage. Most systems will track and store logs on system activities and data manipulation, and they will also provide reports on problems.

 Real World Scenario

Accountability Is More than a Catchphrase

Accountability, like common sense, applies to every aspect of information technology. Several years ago, a company that relied on data that could never be re-created wrote shell scripts to do backups early in the morning when the hosts were less busy. Operators at those machines were told to insert a tape in the drive around midnight and check back at 3:00 a.m. to make certain that a piece of paper had been printed on the printer, signaling the end of the job. If the paper was there, they were to remove the tapes and put them in storage; if the paper was not there, they were to call for support.

The inevitable hard drive crash occurred on one of the hosts one morning, and an IT "specialist" was dispatched to swap it out. The technician changed the hard drive and then asked for the most recent backup tape. To his dismay, the data on the tape was two years old. The machine crash occurred before the backup operation ran, he reasoned, but the odds of rotating two years' worth of tapes was pretty amazing. Undaunted, he asked for the tape from the day before, and found that the data on it was also two years old.

Beginning to sweat, he found the late shift operator for that host and asked her if she was making backups. She assured him that she was and that she was rotating the tapes and putting them away as soon as the paper printed out. Questioning her further on how the data could be so old, she said she could verify her story because she also kept the pieces of paper that appeared on the printer each day. She brought out the stack and handed them to him. They all reported the same thing—*tape in drive is write protected*.

Where did the accountability lie in this true story? The operator was faithfully following the procedures given to her. She thought the fact that the tape was protected represented a good thing. It turned out that all the hosts had been printing the same message, and none of them had been backed up for a long while.

The problem lay not with the operator, but with the training she was given. Had she been shown what correct and incorrect backup completion reports looked like, the data would never have been lost.

Creating Security Zones

Over time, networks can become complex beasts. What may have started as a handful of computers sharing resources can quickly grow to something resembling an electrician's nightmare. The networks may even appear to have lives of their own. It's common for a network to have connections among departments, companies, countries, and public access using private communication paths and through the Internet.

Not everyone in a network needs access to all the assets in the network. The term *security zone* describes design methods that isolate systems from other systems or networks. You can isolate networks from each other using hardware and software. A router is a good example of a hardware solution: You can configure some machines on the network to be in a certain address range and others to be in a different address range. This separation makes the two networks invisible to each other unless a router connects them. Some of the newer data switches also allow you to partition networks into smaller networks or private zones.

When discussing security zones in a network, it's helpful to think of them as rooms. You may have some rooms in your house or office that anyone can enter. For other rooms, access is limited to specific individuals for specific purposes. Establishing security zones is a similar process in a network: Security zones allow you to isolate systems from unauthorized users. Here are the four most common security zones you'll encounter:

- Internet
- Intranet
- Extranet
- Demilitarized zone (DMZ)

The next few sections identify the topologies used to create security zones to provide security. The Internet has become a boon to individuals and to businesses, but it creates a challenge for security. By implementing intranets, extranets, and DMZs, you can create a reasonably secure environment for your organization.

The Internet

The *Internet* is a global network that connects computers and individual networks together. It can be used by anybody who has access to an Internet portal or an Internet service provider (ISP). In this environment, you should have a low level of trust in the people who use the Internet. You must always assume that the people visiting your website may have bad intentions; they may want to buy your product, hire your firm, or bring your servers to a screaming halt. Externally, you have no way of knowing until you monitor their actions. Because the Internet involves such a high level of anonymity, you must always safeguard your data with the utmost precautions.

Figure 1.10 illustrates an Internet network and its connections.

Sometimes the data leaving a network can be as much a sign of trouble as the data entering it. Examining data leaving the network for signs of malicious traffic is a fairly new field of computer security and is known as *extrusion*.

FIGURE 1.10   A typical LAN connection to the Internet

Intranets

Intranets are private networks implemented and maintained by an individual company or organization. You can think of an intranet as an Internet that doesn't leave your company; it's internal to the company, and access is limited to systems within the intranet. Intranets use the same technologies used by the Internet. They can be connected to the Internet but can't be accessed by users who aren't authorized to be part of them; the anonymous user of the Internet is instead an authorized user of the intranet. Access to the intranet is granted to trusted users inside the corporate network or to users in remote locations.

Figure 1.11 displays an intranet network.

FIGURE 1.11   An intranet network

Extranets

Extranets extend intranets to include outside connections to partners. The partners can be vendors, suppliers, or similar parties who need access to your data for legitimate reasons. An extranet allows you to connect to a partner via a private network or a connection using a secure communications channel across the Internet. Extranet connections involve connections between trustworthy organizations.

An extranet is illustrated in Figure 1.12. Note that this network provides a connection between the two organizations. The connection may be through the Internet; if so, these networks would use a tunneling protocol to accomplish a secure connection.

FIGURE 1.12   A typical extranet between two organizations

Demilitarized Zone (DMZ)

A *demilitarized zone (DMZ)* is an area where you can place a public server for access by people you might not trust otherwise. By isolating a server in a DMZ, you can hide or remove access to other areas of your network. You can still access the server using your network, but others aren't able to access further network resources. This can be accomplished using firewalls to isolate your network.

When establishing a DMZ, you assume that the person accessing the resource isn't necessarily someone you would trust with other information. Figure 1.13 shows a server placed in a DMZ. Notice that the rest of the network isn't visible to external users. This lowers the threat of intrusion in the internal network.

 Anytime you want to separate public information from private information, a DMZ is an acceptable option.

The easiest way to create a DMZ is to use a firewall that can transmit in three directions: to the internal network, to the external world (Internet), and to the public information you're sharing (the DMZ). From there, you can decide what traffic goes where; for example, HTTP traffic would be sent to the DMZ, and e-mail would go to the internal network.

FIGURE 1.13   A typical DMZ

Designing Security Zones

Security zone design is an important aspect of computer security. You can use many different approaches to accomplish a good solid design. Some of the design trade-offs involve risk and money. You can create layers of security to protect systems from less-secure connections, and you can use Network Address Translation (NAT) (discussed later) to hide resources. New methods and tools to design secure networks are being introduced on a regular basis. It's important to remember that after you have a good security design, you should revisit it on a regular basis based on what you learn about your security risks.

Working with Newer Technologies

One of the nice things about technology is that it's always changing. One of the bad things about technology is that it's always changing. Several relatively new technologies have become available to help you create a less-vulnerable system. The four technologies this section will focus on are virtualization, virtual local area networks (VLANs), Network Address Translation, and tunneling. These technologies allow you to improve security in your network at little additional cost.

Virtualization Technology

Virtualization is easily the technology du jour, with VMWare, one of the largest vendors of such technology, counting 100% of the Fortune 100 as part of their customer base. In addition to proprietary solutions, there are also open source solutions as well, with Xen being the most well-known example.

Virtualization technology allows you to take any single physical device and hide its characteristics from users—in essence allowing you to run multiple items on one device and make them appear as if they are standalone entities. For example, workstations can only run one operating system at a time. Using virtualization, it is possible for a workstation running Windows XP to also be running Fedora, Red Hat, Windows Server 2003, and any number of other operating systems within virtual windows. The developer working on code can move between windows, cutting and pasting if they choose, and do all they need to do on one machine without needing to run four different workstations. Thanks to virtualization, the workstation can run multiple operating systems, multiple versions of the same operating system, multiple applications, and so on.

Just as a workstation can be virtualized, so, too, can a server. A single server can host multiple logical machines. By using one server to do the function of many, cost savings can be immediately gained in terms of hardware, utility, infrastructure, and so on.

As wonderful as virtualization is, from a security standpoint, it can present challenges. A user accessing the system could have access to everything on the system (not just within their logical machine) if they could override the physical layer protection. As of this writing, the threat of that occurring has been far more rumored than performed, but with virtualization growing in popularity, it is a safe bet that virtual machines will become a popular target of miscreants in coming years.

Virtual Local Area Networks

A *virtual local area network (VLAN)* allows you to create groups of users and systems and segment them on the network. This segmentation lets you hide segments of the network from other segments and thereby control access. You can also set up VLANs to control the paths that data takes to get from one point to another. A VLAN is a good way to contain network traffic to a certain area in a network.

Think of a VLAN as a network of hosts that act as if they're connected by a physical wire even though there is no such wire between them.

On a LAN, hosts can communicate with each other through broadcasts, and no forwarding devices, such as routers, are needed. As the LAN grows, so too does the number of broadcasts. Shrinking the size of the LAN by segmenting it into smaller groups (VLANs) reduces the size of the broadcast domains. The advantages of doing this include reducing the scope of the broadcasts, improving performance and manageability, and decreasing dependence on the physical topology. From the standpoint of this exam, however, the key benefit is that VLANs can increase security by allowing users with similar data sensitivity levels to be segmented together.

Figure 1.14 illustrates the creation of three VLANs in a single network.

Network Address Translation

Network Address Translation (NAT) creates a unique opportunity to assist in the security of a network. Originally, NAT extended the number of usable Internet addresses. Now it allows an organization to present a single address to the Internet for all computer connections. The NAT server provides IP addresses to the hosts or systems in the network and tracks inbound and outbound traffic.

A company that uses NAT presents a single connection to the network. This connection may be through a router or a NAT server. The only information that an intruder will be able to get is that the connection has a single address.

NAT effectively hides your network from the world, making it much harder to determine what systems exist on the other side of the router. The NAT server effectively operates as a firewall for the network. Most new routers support NAT; it provides a simple, inexpensive firewall for small networks.

FIGURE 1.14 A typical segmented VLAN

It's important to understand that NAT acts as a proxy between the local area network (which can be using private IP addresses) and the Internet. Not only can NAT save IP addresses, but it can also act as a firewall.

Most NAT implementations assign internal hosts private IP address numbers and use public addresses only for the NAT to translate to and communicate with the outside world. The private address ranges are as follows:

10.0.0.0–10.255.255.255

172.16.0.0–172.31.255.255

192.168.0.0–192.168.255.255

Figure 1.15 shows a router providing NAT services to a network. The router presents a single address for all external connections on the Internet.

FIGURE 1.15 A typical Internet connection to a local network

 In addition to NAT, Port Address Translation (PAT) is possible. Whereas NAT can use multiple public IP addresses, PAT uses a single one and shares the port with the network. Because it is only using a single port, PAT is much more limited and typically only used on small and home-based networks. Microsoft's Internet Connection Sharing is an example of a PAT implementation.

 IP addressing is a subject on the Network+ exam, as opposed to Security+, but CompTIA still expects you to know the basics. In addition to understanding the concept behind NAT, you should know that subnetting is how networks are divided. RFCs 1466 and 1918 detail subnetting and can be found at http://www.faqs.org/rfcs/.

Tunneling

Tunneling refers to creating a virtual dedicated connection between two systems or networks. You create the tunnel between the two ends by encapsulating the data in a mutually agreed-upon protocol for transmission. In most tunnels, the data passed through the tunnel appears at the other side as part of the network.

Tunneling protocols usually include data security as well as encryption. Several popular standards have emerged for tunneling, with the most popular being the Layer 2 Tunneling Protocol (L2TP).

Tunneling sends private data across a public network by placing (encapsulating) that data into other packets. Most tunnels are virtual private networks (VPNs).

Figure 1.16 shows a connection being made between two networks across the Internet. To each end of the network, this appears to be a single connection.

FIGURE 1.16   A typical tunnel

Internet

Single Private Path or Tunnel
through the Internet

Addressing Business Concerns

An organization or business is well served if it makes a conscious examination of its security situation. This examination includes identifying assets, doing a comprehensive risk assessment, identifying threats, and evaluating vulnerabilities. These four components will help the business principals understand what they're up against and how to cost-effectively address these issues.

The following sections explain the various business requirements you need to address when designing a security topology. The failure to consider any one of these aspects can cause the entire design to be flawed and ineffective.

Real World Scenario

Creating a Corporate Connection to a Business Partner

Your company has just signed an agreement with a large wholesaler to sell your products. The wholesaler has an extensive network that utilizes a great deal of technology, which will benefit you and improve your profitability. You must design a network security topology that will allow you both access to some of each other's systems and information while protecting the confidentiality of your own critical records and information. How might you accomplish this?

A good implementation would connect your network to theirs using a VPN across the Internet. You could use a secure tunneling protocol to ensure that unauthorized parties wouldn't be able to sniff or access information streams between the companies. This approach would create an extranet environment for you and your new business partner.

The challenge lies in creating secure areas in your network that the wholesaler can't access. You can accomplish this by establishing VLANs in your internal network that aren't visible to the extranet. VLANs and network segmentation can be implemented using routers, firewalls, and switches.

Identifying Assets

Every business or organization has valuable assets and resources. These assets must be accounted for, both physically and functionally. *Asset identification* is the process in which a company attempts to place a value on the information and systems it has in place. In some cases, the process may be as simple as counting systems and software licenses. These types of physical asset evaluations are part of the normal accounting procedures a business must perform routinely.

The more difficult part of an asset-identification process is attempting to assign values to information. In some cases, you may only be able to determine what would happen if the information were to become unavailable or lost. If absence of this information would effectively shut down the business, the information is priceless. If you have this type of information, determining which methods and approaches you should take to safeguard it becomes easier.

You wouldn't necessarily assign the same value to the formula for Coca-Cola that you'd assign to your mother's chicken and rice recipe. The Coke formula would be worth a fortune to a person who stole it; they could sell it to competitors and retire. Your mother's recipe would make a nice dinner, but it wouldn't be valuable from a financial perspective.

Assessing Risk

There are several ways to perform a *risk assessment* or *risk analysis*. They range from highly scientific formula-based methods to a conversation with the owner. In general, you should attempt to identify the costs of replacing stolen data or systems, the costs of downtime, and virtually any risk factor you can imagine.

You can move to risk assessment only after completing the asset identification. After you know that databases containing information from freely available sources (such as the U.S. Census Bureau) can always be re-created if need be and shouldn't be viewed in the same light as those containing business-specific data, you can start computing costs.

After you've determined the costs, you can then evaluate the likelihood that certain types of events will occur and the most likely outcome if they do occur. If you work in New York City, what is the likelihood of damage to your business from an earthquake? Will your risk assessment place the high probability of an earthquake on your list of primary concerns?

Identifying Threats

Implementing a security policy requires that you evaluate the risks of both internal and external *threats* to the data and network. It does little good to implement a high-security environment to protect your company from the outside if the threat is mostly internal. If a member of your team brings a disk containing a virus into the office and loads it onto a computer, the virus may spread throughout the entire network and effectively be immune to your external security measures. This is a common problem in schools, libraries, and environments where people regularly use shared resources. If a library offers computers for public use and those computers are in a network, a virus could infect all of the systems throughout the network. External security measures won't prevent potential damage or data loss.

Internal threats also include employee fraud, abuse or alteration of data, and theft of property. Both policies and systems must be put into place to detect and mitigate these possibilities. Investigating and making recommendations to management on procedural changes and policies is a key role for computer security professionals. Figure 1.17 depicts some examples of internal and external threats.

FIGURE 1.17 Internal and external threats to an organization

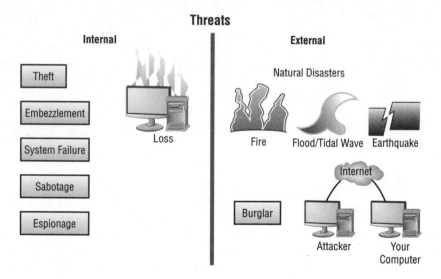

Internal Threats

Most well-publicized *internal threats* involve financial abuses. Some of these abuses are outright fraud or theft. These types of threats, especially in a computer-intensive environment, can be difficult to detect and investigate. They are typically ongoing and involve small transactions over long periods. A recent incident of fraud that occurred in a large software manufacturer involved an accounting professional who generated bogus checks in payment for work that never occurred. Over a few months, this employee was able to make over $100,000 in fraudulent payments to companies that she or relatives had created. It took considerable investigation by computer and financial auditors to determine how this theft occurred. From a computer security perspective, this was an internal threat that was the result of failures in financial, operational, and computer security controls. These types of incidents probably occur more frequently than anyone wants to admit, and many times more often than anyone becomes aware of.

Another incident involved an employee who was using corporate computer resources to operate a financial accounting service. This employee had been running this business for several years. When the company found out, it immediately fired the employee and confiscated his records. During the investigation, the process used to collect evidence inadvertently tainted it. The chain of custody in this case was broken. When the employee went to court over this situation, his attorney was able to have the evidence thrown out of court. Even though the employee was clearly guilty, the judge dismissed the case due to a lack of admissible evidence. The employee then sued the company for wrongful discharge, harassment, and several other charges. He won those suits, and he got his old job back. In this instance, the internal policies and systems put into place to detect, investigate, and correct the problem broke down. It cost the company a huge amount of money and allowed a known embezzler back in.

We'll discuss chains of custody, incident response, and the proper way to conduct investigations in Chapter 9. For now, it's important to know that finding and dealing with internal threats is a key aspect of the computer security job.

External Threats

Many of the internal threats that a company must deal with involve procedures and methods that are standard across industries. *External threats*, on the other hand, are increasing at an alarming rate. Several years ago, most computer incidents were caused by groups of kids or hobbyists who were primarily in it for fun. Most of the time, these incidents were not intentionally malicious in nature. A few of them did involve alteration or destruction of data and records.

Today, many companies take orders online, process payments, track shipments, manage inventory, use online databases, and administer other key information using complicated systems. These systems are connected to other systems that contain private corporate records, trade secrets, strategic plans, and many other types of valuable information.

Unfortunately, when these systems are compromised, an entire business or industry can be compromised. Incidents have occurred where security breaches remained open for years, and the companies involved had no knowledge that a compromise ever took place. One of a professional criminal's greatest joys is creating and exploiting this type of security breach.

Early methods of cracking systems were primitive and labor intensive. Today, software packages exist that find targets automatically and then systematically attack the targets to find their vulnerabilities. Many of these tools use graphical user interfaces that require little technical expertise on the part of the would-be hacker. Many computer systems are being repeatedly and methodically attacked by the curious or by criminals attempting to commit a crime.

The job of a computer security professional in this situation is to detect the attack, find ways to counter it, and assist law-enforcement personnel in investigating the activity. This type of work is interesting and involves many of the skills you'll learn in this book.

Understanding Vulnerabilities

A computer security specialist's main area of concern will probably revolve around the security capabilities of the software and systems used in the business. Until recently, many operating system manufacturers only paid lip service to security. One popular operating system used a logon and password scheme for security. When the logon prompt occurred, all you had to do was click the Cancel button and the system would provide most of the network capabilities and local access to all resources. If the screensaver was password protected, you could either enter the password to unlock the system or reboot the computer to have the system be unsecure. This was worse than having no security. Many users thought they had a secure computer system, but they didn't—and many thefts of data by coworkers occurred as a result.

The *Transmission Control Protocol/Internet Protocol (TCP/IP)* network protocol used by most corporate networks was designed to allow communications in a trustful environment. This protocol was primarily experimental and was used by schools and governmental agencies for research. Although it's robust in its error handling, by its nature it's unsecured. Many modern network attacks occur through the TCP/IP.

Operating systems and applications programs have long been vulnerable to external and internal attacks. Software companies want to sell software that is easy to use, graphically driven, and easily configured. Users want the same thing. Unfortunately, this creates additional security problems in many networks.

One of the most popular products in use today allows e-mail and attachments to begin executing programs or instructions embedded in a message. This functionality allows e-mail messages to have fancy formatting, but it also lets e-mails carry viruses that can damage networks or spread to other networks. The manufacturer of this software is now releasing security updates, but it seems that every time it introduces a security update, someone comes up with a new way around it.

Many operating system manufacturers are completely rethinking security measures. They've recognized that the products they produce can't protect the companies that use them from data loss or abuse. It has become such a problem for many customers that security support is now made available by most operating system and network software manufacturers. In the past, software manufacturers hid security vulnerabilities; now those vulnerabilities are published, and solutions are provided as soon as a vulnerability is discovered. Of course, this situation helps hackers who know that these changes won't be made on many computer systems for a while.

In the most basic sense, progress is the computer security expert's worst nightmare. As a Security+ certification holder, you're part of the team that must evaluate threats to the systems currently installed and proactively be able to anticipate what should be done to keep your systems secure.

Dealing with Telephony Issues

When telephone technology is married with information technology, the result is known as *telephony*. A breach in your telephony infrastructure is just as devastating as any other violation and can lead to the loss of valuable data.

With the exodus from land lines to Voice over IP (VoIP) in order for companies to save money in full swing, it is imperative that you treat this part of the network the same as you would any other. As an example of some of the information available, SecureLogix markets a voice firewall (http://www.securelogix.com/ip-telephony-security.html), and Cisco has published a white paper on IP Telephony Security in Depth (http://www.cisco.com/warp/public/cc/so/cuso/epso/sqfr/safip_wp.pdf).

 From a security standpoint, the biggest problem with VoIP and data being on the same line is that they are then both vulnerable in the event of a PBX (Private Brance Exchange) attack.

Summary

In this chapter, we covered the key elements that an information security specialist should consider. Every organization has a different set of priorities and a different focus when it comes to security. Your responsibility is to take this information and create or maintain a security-oriented environment to address these priorities and concerns.

You'll encounter the following primary areas of responsibility:

- Physical security
- Operational security
- Management and policies

You should consider actions that you perform in this environment to accomplish one or more of the goals of information security:

- Prevention
- Detection
- Response

Security is a set of processes and products. In order for a security program to be effective, all of the following parts must work and be coordinated by the organization:

- Antivirus software
- Access control
- Authentication

Typically, your network will run many different protocols and services. These protocols allow connections to other networks and products. However, they also create potential vulnerabilities that must be understood. You must work to find ways to minimize the vulnerabilities. Many protocols and services offered by modern operating systems are highly vulnerable to attack. New methods of attacking these systems are developed every day.

Security topologies provide a mechanism to design networks that have multiple ways of implementing security. Design goals for a security topology must address these four areas of security to be effective:

- Confidentiality
- Integrity
- Availability
- Accountability

Your network can be made more secure by considering the impact of security zones and access. Here are the three most common security zones you'll encounter in the workplace:

- Internets
- Intranets
- Extranets

You can improve the likelihood of a successful security implementation if you consider putting externally accessed servers into areas called DMZs.

You can take advantage of several technologies to minimize your network's risk of being compromised:

- VLANs
- NAT
- Tunneling

The final part of this chapter discussed business requirements in a security environment:

- Identifying assets
- Assessing risks
- Identifying threats
- Evaluating vulnerabilities

Exam Essentials

Know the various aspects of information security.   Ensuring a secure network involves good design, implementation, and maintenance. The information in your organization is potentially vulnerable to both internal and external threats. Identify these threats and create methods of countering them before they happen.

Identify the potential physical, operational, and management policy decisions that affect your information security efforts.   It isn't good enough to have a plan if the plan is unsound or has gaping holes. You must make sure that the plans you develop and the procedures you follow to ensure security make sense for the organization and are effective in addressing the organization's needs.

Explain the relative advantages of the technologies available to you for authentication.   You have many tools available to establish authentication processes. Some of these tools start with a password and user ID. Others involve physical devices or the physical characteristics of the person who is requesting authentication. This area is referred to as I&A.

Be able to explain the relative capabilities of the technologies available to you for network security.   In most situations, you can create virtual LANs, create connections that are encrypted, and isolate high-risk assets from low-risk assets. You can do so using tunneling, DMZs, and network segmenting.

Identify and describe the goals of information security.   The three primary goals of information security are prevention, detection, and response. Your policies and systems must include these three aspects to be effective. Ideally, you want to prevent a security breach. If a breach happens, you should have methods to detect and respond to it as quickly as possible.

Be able to describe the processes and mechanisms that can be used to implement a secure environment.   Antivirus software, access control, and authentication are the three primary methods you have to implement a secure environment.

Identify the various access control methods used in systems and networks.   Three primary access control methods are used in computer systems today: MAC, DAC, and RBAC. The MAC method establishes all connections and relationships between users statically. The DAC method allows the user to have some control over what information and resources are accessible. The RBAC method sets access levels and permissions based on the role the user plays in a particular situation or job.

Know which services and protocols should be offered and which should not.   Many protocols and services in modern operating systems offer little if any security. These protocols and services may also be vulnerable to attack or offer no encryption in the logon process. Services that should be offered include only those that are necessary for legitimate business needs.

Be able to identify the three aspects of design goals of any security topology.   The design goals of a security topology must take into consideration the need for confidentiality, integrity, and availability. These three aspects are called the CIA of security topology. Additionally, you must consider issues of accountability. Who owns the data or is responsible for verifying that it is accurate?

Know the characteristics of the three types of commonly used security zones.   The three common security zones in place are the Internet, intranets, and extranets. The Internet offers low security. Intranets are considered high security, and extranets may be low to high security. Anytime you connect your network to another network, you increase the vulnerability of your network. One of the primary tools you can use to isolate less-secure resources from more-secure resources is a DMZ.

Be able to identify the differences and characteristics of the technologies available to you. A network can be segmented, and VLANs can be created to improve security. NAT presents only one Internet address to the world, hiding the other elements of the network. Tunneling allows you to make relatively secure connections to other networks using the Internet.

Identify the four business requirements of a network security design.   Identifying assets, assessing risks, identifying threats, and evaluating vulnerabilities are the four primary business requirements that must be considered in a security design.

Hands-On Labs

The labs in this chapter are as follows:

Lab 1.1: Update a Linux System

Lab 1.2: Update a Windows-Based System

Lab 1.1: Update a Linux System

It is important to keep your system current and up-to-date. As soon as a weakness in an operating system becomes known, the number of people trying to exploit that weakness grows at an almost exponential rate. In this exercise, you'll apply patches and updates to an SuSE Linux Enterprise Server (SLES).

To apply patches and updates through YaST, the primary administration tool in SLES, follow these steps:

1. Log in as root and start YaST.

2. Choose Software and then select Online Update.

3. Click Next. YaST retrieves information about new updates. If prompted for a username and password, enter these values, and then choose to install any updates that are found.

   You can also choose to install patches from a CD by selecting Software and Patch CD Update. To specify settings on the server, choose Software and then System Update. Choose Change and then Update Options.

   Finally, the YOU (YaST Online Update) server can be configured by choosing Software and then YOU Server Configuration.

Lab 1.2: Update a Windows-Based System

Whether you are running Windows Server 2003 or 2008, you'll use these steps to look for updates to your system and to begin installing them:

1. Log in as administrator and start Microsoft Internet Explorer.

2. Go to http://v4.windowsupdate.microsoft.com/en/default.asp.

3. Click Express. The system will be checked, and you can choose to install any updates that are found.

Review Questions

1. Of the following types of security, which would be primarily concerned with someone stealing the server from the premises?

    A. Physical security

    B. Operational security

    C. Management and policy

    D. Authentication

2. Upper management has suddenly become concerned about security. As the senior network administrator, you are asked to suggest changes that should be implemented. Which of the following access methods should you recommend if the method is to be one that is primarily based on preestablished access and can't be changed by users?

    A. MAC

    B. DAC

    C. RBAC

    D. Kerberos

3. Your office administrator is being trained to perform server backups. Which authentication method would be ideal for this situation?

    A. MAC

    B. DAC

    C. RBAC

    D. Security tokens

4. You've been assigned to mentor a junior administrator and bring him up to speed quickly. The topic you're currently explaining is authentication. Which method uses a KDC to accomplish authentication for users, programs, or systems?

    A. CHAP

    B. Kerberos

    C. Biometrics

    D. Smart cards

5. Which authentication method sends a challenge to the client that is encrypted and then sent back to the server?

    A. Kerberos

    B. PAP

    C. DAC

    D. CHAP

6. After a careful risk analysis, the value of your company's data has been increased. Accordingly, you're expected to implement authentication solutions that reflect the increased value of the data. Which of the following authentication methods uses more than one authentication process for a logon?

A. Multi-factor

B. Biometrics

C. Smart card

D. Kerberos

7. Which of the following IP addresses is within the private address range?

A. 192.1.1.5

B. 192.168.0.10

C. 192.225.5.1

D. 192.255.255.255

8. After acquiring another company, your organization is in a unique position to create a new—much larger—network from scratch. You want to take advantage of this reorganization to implement the most secure environment that users, and managers, can live with. You've already decided that the only way this will be possible is to implement security zones. Which of the following isn't an example of a type of security zone?

A. Internet

B. Intranet

C. Extranet

D. NAT

9. Which of the following protocols allows an organization to present a single TCP/IP address to the Internet while utilizing private IP addressing across the LAN?

A. NAT

B. VLAN

C. DMZ

D. Extranet

10. You're the administrator for Mercury Technical. Due to several expansions, the network has grown exponentially in size within the past two years. Which of the following is a popular method for breaking a network into smaller private networks that can coexist on the same wiring and yet be unaware of each other?

A. VLAN

B. NAT

C. MAC

D. Security zone

11. Of the following services, which one would be most likely to utilize a retinal scan?

A. Auditing

B. Authentication

C. Access control

D. Data confidentiality

12. One of the vice presidents of the company calls a meeting with information technology after a recent trip to competitors' sites. She reports that many of the companies she visited granted access to their buildings only after fingerprint scans, and she wants similar technology employed at this company. Of the following, which technology relies on a physical attribute of the user for authentication?

A. Smart card

B. Biometrics

C. Mutual authentication

D. Tokens

13. Which technology allows a connection to be made between two networks using a secure protocol?

A. Tunneling

B. VLAN

C. Internet

D. Extranet

14. A new director of information technology has been hired, and you report directly to him. At the first meeting, he assigns you the task of identifying all the company resources that IT is responsible for and assigning a value to each. The process of determining the value of information or equipment in an organization is referred to as which of the following?

A. Asset identification

B. Risk assessment

C. Threat identification

D. Vulnerabilities scan

15. You have been asked to address a management meeting and present the types of threats your organization could face from hackers. Which of the following would best categorize this type of information?

A. Asset identification

B. Risk assessment

C. Threat identification

D. Vulnerabilities

16. Over the years, your company has upgraded its operating systems and networks as it has grown. A recent survey shows that numerous databases on the network haven't been accessed in more than a year. Unfortunately, the survey doesn't identify who created or last accessed those databases. Which aspect of design goals would involve determining who owns a particular database file?

    A. Auditing

    B. Access control

    C. Threat analysis

    D. Accountability

17. A user just complained to you that his system has been infected with a new virus. Which of the following would be a first step to take in addressing and correcting this problem?

    A. Verifying that the most current virus definition file is installed

    B. Reformatting the hard disk

    C. Reinstalling the operating system

    D. Disabling the user's e-mail account

18. You're awakened in the middle of the night by a frantic junior administrator. The caller reports that the guest account—which you have forbidden anyone to use—suddenly logged in and out of the network, and the administrator believes an attack occurred. Which of the following would be the most useful in determining what was accessed during an external attack?

    A. System logs

    B. Antivirus software

    C. Kerberos

    D. Biometrics

19. You want to install a server in the network area that provides web services to Internet clients. You don't want to expose your internal network to additional risks. Which method should you implement to accomplish this?

    A. Install the server in an intranet.

    B. Install the server in a DMZ.

    C. Install the server in a VLAN.

    D. Install the server in an extranet.

20. Your company provides medical data to doctors from a worldwide database. Because of the sensitive nature of the data you work with, it's imperative that authentication be established on each session and be valid only for that session. Which of the following authentication methods provides credentials that are valid only during a single session?

    A. Tokens

    B. Certificate

    C. Smart card

    D. Kerberos

Answers to Review Questions

1. **A.**   Physical security is primarily concerned with the loss or theft of physical assets. This would include theft, fire, and other acts that physically deny a service or information to the organization.

2. **A.**   Mandatory Access Control (MAC) is oriented toward preestablished access. This access is typically established by network administrators and can't be changed by users.

3. **C.**   Role-Based Access Control (RBAC) allows specific people to be assigned to specific roles with specific privileges. A backup operator would need administrative privileges to back up a server. This privilege would be limited to the role and wouldn't be present during the employee's normal job functions.

4. **B.**   Kerberos uses a Key Distribution Center (KDC) to authenticate a principle. The KDC provides a credential that can be used by all Kerberos-enabled servers and applications.

5. **D.**   Challenge Handshake Authentication Protocol (CHAP) sends a challenge to the originating client. This challenge is sent back to the server, and the encryption results are compared. If the challenge is successful, the client is logged on.

6. **A.**   A multi-factor authentication method uses two or more processes for logon. A two-factor method might use smart cards and biometrics for logon.

7. **B.**   The private address range includes IP addresses between 192.168.0.0 and 192.168.255.255.

8. **D.**   Network Address Translation (NAT) is a method of hiding TCP/IP addresses from other networks. The Internet, intranets, and extranets are the three most common security zones in use.

9. **A.**   Network Address Translation (NAT) allows an organization to present a single address to the Internet. Typically, the router or NAT server accomplishes this. The router or NAT server maps all inbound and outbound requests and maintains a table for returned messages.

10. **A.**   Virtual local area networks (VLANs) break a large network into smaller networks. These networks can coexist on the same wiring and be unaware of each other. A router or other routing-type device would be needed to connect these VLANs.

11. **B.**   Authentication is a service that requests the principal user to provide proof of their identity. A retinal scan is a very secure form of evidence used in high-security companies and government agencies.

12. **B.**   Biometric technologies rely on a physical characteristic of the user to verify identity. Biometric devices typically use either a hand pattern or a retinal scan to accomplish this.

13. **A.**   Tunneling allows a network to make a secure connection to another network through the Internet or other network. Tunnels are usually secure and present themselves as extensions of both networks.

14. A.   Asset identification is the process of identifying the types and values of assets in an organization.

15. C.   A threat assessment examines the potential for internal and external threats to your systems and information.

16. D.   Accountability involves identifying who owns or is responsible for the accuracy of certain information in an organization. The department or individual that is accountable for certain information would also be responsible for verifying accuracy in the event of a data-tampering incident.

17. A.   Your first step would be to verify that the user's antivirus software is the most current version. This includes checking the virus definition files.

18. A.   System logs will frequently tell you what was accessed and in what manner. These logs are usually explicit in describing the events that occurred during a security violation.

19. B.   A DMZ is an area in a network that allows access to outside users while not exposing your internal users to additional threats.

20. A.   Tokens are created when a user or system successfully authenticates. The token is destroyed when the session is over.

Chapter

2

Identifying Potential Risks

THE FOLLOWING COMPTIA SECURITY+ EXAM OBJECTIVES ARE COVERED IN THIS CHAPTER:

✓ **1.1 Differentiate among various systems' security threats.**

- Privilege escalation
- Virus
- Worm
- Trojan
- Spyware
- Spam
- Adware
- Rootkits
- Botnets
- Logic bomb

✓ **1.5 Implement security applications.**

- Antivirus
- Anti-spam

✓ **2.1 Differentiate between the different ports and protocols, their respective threats and mitigation techniques.**

- Antiquated protocols
- TCP/IP hijacking
- Null sessions
- Spoofing
- Man-in-the-middle
- Replay

- DoS
- DDoS
- Domain Name Kiting
- DNS poisoning

✓ **2.5 Explain the vulnerabilities and mitigations associated with network devices.**

- Privilege escalation
- Weak passwords
- Back doors
- DoS

✓ **4.2 Carry out vulnerability assessments using common tools.**

- Vulnerability scanners
- OVAL
- Password crackers

✓ **6.6 Explain the concept of and how to reduce the risks of social engineering.**

- *Phishing
- Hoaxes
- Dumpster diving

Everywhere you turn, there are risks. The risks begin the minute you turn a computer on and grow exponentially the moment you slap in a network card. The threat of attack to your network, servers, and workstations can come from many sources. Your job is to implement and maintain measures that can help keep your systems safe from attack. There is a running battle between the people who want to attack your systems and the people who make products and services to help protect your system. Unfortunately, you're right in the middle of these two extremes, and your network and systems constitute the battlefield.

In this chapter, we'll look at several types of attacks, as well as some of the reasons your network is vulnerable. In many instances, the vulnerabilities that you must deal with are a result of the operating system's implementation of networking coupled with the trusting nature of Transmission Control Protocol/Internet Protocol (TCP/IP).

Calculating Attack Strategies

In computing, a lot of the terminology used comes from other fields, such as the military. That seems to be particularly true when it comes to security. Using that line of logic, an *attack* occurs when an unauthorized individual or group of individuals attempts to access, modify, or damage your systems or environment. These attacks can be fairly simple and unfocused, or they can appear to be almost blitzkrieg-like in their intensity.

One main reason for the differences in attacks is that they occur in many ways and for different reasons. Regardless of how they occur, they are generally used to accomplish one or more of these three goals:

- In an *access attack*, someone who should not be able to wants to access your resources.

- During a *modification and repudiation attack*, someone wants to modify information in your systems.

- A *denial-of-service (DoS) attack* is an attempt to disrupt your network and services. When your system becomes so busy responding to illegitimate requests, it can prevent authorized users from having access.

Those who are attacking you might be doing it for the sheer fun of it, they might be criminals attempting to steal from you, or they might be individuals or groups who are using the attack to make a political statement or commit an act of terrorism. Regardless of the motive, your job is to protect the people you work with from these acts of aggression. You are, in many cases, the only person in your organization charged with the responsibility of repulsing these attacks.

The following sections deal with the general types of attacks you'll experience.

 The attacks described in the following sections are considered attack strategies. We'll look at the specific attacks—each of which will fall within one or more of these strategies—later in this chapter, in the section titled "Recognizing Common Attacks."

Understanding Access Attack Types

The goal of an *access attack* is straightforward. An access attack is an attempt to gain access to information that the attacker isn't authorized to have. These types of attacks focus on breaching the confidentiality of information. They occur either internally or externally; they might also occur when physical access to the information is possible.

Dumpster diving is a common physical access method. Companies normally generate a huge amount of paper, most of which eventually winds up in Dumpsters or recycle bins. Dumpsters may contain information that is highly sensitive in nature. In high-security and government environments, sensitive papers are either shredded or burned. Most businesses don't do this. In addition, the advent of "green" companies has created an increase in the amount of recycled paper, which can often contain all kinds of juicy information about a company and its individual employees.

A second common method used in access attacks is to capture information en route between two systems; rather than paper, data is found in such attacks. There are several common types of access attacks:

Eavesdropping *Eavesdropping* is the process of listening in on or overhearing parts of a conversation, including listening in on your network traffic. This type of attack is generally passive. For example, a coworker might overhear your dinner plans because your speakerphone is set too loud or you're yelling into your cell phone. The opportunity to overhear a conversation is coupled with the carelessness of the parties in the conversation.

Snooping *Snooping* occurs when someone looks through your files hoping to find something interesting. The files may be either electronic or on paper. In the case of physical snooping, people might inspect your Dumpster, recycling bins, or even your file cabinets; they can look under the keyboard for Post-it notes or look for scraps of paper tacked to your bulletin board. Computer snooping, on the other hand, involves someone searching through your electronic files trying to find something interesting.

Interception *Interception* can be either an active or a passive process. In a networked environment, a passive interception would involve someone who routinely monitors network traffic. Active interception might include putting a computer system between the sender and receiver to capture information as it's sent. The process is usually covert. The last thing a person on an intercept mission wants is to be discovered. Intercept missions can occur for years without the knowledge of the parties being monitored.

Government agencies routinely run intercept missions to gather intelligence about the capabilities and locations of enemies. For instance, the FBI has several products that they install on ISPs' systems to gather and process e-mail, looking for keywords. These keyword searches become the basis of an investigation.

The major difference between these types of attacks is how they're accomplished. The ultimate objective is to gain unauthorized access to information.

 Real World Scenario

Survey Your Surroundings

As an administrator, you've no doubt heard countless horror stories of data being accessed as a result of stupidity. Users write their passwords on scraps of paper and tape them to the monitor because the length/complexity requirements have made the passwords too difficult to remember. Other users go home without logging out and never return; the terminal stays logged in indefinitely, allowing an attacker to sit at it and copy key files. These stories may sound too unrealistic to believe, but there is some truth to them.

For this scenario, you'll need to put yourself in the position of an outsider wanting to find any sliver of data that can be used to allow you to gain access to a network. That sliver of data could be a user's password, the name and location of a data file, or anything else of a sensitive nature. From that perspective, see if you can answer these questions:

- How often do users change their passwords, and how do they go about memorizing their new ones for the first few days? Do they write them down and carry them in their belongings? Do they stick a piece of paper in a drawer (and if so, is it locked)?

- What happens to sensitive information that's printed? Is it shredded or just tossed in the wastebasket? Who collects the trash—a contracted service provider or the city?

- Crucial data, such as backup sets, are stored off-site. Where are they stored? Would it be easier to break in and get that data than to break into the network? How many people know where the backup sets are?

These are a few of the questions you must ask as an administrator in order to keep your data safe. Your answers can help you determine whether you need to make the workplace more secure. Throughout this book, I'll introduce topics for you to think about and apply to your own environment.

Recognizing Modification and Repudiation Attacks

Modification attacks involve the deletion, insertion, or alteration of information in an unauthorized manner that is intended to appear genuine to the user. These attacks can be hard to detect. They're similar to access attacks in that the attacker must first get to the data on the servers, but they differ from that point on. The motivation for this type of attack may be to plant information, change grades in a class, fraudulently alter credit card records, or something similar. Website defacements are a common form of modification attack; they involve someone changing web pages in a malicious manner.

A variation of a modification attack is a *repudiation attack*. Repudiation attacks make data or information appear to be invalid or misleading (which can be even worse). For example, someone might access your e-mail server and send inflammatory information to others under the guise of one of your top managers. This information might prove embarrassing to your company and possibly do irreparable harm. Repudiation attacks are fairly easy to accomplish because most e-mail systems don't check outbound mail for validity. Repudiation attacks, like modification attacks, usually begin as access attacks.

> The opposite of repudiation is *nonrepudiation*. When you purchase something from an online vendor, the vendor often asks for information—such as the PIN on your credit card, not just the credit card number—to prove that you are who you say you are. By proving your identity, the company has nonrepudiated evidence that the sale is valid.

A common type of repudiation attack involves a customer who claims that they never received a service for which they were billed. In this situation, the burden of proof that the information used to generate the invoice is accurate is on the company. If an external attacker has modified the data, verifying the information may be difficult.

Identifying Denial-of-Service and Distributed Denial-of-Service Attacks

Denial-of-service (DoS) attacks prevent access to resources by users authorized to use those resources. An attacker may attempt to bring down an e-commerce website to prevent or deny usage by legitimate customers. DoS attacks are common on the Internet, where they have hit large companies such as Amazon, Microsoft, and AT&T. These attacks are often widely publicized in the media. Most simple DoS attacks occur from a single system, and a specific server or organization is the target.

> There isn't a single type of DoS attack, but a variety of similar methods that have the same purpose. It's easiest to think of a DoS attack by imagining that your servers are so busy responding to false requests that they don't have time to service legitimate requests. Not only can the servers be physically busy, but the same result can occur if the attack consumes all the available bandwidth.

Several types of attacks can occur in this category. These attacks can deny access to information, applications, systems, or communications. A DoS attack on an application may bring down a website while the communications and systems continue to operate. A DoS attack on a system crashes the operating system (a simple reboot may restore the server to normal operation). A DoS attack against a network is designed to fill the communications channel and prevent access by authorized users. A common DoS attack involves opening as many TCP sessions as possible; this type of attack is called a TCP SYN flood DoS attack.

Two of the most common types of DoS attacks are the *ping of death* and the *buffer overflow*. The ping of death crashes a system by sending *Internet Control Message Protocol* (ICMP) packets (think echoes) that are larger than the system can handle. Buffer overflow attacks, as the name implies, attempt to put more data (usually long input strings) into the buffer than it can hold. Code Red, Slapper, and Slammer are all attacks that took advantage of buffer overflows, and sPing is an example of a ping of death.

In a *null session attack*, a user logs into Windows-based computers as a null user (bypassing basic authentication). This type of access is often used to launch a DoS attack.

A *distributed denial-of-service (DDoS) attack* is similar to a DoS attack. A DDoS attack amplifies the concepts of a DoS by using multiple computer systems to conduct the attack against a single organization. These attacks exploit the inherent weaknesses of dedicated networks such as DSL and cable. These permanently attached systems usually have little, if any, protection. An attacker can load an attack program onto dozens or even hundreds of computer systems that use DSL or cable modems. The attack program lies dormant on these computers until they get an attack signal from a master computer. The signal triggers the systems, which launch an attack simultaneously on the target network or system. Figure 2.1 shows an attack occurring and the master controller orchestrating the attack. The master controller may be another unsuspecting user. The systems taking direction from the master control computer are referred to as *zombies*. These systems merely carry out the instruction they've been given by the master computer.

Software running on zombie computers is often known as a *botnet*. Bots, by themselves, are but a form of software that runs automatically and autonomously (Google uses the Googlebot to find web pages and bring back values for the index), but *botnet* has come to be the word used to describe malicious software running on a zombie.

Remember that the difference between a DoS attack and a DDoS attack is that the latter uses multiple computers—all focused on one target.

The nasty part of this type of attack is that the machines used to carry out the attack belong to normal computer users. The attack gives no special warning to those users. When the attack is complete, the attack program may remove itself from the system or infect the unsuspecting user's computer with a virus that destroys the hard drive, thereby wiping out the evidence.

FIGURE 2.1   Distributed denial-of-service attack

Can You Prevent Denial Attacks?

In general, there is little you can do to prevent DoS or DDoS attacks. Your best method of dealing with these types of attacks involves countermeasures and prevention. Many operating systems are particularly susceptible to these types of attacks. Fortunately, most operating system manufacturers have implemented updates to minimize their effects. Make sure your operating system and the applications you use are up-to-date.

Recognizing Common Attacks

Most attacks are designed to exploit potential weaknesses, which can be in the implementation of programs or in the protocols used in networks. Many types of attacks require a high level of sophistication and are rare, but you need to know about them so that, should they occur, you can identify what has happened in your network.

In the following sections, we'll look at some common attacks more closely.

Back Door Attacks

The term *back door attack* can have two different meanings. The original term *back door* referred to troubleshooting and developer hooks into systems. During the development of a complicated operating system or application, programmers add back doors or maintenance hooks. Back doors allow them to examine operations inside the code while the code is running. The back doors are stripped out of the code when it's moved to production. When a software manufacturer discovers a hook that hasn't been removed, it releases a maintenance upgrade or patch to close the back door. These patches are common when a new product is initially released.

The second type of back door refers to gaining access to a network and inserting a program or utility that creates an entrance for an attacker. The program may allow a certain user ID to log on without a password or gain administrative privileges. Figure 2.2 shows how a back door attack can be used to bypass the security of a network. In this example, the attacker is using a back door program to utilize resources or steal information.

FIGURE 2.2   A back door attack in progress

A back door attack is usually either an access or modification attack. A number of tools exist to create back door attacks on systems. One of the more popular is Back Orifice. Another popular back door program is NetBus. Fortunately, most conventional antivirus software will detect and block these types of attacks.

Back Orifice and NetBus are remote administration tools used by attackers to take control of Windows-based systems. These packages are typically installed using a Trojan horse program. Back Orifice and NetBus allow a remote user to take full control of systems on which they are installed. They run on all of the current Windows operating systems.

Spoofing Attacks

A *spoofing attack* is an attempt by someone or something to masquerade as someone else. This type of attack is usually considered an access attack. A common spoofing attack that was popular for many years on early Unix and other timesharing systems involved a programmer writing a fake logon program. It would prompt the user for a user ID and password. No matter what the user typed, the program would indicate an invalid logon attempt and then transfer control to the real logon program. The spoofing program would write the logon and password into a disk file, which was retrieved later.

The most popular spoofing attacks today are *IP spoofing* and *DNS spoofing*. With IP spoofing, the goal is to make the data look as if it came from a trusted host when it didn't (thus spoofing the IP address of the sending host). With DNS spoofing, the DNS server is given information about a name server that it thinks is legitimate when it isn't. This can send users to a website other than the one they wanted to go to, reroute mail, or do any other type of redirection wherein data from a DNS server is used to determine a destination. Another name for this is *DNS poisoning*.

Always think of spoofing as fooling. Attackers are trying to fool the user, system, and/or host into believing they're something they aren't. Because the word *spoof* can describe any false information at any level, spoofing can occur at any level of network.

Another DNS weakness is *Domain Name Kiting*. When a new domain name is issued, there is a five-day grace period before you must technically pay for it. Those engaged in kiting can delete the account within the five days and re-register it again—allowing them to have accounts that they never have to pay for.

Figure 2.3 shows a spoofing attack occurring as part of the logon process on a computer network. The attacker in this situation impersonates the server to the client attempting to log in. No matter what the client attempts to do, the impersonating system will fail the login. When this process is finished, the impersonating system disconnects from the client. The client then logs in to the legitimate server. In the meantime, the attacker now has a valid user ID and password.

The important point to remember is that a spoofing attack tricks something or someone into thinking something legitimate is occurring.

Man-in-the-Middle Attacks

Man-in-the-middle attacks tend to be fairly sophisticated. This type of attack is also an access attack, but it can be used as the starting point for a modification attack. The method used in these attacks clandestinely places a piece of software between a server and the user that neither the server administrators nor the user is aware of. The software intercepts data and then sends the information to the server as if nothing is wrong. The server responds back to the software, thinking it's communicating with the legitimate client. The attacking software continues sending information on to the server, and so forth.

FIGURE 2.3   A spoofing attack during logon

Attacker now has logon and password.

If communication between the server and user continues, what's the harm of the software? The answer lies in whatever else the software is doing. The man-in-the-middle software may be recording information for someone to view later, altering it, or in some other way compromising the security of your system and session.

A man-in-the-middle attack is an active attack. Something is actively intercepting the data and may or may not be altering it. If it's altering the data, the altered data masquerades as legitimate data traveling between the two hosts.

Figure 2.4 illustrates a man-in-the-middle attack. Notice how both the server and client assume that the system they're talking to is the legitimate system. The man in the middle appears to be the server to the client, and it appears to be the client to the server.

In recent years, the threat of man-in-the-middle attacks on wireless networks has increased. Because it's no longer necessary to connect to the wire, a malicious rogue can be outside the building intercepting packets, altering them, and sending them on. A common solution to this problem is to enforce a secure wireless authentication protocol such as WPA2.

FIGURE 2.4   A man-in-the-middle attack occurring between a client and a web server

An older term generically used for all man-in-the-middle attacks was *TCP/IP hijacking*. TCP/IP hijacking is addressed in detail later in this chapter.

Replay Attacks

Replay attacks are becoming quite common. They occur when information is captured over a network. A replay attack is a kind of access or modification attack. In a distributed environment, logon and password information is sent between the client and the authentication system. The attacker can capture the information and replay it again later. This can also occur with security certificates from systems such as Kerberos: The attacker resubmits the certificate, hoping to be validated by the authentication system and circumvent any time sensitivity.

Figure 2.5 shows an attacker presenting a previously captured certificate to a Kerberos-enabled system. In this example, the attacker gets legitimate information from the client and records it. Then, the attacker attempts to use the information to enter the system. The attacker later relays information to gain access.

FIGURE 2.5 A replay attack occurring

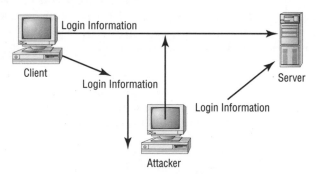

If this attack is successful, the attacker will have all the rights and privileges from the original certificate. This is the primary reason that most certificates contain a unique session identifier and a time stamp: If the certificate has expired, it will be rejected and an entry should be made in a security log to notify system administrators.

Password-Guessing Attacks

Password-guessing attacks occur when an account is attacked repeatedly. This is accomplished by utilizing applications known as *password crackers,* which send possible passwords to the account in a systematic manner. The attacks are initially carried out to gain passwords for an access or modification attack. There are two types of password-guessing attacks:

Brute-force attack   A *brute-force attack* is an attempt to guess passwords until a successful guess occurs. This type of attack usually occurs over a long period. To make passwords more difficult to guess, they should be much longer than two or three characters (six should be the bare minimum), be complex, and have password lockout policies.

Dictionary attack   A *dictionary attack* uses a dictionary of common words to attempt to find the user's password. Dictionary attacks can be automated, and several tools exist in the public domain to execute them.

Not all attacks are only brute-force or dictionary based. A number of hybrids also exist that will try combinations of these two methods. One of the more common techniques involves using *rainbow* tables—values of hashes—to identify the *salt* (random bits added to the password) used in creating the stored value.

Some systems will identify whether an account ID is valid and whether the password is wrong. Giving the attacker a clue as to a valid account name isn't a good practice. If you can enable your authentication to either accept a valid ID/password group or require the entire logon process again, you should.

Privilege Escalation

Privilege escalation can be the result of an error on an administrator's part in assigning too high a permission set to a user, but it's more often associated with bugs left in software. When creating a software program, developers will occasionally leave a back door in the program that allows them to become a root user should they need to fix something during the debugging phase.

After debugging is done and before the software goes live, these abilities are removed. If a developer forgets to remove the back door in the live version and the method of accessing them gets out, it leaves the ability for a miscreant to take advantage of the system.

To understand privilege escalation, think of cheat codes in video games. Once you know the game's code, you can enter it and become invincible. Similarly, someone might take advantage of a hidden cheat in a software application you are using to become root.

Identifying TCP/IP Security Concerns

As a security professional, one of your biggest problems is working with TCP/IP. You could say that the ease of connectivity TCP/IP offers is one of the most significant difficulties we face. Virtually all large networks, including the Internet, are built on the TCP/IP protocol suite. It has become an international standard.

TCP/IP was designed to connect disparate computer systems into a robust and reliable network. It offers a richness of capabilities and support for many different protocols. After TCP/IP has been installed, it will generally operate reliably for years.

 Real World Scenario

Responding to an Attack

As a security administrator, you know all about the different types of attacks that can occur, and you're familiar with the value assigned to the data on your system. Now imagine that the log files indicate that an intruder entered your system for a lengthy period last week while you were away on vacation.

The first thing you should do is make a list of questions you should begin asking to deal with the situation, using your network as a frame of reference. The following list includes some of the questions you should be thinking of:

1. How can you show that a break-in really occurred?

2. How can you determine the extent of what was done during the entry?

3. How can you prevent further entry?

4. Whom should you inform in your organization?

5. What should you do next?

Answers to these questions will be addressed throughout this book. The most important question on the list, though, is whom you should inform in your organization. It's important to know the escalation procedures without hesitation and be able to act quickly.

TCP/IP has been a salvation for organizations that need to connect different systems together to function as a unified whole. Unfortunately, a downside that comes with being an easy-to-use, well-documented network that has been around for many years is numerous holes. You can easily close most of these holes in your network, but you must first know about them.

You need to have a good understanding of the processes TCP/IP uses in order to know how attacks to TCP/IP work. The emphasis in this section is on the types of connections and services. If you're weak in those areas, you'll do well to supplement your study with basic networking information that can be found on the Web.

The following sections delve into issues related to TCP/IP and security. Many of these issues will be familiar to you if you've taken the Network+ or Server+ exam from CompTIA. If there are any gaps in your knowledge of the topics, however, be sure to read the sections carefully.

Working with the TCP/IP Suite

The TCP/IP suite is broken into four architectural layers:

- Application layer
- Host-to-Host or Transport layer
- Internet layer
- Network Interface layer

Computers using TCP/IP use the existing physical connection between the systems. TCP/IP doesn't concern itself with the network topology, or physical connections. The network controller that resides in a computer or host deals with the physical protocol, or topology. TCP/IP communicates with that controller and lets the controller worry about the network topology and physical connection.

In TCP/IP parlance, a computer on the network is a *host*. A host is any device connected to the network that runs a TCP/IP protocol suite, or stack. Figure 2.6 shows the four layers in a TCP/IP protocol stack. Notice that this drawing includes the physical, or network, topology. Although it isn't part of the TCP/IP protocol, the topology is essential to conveying information on a network.

FIGURE 2.6   The TCP/IP protocol architecture layers

The four layers of TCP/IP have unique functions and methods for accomplishing work. Each layer talks to the layers that reside above and below it. Each layer also has its own rules and capabilities.

The following sections discuss the specific layers of the TCP/IP protocol as well as the common protocols used in the stack and how information is conveyed between the layers. I also discuss some of the more common methods used to attack TCP/IP-based networks. Finally, I briefly discuss *encapsulation*, the process used to pass messages between the layers in the TCP/IP protocol.

The Application Layer

The *Application layer* is the highest layer of the suite. It allows applications to access services or protocols to exchange data. Most programs, such as web browsers, interface with TCP/IP at this level. The most commonly used Application layer protocols are as follows:

Hypertext Transfer Protocol   *Hypertext Transfer Protocol (HTTP)* is the protocol used for web pages and the World Wide Web. HTTP applications use a standard language called *Hypertext Markup Language (HTML)*. HTML files are normal text files that contain special coding that allows graphics, special fonts, and characters to be displayed by a web browser or other web-enabled applications.

File Transfer Protocol   *File Transfer Protocol (FTP)* is an application that allows connections to FTP servers for file uploads and downloads. FTP is a common application used to transfer files between hosts on the Internet.

Simple Mail Transfer Protocol   *Simple Mail Transfer Protocol (SMTP)* is the standard protocol for e-mail communications. SMTP allows e-mail clients and servers to communicate with each other for message delivery.

Telnet   *Telnet* is an interactive terminal emulation protocol. It allows a remote user to conduct an interactive session with a Telnet server. This session can appear to the client as if it were a local session.

Domain Name Service   *Domain Name Service (DNS)* allows hosts to resolve hostnames to an Internet Protocol (IP) address. IP is discussed in the section on the Internet layer.

Routing Information Protocol   *Routing Information Protocol (RIP)* allows routing information to be exchanged between routers on an IP network.

Simple Network Management Protocol   *Simple Network Management Protocol (SNMP)* is a management tool that allows communications between network devices and a management console. Most routers, bridges, and intelligent hubs can communicate using SNMP.

Post Office Protocol   *Post Office Protocol (POP)* is a protocol used in many e-mail systems. It allows for advanced features and is a standard interface in many e-mail servers. POP is used for receiving e-mail.

One of the key things to know when securing any network is that you are only running the protocols needed for operations. Make certain that *antiquated protocols*—those once needed but now no longer used are removed. If you do not, you are leaving an opening for an attacker to access your system through weaknesses in that protocol.

The Host-to-Host or Transport Layer

The *Host-to-Host layer*, also called the *Transport layer*, provides the Application layer with session and datagram communications services. The *TCP* and *User Datagram Protocol (UDP)* operate at this layer. These two protocols provide a huge part of the functionality of the TCP/IP network:

TCP   *TCP* is responsible for providing a reliable one-to-one, connection-oriented session. TCP establishes a connection and ensures that the other end receives any packets. Two hosts communicate packet results to each other. TCP also makes sure that packets are decoded and sequenced properly. This connection is persistent during the session. When the session ends, the connection is broken.

UDP   *UDP* provides an unreliable connectionless communication method between hosts. UDP protocol is considered a best-effort protocol, but it's considerably faster than TCP. The sessions don't establish a synchronized session like the kind used in TCP, and UDP doesn't guarantee error-free communications. The primary purpose of UDP is to send small packets of information. The application is responsible for acknowledging the correct reception of the data.

The Internet Layer

The *Internet layer* is responsible for routing, IP addressing, and packaging. The Internet layer protocols accomplish most of the behind-the-scenes work in establishing the ability to exchange information between hosts. Here are the four standard protocols of the Internet layer:

Internet Protocol   *Internet Protocol (IP)* is a routable protocol, and it's responsible for IP addressing. IP also fragments and reassembles message packets. IP only routes information; it doesn't verify it for accuracy. Accuracy checking is the responsibility of TCP. IP determines if a destination is known and, if so, routes the information to that destination. If the destination is unknown, IP sends the packet to the router, which sends it on.

Address Resolution Protocol   *Address Resolution Protocol (ARP)* is responsible for resolving IP addresses to Network Interface layer addresses, including hardware addresses. ARP can resolve an IP address to a *Media Access Control (MAC)* address. MAC addresses are used to identify hardware network devices such as a network interface card (NIC).

You'll notice the acronym *MAC* used a lot. It's also used to identify *Mandatory Access Control*, which defines how access control operates in an authentication model. You'll also see *MAC* used in cryptography, where it stands for *Message Authentication Code*. This MAC verifies that an algorithm is accurate.

Internet Control Message Protocol   *Internet Control Message Protocol (ICMP)* provides maintenance and reporting functions. It's used by the Ping program. When a user wants to test connectivity to another host, they can enter the PING command with the IP address, and the user's system will test connectivity to the other host's system. If connectivity is good, ICMP will return data to the originating host. ICMP will also report if a destination is unreachable. Routers and other network devices report path information between hosts with ICMP.

Internet Group Management Protocol   *Internet Group Management Protocol (IGMP)* is responsible primarily for managing IP multicast groups. IP multicasts can send messages or packets to a specified group of hosts. This is different from a broadcast, which all users in a network receive.

The Network Interface Layer

The lowest level of the TCP/IP suite is the *Network Interface layer.* This layer is responsible for placing and removing packets on the physical network through communications with the network adapters in the host. This process allows TCP/IP to work with virtually any type of network topology or technology with little modification. If a new physical network topology were installed—say, a 10GB Fiber Ethernet connection—TCP/IP would only need to know how to communicate with the network controller in order to function properly. TCP/IP can also communicate with more than one network topology simultaneously. This allows the protocol to be used in virtually any environment.

Understanding Encapsulation

One of the key points in understanding this layering process is the concept of *encapsulation*. Encapsulation allows a transport protocol to be sent across the network and utilized by the equivalent service or protocol at the receiving host. Figure 2.7 shows how e-mail is encapsulated as it moves from the application protocols through the transport and Internet protocols. Each layer adds header information as the e-mail moves down the layers.

Transmission of the packet between the two hosts occurs through the physical connection in the network adapter. Figure 2.8 illustrates this process between two hosts. What's shown in the figure isn't comprehensive but illustrates the process of message transmission.

After it is encapsulated, the message is sent to the server. Notice that in Figure 2.8 the message is sent via the Internet; it could have just as easily been sent locally. The e-mail client doesn't know how the message is delivered, and the server application doesn't care how the message got there. This makes designing and implementing services such as e-mail possible in a global or Internet environment.

FIGURE 2.7   The encapsulation process of an e-mail message

FIGURE 2.8   An e-mail message that an e-mail client sent to an e-mail server across the Internet

Working with Protocols and Services

It's imperative that you have a basic understanding of protocols and services to pass this exam. Although it isn't a requirement, CompTIA recommends that you already hold the Network+ certification before undertaking this exam. In case you're weak in some areas, the following sections will discuss in more detail how TCP/IP hosts communicate with each other. I'll discuss the concepts of ports, handshakes, and application interfaces. The objective isn't to make you an expert on this subject, but to help you understand what you're dealing with when attempting to secure a TCP/IP network.

Well-Known Ports

Simply stated, *ports* identify how a communication process occurs. Ports are special addresses that allow communication between hosts. A port number is added from the originator, indicating which port to communicate with on a server. If a server has this port defined and available for use, it will send back a message accepting the request. If the port isn't valid, the server will refuse the connection. The *Internet Assigned Numbers Authority (IANA)* has defined a list of ports called *well-known ports*.

 You can see the full description of the ports defined by IANA on the following website: www.iana.org. Many thousands of ports are available for use by servers and clients.

A port is nothing more than a bit of additional information added to either the TCP or UDP message. This information is added in the header of the packet. The layer below it encapsulates the message with its header.

Many of the services you'll use in the normal course of utilizing the Internet use the TCP port numbers identified in Table 2.1. Table 2.2 identifies some of the more common, well-known UDP ports.

TABLE 2.1   Well-Known TCP Ports

TCP Port Number	Service
20	FTP (data channel)
21	FTP (control channel)
22	SSH
23	Telnet
25	SMTP
49	TACACS authentication service
80	HTTP (used for the World Wide Web)
110	POP3
119	NNTP
139	NetBIOS session service
143	IMAP
389	LDAP
443	HTTPS (used for secure web connections)

TABLE 2.2   Well-Known UDP Ports

UDP Port Number	Service
53	DNS name queries
69	Trivial File Transfer Protocol (TFTP)
137	NetBIOS name service
138	NetBIOS datagram service
161	SNMP
162	SNMP trap

The early documentation for these ports specified that ports below 1024 were restricted to administrative uses. However, enforcement of this restriction has been voluntary and is creating problems for computer security professionals. As you can see, each of these ports potentially requires different security considerations, depending on the application they're assigned for. All the ports allow access to your network; even if you establish a firewall, you must have these ports open if you want to provide e-mail or web services.

TCP Three-Way Handshake

TCP, which is a *connection-oriented* protocol, establishes a session using a *three-way handshake*. A host called a *client* originates this connection. The client sends a TCP segment, or message, to the server. This client segment includes an *Initial Sequence Number (ISN)* for the connection and a window size. The server responds with a TCP segment that contains its ISN and a value indicating its buffer, or window size. The client then sends back an acknowledgment of the server's sequence number.

Figure 2.9 shows this three-way handshake occurring between a client and a server. When the session or connection is over, a similar process occurs to close the connection.

A web request uses the TCP connection process to establish the connection between the client and the server. After this occurs, the two systems communicate with each other; the server uses TCP port 80. The same thing occurs when an e-mail connection is made, with the difference being that the client (assuming it's using POP3) uses port 110.

FIGURE 2.9   The TCP connection process

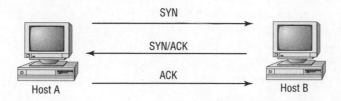

In this way, a server can handle many requests simultaneously. Each session has a different sequence number even though all sessions use the same port. All the communications in any given session use this sequence number to keep the sessions from becoming confused.

Application Programming Interface

Interfacing to TCP/IP is much simpler than interfacing to earlier network models. A well-defined and well-established set of *Application Programming Interfaces (APIs)* is available from most software companies. APIs allow programmers to create interfaces to the protocol. When a programmer needs to create a web-enabled application, they can call or use one of these APIs to make the connection, send or receive data, and end the connection. The APIs are prewritten, and they make the job considerably easier than manually coding all of the connection information.

Microsoft uses an API called a *Windows socket (WinSock)* to interface to the protocol. It can access either TCP or UDP protocols to accomplish the needed task. Figure 2.10 illustrates how the Windows socket connects to the TCP/IP protocol suite.

FIGURE 2.10 The Windows socket interface

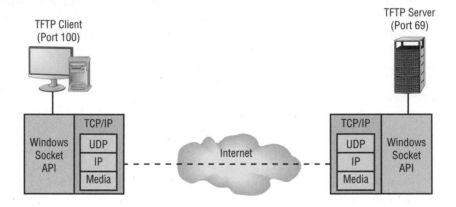

Recognizing TCP/IP Attacks

Attacks on TCP/IP usually occur at the host-to-host or Internet layer, although any layer is potentially vulnerable. TCP/IP is susceptible to attacks from both outside and inside an organization.

The opportunities for external attacks are somewhat limited by the devices in the network, including the router. The router blocks many of the protocols from exposure to the Internet. Some protocols, such as ARP, aren't routable and aren't generally vulnerable to outside attacks. Other protocols, such as SMTP and ICMP, pass through the router and form a normal part of Internet and TCP/IP traffic. TCP, UDP, and IP are all vulnerable to attack.

Your network is easily exposed to inside attacks. Any network-enabled host has access to the full array of protocols used in the network. A computer with a network card has the ability to act as a network sniffer with the proper configuration and software.

The following sections introduce you to the specific attacks that a TCP/IP-based network is susceptible to when off-the-shelf software or shareware is used.

Sniffing the Network

A *network sniffer*, or *scanner*, is a device that captures and displays network traffic. Your existing computers have the ability to operate as sniffers. Network cards usually only pass information up to the protocol stack if the information is intended for the computer on which they're installed; any network traffic not intended for that computer is ignored. Most NICs can be placed into what is called *promiscuous mode*, which allows the NIC to capture all information that it sees on the network. Devices such as routers, bridges, and switches are used to separate or segment networks within a larger network (known as virtual LANs, or VLANs). Any traffic in a particular segment is visible to all stations in that segment.

Adding a network sniffer such as the one included by Microsoft in its Systems Management Server (SMS) package allows any computer to function as a network sniffer. This software is widely available and is very capable. A number of public domain or shareware sniffers are also available online, such as Wireshark (http://www.wireshark.org).

By using a sniffer, an internal attacker can capture all the information transported by the network. Many advanced sniffers can reassemble packets and create entire messages, including user IDs and passwords. This vulnerability is particularly acute in environments where network connections are easily accessible to outsiders. For example, an attacker could put a laptop or a portable computer in your wiring closet and attach it to your network.

Scanning Ports

A TCP/IP network makes many of the ports available to outside users through the router. These ports respond in a predictable manner when queried. For example, TCP attempts synchronization when a session initiation occurs. An attacker can systematically query your network to determine which services and ports are open. This process is called *port scanning*, and it is part of fingerprinting a network; it can reveal a great deal about your systems. Port scans are possible both internally and externally. Many routers, unless configured appropriately, will let all protocols pass through them.

 Port scans help in identifying what services are running on a network.

Individual systems within a network might also have applications and services running that the owner doesn't know about. These services could potentially allow an internal attacker to gain access to information by connecting to the port associated with those services. Many Microsoft Internet Information Server (IIS) users don't realize the weak security that this product offers. If they didn't install all of the security patches when they installed IIS on their desktops, attackers can exploit the weaknesses of IIS and gain access to information. This has been done in many cases without the knowledge of the owner. These attacks might not technically be considered TCP/IP attacks, but they are because the inherent trust of TCP is used to facilitate the attacks.

After they know the IP addresses of your systems, external attackers can attempt to communicate with the ports open in your network, sometimes simply by using Telnet.

> To check whether a system has a particular protocol or port available, all you have to do is use the `telnet` command and add the port number. For example, you can check to see if a particular server is running an e-mail server program by entering `telnet www.youreintrouble.com 25`. This initiates a Telnet connection to the server on port 25. If the server is running SMTP, it will immediately respond with logon information. It doesn't take much to figure out how to talk to SMTP; the interface is well documented. If an e-mail account didn't have a password, this system is now vulnerable to attack.

This process of port scanning can be expanded to develop a footprint of your organization. If your attacker has a single IP address of a system in your network, they can probe all the addresses in the range and probably determine what other systems and protocols your network is utilizing. This allows the attacker to gain knowledge about the internal structure of your network.

> A study done by the University of Maryland's A. James Clark School of Engineering found that 38 percent of attacks were preceded by vulnerability scans. The combination of port scans with vulnerability scans created a lethal combination that often led to an attack.

In addition to scanning, network mapping allows you to visually see everything that is available. The most well-known network mapper is nmap, which can run on all operating systems and is found at `http://nmap.org/`.

TCP Attacks

TCP operates using synchronized connections. The synchronization is vulnerable to attack; this is probably the most common attack used today. As you may recall, the synchronization, or handshake, process initiates a TCP connection. This handshake is particularly vulnerable to a DoS attack referred to as a *TCP SYN flood attack*. The protocol is also susceptible to access and *modification attacks*, which are briefly explained in the following sections.

TCP SYN or TCP ACK Flood Attack

The *TCP SYN flood*, also referred to as the *TCP ACK attack*, is common. The purpose is to deny service. The attack begins as a normal TCP connection: The client and server exchange information in TCP packets. Figure 2.11 illustrates how this attack occurs. Notice that the

TCP client continues to send ACK packets to the server. The ACK packets tell the server that a connection is requested. The server responds with an ACK packet to the client. The client is supposed to respond with another packet accepting the connection, and a session is established.

FIGURE 2.11   TCP SYN flood attack

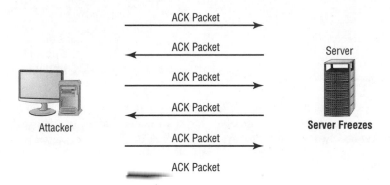

In this attack, the client continually sends and receives the ACK packets but doesn't open the session. The server holds these sessions open, awaiting the final packet in the sequence. This causes the server to fill up the available sessions and deny other clients the ability to access the resources.

This attack is virtually unstoppable in most environments without working with upstream providers. Many newer routers can track and attempt to prevent this attack by setting limits on the length of an initial session to force sessions that don't complete to close out. This type of attack can also be undetectable. An attacker can use an invalid IP address, and TCP won't care because TCP will respond to any valid request presented from the IP layer.

TCP Sequence Number Attack

TCP sequence number attacks occur when an attacker takes control of one end of a TCP session. This attack is successful when the attacker kicks the attacked end off the network for the duration of the session. Each time a TCP message is sent, either the client or the server generates a sequence number. In a TCP sequence number attack, the attacker intercepts and then responds with a *sequence number* similar to the one used in the original session. This attack can either disrupt or hijack a valid session. If a valid sequence number is guessed, attackers can place themselves between the client and server. Figure 2.12 illustrates a sequence number attack in process against a server. In this example, the attacker guesses the sequence number and replaces a real system with one of their own.

In this case, the attacker effectively hijacks the session and gains access to the session privileges of the victim's system. The victim's system may get an error message indicating that it has been disconnected, or it may reestablish a new session. In this case, the attacker gains the connection and access to the data from the legitimate system. The attacker then has access to the privileges established by the session when it was created.

FIGURE 2.12 TCP sequence number attack

This weakness is again inherent in the TCP protocol, and little can be done to prevent it. Your major defense against this type of attack is knowing that it's occurring. Such an attack is also frequently a precursor to a targeted attack on a server or network.

TCP/IP Hijacking

TCP/IP hijacking, also called *active sniffing*, involves the attacker gaining access to a host in the network and logically disconnecting it from the network. The attacker then inserts another machine with the same IP address. This happens quickly and gives the attacker access to the session and to all the information on the original system. The server won't know this has occurred and will respond as if the client is trusted. Figure 2.13 shows how TCP/IP hijacking occurs. In this example, the attacker forces the server to accept its IP address as valid.

TCP/IP hijacking presents the greatest danger to a network because the hijacker will probably acquire privileges and access to all the information on the server. As with a sequence number attack, there is little you can do to counter the threat. Fortunately, these attacks require fairly sophisticated software and are harder to engineer than a DoS attack such as a TCP SYN attack.

FIGURE 2.13 TCP/IP hijacking attack

UDP Attacks

A *UDP attack* attacks either a maintenance protocol or a UDP service in order to overload services and initiate a DoS situation. UDP attacks can also exploit UDP protocols.

One of the most popular UDP attacks is the ping of death discussed earlier in the section "Identifying Denial-of-Service and Distributed Denial-of-Service Attacks."

UDP packets aren't connection oriented and don't require the synchronization process described in the previous section. UDP packets, however, are susceptible to interception, and UDP can be attacked. UDP, like TCP, doesn't check the validity of IP addresses. The nature of this layer is to trust the layer below it, the IP layer.

The most common UDP attacks involve *UDP flooding*. UDP flooding overloads services, networks, and servers. Large streams of UDP packets are focused at a target, causing the UDP services on that host to shut down. UDP floods also overload the network bandwidth and cause a DoS situation to occur.

ICMP Attacks   *ICMP attacks* occur by triggering a response from the ICMP protocol to a seemingly legitimate maintenance request. From earlier discussions, you'll recall that ICMP is often associated with echoing.

ICMP supports maintenance and reporting in a TCP/IP network. It is part of the IP level of the protocol suite. Several programs, including Ping, use the ICMP protocol. Until fairly recently, ICMP was regarded as a benign protocol that was incapable of much damage. However, it has now joined the ranks of protocols used in common attack methods for DoS attacks. Two primary methods use ICMP to disrupt systems: *smurf attacks* and *ICMP tunneling*.

Smurf Attacks   *Smurf attacks* can create havoc in a network. A smurf attack uses IP spoofing and broadcasting to send a ping to a group of hosts in a network. An ICMP ping request (type 8) is answered with an ICMP ping reply (type 0) if the targeted system is up, otherwise an unreachable message is returned. If a broadcast is sent to a network, all of the hosts will answer back to the ping. The result is an overload of the network and the target system.

Figure 2.14 shows a smurf attack under way in a network. The attacker sends a broadcast message with a legal IP address. In this case, the attacking system sends a ping request to the broadcast address of the network. The request is sent to all the machines in a large network. The reply is then sent to the machine identified with the ICMP request (the spoof is complete). The result is a DoS attack that consumes the network bandwidth of the replying system, while the victim system deals with the flood of ICMP traffic it receives.

The primary method of eliminating smurf attacks involves prohibiting ICMP traffic through a router. If the router blocks ICMP traffic, smurf attacks from an external attacker aren't possible.

FIGURE 2.14   A smurf attack under way against a network

Attacker

Attacker sends ICMP broadcast
to network with false IP address.

Internet

Network overloads victim
with ICMP response.

Victim

ICMP Tunneling   ICMP messages can contain data about timing and routes. A packet can be used to hold information that is different from the intended information. This allows an ICMP packet to be used as a communications channel between two systems. The channel can be used to send a Trojan horse or other malicious packet. This is a relatively new opportunity to create havoc and mischief in networks.

The countermeasure for ICMP attacks is to deny ICMP traffic through your network. You can disable ICMP traffic in most routers, and you should consider doing so in your network.

Many of the newer SOHO router solutions (and some of the personal firewall solutions on end-user workstations) close down the ICMP ports by default. Keep this in mind, as it can drive you nuts when you are trying to see if a brand-new station/server/router is up and running.

Understanding Software Exploitation

The term *software exploitation* refers to attacks launched against applications and higher-level services. They include gaining access to data using weaknesses in the data access objects of a database or a flaw in a service. This section briefly outlines common exploitations that have been successful in the past. The following exploitations can be introduced using viruses, as in the case of the Klez32 virus, or by using access attacks described earlier in this chapter:

Database exploitation   Many database products allow sophisticated access queries to be made in the client/server environment. If a client session can be hijacked or spoofed, the attacker can formulate queries against the database that disclose unauthorized information.

For this attack to be successful, the attacker must first gain access to the environment through one of the attacks outlined previously.

Application exploitation   The macro virus is another example of software exploitation. A macro virus is a set of programming instructions in a language such as VBScript that commands an application to perform illicit actions. Users want more powerful tools, and manufacturers want to sell users what they want. The macro virus takes advantage of the power offered by word processors, spreadsheets, or other applications. This exploitation is inherent in the product, and all users are susceptible to it unless they disable all macros.

E-mail exploitation   Hardly a day goes by without another e-mail virus being reported. This is a result of a weakness in many common e-mail clients. Modern e-mail clients offer many shortcuts, lists, and other capabilities to meet user demands. A popular exploitation of e-mail clients involves accessing the client address book and propagating viruses. There is virtually nothing a client user can do about these exploitations, although antivirus software that integrates with your e-mail client does offer some protection. To be truly successful, the software manufacturer must fix the weaknesses—an example is Outlook's option to protect against access to the address book. This type of weakness isn't a bug, in many cases, but a feature that users wanted.

Teach users to exercise discretion when opening any e-mail attachment.

Spyware   *Spyware* differs from other malware in that it works—often actively—on behalf of a third party. Rather than self-replicating, like viruses and worms, spyware is spread to machines by users who inadvertently ask for it. The users often do not know they have asked for it, but have acquired it by downloading other programs, visiting infected sites, and so on.

New Attacks on the Way

The discussion of attacks in this section isn't comprehensive. New methods are being developed even as you read this book. Your first challenge in these situations is to recognize that you're fighting the battle on two fronts.

The first front involves the inherent open nature of TCP/IP and its protocol suite. TCP/IP is a robust and rich environment. This richness allows many opportunities to exploit the vulnerabilities of the protocol suite. The second front of this battle involves the implementation of TCP/IP by various vendors. A weak TCP/IP implementation will be susceptible to all forms of attacks, and there is little you'll be able to do about it except to complain to the software manufacturer. Fortunately, most of the credible manufacturers are now taking these complaints seriously and doing what they can to close the holes they have created in your systems. Keep your updates current because this is where most of the corrections for security problems are implemented.

The spyware program monitors the user's activity and responds by offering unsolicited pop-up advertisements (sometimes known as *adware*), gathers information about the user to pass on to marketers, or intercepts personal data such as credit card numbers. One thing separating spyware from most other malware is that it almost always exists to provide commercial gain. The operating systems from Microsoft are the ones most affected by spyware, and Microsoft has released Microsoft AntiSpyware to combat the problem.

Rootkits   Recently, *rootkits* have become the software exploitation program du jour. Rootkits are software programs that have the ability to hide certain things from the operating system. With a rootkit, there may be a number of processes running on a system that do not show up in Task Manager or connections established or available that do not appear in a `netstat` display—the rootkit masks the presence of these items. The rootkit is able to do this by manipulating function calls to the operating system and filtering out information that would normally appear.

Unfortunately, many rootkits are written to get around antivirus and antispyware programs that are not kept up-to-date. The best defense you have is to monitor what your system is doing and catch the rootkit in the process of installation.

As these new threats have developed, so have some excellent programs for countering them. Within any search engine, you can find a rootkit analyzer for your system, including Spybot, Spyware Doctor, and AdAware.

One of the most important measures you can take to proactively combat software attacks is to know common file extensions and the applications they're associated with. For example, the `.scr` filename extension is used for screensavers, and viruses are often distributed through the use of these files. No legitimate user should be sending screensavers via e-mail to your users, and all attachments with the `.scr` filename extension should be banned from entering the network.

Table 2.3, while not comprehensive, contains the most common filename extensions for files that should and should not, as a general rule, be allowed into the network as e-mail attachments.

TABLE 2.3   Common Filename Extensions for E-mail Attachments

Should Be Allowed	Should *Not* Be Allowed
.doc	.bat
.pdf	.com
.txt	.exe
.xls	.hlp

TABLE 2.3   Common Filename Extensions for E-mail Attachments *(continued)*

Should Be Allowed	Should *Not* Be Allowed
.zip	.pif
	.scr

Understanding OVAL

The *Open Vulnerability and Assessment Language (OVAL)* is a community standard written in XML that strives to promote open and publicly available security content. It consists of a language, interpreter, and repository and is meant to standardize information between security tools.

As of this writing, version 5.4 is available, and you can find it at http://oval.mitre.org.

Surviving Malicious Code

Malicious code refers to a broad category of software threats to your network and systems, including viruses, Trojan horses, bombs, and worms. Your users depend on you to help keep them safe from harm and to repulse these attacks. When successful, these attacks can be devastating to systems, and they can spread through an entire network. One such incident involved the Melissa virus that effectively brought the entire Internet down for a few days in March 1999. This virus spread to millions of Outlook and Outlook Express users worldwide. Variants of this virus are still propagating through the Internet.

The following sections will briefly introduce you to the types of malicious code you'll encounter. I'll also explain the importance of antivirus software.

Viruses

A *virus* is a piece of software designed to infect a computer system. The virus may do nothing more than reside on the computer. A virus may also damage the data on your hard disk, destroy your operating system, and possibly spread to other systems. Viruses get into your computer in one of three ways: on contaminated media (floppy, USB drive, or CD-ROM), through e-mail and peer-to-peer sites, or as part of another program.

Viruses can be classified as polymorphic, stealth, retroviruses, multipartite, armored, companion, phage, and macro viruses. Each type of virus has a different attack strategy and different consequences.

Estimates for losses due to viruses are in the billions of dollars. These losses include financial loss as well as lost productivity.

The following sections will introduce the symptoms of a virus infection, explain how a virus works, and describe the types of viruses you can expect to encounter and how they generally behave. I'll also discuss how a virus is transmitted through a network and look at a few hoaxes.

Symptoms of a Virus Infection

Many viruses will announce that you're infected as soon as they gain access to your system. They may take control of your system and flash annoying messages on your screen or destroy your hard disk. When this occurs, you'll know that you're a victim. Other viruses will cause your system to slow down, cause files to disappear from your computer, or take over your disk space.

You should look for some of the following symptoms when determining if a virus infection has occurred:

- The programs on your system start to load more slowly. This happens because the virus is spreading to other files in your system or is taking over system resources.

- Unusual files appear on your hard drive, or files start to disappear from your system. Many viruses delete key files in your system to render it inoperable.

- Program sizes change from the installed versions. This occurs because the virus is attaching itself to these programs on your disk.

- Your browser, word processing application, or other software begins to exhibit unusual operating characteristics. Screens or menus may change.

- The system mysteriously shuts itself down or starts itself up and does a great deal of unanticipated disk activity.

- You mysteriously lose access to a disk drive or other system resources. The virus has changed the settings on a device to make it unusable.

- Your system suddenly doesn't reboot or gives unexpected error messages during startup.

This list is by no means comprehensive.

How Viruses Work

A virus, in most cases, tries to accomplish one of two things: render your system inoperable or spread to other systems. Many viruses will spread to other systems given the chance and then render your system unusable. This is common with many of the newer viruses.

If your system is infected, the virus may try to attach itself to every file in your system and spread each time you send a file or document to other users. Figure 2.15 shows a virus spreading from an infected system either through a network or by removable media. When you give removable media to another user or put it into another system, you then infect that system with the virus.

FIGURE 2.15   Virus spreading from an infected system using the network or removable media

Many newer viruses spread using e-mail. The infected system attaches a file to any e-mail that you send to another user. The recipient opens this file, thinking it's something you legitimately sent them. When they open the file, the virus infects the target system. The virus might then attach itself to all the e-mails the newly infected system sends, which in turn infects the recipients of the e-mails. Figure 2.16 shows how a virus can spread from a single user to literally thousands of users in a very short time using e-mail.

Types of Viruses

Viruses take many different forms. The following sections briefly introduce these forms and explain how they work. These are the most common types, but this isn't a comprehensive list.

The best defense against a virus attack is up-to-date antivirus software installed and running. The software should be on all workstations as well as the server.

Armored Virus

An *armored virus* is designed to make itself difficult to detect or analyze. Armored viruses cover themselves with protective code that stops debuggers or disassemblers from examining critical elements of the virus. The virus may be written in such a way that some aspects of the programming act as a decoy to distract analysis while the actual code hides in other areas in the program.

From the perspective of the creator, the more time it takes to deconstruct the virus, the longer it can live. The longer it can live, the more time it has to replicate and spread to as many machines as possible. The key to stopping most viruses is to identify them quickly and educate administrators about them—the very things that the armor intensifies the difficulty of accomplishing.

FIGURE 2.16 An e-mail virus spreading geometrically to other users

Companion Virus

A *companion virus* attaches itself to legitimate programs and then creates a program with a different filename extension. This file may reside in your system's temporary directory. When a user types the name of the legitimate program, the companion virus executes instead of the real program. This effectively hides the virus from the user. Many of the viruses that are used to attack Windows systems make changes to program pointers in the Registry so that they point to the infected program. The infected program may perform its dirty deed and then start the real program.

Macro Virus

A *macro virus* exploits the enhancements made to many application programs. Programmers can expand the capability of applications such as Word and Excel. Word, for example, supports a mini-BASIC programming language that allows files to be manipulated automatically. These programs in the document are called *macros*. For example, a macro can tell your word processor to spell-check your document automatically when it opens. Macro viruses can infect all the documents on your system and spread to other systems via e-mail or other methods. Macro viruses are the fastest growing exploitation today.

Multipartite Virus

A *multipartite virus* attacks your system in multiple ways. It may attempt to infect your boot sector, infect all of your executable files, and destroy your application files. The hope here is that you won't be able to correct all the problems and will allow the infestation to continue. The multipartite virus in Figure 2.17 attacks your boot sector, infects application files, and attacks your Microsoft Word documents.

Phage Virus

A *phage virus* modifies and alters other programs and databases. The virus infects all of these files. The only way to remove this virus is to reinstall the programs that are infected. If you miss even a single incident of this virus on the victim system, the process will start again and infect the system once more.

FIGURE 2.17   A multipartite virus commencing an attack on a system

Polymorphic Virus

Polymorphic viruses change form in order to avoid detection. These types of viruses attack your system, display a message on your computer, and delete files on your system. The virus will attempt to hide from your antivirus software. Frequently, the virus will encrypt parts of itself to avoid detection. When the virus does this, it's referred to as *mutation*. The mutation process makes it hard for antivirus software to detect common characteristics of the virus. Figure 2.18 shows a polymorphic virus changing its characteristics to avoid detection. In this example, the virus changes a signature to fool antivirus software.

Retrovirus

A *retrovirus* attacks or bypasses the antivirus software installed on a computer. You can consider a retrovirus to be an anti-antivirus. Retroviruses can directly attack your antivirus software and potentially destroy the virus definition database file. Destroying this information without your knowledge would leave you with a false sense of security. The virus may also directly attack an antivirus program to create bypasses for itself.

FIGURE 2.18   The polymorphic virus changing its characteristics

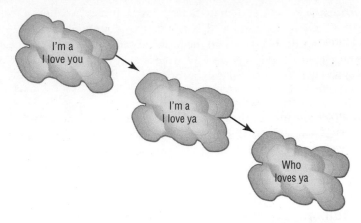

Stealth Virus

A *stealth virus* attempts to avoid detection by masking itself from applications. It may attach itself to the boot sector of the hard drive. When a system utility or program runs, the stealth virus redirects commands around itself in order to avoid detection. An infected file may report a file size different from what is actually present in order to avoid detection. Figure 2.19 shows a stealth virus attaching itself to the boot sector to avoid detection. Stealth viruses may also move themselves from fileA to fileB during a virus scan for the same reason.

An updated list of the most active viruses and spyware is on the Panda Software site at http://enterprise.pandasoftware.com.

FIGURE 2.19   A stealth virus hiding in a disk boot sector

← This is a disk

Virus Transmission in a Network

Upon infection, some viruses destroy the target system immediately. The saving grace is that the infection can be detected and corrected. Some viruses won't destroy or otherwise tamper with a system; they use the victim system as a carrier. The victim system then infects servers, file shares, and other resources with the virus. The carrier then infects the target system again. Until the carrier is identified and cleaned, the virus continues to harass systems in this network and spread.

Present Virus Activity

New viruses and threats are released on a regular basis to join the cadre of those already in existence. From an exam perspective, you need only be familiar with the world as it existed at the time the questions were written. From an administration standpoint, however, you need to know what is happening today.

To find this information, visit the CERT/CC Current Activity web page at http://www.us-cert .gov/current/current_activity.html. Here you'll find a detailed description of the most current viruses as well as links to pages on older threats.

Identifying Hoaxes

Network users have plenty of real viruses to worry about. Yet some people find it entertaining to issue phony threats to keep people on their toes. Some of the more popular hoaxes that have been passed around are the Good Time and the Irina viruses. Millions of users received e-mails about these two viruses, and the symptoms sounded awful.

Both of these viruses claimed to do things that are impossible to accomplish with a virus. When you receive a virus warning, you can verify its authenticity by looking on the website of the antivirus software you use, or you can go to several public systems. One of the more helpful sites to visit to get the status of the latest viruses is the CERT organization (www.cert.org). CERT monitors and tracks viruses and provides regular reports on this site.

When you receive an e-mail you suspect is a hoax, check the CERT site before forwarding the message to anyone else. The creator of the hoax wants to create widespread panic, and if you blindly forward the message to coworkers and acquaintances, you're helping the creator accomplish their task. For example, any e-mail that says "forward to all your friends" is a candidate for hoax research. Disregarding the hoax allows it to die a quick death and keeps users focused on productive tasks.

Symantec and other vendors maintain pages devoted to bogus hoaxes (www.symantec.com/business/security_response/threatexplorer/risks/hoaxes .jsp). You can always check there to verify whether an e-mail you've received is indeed a hoax.

While *spam* is not truly a virus or a hoax, it is one of the most annoying things an administrator can contend with. Spam is defined as any unwanted, unsolicited e-mail, and not only can the sheer volume of it be irritating, it can often open the door to larger problems. Some of the sites advertised in spam may be infected with viruses, worms, and other unwanted programs. If users begin to respond to spam by visiting those sites, then your problems will only multiply.

There are numerous anti-spam programs available and they can be run by users as well as administrators. One of the biggest problems with many of these applications is false-positives: they will occasionally flag legitimate e-mail as spam and stop it from being delivered.

Just as you can, and must, install good antivirus software programs, you should also consider similar measures for spam. Filtering the messages out and preventing them from ever entering the network is the most effective method of dealing with the problem. Recently, the word spam has found its way into other forms of unwanted messaging beyond email, giving birth to the acronyms SPIM (spam over Instant Messaging) and SPIT (spam over Internet Telephony).

Trojan Horses

Trojan horses are programs that enter a system or network under the guise of another program. A Trojan horse may be included as an attachment or as part of an installation program. The Trojan horse could create a back door or replace a valid program during installation. It would then accomplish its mission under the guise of another program. Trojan horses can be used to compromise the security of your system, and they can exist on a system for years before they're detected.

The best preventive measure for Trojan horses is to not allow them entry into your system. Immediately before and after you install a new software program or operating system, back it up! If you suspect a Trojan horse, you can reinstall the original programs, which should delete the Trojan horse. A port scan may also reveal a Trojan horse on your system. If an application opens a TCP or UDP port that isn't regularly used in your network, you can notice this and begin corrective action.

Is a Trojan horse also a virus? A Trojan horse is anything that sneaks in under the guise of something else. Given that general definition, it's certainly possible that a virus can (and usually does) sneak in, but this description most often fits the definition of a companion virus. The primary distinction, from an exam perspective, is that with a Trojan horse you always intentionally obtained something (usually an application) and didn't know an unpleasant freeloader was hidden within. An example is spyware, which is often installed (unknown to you) as part of another application.

Logic Bombs

Logic bombs are programs or snippets of code that execute when a certain predefined event occurs. A bomb may send a note to an attacker when a user is logged on to the Internet and is using a word processor. This message informs the attacker that the user is ready for an attack.

Figure 2.20 shows a logic bomb in operation. Notice that this bomb doesn't begin the attack but tells the attacker that the victim has met the needed criteria or state for an attack to begin. Logic bombs may also be set to go off on a certain date or when a specified set of circumstances occurs.

In the attack depicted in Figure 2.20, the logic bomb sends a message back to the attacking system that it has loaded successfully. The victim system can then be used to initiate an attack such as a DDoS attack, or it can grant access at the time of the attacker's choosing.

FIGURE 2.20   A logic bomb being initiated

1. Attacker implants logic bomb.
2. Victim reports installation.
3. Attacker sends attack message.
4. Victim does as logic bomb indicates.

Worms

A *worm* is different from a virus in that it can reproduce itself, it's self-contained, and it doesn't need a host application to be transported. Many of the so-called viruses that have made the papers and media were, in actuality, worms and not viruses. However, it's possible for a worm to contain or deliver a virus to a target system.

The Melissa virus (which was actually a worm) spread itself to more than 100,000 users in a relatively short period when it first came out, according to CERT. One site received more than 32,000 copies of the Melissa virus in a 45-minute period.

Worms by their nature and origin are supposed to propagate and will use whatever services they're capable of to do that. Early worms filled up memory and bred inside the RAM of the target computer. Worms can use TCP/IP, e-mail, Internet services, or any number of means to reach their target.

Antivirus Software

The primary method of preventing the propagation of malicious code involves the use of *antivirus software*. Antivirus software is an application that is installed on a system to protect it and to scan for viruses as well as worms and Trojan horses. Most viruses have characteristics that are common to families of virus. Antivirus software looks for these characteristics, or fingerprints, to identify and neutralize viruses before they impact you.

More than 60,000 known viruses, worms, bombs, and other malicious code have been defined. New ones are added all the time. Your antivirus software manufacturer will usually work very hard to keep the definition database files current. The definition database file contains all of the known viruses and countermeasures for a particular antivirus software product. You probably won't receive a virus that hasn't been seen by one of these companies. If you keep the virus definition database files in your software up-to-date, you probably won't be overly vulnerable to attacks.

 The best method of protection is to use a layered approach. Antivirus software should be at the gateways, at the servers, and at the desktop. If you want to go one step further, you can use software at each location from different vendors to make sure you're covered from all angles.

The second method of preventing viruses is education. Teach your users not to open suspicious files and to open only those files that they're reasonably sure are virus free. They need to scan every disk, e-mail, and document they receive before they open them.

 Real World Scenario

A Virus Out of Control

A large private university has over 30,000 students taking online classes. These students use a variety of systems and network connections. The instructors of this university are being routinely hit with the Klez32 virus. Klez32 (specifically, in this case, the W32/Klez. mm virus) is a well-known and documented virus. It uses Outlook or Outlook Express to spread. It grabs a name randomly from the address book and uses that name in the header. The worm then uses a mini-mailer and mails the virus to all the people in the address book. When one of these users opens the file, the worm attempts to disable their antivirus software and spread to other systems. Doing so opens the system to an attack from other viruses, which might follow later.

You've been appointed to the IT department at this school, and you've been directed to solve this problem. Ponder what you can do about it.

The best solution would be to install antivirus software that scans and blocks all e-mails that come through the school's servers. You should also inspect outgoing e-mail and notify all internal users of the system when they attempt to send a virus-infected document using the server.

These two steps—installing antivirus scanners on the external and internal connections and notifying unsuspecting senders—would greatly reduce the likelihood that the virus could attack either student or instructor computers.

Understanding Social Engineering

In the previous sections, you learned how attacks work. You also learned about TCP/IP and some of its vulnerabilities. And you were exposed to the issues that your users will face so you can help them from a technical perspective. A key method of attack that you must guard against is called social engineering.

Social engineering is a process in which an attacker attempts to acquire information about your network and system by social means, such as talking to people in the organization. A social engineering attack may occur over the phone, by e-mail, or in person. The intent is to acquire access information, such as user IDs and passwords.

 Always think of a social engineering attack as one that involves people who are unwitting.

These types of attacks are relatively low-tech and are more akin to con jobs. Take the following example: Your help desk gets a call at 4:00 a.m. from someone purporting to be the vice president of your company. She tells the help desk personnel that she is out of town to attend a meeting, her computer just failed, and she is sitting in a Kinko's trying to get a file from her desktop computer back at the office. She can't seem to remember her password and user ID. She tells the help desk representative that she needs access to the information right away or the company could lose millions of dollars. Your help desk rep knows how important this meeting is and gives the vice president her user ID and password over the phone. You've been hit!

Another common approach is initiated by a phone call or e-mail from someone claiming to be your software vendor, telling you that they have a critical fix that must be installed on your computer system. If this patch isn't installed right away, your system will crash, and you'll lose all your data. For some reason, you've changed your maintenance account password, and they can't log on. Your systems operator gives the password to the person. You've been hit again.

 Users are bombarded with e-mails and messages on services such as AOL asking them to confirm the password they use. These attacks appear to come from the administrative staff of the network. The attacker already has the user ID or screen name; all they need to complete the attack is the password. Make sure your users never give their user IDs or passwords. Either case potentially completes an attack.

With social engineering, the villain doesn't always have to be seen or heard to conduct the attack. The use of e-mail was mentioned earlier, and in recent years, the frequency of attacks via instant messaging has also increased. Attackers can send infected files over Instant Messaging (IM) as easily as they can over e-mail. A recent virus on the scene accesses a user's IM client and uses the infected user's buddy list to send messages to other users and infect their machines as well.

Phishing is a form of social engineering in which you simply ask someone for a piece of information that you are missing by making it look as if it is a legitimate request. An e-mail might look as if it is from a bank and contain some basic information, such as the user's name. In the e-mail, it will often state that there is a problem with the person's account or access privileges. They will be told to click a link to correct the problem. After they click the link—which goes to a site other than the bank's—they are asked for their username, password, account information, and so on. The person instigating the phishing can then use the values entered there to access the legitimate account.

One of the best counters to phishing is to simply mouse over the Click Here link and read the URL. Almost every time it is pointing to an adaptation of the legitimate URL as opposed to a link to the real thing.

The only preventive measure in dealing with social engineering attacks is to educate your users and staff to never give out passwords and user IDs over the phone or via e-mail, or to anyone who isn't positively verified as being who they say they are. Social engineering is a recurring topic that will appear several times throughout this book as it relates to the subject being discussed.

 Real World Scenario

A Security Analogy

In this chapter, a number of access methods were discussed. Sometimes it can be confusing to keep them all straight. To put the main ones somewhat in perspective think of it in terms of a stranger who wants to gain access to your house. There are any number of types of individuals who may want to get in your house without your knowing it:

▪   A thief wanting to steal any valuables you may have

▪   Teenagers wanting to do something destructive on a Saturday night

▪   Homeless people looking to get in out of the cold and find some food

▪   A neighbor who has been drinking and accidentally pulls in the wrong driveway and starts to come in, thinking it is their house

▪   A professional hit man wanting to lie in wait for you to come home

There are many more, but these represent a good cross section of individuals, each of whom has different motives and motivational levels for trying to get in.

To keep the thief out, you could post security signs all around your house and install a home alarm. He might not know if you really have ABC Surveillance active monitoring—as the signs say—but he might not want to risk it and go away looking for an easier target to hit. In the world of computer security, encryption acts like your home alarm and monitoring software, alerting you (or your monitoring company) to potential problems when they arise.

The teenagers are just wanting to do damage anywhere, and your house is as good as the next one. Installing motion lights above the doors and around the side of the house is really all you need to make them drive farther down the road. In the world of computer security, good passwords—and policies that are enforced—will keep these would-be intruders out.

The homeless also have no particular affection for your home as opposed to the next. You can keep them out by using locks on your doors and windows and putting a fence around your yard. If they can't get in the fence, they can't approach the house, and if they do manage that, they are confronted by the locks. Firewalls serve this purpose in the world of computer security.

The neighbor just made a legitimate error. That happens. I once went into the wrong person's tent when camping because they all look the same. To make yours look different, you can add banners and warnings to the login routines stating, for example, that this is ABC server and you must be an authorized user to access.

This leaves the hit man. He has been paid to do a job, and that job entails gaining access to your home. No matter how good the locks are on your house, no matter how many motion lights you put up, if someone's sole purpose in life is to gain access to your house, they will find a way to do it. The same is true of your server. You can implement measures to keep everyone else out, but if someone spends their entire existence dedicated to getting access to that server, they will do it if it entails putting on a heating and air conditioning uniform and walking past the receptionist, pointing two dozen computers to hashing routines that will crack your passwords, or driving a tank through the side of the building. Your job is to handle all the reasonable risks that come your way. Some, however, you have to acknowledge have only a very slim chance of ever truly being risks, and some, no matter what precautions you take, will not go away.

Introducing Auditing Processes and Files

Most systems generate *security logs* and *audit files* of activity. These files do absolutely no good if they aren't periodically reviewed for unusual events. Many web servers provide message auditing, as do logon, system, and application servers.

The amount and volume of information these files contain can be overwhelming. You should establish a procedure to review them on a regular basis.

 A rule of thumb is to never start auditing by trying to record everything because the sheer volume of the entries will make the data unusable. Approach auditing from the opposite perspective: Begin auditing only a few key things, and then expand the audits as you find you need more data.

Audit files and security logs may also be susceptible to access or modification attacks. The files often contain critical system information, including resource sharing, security status, and so on. An attacker may be able to use this information to gather more detailed data about your network.

In an access attack, these files can be deleted, modified, and scrambled to prevent system administrators from knowing what happened in the system. A logic bomb could, for example, delete these files when it completes. Administrators might know that something happened, but they would get no clues or assistance from the log and audit files.

You should consider periodically inspecting systems to see what software is installed and whether passwords are posted on sticky notes on monitors or keyboards. A good way to do this without attracting attention is to clean all the monitor faces. While you're cleaning the monitors, you can also verify that physical security is being upheld. If you notice a password on a sticky note, you can "accidentally" forget to put it back. You should also notify that user that this is an unsafe practice and not to continue it.

You should also consider obtaining a vulnerability scanner and running it across your network. A *vulnerability scanner* is a software application that checks your network for any known security holes; it's better to run one on your own network before someone outside the organization runs it against you. One of the best-known vulnerability scanners is Nessus.

Summary

This chapter focused on the types of attacks you'll encounter and your network's vulnerabilities:

- Types of attack
- TCP/IP
- Malicious code
- Social engineering

Denial of service, distributed denial of service, back door attacks, spoofing attacks, man-in-the-middle attacks, and replay attacks are all types of attacks you may encounter. Each takes advantage of inherent weaknesses in the network technologies most commonly used today.

TCP/IP is particularly vulnerable to attacks at the Host-to-Host (or Transport) layer and the IP layer. Transport layer attacks are designed to take advantage of the synchronization method used by TCP, the unsynchronized characteristics of UDP, and the maintenance messages generated by ICMP.

Common attacks on TCP include the SYN or ACK flood attack, TCP sequence number attack, and TCP/IP hijacking.

UDP is vulnerable to flooding attacks. Flooding attacks are DoS attacks, and they're designed to prevent access by authorized users.

TCP/IP uses protocols and services at each layer of the network model. These protocols and services offer ports to receive and send messages to other services or applications. The ports are vulnerable to attack depending on the protocol. Thousands of ports are available for use in TCP/IP. The ports numbered below 1024 are considered well known, and they usually require administrative access to be used.

Applications interface with the TCP/IP suite using either APIs or Windows sockets. These interfaces are well established and published.

Each layer of the protocol suite communicates with the layers above and below it. The process of preparing a message for transmission involves adding headers as the packet moves down this stream. This process is called encapsulation.

Malicious code describes an entire family of software that has nefarious intentions for your networks and computers. This includes viruses, Trojan horses, logic bombs, and worms. Viruses and worms are becoming a major problem on the Internet. The best prevention methods available include antivirus software and user education.

The process of using human intelligence to acquire access to information and systems is called social engineering. Social engineering involves someone contacting a member of an organization and attempting to con them out of account and password information. The best method of minimizing social engineering attacks is user education and positive verification of the identity of the person committing the attack.

Audit files and system logs are very effective for tracking activity in a network or on a server. They should be reviewed regularly to identify if unauthorized activity is occurring. Systems should be routinely inspected to verify whether physical security procedures are being followed.

Exam Essentials

Be able to describe the various types of attacks to which your systems are exposed. Your network is vulnerable to DoS attacks caused by either a single system or multiple systems. Multiple system attacks are called DDoS. Your systems are also susceptible to access, modification, and repudiation attacks.

Be able to describe the methods used to conduct a back door attack. Back door attacks occur using either existing maintenance hooks or developmental tools to examine the internal operations of a program. These hooks are usually removed when a product is prepared for market or production. Back door attacks also refer to inserting into a machine a program or service that allows authentication to be bypassed and access gained.

Know how a spoofing attack occurs.   Spoofing attacks occur when a user or system masquerades as another user or system. Spoofing allows the attacker to assume the privileges and access rights of the real user or system.

Be able to describe a man-in-the-middle attack.   Man-in-the-middle attacks are based on the principle that a system can be placed between two legitimate users to capture or exploit the information being sent between them. Both sides of the conversation assume that the man in the middle is the other end and communicate normally. This creates a security breach and allows unauthorized access to information.

Be able to describe a replay attack.   A replay attack captures information from a previous session and attempts to resend it to gain unauthorized access. This attack is based on the premise that if it worked once, it will work again. This is especially effective in environments where a user ID and password are sent in the clear across a large network.

Be able to describe a TCP/IP hijacking.   TCP/IP hijacking occurs when an unauthorized system replaces the authorized system without being detected. This allows access privileges to be kept in the session. Hijacking attacks are hard to detect because everything appears to be normal except the hijacked system. Hijacking attacks take advantage of the sequencing numbers used in TCP sessions.

Know how social engineering occurs.   Social engineering is a process in which an unauthorized person attempts to gain access to information by asking the help desk or other employees for account and password information. This assault typically occurs when an attacker acts as someone who would legitimately have a right to that information.

Be able to describe the two methods used in password guessing.   The two methods used to guess passwords are brute force and dictionary. Brute-force attacks work by trying to randomly guess a password repeatedly against a known account ID. In a dictionary attack, a dictionary of common words is used to attempt to find a user's password.

Know how software exploitation occurs.   Software exploitation involves using features or capabilities of a software product in a manner either unplanned for or unanticipated by the software manufacturer. In many cases, the original feature enhanced the functionality of the product but, unfortunately, creates a potential vulnerability.

Know the characteristics and types of viruses used to disrupt systems and networks.   Several different types of viruses are floating around today. The most common ones are polymorphic viruses, stealth viruses, retroviruses, multipartite viruses, and macro viruses.

Be able to explain the characteristics of Trojan horses and logic bombs.   Trojan horses are programs that enter a system or network under the guise of another program. Logic bombs are programs or snippets of code that execute when a certain predefined event occurs.

Know how worms operate.   Worms attack systems and attempt to procreate and propagate. Worms spread using files, e-mail, and physical media, such as a USB drive. A worm will also frequently contain a virus that causes the destruction of a system.

Be able to describe how antivirus software operates.   Antivirus software looks for a signature in the virus to determine what type of virus it is. The software then takes action to neutralize the virus based on a virus definition database. Virus definition database files are regularly made available on vendor sites.

Know how audit files can help detect unauthorized activity on a system or network.   Most operating systems provide a number of audit files to record the results of activities. These log files will frequently contain unsuccessful logon attempts as well as reports of excessive network traffic. They should be reviewed on a regular basis to determine what is happening on a system or a network.

Hands-On Labs

The labs in this chapter are as follows:

Lab 2.1: Identify Running Processes on a Windows-Based Machine

Lab 2.2: Identify Running Processes on a Linux-Based Machine

Lab 2.1: Identify Running Processes on a Windows-Based Machine

It is important to know what processes are running on a machine at any given time. In addition to the programs that a user may be using, there are always many others that are required by the operating system, the network, or other applications.

All recent versions of Windows include the Task Manager to allow you to see what is running. To access this information, follow these steps:

1. Right-click an empty location in the Windows Taskbar.

2. Choose Task Manager from the pop-up menu that appears.

3. The Task Manager opens to Applications by default and shows what the user is actually using. Click the Processes tab. Information about the programs that are needed for the running applications is shown, as well as all other processes running. (If the Show Processes From All Users check box appears beneath this tab, be sure to click it.) Many of the names of the processes appear cryptic, but definitions for most (good and bad) can be found at http://www.liutilities.com/products/wintaskspro/processlibrary/.

4. Examine the list and look for anything out of the ordinary. After doing this a few times, you will become familiar with what is normally there and will be able to spot oddities quickly.

5. Notice the values in the CPU column. Those values will always total 100, with System Idle Processes typically making up the bulk. High numbers on another process can indicate that there is a problem with it. If the numbers do not add up to 100, it can be a sign that a rootkit is masking some of the display.

6. Close the Task Manager.

Lab 2.2: Identify Running Processes on a Linux-Based Machine

Most versions of Linux include a graphical utility to allow you to see the running processes. Those utilities differ based on the distribution of Linux you are using and the desktop that you have chosen.

All versions of Linux, however, do offer a command line and the ability to use the ps utility. Because of that, this method is employed in this lab. To access this information, follow these steps:

1. Open a shell window, or otherwise access a command prompt.

2. Type ps -ef | more.

3. The display shows the processes running for all users. The names of the processes appear in the rightmost column, and the processor time will be in the column closest to it. The names are cryptic, but definitions for most can be found by using the man command followed by the name of the process. Those that are application specific can usually be found through a web search.

4. Examine the list and look for anything out of the ordinary. After doing this a few times, you will become familiar with what is normally there and will be able to spot oddities quickly.

5. Pay particular attention to those processes associated with the root user (the user appears in the first column). Because the root user has the power to do anything, only necessary daemons and processes should be associated with that user.

6. Exit the shell.

Review Questions

1. Which type of attack denies authorized users access to network resources?

   A. DoS

   B. Worm

   C. Logic bomb

   D. Social engineering

2. As the security administrator for your organization, you must be aware of all types of attacks that can occur and plan for them. Which type of attack uses more than one computer to attack the victim?

   A. DoS

   B. DDoS

   C. Worm

   D. UDP attack

3. A server in your network has a program running on it that bypasses authorization. Which type of attack has occurred?

   A. DoS

   B. DDoS

   C. Back door

   D. Social engineering

4. An administrator at a sister company calls to report a new threat that is making the rounds. According to him, the latest danger is an attack that attempts to intervene in a communications session by inserting a computer between the two systems that are communicating. Which of the following types of attacks does this constitute?

   A. Man-in-the-middle attack

   B. Back door attack

   C. Worm

   D. TCP/IP hijacking

5. You've discovered that an expired certificate is being used repeatedly to gain logon privileges. Which type of attack is this most likely to be?

   A. Man-in-the-middle attack

   B. Back door attack

   C. Replay attack

   D. TCP/IP hijacking

6. A junior administrator comes to you in a panic. After looking at the log files, he has become convinced that an attacker is attempting to use an IP address to replace another system in the network to gain access. Which type of attack is this?

    A. Man-in-the-middle attack

    B. Back door attack

    C. Worm

    D. TCP/IP hijacking

7. A server on your network will no longer accept connections using the TCP protocol. The server indicates that it has exceeded its session limit. Which type of attack is probably occurring?

    A. TCP ACK attack

    B. Smurf attack

    C. Virus attack

    D. TCP/IP hijacking

8. A smurf attack attempts to use a broadcast ping on a network; the return address of the ping may be a valid system in your network. Which protocol does a smurf attack use to conduct the attack?

    A. TCP

    B. IP

    C. UDP

    D. ICMP

9. Your help desk has informed you that it received an urgent call from the vice president last night requesting his logon ID and password. What type of attack is this?

    A. Spoofing

    B. Replay attack

    C. Social engineering

    D. Trojan horse

10. A user calls you in a panic. He is receiving e-mails from people indicating that he is inadvertently sending viruses to them. Over 200 such e-mails have arrived today. Which type of attack has most likely occurred?

    A. SAINT

    B. Back door attack

    C. Worm

    D. TCP/IP hijacking

11. Your system has just stopped responding to keyboard commands. You noticed that this occurred when a spreadsheet was open and you dialed in to the Internet. Which kind of attack has probably occurred?

    A. Logic bomb

    B. Worm

    C. Virus

    D. ACK attack

12. You're explaining the basics of security to upper management in an attempt to obtain an increase in the networking budget. One of the members of the management team mentions that they've heard of a threat from a virus that attempts to mask itself by hiding code from antivirus software. What type of virus is he referring to?

    A. Armored virus

    B. Polymorphic virus

    C. Worm

    D. Stealth virus

13. What kind of virus could attach itself to the boot sector of your disk to avoid detection and report false information about file sizes?

    A. Trojan horse virus

    B. Stealth virus

    C. Worm

    D. Polymorphic virus

14. A mobile user calls you from the road and informs you that his laptop is exhibiting erratic behavior. He reports that there were no problems until he downloaded a tic-tac-toe program from a site that he had never visited before. Which of the following terms describes a program that enters a system disguised in another program?

    A. Trojan horse virus

    B. Polymorphic virus

    C. Worm

    D. Armored virus

15. Your system has been acting strangely since you downloaded a file from a colleague. Upon examining your antivirus software, you notice that the virus definition file is missing. Which type of virus probably infected your system?

    A. Polymorphic virus

    B. Retrovirus

    C. Worm

    D. Armored virus

16. Internal users are reporting repeated attempts to infect their systems as reported to them by pop-up messages from their virus scanning software. According to the pop-up messages, the virus seems to be the same in every case. What is the most likely culprit?

    A. A server is acting as a carrier for a virus.

    B. You have a worm virus.

    C. Your antivirus software has malfunctioned.

    D. A DoS attack is under way.

17. Your system log files report an ongoing attempt to gain access to a single account. This attempt has been unsuccessful to this point. What type of attack are you most likely experiencing?

    A. Password guessing attack

    B. Back door attack

    C. Worm attack

    D. TCP/IP hijacking

18. A user reports that he is receiving an error indicating that his TCP/IP address is already in use when he turns on his computer. A static IP address has been assigned to this user's computer, and you're certain this address was not inadvertently assigned to another computer. Which type of attack is most likely underway?

    A. Man-in-the-middle attack

    B. Back door attack

    C. Worm

    D. TCP/IP hijacking

19. You're working late one night, and you notice that the hard disk on your new computer is very active even though you aren't doing anything on the computer and it isn't connected to the Internet. What is the most likely suspect?

    A. A disk failure is imminent.

    B. A virus is spreading in your system.

    C. Your system is under a DoS attack.

    D. TCP/IP hijacking is being attempted.

20. You're the administrator for a large bottling company. At the end of each month, you routinely view all logs and look for discrepancies. This month, your e-mail system error log reports a large number of unsuccessful attempts to log on. It's apparent that the e-mail server is being targeted. Which type of attack is most likely occurring?

    A. Software exploitation attack

    B. Back door attack

    C. Worm

    D. TCP/IP hijacking

Answers to Review Questions

1. A.   A DoS attack is intended to prevent access to network resources by overwhelming or flooding a service or network.

2. B.   A DDoS attack uses multiple computer systems to attack a server or host in the network.

3. C.   In a back door attack, a program or service is placed on a server to bypass normal security procedures.

4. A.   A man-in-the-middle attack attempts to fool both ends of a communications session into believing the system in the middle is the other end.

5. C.   A replay attack attempts to replay the results of a previously successful session to gain access.

6. D.   TCP/IP hijacking is an attempt to steal a valid IP address and use it to gain authorization or information from a network.

7. A.   A TCP ACK attack creates multiple incomplete sessions. Eventually, the TCP protocol hits a limit and refuses additional connections.

8. D.   A smurf attack attempts to use a broadcast ping (ICMP) on a network. The return address of the ping may be a valid system in your network. This system will be flooded with responses in a large network.

9. C.   Someone trying to con your organization into revealing account and password information is launching a social engineering attack.

10. C.   A worm is a type of malicious code that attempts to replicate using whatever means are available. The worm may not have come from the user's system; rather, a system with the user's name in the address book has attacked these people.

11. A.   A logic bomb notifies an attacker when a certain set of circumstances has occurred. This may in turn trigger an attack on your system.

12. A.   An armored virus is designed to hide the signature of the virus behind code that confuses the antivirus software or blocks it from detecting the virus.

13. B.   A stealth virus reports false information to hide itself from antivirus software. Stealth viruses often attach themselves to the boot sector of an operating system.

14. A.   A Trojan horse enters with a legitimate program to accomplish its nefarious deeds.

15. B.   Retroviruses are often referred to as anti-antiviruses. They can render your antivirus software unusable and leave you exposed to other, less-formidable viruses.

16. A.   Some viruses won't damage a system in an attempt to spread into all the other systems in a network. These viruses use that system as the carrier of the virus.

17. A. A password guessing attack occurs when a user account is repeatedly attacked using a variety of different passwords.

18. D. One of the symptoms of a TCP/IP hijacking attack may be the unavailability of a TCP/IP address when the system is started.

19. B. A symptom of many viruses is unusual activity on the system disk. This is caused by the virus spreading to other files on your system.

20. A. A software exploitation attack attempts to exploit weaknesses in software. A common attack attempts to communicate with an established port to gain unauthorized access. Most e-mail servers use port 25 for e-mail connections using SMTP.

Chapter

3

Infrastructure and Connectivity

THE FOLLOWING COMPTIA SECURITY+ EXAM OBJECTIVES ARE COVERED IN THIS CHAPTER:

✓ **1.2 Explain the security risks pertaining to system hardware and peripherals.**

- Removable storage
- Network attached storage

✓ **1.4 Carry out the appropriate procedures to establish application security.**

- ActiveX
- Java
- Scripting
- Browser
- Buffer overflows
- Cookies
- SMTP open relays
- P2P
- Input validation
- Cross-site scripting (XXS)

✓ **1.5 Implement security applications.**

- Popup blockers

✓ **2.3 Determine the appropriate use of network security tools to facilitate network security.**

- Proxy servers

✓ **2.4 Apply the appropriate network tools to facilitate network security.**

- Proxy servers

✓ **2.5 Explain the vulnerabilities and mitigations associated with network devices.**

- Default accounts

✓ **2.6 Explain the vulnerabilities and mitigations associated with various transmission media.**

- Vampire taps

✓ **3.7 Deploy various authentication models and identify the components of each.**

- RADIUS
- RAS
- Remote access policies
- Remote authentication
- VPN
- 802.1x
- TACACS

The previous two chapters focused more on theoretical concepts than purchasable components. They created the foundation on which the topics in this chapter will build as the discussion moves into actual implementation. Bear in mind that even though a variety of products exist to satisfy every need of the market, none are as successful as they need to be without education and training. One of your top priorities should always be to make certain your users understand every aspect of the security policies.

This chapter introduces the hardware used within the network. Your network is composed of a variety of *media* and devices that both facilitate communications and provide security. Some of these devices (such as routers, modems, and PBX systems) provide external connectivity from your network to other systems and networks. Some of the devices (such as CD-Rs, disks, USB thumb drives, and tape) provide both internal archival storage and working storage for your systems.

To provide reasonable security, you must know how these devices work and how they provide, or fail to provide, security. This chapter deals with issues of infrastructure and media. They're key components of the Security+ exam, and it's necessary that you understand them to secure your network. Like many certification exams, though, the Security+ test requires you to know not only current technologies, but some legacy components as well. Although there aren't a whole lot of bus-based coaxial LANs being implemented today, you need to know the basics for this certification.

 There is some overlap between the topics here and in other chapters, just as the Security+ exam objectives overlap one another in many places. In instances where a topic has already been addressed in an earlier chapter, I include references to that information.

Understanding Infrastructure Security

As the name implies, an *infrastructure* is the basis for all the work occurring in your organization. *Infrastructure security* deals with the most basic aspect of how information flows and how work occurs in your network and systems. When discussing infrastructures, keep in mind that this includes servers, networks, network devices, workstations, and the processes in place to facilitate work.

To evaluate the security of your infrastructure, you must examine the hardware and its characteristics as well as the software and its characteristics. Each time you add a device, change configurations, or switch technologies, you're potentially altering the fundamental security capabilities of your network. Just as a chain is no stronger than its weakest link, it can also be said that a network is no more secure than its weakest node.

Networks are tied together using the Internet and other network technologies, thereby making them vulnerable to any number of attacks. The job of a security professional is to eliminate the obvious threats, to anticipate how the next creative assault on your infrastructure might occur, and to be prepared to neutralize it before it happens.

The following sections deal with the hardware and software components that make up a network.

Working with Hardware Components

Network hardware components include physical devices such as routers, servers, firewalls, workstations, and switches. Figure 3.1 depicts a typical network infrastructure and some of the common hardware components in the environment. From a security perspective, this infrastructure is much more than just the sum of all its parts. You must evaluate your network from the standpoint of each and every device within it. It cannot be overstated: The complexity of most networks makes securing them extremely complicated. To provide reasonable security, you must evaluate every device to determine its unique strengths and vulnerabilities.

FIGURE 3.1   A typical network infrastructure

Notice in this figure that the network we'll be evaluating has Internet connections. Internet connections expose your network to the highest number of external threats. These threats can come from virtually any location worldwide.

Network infrastructure devices are covered in detail later in this chapter.

 Real World Scenario

Compile an Infrastructure List

As an administrator, you have to deal with a variety of devices every day. Not only must you attend to the needs of the servers, but you must also maintain Internet access, manage a plethora of users and workstations, and keep everything running smoothly. You can have firewall after firewall in place, but if you're connecting a computer or a network that isn't with minimal safeguards, that connection becomes the baseline of your security.

In this scenario, survey your network and compile an infrastructure list. Make a note of all the devices that are connected—permanently or intermittently—to your network. See if you can answer these questions:

1. How many servers are there? What is the function of each, and what level of security applies to each?

2. How many workstations are there? What operating systems are they running? How do they connect to the network (cabling, wireless, dial-in)?

3. How does data leave the network (routers, gateways)? How secure is each of those devices? Are firewalls or other devices impeding traffic?

4. What else is connected to the network (modems and so on) that can be used to access it?

In all honesty, this information should already exist and be readily accessible. If your organization is like most others, though, the information doesn't exist, and devices are added as needed with the intent of creating documentation at some future point in time. There is no better time than the present to create it.

One issue to watch out for is the "It can't happen to me/us!" attitude many seem to have. Be prepared to handle it by explaining that it can indeed happen and you need to be actively doing all you can to prevent it.

Working with Software Components

Hardware exists to run software. The software is intended to make the hardware components easy to configure and easy to support. To a certain extent, however, that software can also make the hardware easy to bypass.

The network infrastructure illustrated in Figure 3.1 includes servers, workstations running operating systems, a router, a firewall (and there may be some that run as applications on servers), and dedicated devices that have their own communications and control programs. This situation leaves networks open to attacks and security problems because many of these systems work independently.

Many larger organizations have built a single area for network monitoring and administrative control of systems. This centralization lets you see a larger overall picture of the network, and it lets you take actions on multiple systems or network resources if an attack is under way. Such a centralized area is called a *Network Operations Center (NOC)*. Using a NOC makes it easier to see how an attack develops and to provide countermeasures. Unfortunately, a NOC is beyond the means of most medium-sized and small businesses. NOCs are expensive and require a great deal of support: factors beyond the economy or scale of all but the largest businesses. After a NOC is developed and implemented, the job doesn't stop there—the NOC must be constantly evaluated and changed as needed.

If your organization does not employ a dedicated security professional but you still need to implement security measures, one approach is to outsource to a *Managed Security Service Provider (MSSP)*. MSSPs offer overall security services to small companies and can be more cost effective than adding a dedicated individual to the payroll.

AT&T Wireless NOCs

AT&T Wireless maintains a huge NOC for each of the cell centers it manages. These centers provide 24/7 real-time monitoring of all devices in the cellular and computer network they support. The operators in the NOC can literally reach out and touch any device in the network to configure, repair, and troubleshoot it. A single NOC has dozens of people working around the clock to keep on top of the network. When an AT&T Wireless center goes down, it effectively takes down the cell-phone service for an entire region. As you can imagine, this is horrendously expensive, and the company doesn't let it happen often. There are several NOC facilities in the United States, and one region can support or take over operations for another region if that center becomes inoperable.

Understanding the Different Network Infrastructure Devices

Connecting all these components requires physical devices. Large multinational corporations, as well as small and medium-sized corporations, are building networks of enormous complexity and sophistication. These networks work by utilizing miles of both wiring and *wireless technologies.* If the network is totally wire and fiber based or totally wireless, the method of transmitting data from one place to another opens vulnerabilities and opportunities for exploitation. Vulnerabilities appear whenever an opportunity exists to intercept information from the media.

The devices briefly described here are the components you'll typically encounter in a network.

Many network devices contain firmware that you interact with during configuration. For security purposes, you must authenticate in order to make configuration changes and do so initially by using the default account(s). Make sure the default password is changed after the installation on any network device, or you are leaving that device open for anyone recognizing the hardware to access it using the known factory password.

Firewalls

Firewalls are one of the first lines of defense in a network. There are different types of firewalls, and they can be either stand-alone systems or included in other devices such as routers or servers. You can find firewall solutions that are marketed as hardware only and others that are software only. Many firewalls, however, consist of add-in software that is available for servers or workstations.

Although solutions are sold as "hardware only," the hardware still runs some sort of software. It may be hardened and in ROM to prevent tampering, and it may be customized—but software is present nonetheless.

The basic purpose of a firewall is to isolate one network from another. Firewalls are becoming available as appliances, meaning they're installed as the primary device separating two networks. *Appliances* are freestanding devices that operate in a largely self-contained manner, requiring less maintenance and support than a server-based product.

Firewalls function as one or more of the following:

- Packet filter
- Proxy firewall
- Stateful inspection firewall

To understand the concept of a firewall, it helps to know where the term comes from. In days of old, dwellings used to be built so close together that if a fire broke out in one, it could easily destroy a block or more before it could be contained. To decrease the risk of this happening, firewalls were built between buildings. The firewalls were huge brick walls that separated the buildings and kept a fire confined to one side. The same concept of restricting and confining is true in network firewalls. Traffic from the outside world hits the firewall and isn't allowed to enter the network unless otherwise invited.

The firewall shown in Figure 3.2 effectively limits access from outside networks, while allowing inside network users to access outside resources. The firewall in this illustration is also performing proxy functions, discussed later.

FIGURE 3.2   A proxy firewall blocking network access from external networks

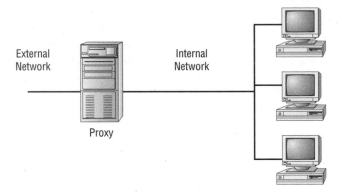

The following sections discuss three of the most common functions that firewalls perform.

Although firewalls are often associated with outside traffic, you can place a firewall anywhere. For example, if you want to isolate one portion of your internal network from others, you can place a firewall between them.

Packet Filter Firewalls

A firewall operating as a *packet filter* passes or blocks traffic to specific addresses based on the type of application. The packet filter doesn't analyze the data of a packet; it decides whether to pass it based on the packet's addressing information. For instance, a packet filter may allow web traffic on port 80 and block Telnet traffic on port 23. This type of filtering is included in many routers. If a received packet request asks for a port that isn't authorized, the filter may reject the request or simply ignore it. Many packet filters can also specify which IP addresses can request which ports and allow or deny them based on the security settings of the firewall.

Packet filters are growing in sophistication and capability. A packet filter firewall can allow any traffic that you specify as acceptable. For example, if you want web users to access your site, then you configure the packet filter firewall to allow data on port 80 to enter. If every network were exactly the same, firewalls would come with default port settings hard-coded, but networks vary, so the firewalls don't include such settings.

 Real World Scenario

Decide Which Traffic to Allow Through

As an administrator, you need to survey your network and decide which traffic should be allowed through the firewall. What traffic will you allow in, and what will you block at the firewall?

Table 3.1 lists only the most common TCP ports. In the table, check the boxes in the last two columns, indicating whether you'll allow data using this port through the firewall.

TABLE 3.1   Ports Allowed through the Firewall

TCP Port Number	Service	Yes	No
20	FTP (data channel)		
21	FTP (control channel)		
23	Telnet		
25	Simple Mail Transfer Protocol (SMTP)		
49	TACACS authentication service		
80	HTTP (used for World Wide Web)		
110	POP3		
119	NNTP		
137, 138, and 139	NetBIOS session service		
143	IMAP		
389	LDAP		
443	HTTPS (used for secure web connections)		
636	LDAP (SSL)		

Proxy Firewalls

A *proxy firewall* can be thought of as an intermediary between your network and any other network. Proxy firewalls are used to process requests from an outside network; the proxy firewall examines the data and makes rule-based decisions about whether the request should be forwarded or refused. The proxy intercepts all the packages and reprocesses them for use internally. This process includes hiding IP addresses.

 When you consider the concept of hiding IP addresses, think of Network Address Translation (NAT) as it was discussed in the section "Working with Newer Technologies" in Chapter 1, "General Security Concepts."

The proxy firewall provides better security than packet filtering because of the increased intelligence that a proxy firewall offers. Requests from internal network users are routed through the proxy. The proxy, in turn, repackages the request and sends it along, thereby isolating the user from the external network. The proxy can also offer caching, should the same request be made again, and can increase the efficiency of data delivery.

A proxy firewall typically uses two network interface cards (NICs). This type of firewall is referred to as a *dual-homed* firewall. One of the cards is connected to the outside network, and the other is connected to the internal network. The proxy software manages the connection between the two NICs. This setup segregates the two networks from each other and offers increased security. Figure 3.3 illustrates a dual-homed firewall segregating two networks from each other.

FIGURE 3.3   A dual-homed firewall segregating two networks from each other

Real World Scenario

Dual-Homed Proxy Firewall

You're the network administrator of a small network. You're installing a new firewall server. After you complete the installation, you notice that the network doesn't appear to be routing traffic through the firewall and that inbound requests aren't being blocked. This situation presents a security problem for the network because you've been getting unusual network traffic lately.

The most likely solution to this problem deals with the fact that the server offers the ability to use IP forwarding in a dual-homed server. IP forwarding bypasses your firewall and uses the server as a router. Even though the two networks are effectively isolated, the new router is doing its job well, and it's routing IP traffic.

You'll need to verify that IP forwarding and routing services aren't running on this server.

 Anytime you have a system that is configured with more than one IP address, it can be said to be *multihomed*.

The proxy function can occur at either the application level or the circuit level. *Application-level proxy* functions read the individual commands of the protocols that are being served. This type of server is advanced and must know the rules and capabilities of the protocol used. An implementation of this type of proxy must know the difference between GET and PUT operations, for example, and have rules specifying how to execute them. A *circuit-level proxy* creates a circuit between the client and the server and doesn't deal with the contents of the packets that are being processed.

A unique application-level proxy server must exist for each protocol supported. Many proxy servers also provide full *auditing*, *accounting*, and other usage information that wouldn't normally be kept by a circuit-level proxy server.

Stateful Inspection Firewalls

The last section on firewalls focuses on the concept of stateful inspection. *Stateful inspection* is also referred to as *stateful packet filtering*. Most of the devices used in networks don't keep track of how information is routed or used. After a packet is passed, the packet and path are forgotten. In stateful inspection (or stateful packet filtering), records are kept using a state table that tracks every communications channel. Stateful inspections occur at all levels of the network and provide additional security, especially in connectionless protocols such as *User Datagram Protocol (UDP)* and *Internet Control Message Protocol (ICMP)*. This adds complexity to the process. Denial-of-service (DoS) attacks present a challenge because flooding techniques are used to overload the state table and effectively cause the firewall to shut down or reboot.

For the exam, remember that pure packet filtering has no real intelligence. It allows data to pass through a port if that port is configured and otherwise discards it—it doesn't examine the packets. Stateful packet filtering, however, has intelligence in that it keeps track of every communications channel.

Hubs

One of the simplest devices in a network is a hub. Although it's possible to load software to create a managed hub, in its truest sense, a *hub* is nothing more than a device allowing many hosts to communicate with each other through the use of physical ports. Broadcast traffic can traverse the hub, and all data received through one port is sent to all other ports. This arrangement creates an extremely unsecure environment should an intruder attach to a hub and begin intercepting data.

Broadcasts are messages sent from a single system to the entire network. *Multicasting* sends a message to multiple addresses. *Unicasts* are multicast formatted but oriented at a single system.

Some of the more expensive hubs do allow you to enable *port security*. If this is enabled, each port takes note of the first MAC address it hears on that port. If the MAC address changes, the hub disables the port. Port security increases the level of security on the LAN, but it can also increase the administrator's workload if you reconfigure your environment often.

For exam purposes, think of hubs as, by default, being unsecure LAN devices that should be replaced with switches for security and increased throughput.

Modems

A *modem* is a hardware device that connects the digital signals from a computer to an analog telephone line. It allows the signals to be transmitted longer distances than are normally possible. The word *modem* is an amalgam of the words *modulator* and *demodulator*, which are the two functions that occur during transmission.

Modems present a unique set of challenges from a security perspective. Most modems answer any call made to them when connected to an outside line. After the receiving modem answers the phone, it generally synchronizes with a caller's modem and makes a connection. A modem, when improperly connected to a network, can allow instant unsecured access to the system's or network's data and resources. If a physical security breach occurs, a modem can be used as a remote network connection that allows unrestricted access. This can occur with no knowledge on the part of the system's owner or the network administrators.

Many PCs being built and delivered today come with internal modems. Unless the modems are specifically needed, they should be disabled or removed from network workstations. If this isn't possible, they should be configured not to auto-answer incoming calls. In other words, you must eliminate as many features of the modem as possible in order to increase security.

Many preconfigured administrative systems provide modem connections for remote maintenance and diagnostics. These connections should either be password-protected or have a cut-off switch so they don't expose your network to security breaches.

Remote Access Services

Remote Access Services (RAS) refers to any server service that offers the ability to connect remote systems. The current Microsoft product for Windows-based clients is called *Routing and Remote Access Services (RRAS),* but it was previously known as *Remote Access Services (RAS)*. Because of this, you'll encounter the term *RAS* used interchangeably to describe both the Microsoft product and the process of connecting to remote systems.

Figure 3.4 depicts a dial-up connection being made from a workstation to a network using a RAS server on the network. In this case, the connection is being made between a Windows-based system and a Windows server using *Plain Old Telephone Service (POTS)* and a modem.

FIGURE 3.4   A RAS connection between a remote workstation and a Windows server

The RAS connection is accomplished via dial-up or network technologies such as VPNs, ISDN, DSL, and cable modems. RAS connections may be secure or in the clear, depending on the protocols that are used in the connection.

A popular method of remote access is through the use of PC Anywhere and similar remote connection/virtual network programs. A major issue with Virtual Network Computing (VNC) is that you are leaving a door into the network open that anyone may stumble upon.

By default, most of these programs start the server service automatically, and it is running even when it is not truly needed. It is highly recommended that you configure the service as a manual start service and launch it *only* when needed to access the host. At all other times, that service should be shut down.

Routers

The primary instrument used for connectivity between two or more networks is the *router*. Routers work by providing a path between the networks. A router has two connections that are used to join the networks. Each connection has its own address and appears as a valid address in its respective network. Figure 3.5 illustrates a router connected between two LANs.

FIGURE 3.5   Router connecting two LANs

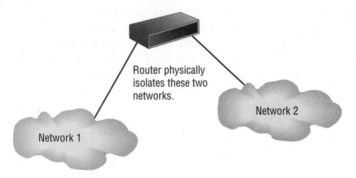

Router physically isolates these two networks.

Network 2

Network 1

Routers are intelligent devices, and they store information about the networks to which they're connected. Most routers can be configured to operate as packet-filtering firewalls. Many of the newer routers also provide advanced firewall functions.

Routers, in conjunction with a Channel Service Unit/Data Service Unit (CSU/DSU), are also used to translate from *LAN framing* to *WAN framing* (for example, a router that connects a 100BaseT network to a T1 network). This is needed because the network protocols are different in LANs and WANs. Such routers are referred to as *border routers*. They serve as the outside connection of a LAN to a WAN, and they operate at the border of your network. Like the border patrols of many countries, border routers decide who can come in and under what conditions.

Dividing internal networks into two or more subnetworks is a common use for routers. Routers can also be connected internally to other routers, effectively creating *zones* that operate autonomously. Figure 3.6 illustrates a corporate network that uses the combination of a border router for connection to an ISP and internal routers to create autonomous networks for communications. This type of connection keeps local network traffic off the backbone of the corporate network and provides additional security to internal users.

Because broadcasts don't traverse routers, network segmentation decreases traffic.

FIGURE 3.6 A corporate network implementing routers for segmentation and security

Routers establish communication by maintaining tables about destinations and local connections. A router contains information about the systems connected to it and where to send requests if the destination isn't known. These tables grow as connections are made through the router.

Routers communicate routing and other information using three standard protocols:

- *Routing Information Protocol (RIP)* is a simple protocol that is part of the TCP/IP protocol suite. Routers that use RIP routinely broadcast the status and routing information of known routers. RIP also attempts to find routes between systems using the smallest number of hops or connections.

- *Border Gateway Protocol (BGP)* allows groups of routers to share routing information.

- *Open Shortest Path First (OSPF)* allows routing information to be updated faster than with RIP.

In the Cisco world, *Interior Gateway Routing Protocol (IGRP)* and *Enhanced Interior Gateway Routing Protocol (EIGRP)* are commonly used. These are distance vector protocols that automatically/mathematically compute routes and choose the best one.

Routers are your first line of defense, and they must be configured to pass only traffic that is authorized by the network administrators. In effect, a router can function as a firewall if it's configured properly. The best approach is layered; a router shouldn't take the place of a firewall but simply augment it.

The routes themselves can be configured as static or dynamic. If they are static, then they are edited manually and stay that way until changed. If they are dynamic, then they learn of other routers around them and use information about those to build their routing tables.

In the labs at the end of this chapter, you'll check for the presence of a routing table and view the entries.

Switches

Switches are multiport devices that improve network efficiency. A switch typically has a small amount of information about systems in a network. Using switches improves network efficiency over hubs because of the virtual circuit capability. Switches also improve network security because the virtual circuits are more difficult to examine with network monitors. You can think of a switch as a device that has some of the best capabilities of routers and hubs combined.

The switch maintains limited routing information about systems in the internal network and allows connections to systems like a hub. Figure 3.7 shows a switch in action between two workstations in a LAN. The connection isn't usually secure or encrypted; however, it doesn't leave the switched area and become part of the overall broadcast traffic as typically happens on a star-based or bus-based LAN.

FIGURE 3.7   Switching between two systems

Telecom/PBX Systems

Telecommunications (or *telecom*) capabilities have undergone radical changes in the last 10 years. The telephone systems and technologies available to deal with communications have given many small businesses fully integrated voice and data services at reasonable prices.

These changes have complicated the security issues that must be handled. One of the primary tools in communications systems is the *private branch exchange (PBX)* system. PBX systems now allow users to connect voice, data, pagers, networks, and almost any other conceivable application into a single telecommunications system. In short, a PBX system allows a company to be its own phone company.

The technology is developing to the point where all communications occur via data links to phone companies using standard data transmission technologies, such as T1 or T3. This means that both voice and data communications are occurring over the same network connection to a phone company or a provider. This allows a single connection for all communications to a single provider of these services.

Potentially, your phone system is a target for attack. Figure 3.8 shows a PBX system connected to a phone company using a T1 line. The phone company, in this illustration, is abbreviated *CO* (for central office). The phone company systems that deal with routing and switching of calls and services are located at the CO.

FIGURE 3.8   A modern digital PBX system integrating voice and data onto a single network connection

If your phone system is part of your data communications network, an attack on your network will bring down your phone system. This event can cause the stress level in a busy office to increase dramatically.

Find the Holes

The United States Department of Commerce, in conjunction with the National Institute of Standards and Technology, has posted an excellent article titled "Vulnerability Analysis: Finding Holes in Your PBX Before Someone Else Does" at http://csrc.nist.gov/publications/nistpubs/800-24/sp800-24pbx.pdf. This document walks through system architecture, hardware, maintenance, and other issues relevant to daily administration as well as exam study.

The security problems in this situation also increase because you must work to ensure security for your voice communications. At the time the exam questions were written, there were no incidents you needed to be aware of involving phone systems being attacked by malicious code. Since then, some Voice over IP (VoIP) attacks have been reported, and such attacks will probably become a greater concern in the near future.

For the exam, know that because a PBX has many of the same features as other network components, it's subject to the same issues, such as leaving TCP ports open. The PBX should be subject to audit and monitoring like every other network component.

Imagine that someone left a voice message for the president of your company. A *phreaker* (someone who abuses phone systems, as opposed to data systems) might intercept this message, alter it, and put it back. The result of this prank could be a calamity for the company (or at least for you). Make sure the default password is changed after the installation has occurred on the maintenance and systems accounts for a PBX, as you would for any network device.

Virtual Private Networks

A *virtual private network (VPN)* is a private network connection that occurs through a public network. A private network provides security over an otherwise unsecure environment. VPNs can be used to connect LANs together across the Internet or other public networks. With a VPN, the remote end appears to be connected to the network as if it were connected locally. A VPN requires either special hardware to be installed or a VPN software package running on servers and workstations.

VPNs typically use a tunneling protocol such as Layer 2 Tunneling Protocol (L2TP), IPSec, or Point-to-Point Tunneling Protocol (PPTP). Figure 3.9 shows a remote network being connected to a LAN using the Internet and a VPN. This connection appears to be a local connection, and all message traffic and protocols are available across the VPN.

FIGURE 3.9   Two LANs being connected using a VPN across the Internet

VPNs are becoming the connection of choice when establishing an extranet or intranet between two or more remote offices. The major security concern when using a VPN is encryption. PPTP offers some encryption capabilities, although they're weak. IPSec offers higher security, and it's becoming the encryption system used in many secure VPN environments.

 Even though a VPN is created through the Internet or other public network, the connection logically appears to be part of the local network. This is why a VPN connection used to establish a connection between two private networks across the Internet is considered a private connection or an extranet.

As mentioned earlier, VPNs are used to make connections between private networks across a public network, such as the Internet. These connections aren't guaranteed to be secure unless a tunneling protocol (such as PPTP) and an encryption system (such as IPSec) are used. A wide range of options, including proprietary technologies, is available for VPN support. Many of the large ISPs and data communications providers offer dedicated hardware with VPN capabilities. Many servers also provide software VPN capabilities for use between two networks.

VPN systems can be dedicated to a certain protocol, or they can pass whatever protocols they see on one end of the network to the other end. A pure VPN connection appears as a dedicated wired connection between the two network ends.

Wireless Access Points

It does not take much to build a wireless network. On the client side, you need a wireless network card (NIC) in place of the standard wired NIC. On the network side, you need something to communicate with the clients.

The primary method of connecting a wireless device to a network is via a wireless portal. A *wireless access point* (WAP) is a low-power transmitter/receiver, also known as a *transceiver*, which is strategically placed for access. The portable device and the access point communicate using one of several communications protocols, including *IEEE 802.11* (also known as Wireless Ethernet).

Wireless communications, as the name implies, don't use wires as the basis for communication. Most frequently, they use a portion of the *radio frequency (RF) spectrum called microwave*. Wireless communication methods are becoming more prevalent in computing because the cost of the transmitting and receiving equipment has fallen drastically over the last few years. Wireless also offers mobile connectivity within a campus, a building, or even a city. Most wireless frequencies are shared frequencies in that more than one person may be using the same frequency for communication.

Figure 3.10 illustrates a wireless portal being used to connect a computer to a company network. Notice that the portal connects to the network and is treated like any other connection used in the network.

Wireless communications, although convenient, can also be less than secure. While many WAPs now ship with encryption on, you will still want to verify that this is the case with your network.

FIGURE 3.10   Wireless access point and workstation

Real World Scenario

Estimating Signal Strength

One of the most troublesome aspects of working with wireless networks is trying to compute the strength of the signal between the WAP and the client(s). It's often joked that a hacker can stand outside a building and tap into your network but a user within the building can't get a strong enough signal to stay on the network.

Think of the signal in terms of any other radio signal—its strength is reduced significantly by cinderblock walls, metal cabinets, and other barriers. The signal can pass through glass windows and thin walls with no difficulty.

When you're laying out a network, it's highly recommended that you install a strength meter on a workstation—many are free to download—and use it to evaluate the intensity of the signal you're receiving. If the signal is weak, you can add additional WAPs and repeaters to the network, just as you would on a wired network.

At a bare minimum, Wired Equivalent Privacy (WEP) should be used across the wireless network. WEP is discussed further in Chapter 7, "Cryptography Basics, Methods, and Standards." Wi-Fi Protected Access (WPA) was created by the Wi-Fi Alliance—an industry trade group—to address many of the holes in security based on 802.11i. You can find more information about WPA at `http://www.wi-fi.org/knowledge_center/wpa/`.

Monitoring and Diagnosing Networks

Network monitoring is an area as old as data communications. It is the process of using a data-capture device or other method to intercept information from a network. Network monitors come in two forms: *sniffers* and *intrusion detection systems (IDSs)*. These tools allow you to examine the activity on your network or, in the case of an IDS, add intelligence to the process, monitor system logs, monitor suspicious activities, and take corrective action when needed.

The concepts of network monitoring and IDS are briefly covered here. They're discussed in greater detail in Chapter 4, "Monitoring Activity and Intrusion Detection."

Network Monitors

Network monitors, otherwise called *sniffers*, were originally introduced to help troubleshoot network problems. Simple network configuration programs like IPCONFIG don't get down on the wire and tell you what is physically happening on a network. Examining the signaling and traffic that occurs on a network requires a network monitor. Early monitors were bulky and required a great deal of expertise to use. Like most things in the computer age, they have gotten simpler, smaller, and less expensive. Network monitors are now available for most environments, and they're effective and easy to use.

Today, a network-monitoring system usually consists of a PC with a NIC (running in promiscuous mode) and monitoring software. The monitoring software is menu driven, is easy to use, and has a big help file. The traffic displayed by sniffers can become overly involved and require additional technical materials; you can buy these materials at most bookstores, or you can find them on the Internet for free. With a few hours of work, most people can make network monitors work efficiently and use the data they present.

Windows Server products include a service called Network Monitor that you can use to gain basic information about network traffic. A more robust, detailed version of Network Monitor is included with Systems Management Server (SMS).

Sniffer is a trade name, like Kleenex. It's the best-known network monitor, so everyone started calling network monitoring hardware *sniffers*.

Intrusion Detection Systems

An *intrusion detection system (IDS)* is software that runs on either individual workstations or network devices to monitor and track network activity. By using an IDS, a network administrator can configure the system to respond just like a burglar alarm. IDSs can be configured to evaluate systems logs, look at suspicious network activity, and disconnect sessions that appear to violate security settings.

Many vendors have oversold the simplicity of these tools. They're quite involved and require a great deal of planning and maintenance to work effectively. Many manufacturers are selling IDSs with firewalls, and this area shows great promise. Firewalls by themselves will prevent many common attacks, but they don't usually have the intelligence or the reporting capabilities to monitor the entire network. An IDS, in conjunction with a firewall, allows both a reactive posture with the firewall and a preventive posture with the IDS.

Figure 3.11 illustrates an IDS working in conjunction with a firewall to increase security.

FIGURE 3.11   An IDS and a firewall working together to secure a network

In the event the firewall is compromised or penetrated, the IDS can react by disabling systems, ending sessions, and even potentially shutting down your network. This arrangement provides a higher level of security than either device provides by itself.

Securing Workstations and Servers

Workstations are particularly vulnerable in a network. Most modern workstations, regardless of their operating systems, communicate using services such as file sharing, network services, and applications programs. Many of these programs have the ability to connect to other workstations or servers.

> Because a network generally consists of a minimal number of servers and a large number of workstations, it's often easier for a hacker to find an unsecure workstation and enter there first. Once the hacker has gained access to the workstation, it becomes easier to access the network since they're now inside the firewall.

These connections are potentially vulnerable to interception and exploitation. The process of making a workstation or a server more secure is called *platform hardening*. The process of hardening the operating system is referred to as *OS hardening*. (OS hardening is part of platform hardening, but it deals only with the operating system.) Platform hardening procedures can be categorized into three basic areas:

- Remove unused software, services, and processes from the workstations (for example, remove the server service from a workstation). These services and processes may create opportunities for exploitation.

- Ensure that all services and applications are up-to-date (including available service and security packs) and configured in the most secure manner allowed. This may include assigning passwords, limiting access, and restricting capabilities.

- Minimize information dissemination about the operating system, services, and capabilities of the system. Many attacks can be targeted at specific platforms once the platform has been identified. Many operating systems use default account names for administrative access. If at all possible, these should be changed. During a new installation of Windows Vista or Windows XP, the first user created is automatically added to the administrators group. Windows Vista then goes one step further and automatically disables the actual administrator account once another account belonging to the administrators group has been created.

> One way to prevent users from making changes in the Microsoft operating systems is to lock their configuration settings. This is possible with Windows clients through the use of group policies.

Most modern server products also offer workstation functionality. In fact, many servers are virtually indistinguishable from workstations. Linux functions as both a workstation and a server in most cases.

Most successful attacks against a server will also work against a workstation, and vice versa. Additionally, servers run dedicated applications, such as SQL Server or a full-function web server.

> ### ⊕ Real World Scenario
>
> #### Users Installing Unauthorized Software
>
> Members of your information systems (IS) department are screaming about the amount of unauthorized software that is being installed on many of the Windows clients on your network. What advice can you offer them on how to minimize the impact of this software?
>
> All newer Windows clients allow permissions to be established to prevent software installation. You should evaluate the capabilities of the settings in the workstations for security. This process is referred to as *locking down* a desktop. You can lock down most desktops to prevent the installation of software. Doing so may also prevent users from automatically upgrading software and may create additional work for the IS department. You'll need to evaluate both issues to determine the best approach to take and then make your recommendation to the IS department.

An early version of Internet Information Services (IIS) included a default mail system as a part of its installation. This mail system was enabled unless specifically disabled. It suffered from most of the vulnerabilities to virus and worm infections discussed in Chapter 2. Make sure your system runs only the services, protocols, and processes you need. Turn off or disable things you don't need.

When you're looking for ways to harden a server, never underestimate the obvious. You should always apply all patches and fixes that have been released for the operating system. Additionally, you should make certain you aren't running any services that aren't needed on the machine.

Understanding Mobile Devices

Mobile devices, including pagers and personal digital assistants (PDAs), are popular. Many of these devices use either RF signaling or cellular technologies for communication. If the device uses the Wireless Application Protocol (WAP), the device in all likelihood doesn't have security enabled. Several levels of security exist in the WAP protocol:

- *Anonymous authentication*, which allows virtually anyone to connect to the wireless portal

- *Server authentication*, which requires the workstation to authenticate against the server

- *Two-way (client and server) authentication*, which requires both ends of the connection (client and server) to authenticate to confirm validity

Real World Scenario

Look for Ways to Harden Your Servers

Armed with a list of the different types of servers on your network (from Lab 3.1), look for ways in which they can be hardened:

1. Are there services running on them that aren't needed?

2. Have the latest patches and fixes been applied?

3. Are there known issues with this operating system?

4. Are there known issues with the services or applications that are running?

One of the first tasks you should do is to go to a search engine and enter the word *hardening* along with the exact operating system you're running.

> **NOTE**   WAP is covered in detail in Chapter 4.

Many new wireless devices are also capable of using certificates to verify authentication. Figure 3.12 shows a mobile systems network; this network uses both encryption and authentication to increase security.

FIGURE 3.12   A mobile environment using WAP security

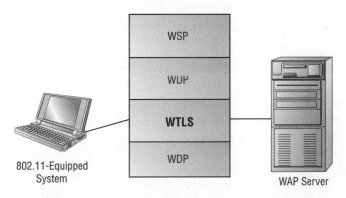

Security is managed at the WTLS layer.

WSP

WDP

WTLS

WDP

802.11-Equipped
System

WAP Server

The *Wireless Session Protocol (WSP)* manages the session information and connection between the devices. The *Wireless Transaction Protocol (WTP)* provides services similar to TCP and UDP for WAP. The *Wireless Datagram Protocol (WDP)* provides the common interface between devices. *Wireless Transport Layer Security (WTLS)* is the security layer of the Wireless Application Protocol and is discussed in detail in Chapter 4.

Understanding Remote Access

One of the primary purposes for having a network is the ability to connect systems. As networks have grown, many technologies have come on the scene to make this process easier and more secure. A key area of concern relates to the connection of systems and other networks that aren't part of your network. The following sections discuss the more common protocols used to facilitate connectivity among remote systems.

Ancient History: the Serial Line Internet Protocol

Serial Line Internet Protocol (SLIP) is an older protocol that was used in early remote access environments. SLIP was originally designed to connect Unix systems in a dial-up environment, and it supports only serial communications.

A very simple protocol, SLIP could only be used to pass TCP/IP traffic and wasn't secure or efficient. While some systems still support SLIP, it is strictly used for legacy systems.

Any authentication done for a remote user is known as *remote authentication*. This authentication is commonly done using TACACS or RADIUS.

Using Point-to-Point Protocol

Introduced in 1994, *Point-to-Point Protocol (PPP)* offers support for multiple protocols including AppleTalk, IPX, and DECnet. PPP works with POTS, Integrated Services Digital Network (ISDN), and other faster connections such as T1. PPP doesn't provide data security, but it does provide authentication using *Challenge Handshake Authentication Protocol (CHAP)*.

Figure 3.13 shows a PPP connection over an ISDN line. In the case of ISDN, PPP would normally use one 64Kbps B channel for transmission. PPP allows many channels in a network connection (such as ISDN) to be connected or bonded together to form a single virtual connection.

FIGURE 3.13   PPP using a single B channel on an ISDN connection

PPP works by encapsulating the network traffic in a protocol called *Network Control Protocol (NCP)*. Authentication is handled by *Link Control Protocol (LCP)*. A PPP connection allows remote users to log on to the network and have access as though they were local users on the network. PPP doesn't provide for any encryption services for the channel.

As you might have guessed, the unsecure nature of PPP makes it largely unsuitable for WAN connections. To counter this issue, other protocols have been created that take advantage of PPP's flexibility and build on it. A dial-up connection using PPP works well because it isn't common for an attacker to tap a phone line. You should make sure all your PPP connections use secure channels, dedicated connections, or dial-up connections.

Remote users who connect directly to a system using dial-up connections don't necessarily need to have encryption capabilities enabled. If the connection is direct, the likelihood that anyone would be able to tap an existing phone line is relatively small. However, you should make sure that connections through a network use an encryption-oriented tunneling system.

Working with Tunneling Protocols

Tunneling protocols add a capability to the network: the ability to create tunnels between networks that can be more secure, support additional protocols, and provide virtual paths between systems. The best way to think of tunneling is to imagine sensitive data being encapsulated in other packets that are sent across the public network. Once they're received at the other end, the sensitive data is stripped from the other packets and recompiled into its original form.

The most common protocols used for tunneling are as follows:

Point-to-Point Tunneling Protocol   *Point-to-Point Tunneling Protocol (PPTP)* supports encapsulation in a single point-to-point environment. PPTP encapsulates and encrypts PPP packets. This makes PPTP a favorite low-end protocol for networks. The negotiation between the two ends of a PPTP connection is done in the clear. After the negotiation is performed, the channel is encrypted. This is one of the major weaknesses of the PPTP protocol. A *packet-capture device*, such as a sniffer, that captures the negotiation process can potentially use that information to determine the connection type and information about how the tunnel works. Microsoft developed PPTP and supports it on most of the company's products. PPTP uses port 1723 and TCP for connections.

Layer 2 Forwarding   *Layer 2 Forwarding (L2F)* was created by Cisco as a method of creating tunnels primarily for dial-up connections. It's similar in capability to PPP and shouldn't be used over WANs. L2F provides authentication, but it doesn't provide encryption. L2F uses port 1701 and TCP for connections.

Layer 2 Tunneling Protocol   Relatively recently, Microsoft and Cisco agreed to combine their respective tunneling protocols into one protocol: *Layer 2 Tunneling Protocol (L2TP)*. L2TP is a hybrid of PPTP and L2F. It's primarily a point-to-point protocol. L2TP supports multiple network protocols and can be used in networks besides TCP/IP. L2TP works over IPX, SNA, and IP, so it can be used as a bridge across many types of systems. The major problem with L2TP is that it doesn't provide data security: The information isn't encrypted. Security can be provided by protocols such as IPSec. L2TP uses port 1701 and UDP for connections.

Secure Shell   *Secure Shell (SSH)* is a tunneling protocol originally designed for Unix systems. It uses encryption to establish a secure connection between two systems. SSH also provides alternative, security-equivalent programs for such Unix standards as Telnet, FTP, and many other communications-oriented applications. SSH is now available for use on Windows systems as well. This makes it the preferred method of security for Telnet and other cleartext-oriented programs in the Unix environment. SSH uses port 22 and TCP for connections.

Internet Protocol Security   *Internet Protocol Security (IPSec)* isn't a tunneling protocol, but it's used in conjunction with tunneling protocols. IPSec is oriented primarily toward LAN-to-LAN connections, but it can also be used with dial-up connections. IPSec provides secure authentication and encryption of data and headers; this makes it a good choice for security. IPSec can work in either Tunneling mode or Transport mode. In Tunneling mode, the data or payload and message headers are encrypted. Transport mode encrypts only the payload.

 Real World Scenario

Connecting Remote Network Users

Your company wants to support network connections for remote users. These users will use the Internet to access desktop systems and other resources in the network. What would you advise the company to consider?

You should advise your organization to implement a tunneling protocol that supports security. A good solution would be a VPN connection that uses IPSec. You might also want to explore protocols like SSL, TLS, and SSH as alternatives. All of these protocols offer security as a part of their connection process.

Using 802.1x Wireless Protocols

The *IEEE 802.1x* protocols represent a broad range of wireless protocols for wireless communications. There are two major families of standards for wireless communications: the 802.11 family and the 802.16 family. The *802.11* protocols are primarily short-range systems suitable for use in buildings and campus environments. The *802.16* standard was finalized in the fall of 2002 and defines the development and deployment of broadband wireless metropolitan-area networks.

The 802.11 standards are discussed in detail in Chapter 4, "Monitoring Activity and Intrusion Detection."

Working with RADIUS

Remote Authentication Dial-In User Service (RADIUS) is a mechanism that allows authentication of dial-in and other network connections. The RADIUS protocol is an IETF standard, and it has been implemented by most of the major operating system manufacturers. A RADIUS server can be managed centrally, and the servers that allow access to a network can verify with a RADIUS server whether an incoming caller is authorized. In a large network with many connections, this allows a single server to perform all authentications.

Figure 3.14 shows an example of a RADIUS server communicating with an ISP to allow access to a remote user. Notice that the remote server is functioning as a client to the RADIUS server. This allows centralized administration of access rights.

You should use RADIUS when you want to improve network security by implementing a single service to authenticate users who connect remotely to the network. Doing so gives you a single source for the authentication to take place. Additionally, you can implement auditing and accounting on the RADIUS server.

FIGURE 3.14   The RADIUS client manages the local connection and authenticates against a central server.

The major difficulty with a single-server RADIUS environment is that the entire network may refuse connections if the server malfunctions. Many RADIUS systems allow multiple servers to be used to increase reliability. All of these servers are critical components of the infrastructure, and they must be protected from attack.

TACACS/+

Terminal Access Controller Access Control System (TACACS) is a client-server-oriented environment, and it operates in a manner similar to how RADIUS operates. Extended TACACS (XTACACS) replaced the original and combined authentication and authorization with logging to enable auditing.

The most current method or level of TACACS is TACACS/+, and this replaces the previous two incarnations. TACACS/+ allows credentials to be accepted from multiple methods, including Kerberos. The TACACS client/server process occurs in the same manner as the RADIUS process illustrated in Figure 3.14.

Cisco has widely implemented TACACS/+ for connections. TACACS/+ is expected to become widely accepted as an alternative to RADIUS.

Remember: RADIUS and TACACS can be used to authenticate connections.

Securing Internet Connections

The Internet is perhaps the area of largest growth for networks. The Internet is a worldwide network that offers the capability of instantaneous connections between networks, no matter where they're located. The technology started as a research project funded by the Department of Defense and has grown at an enormous rate. Within a few years, virtually every computer in the world is expected to be connected to the Internet. This situation creates a security nightmare and is one of the primary reasons the demand for professionals trained in information and computer security is expected to grow exponentially.

The following sections describe ports and sockets and then some of the more common protocols, including e-mail, web, and FTP.

Working with Ports and Sockets

As we've already discussed, the primary method of connection between systems using the Internet is the TCP/IP protocol. This protocol establishes connections and circuits using a combination of the IP address and a port. A *port* is an interface that is used to connect to a device. *Sockets* are a combination of the IP address and the port. For example, if you attempt to connect to a remote system with the IP address 192.168.0.100, which is running a website, you'll use port 80 by default. The combination of these two elements gives you a socket. The full address and socket description would then be 192.168.0.100:80.

IP is used to route the information from one host to another through a network. The four layers of TCP/IP encapsulate the information into a valid IP packet that is then transmitted across the network. Figure 3.15 illustrates the key components of a TCP packet requesting the home page of a website. The data will be returned from the website to port 1024 on the originating host.

FIGURE 3.15   A TCP packet requesting a web page from a web server

The destination port indicates port 80.

This is the default for an HTTP Server. The return port to the client is 1024.

Source Port 1024				Destination Port 80
Sequence Number				
Acknowledgment Number				
Offset	Reserved	Flags	Window	
Checksum			Urgent Pointer	
Options			Padding	
Data			**GET/**	

The command GET/ instructs the server to send data.

The source port is the port that is addressed on the destination. The destination port is the port to which the data is sent. In the case of a web application, the data for port addresses would both contain 80. A number of the fields in this packet are used by TCP for verification and integrity, and you need not be concerned with them at this time.

However, the data field contains the value Get/. This value requests the home or starting page from the web server. In essence, this command or process requested the home page of the site 192.168.0.100 port 80. The data is formed into another data packet that is passed down to IP and sent back to the originating system on port 1024.

The connections to most services using TCP/IP are based on this port model. Many of the ports are well documented, and the protocols to communicate with them are well known. If a vendor has a technological weakness or implements security poorly, the vulnerability will become known and exploited in a short time.

Working with E-Mail

E-mail is one of the most popular applications in use on the Internet. Several good e-mail servers and clients are available. Figure 3.16 demonstrates the process of transferring an e-mail message.

FIGURE 3.16 E-mail connections between clients and a server

The most common e-mail systems use the following protocols, which use the TCP protocol for session establishment:

Simple Mail Transport Protocol *Simple Mail Transport Protocol (SMTP)* is a mail delivery protocol that is used to send e-mail between an e-mail client and an e-mail server as well as between e-mail servers. Messages are moved from client to server to client via the Internet. Each e-mail message can take a different path from the client to the server. In the case of Figure 3.16, the clients are on two different e-mail servers; they could both be on the same server, and the process would appear transparent to the user. SMTP uses port 25 and TCP for connections.

Post Office Protocol *Post Office Protocol (POP)* is a newer protocol that relies on SMTP for message transfer to receive e-mail. POP provides a message store that can be used to store and forward messages. If a server isn't operating, the originating server can store a message and try to resend it later. POP3, the newest version of POP, allows messages to be transferred from the waiting post office to the e-mail client. The current POP standard uses port 109 for POP2 and 110 for POP3. The POP protocol uses TCP for connections.

Internet Message Access Protocol *Internet Message Access Protocol (IMAP)* is the newest player in the e-mail field, and it's rapidly becoming the most popular. Like POP, IMAP has a store-and-forward capability. However, it has much more functionality. IMAP allows messages to be stored on an e-mail server instead of being downloaded to the client. It also allows messages to be downloaded based on search criteria. Many IMAP implementations also allow connections using web browsers. The current version of IMAP (IMAP 4) uses port 143 and TCP for connections.

S/MIME and *PGP* are two of the more popular methods of providing security for e-mails. These are covered in detail in Chapter 7.

Working with the Web

When two hosts communicate across the Web, data is returned from the host using *Hypertext Markup Language (HTML)*. HTML is nothing more than a coding scheme to allow text and pictures to be presented in a specific way in a web browser. HTML can be created any number of ways, including via manual coding and in graphical design programs. HTML files are read, interpreted by your browser, and displayed on your system. If you want to see what HTML looks like, you can set your browser to view source code—you'll see things similar to word-processor coding for virtually every characteristic of the web page you're viewing.

Websites are collections of these pages, which are called into your browser when you click a link or scroll through the pages. Most developers want more than the ability to display pages and pages of colored text on your computer. To make creative and sophisticated websites possible, web browsers have become more complicated, as have web servers. Current browsers include audio, visuals, animations, live chats, and almost any other feature you can imagine.

Figure 3.17 illustrates some of the content that can be delivered over the Internet via a web server.

FIGURE 3.17 A web server providing streaming video, animation, and HTML data to a client

This ability to deliver content over the Web is accomplished in one of several ways. The most common approach involves installing applications that talk through the server to your browser. The applications require additional ports to be opened through your firewall and routers. Unfortunately, doing so inherently creates security vulnerabilities.

Each port you leave open in your network increases your vulnerability. If you open the ports necessary to use the popular program NetMeeting, you're exposing your users to additional opportunities for attack. NetMeeting has had a number of security vulnerabilities in the past, and it will probably have more in the future.

Each of the popular web services is now offered in conjunction with web-enabled programs such as Flash and Java. These services use either a socket to communicate or a program that responds to commands through the browser. If your browser can be controlled by an application, your system is at great risk of being coerced into giving attackers information you don't want them to have. Servers are also vulnerable to this issue because they must process requests from browsers for information or data. A little research into the vulnerabilities of a proposed new service may save you a lot of time later should you become the target of an attack.

> While HTML remains popular, *Extensible Markup Language (XML)* is quickly becoming adopted by many. Although it's not a replacement for HTML, XML offers many capabilities that HTML does not. These include the ability to describe the information (and not just display it). By being able to describe the data, it can display it across several platforms, systems, and so forth.

The best solution for many of the vulnerabilities that exist on the Web is to implement secure web connections—the topic of our next section.

Secure Web Connections

There are two common ways to provide secure connections between a web client and a web server:

Secure Sockets Layer and Transport Layer Security   *Secure Sockets Layer (SSL)* and *Transport Layer Security (TLS)* are two common protocols used to convey information between a web client and a server. The SSL protocol uses an encryption scheme between the two systems. The client initiates the session, the server responds, indicating that encryption is needed, and then they negotiate an appropriate encryption scheme. TLS is a newer protocol that merges SSL with other protocols to provide encryption. TLS supports SSL connections for compatibility, but it also allows other encryption protocols, such as Triple DES, to be used. SSL/TLS uses port 443 and TCP for connections.

HTTP/S   *HTTP Secure (HTTP/S)* is a protocol that is used for secure connections between two systems that use the Web. It protects the connection, and all traffic between the two systems is encrypted. HTTP/S uses SSL or TLS for connection security, and it uses port 443 and TCP for connections.

> Don't confuse Secure HTTP (S-HTTP) with HTTP/S. S-HTTP is a different protocol that lets systems negotiate an encryption connection between each other. S-HTTP can provide some of the capabilities of HTTP/S, but it isn't as secure.

Vulnerabilities of Web Add-ins

The growth of the Web and demands from users for more features has spurred the creation of a new set of vulnerabilities that must be evaluated and managed. Increasingly, web browsers and other web-enabled technologies allow servers to send instructions to the client to provide multimedia and other capabilities. This is creating a problem for security professionals because these protocols offer potential weaknesses.

The following sections discuss the more common web-based applications, such as JavaScript and applets, and the vulnerabilities you should be aware of. These vulnerabilities can include malicious code, viruses, and exploitations.

ActiveX

ActiveX is a technology that was implemented by Microsoft to customize controls, icons, and other features, which increases the usability of web-enabled systems. ActiveX runs on the client. It uses a method called *Authenticode* for security. Authenticode is a type of certificate technology that allows ActiveX components to be validated by a server.

ActiveX components are downloaded to the client hard disk, potentially allowing additional security breaches. Web browsers can be configured so that they require confirmation to accept an ActiveX control. However, many users don't understand these confirmation messages when they appear, and they automatically accept the components. Automatically accepting an ActiveX component or control creates the opportunity for security breaches on a client system when the control is used because an ActiveX control contains programming instructions that can contain malicious code or create vulnerabilities in a system.

> It's highly recommended that browsers be configured so that they do not allow ActiveX to run without prompting the user because of the potential security hole that could be opened.

Buffer Overflows

Buffer overflows occur when an application receives more data than it's programmed to accept. This situation can cause an application to terminate or to write data beyond the end of the allocated space. Termination may leave the system sending the data with temporary access to privileged levels in the attacked system, while overwriting can cause important data to be lost. This exploitation is usually a result of a programming error in the development of the software.

Buffer overflows, while a less common source of exploitation than in the past, still crop up.

Common Gateway Interface

Common Gateway Interface (CGI) is an older form of scripting that was used extensively in early web systems. CGI scripts were used to capture data from a user using simple forms. They aren't widely used in new systems and are being replaced by Java, ActiveX, and other technologies.

CGI scripts run on the web server and interact with the client browser. CGI is often frowned upon in new applications because of its security issues, but it's still widely used in older systems. Vulnerabilities in CGI are the result of its inherent ability to do what it is told. If a CGI script is written to wreak havoc (or carries extra code added to it by a miscreant) and it is executed, your systems will suffer. The best protection against any weaknesses is to not run applications written in CGI but rather to opt for those written in the newer languages where possible.

Cookies

Cookies are text files that a browser maintains on the user's hard disk in order to provide a persistent, customized web experience for each visit. A cookie typically contains information about the user. For example, a cookie can contain a client's history to improve customer service. If a bookstore wants to know your buying habits and what types of books you last viewed at its site, it can load this information into a cookie on your system. The next time you return to that store, the server can read your cookie and customize what it presents to you. Cookies can also be used to time-stamp a user to limit access. A financial institution may send your browser a cookie once you've authenticated. The server can read the cookie to determine when a session is expired.

Obviously, cookies are considered a risk because they have the potential to contain your personal information, which could get into the wrong hands. If security is your utmost concern, the best protection is to not allow cookies to be accepted. Almost every browser offers the option of enabling or disabling cookies. If you enable them, you can usually choose whether to accept/reject all or only those from an originating server.

Cross-site scripting (XSS)

Using a client-side scripting language, it is possible for a ne'er-do-well to trick a user into visiting their site and having code then execute locally. When this is done, it is known as *cross-site scripting*. As an example, UserA may get a message telling him that he needs to make changes to his XYZ account, but the link in the message is not really to the XYZ site (a phishing ploy). When he clicks on the link, a JavaScript routine begins to run on his machine. Since the script is running on UserA's system, it has his permissions and can begin doing such things as running malevolent routines to send/delete/alter data.

The best protection against cross-site scripting is to disable the running of scripts.

Input Validation

Anytime a user must supply values in a session, validation of the data entered should be done. Many vendors, however, have fallen prey to *input validation* vulnerabilities within their code. In some instances, empty values have been accepted, while others have allowed privilege escalation if certain backdoor passwords were used.

The best protection against input validation vulnerabilities is for developers to follow best practices and always validate all values entered. As an administrator, when you learn of an input validation vulnerability with any application on your system, you should immediately stop using it until a patch has been released and installed.

Java Applets

A *Java applet* is a small, self-contained Java script that is downloaded from a server to a client and then run from the browser. The client browser must have the ability to run Java applets in a virtual machine on the client. Java applets are used extensively in web servers today, and they're becoming one of the most popular tools used for website development.

Java-enabled applications can accept programmed instructions (Java scripts) from a server and control certain aspects of the client environment. Java requires you to download a virtual machine in order to run the Java applications or applets. Java scripts run on the client.

The applets run in a restricted area of memory called the *sandbox*. The sandbox limits the applet's access to user areas and system resources. An applet that runs in the sandbox is considered *safe*, meaning it won't attempt to gain access to sensitive system areas. Errors in the Java virtual machine that runs in the applications may allow some applets to run outside of the sandbox. When this occurs, the applet is unsafe and may perform malicious operations. Attackers on client systems have exploited this weakness. From a user's stand-point, the best defense is to make certain you run only applets from reputable sites you're familiar with. From an administrator's standpoint, you should make certain programmers adhere to programming guidelines when creating the applets.

JavaScript

JavaScript is a programming language that allows access to system resources of the system running a script. A JavaScript script is a self-contained program that can be run as an execut-able file in many environments. These scripts can interface with all aspects of an operating system, just as programming languages such as the C language can. This means that JavaScript scripts, when executed, can potentially damage systems or be used to send information to unauthorized persons. JavaScript scripts can be downloaded from a website and executed.

Popups

While not technically an add-in, popups (also known as pop-ups) are both frustrating and chancy. Whenever a user visits a website and another instance (either another tab or another browser window) is opened in the foreground, it is called a popup; if it opens in the background, it is called a popunder. Both popups and popunders are opening pages or sites that you did not specifically request and may only display ads or bring up applets that should be avoided.

Popup blockers are used to prevent both popups and popunders from appearing. While older browsers did not incorporate an option to block popups, most newer browsers now have that capability built in.

Signed Applets

Signed applets are similar to Java applets, with two key differences: A signed applet doesn't run in the Java sandbox, and it has higher system access capabilities. Signed applets aren't usually downloaded from the Internet; this type of applet is typically provided by in-house or custom-programming efforts. These applets can also include a digital signature to verify authenticity. If the applet is verified as authentic, it will be installed. Users should never download a signed applet unless they're sure the provider is trusted. A signed applet from an untrustworthy provider has the same security risks as an unsigned applet.

A vulnerability reveals itself when an applet is always assumed to be safe because it is signed. Being signed, it may have the ability to do things outside the realm of normal applets, such as execute programs. A disgruntled programmer can create a malicious signed applet and wreak havoc until stopped.

Most web browsers have settings that can be used to control Java access. This allows clients to control resource access using Java applets or scripts.

SMTP Relay

SMTP relay is a feature designed into many e-mail servers that allows them to forward e-mail to other e-mail servers. Initially, the SMTP relay function was intended to help bridge traffic between systems. This capability allows e-mail connections between systems across the Internet to be made easily.

Unfortunately, this feature has been used to generate a great deal of spam on the Internet. An e-mail system that allows this type of forwarding to occur is referred to as an *open relay*. Unscrupulous individuals can use open relays to send advertisements and other messages through open relay servers. SMTP relaying should be disabled on your network unless it's limited to the e-mail servers in your domain.

 Real World Scenario

SMTP Relaying in Action

You've just received a call from a client indicating that their e-mail server is acting peculiarly. When you arrive at the site, you notice that there are more than 20,000 e-mails in the outbound mail folder and that the system has no disk space available. When you shut down the e-mail software, you delete these files and restart the e-mail server. You see that the outbound mail folder begins to fill up again. What problem could this server be encountering?

E-marketers may be using the server as a relay. This hijacking will continue until you disable the SMTP relay capabilities in the server. Many older systems don't allow SMTP relaying to be turned off; such servers must be upgraded or replaced to prevent this from continuing.

Working with File Transfer Protocol

File Transfer Protocol (FTP) was the most common protocol used to transfer files between systems on the Internet for many years, and it's available on most major server environments.

The Internet has replaced many of the functions FTP served in the past. FTP is still commonly used, but it's becoming less popular as other methods of file downloading are made available. Most popular browsers allow an FTP site to be accessed as a website, and HTTP supports file transfer capabilities. A browser provides a graphical interface that users can use without having to be exposed to the command structure that FTP uses by default.

The following sections discuss FTP, its vulnerabilities, and ways to secure it.

Blind/Anonymous FTP

Early FTP servers didn't offer formal security—security was based on the honor system. In most cases, the honor system was used strictly for downloading files from an FTP server to a client; a client couldn't upload files without using a different logon ID. In some cases, the opposite situation existed, and a client could "blindly" upload files for others but could not download—or even see—any files.

Most logons to an FTP site used the anonymous logon; by convention, the logon ID was anonymous, and the password was the user's e-mail address. This honor system is still used in systems that want to allow public access to files, and it simplifies administration because only one account is used.

The cost of this implementation, however, is the risk that is taken on. In this situation, the only security offered is what is configured by the operating system.

Secure FTP

Secure FTP (S/FTP) is accomplished using a protocol called *Secure Shell (SSH)*—a type of tunneling protocol that allows access to remote systems in a secure manner. As discussed earlier, SSH allows connections to be secured by encrypting the session between the client and the server. SSH is available for Unix and other systems that provide capabilities similar to FTP.

Sharing Files

File sharing is accomplished by storing files at an assigned location on the server or workstation. When files are stored on a workstation, the connection is referred to as a *peer-to-peer connection*. The assigned location is typically a subdirectory located on one of the disk drives on the server or another workstation.

In an FTP connection, you can upload a file from a client using the PUT command. You download using the GET command. Most modern servers and applications allow an application program to access shared files at the record level. This type of sharing allows multiuser applications, such as databases, to function. Web browsers typically accept files from a web server by downloading them from the server. These downloaded files are then processed through the browser and displayed to the user.

FTP's Vulnerability

FTP has a major flaw: The user ID and password aren't encrypted and are subject to packet capture. This creates a major security breach—especially if you're connecting to an FTP server across the Internet. There is also a problem if you're allowing the use of the anonymous version of FTP: *Trivial File Transfer Protocol (TFTP)*.

Real World Scenario

Remote File Transfers

Your organization has a large number of remote users who transfer files to your system across the Internet. These file transfers are an essential part of your business, and they must be allowed to continue. You want to provide additional security to your users so that information won't be compromised. How might you accomplish this?

You could implement SSH or other secure protocols for FTP file transfers. Doing so would allow information to be sent across the Internet in a secure manner. You may also be able to use TLS, SSL, or another secure format.

Understanding Network Protocols

Your network may have network protocols running in addition to TCP/IP, and each of these protocols may be vulnerable to outside attack. Some protocols (such as NetBEUI, DLC, and other more primitive protocols) aren't routable and, therefore, aren't subject to attack. Of course, there is a great big "unless": If your router or firewall is configured to pass them, some of these protocols can be imbedded in TCP/IP and may be passed to other systems.

The major protocols used by TCP/IP for maintenance and other activities include those discussed in the following list:

Simple Network Management Protocol TCP/IP uses *Simple Network Management Protocol (SNMP)* to manage and monitor devices in a network. Many copiers, fax machines, and other smart office machines use SNMP for maintenance functions. This protocol travels through routers quite well and can be vulnerable to attack. Although such an attack might not be dangerous, think about what could happen if your printer suddenly went online and started spewing paper all over the floor.

SNMP was upgraded as a standard to SNMPv2, which provides security and improved remote monitoring. SNMP is currently undergoing a revision; although a new standard (SNMPv3) is out, although most systems still use SNMPv2.

Internet Control Message Protocol TCP/IP uses *Internet Control Message Protocol (ICMP)* to report errors and reply to requests from programs such as Ping and Traceroute. ICMP is one of the favorite protocols used for DoS attacks. Many businesses have disabled ICMP through the router to prevent these types of situations from occurring.

Real World Scenario

Using ICMP to Deal with Smurf Attacks

Your organization has been repeatedly hit by smurf attacks. These attacks have caused a great deal of disruption, and they must be stopped. What could you suggest to minimize these attacks?

You should recommend disabling ICMP traffic at the point where your network connects to the Internet. You can do this by disabling the protocol on your router and blocking this traffic in firewall systems. Doing so won't completely eliminate the problem, but it will greatly reduce the likelihood of a successful attack occurring using ICMP. This step will also prevent people from gaining information about your network because any programs (such as Ping) that request information from your network systems will no longer function.

Internet Group Management Protocol   TCP/IP uses *Internet Group Management Protocol (IGMP)* to manage group or multicasting sessions. It can be used to address multiple recipients of a data packet: The sender initiates broadcast traffic, and any client who has broadcasting enabled receives it. (*Broadcasts* are messages sent from a single system to the entire network—the systems could be inside your network or throughout the world.) This process, called *multicasting*, can consume huge amounts of bandwidth in a network and possibly create a DoS situation. Most network administrators disable the reception of broadcast and multicast traffic from outside their local network.

A *unicast* is IGMP traffic that is oriented at a single system. TCP/IP primarily uses a unicast method of communication: A message is sent from a single system to another single system.

 Every one of these major protocols used by TCP/IP presents a potential problem for security administrators. Make sure you use what you need and disable what you don't.

The Basics of Cabling, Wires, and Communications

Nothing happens in a network until data is moved from one place to another. Naturally, this requires some type of cable, wire, or transmission media. The following sections explore the realm of wiring from a technical and a security perspective. Specifically, you'll learn about coaxial cable, UTP/STP, fiber optics, infrared, radio frequency, and microwave media.

Coax

Coaxial cable, or *coax*, is one of the oldest media used in networks. Coax is built around a center conductor or core that is used to carry data from point to point. The center conductor has an insulator wrapped around it, a shield over the insulator, and a nonconductive sheath around the shielding. This construction, depicted in Figure 3.18, allows the conducting core to be relatively free from outside interference. The shielding also prevents the conducting core from emanating signals externally from the cable.

FIGURE 3.18   Coaxial cable construction

Center pin

Center conductor   Braid

BNC connector

Sheath

Center insulator

    Before you read any further, accept the fact that the odds are incredibly slim that you will ever need to know about coax for a new installation in the real world. If you do come across it, it will be in an existing installation, and one of the first things you'll recommend is that it be changed. That said, you do need to know about coax for this exam.

Connections to a coax occur through a wide variety of connectors, often referred to as *plumbing*. These connectors provide a modular design that allows for easy expansion. The three primary connections used in this case are the T-connector, the inline connector, and the terminating connector (also known as a *terminating resistor* or *terminator*). Figure 3.19 shows some of these common connectors in a coaxial cable–based network.

FIGURE 3.19   Common BNC connectors

BNC male connector

BNC inline connector

BNC female connector

BNC T-connector

Coax supports both baseband and broadband signaling. *Baseband* signaling means that a single channel is carried through the coax, and *broadband* refers to multiple channels on the coax. Figure 3.20 illustrates this difference. Baseband signaling is similar in concept to a speaker wire. The speaker wire in your stereo connects one channel from the amplifier to the speaker. Broadband is similar to the cable TV connection in your home. The cable from the cable company carries hundreds of channels. Your TV set uses a tuner to select the channel you choose to watch.

In a coax network, some type of device must terminate all the coax ends. Figure 3.21 shows this termination process in more detail. Coax is present in many older networks and tends to provide reliable service once it's installed. However, if a terminator, NIC, T-connector, or inline connector malfunctions or becomes disconnected, the entire segment of wire in that network will malfunction, and network services will cease operation. Coax also tends to become brittle over time, and it can fail when handled. In addition, coax is expensive per foot when compared to UTP cable. These are the primary reasons that coax is falling from favor as a primary network media.

Coax has two primary vulnerabilities from a security perspective. The most common is the addition of a T-connector attached to a network sniffer. This sniffer would have unrestricted access to the signaling on the cable. The second and less common method involves a connection called a *vampire tap*. A vampire tap is a type of connection that hooks directly into a coax by piercing the outer sheath and attaching a small wire to the center conductor or core. This type of attachment allows a tap to occur almost anywhere in the network. Taps can be hard to find because they can be anywhere in the cable. Figure 3.22 shows the two common methods of tapping a coax cable. The T-connector is a standard connector that can be used any place there is a connector on the cable. An *inductive pickup* or *RF collar* can be placed around a coaxial cable to capture any stray RF that isn't blocked by the coax's shield.

FIGURE 3.20   Broadband versus baseband signaling

FIGURE 3.21   Network termination in a coax network

Unshielded Twisted Pair and Shielded Twisted Pair

Unshielded Twisted Pair (UTP) and *Shielded Twisted Pair (STP)* are the most prevalent media installed today. UTP cabling and STP cabling are similar in function, with the exception that STP wraps a shield, like a coax, over the wires. STP is popular, but UTP is by far the most popular cabling in use.

FIGURE 3.22   A vampire tap and a T-connector on a coax

Vampire Tap

The screw fang
pierces the shielding
and connects with the core.

BNC
Connector

Coax

Coax

BNC
Connector

T-Connector

Figure 3.23 illustrates the difference between UTP and STP cable. Notice that the STP cable has a single shield around all the pairs. Some versions of STP also have shields around each pair of wires. This is much less common in computer networks, but it reduces electrical interference susceptibility in the cable.

This discussion will revolve around UTP, but STP operates the same way. UTP cabling comes in seven grades or categories, which are listed in Table 3.2.

FIGURE 3.23   STP and UTP cable construction

STP

UTP

shield

TABLE 3.2   The Common UTP/STP Cable Specifications

Category	Speed	Usage
Category 1	Voice-grade cable	Used strictly for telephone (POTS) and modems.
Category 2	4Mbps	Used extensively in older mainframe systems and some Token Ring networks.
Category 3	10Mbps Ethernet	Used in 10Base-T networks for voice and data.
Category 4	16–20Mbps	Used extensively in 16MB Token Ring networks.
Category 5	1000Mbps	Used in 10-, 100-, and 1000Base-T and similar networks. The most common wiring in newer networks.
Category 6	1000Mbps	Used in high-speed network installations for broadband. Not yet common.
Category 7	1000Mbps	Used in very high-speed network installations. Not available—proposed standard.

The most common cable standard used at this time is Category 5 (CAT 5). CAT 3 is common in older twisted-pair networks. The limit of a cable segment length of twisted pair for use with Ethernet is 100 meters; beyond this length, the attenuation of the cables may cause reliability problems.

UTP and STP cabling isn't as secure as coax because it can be easily tapped into, and it's used primarily for internal wiring. It's more difficult to splice into a twisted-pair cable, but three-way breakout boxes are easy to build or buy. The common networks that use UTP are 10Base-T, 100Base-T, and 1000Base-T. These networks use hubs for distribution, and hubs allow sniffers to be easily connected. Many modern networks include switches, and network monitoring doesn't work properly through a switch unless the switch is configured to allow it. Remember that each circuit through a switch is dedicated when switched and won't be seen on the other ports. Figure 3.24 illustrates a hub in a 10Base-T network and a sniffer attached to the hub. The sniffer in this situation is a portable PC with a NIC for the network protocol.

Fiber Optic

Fiber-optic technology takes network bandwidth to new levels of performance. Telecommunications and data communication providers worldwide have laid fiber cables extensively. At one point, the industry claimed that fiber would surpass wire as the preferred method of making network connections. Fiber optics and its assembly continue to be very expensive when compared to wire, and this technology isn't common on the desktop.

FIGURE 3.24   10Base-T network with a sniffer attached at the hub

 Because fiber-optic cabling uses light in place of an electrical signal, it's less likely than other implementations to be affected by interference problems.

Fiber, as a media, is relatively secure because it can't be tapped easily. Fiber's greatest security weakness is at the connections to the fiber-optic transceivers. Passive connections can be made at the connections, and signals can be tapped from there. The other common security issue associated with fiber optics is that fiber connections are usually bridged to wire connections. Figure 3.25 shows how a fiber connection to a transceiver can be tapped. This type of splitter requires a signal regenerator for the split to function, and it can be easily detected.

FIGURE 3.25   An inline fiber splitter

Infrared

Infrared (IR) uses a type of radiation for communications. This infrared radiation allows a point-to-point connection to be made between two IR transceiver-equipped devices. IR connections tend to be slow and are used for limited amounts of data. Many newer laptop PCs, PDAs, and portable printers now come equipped with IR devices for wireless communications.

IR is line of sight; it isn't secure and can be easily intercepted. But the interception device must be either in position between the two connections or in an area where a reflection has occurred. (IR can be bounced off windows and mirrors, as can other radiation.)

Radio Frequencies

Radio frequency (RF) communications have had an interesting love/hate relationship with data communication. Early data communications systems, such as teletypes, used extensive networks of high-powered shortwave transmitters to send information and data. Most of the early news feeds were broadcast on shortwave frequencies and received around the world by news offices. These connections were also used for early facsimile transmission of weather maps and other graphically oriented images. The transmitters were very expensive, and large numbers of personnel were required to manage and maintain them. Telephone connections largely replaced this means of communications, but teleprinters are still in use today.

RF transmissions use antennas to send signals across the airwaves. These signals can be easily intercepted. Anyone can connect a shortwave receiver to the sound card of a PC to intercept, receive, and record shortwave and higher-frequency transmissions. Figure 3.26 illustrates a shortwave transmission between two ground sites used for text transmission. This is an active pastime—tens of thousands of hobbyists worldwide are eavesdropping.

Microwave Systems

Microwaves use the RF spectrum, but they have some interesting characteristics and capabilities. The microwave frequency spectrum includes many types of communications; some involve huge amounts of data and information, and others involve small amounts. Common applications of microwave today include cellular phones, police and aircraft communications, fax, and broadband telecommunications systems. The equipment to communicate on these frequencies is usually very small and power efficient.

Much of the telecommunications system we use today is built on microwave technology. Microwave has the ability to carry enormous amounts of data, communicate line of sight, and use broad power ranges. Figure 3.27 illustrates a cell network in a metropolitan area. A typical cell network is capable of handling hundreds of calls simultaneously, and cell usage is growing at a fast rate worldwide.

FIGURE 3.26   RF communications between two ground stations

Many people use cell phones for data communications. Most users assume that cell connections are private when in fact they may not be. Communications on a cell network can be intercepted using off-the-shelf equipment. Analog cellular communications can be easily understood, whereas digital cellular service requires additional equipment to decode transmissions.

A relative newcomer on the microwave communications scene involves wireless networks. Some of the wireless networks allow pagers, PDAs, and internal or private networks. Wireless networks operate in the 2.5 to 5.0GHz spectrum. When implementing wireless networks, you would be wise to make sure you implement or install communications security devices or encryption technology to prevent the unauthorized disclosure of information in your network. Many of the newer devices include encryption protocols similar to IPSec.

FIGURE 3.27   Cellular network in a metropolitan area

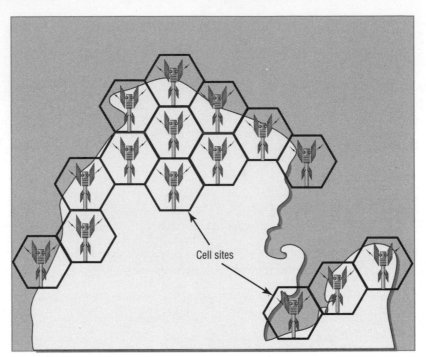

Cell sites

Employing Removable Storage

Computer systems have become modular over the last few years, and one of the benefits is removable media. *Removable storage* (commonly known as *removable media)* refers to any type of storage device (such as a floppy drive, magnetic tape cartridge, or CD-ROM) that can be removed from the system. Disk drives that once cost thousands of dollars now cost hundreds or even less. What once took up a whole room can easily be put in a coat pocket.

It's important to remember that removable media is subject to viruses, physical damage, and theft. If a CD-ROM is stepped on or scratched, it probably won't work properly. If it's stolen, it won't be available, and the information it contained will be gone forever. That information could include customer lists, IP addresses, databases, financial spreadsheets, or anything else of a sensitive nature.

The following sections discuss the most common types of removable media in use today and the physical and operational measures necessary to safeguard them.

CD-R/DVD-R

The *CD Recordable (CD-R)* is a relatively new technology that allows CDs to be made or burned on a computer system. CD-Rs operate like regular CDs, and they can be burned quickly. Most new computer systems come standard with a CD-R burner or CD-R drive. You can quickly back up data to or restore data from the CD-R.

CD-Rs are susceptible to computer viruses, and an infected file on the computer that is transferred to the CD-R will infect another system when the file is downloaded. All files need to be scanned for viruses before being written to or read from a CD-R. Data theft is also easy with a CD-R; an attacker can get on a system that has a CD-R and copy data from hard disks or servers. Some older CD-Rs are susceptible to erasure by sustained exposure to sunlight, so it's generally a good idea to keep CD-Rs out of environments that are high in ultraviolet (UV) light.

Whether the removable media you use is tape, CD-R, hard drives, or other media, you should bear in mind that one of the biggest vulnerabilities you face is the theft of that media and the data it holds. The best protection you have is to keep a close watch over the media; make sure it's securely and safely locked up when not in use.

While the exam focuses on CD-R, you should know that CD-RW (offering the ability to write) has surpassed CD-R and is now being eclipsed by read and write DVD. The enormous storage capacity of DVD/DVD-R, and its ease of use, is quickly making it a favorite when it comes to holding large amounts of important data. A single-layer DVD can store approximately seven times what a CD can (4.7GB), which makes it much more convenient for large backups and archives.

Diskettes

Most computer systems provide the capability to accept floppy and other types of *diskettes*. Diskettes have properties similar to hard drives, although they usually store smaller amounts of data. They're one of the primary carriers of computer viruses, and they can be used to make copies of small files from hard disks.

Diskette drives are rugged and can take all kinds of physical abuse. However, if the media in the drive is scratched, the data will be lost. Diskettes are also sensitive to erasure by magnetic fields.

Flash Cards

Flash cards, also referred to as *memory sticks*, are small memory cards that can be used to store information. A system that has a flash card interface usually treats flash cards like a hard drive. Flash cards can carry viruses, and they can be used to steal small amounts of information from systems that support them.

Flash cards are coming down in price and are becoming standard on many computer systems. Most PDA devices accept flash cards, making them susceptible to viruses that are targeted at PDAs.

Hard Drives

Hard drives today are small and can store a great deal of data. Usually, hard drives can be quickly removed from systems, and portable hard drives can be easily attached. Software that creates an exact copy, or *image*, of a drive can be used to download a system onto a hard drive in minutes. Many of the hard drives available today use USB or parallel ports to connect, and most operating systems will install them automatically using Plug and Play technology.

An attacker can attach a USB hard drive and then copy files from a workstation; this can happen in a matter of minutes with little possibility of detection. Another aspect of hard drive security involves the physical theft or removal of the drives. If a drive containing key information is stolen, it may be difficult to replace unless a recent backup has been performed. Hard drives are also susceptible to viruses because they're the primary storage devices for most computers. Additionally, hard drives are susceptible to vibration damage—dropping a hard drive will usually result in premature failure of the unit.

Network Attached Storage

Not all removable media needs to be directly connected to the workstation. There is growing acceptance of network attached storage in businesses today for such purposes as backups, archives, and just allowing storage to grow. Most *network attached storage (NAS)* devices are simply computers dedicated to the task of storing files for users on the network. The users connect to the NAS units typically through Network File System (NFS) or Server Message Blocks (SMB) communication with network file servers.

 An excellent whitepaper on using NAS to address file storage growth can be found at http://www.sun.com/storagetek/white-papers/IDC_NAS_FINAL_112906.pdf.

Smart Cards

Smart cards are generally used for access control and security purposes. The card itself usually contains a small amount of memory that can be used to store permissions and access information.

Smart cards are difficult to counterfeit, but they're easy to steal. Once a thief has a smart card, they have all the access the card allows. To prevent this, many organizations don't put any identifying marks on their smart cards, making it harder for someone to utilize them. A password or PIN is required to activate many modern smart cards, and encryption is employed to protect the contents.

Many European countries are beginning to use smart cards instead of magnetic-strip credit cards because they offer additional security and can contain more information.

> When you think of a smart card, always remember that this tool can be used for authentication as well as storage. Not only can the card identify you, it can hold relevant information as well. As an analogy, think of a smart card as a debit card that has an updated total of your bank account balance on it as opposed to a credit card that has only your account number.

 Real World Scenario

Working with Smart Cards

You've been asked to help troubleshoot a problem that is occurring in your school's computer lab. Students are complaining about viruses that are infecting the floppy disks they bring to school. How can you help remedy this situation?

You should ensure that all the systems in your school lab computers are running antivirus software and that this software is kept up-to-date. Doing so will prevent known viruses from entering the school's system and being transferred to student files. You may also want to evaluate whether the school computers should have removable media installed on their systems. Several manufacturers now sell systems called *thin clients* that don't provide any disk storage or removable media on their workstations. Thin clients use dedicated servers to download applications, data, and any other information they need to have in order to run. This eliminates the danger of viruses being introduced from student disks.

Tape

One of the oldest forms of removable media is magnetic *tape*. Magnetic tapes come in a variety of types and sizes. Older tapes were reel-to-reel and were bulky and sensitive to environmental factors such as heat and moisture. Newer tapes are cartridge or cassette oriented and are smaller and much more durable. With some of the new tape technologies, you can store on a single tape what once would have required a 10-foot-by-10-foot tape vault.

Magnetic tapes have become very fast, and they can hold enormous amounts of data. They're commonly used to back up systems and archive old data. The major concern with tape involves physical security—a tape is easy to remove from the premises undetected.

Tape can be restored to another system, and all the contents will be available for review and alteration. It's relatively easy to edit a document, put it back on the tape, and then restore the bogus file back to the original computer system. This, of course, creates an integrity issue that may be difficult to detect.

Tapes can also become infected with viruses, and they can infect a system during the data recovery process. Files going onto a tape drive should be scanned to ensure that they're virus free.

One of the biggest issues when using tape has always been trying to figure out the best way to rotate sets of backups.

 Real World Scenario

Understanding Tape Rotation Schemes

As an administrator, you know the importance of backups and having more than one set of data available to restore. In this exercise, you'll use the Web to research some of the most commonly implemented tape-rotation schemes and compare/contrast them.

Using the Web, research these methods of tape rotation and look for the differences between them:

1. Tower of Hanoi

2. Grandfather-Father-Son (GFS)

3. Round Robin

You should discover that all of these are valid methods of rotating tape sets in order to maintain multiple copies that can be restored after a disaster. One method isn't monumentally better than another, and you'll want to identify the one that would work best in your implementation.

 While tape used to be the standard for removable media, it is quickly being replaced in the market by newer technologies for backups. You need to know about tape for this exam, but for the real world, you should know that it isn't being deployed at anywhere near the rate it used to be.

Thumb Drives

Thumb drives and flash cards come from the same family. In fact, *thumb drives* are nothing more than USB flash cards that allow you to store a large quantity of data on something that easily fits into your pocket. Because of their size and versatility, thumb drives have become the de facto standard for removable media, and they have replaced diskettes and other storage in many settings.

Being nothing more than storage media, thumb drives are susceptible to holding the same malware as other forms of removable media.

Summary

In this chapter, I covered the key elements of the network infrastructure and the various components involved in networking. Your infrastructure is the backbone and key to all the security capabilities of your network.

Your infrastructure includes the hardware and software necessary to run your network. The key elements used in security are routers and firewalls. Proper configuration is the key to providing services the way your network needs them. If your network security devices are improperly configured, you may be worse off than if you didn't have them at all. It's a dangerous situation when you think you're secure but in actuality you aren't.

Networks are becoming more complicated, and they're being linked to other networks at an accelerated speed. Several tools are available to help you both link and secure your networks:

- VPNs
- Tunneling protocols
- Remote access

The connections you make using TCP/IP are based primarily on IP addresses. When coupled with a port, these addresses form a socket. Sockets are the primary method used to communicate with services and applications such as the Web and Telnet. Most services have standard sockets that operate by default. Sockets are changeable for special configurations and additional security. Changing default ports requires that users know which ports provide which services.

Network monitors are primarily troubleshooting tools, and they can be used to eavesdrop on networks. Intrusion detection systems take an active role and can control traffic and systems. IDSs use extensive rule-based procedures to check audit files and network traffic, and they can make decisions based upon those rules. In conjunction with a firewall, an IDS can offer high levels of security.

The communication media you use will determine the security of communication from the physical perspective. Several different types of media are available for networks, including:

- Coax
- UTP/STP

- Fiber optic
- Infrared
- RF
- Microwave

Each provides a unique challenge that requires attention to ensure that security requirements are met.

Removable media can be a carrier or storage vessel for viruses. Make sure it is scanned with antivirus software to verify that it remains clean. Removable media is also easily transported and can disappear. Physical security measures are important to prevent this from happening.

Exam Essentials

Be able to describe the various components and the purpose of an infrastructure. Your network's infrastructure is the backbone of your systems and network operations. The infrastructure includes all the hardware, software, physical security, and operational security methods in place. The key components of your infrastructure include devices such as routers, firewalls, switches, modems, telecommunications systems, and the other devices used in the network.

Know the characteristics of the connectivity technologies available to you and the security capabilities associated with each. Remote access, PPP, tunneling protocols, and VPNs are your primary tools. PPTP and L2TP are two of the most common protocols used for tunneling. IPSec, although not a tunneling protocol, provides encryption to tunneling protocols; it's often used to enhance tunnel security.

Familiarize yourself with the technologies used by TCP/IP and the Internet. IP addresses and port numbers are combined to create an interface called a socket. Most TCP and UDP protocols communicate using this socket as the primary interface mechanism. Clients and servers communicate using ports. Ports can be changed to enhance security. Web services use HTML and other technologies to allow rich and animated websites. These technologies potentially create security problems because they may have individual vulnerabilities. Verify the problems that exist from a security perspective before enabling these technologies on your systems.

Be able to describe the two primary methods used for network monitoring. The primary methods used for network monitoring are sniffers and IDSs. Sniffers are passive and can provide real-time displays of network traffic. They're intended to be used primarily for troubleshooting purposes, but they're one of the tools used by attackers to determine what protocols and systems you're running. IDSs are active devices that operate to alert administrators of attacks and unusual events. This is accomplished by automatically reviewing log files and system traffic and by applying rules that dictate how to react to events. An IDS, when used in conjunction with firewalls, can provide excellent security for a network.

Understand the various types and capabilities of the media used in a network.   Network media is wire, fiber, or wireless based. Each type of media presents challenges to security that must be evaluated. Never assume that a wireless connection is secure.

Be able to describe the vulnerabilities of removable media and what steps must be taken to minimize the risks.   Removable media are used for backup, archives, and working storage. The capacity and capabilities of these types of devices have increased dramatically over the last few years. Most removable media is small and easily hidden, so physical security measures are necessary to keep someone from walking off with them. In addition, media can be copied to other systems, presenting confidentiality issues. Make sure you know how to safeguard this technology.

Hands-On Labs

The labs in this chapter are as follows:

Lab 3.1: Examine the Windows Routing Table

Lab 3.2: Examine the Linux Routing Table

Lab 3.1: Examine the Windows Routing Table

Routing tables identify the network destination, netmask, gateway, and interface to use as well as the metric associated with it. For this lab, you'll look for the presence of a routing table on a Windows-based host (XP or 2000/2003):

1. Open a command prompt by choosing Start ➢ Run and enter **CMD** at the Run prompt.

2. Enter the command **route print**.

3. If any routing tables exist, active routes are displayed. Carefully look at the display and notice how data is routed between this network and others.

4. In some versions of Windows, the display breaks out the active routes and persistent routes. Persistent routes survive a reboot and are always configured. You can make a route persistent by creating it with the –p parameter.

5. Enter the command **route**.

Read the help message displayed, and examine the different parameters available for setting and removing routes.

Lab 3.2: Examine the Linux Routing Table

For this lab, you'll look for the presence of a routing table on a Linux-based host and examine the entries in it:

1. Open a shell prompt.

2. Enter the command **route**. If you receive a message indicating that the command is not found, use **su** to become the root user and run the command again.

3. If any routing tables exist, active routes are displayed. Carefully look at the display and notice how data is routed between this network and others.

4. Enter the command **route –help**.

Read the help message displayed, and examine the different parameters you can use to set and remove routes.

Review Questions

1. Which of the following devices is the most capable of providing infrastructure security?

    A. Hub

    B. Switch

    C. Router

    D. Modem

2. Upper management has decreed that a firewall must be put in place immediately, before your site suffers an attack similar to one that struck a sister company. Responding to this order, your boss instructs you to implement a packet filter by the end of the week. A packet filter performs which function?

    A. Prevents unauthorized packets from entering the network

    B. Allows all packets to leave the network

    C. Allows all packets to enter the network

    D. Eliminates collisions in the network

3. Which device stores information about destinations in a network?

    A. Hub

    B. Modem

    C. Firewall

    D. Router

4. As more and more clients have been added to your network, the efficiency of the network has decreased significantly. You're preparing a budget for next year, and you specifically want to address this problem. Which of the following devices acts primarily as a tool to improve network efficiency?

    A. Hub

    B. Switch

    C. Router

    D. PBX

5. Which device is used to connect voice, data, pagers, networks, and almost any other conceivable application into a single telecommunications system?

    A. Router

    B. PBX

    C. HUB

    D. Server

6. Most of the sales force have been told that they should no longer report to the office on a daily basis. From now on, they're to spend the majority of their time on the road calling on customers. Each member of the sales force has been issued a laptop computer and told to connect to the network nightly through a dial-up connection. Which of the following protocols is widely used today as a transport protocol for Internet dial-up connections?

    A. SMTP

    B. PPP

    C. PPTP

    D. L2TP

7. Which protocol is unsuitable for WAN VPN connections?

    A. PPP

    B. PPTP

    C. L2TP

    D. IPSec

8. You've been given notice that you'll soon be transferred to another site. Before you leave, you're to audit the network and document everything in use and the reason why it's in use. The next administrator will use this documentation to keep the network running. Which of the following protocols isn't a tunneling protocol but is probably used at your site by tunneling protocols for network security?

    A. IPSec

    B. PPTP

    C. L2TP

    D. L2F

9. A socket is a combination of which components?

    A. TCP and port number

    B. UDP and port number

    C. IP and session number

    D. IP and port number

10. You're explaining protocols to a junior administrator shortly before you leave for vacation. The topic of Internet mail applications comes up, and you explain how communications are done now as well as how you expect them to be done in the future. Which of the following protocols is becoming the newest standard for Internet mail applications?

    A. SMTP

    B. POP

    C. IMAP

    D. IGMP

11. Which protocol is primarily used for network maintenance and destination information?

    A. ICMP

    B. SMTP

    C. IGMP

    D. Router

12. You're the administrator for Mercury Technical. A check of protocols in use on your server brings up one that you weren't aware was in use; you suspect that someone in HR is using it to send messages to multiple recipients. Which of the following protocols is used for group messages or multicast messaging?

    A. SMTP

    B. SNMP

    C. IGMP

    D. L2TP

13. Which device monitors network traffic in a passive manner?

    A. Sniffer

    B. IDS

    C. Firewall

    D. Web browser

14. Security has become the utmost priority at your organization. You're no longer content to act reactively to incidents when they occur—you want to start acting more proactively. Which system performs active network monitoring and analysis and can take proactive steps to protect a network?

    A. IDS

    B. Sniffer

    C. Router

    D. Switch

15. Which media is broken down into seven categories depending on capability?

    A. Coax

    B. UTP

    C. Infrared

    D. Fiber-optic cable

16. You're the network administrator for MTS. Within five months, your company will leave its rented office space and move into a larger facility. As the company has grown, so too has the value of its data. You're in a unique position to create a network layout at the new facility from scratch and incorporate needed security precautions. Which media is the least susceptible to interception or tapping?

    A. Coax

    B. UTP

    C. STP

    D. Fiber

17. Which media offers line-of-sight broadband and baseband capabilities?

    A. Coax

    B. Infrared

    C. Microwave

    D. UTP

18. An evaluation is under way of the current forms of removable media allowed within the company. Once the evaluation has been completed, the policies and procedures for network and computer usage will be updated. Which of the following media should the policies dictate be used primarily for backup and archiving purposes?

    A. Tape

    B. CD-R

    C. Memory stick

    D. Removable hard drives

19. Which media is susceptible to viruses?

    A. Tape

    B. Memory stick

    C. CD-R

    D. All of the above

20. You want to begin using a media format that can store personal information and is difficult to copy or counterfeit. Which of the following devices should be used for this purpose?

    A. CD-R

    B. Smart card

    C. Flash card

    D. Tape

Answers to Review Questions

1. **C.** Routers can be configured in many instances to act as packet-filtering firewalls. When configured properly, they can prevent unauthorized ports from being opened.

2. **A.** Packet filters prevent unauthorized packets from entering or leaving a network. Packet filters are a type of firewall that block specified port traffic.

3. **D.** Routers store information about network destinations in routing tables. Routing tables contain information about known hosts on both sides of the router.

4. **B.** Switches create virtual circuits between systems in a network. These virtual circuits are somewhat private and reduce network traffic when used.

5. **B.** Many modern PBX (private branch exchange) systems integrate voice and data onto a single data connection to your phone service provider. In some cases, this allows an overall reduction in cost of operations. These connections are made using existing network connec-tions book as a T1 or T3 network.

6. **B.** PPP can pass multiple protocols and is widely used today as a transport protocol for dial-up connections.

7. **A.** PPP provides no security, and all activities are unsecure. PPP is primarily intended for dial-up connections and should never be used for VPN connections.

8. **A.** IPSec provides network security for tunneling protocols. IPSec can be used with many different protocols besides TCP/IP, and it has two modes of security.

9. **D.** A socket is a combination of IP address and port number. The socket identifies which application will respond to the network request.

10. **C.** IMAP is becoming the most popular standard for e-mail clients and is replacing POP protocols for mail systems. IMAP allows mail to be forwarded and stored in information areas called stores.

11. **A.** ICMP is used for destination and error reporting functions in TCP/IP. ICMP is routable and is used by programs such as Ping and Traceroute.

12. **C.** IGMP is used for group messaging and multicasting. IGMP maintains a list of sys-tems that belong to a message group. When a message is sent to a particular group, each system receives an individual copy.

13. **A.** Sniffers monitor network traffic and display traffic in real time. Sniffers, also called network monitors, were originally designed for network maintenance and troubleshooting.

14. **A.** An IDS is used to protect and report network abnormalities to a network administrator or system. It works with audit files and rule-based processing to determine how to act in the event of an unusual situation on the network.

15. B.   UTP is broken down into seven categories that define bandwidth and performance. The most common category is CAT 5, which allows 1000Mbps bandwidth. CAT 5 cabling is most frequently used with 100Base-T networks.

16. D.   Fiber networks are considered the most secure, although they can be tapped. Fiber networks use a plastic or glass conductor and pass light waves generated by a laser.

17. C.   Microwave communications systems can offer huge bandwidth and operate with either baseband or broadband capabilities. Baseband communication uses a single channel, whereas broadband is a multichannel environment.

18. A.   The most common backup and archiving media in large systems is tape. Of the choices given, tape provides the highest-density storage in the smallest package. CD-Rs and removable hard drives may also be used, but they generally don't have the storage capacity of equivalent tape cartridges.

19. D.   All of these devices can store and pass viruses to uninfected systems. Make sure that all files are scanned for viruses before they're copied to these media.

20. B.   Smart cards are used for access control, and they can contain a small amount of information. Smart cards are replacing magnetic cards, in many instances because they can store additional personal information and are harder to copy or counterfeit.

Chapter

4

Monitoring Activity and Intrusion Detection

THE FOLLOWING COMPTIA SECURITY+ EXAM OBJECTIVES ARE COVERED IN THIS CHAPTER:

✓ **1.4 Carry out the appropriate procedures to establish application security.**

- Instant messaging

✓ **1.5 Implement security applications.**

- HIDS
- Personal software firewalls

✓ **2.3 Determine the appropriate use of network security tools to facilitate network security.**

- NIDS
- NIPS
- Firewalls
- Honeypot
- Protocol analyzers

✓ **2.4 Apply the appropriate network tools to facilitate network security.**

- NIDS
- Firewalls
- Protocol analyzers

✓ **2.7 Explain the vulnerabilities and implement mitigations associated with wireless networking.**

- Data emanation
- War driving
- SSID broadcast

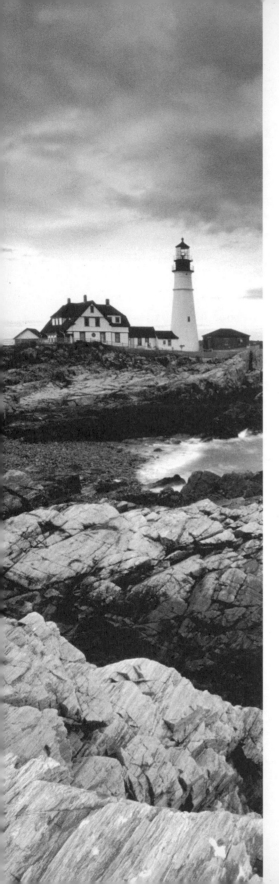

- Blue jacking
- Bluesnarfing
- Rogue access points
- Weak encryption

✓ **4.2 Carry out vulnerability assessments using common tools.**

- Port scanners
- Vulnerability scanners
- Protocol analyzers
- Network mappers

✓ **4.4 Use monitoring tools on systems and networks and detect security-related anomalies.**

- Protocol analyzers

✓ **4.5 Compare and contrast various types of monitoring methodologies.**

- Behavior-based
- Signature-based
- Anomaly-based

✓ **4.6 Execute proper logging procedures and evaluate the results.**

- Security application
- DNS
- System
- Performance
- Access
- Firewall
- Antivirus

✓ **6.3 Differentiate between and execute appropriate response procedures.**

- Forensics
- Chain of custody
- First responders
- Damage and loss control
- Reporting—disclosure of

If it were not for the need to provide a connection path to share data, resources, and services, no one would ever install a network. This very connectivity—this need for convenience—forms the basis of the problems we face in providing a secure environment for our systems. This chapter deals with a number of faculties, including intrusion detection, detection methods, wireless technologies, and instant messaging. Additionally, this chapter discusses signal analysis and network monitoring.

Monitoring the Network

The basics of network monitoring were introduced earlier (in Chapter 2). This chapter picks up that topic and examines more of the specifics and details of network monitoring.

Your network is vulnerable to all sorts of attacks and penetration efforts. Network-monitoring techniques help you track what is happening in your network. Monitoring can occur in real time (for example, when using a network sniffer) or by following events using log files and security systems (a task made simpler by using an intrusion detection system [IDS]).

More than likely, the building you occupy has a perimeter security system. This system might not keep a determined burglar from breaking in, but it will keep out most people. Most office buildings also have video cameras, motion detectors, and other devices to detect intruders and notify authorities about a break-in. In addition, your building probably has fire and smoke detectors, water sensors, and any number of other safety and security devices installed. All of this equipment, working together, provides a reasonably safe work environment. Your computers and network need the same sorts of things.

Network monitoring helps ensure a safe environment. You can help secure your computer's environment by installing tools to automatically monitor it and report unusual events that occur. You can monitor your network by reviewing system logs on a regular basis or by installing complex software that performs these activities for you and then reports anything unusual. This process is much like the fire-suppression system in your building. When a fire is detected, elevators return to the basement, sprinklers automatically activate, and the local fire department is notified. When a computer security breach occurs, the network needs to isolate the affected systems, notify the administrator(s), and even attempt (if necessary) to shut down the systems.

Monitoring your network on a regular basis is important to determine what types of events are occurring. Without this information, you're shooting in the dark. As a security professional, you should primarily deal with what is happening in your network as it occurs. You also want to establish preventive measures to reduce the fear of the unknown.

The following sections introduce you to the types of network traffic you'll encounter on most networks. These include a wide variety of protocols, such as TCP/IP, IPX, and Net-BEUI. Each one operates with its own rules and methods. In general, these protocols don't interact with each other, and they're oblivious to the existence of the other protocols.

> With each passing day, it is harder and harder to find networking protocols in use other than TCP/IP. It has become the de facto networking protocol and is now the standard default in almost every operating system, including those from Microsoft and Novell. For the exam, however, you should know general information about all the protocols discussed in this book.

Recognizing the Different Types of Network Traffic

The following sections briefly explain the protocols and services that are common in networks. The most common protocol used in wide area networks (WANs) today is TCP/IP, which is why it is discussed first. Some networks also run protocols unique to Novell, Microsoft, Network File Systems, and AppleTalk, and these protocols are discussed as well. The following sections introduce you to these protocols and identify potential threats to your networks.

TCP/IP

As you might recall, the TCP/IP suite supports a wide variety of protocols used to transport information inside and outside the local area network (LAN). The protocols that are most susceptible to attacks are IP, TCP, UDP, ICMP, and IGMP, which were briefly mentioned in Chapter 2, "Identifying Potential Risks." The important thing to remember is that each of these protocols may be vulnerable because of the unsecure nature of TCP/IP or a weakness in the software manufacturer's implementation of the protocol.

It's important to know which TCP and UDP ports are open in order to understand what services your server is allowing.

> Lab 4.1 shows how to view the active TCP and UDP ports.

Novell Protocols

Novell, Inc., has long been a significant player in the network environment. Its NetWare product line was once the server network operating system (NOS) used throughout the majority of all office buildings. Novell is a longtime rival of Microsoft, and the company has a large and loyal following.

NetWare, a server-based networking environment/operating system, offers network protocols, services, and applications. NetWare is susceptible to DoS attacks, as are most TCP/IP-based environments. In addition to TCP/IP, NetWare supports two other proprietary protocols:

IPX/SPX   *Internetwork Packet Exchange (IPX)* and *Sequenced Packet Exchange (SPX)* are two of the proprietary protocols unique to Novell 4.*x* and earlier NetWare networks. IPX and SPX are still in use, but they're not as widespread as they once were. These protocols are fast, efficient, and well documented. They're also susceptible to communications interception using internal monitoring.

Microsoft desktop operating systems often include the ability to communicate using IPX/SPX so that the workstations can exist on NetWare-based networks. Because IPX/SPX is proprietary to Novell, Microsoft created NWLink, an IPX-/SPX-compatible protocol that it owns.

NDS and eDirectory   Novell introduced a directory management service called *NetWare Directory Services (NDS)* to manage all the resources in a network. The acronym NDS was later changed to *Novell Directory Services*. NDS provides a database of all network objects or resources. Figure 4.1 shows an NDS tree. The key point to remember here is that NDS is a network-based service. Notice that the NDS tree treats print devices, disk volumes, users, and groups as *leaf objects*, or resources, in the tree. Earlier versions of NetWare used bindery services; the bindery kept track of resources on a server-by-server basis.

FIGURE 4.1   A typical NDS tree structure

Chapter 5, "Implementing and Maintaining a Secure Network," examines NDS and eDirectory.

In the most recent versions of NetWare, NDS has been expanded and renamed *eDirectory*. Novell changed the environment so that it now operates using TCP/IP as the native network protocol.

Novell also provides a number of applications, tools, and products that compare favorably to other network-based products. Two of the more popular Novell products are GroupWise, an e-mail and collaboration system similar to Microsoft Exchange, and a software and configuration distribution product known as ZENworks.

The last version of NetWare to be released was 6.5. All versions above 5.0 use TCP/IP as their default networking protocol rather than IPX/SPX. Novell is now in the process of converting its products to Linux (which has always used TCP/IP as the default). *Open Enterprise Server (OES)* is a shell that runs on top of NetWare or Linux and allows Novell's remaining proprietary tools to run on both operating systems.

Microsoft Protocols

Microsoft and IBM were early leaders in PC network technologies. Early PC systems supported a rudimentary peer-to-peer networking environment that was fast and required little overhead. Of course, networks in those days were simple, and high levels of functionality weren't expected. The two original network protocols available for PCs were NetBIOS and NetBEUI.

The following sections include brief discussions of each of these protocols, plus Windows Internet Naming Service (WINS). Although WINS isn't technically a protocol, it's an integral part of the traffic on a Microsoft network.

Over the years, Microsoft has introduced a number of other protocols and services to facilitate communication among Windows network systems. Microsoft has stated that future network products will utilize TCP/IP, which is now replacing most of these protocols.

NetBIOS

Network Basic Input Output System (NetBIOS) is the native protocol of Windows PCs. NetBIOS provides a 15-character naming convention for resources on the network. It's a broadcast-oriented network protocol in that all traffic is available to all devices in a LAN. The protocol can be transported over NetBEUI, TCP/IP, or IPX/SPX.

The biggest vulnerability with NetBIOS is that it opens ports for file and print sharing. These ports (which can include 135 through 139 and 445) can be accessed across the Internet as well as by devices on the local LAN.

NetBEUI

The *NetBIOS Extended User Interface (NetBEUI)* is used to transport NetBIOS traffic in a LAN. NetBEUI and NetBIOS were originally packaged as a single product, beginning with the release of Windows for Workgroups. As network technologies advanced, NetBIOS was turned into a separate protocol. Figure 4.2 shows a network running only NetBEUI.

FIGURE 4.2   NetBEUI network using a VPN over a TCP/IP network

NetBEUI is a nonroutable protocol, meaning that it can't be sent across routers. NetBEUI traffic is easy to intercept internally using a network sniffer.

WINS Service

The *Windows Internet Naming Service (WINS)* translates NetBIOS names to TCP/IP addresses. WINS runs as a service on a server. It provides name translation for networks, similar in nature to DNS. If WINS isn't available, a Windows system can use a local file, LMHOSTS, to resolve NetBIOS names to TCP/IP addresses. In Figure 4.3, a WINS server provides a NetBIOS name to TCP/IP addresses in a LAN. This resolution process has been coupled by DNS with Windows Server products.

FIGURE 4.3   WINS Server resolving TCP/IP addresses to names

Because WINS is providing a service to clients who request information from it, it's susceptible to DoS attacks. When left unpatched, it is also available for remote code execution.

Network File System Protocol

Network File System (NFS) is the default file-sharing protocol for Unix systems. NFS allows a remote user to mount drives on a machine in the network. To be secure, NFS requires special configuration and is, in many ways, more of a Linux+ topic than Security+. NFS is equivalent to Distributed File System (DFS), which tends to exist outside of the Unix world. Figure 4.4 shows a remote system mounting a drive on a local machine using NFS.

FIGURE 4.4   An NFS device being mounted by a remote Unix system

    NFS is also discussed in Chapter 5.

The Apple Protocol

Apple Computers has been a network player for many years. The Apple networking protocol, *AppleTalk*, is a routable protocol (although it has a lot of routing overhead), and it has been a standard on Apples and Apple printers for many years. Most manufacturers of network products support the AppleTalk protocol, which isn't intended for secure applications. Modern Macintosh systems can also use TCP/IP for connections.

Most of AppleTalk's vulnerabilities don't center around the protocol itself, but instead are exploitations of programs that offer this service. For example, there are known vulnerabilities with programs that allow Linux to offer AppleTalk, but those weaknesses are with the programs themselves and not with AppleTalk per se.

Monitoring Network Systems

Several monitoring mechanisms are available to track traffic. Monitoring can occur on individual systems, on servers, or as a separate component of the network. The connection used when monitoring occurs on a network is called a *tap*. Figure 4.5 illustrates some of the places where a network tap can occur. Each location presents a different view of the network. For an effective security process, multiple taps are probably needed.

FIGURE 4.5   Tap locations used to monitor network traffic

Your system faces both internal and external threats. If all your monitoring activities are oriented toward external threats, discovering internal security breaches as they occur may be difficult. You must always strive to achieve a good balance between the two and be willing to increase measures in one direction or another as needed. For example, should you learn that the company is about to downsize 25 percent of the workforce, then it would be prudent to increase security measures targeted at minimizing internal breaches. Following a rash of intrusions at companies in the same business as yours, increasing external security measures should be the top priority.

Always remember that common sense is the most important tool you have in answering exam questions as well as facing real-world scenarios.

In a busy network, identifying the types of activities that are occurring is difficult because of the sheer volume of traffic. Heavy traffic makes it necessary to dedicate personnel to monitoring. Network activity is also reported in system logs and audit files. Although it's a good practice to periodically review these files, doing so can be a daunting and extremely boring undertaking. Automated tools, which make this process more manageable, are coming to the market.

Understanding Intrusion Detection Systems

Imagine that you have just come home from vacation. While you were gone, someone entered your house without your permission. How will you know it? Will the alarm be sounding, or will you notice the front door unlocked? Will you need to spot something missing, or will a rug out of place tip you off?

Real World Scenario

Know the Resources Available in Linux

Security information is readily found at a number of Linux-related sites. The first to check, and stay abreast of, is always the distribution vendor's site. Its pages usually provide an overview of Linux-related security issues with links to other relevant pages. You should also keep abreast of issues and problems posted at http://www.cert.org and http://www.linuxsecurity.com.

You can find information on any Linux command through a number of utilities inherent in Linux:

- The man tool offers pages on each utility. For example, to find information about the setfacl tool, you can type **mansetfacl**.

- Most utilities have the built-in option of –help to offer information. From the command line, you can type **setfacl –help** to see a quick list of available options.

- The info utility shows the man pages as well.

- The whatis utility can show if there is more than one set of documentation on the system for the utility.

- The whereis utility lists all the information it can find about locations associated with a file.

- The apropos utility uses the whatis database to find values and returns the short summary information.

In the original *Walking Tall* movies, the sheriff put small strips of clear tape on the hood of his car. Before getting in the vehicle, he would check the difficult-to-detect tape to see if it was broken—if it was, it tipped him off that someone had been messing beneath the hood, and that saved his life. Do you have clear tape on your network?

Intrusion detection systems (IDSs) are becoming integral parts of network monitoring. IDS is a relatively new technology, and it shows a lot of promise in helping to detect network intrusions. *Intrusion detection (ID)* is the process of monitoring events in a system or network to determine if an intrusion is occurring. An *intrusion* is defined as any activity or action that attempts to undermine or compromise the confidentiality, integrity, or availability of resources. Firewalls, as you may recall, were designed to prevent access to resources by an attacker. An IDS reports and monitors intrusion attempts.

It should be inherently understood that every network, regardless of size, should utilize a firewall. On a home-based network, a personal software firewall can be implemented to provide protection against attacks.

Several key terms are necessary to explain the technology and facilitate the discussion in this section:

Activity   An *activity* is an element of a data source that is of interest to the operator. This could include a specific occurrence of a type of activity that is suspicious. An example might be a TCP connection request that occurs repeatedly from the same IP address.

Administrator   The *administrator* is the person responsible for setting the security policy for an organization. They're responsible for making decisions about the deployment and configuration of the IDS. The administrator should make decisions regarding alarm levels, historical logging, and session monitoring capabilities. They're also responsible for determining the appropriate responses to attacks and ensuring that those responses are carried out.

Most organizations have an escalation chart. The administrator is rarely at the top of the chart but is always expected to be the one doing the most to keep incidents under control.

Alert   An *alert* is a message from the analyzer indicating that an event of interest has occurred. The alert contains information about the activity as well as specifics of the occurrence. An alert may be generated when an excessive amount of *Internet Control Message Protocol* (ICMP) traffic is occurring or when repeated logon attempts are failing. A certain level of traffic is normal for a network. Alerts occur when activities of a certain type exceed a preset threshold. For instance, you might want to generate an alert every time someone from inside your network pings the outside using the Ping program.

Analyzer   The *analyzer* is the component or process that analyzes the data collected by the sensor. It looks for suspicious activity among all the data collected. Analyzers work by monitoring events and determining whether unusual activities are occurring, or they can use a rule-based process that is established when the IDS is configured.

Data source   The *data source* is the raw information that the IDS uses to detect suspicious activity. The data source may include audit files, system logs, or the network traffic as it occurs.

Event   An *event* is an occurrence in a data source that indicates that a suspicious activity has occurred. It may generate an alert. Events are logged for future reference. They also typically trigger a notification that something unusual may be happening in the network. An IDS might begin logging events if the volume of inbound e-mail connections suddenly spiked; this event might be an indication that someone was probing your network. The event might trigger an alert if a deviation from normal network traffic patterns occurred or if an activity threshold was crossed.

Manager   The *manager* is the component or process the operator uses to manage the IDS. The IDS console is a manager. Configuration changes in the IDS are made by communicating with the IDS manager.

Notification *Notification* is the process or method by which the IDS manager makes the operator aware of an alert. This might include a graphic display highlighting the traffic or an e-mail sent to the network's administrative staff.

Operator The *operator* is the person primarily responsible for the IDS. The operator can be a user, administrator, and so on, as long as they're the primary person responsible.

Sensor A *sensor* is the IDS component that collects data from the data source and passes it to the analyzer for analysis. A sensor can be a device driver on a system, or it can be an actual black box that is connected to the network and reports to the IDS. The important thing to remember is that the sensor is a primary data collection point for the IDS.

The IDS, as you can see, has many different components and processes that work together to provide a real-time picture of your network traffic. Figure 4.6 shows the various components and processes working together to provide an IDS. Remember that data can come from many different sources and must be analyzed to determine what's occurring. An IDS isn't intended as a true traffic-blocking device, though some IDSs can also perform this function; it's intended to be a traffic-auditing device.

FIGURE 4.6   The components of an IDS working together to provide network monitoring

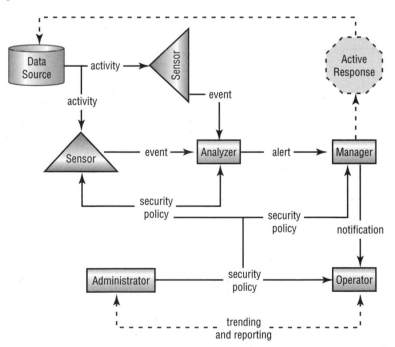

IDSs use two primary approaches:

Signature-based-detection IDS A *signature-based* system, also commonly known as *misuse-detection IDS (MD-IDS)*, is primarily focused on evaluating attacks based on attack signatures and audit trails. Attack signatures describe a generally established method of attacking a system. For example, a TCP flood attack begins with a large number of incomplete TCP sessions. If the MD-IDS knows what a TCP flood attack looks like, it can make an appropriate report or response to thwart the attack.

Figure 4.7 illustrates a signature-based IDS in action. Notice that this IDS uses an extensive database to determine the signature of the traffic. This process resembles an antivirus software process.

FIGURE 4.7 A signature-based IDS in action

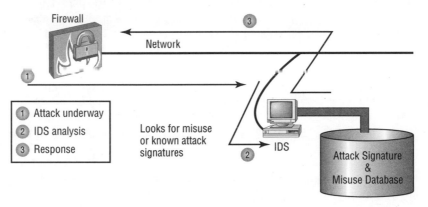

Anomaly-detection IDS An *anomaly-detection IDS (AD-IDS)* looks for anomalies, meaning it looks for things outside of the ordinary. Typically, a training program learns what the normal operation is and then can spot deviations from it. An AD-IDS can establish the baseline either by being manually assigned values or through automated processes that look at traffic patterns. One method is *behavior-based*, which looks for unusual behavior and then acts accordingly.

IDSs are primarily focused on reporting events or network traffic that deviate from historical work activity or network traffic patterns. For this reporting to be effective, administrators should develop a baseline or history of typical network traffic. This baseline activity provides a stable, long-term perspective on network activity. An example might be a report generated when a higher-than-normal level of ICMP responses is received in a specified time period. Such activity may indicate the beginning of an ICMP flood attack. The system may also report when a user who doesn't normally access the network using a VPN suddenly requests administrative access to the system. Figure 4.8 demonstrates an AD-IDS tracking and reporting excessive traffic in a network. The AD-IDS process frequently uses artificial intelligence or expert system technologies to learn about normal traffic for a network.

FIGURE 4.8   AD-IDS using expert system technology to evaluate risks

AD-IDS System

The best solution to creating a secure network is to place IDS in front of and behind the firewall. This double security provides as much defense as possible.

Whenever there is an attack, there is almost always something created that identifies it—an entry in the login report, an error in a log, and so forth. Those items represent intrusion signatures, and you can learn from them and instruct IDS to watch for and prevent repeat performances of those items.

MD-IDS and AD-IDS are merging in most commercial systems. They provide the best opportunity to detect and thwart attacks and unauthorized access. Unlike a firewall, the IDS exists to detect and report unusual occurrences in a network, not block them.

The next sections discuss network-based and host-based implementations of IDS and the capabilities they provide. I'll also introduce honeypots and incident response.

Working with a Network-Based IDS

A *network-based IDS (N-IDS)* approach to IDS attaches the system to a point in the network where it can monitor and report on all network traffic. This can be in front of or behind the firewall, as shown in Figure 4.9.

The best solution to creating a secure network is to place IDS in front of and behind the firewall. This double security provides as much defense as possible.

Placing the N-IDS in front of the firewall provides monitoring of all network traffic going into the network. This approach allows a huge amount of data to be processed, and it lets you see all the traffic coming into the network. Putting the N-IDS behind the firewall only allows you to see the traffic that penetrates the firewall. Although this approach reduces the amount of data processed, it doesn't let you see all the attacks that might be developing.

FIGURE 4.9   N-IDS placement in a network determines what data will be analyzed.

The N-IDS can be attached to a switch or a hub, or it can be attached to a tap. Many hubs and switches provide a monitoring port for troubleshooting and diagnostic purposes. This port may function in a manner similar to a tap. The advantage of the tap approach is that the IDS is the only device that will be using the tap. Figure 4.10 illustrates a connection to the network using a hub.

FIGURE 4.10   A hub being used to attach the N-IDS to the network

> *Port spanning,* also known as *port mirroring,* copies the traffic from all ports to a single port and disallows bidirectional traffic on that port. Cisco's Switched Port Analyzer (SPAN) is one example of a port spanning implementation.

In either case, the IDS monitors and evaluates all the traffic to which it has access.

Two basic types of responses can be formulated at the network level: passive and active. They're briefly explained in the following sections.

> ### 🌐 Real World Scenario
>
> #### Working with Network Audit Files
>
> You're the network administrator of a relatively busy network. Your company has gone through a couple of cutbacks, and your staffing is limited. You want to make sure that your network stays as secure as you can make it. What can you do to ease your workload?
>
> You should consider two primary possibilities to protect your network: Either install an IDS or reduce the logging levels of your network audit files. An alternative is to install an audit log-collection system with filtering.
>
> You might be able to reduce the amount of logged traffic in your audit files by changing the settings that determine what you audit. However, changing audit rules would prevent you from seeing what's happening on your network because most events wouldn't be logged.
>
> Installing an IDS would allow you to establish rules that would provide a higher level of automation than you could achieve by reviewing audit files. Your best solution might be to convince your company to invest in an IDS. An IDS could send you an e-mail or alert you when an event was detected.

Implementing a Passive Response

A *passive response* is the most common type of response to many intrusions. In general, passive responses are the easiest to develop and implement. The following list includes some passive response strategies:

Logging *Logging* involves recording that an event has occurred and under what circumstances it occurred. Logging functions should provide sufficient information about the nature of the attack to help administrators determine what has happened and to assist in evaluating the threat. This information can then be used to devise methods to counter the threat.

Notification *Notification* communicates event-related information to the appropriate personnel when an event has occurred. This includes relaying any relevant data about the event to help evaluate the situation. If the IDS is manned full time, messages can be displayed on the manager's console to indicate that the situation is occurring.

Shunning *Shunning* or ignoring an attack is a common response. This might be the case if your IDS notices an Internet Information Server (IIS) attack occurring on a system that's running another web-hosting service, such as Apache. The attack won't work because Apache doesn't respond the same way that IIS does, so why pay attention to it? In a busy network, many different types of attacks can occur simultaneously. If you aren't worried about an attack succeeding, why waste energy or time investigating it or notifying someone about it? The IDS can make a note of it in a log and move on to other more pressing business.

Remember that passive responses are the most commonly implemented. They are the least costly and the easiest to put into practice.

Implementing an Active Response

An *active response* involves taking an action based on an attack or threat. The goal of an active response is to take the quickest action possible to reduce an event's potential impact. This type of response requires plans for how to deal with an event, clear policies, and intelligence in the IDS in order to be successful. An active response will include one of the reactions briefly described here:

Terminating processes or sessions   If a flood attack is detected, the IDS can cause the subsystem, such as TCP, to force resets to all the sessions that are under way. Doing so frees up resources and allows TCP to continue to operate normally. Of course, all valid TCP sessions are closed and will need to be reestablished—but at least this will be possible, and it may not have much effect on the end users. The IDS evaluates the events and determines the best way to handle them. Figure 4.11 illustrates TCP being directed to issue RST or reset commands from the IDS to reset all open connections to TCP. This type of mechanism can also terminate user sessions or stop and restart any process that appears to be operating abnormally.

FIGURE 4.11   IDS instructing TCP to reset all connections

Network configuration changes   If a certain IP address is found to be causing repeated attacks on the network, the IDS can instruct a border router or firewall to reject any requests or traffic from that address. This configuration change can remain in effect permanently or for a specified period. Figure 4.12 illustrates the IDS instructing the firewall to close port 80 for 60 seconds to terminate an IIS attack.

If the IDS determines that a particular socket or port is being attacked, it can instruct the firewall to block that port for a specified amount of time. Doing so effectively eliminates the attack but may also inadvertently cause a self-imposed DoS situation to occur by eliminating legitimate traffic. This is especially true for port 80 (HTTP or web) traffic.

Deception   A *deception* active response fools the attacker into thinking the attack is succeeding while the system monitors the activity and potentially redirects the attacker to a system that is designed to be broken. This allows the operator or administrator to gather data about how the attack is unfolding and the techniques being used in the attack. This process is referred to as *sending them to the honeypot*, and it's described later in the section "Utilizing Honeypots." Figure 4.13 illustrates a honeypot where a deception has been successful.

FIGURE 4.12   IDS instructing the firewall to close port 80 for 60 seconds to thwart an IIS attack

FIGURE 4.13   A network honeypot deceives an attacker and gathers intelligence.

The advantage of this type of response is that all activities are watched and recorded for analysis when the attack is completed. This is a difficult scenario to set up, and it's dangerous to allow a hacker to proceed into your network, even if you're monitoring the events.

This approach is frequently used when an active investigation is under way by law enforcement and they're gathering evidence to ensure a successful prosecution of the attacker. Deception allows you to gather documentation without risking live data.

> Remember that active responses are the least commonly implemented. Those that are the most effective are the most costly, and the hardest to put into practice.

Working with a Host-Based IDS

A *host-based IDS (HIDS)* is designed to run as software on a host computer system. These systems typically run as a service or as a background process. HIDSs examine the machine logs, system events, and applications interactions; they normally don't monitor incoming network traffic to the host. HIDSs are popular on servers that use encrypted channels or channels to other servers.

Figure 4.14 illustrates an HIDS installed on a server. Notice that the HIDS interacts with the logon audit and kernel audit files. The kernel audit files are used for process and application interfaces.

FIGURE 4.14 A host-based IDS interacting with the operating system

H-IDS System

Two major problems with HIDS aren't easily overcome. The first problem involves a compromise of the system. If the system is compromised, the log files the IDS reports to may become corrupt or inaccurate. This may make fault determination difficult or the system unreliable. The second major problem with HIDS is that it must be deployed on each system that needs it. This can create a headache for administrative and support staff.

One of HIDS's major benefits is the potential to keep checksums on files. These checksums can be used to inform system administrators that files have been altered by an attack. Recovery is simplified because it's easier to determine where tampering has occurred.

Host-based IDSs typically respond in a passive manner to an incident. An active response would theoretically be similar to those provided by a network-based IDS.

Working with NIPS

As opposed to *Network Intrusion Detection Systems (NIDSs)*, *Network Intrusion Prevention Systems (NIPSs)* focus on *prevention*. These systems focus on signature matches and then take a course of action. For example, if it appears as if an attack might be underway, packets can be dropped, ignored, and so forth. In order to be able to do this, the NIPS must be able to *detect* the attack occurring, and thus it can be argued that NIPS is a subset of NIDS.

The line continues to blur between technologies. For example, NIST now refers to its releases as IDPS. While it is important to stay current on the terminology in the real world, know that the exam is frozen in time and you should be familiar with the older terminology for the questions you will face on it.

Log Files in Linux

There are a number of logs to check for entries that might indicate an intrusion. The primary ones you should examine are listed here:

`/var/log/faillog`   Open a shell prompt and use the `faillog` utility to view a list of users' failed authentication attempts.

`/var/log/lastlog`   Open a shell prompt and use the `lastlog` utility to view a list of all users and when they last logged in.

`/var/log/messages`   Use `grep`, or a derivative thereof, to find login-related entries in this file.

`/var/log/wtmp`   Open a shell prompt and use the `last` command to view a list of users who have authenticated to the system.

Utilizing Honeypots

A *honeypot* is a computer that has been designated as a target for computer attacks. The best way to visualize a honeypot is to think of Winnie the Pooh and the multiple times the cartoon bear has become stuck while trying to get the honey out of the jugs it is stored in. By getting stuck, he has incapacitated himself and become an easy target for anyone trying to find him.

Two of the most popular honeypots for Linux are honeyd (http://honeyd .org) and thp (http://www.alpinista.org/thp).

The purpose of a honeypot is to allow itself to succumb to an attack. During the process of "dying," the system can be used to gain information about how the attack developed and what methods were used to institute the attack. The benefit of a honeypot system is that it draws attackers away from a higher-value system or allows administrators to gain intelligence about an attack strategy. See Figure 4.13 for a diagram of a honeypot implementation.

Honeypots aren't normally secured or locked down. If they come straight out of the box with an operating system and applications software, they may be configured as is. Elaborate honeypot systems can contain information and software that might entice an attacker to probe deeper and take over the system. If not configured properly, a honeypot system can be used to launch attacks against other systems.

There are several initiatives in the area of honeypot technology. One of the more interesting involves the Honeynet Project, which created a synthetic network that can be run on a single computer system and is attached to a network using a normal network interface card (NIC). The system looks like an entire corporate network, complete with applications and data, all of which are fake. As part of the Honeynet Project, the network was routinely scanned, worms were inserted, and attempts were made to contact other systems to infest them—all over the course of a three-day period. At the end of day three, the system had been infected by no fewer than three worms. This infestation happened without any advertising by the Honeynet Project.

Additional information is available on the Honeynet Project at `http://www` `.honeynet.org/misc/project.html`.

Before you even consider implementing a honeypot or a honeynet-type project, you need to understand the concepts of *enticement* and *entrapment*:

Enticement   *Enticement* is the process of luring someone into your plan or trap. You might accomplish this by advertising that you have free software, or you might brag that no one can break into your machine. If you invite someone to try, you're enticing them to do something that you want them to do.

Entrapment   *Entrapment* is the process in which a law enforcement officer or a government agent encourages or induces a person to commit a crime when the potential criminal expresses a desire not to go ahead. Entrapment is a valid legal defense in a criminal prosecution.

While enticement is legally acceptable, entrapment isn't. Your legal liabilities are probably small in either case, but you should seek legal advice before you implement a honeypot on your network. You may also want to contact law enforcement or the prosecutor's office if you want to pursue legal action against attackers.

Some security experts use the term *tar pit in place of honeypot*. The two phrases are interchangeable.

Understanding Incident Response

Forensics refers to the process of identifying what has occurred on a system by examining the data trail. *Incident response* encompasses forensics and refers to the process of identifying, investigating, repairing, documenting, and adjusting procedures to prevent another incident. Simply, an *incident* is the occurrence of any event that endangers a system or network. We need to discuss responses to two types of incidents: internal incidents and incidents involving law enforcement professionals. Figure 4.15 illustrates the interlocked relationship of these processes in an incident response. Notice that all the steps, including the first step, are related. Incidents are facts of life. You want to learn from them, and you want your organization to learn from them.

It's a good idea to include the procedures you'll generally follow in an *incident response plan (IRP)*. The IRP outlines what steps are needed and who is responsible for deciding how to handle a situation. Carnegie Mellon pioneered this process.

FIGURE 4.15   Incident response cycle

Law enforcement personnel are governed by the rules of evidence, and their response to an incident will be largely out of your control. You need to carefully consider involving law enforcement before you begin. There is no such thing as dropping charges. Once they begin, law enforcement professionals are required to pursue an investigation.

The term *incident* has special meanings in different industries. In the banking and financial areas, it's very specific and involves something that includes the loss of money. You wouldn't want to call a hacker attempt an *incident* if you were involved in a bank network because this terminology would automatically trigger an entirely different type of investigation.

The next five sections deal with the phases of a typical incident response process. The steps are generic in this example. Each organization will have a specific set of procedures that will generally map to these steps.

An important concept to keep in mind when working with incidents is the *chain of custody*. When you begin to collect evidence, you must keep track of that evidence at all times and show who has it, who has seen it, and where it has been. The evidence must always be within your custody, or you're open to dispute about whether it has been tampered with.

Step One: Identifying the Incident

Incident identification is the first step in determining what has occurred in your organization. An internal or external attack may have been part of a larger attack that has just surfaced, or it may be a random probe or scan of your network.

An event is often an IDS-triggered signal. Operations personnel will determine if an *event* becomes an *incident*.

Many IDSs trigger false positives when reporting incidents. False positives are events that aren't really incidents. Remember that an IDS is based on established rules of acceptance (deviations from which are known as *anomalies*) and attack signatures. If the rules aren't set up properly, normal traffic may set off the analyzer and generate an event. You don't want to declare an emergency unless you're sure you have one.

One problem that can occur with manual network monitoring is overload. Over time, a slow attack may develop that increases in intensity. Manual processes typically will adapt, and they may not notice the attack until it's too late to stop it. Personnel tend to adapt to changing environments if the changes occur over a long period of time. An automated monitoring system, such as an IDS, will sound the alarm when a certain threshold or activity level occurs.

When a suspected incident pops up, *first responders* are those who must ascertain if it truly is an incident or a false alarm. Depending upon your organization, the first responder may only be the main security administrator, or could consist of a team of network and system administrators.

After you've determined that you indeed have an incident on your hands, you need to consider how to handle it. This process, called *escalation*, involves consulting policies, consulting appropriate management, and determining how best to conduct an investigation into the incident. Make sure that the methods you use to investigate the incident are consistent with corporate and legal requirements for your organization. Bring your human resources and legal departments into the investigation early, and seek their guidance whenever questions involving their areas of expertise appear.

A key aspect, often overlooked by system professionals, involves information control. When an incident occurs, who is responsible for managing the communications about the incident? Employees in the company may naturally be curious about a situation. A single spokesperson needs to be designated. Remember, what 1 person knows, 100 people know.

Step Two: Investigating the Incident

The process of investigating an incident involves searching logs, files, and any other sources of data about the nature and scope of the incident. If possible, you should determine whether this is part of a larger attack, a random event, or a false positive. False positives are common in an IDS environment and may be the result of unusual traffic in the network. It may be that your network is being pinged by a class of computer security students to demonstrate the return times, or it may be that an automated tool is launching an attack.

 It is sad but true: One reason administrators don't put as much security on networks as they could is because they do not want to have to deal with the false positives. While this is a poor excuse, it is still often used by administrators. As a security administrator, you must seek a balance between being overwhelmed with too much unneeded information and knowing when something out of the ordinary is occurring. It is an elusive balance that is easier to talk about than find, but it's one you must strive for.

You might find that the incident doesn't require a response if it can't be successful. Your investigation might conclude that a change in policies is required to deal with a new type of threat. These types of decisions should be documented, and if necessary, reconfigurations should be made to deal with the change.

 Real World Scenario

What If the Intrusion Is Now?

Suppose a junior administrator rushes into your office and reports that an alert just notified him that the guest user account has logged in remotely. A suspected attack is occurring this very moment. What should you do?

You should respond to an attack that's occurring at this moment the same way you would respond to one that happened before you knew about it. You need to determine what the account is doing and try to figure out who they are and where they're coming from. As you collect any information, you should treat it as evidence and keep careful watch over it.

Although collecting as much information as possible is important, no one can be blamed for trying to protect their data. Damage and loss control are critical, while it may be admirable to catch a crook deleting your data, if you can keep the data from being deleted, you will stand a much better chance of still being employed tomorrow. As soon as it becomes apparent that data is at risk, you should disconnect the user. Catching a bad guy is a noble task, but the security of the data should be considered paramount.

 Real World Scenario

The E-Mail Incident

You're the administrator of a small network. This network has an old mail server that is used for internal and external e-mail. You periodically investigate log and audit files to determine the status of your systems and servers. Recently, you noticed that your e-mail log file has been reporting a large number of undeliverable or bounced e-mails. The addresses appear to be random. Upon examining the e-mail system, you notice that the outbound mail folder seems to be sending mail every second. A large number of files are being sent. After inspecting the workstations in the business, you determine that several of them have out-of-date antivirus software. How should you handle this situation?

For starters, you may have one or more viruses or worms in your system. This type of virus sounds like a Simple Mail Transfer Protocol (SMTP) virus. Outlook and Outlook Express are the most popular virus spreaders in use today. A virus like Klez32 can gain access to the address directory and propagate itself using SMTP.

You should investigate why the antivirus software is out-of-date, upgrade these systems as appropriate, and add server-based and mail-server virus-protection capabilities to your network.

Step Three: Repairing the Damage

One of your first considerations after an incident is to determine how to restore access to resources that have been compromised. Then, of course, you must reestablish control of the system. Most operating systems provide the ability to create a disaster-recovery process using distribution media or system state files.

After a problem has been identified, what steps will you take to restore service? In the case of a DoS attack, a system reboot may be all that is required. Your operating system manufacturer will typically provide detailed instructions or documentation on how to restore services in the event of an attack.

If a system has been severely compromised, as in the case of a worm, it might not be possible to repair it. It may need to be regenerated from scratch. Fortunately, antivirus software packages can repair most of the damage done by the viruses you encounter. But what if you come across something new? You might need to start over with a new system. In that case, you're highly advised to do a complete disk drive format or repartition to ensure that nothing is lurking on the disk, waiting to infect your network again.

 Real World Scenario

The Virus That Won't Stop

A virus recently hit a user in your organization through an e-mail attachment. The user updated all the programs in his computer and also updated his antivirus software; however, he's still reporting unusual behavior in his computer system. He's also receiving complaints from people in his e-mail address book because he's sending them a virus. You've been asked to fix the problem.

The user has probably contracted a worm that has infected the system files in his computer. You should help him back up his user files to removable media. Then, completely reformat his drives and reinstall the operating system and applications. After you've replaced these, you can install new antivirus software and scan the entire system. When the scan is complete, help the user reinstall data files and scan the system again for viruses. This process should eliminate all viruses from system, application, and data files.

 Just as every network, regardless of size, should have a firewall, it should also be protected by antivirus software that is enabled and current. ClamAV is an open source solution once available only for Unix-based systems that is now available for most operating systems.

Step Four: Documenting and Reporting the Response

During the entire process of responding to an incident, you should document the steps you take to identify, detect, and repair the system or network. This information is valuable; it needs to be captured in case an attack like this occurs again. The documentation should be accessible by the people most likely to deal with this type of problem. Many help-desk software systems provide detailed methods you can use to record procedures and steps. These types of software products allow for fast access.

If appropriate, you should report/disclose the incident to legal authorities and CERT (www.cert.org) so that others can be aware of the type of attack and help look for proactive measures to prevent this from happening again. At the CERT site, you can find detailed steps to take to recover after your computer has been compromised; this is located at http://www.cert.org/tech_tips/win-UNIX-system_compromise.html.

You might also want to inform the software or system manufacturer of the problem and how you corrected it. Doing so might help them inform or notify other customers of the threat and save time for someone else.

 Real World Scenario

How Incident Response Plans Work

Emergency management (EM) personnel routinely stage fake emergencies to verify that they know what they should do in the event of an actual emergency. For example, if you live in a town with a train track that is routinely used by railcars carrying toxic chemicals, it isn't uncommon for EM personnel to stage a fake spill every couple of years. Those organizing the practice won't tell those responding what type of spill it is, or the severity of it, until they arrive at the scene. The organizers monitor and evaluate the responses to see that they're appropriate and where they can be improved.

Responding to security incidents requires the same type of focus and training. You should plan a fake incident at your site, inform all those who will be involved that it's coming, and then evaluate their response. You should evaluate the following items:

1. Was the evidence gathered and chain of custody maintained?

2. Did the escalation procedures follow the correct path?

3. Given the results of the investigation, would you be able to find and prosecute the culprit?

4. What was done that should not be done?

5. What could be done better?

Practice makes perfect, and there is no better time to practice your company's response to an emergency than before one really occurs.

Step Five: Adjusting Procedures

After an incident has been successfully managed, it's a worthwhile step to revisit the procedures and policies in place in your organization to determine what changes, if any, need to be made.

Answering simple questions can sometimes be helpful when you're resolving problems. The following questions might be included in a policy or procedure manual:

- How did the policies work or not work in this situation?

- What did we learn about the situation that was new?

- What should we do differently next time?

These simple questions can help you adjust procedures. This process is called a *postmortem*, and it's the equivalent of an autopsy.

Working with Wireless Systems

Wireless systems, plainly put, are systems that don't use wires to send information but rather transmit it through the air. The growth of wireless systems creates several opportunities for attackers. These systems are relatively new, they use well-established communications mechanisms, and they're easily intercepted.

The following sections discuss the various types of wireless systems that you'll encounter and mention some of the security issues associated with this technology. Specifically, they deal with Wireless Transport Layer Security (WTLS), the IEEE 802 wireless standards, WEP/WAP applications, and the vulnerabilities that each presents.

Wireless Transport Layer Security

Wireless Transport Layer Security (WTLS) is the security layer of the Wireless Application Protocol (WAP), discussed in the section "WEP/WAP." WTLS provides authentication, encryption, and data integrity for wireless devices. It's designed to utilize the relatively narrow bandwidth of these types of devices, and it's moderately secure. WTLS provides reasonable security for mobile devices, and it's being widely implemented in wireless devices.

Figure 4.16 illustrates WTLS as part of the WAP environment. WAP provides the functional equivalent of TCP/IP for wireless devices. Many devices, including newer cell phones and PDAs, include support for WTLS as part of their networking protocol capabilities.

The term *gap in the WAP* is used to describe the security concern that exists when converting between WAP and SSL/TLS.

FIGURE 4.16   WTLS used between two WAP devices

IEEE 802.11*x* Wireless Protocols

The *IEEE 802.11x* family of protocols provides for wireless communications using radio frequency transmissions. The frequencies in use for 802.11 standards are the 2.4GHz and the 5GHz frequency spectrum. Several standards and bandwidths have been defined for use in wireless environments, and—with the exception of 802.11a—tend to be compatible with each other:

802.11   The *802.11* standard defines wireless LANs transmitting at 1Mbps or 2Mbps bandwidths using the 2.4GHz frequency spectrum and using either frequency-hopping spread spectrum (FHSS) or direct-sequence spread spectrum (DSSS) for data encoding.

802.11a   The *802.11a* standard provides wireless LAN bandwidth of up to 54Mbps in the 5GHz frequency spectrum. The 802.11a standard also uses orthogonal frequency division multiplexing (OFDM) for encoding rather than FHSS or DSSS.

802.11b   The *802.11b* standard provides for bandwidths of up to 11Mbps (with fallback rates of 5.5, 2, and 1Mbps) in the 2.4GHz frequency spectrum. This standard is also called *Wi-Fi* or *802.11 high rate*. The 802.11b standard uses only DSSS for data encoding.

802.11g   The *802.11g* standard provides for bandwidths of up to 54Mbps in the 2.4GHz frequency spectrum. While able to obtain faster speeds, it also suffers from the same interference problems inherent with 802.11b—having to share the spectrum with other devices using that frequency.

802.11n   The *802.11n* standard provides for bandwidths of up to 300Mbps in the 5GHz frequency spectrum (it can also communicate at 2.4GHz for compatibility). The advantage of this standard is that it offers higher speed and a frequency that does not have as much interference.

Three technologies are used to communicate in the 802.11 standard and provide backward compatibility with 802.11b:

Direct-sequence spread spectrum   *Direct-sequence spread spectrum (DSSS)* accomplishes communication by adding the data that is to be transmitted to a higher-speed transmission.

The higher-speed transmission contains redundant information to ensure data accuracy. Each packet can then be reconstructed in the event of a disruption.

Frequency-hopping spread spectrum   *Frequency-hopping spread spectrum (FHSS)* accomplishes communication by hopping the transmission over a range of predefined frequencies. The changing or hopping is synchronized between both ends and appears to be a single transmission channel to both ends.

Orthogonal frequency division multiplexing   *Orthogonal frequency division multiplexing (OFDM)* accomplishes communication by breaking the data into subsignals and transmitting them simultaneously. These transmissions occur on different frequencies or subbands.

The mathematics and theories of these transmission technologies are beyond the scope of this book.

WEP/WAP

Wireless systems frequently use the Wireless Application Protocol (WAP) for network communications. Wired Equivalent Privacy (WEP) is intended to provide the equivalent security of a wired network protocol. The following sections briefly discuss these two terms and provide you with an understanding of their relative capabilities.

Wireless Application Protocol

The *Wireless Application Protocol (WAP)* is the technology designed for use with wireless devices. WAP has become a standard adopted by many manufacturers, including Motorola and Nokia. WAP functions are equivalent to TCP/IP functions in that they're trying to serve the same purpose for wireless devices. WAP uses a smaller version of HTML called *Wireless Markup Language (WML)*, which is used for Internet displays. WAP-enabled devices can also respond to scripts using an environment called *WMLScript*. This scripting language is similar to Java, which is a programming language.

The ability to accept web pages and scripts produces the opportunity for malicious code and viruses to be transported to WAP-enabled devices. No doubt this will create a new set of problems, and antivirus software will be needed to deal with them.

WAP systems communicate using a WAP gateway system, as depicted in Figure 4.17. The gateway converts information back and forth between HTTP and WAP as well as encodes and decodes between the security protocols. This structure provides a reasonable assurance that WAP-enabled devices can be secured. If the interconnection between the WAP server and the Internet isn't encrypted, packets between the devices may be intercepted, creating a potential vulnerability. This vulnerability is called a *gap in the WAP*.

Wired Equivalent Privacy

Wired Equivalent Privacy (WEP) is a security standard for wireless devices. WEP encrypts data to provide data security. The protocol has always been under scrutiny for not being as secure as initially intended.

FIGURE 4.17   A WAP gateway enabling a connection to WAP devices by the Internet

WEP is vulnerable due to weaknesses in the way the encryption algorithms are employed. These weaknesses allow the algorithm to potentially be cracked in as few as five minutes using available PC software. This makes WEP one of the more vulnerable protocols available for security.

Wi-Fi Protected Access

The *Wi-Fi Protected Access* (WPA) and *Wi-Fi Protected Access 2* (WPA2) technologies were designed to address the core problems with WEP. These technologies implement the 802.11i standard. The difference between WPA and WPA2 is that the former implements most—but not all—of 802.11i in order to be able to communicate with older wireless cards (which might still need an update through their firmware in order to be compliant), while WPA2 implements the full standard and is not compatible with older cards.

Wireless Vulnerabilities to Know

Wireless systems are vulnerable to all the different attacks that wired networks are vulnerable to. However, because these protocols use radio frequency signals for *data emanation*, they have an additional weakness: All radio frequency signals can be easily intercepted. To intercept 802.11x traffic, all you need is a PC with an appropriate 802.11x card installed. Many networks will regularly broadcast their name (known as an *SSID broadcast*) to announce their presence. Simple software on the PC can capture the link traffic in the WAP and then process this data in order to decrypt account and password information.

An additional aspect of wireless systems is the *site survey*. Site surveys involve listening in on an existing wireless network using commercially available technologies. Doing so allows intelligence, and possibly data capture, to be performed on systems in your wireless network.

The term *site survey* initially meant determining whether a proposed location was free from interference. When used by an attacker, a site survey can determine what types of systems are in use, the protocols used, and other critical information about your network. It's the primary method used to gather data about wireless networks. Virtually all wireless networks are vulnerable to site surveys.

If wireless portals are installed in a building, the signals will frequently radiate past the inside of the building, and they can be detected and decoded outside the building using inexpensive equipment. The term *war driving* refers to driving around town with a laptop looking for WAPs that can be communicated with. The network card on the laptop is set to promiscuous mode, and it looks for signals coming from anywhere. After intruders gain access, they may steal Internet access or start damaging your data.

Weak encryption was an issue with earlier access points, but most of the newer wireless controllers use special ID numbers (SSID) and must be configured in the network cards to allow communications. However, using ID number configurations doesn't necessarily prevent wireless networks from being monitored, and one particularly mischievous undertaking involves taking advantage of *rogue access points*. Any wireless access point added to your network that has not been authorized is considered a rogue. The rogue may be added by an attacker, or could have been innocently added by a user wanting to enhance their environment—the problem with the user doing so is that there is a good chance they will not implement the security you would, and this could open the system up for a man-in-the-middle attack. Educate and train users about the wireless network and the need to keep it secure, just as you would train and educate them about any other security topic. Be sure to change the default settings on all wireless devices.

 Never assume that a wireless connection is secure. The emissions from a wireless portal may be detectable through walls and for several blocks from the portal. Interception is easy to accomplish, given that RF is the medium used for communication. Newer wireless devices offer data security, and you should use it. You can set newer WAPs and wireless routers to non-broadcast in addition to configuring WEP at a higher encryption level.

With the popularity of Bluetooth on the rise, two additional vulnerabilities have been added: *blue jacking* and *bluesnarfing*. Blue jacking is the sending of unsolicited messages (think spam) over the Bluetooth connection. While annoying, it is basically considered harmless.

Bluesnarfing is the gaining of unauthorized access through a Bluetooth connection. This access can be gained through a phone, PDA, or any device using Bluetooth. Once access has been gained, the attacker can copy any data in the same way they would with any other unauthorized access.

 The Bluetooth standard has addressed weaknesses in the technology, and it continues to get more secure. One of the simplest ways to secure Bluetooth devices is to not set their attribute to discoverable.

Understanding Instant Messaging's Features

Instant messaging (IM) has become a hugely popular application on the Internet. Millions of users are estimated to be using instant messaging worldwide. America Online and Microsoft provide IM services to their subscribers. Their services are free and easily accessible.

IM users can send photos, play network games, conduct chats, send e-mail, and even have IM conferences. IM functionality in no small part explains its growth. Besides, it's just fun. Clients use software to connect to IM servers to communicate. These servers might be synchronized worldwide to allow instantaneous communications between any two users in the world. Figure 4.18 shows clients connecting to an IM server system similar to the ones used by Microsoft and AOL.

FIGURE 4.18   An IM network with worldwide users

The next sections deal with the vulnerabilities inherent in IM as well as ways to control privacy.

Understanding IM Vulnerabilities

Attacks using IM are becoming common. Many of the attacks are intended to disrupt existing systems by interjecting or flooding a channel with garbage data. This is also called *jamming,* and it's one of the favorite techniques used to disrupt public channel communications systems, including instant messaging systems.

Malicious code, Trojan horse programs, and traditional DoS attacks can also compromise IM clients. IM is supposed to be easy to use, highly interactive, and intuitive for average users. Unfortunately, users frequently don't pay attention to security-related issues when they're using IM.

Most IM systems allow broadcasts and, in fact, sell this capability to businesses. The broadcasting capability allows an attacker to potentially send a "bait message" to millions of people simultaneously throughout the world. These broadcasts may announce sites offering free pornography or the opportunity to make millions of dollars in minutes. The acronym SPIM has even been added recently to the vernacular to describe spam over instant messaging.

When they go to these sites, unsuspecting individuals can be flooded with literally hundreds of windows that open simultaneously on the client system. When the user closes one window, two, three, or more windows open. In short, this is a DoS attack against a client. You can go into a chat room or a conversation area on a busy network, such as AOL or MSN, and watch the amount of jamming that occurs on these channels.

The best protection against this type of attack includes using antivirus software, not visiting sites that are advertised in this manner, and not opening suspicious files.

Controlling Privacy

Many users take privacy for granted. Unfortunately, IM systems weren't intended for confidential purposes.

Although most IM providers have made improvements in this area, never assume that information being sent using an IM system is private. Attachments, if sensitive, should be encrypted before you send them across an IM system.

IM is commonly used for people to meet each other. People frequently use IM to exchange phone numbers, addresses, and other personal information. If made available on the Internet, this information might create an unsafe situation for an individual. Even the disclosure of an e-mail address could cause an increase in unwanted e-mails from other people on the Internet.

A malformed MIME message can cause a buffer overflow. As simplistic as it sounds, this has been known to make servers crash.

Working with 8.3 File Naming

Early PC systems used a standard naming convention for files called the *8.3 format*. This format allowed eight characters for the filename and three characters for the file type or extension. Certain file extensions told the operating system to immediately start executing a file (for example, .bat, .com, and .exe).

Modern systems have expanded the 8.3 format to allow longer and user-friendlier filenames. They still maintain the file extension type and hide it from the user.

If a file type is indicated—for instance, a filename has a .jpg extension—the system automatically opens the program that has been registered to be associated with the file. Table 4.1 shows some of the common file types used in PC systems today.

TABLE 4.1 Common Executable File Types That PC Systems Use

Extension	Type
.bat	Batch files
.com	Command files
.exe	Executable files
.js	JavaScript
.vbs	Visual Basic Script

Many operating systems, including Windows environments, hide the file extension from the user. A user may receive a file named `mycatspicture` and assume that it's a JPEG or other picture. Unfortunately, the actual file type isn't usually shown to the user when they contemplate opening it. If the file is an executable or a script, it will start executing using the appropriate language or command processor. If this file is a Trojan horse, a worm, or some other form of malicious code, the system has potentially been compromised.

Files can even appear to have more than one filename extension. A file may indicate that it's `mycatspicture.jpg` when it's actually `mycatspicture.jpg.exe`. This file will start executing when it's opened and may expose the system to malicious code.

From a user's perspective, the simpler things are, the easier they are to work with. However, from an administrator's perspective, you want to know as much as you can. Windows XP, like its most recent predecessors, by default hides known file extensions as well as certain files and folders.

Understanding Protocol Analyzers

The terms *Protocol analyzing* and *packet sniffing* are interchangeable. They refer to the process of monitoring the data that is transmitted across a network. The software that performs the operation is called either an *analyzer* or a *sniffer*. Sniffers are readily available on the Internet. These tools were initially intended for legitimate network-monitoring processes, but they can also be used to gather data for illegal purposes.

IM traffic, for example, uses the Internet and is susceptible to packet-sniffing activities. Any information contained in an IM session is potentially vulnerable to interception. Make sure users understand that sensitive information should not be sent using this method.

One of the most well-known tools for analyzing network traffic in real time is snort (`http://www.snort.org`). Lab 4.3 walks through the installation of this tool.

Understanding Signal Analysis and Intelligence

The terms *signal analysis* and *signal intelligence* refer to capturing and analyzing electronic signals. Military and governmental agencies have been doing this since the beginning of the electronic age. The purpose of analysis and intelligence is to identify and evaluate the enemy, identify and track communications patterns, and identify what types of technologies are being used to send them.

This is a game of patience and persistence. People who want to attack your system are also performing analysis and intelligence. They're trying to discover what your communications topology and infrastructure look like, what your critical or sensitive circuits are, and what you use them to do.

Attackers have many tools at their disposal; most of them are relatively easy to use. Your job is to act as a counterintelligence agent and, where possible, prevent them from gaining access to this information.

Your enemy has several common methods to gain intelligence about your network and your potential vulnerabilities. The following sections describe two of these methods.

Footprinting

Footprinting is the process of systematically identifying the network and its security posture. An attacker may be able to gain knowledge of the systems you use, the protocols you run, the servers you operate, and what additional software is being used by systems such as web servers, mail servers, and the like.

A simple method of footprinting might examine the source code of your website. Web servers often have plug-ins or options installed that allow entrance into a network using buffer overflows or command processing. Attackers may also be able to gain insights into your business by doing online searches of business records and filings.

For example, EDGAR, an online business research website, maintains a database of publicly available information about businesses. Your company's annual report may brag about the new infrastructure that was installed last year. Strategic relationships with business partners may provide intelligence about your business. Similar information can help attackers infiltrate your system: They can go to VeriSign/InterNic and determine the root IP address for your network as well as obtain contact information to attempt social engineering attacks. In short, anything online or in print is a potential source of information.

An attacker can query DNS servers to determine what types of records are stored about your network. This information might provide insight into the type of e-mail system you're using. Most DNS servers readily provide this information when a proper query is formed.

Individually, none of this information is damaging or discloses much about your business. Collectively, though, it may provide key pieces to the jigsaw puzzle that is your organization.

Scanning

Scanning is the process that attackers use to gather information about how your network is configured. They scan your network and look for paths to systems in your network using programs such as Traceroute. Traceroute can provide a detailed picture of your network, right to the demilitarized zone (DMZ).

After an attacker has a general layout of your network, they can then switch to a scan. Scans can start with a simple ping of systems with addresses near your web or mail server. If any of these machines respond, the attacker knows that you have ICMP running and, by default, TCP/IP.

After they know what systems are "alive" in your network, they can systematically attempt to find out what ports are running on these systems; this is known as a *port scan*. Using the information gained from the port scanner to know what ports are running , the attacker may try a few simple probes of your system to determine what vulnerabilities might provide an opportunity for attack. A *vulnerability scanner* is used to analyze the results from the probe.

 One of the most well-known port scanners is nmap, while warscan can be used to test exploits that are found. Both of these can be readily found on the Internet.

After the scanning process is complete, the attacker may next choose enumeration. Enumeration will most likely provide the attacker with enough information to implement a *network mapper* and attack the target. The attack is the next step but might only provide the attacker with a low-level (non-root) account. If this is the case, the attacker will attempt privilege escalation. If the attacker is successful with privilege escalation, they will essentially own the computer.

While it may seem as if an attacker must have a great many tools at his disposal—protocol analyzer, port scanner, vulnerability scanner, and network mapper to name but a few—the reality is that many of these tools are bundled together or found on the same site. BackTrack (http://remote-exploit.org/backtrack.html), for example, combines all of these tools into a single application that is run from a CD.

Practicing good security techniques—such as those discussed in this chapter, and this book—can prevent events of this type from occurring.

Summary

This chapter covered most of the major points concerning communications monitoring, IDS, wireless technologies, and instant messaging. Your network infrastructure is vulnerable, but the situation isn't hopeless. Tools exist to help you do your job.

Many different protocols may exist in your network. Each protocol has its own strengths and weaknesses. You must know what they are and how to deal with them. Network product vendors have become forthcoming about their products' vulnerabilities; make sure you consult them to determine what problems exist. Protocols such as NetBEUI and NetBIOS aren't routable protocols, but they can be encapsulated in TCP/IP traffic and shipped to other networks using VPN technology.

The primary tools used to detect attacks are network monitors and intrusion detection systems. Network monitors involve manual monitoring and can be difficult to use. IDSs identify and respond to attacks using defined rules or logic. These systems can track either anomalies in network traffic or misuses of protocols. IDSs can also be established to monitor an entire network or used to monitor a host. These systems are referred to as either NIDSs or HIDSs. NIDSs can make active or passive responses, whereas HIDSs are usually only capable of passive responses.

A honeypot is a system designed to entice or entrap an attacker. Enticement means inviting or luring an attacker to the system. Entrapment is the process of encouraging an attacker to perform an act, even if they don't want to do it. Entrapment is a valid legal defense in criminal proceedings.

An incident is an attack or theft of data in your network. The steps in incident response include identifying, investigating, repairing, and documenting the incident, and afterward adjusting procedures to help in future incidents.

Wireless systems are becoming increasingly popular and standardized. The most common protocol implemented in wireless systems is WAP. The security layer for WAP is WTLS. WAP is equivalent to TCP/IP for wireless systems.

The standards for wireless systems are developed by the IEEE. The most common standards are 802.11, 802.11a, 802.11b, and 802.11g. These standards use the 2.4GHz or 5GHz frequency spectrum. Several communications technologies are available to send messages between wireless devices.

Wireless networks are vulnerable to site surveys. Site surveys can be accomplished using a PC and an 802.11x card. The term *site survey* is also used in reference to detecting interference in a given area that might prevent 802.11x from working.

Instant messaging is a growing application on the Internet. IM uses synchronized servers to provide instantaneous communications, such as chatting, between users on a global basis. IM is vulnerable to malicious code and packet sniffing. Information that is sensitive should be encrypted before being sent, or other methods should be found to send it.

The process of gathering information about a computer network uses methodologies called signal analysis and signal intelligence. These methods have been used by governmental agencies for many years. As a security expert, your job is to act as a counterintelligence agent to prevent sensitive information from falling into the wrong hands. The methods used to gain information about your environment include footprinting and scanning.

Exam Essentials

Be able to identify and describe the two types of intrusion detection systems in use.   The two types of IDSs in use are host-based (HIDS) and network-based (NIDS). Host-based IDS works strictly on the system on which it's installed. Network-based IDS monitors the entire network.

Be able to identify and explain the terms and functions in an IDS environment.   These terms include *activity*, *administrator*, *alert*, *analyzer*, *data source*, *event*, *manager*, *notification*, *operator*, and *sensor*. For simplicity's sake, some of these systems are combined in IDSs, but they're all functions that must be performed to be effective.

Know the difference between an active response and a passive response.   An active response allows an IDS to manage resources in the network if an incident occurs. Passive responses involve notification and reporting of attacks or suspicious activities.

Be able to explain the purpose of a honeypot.   A honeypot is a system that is intended to be used to gather information or designed to be broken. Honeypot systems are used to gather evidence in an investigation and to study attack strategies.

Know the aspects needed to form an effective incident response.   The stages of an incident response are identification, investigation, repair, and documentation. Communication and escalation plans are also part of an effective incident response approach. The process and methods used to respond to incidents should be developed into an incident response plan that can be used as a guideline for all incident response activities.

Know the protocols and components of a wireless system.   The backbone of most wireless systems is WAP. WAP can use the WEP protocol to provide security in a wireless environment. WTLS is the security layer of WAP. WAP and TCP/IP perform similarly.

Know the capabilities and limitations of the 802.11x network standards.   The current standards for wireless protocols are 802.11, 802.11a, 802.11b, and 802.11g. The 802.11n standard is undergoing review and isn't yet a formal standard.

Know the vulnerabilities of wireless networks.   The primary method of gaining information about a wireless network is a site survey. Site surveys can be accomplished with a PC and an 802.11 card. Wireless networks are subject to the same attacks as wired networks.

Know the capabilities and security issues associated with instant messaging.   IM is a rapidly growing interactive communications capability on the Internet. IM is susceptible to sniffing, jamming, and viruses. Never assume that an IM session is confidential. Viruses can be sent using attachments in IM, just as with e-mail. Antivirus software can help filter for known viruses.

Know the limits of the 8.3 naming convention.   Early PC systems used a standard naming convention for files called the 8.3 format. This format allowed for only eight characters to be used for the filename and three characters for the file type or extension.

Hands-On Labs

The labs in this chapter are as follows:

Lab 4.1: View the Active TCP and UDP Ports

Lab 4.2: Run Windows Network Monitor

Lab 4.3: Install snort in Linux

Lab 4.4: Make File Extensions Visible in Windows XP

Lab 4.5: Monitor Network Traffic in Linux

Lab 4.1: View the Active TCP and UDP Ports

As an administrator, you should know what ports are active on your server. The following lab will display this information:

1. Go to a command prompt. On a Windows-based server, enter **CMD** at the Run prompt; on a Linux server, open a command window.

2. Enter the command **netstat**.

3. Few items should appear. Now enter the command **netstat -a**. The –a parameter tells the netstat command to display all the information.

4. Note the ports that are listed.

5. View the services file (*systemroot*\system32\drivers\etc\services in Windows or /etc/services in Linux). Although the file is not actively read by the system, this file lists the services and the ports used for the most common network operations.

Lab 4.2: Run Windows Network Monitor

As an administrator of a Windows-based network, you should be familiar with Network Monitor. The following lab will run you through a sample session with it.

On a Windows-based server, follow these steps:

1. Choose Start ➢ Programs ➢ Administrative Tools ➢ Network Monitor (if it does not appear there, as it differs based upon the version of Windows Server you are running, check Microsoft Network Monitor).

2. Capture traffic data.

3. Go to the Desktop and open Network Neighborhood or My Network Places (depending on the version of Windows Server you're using).

4. Double-click a domain or workstation that appears in the list (the number that appears depends on your network) and continue to expand the object as deep as you can— shares, files, and so on.

5. Return to Network Monitor and stop the capture.

6. Open the Details windows and see how much traffic the browsing operation generated.

Lab 4.3: Install snort in Linux

The de facto standard for intrusion detection in Linux is snort. To install the package on a SuSE server, follow these steps:

1. Log in as root and start YaST.

2. Choose Software and then Install and Remove Software. Search for snort.

3. Check the box when the package appears.

4. Click Accept. If any dependency messages appear, click Continue to add them as well.

5. Swap CDs as prompted and exit YaST upon completion.

6. To use the snort utility, open a terminal session and type **snort**. This generates an error message that lists all the options that you can use with the utility.

Lab 4.4: Make File Extensions Visible in Windows XP

By default, the extensions for known file types do not appear in many Windows-based operating systems, such as Windows XP. Knowing what the extension is, however, can help you readily identify what type of file it is—executable, document, and so on. To make file extensions visible, follow these steps:

1. Click Start ➢ Control Panel ➢ Folder Options.

2. Choose the View tab.

3. Choose the Show Hidden Files and Folders radio button.

4. Deselect the Hide Extensions for Known File Types check box.

5. Click OK and exit from Control Panel. You'll now be able to see the extensions on file-names.

Lab 4.5: Monitor Network Traffic in Linux

There are a number of ways in which network traffic can be monitored, but the best approach is to use ntop. The following steps install this utility and illustrate its usage on a SuSE server:

1. Log in as root and start YaST.

2. Choose Software and then Install and Remove Software. Search for ntop and choose to install the package.

3. Exit YaST upon completion of the installation.

4. Open a terminal session and type **rcntop start** to start the ntop daemon. A message appears that states that the administrator password has not yet been set.

5. Type **ntop -A -u wwwrun**.

6. Enter a password for the administrative user. Reenter the password when prompted. Check to see if ntop is running (**ps -ef | grep ntop**). If it is not, repeat the command in step 5.

7. Open Konqueror and go to http://localhost:3000.

8. On the first line of ntop, pick All Protocols.

9. On the second line, pick Traffic, and you will see a summary of all traffic that has occurred since the program has been running. Select Throughput and Activity to gather statistics on those items.

10. You can log the data (Admin, Log) and shut down ntop (Admin, Shutdown) from this interface as well.

Review Questions

1. Which of the following can be used to monitor a network for unauthorized activity? (Choose two.)

   A. Network sniffer

   B. NIDS

   C. HIDS

   D. VPN

2. You're the administrator for Acme Widgets. After attending a conference on buzzwords for management, your boss informs you that an IDS should be up and running on the network by the end of the week. Which of the following systems should be installed on a host to provide IDS capabilities?

   A. Network sniffer

   B. NIDS

   C. HIDS

   D. VPN

3. Which of the following is an active response in an IDS?

   A. Sending an alert to a console

   B. Shunning

   C. Reconfiguring a router to block an IP address

   D. Making an entry in the security audit file

4. A junior administrator bursts into your office with a report in his hand. He claims that he has found documentation proving that an intruder has been entering the network on a regular basis. Which of the following implementations of IDS detects intrusions based on previously established rules that are in place on your network?

   A. MD-IDS

   B. AD-IDS

   C. HIDS

   D. NIDS

5. Which IDS function evaluates data collected from sensors?

   A. Operator

   B. Manager

   C. Alert

   D. Analyzer

6. During the creation of a new set of policies and procedures for network usage, your attention turns to role definition. By default, which of the following roles is responsible for reporting the results of an attack to a system operator or administrator?

   A. Alert

   B. Manager

   C. Analyzer

   D. Data source

7. What is a system that is intended or designed to be broken into by an attacker called?

   A. Honeypot

   B. Honeybucket

   C. Decoy

   D. Spoofing system

8. An emergency meeting of all administrators has been called at MTS. It appears that an unauthorized user has been routinely entering the network after hours. A response to this intrusion must be formulated by those assembled. What is the process of formulating a reaction to a computer attack officially called?

   A. Incident response

   B. Evidence gathering

   C. Entrapment

   D. Enticement

9. Which of the following is *not* a part of an incident response?

   A. Identification

   B. Investigating

   C. Entrapment

   D. Repairing

10. Which protocol is mainly used to enable access to the Internet from a mobile phone or PDA?

   A. WEP

   B. WTLS

   C. WAP

   D. WOP

11. Which protocol operates on 2.4GHz and has a bandwidth of 1Mbps or 2Mbps?

   A. 802.11

   B. 802.11a

   C. 802.11b

   D. 802.11g

12. You're outlining your plans for implementing a wireless network to upper management. Suddenly, a paranoid vice president brings up the question of security. Which protocol was designed to provide security to a wireless network and can be considered equivalent to the security of a wired network?

   A. WAP

   B. WTLS

   C. WPA2

   D. IR

13. Which of the following is a primary vulnerability of a wireless environment?

   A. Decryption software

   B. IP spoofing

   C. A gap in the WAP

   D. Site survey

14. As the administrator for MTS, you want to create a policy banning the use of instant messaging, but you're receiving considerable opposition from users. To lessen their resistance, you decide to educate them about the dangers inherent in IM. To which of the following types of attacks is IM vulnerable?

   A. Malicious code

   B. IP spoofing

   C. Man-in-the-middle attacks

   D. Replay attacks

15. What is the process of identifying the configuration of your network called?

   A. Footprinting

   B. Scanning

   C. Jamming

   D. Enumeration

16. During the annual performance review, you explain to your manager that this year you want to focus on looking at multiple sources of information and determining what systems your users may be using. You think this is a necessary procedure for creating a secure environment. What is the process of identifying your network and its security posture called?

   A. Footprinting

   B. Scanning

   C. Jamming

   D. Enumeration

17. When an event is detected when it is happening, it is being detected in:

    A. Present time

    B. Here-and-now

    C. Active time

    D. Real time

18. A user calls with a problem. Even though she has been told not to use instant messaging, she has been doing so. For some reason, she is now experiencing frequent interrupted sessions. You suspect an attack and inform her of this. What is the process of disrupting an IM session called?

    A. Jamming

    B. Broadcasting

    C. Incident response

    D. Site survey

19. You've just received a call from an IM user in your office who visited an advertised website. The user is complaining that his system is unresponsive and about a million web browser windows have opened on his screen. What type of attack has your user experienced?

    A. DoS

    B. Malicious code

    C. IP spoofing

    D. Site survey

20. A fellow administrator is reviewing the log files for the month when he calls you over. A number of IDS entries don't look right to him, and he wants to focus on those incidents. Which of the following terms best describes an occurrence of suspicious activity within a network?

    A. Event

    B. Occurrence

    C. Episode

    D. Enumeration

Answers to Review Questions

1. A, B.   Network sniffers and NIDSs are used to monitor network traffic. Network sniffers are manually oriented, whereas an NIDS can be automated.

2. C.   A host-based IDS (HIDS) is installed on each host that needs IDS capabilities.

3. C.   Dynamically changing the system's configuration to protect the network or a system is an active response.

4. A.   By comparing attack signatures and audit trails, a misuse-detection IDS determines whether an attack is occurring.

5. D.   The analyzer function uses data sources from sensors to analyze and determine whether an attack is under way.

6. B.   The manager is the component that the operator uses to manage the IDS. The manager may be a graphical interface, a real-time traffic screen, or a command-line-driven environment.

7. A.   A honeypot is a system that is intended to be sacrificed in the name of knowledge. Honeypot systems allow investigators to evaluate and analyze the attack strategies used. Law enforcement agencies use honeypots to gather evidence for prosecution.

8. A.   Incident response is the process of determining the best method of dealing with a computer security incident.

9. C.   Entrapment is the process of encouraging an individual to perform an unlawful act that they wouldn't normally have performed.

10. C.   Wireless Application Protocol (WAP) is an open international standard for applications that use wireless communication.

11. A.   802.11 operates on 2.4GHZ. This standard allows for bandwidths of 1Mbps or 2Mbps.

12. C.   Wi-Fi Protected Access 2 (WPA2) was intended to provide security that's equivalent to the security on a wired network and implements elements of the 802.11i standard.

13. D.   A site survey is the process of monitoring a wireless network using a computer, wireless controller, and analysis software. Site surveys are easily accomplished and hard to detect.

14. A.   IM users are highly susceptible to malicious code attacks such as worms, viruses, and Trojan horses. Ensure that IM users have up-to-date antivirus software installed.

15. B.   Scanning is the process of gathering data about your network configuration and determining which systems are live.

16. A.   Footprinting involves identifying your network and its security posture. Footprinting is done using multiple sources of information to determine what systems you may be using.

17. D.   When an event is detected when it is happening, is is said to be detected in *Real time*.

18. A.   Jamming is the process of intentionally disrupting communications in an IM session. *Jamming* is a loosely defined term, and it refers to any intentional disruption that isn't a DoS attack.

19. A.   Your user has just encountered an application-level DoS attack. This type of attack is common and isn't usually fatal, but it's very annoying. Your user should restart his system, verify that the website didn't transmit a virus, and stay away from broadcasted websites.

20. A.   An IDS will announce an event through an alert when suspicious activity is encountered.

Chapter

5

Implementing and Maintaining a Secure Network

THE FOLLOWING COMPTIA SECURITY+ EXAM OBJECTIVES ARE COVERED IN THIS CHAPTER:

✓ **1.3 Implement OS hardening practices and procedures to achieve workstation and server security.**

- Hotfixes
- Service packs
- Patches
- Patch management
- Group policies
- Security templates
- Configuration baselines

✓ **2.1 Differentiate between the different ports and protocols, their respective threats and mitigation techniques.**

- DNS poisoning
- ARP poisoning

✓ **2.3 Determine the appropriate use of network security tools to facilitate network security.**

- Internet content filters

✓ **2.4 Apply the appropriate network tools to facilitate network security.**

- Internet content filters

✓ **3.7 Deploy various authentication models and identify the components of each.**

- LDAP

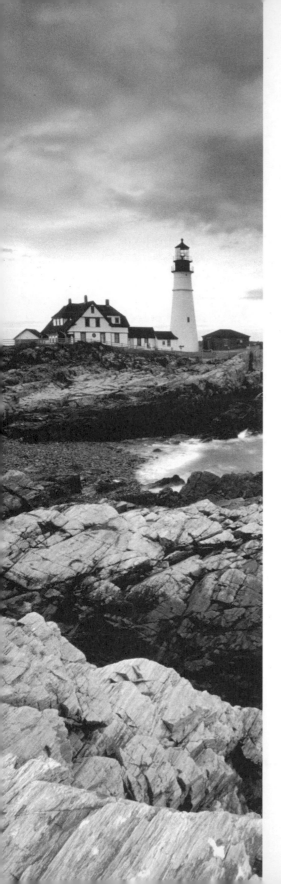

✓ **4.3 Within the realm of vulnerability assessments, explain the proper use of penetration testing versus vulnerability scanning.**

✓ **4.4 Use monitoring tools on systems and networks and detect security-related anomalies.**

- ▪ Performance monitor
- ▪ Systems monitor
- ▪ Performance baseline

✓ **4.7 Conduct periodic audits of system security settings.**

- ▪ Group policies

✓ **5.1 Explain general cryptography concepts.**

- ▪ Whole disk encryption

The operating systems, applications, and network products you deal with are usually secure when they're implemented the way the manufacturer intends. This chapter deals with the process of ensuring that the products you use are as secure as they can be.

The primary focus of this chapter is hardening. *Hardening* refers to the process of reducing or eliminating weaknesses, securing services, and attempting to make your environment immune to attacks. Typically, when you install operating systems, applications, and network products, the defaults from the manufacturer are to make the product as simple to use as possible and allow it to work with your existing environment as effortlessly as possible. That isn't always the best scenario when it comes to security.

In this chapter, you'll learn the general process involved in securing or hardening the systems, network, and applications that are typically found in a business. This chapter also develops the issues of threats to your network and the concept of developing a security baseline.

Overview of Network Security Threats

Network threats involve many facets of the network and organization. You've seen that your systems and information are susceptible to attacks and disruption based on internal, external, and design factors in the systems you support. Ensuring that your systems and applications are kept up-to-date and making sure your security procedures are in place and followed meticulously can minimize many of these threats. Most of the exploitation attacks that occur to programs such as Outlook, Outlook Express, and Exchange are fixed as soon as they're discovered, if not shortly thereafter. As an administrator, you must apply fixes and patches immediately after they have been thoroughly tested in a lab environment; doing so makes it harder for attackers to learn about your systems and exploit known weaknesses.

One of the organizations that tracks and reports security problems is the CERT Coordination Center (CERT/CC). CERT/CC is a part of the Software Engineering Institute (SEI) at Carnegie-Mellon University. SEI is a federally funded research institution with a strong emphasis on computer security–related topics. CERT/CC (http://www.cert.org/stats/fullstats.html) provides interesting perspectives on the growth of computer-related incidents but stopped making numbers available after 2003 since "attacks against Internet-connected systems have become so commonplace that counts of the number of incidents reported provide little information with regard to assessing the scope and impact of attacks."

CERT/CC provides a great deal of current threat analysis and future analysis in the computer security area. The website for CERT/CC is http://www.cert.org.

In the past, the computer industry hasn't taken the issue of computer security as seriously as it should. This attitude has caused a great deal of frustration on the part of users and administrators who are attempting to protect assets. The important thing to remember is that until recently, many software manufacturers have only paid lip service to the problem of operating system and application vulnerabilities.

According to the Internet Storm Center (http://isc.sans.org), a computer connected to the Internet has an average of 5 minutes before it falls under some form of attack.

A penetration test is the best way to tell what services are really running on your system. *Penetration testing* involves trying to get access to your system from an attacker's perspective. Typically, you perform this test from a system on the Internet and try to see if you can break in or, at a minimum, get access to services running on your system.

Just short of penetration testing is *vulnerability testing*. In a vulnerability test, you typically run a software program that contains a database of known vulnerabilities against your system to identify weaknesses. Two of the most well-known vulnerability scanners are Nessus (http://www.nessus.org/nessus/) and the NMAP port scanner (http://nmap.org/).

Defining Security Baselines

One of the first steps in developing a secure environment is to develop a baseline of the minimum security needs of your organization. A *security baseline* defines the level of security that will be implemented and maintained. You can choose to set a low baseline by implementing next to no security or a high baseline that doesn't allow users to make any changes at all to the network or their systems. In practice, most implementations fall between the two extremes; you must determine what is best for your organization.

The security baseline, which can also be called a *performance baseline*, provides the input needed to design, implement, and support a secure network. Developing the baseline includes gathering data on the specific security implementation of the systems with which you'll be working.

One of the newest standards for security is *Common Criteria (CC)*. (As of this writing, the latest version of the standard is 3.1, and it's available for viewing at http://www.commoncriteriaportal.org. The website also maintains a registry of products certified by CC.) This document is a joint effort between Canada, France, Germany, the Netherlands, the United Kingdom, and the United States. The standard outlines a comprehensive set of evaluation criteria, broken down into seven *Evaluation Assurance Levels (EALs)*. EAL 1 to EAL 7 are discussed here:

EAL 1   EAL 1 is primarily used when the user wants assurance that the system will operate correctly but threats to security aren't viewed as serious.

EAL 2   EAL 2 requires product developers to use good design practices. Security isn't considered a high priority in EAL 2 certification.

EAL 3   EAL 3 requires conscientious development efforts to provide moderate levels of security.

EAL 4   EAL 4 requires positive security engineering based on good commercial development practices. It is anticipated that EAL 4 will be the common benchmark for commercial systems.

EAL 5   EAL 5 is intended to ensure that security engineering has been implemented in a product from the early design phases. It's intended for high levels of security assurance. The EAL documentation indicates that special design considerations will most likely be required to achieve this level of certification.

EAL 6   EAL 6 provides high levels of assurance of specialized security engineering. This certification indicates high levels of protection against significant risks. Systems with EAL 6 certification will be highly secure from penetration attackers.

EAL 7   EAL 7 is intended for extremely high levels of security. The certification requires extensive testing, measurement, and complete independent testing of every component.

EAL certification has replaced the Trusted Computer Systems Evaluation Criteria (TCSEC) system for certification. The recommended level of certification for commercial systems is EAL 4.

 Real World Scenario

Implementing a Secure Server Environment

You've been appointed to the panel that will make decisions regarding the purchase of a new server for your organization. The new server needs to be relatively secure and suitable for storing sensitive information. It will also be part of an e-commerce environment. How can you assist the panel?

You can be of real value to the panel by determining the operating systems that have been certified for the common criteria. You can visit the website http://www.commoncriteriaportal .org/products_OS.html#OS to identify which operating systems and products have been EAL 4 certified. Encourage your IT staff members to make their decision based on the data available about security as opposed to vendor claims. Most vendors claim to have a secure environment when in fact they don't. The CC certification proves that an impartial third party did an evaluation.

Currently, only a few operating systems have been approved at the EAL 4 level, and even though an operating system straight out of the box may be, that doesn't mean your own individual implementation of it is functioning at that level. If your implementation doesn't use the available security measures, then you're operating below that level.

As an administrator, you should know and thoroughly understand that just because the operating system you have is capable of being certified at a high level of security doesn't mean that your implementation is at that level.

 Real World Scenario

Security from a Windows Server 2003 Administrator's View

As a security administrator, you'll need to evaluate the security issues for Windows Server 2003:

1. Go to http://www.microsoft.com/technet/security/prodtech/windowsserver2003/ W2003HG/SGCH00.mspx.

2. Beneath the Download link (on the right), choose Get the Windows Server 2003 Security Guide. Read it and pay particular attention to the Threats and Counter-measures discussion.

3. Go to http://www.microsoft.com/technet/community/columns/sectip/st0805.mspx and read the Security and Compliance Solutions Guidance list posted there. Clicking on Security Tip of the Month columns will open up a plethora of useful articles.

 It cannot be overstated enough—the network is only as strong as its weakest component. If users can install software, delete files, and change configurations, then the actions they perform can also be performed by illicit software programs such as viruses and malware as well.

Hardening the OS and NOS

Any network is only as strong as its weakest component. Sometimes, the most obvious components are overlooked, and it's your job as a security administrator to make certain that doesn't happen. You must ensure that the operating systems running on the workstations and on the network servers are as secure as they can be.

Hardening an operating system (OS) or network operating system (NOS) refers to the process of making the environment more secure from attacks and intruders. The following sections discuss hardening an OS and the methods of keeping it hardened as new threats emerge. They will also discuss some of the vulnerabilities of the more popular operating systems and what can be done to harden those OSs.

The current exam doesn't test specifics of operating system hardening. However, you should know and understand the general principles of hardening. Each product has a different set of procedures and methods to accomplish this. Review your software and hardware vendors' websites, literature, and installation documentation to more fully understand these procedures.

Configuring Network Protocols

Configuring an OS's network protocols properly is a major factor in hardening. PC systems today primarily use TCP/IP, but for the exam, you should pretend that they use three primary network protocols:

- NetBIOS Extended User Interface (NetBEUI)
- Transmission Control Protocol/Internet Protocol (TCP/IP)
- Internetwork Packet Exchange/Sequenced Packet Exchange (IPX/SPX)

Each of these protocols can transport the Microsoft native networking protocol Network Basic Input/Output System (NetBIOS) across networks. NetBIOS protocol–enabled systems periodically announce names, service types, and other information on the networks bound to them. NetBIOS is also used for programming interfaces and other purposes.

For several years, Microsoft has been suggesting that TCP/IP be the primary network protocol used in networks. The company is concentrating more effort in making this protocol secure.

In looking at the large picture, don't overlook the simple things. Applications such as Netscape, Internet Explorer, and Office are susceptible to exploitation. Make sure that all your applications are up to the current release level and that all security patches have been installed.

Firefox is a browser gaining market acceptance because there are currently fewer exploits for it than other browsers.

In the following sections, we'll look at how network protocols are configured, how they're installed, and how they operate in a PC environment.

Network Binding

Binding is the process of tying a network protocol to another network protocol or to a network interface card (NIC). In a Microsoft network, NetBIOS can be bound to any of the three protocols mentioned in the previous section.

For example, binding NetBIOS to TCP/IP encapsulates NetBIOS messages into TCP/IP packets. TCP/IP can then be used to send NetBIOS traffic across the network. This binding process is where you'll find the security vulnerability. The problem lies in the fact that NetBIOS information becomes encapsulated in TCP/IP packets, making them vulnerable to sniffing (listening in on network traffic). Figure 5.1 illustrates the process of network binding. If the TCP/IP packet is intercepted, critical systems information, including passwords, can be discovered.

FIGURE 5.1   NetBIOS binding to the TCP/IP network protocol

Make sure your network protocols and adapters have the proper binding configurations. Don't bind NetBIOS to a protocol unless necessary. Figure 5.2 shows the network binding of a typical Windows XP system. When two computers, such as a server and a client, attempt to communicate with each other, they must first find a common language. They do so by trying different protocols based on the binding order. (Internet Protocol [TCP/IP] is the only default in the latest operating systems from Microsoft.) For that reason, the protocols most commonly used on the server/client should be at the top of the binding list.

FIGURE 5.2   Network binding in a Windows XP system

NetBEUI

NetBEUI is a proprietary protocol developed by Microsoft for Windows networks. If your entire network is configured for NetBEUI, the network will be almost invulnerable to outside attack. This is the case because NetBEUI isn't routable, so you can't connect it to an outside network using a router.

NetBEUI is not available by default on Windows XP Professional or Microsoft Windows Vista.

Tools such as Network Neighborhood, Explorer, and file sharing use NetBIOS for communications. Virtually all internal networking functions operate properly if NetBEUI is used for internal networking. NetBEUI wasn't designed to provide any security capabilities, and its packets disclose a great deal about system configuration, services running, and other information that can be used to identify weaknesses in a system. NetBEUI, isn't however, intended for large networks and is less efficient than Internetwork Packet Exchange/Sequenced Packet Exchange (IPX/SPX) or TCP/IP in such an environment.

TCP/IP

TCP/IP is vulnerable to all the threats discussed in Chapter 2, "Identifying Potential Risks." If your system is connected to the Internet or other large-scale networks, the security of the system is tied to the vulnerability of the TCP/IP network protocol.

The current implementations of TCP/IP are relatively secure. Earlier versions of TCP/IP, as implemented by Microsoft, Novell, Apple, and other vendors, had a huge number of technical problems and security vulnerabilities. The security of the network, regardless of the manufacturer, is only as good as the implementation the manufacturer accomplishes.

Don't jump to the conclusion that all Internet vulnerabilities are weaknesses within TCP/IP. After so many years of development and implementation, the stack is now relatively secure. Many of the newer vulnerabilities are in the operating systems and applications that use TCP/IP as the transport.

IPX/SPX

IPX/SPX is an efficient, routable protocol that was originally designed for use with Novell NetWare systems. The routers in use today don't generally route IPX/SPX unless they're specifically configured to do so. NetBIOS can be bound to IPX/SPX, and it won't be vulnerable to external attack unless this protocol is routed.

Hardening Microsoft Windows Vista

Security is such a driving component of computing today that it was one of the catalysts behind the development of the most recent version of Microsoft's workstation product. A new feature in this operating system is the ability to apply parental controls to accounts. To do so, choose the Set Up Parental Controls for Any User applet from the Control Panel, choose the user you want to apply them to, and click the On, Enforce Current Settings radio button.

From this same applet, you can also choose the Windows Vista web filter and set a web restriction level or the Time limits settings and restrict hours that the computer can be used. The former also allows you to block file downloads as well as choose websites to allow/block, and is an example of an *Internet content filter.*

Internet content filters, while not included with every operating system by default, are plentiful and can be readily found for any operating system with a simple web search. It is highly recommended that you place content filters on all servers (NAT, proxy, etc.) facilitating client access as well as on the workstations themselves. This provides two levels of security that can keep errant pages out.

However, the Security applet, beneath the Control Panel, is the main interface for security features in Vista. From here, you can configure Windows Firewall, automatic scans of your computer, and Windows Defender. One of the newest security features that is available only in the Enterprise and Ultimate versions of Vista is Bitlocker. Bitlocker is a *whole disk encryption* feature that can encrypt an entire volume with 128-bit encryption. When the entire volume is encrypted, the data is not accessible to someone who might boot another operating system in an attempt to bypass the computer's security.

The Microsoft security website is at http://www.microsoft.com/security/, and it is the first place to turn to for up-to-date information on operating system issues.

Hardening Microsoft Windows XP

Windows XP functioned as a replacement for both the Windows 9x family and Windows 2000 Professional. There are multiple versions of Windows XP, including the Home, Media Center, and Professional editions, but Microsoft is currently planning to discontinue supporting it in the near future in favor of Windows Vista.

The Windows XP Home edition was intended specifically to replace Windows 9x clients, while Media Center added entertaining options (such as a remote control for TV) and Windows XP Professional was designed for the corporate environment. Windows XP Professional has the ability to take advantage of the security possible from Windows 200x servers running Active Directory.

The service packs fix minor security openings within the operating system, and as of this writing, three such service packs have been released.

One of the best tools to use when looking for possible illicit activity on a workstation is *Systems Monitor* (also known as *System Monitor*). This utility can be used to examine activity on any counter, and excessive processor usage is one worth paying attention to if you suspect the workstation is affected or being illegitimately accessed. In previous versions of Windows-based operating systems, this utility was a standalone menu choice. With Windows XP, it became a subcomponent (a snap-in) in the Performance Console. To access it, choose Start ➤ Run ➤ and type `perfmon.msc`. By default, System Monitor comes up showing three counters: Pages/sec, Avg. Disk Queue Length, and % Processor Time. To add more counters, right click in the right pane and choose Add Counters from the popup menu.

Hardening Windows Server 2003

At the time the questions for this exam were written, Windows Server 2008 had only recently been released. As a result, the exam does not include questions specific to Windows Server 2008.

Windows Server 2003 was released in four variants:

- Web edition
- Standard edition
- Enterprise edition
- Datacenter edition

This product introduced the following features to the Microsoft server line:

- Internet connection firewall
- Secure authentication (locally and remotely)
- Secure wireless connections
- Software restriction policies
- Secure Web Server (IIS 6)
- Encryption and cryptography enhancements
- Improved security in VPN connections
- PKI and X.509 certificate support

In short, the goal was to make a product that is both secure and flexible. Since a server is only as secure as the workstations connected to it, one of the best ways to keep the network safe is by utilizing *Group Policies* and regularly reviewing them. Group Policies replace System Policies, which existed in Microsoft operating systems prior to Windows 2000.

With a Group Policy, you create restrictions that will apply to workstations when users authenticate. Upon each authentication, those restrictions are then applied as Registry settings, providing an efficient way to manage a large number of computers.

The restrictions you set come from choices within template files and can be as simple as not allowing the user to access Solitaire, to removing their ability to access the other networks. *Security templates* are those template files that hold Registry setting choices that relate to security settings.

Not every configuration setting needs to be downloaded through the domain. Every current Microsoft operating system also includes *local policies*—settings that apply to the workstation when the user has yet to authenticate with the network. The purpose of these policies are to restrict the user locally, just as you would across the network, when they have yet to log into the domain. To see the local polices, choose Start ➤ Run ➤ and type **secpol.msc**.

You should routinely monitor the settings made throughout your network in local and Group Policies and tweak them as needed.

Hardening Microsoft Windows 2000

Windows 2000 entered the market at the millennium. It includes workstation and several server versions. The market has embraced these products, and they offer reasonable security when updated. Windows 2000 provides a Windows Update icon on the Start menu; this icon allows you to connect to the Microsoft website and automatically download and install updates. A large number of security updates are available for Windows 2000—make sure they're applied.

In the Windows environment, the *Services* manager or applet is one of the primary methods (along with policies) used to disable a service.

The server and workstation products operate in a manner similar to Windows NT 4. These products run into the most security-related problems when they're bundled with services that Microsoft has included with them. Some of the more attack-prone services include Internet Information Server (IIS), File Transfer Protocol (FTP), and other common web technologies. Make sure these services are disabled if they aren't needed, and keep them up-to-date with the most recent security and service packs.

Many security updates have been issued for Windows 2000. The Microsoft TechNet and Security websites provide tools, white papers, and materials to help secure Windows 2000 systems.

You can find the Microsoft TechNet website at http://technet.microsoft.com/default.aspx. This is one of the first places to turn for technical information on Microsoft products.

Windows 2000 includes extensive system logging, reporting, and monitoring tools. They help make the job of monitoring security fairly easy. In addition, Windows 2000 provides a great deal of flexibility in managing groups of users, security attributes, and access control to the environment.

The *Event Viewer* is the major tool for reviewing logs in Windows 2000. Figure 5.3 shows an example Event Viewer. Using Event Viewer, an administrator can log a number of different types of events and configure the level of events that are logged.

FIGURE 5.3   Event Viewer log of a Windows 2000 system

Another important security tool is *Performance Monitor*. As an administrator of a Windows 2000 network, you must know how to use Performance Monitor. This tool can be a lifesaver when you're troubleshooting problems and looking for resource-related issues.

Windows 2000 servers can run a technology called *Active Directory (AD)*, which lets you control security configuration options of Windows 2000 systems in a network. Unfortunately, the full power of AD doesn't work unless all the systems in the network are running Windows 2000 or higher.

Hardening Unix/Linux

The Unix environment and its derivatives are some of the most-installed server products in the history of the computer industry. Over a dozen different versions of Unix are available; the most popular is a free version derivative called *Linux*.

Unix was created in the 1970s. The product designers took an *open-systems* approach, meaning that the entire source code for the operating system was readily available for most versions. This open-source philosophy has allowed tens of thousands of programmers, computer scientists, and systems developers to tinker with and improve the product.

The National Security Agency (NSA) has released a set of enhancements to provide additional security for Linux systems. These enhancements are bundled in a set of tools called *Security Enhanced Linux (SELinux)*. SELinux uses mandatory access control methods as part of the mechanisms for improved security. You can find information on it at http://www.nsa.gov/selinux/.

Linux and Unix, when properly configured, provide a high level of security. The major challenge with the Unix environment is configuring it properly.

Unix includes the capacity to handle and run almost every protocol, service, and capability designed. You should turn off most of the services when they aren't needed by running a script during system startup. The script will configure the protocols, and it will determine which services are started.

All Unix security is handled at the file level. Files and directories need to be established properly to ensure correct access permissions. The file structure is hierarchical by nature, and when a file folder access level is set, all subordinate file folders usually inherit this access. This inheritance of security is established by the systems administrator or by a user who knows how to adjust directory permissions.

Keeping patches and updates current is essential in the Unix environment. You can accomplish this by regularly visiting the developer's website for the version/flavor you're using and downloading the latest fixes.

Linux also provides a great deal of activity logging. These logs are essential in establishing patterns of intrusion.

An additional method of securing Linux systems is accomplished by adding *TCP wrappers*, which are low-level logging packages designed for Unix systems. Wrappers provide additional detailed logging on activity using a specific protocol. Each protocol or port must have a wrapper installed for it. The wrappers then record activities and deny access to the service or server.

Linux is considered an *open-source program*. This means that all of the source code for the system is available for examination and modification. This typically requires a high level of programming expertise. Vendors such as Sun, IBM, and HP have implemented Unix-based or Linux-based systems to simplify the process. In most cases, they make the modifications available to customers.

As an administrator of a Unix or Linux network, you're confronted with a large number of configuration files and variables that you must work with in order to keep all hosts communicating properly.

Hardening Novell NetWare

Novell was one of the first companies to introduce a network operating system (NOS) for desktop computers, called NetWare. Early versions of NetWare provided the ability to connect

PCs into primitive but effective LANs. The most recent version of NetWare, version 6.5, includes file sharing, print sharing, support for most clients, and fairly tight security.

NetWare functions as a server product. The server has its own NOS. The NetWare software also includes client applications for a number of different types of systems, including Macintoshes and PCs. You can extend the server services by adding NetWare Loadable Modules (NLMs) to the server. These modules allow executable code to be patched or inserted into the OS.

What Microsoft calls service packs—updates to the core operating system—Novell calls support packs. The support packs fix known problems with the OS and occasionally add additional functionality.

NetWare version 6.*x* is primarily susceptible to denial of service (DoS) types of attacks, as opposed to exploitation and other attacks. NetWare security is accomplished through a combination of access controls, user rights, security rights, and authentication.

The heart of NetWare security is the *Novell Directory Service (NDS)* or eDirectory (for newer Novell implementations). NDS and eDirectory maintain information about rights, access, and usage on a NetWare-based network.

A number of additional capabilities make NetWare a product worth evaluating in implementation. These include e-commerce products, document retrieval, and enhanced network printing.

Prior to version 5, NetWare defaulted to the proprietary IPX/SPX protocol for networking. All newer versions of NetWare default to TCP/IP.

Hardening Apple Macintosh

Macintosh systems seem to be the most vulnerable to physical access attacks targeted through the console. The network implementations are as secure as any of the other systems discussed in this chapter.

Macintosh security breaks down in its access control and authentication systems. Macintosh uses a simple 32-bit password encryption scheme that is relatively easy to crack. The password file is located in the Preference folder; if this file is shared or is part of a network share, it may be vulnerable to decryption.

Macintosh systems also have several proprietary network protocols that aren't intended for routing. Recently, Macintosh systems have implemented TCP/IP networking as an integral part of the operating system.

To secure the system, you should verify that it is not configured to automatically log in a user at startup. Every system must require a username and password in order to gain access to the Mac itself, as well as to the network.

You should also configure a screensaver to automatically deploy after a few moments of inactivity. The screensaver can be any that you want to use as long as it requires a password to resume the session.

 OS X, the successor to Macintosh, is a descendant of BSD-based Unix. As such, the information described in "Hardening Unix/Linux" applies.

Hardening Filesystems

Several filesystems are involved in the operating systems we've discussed, and they have a high level of interoperability between them—from a network perspective, that is. Through the years, the different vendors have implemented their own sets of file standards. Some of the more common filesystems are listed here:

Microsoft FAT   Microsoft's earliest filesystem was referred to as *File Allocation Table (FAT)*. FAT is designed for relatively small disk drives. It was upgraded first to FAT-16 and finally to FAT-32. FAT-32 allows large disk systems to be used on Windows systems. FAT allows only two types of protection: share-level and user-level access privileges. If a user has write or change access to a drive or directory, they have access to any file in that directory. This is very unsecure in an Internet environment.

 It is rare to find FAT used in the corporate world these days, but you should still know about it for the exam.

Microsoft NTFS   *The New Technology File System (NTFS)* was introduced with Windows NT to address security problems. Before Windows NT was released, it had become apparent to Microsoft that a new filing system was needed to handle growing disk sizes, security concerns, and the need for more stability. NTFS was created to address those issues.

Although FAT was relatively stable if the systems that were controlling it kept running, it didn't do so well when the power went out or the system crashed unexpectedly. One of the benefits of NTFS was a transaction-tracking system, which made it possible for Windows NT to back out of any disk operations that were in progress when Windows NT crashed or lost power.

With NTFS, files, directories, and volumes can each have their own security. NTFS's security is flexible and built in. Not only does NTFS track security in access control lists (ACLs), which can hold permissions for local users and groups, but each entry in the ACL can specify what type of access is given—such as Read-Only, Change, or Full Control. This allows a great deal of flexibility in setting up a network. In addition, special file-encryption programs were developed to encrypt data while it was stored on the hard disk.

Microsoft strongly recommends that all network shares be established using NTFS.

Novell NetWare Storage Services   Novell, like Microsoft, implemented a proprietary file structure. Novell's is called *NetWare File System*. This system allows complete control of every file resource on a NetWare server. The NetWare File System was upgraded to *NetWare Storage Service (NSS)* in version 6. NSS provides higher performance and larger file storage capacities than the NetWare File System. NSS, like its predecessor, uses the NDS or eDirectory to provide authentication for all access.

Unix Filesystem   The Unix filesystem is a completely hierarchical filesystem. Each file, filesystem, and subdirectory has complete granularity of access control. The three primary attributes in a Unix file or directory are Read, Write, and Execute. The ability to individually create these capabilities, as well as to establish inheritance to subdirectories, gives Unix the highest level of security available for commercial systems. The major difficulty with Unix is that establishing these access-control hierarchies can be time consuming when the system is initially configured. Figure 5.4 illustrates this hierarchical file structure. Most current operating systems have embraced this method of file organization.

FIGURE 5.4   Hierarchical file structure used in Unix and other operating systems

Unix Network Filesystems   *Network File System (NFS)* is a Unix protocol that allows systems to mount filesystems from remote locations. This ability allows a client system to view the server or remote desktop storage as a part of the local client. NFS, while functional, is difficult to secure. The discussion of this protocol is beyond the scope of this book; the major issue lies in Unix's inherent trust of authentication processes. NFS was originally implemented by Sun Microsystems, and it has become a standard protocol in Unix environments.

 Don't confuse NetWare File System with Network File System; they're two entirely different technologies.

Apple File Sharing   *Apple File Sharing (AFS)* was intended to provide simple networking for Apple Macintosh systems. This system used a proprietary network protocol called *AppleTalk*. An AppleTalk network isn't routed through the Internet and isn't considered secure. AFS allows the file owner to establish password and access privileges. This process is similar to the Unix filesystem. OS X, the newest version of the Macintosh operating system, has more fully implemented a filesystem that is based on the Unix model. In general, Apple networking is considered as secure as the other implementations discussed in the section. The major weakness of the operating system involves physical control of the systems.

Each of these filesystem implementations requires careful consideration when you're implementing it in a network. You must evaluate their individual capabilities, limitations, and vulnerabilities when you're choosing which protocols or systems to implement.

Most OS providers support multiple protocols and methods. Turn off any protocols that aren't needed because each protocol or filesystem running on a workstation or server increases your vulnerability and exposure to attack, data loss, or DoS attacks.

 If at all possible, don't share the root directories of a disk drive. Doing so allows access to system files, passwords, and other sensitive information. Establish shares off hard drives that don't contain system files.

 Windows systems often have hidden administrative shares with names that end with a dollar sign character (C$, admin$, etc.). These are created for use in managing the computer on the network, and can only be permanently disabled through Registry edits. You can temporarily disable them with the Computer Management console, but they will return on reboot. For the purpose of this exam, simply know they exist and are needed for full network functionality.

Make sure you periodically review the manufacturers' support websites and other support resources that are available to apply current updates and security patches to your systems. Doing this on a regular basis will lower your exposure to security risks.

Updating Your Operating System

Operating system manufacturers typically provide product updates. For example, Microsoft provides a series of regular updates for Windows (a proprietary system) and other applications. However, in the case of public source systems (such as Linux), the updates may come from a newsgroup, the manufacturer of the version you're using, or a user community.

In both cases, public and private, updates help keep operating systems up to the most current revision level. Researching updates is important; when possible, so is getting feedback from other users before you install an update. In a number of cases, a service pack or update has rendered a system unusable. Make sure your system is backed up before you install updates.

Be sure to test updates on test systems before you implement them on production systems.

Three different types of updates are discussed here: hotfixes, service packs, and patches.

Hotfixes

Hotfixes are used to make repairs to a system during normal operation, even though they might require a reboot. A hotfix may entail moving data from a bad spot on the disk and remapping the data to a new sector. Doing so prevents data loss and loss of service. This type of repair may also involve reallocating a block of memory if, for example, a memory problem occurred. This allows the system to continue normal operations until a permanent repair can be made. Microsoft refers to a bug fix as a *hotfix*. It involves the replacement of files with an updated version.

Service Packs and Support Packs

A *service pack* or *support pack* (depending upon the vendor) is a comprehensive set of fixes consolidated into a single product. A service pack may be used to address a large number of bugs or to introduce new capabilities in an OS. When installed, a service pack usually contains a number of file replacements.

Make sure you check related websites to verify that the service pack works properly. Sometimes a manufacturer will release a service pack before it has been thoroughly tested. An untested service pack can cause extreme instability in an operating system or, even worse, render it inoperable.

One large OS manufacturer released a service pack for a popular server product three times before it was right. When installed, this service pack caused many systems to become inoperable. The service pack took down the entire server farm of a large ISP. Many users lost their servers for several days while everything was sorted out and repaired.

Patches

A *patch* is a temporary or quick fix to a program. Patches may be used to temporarily bypass a set of instructions that have malfunctioned. Several OS manufacturers issue patches that can either be manually applied or applied using a disk file to fix a program.

When you're working with customer support on a technical problem with an OS or applications product, customer service may have you go into the code and make alterations to the binary files that run on your system. Double-check each change to prevent catastrophic failures due to improperly entered code.

Patches fix problems, but they also add the potential for new problems. Most manufacturers would rather release a new program than patch an existing program. A new release can repair multiple problems.

When more data is known about the problem, a service pack or hotfix may be issued to fix the problem on a larger scale. Patching is becoming less common, but it's still very much a way of life for many vendors and administrators.

Hardening Network Devices

The discussions up to this point have dealt with how to establish security baselines and update operating systems. We've also briefly discussed filesystems. The next sections deal with keeping your network devices up-to-date. The routers, gateways, firewalls, and other devices that run the network are also vulnerable to attack.

We'll look at how to update and configure your network devices. The focus will be on applications and routers, with coverage of other devices as they apply to this topic.

Updating Network Devices

As a security administrator, you should make sure that software for devices such as routers and switches is kept up-to-date. These devices usually contain a ROM-based (read-only memory) OS and applications. They may also have floppy drives and CD drives that you can use to update their software.

Make sure you periodically visit the manufacturers' websites for the devices in your network and regularly apply the updates that they publish.

Routers are your front line of defense against external attacks. New exploits and methods to attack network devices are being introduced as quickly as new features are released. Fortunately, most network devices have a limited scope of function, unlike general-purpose servers. This narrow scope allows manufacturers to improve network device security rather quickly.

Many of these devices contain proprietary operating systems to manage the functions in the router. Devices such as hubs and switches are generally preconfigured out of the box, though most higher-end switches allow configuration options to be established. Firewalls, on the other hand, provide the primary screening of network traffic once the data has passed through the router. Firewalls are constantly being upgraded to allow increased sophistication and capability.

Routers have become increasingly complex, as have firewalls and other devices in your network. If they aren't kept up-to-date, they will become vulnerable to new attacks or exploits.

Many of the newer routers also allow you to add and expand features. Some of these features deal with security and access. You should make sure your network is kept up-to-date. Network device manufacturers upgrade the functionality of their equipment to deal with new threats and protocols on a regular basis; these upgrades are sometimes free. When a new option is released, an entire upgrade of the firmware may be needed. If such an upgrade is needed, you'll be charged for it in most cases.

Many router manufacturers provide service for their routers piece by piece. They allow the buyer to mix and match the specific protocols, capabilities, and functionality to suit the mission the equipment is being used to accomplish. In some cases, the basic router may only cost $1,000, but the upgrades and feature packs to add additional features may cost thousands more. The advantage is that customers can configure equipment with only the options they need, and they can upgrade at a later time when they need to do so.

Configuring Routers and Firewalls

Many ISPs and other providers will work with you to install and configure the features you need for your network. These features can usually be implemented using either a web-based interface or a terminal-based interface. Proper configuration of these devices is essential to ensure that your network operates smoothly and efficiently. Routers, in particular, have a large number of configuration options, including basic firewall and security support. Several network device manufacturers, such as Cisco, offer certification and training programs.

 The Cisco Certified Internetwork Expert (CCIE) certification is considered one of the most difficult certifications in the industry. Not only are candidates required to take multiple-choice tests similar to the Security+ exam, they're also required to demonstrate hands-on troubleshooting in a lab setting.

Several network product manufacturers are introducing preconfigured firewalls to customers. The firewalls are being referred to as *appliances*. The appliances, like any other computer system, will require updates and maintenance. This technology promises to make networks easier to protect: You'll be able to buy a firewall appliance that can be simply plugged in and turned on. This will allow firewall systems, which are complex, to be easily installed and maintained in smaller networks.

The two most essential operational aspects of network device hardening involve ensuring that your network devices run only necessary protocols, services, and access control lists. The next two sections describe these capabilities from a security perspective.

Enabling and Disabling Services and Protocols

Many routers offer the ability to provide *Dynamic Host Configuration Protocol (DHCP)* services, packet filtering, service protocol configuration options, and other services for use in a network. Make sure your router is configured to allow only the protocols and services you'll need for your network. Leaving additional network services enabled may cause difficulties and can create vulnerabilities in your network. As much as possible, configure your network devices as restrictively as you can. This additional layer of security costs you nothing, and it makes it that much harder for an intruder to penetrate your system.

Working with Access Control Lists

Access control lists (ACLs) enable devices in your network to ignore requests from specified users or systems or to grant them certain network capabilities. You may find that a certain IP address is constantly scanning your network, and you can block this IP address. If you block it at the router, the IP address will automatically be rejected any time it attempts to utilize your network.

ACLs allow a stronger set of access controls to be established in your network. The basic process of ACL control allows the administrator to design and adapt the network to deal with specific security threats.

Hardening Applications

As we've explained, a good way to begin securing a network is to make sure every system in the network is up-to-date and to verify that only the protocols you need are enabled. Unfortunately, these steps aren't enough. Your servers and workstations also run applications and services. Server services (especially web, e-mail, and media servers) are particularly vulnerable to exploitation and attack. These applications must also be hardened to make them as difficult as possible to exploit.

The following sections deal with hardening your applications, both on the desktop and at the server, to provide maximum security.

Hardening Web Servers

Web servers are favorite areas for attackers to exploit. Microsoft's Internet Information Server (IIS), a common web server, continually makes it into the news. IIS, like most web servers, provides connections for web browsers.

Web servers were originally simple and were used primarily to provide HTML text and graphics content. Modern web servers allow database access, streaming media, and virtually every other type of service that can be contemplated. This diversity gives websites the ability to provide rich and complex capabilities to web surfers.

Every service and capability supported on a website is potentially a target for exploitation. Make sure they're kept to the most current software standards. You must also make certain that you're allowing users to have only the minimal permissions necessary to accomplish their tasks. If users are accessing your server via an anonymous account, then common sense dictates that you must make certain the anonymous account has only the permissions needed to view web pages and nothing more.

Two particular areas of interest with web servers are filters and controlling access to executable scripts. *Filters* allow you to limit the traffic that is allowed through. Limiting traffic to only that which is required for your business can help ward off attacks.

A good set of filters can also be applied to your network to prevent users from accessing sites other than those that are business related. Not only does this increase productivity, it also decreases the likelihood of users obtaining a virus from a questionable site.

Executable scripts, such as *Common Gateway Interface (CGI)* scripts, often run at elevated permission levels. Under most circumstances this isn't a problem because the user is returned to their regular permission level at the conclusion of the execution. Problems arise, however, if the user can break out of the script while at the elevated level. From an administrator's standpoint, the best course of action is to verify that all scripts on your server have been thoroughly tested, debugged, and approved for use.

The IUSR_*computername* account is created when services are installed on IIS and used to represent the anonymous user. Rights assigned to this account apply to all anonymous web users.

Hardening E-Mail Servers

E-mail servers provide the communications backbone for many businesses. They typically run either as an additional service on an existing server or as dedicated systems.

Putting an active virus scanner on e-mail servers can reduce the number of viruses introduced into your network as well as prevent viruses from being spread by your e-mail server. Figure 5.5 illustrates an e-mail virus scanner being added to a server. In this implementation, the scanner filters incoming e-mails that are suspicious and informs e-mail users of a potential system compromise. This feature will no doubt become a standard feature of most e-mail servers in the near future; it's very effective in preventing the spread of viruses via e-mail.

FIGURE 5.5   E-mail virus scanner on an e-mail server

Several servers use data stores, or storage, to allow collaboration, meeting scheduling, conferencing, and other functions. The functionality and capabilities of these servers is increasing on a regular basis. Keep them up-to-date and current.

 Real World Scenario

Using ACLs to Address Spam

You've been observing repeated attempts by a TCP/IP address to connect to your e-mail server. These failed connection attempts appear in your e-mail system logs. The intruder continually attempts to access port 25.

E-mail servers are being inundated by automated systems that attempt to use them to send spam. Most e-mail servers have implemented measures to prevent this. However, the threats are becoming increasingly more sophisticated. You may be able to reduce these attempts to access your system by entering the TCP/IP addresses in your router's ACL Deny list. Doing so will cause your router to ignore connection requests from these IP addresses, effectively improving your security.

Hardening FTP Servers

File Transfer Protocol (FTP) servers aren't intended for high-security applications because of their inherent weaknesses. Most FTP servers allow you to create file areas on any drive on the system. You should create a separate drive or subdirectory on the system to allow file transfers. If possible, use virtual private network (VPN) or Secure Shell (SSH) connections for FTP-type activities. FTP isn't notable for security, and many FTP systems send account and password information across the network unencrypted. FTP is one of the tools frequently used to exploit systems.

From an operational security perspective, you should use separate logon accounts and passwords for FTP access. Doing so will prevent system accounts from being disclosed to unauthorized individuals. Also make sure that all files stored on an FTP server are scanned for viruses.

You should *always* disable the anonymous user account. To make FTP usage easier, most servers default to allowing anonymous access. However, from a security perspective, the last thing you want is to allow anonymous users to copy files to and from your servers. Disabling anonymous access requires the user to be a known, authenticated user in order to access the FTP server.

As mentioned, for web access with various versions of IIS, the `IUSR_` *computername* account is created when services are installed and used to represent the anonymous user. Rights assigned to this account apply to all anonymous users.

The best way to secure FTP is to replace it altogether. Instead of using FTP, the same functionality can be found in more secure services such as Secure File Transfer Protocol (SFTP).

Hardening DNS Servers

Domain Name Service (DNS) servers resolve hostnames to IP addresses. This service allows a website name such as www.sybex.com to be resolved to an IP address such as 192.168.1.110.

A registrar manages your domain name. Most registrars require an annual renewal fee. If these fees aren't paid, another company will be able to hijack your domain name. Such hijacking has embarrassed many organizations.

DNS servers can be used internally for private functions as well as externally for public lookups. DNS-related attacks aren't common, but they generally come in one of three types:

Domain Name Service Denial of Service attacks   *Domain Name Service Denial of Service (DNS DoS)* attacks are primarily aimed at DNS servers. The intention is to disrupt the operations of the server, thereby making the system unusable. To address these attacks, make sure your DNS server software and the operating system software are kept up-to-date. Doing so will tend to minimize the impact of DNS DoS attacks.

Network footprinting   *Footprinting* is the act of gathering data about a network in order to find ways someone might intrude. When you footprint, you're looking for vulnerabilities and any means of entry. A great deal of information about your network is stored in

DNS servers. By using one of the common DNS lookup programs, such as NSLOOKUP, an attacker can learn about your network configuration. DNS entries typically include information pertaining to domain names and mail, web, commerce, and other key servers in your network. Keep the amount of information stored about your network in external DNS servers to a bare minimum.

Compromising record integrity   DNS lookup systems usually involve either a primary or a primary and a secondary DNS server. If you make a change to a primary or secondary server, the change propagates to other trusted DNS servers. If a bogus record is inserted into a DNS server, the record will point to the location the attacker intends rather than to a legitimate site. Imagine the embarrassment to a corporation when its website visitors are redirected to a competitor or, even worse, to a porno site. Make sure all DNS servers require authentication before updates are made or propagated. Doing so will help ensure that unauthorized records aren't inserted into your servers.

DNS poisoning is a problem that existed in early implementations of DNS. It hasn't been a serious problem for a while, but you should be aware of it for the exam. With DNS poisoning (also known as *cache poisoning*), a daemon caches DNS reply packets, which sometimes contain other information (data used to fill the packets). The extra data can be scanned for information useful in a break-in or man-in-the-middle attack.

A similar attack, *Address Resolution Protocol (ARP) poisoning,* tries to convince the network that the attacker's MAC address is the one associated with an IP address so that traffic sent to that IP address is wrongly sent to the attacker's machine.

Hardening NNTP Servers

Network News Transfer Protocol (NNTP) servers provide the capability for delivering network news messages. NNTP servers are also commonly used for internal communications in a company or community. These newsgroup servers should require authentication before accepting a posting or allowing a connection to be made.

NNTP servers in many public settings have become overwhelmed with junk mail. Moderators, as well as automated tools called *robots*, are usually used to screen as much of this junk as possible from subscribers. Newsgroups that don't use these types of approaches have become virtually useless as communication tools.

NNTP servers can become overwhelmed by spam and DoS attacks. Many newsgroups started out as small groups of users who shared a common interest. Typically, newsgroups use a moderator to ensure that spam messages aren't propagated to subscribers of the newsgroup.

However, some newsgroups have grown to include tens of thousands of members worldwide, and the amount of traffic or messages on these servers has long since surpassed the level that moderators can manage.

 WARNING   Use caution when signing newsgroups with your real e-mail account. Many spammers use this information to send junk mail, so you may be inundated with spam.

Several scanning programs are now available to help reduce the amount of junk mail these systems process. Of course, as with all good countermeasures, someone always comes up with a way to neutralize their effectiveness.

Hardening File and Print Servers and Services

File and print servers are primarily vulnerable to DoS and access attacks. DoS attacks can be targeted at specific protocols and overwhelm a port with activity. Make sure these servers run only the protocols needed to support the network.

In a network that has PC-based systems, make sure NetBIOS services are disabled on servers or that an effective firewall is in place between the server and the Internet. Many of the popular attacks that are occurring on systems today take place through the NetBIOS services, via ports 135, 137, 138, and 139. On Unix systems, make sure port 111, the Remote Procedure Call (RPC) port, is closed.

 NOTE   *Remote Procedure Call (RPC)* is a programming interface that allows a remote computer to run programs on a local machine. It has created serious vulnerabilities in systems that have RPC enabled.

Directory sharing should be limited to what is essential to perform systems functions. Make sure any root directories are hidden from browsing. It's better to designate a subfolder or subdirectory off the root directory and share it rather than a root directory. Figure 5.6 illustrates a network share connection. Notice that when a user connects to the network-shared directory, they aren't aware of where this share actually is in the hierarchy of the filesystem.

FIGURE 5.6   Network share connection

You should always apply the most restrictive access necessary for a shared directory.

 Never share the root or parent directory of a disk drive. Doing so creates a potential vulnerability for every file on the system. Instead, share subdirectories.

If an attacker penetrates a root directory, all the subdirectories under that directory are vulnerable. If a subdirectory is penetrated, only the directories that reside below it are exposed—in most cases.

Hardening DHCP Services

Dynamic Host Configuration Protocol (DHCP) is used in many networks to automate the assignment of IP addresses to workstations. DHCP services can be provided by many different types of devices, including routers, switches, and servers. The DHCP process involves leasing a TCP/IP address to a workstation for a specified time. DHCP can also provide other network configuration options to a workstation.

In a given network or segment, only one DHCP server should be running. If more than one is running, they will clash with each other over which one provides the address. This can cause duplication of TCP/IP addresses and potentially lead to addressing conflicts.

DHCP-enabled clients can be serviced by a Network Address Translation (NAT) server. (See Chapter 1, "General Security Concepts," for a discussion of NAT servers.) DHCP usage should be limited to workstation systems.

 An exception to only having one DHCP server running in the network would be if you are implementing redundant DHCP services without overlapping scopes.

Working with Data Repositories

Many of the systems that are being used in networks today rely heavily on stored data. The data is usually kept in servers that provide directory services and database services. These systems are referred to as *data repositories*. The following sections discuss some of the more common data repositories in use. Most data repositories are enabled by some form of database technology.

Directory Services

Directory services are tools that help organize and manage complex networks. They allow data files, applications, and other information to be quickly and easily relocated within a network. This greatly simplifies administrative tasks, and it allows programmers and developers to better utilize network resources. The more current methods treat data and other network resources as objects. This object-oriented approach allows information to be stored and accessed based on certain characteristics or attributes.

 Real World Scenario

Where Did All These Strange IP Addresses Originate?

Some of your computer users have suddenly started calling you to indicate that after rebooting their systems, they can no longer access network services or the Internet. After investigating the situation, you discover that the IP addresses they're using are invalid for your network. The IP addresses are valid, but they aren't part of your network. You've inspected your DHCP server and can't find a reason for this. What should you investigate next?

You should investigate whether someone has configured another server or device in your network with an active DHCP server. If so, the illicit DHCP server is now leasing addresses to the users instead of the addresses coming from your server, or the systems can't reach your DHCP server and are getting an Automatic Private IP Addressing (APIPA) address.

This happens when administrators or developers are testing pilot systems. Make sure all test systems are isolated from your production network either by a router or by some other mechanism. These servers are referred to as *rogue servers,* and they can cause much confusion in a DHCP environment.

In addition to creating and storing data, directory services must publish appropriate data to users. Perhaps the best way to visualize this function is to think of it as the yellow and white pages of a business phone directory. A business wants its name and phone number published in a list that's in alphabetical order. The business also likely wants its name listed in one or more categories in the directory. If you were a computer consultant, you might want your name and phone number listed under computer consultants, computer trainers, and other areas. This is what a directory can accomplish for you.

Most directory services have implemented a model of hierarchy similar to the one illustrated in Figure 5.7. This hierarchy allows an object to be uniquely identified to directory users.

Security for directory services is critical, and it's typically accomplished by using both authentication and access control. You wouldn't want your directory entry to show up just anywhere, would you?

The following sections briefly describe some of the directory services used in networking today. LDAP, Active Directory, and eDirectory are becoming more widely used and are sure to become even more targeted for misuse in the future.

FIGURE 5.7   Directory structure showing unique identification of a user

mail: John@sybex.com

Lightweight Directory Access Protocol

Lightweight Directory Access Protocol (LDAP) is a standardized directory access protocol that allows queries to be made of directories (specifically, pared-down X.500-based directories). If a directory service supports LDAP, you can query that directory with an LDAP client, but it's LDAP that is growing in popularity and is being used extensively in online white and yellow pages.

LDAP is the main access protocol used by Active Directory (discussed next). It operates, by default, at port 389. The LDAP syntax uses commas between names.

Active Directory

Microsoft implemented a directory service called *Active Directory (AD)* with Windows 2000. For Microsoft products, AD is the backbone for all security, access, and network implementations. AD gives administrators full control of resources. It's a proprietary directory service that provides services for other directory services, such as LDAP. One or more servers manage AD functions; these servers are connected in a tree structure that allows information to be shared or controlled through the entire AD structure.

In conjunction with Active Directory, LDAP uses four different name types:

Distinguished Name   A *Distinguished Name (DN)* exists for every object in AD. These values can't be duplicates and must be unique. This is the full path of the object, including any containers.

Relative Distinguished Name   A *Relative Distinguished Name (RDN)* doesn't need to be a wholly unique value as long as there are no duplicates within the organizational unit (OU). As such, an RDN is the portion of the name that is unique within its container.

User Principal Name   A *User Principal Name (UPN)* is often referred to as a *friendly name*. It consists of the user account and the user's domain name and is used to identify the user (think of an e-mail address).

Canonical Name   The *Canonical Name (CN)* is the DN given in a top-down notation.

X.500

The *International Telecommunications Union (ITU),* an international standards group for directory services in the late 1980s, implemented the *X.500 standard*, which was the basis for later models of directory structure such as LDAP. The major problem in the industry implementing a full-blown X.500 structure revolved around the complexity of the implementation. Novell was one of the first manufacturers to implement X.500 in its NetWare NDS product.

eDirectory

eDirectory is the backbone for new Novell networks. It stores information on all system resources and users and any other relevant information about systems attached to a NetWare server. eDirectory is an upgrade and replacement for NDS, and it has gained wide acceptance in the community.

Databases and Technologies

One key reason computers are installed is for their ability to store, access, and modify data. The primary tool for data management is the database. Databases have become increasingly more sophisticated, and their capabilities have grown dramatically over the last 10 years. This growth has created opportunities to view data in new ways; it has also created problems for both designers and users of these products.

This section briefly discusses database technologies and some of the common issues associated with vulnerabilities in database systems.

The *relational database* has become the most common approach to database implementation. This technology allows data to be viewed in dynamic ways based on the user's or administrator's needs. The most common language used to speak to databases is called *Structured Query Language (SQL)*. SQL allows queries to be configured in real time and passed to database servers. This flexibility causes a major vulnerability when it isn't implemented securely.

 Don't confuse the acronym *SQL* with Microsoft's database product *SQL Server*. SQL Server implements Structured Query Language, or SQL, as do most other databases.

For instance, you might want to get the phone numbers of all the customers who live in a certain geographic area and have purchased products from you in the last two years. In a manual system, you would first need to determine which customers live in the area you want. You would perform a manual search of customer records, and then you would identify which customers have made purchases. This type of process could be very involved and time consuming.

In a relational database environment, you could query the database to find all records that meet your criteria and then print them. The command to do this might be a single line of code, or it might require thousands of instructions. Obviously, the increase in productivity is a worthwhile investment.

Corporate or organizational data is one of an organization's most valuable possessions. It usually resides either in desktop systems or in large centralized database servers. This information makes the servers tempting targets for industrial espionage and damage.

Database servers suffer from all the vulnerabilities we've discussed to this point. Additionally, the database itself is a complex set of programs that work together to provide access to data.

Early database systems connected the end user directly to the data through applications programs. These programs were intended to allow easy data access and to allow transactions to be performed against the database. In a private network, physical security was usually all that was needed to protect the data.

As the Internet has grown, businesses have allowed customer access to data such as catalogs, order status, online ordering, and virtually any other capabilities they want. This increased interoperability has added more coding, more software, and increased complexity to the database issue. Software manufacturers work hard to keep up with customer demands. Unfortunately, they frequently release software that is prone to security problems. The increase in demand for database-oriented systems and the security problems introduced by software developers and manufacturers have been the biggest area of vulnerability for database servers.

Databases need patching just like other applications. You should configure them to use access controls and provide their own levels of security.

To improve system performance, as well as to improve the security of databases, companies have implemented the tiered model of systems. Three different models are explained here:

One-tier model   In a *one-tier model*, or *single-tier environment,* the database and the application exist on a single system. This is common on desktop systems running a stand-alone database. Early Unix implementations also worked in this manner; each user would sign on to a terminal and run a dedicated application that accessed the data.

Two-tier model   In a *two-tier model*, the client PC or system runs an application that communicates with the database that is running on a different server. This is a common implementation, and it works well for many applications.

Three-tier model   The *three-tier model* effectively isolates the end user from the database by introducing a *middle-tier server.* This server accepts requests from clients, evaluates them, and then sends them on to the database server for processing. The database server sends the data back to the middle-tier server, which then sends the data to the client system. This approach is becoming common in business today. The middle server can also control access to the database and provide additional security.

The three models provide increasing capability and complexity. You must individually manage each system and keep it current for this system to provide security.

Summary

This chapter introduced you to the concept of hardening operating systems, network devices, and applications. To secure a network, each of the elements in its environment must be individually evaluated. Remember, your network is no more secure than its weakest link.

Security baselines provide a standardized method for evaluating the security capabilities of particular products. Never consider an operating system or application to be secured unless it has been certified using the EAL standard, which provides seven levels of certification. Common Criteria has replaced TCSEC as the primary security certification. EAL 4 is the level recommended to provide reasonable security for commercial operating systems.

The number of vulnerabilities is rapidly increasing. The increase is partially due to the fact that many systems manufacturers didn't take security issues seriously enough in the past. This attitude is changing, and many of the larger manufacturers now realize the damage that security leaks cause to their users.

The process of making a server or an application resistant to attack is called hardening. One of the major methods of hardening an operating system is to disable any protocols that aren't needed in the system. Keeping systems updated also helps improve security.

The common protocols used in PC-based networks are NetBEUI, IPX/SPX, and TCP/IP. Each of these protocols creates unique security challenges that must be addressed. Unused protocols should be disabled on all devices: Each protocol used increases the potential vulnerability of your environment. ACLs are being implemented in network devices and systems to enable the control of access to systems and users; ACLs allow individual systems, users, or IP addresses to be ignored.

Large-scale networks often use Unix networks and additional protocols, such as NFS. NFS is difficult to secure, and it shouldn't be used in external networks. Additional security is available in this environment if secure VPN connections are used.

The FAT filesystem provides user-level and share-level security. As a result, FAT is largely unsuitable as a filesystem for use in secure environments. NTFS provides security capabilities similar to Unix, and it allows control of individual files using various criteria.

Manufacturers and venders provide product updates to improve security and to fix errors in the products they support. The three primary methods of upgrading systems are hotfixes, service packs, and patches. Hotfixes are usually meant as temporary fixes to a system until a permanent fix can be found. Microsoft also refers to its bug patches as hotfixes. Service packs usually contain multiple fixes to a system. Patches are used to temporarily fix a program until a permanent fix can be applied. Manufacturers tend to replace entire programs rather than patching or hotfixing systems. When you're installing a patch, make sure you follow the directions to the letter; an improperly installed patch can render a system unusable.

Network devices are becoming increasingly complicated, and they require that updates be applied on a regular basis. The update process is usually accomplished using either a terminal-based or a web-based utility. Intruders are increasingly targeting routers and other devices for attack; make sure they're kept to the current software release.

Application hardening helps ensure that vulnerabilities are minimized. Make sure you run only the applications and services that are needed to support your environment. Attackers can target application protocols. Many of the newer systems offer a rich environment for end users, and each protocol increases your risk.

Directory services allow information to be shared in a structured manner with large numbers of users. These services must be secure in order to prevent impersonation or embarrassment. The more common directory services used are LDAP, AD, X.500, and eDirectory.

Database technologies are vulnerable to attacks due to the nature of the flexibility they provide. Make sure database servers and applications are kept up-to-date. To provide increased security, many environments have implemented multi-tiered approaches to data access.

Exam Essentials

Be able to describe the process of hardening an operating system.   Make sure all the products used in a network are kept up-to-date with the most current release. Apply service packs and security updates on a regular basis.

Be able to identify the capabilities of the various filesystems used.   Different filesystems have different security capabilities. The least secure is FAT, which provides only share-level and user-level security. Most of the truly networked filesystems provide access down to the individual file or directory level. The method used by Unix allows each individual file to have Read, Write, or Execute permissions for security. The filesystem can be configured when the system is installed. Unix filesystems are considered the most secure for commercial applications.

Know the types of updates used in systems.   The three common methods for updating are hotfixes, service packs, and patches. Hotfixes are usually applied to a system in real time in order to continue operations until a permanent fix can be made. Service packs are groups of updates for a system or application. Service packs typically replace entire programs. Patches are made to systems to solve a problem or to bypass a particular malfunctioning system.

Be able to discuss the methods of turning off unneeded protocols and services.   In the Unix environment, a script file for protocols and services is run at startup. Commenting out protocols that aren't needed is the primary method used to turn off protocols in Unix. In the Windows environment, the Services manager is one of the primary methods (along with policies) used to disable a service.

Know how ACLs work.   Access control lists (ACLs) are used to identify systems and specify which users, protocols, or services are allowed. ACL-based systems can be used to prevent unauthorized users from accessing vulnerable services.

Be able to discuss the weaknesses and vulnerabilities of the various applications that run on a network.   Web, e-mail, and other services present unique security challenges that must be considered. Turn off services that aren't needed. Make sure applications are kept up-to-date with security and bug fixes. Implement these services in a secure manner, as the manufacturer intended; this is the best method for securing applications.

Be able to identify the purpose and common protocols used for directory services. The most commonly implemented directory service is LDAP. LDAP allows users to globally publish information that they want others to know. This process is done using an LDAP server or service. Other directory services are DNS, AD, eDirectory, and X.500. Most directory services are implemented in a hierarchical manner that allows objects to be uniquely identified.

Hands-On Labs

The labs in this chapter are as follows:

Lab 5.1: Install OpenLDAP on a SuSE Server

Lab 5.2: Work with Performance Monitor and Windows

Lab 5.3: Work with Unix/Linux Networking

Lab 5.1: Install OpenLDAP on a SuSE Server

OpenLDAP is the primary LDAP service in use in Linux implementations. To install Open-LDAP on the SuSE server, follow these steps:

1. Start YaST as the root user.

2. Choose Software and then Install and Remove Software.

3. Type `openldap` in the Search field and click Search.

4. Check the `openldap2`, `openldap2-client`, and `yast2-ldap-server` packages and click Accept. Insert any SLES CDs needed if prompted.

5. Back in YaST, choose Network Services, then LDAP Server. A prompt may appear informing you that you must start LDAP—if this is the case, choose to do so.

6. Click Configure, and you are automatically able to edit the configuration files entries through the YaST interface.

7. Click Finish.

Lab 5.2: Work with Performance Monitor and Windows

Performance Monitor's objects and counters are specific; you can use Performance Monitor as a general troubleshooting tool as well as a security-troubleshooting tool. For instance, you can see where resources are being utilized and where the activity is coming from. In this lab, you'll use the Performance Monitor tool to become more familiar with its functionality:

1. Select Start ➢ Settings ➢ Control Panel ➢ Administrative Tools and choose Performance.

2. Click the Add Counters button, and choose to add the Processor Performance object.

3. Add the %Processor Time counter, and then click Close.

4. Choose Start ➢ Search ➢ For Files and Folders and click the Search Now button without specifying any particular files to look for. Quickly change to Performance Monitor and watch the impact of this search on the processor. This action is time consuming and therefore will help you notice the changes that take place in Performance Monitor.

5. Run the same operation again, but this time change your view within Performance Monitor to histogram (click the two buttons to the left of the plus sign [+]).

6. Run the same operation again, and change your view within Performance Monitor to report (click the button directly to the left of the plus sign [+]).

7. Exit Performance Monitor.

Lab 5.3: Work with Unix/Linux Networking

As a security administrator, you should know about the default networking files and their purpose. In this lab, you'll work from the command line and look at the values of some key variables. These text files hold configuration values that can be used to set networking parameters.

1. From a command prompt, change to the /etc directory.

2. View the contents of the HOSTNAME file by typing the following at the command prompt: `cat HOSTNAME`. The value shown holds the name of the host and domain on a single line (in some implementations, the name of the file is lowercase rather than uppercase).

3. View the contents of the hosts file by typing `cat hosts`. This is an ASCII file used to list IP addresses and text names of known hosts. The use of this file predates DNS; you can use it in place of DNS on small networks.

4. View the contents of the networks file by typing `cat networks`. This file lists the known networks with which this host can communicate.

5. Exit the command line.

Review Questions

1. Which of the following terms refers to the process of establishing a standard for security?

    A. Baselining

    B. Security evaluation

    C. Hardening

    D. Methods research

2. You've been chosen to lead a team of administrators in an attempt to increase security. You're currently creating an outline of all the aspects of security that will need to be examined and acted upon. Which of the following terms describes the process of improving security in an NOS?

    A. Common Criteria

    B. Hardening

    C. Encryption

    D. Networking

3. What is the method of establishing a protocol connection to a controller called?

    A. Linkage

    B. Networking

    C. Binding

    D. Access control

4. You're evaluating the protocols in use on your network. After evaluation, you'll make a recommendation to the vice president of IT on protocols that should be removed from the systems. Which of the following protocols shouldn't be bound to TCP/IP, if at all possible, because it's a well-established target of attackers?

    A. IPX/SPX

    B. SMTP

    C. NetBIOS

    D. LDAP

5. What tool is used in Windows Vista to encrypt an entire volume?

    A. Bitlocker

    B. Syslock

    C. Drive Defender

    D. NLock

6. Your organization has created a new overseer position, and licensing has suddenly become an issue. Licenses need to be in existence and able to be readily produced for all proprietary software. Which of the following operating systems is an open-source product and not considered proprietary?

    A. Windows 2000

    B. Novell NetWare

    C. Linux

    D. Mac OS

7. Which filesystem was primarily intended for desktop system use and offers limited security?

    A. NTFS

    B. NFS

    C. FAT

    D. AFS

8. Your company has acquired a competitor's business. You've been assigned the role of formulating a strategy by which the servers on your existing network will communicate with those on the newly acquired network. All you know about the competitor is that it's using Novell's newest filesystem and it's a proprietary environment for servers. Which filesystem is used in NetWare servers?

    A. NSS

    B. NTFS

    C. AFS

    D. FAT

9. Which filesystem allows remote mounting of filesystems?

    A. NTFS

    B. FAT

    C. AFS

    D. NFS

10. The administrator at MTS was recently fired, and it has come to light that he didn't install updates and fixes as they were released. As the newly hired administrator, your first priority is to bring all networked clients and servers up-to-date. What is a bundle of one or more system fixes in a single product called?

    A. Service pack

    B. Hotfix

    C. Patch

    D. System install

11. Which of the following statements is *not* true?

   A. You should never share the root directory of a disk.

   B. You should share the root directory of a disk.

   C. You should apply the most restrictive access necessary for a shared directory.

   D. Filesystems are frequently based on hierarchical models.

12. Your company does electronic monitoring of individuals under house arrest around the world. Because of the sensitive nature of the business, you can't afford any unnecessary downtime. What is the process of applying a repair to an operating system while the system stays in operations called?

   A. Upgrading

   B. Service pack installation

   C. Hotfix

   D. File update

13. What is the process of applying manual changes to a program called?

   A. Hotfix

   B. Service pack

   C. Patching

   D. Replacement

14. A newly hired junior administrator will assume your position temporarily while you attend a conference. You're trying to explain the basics of security to her in as short a period of time as possible. Which of the following best describes an ACL?

   A. ACLs provide individual access control to resources.

   B. ACLs aren't used in modern systems.

   C. The ACL process is dynamic in nature.

   D. ACLs are used to authenticate users.

15. What product verifies that files being received by an SMTP server contain no suspicious code?

   A. E-mail virus filter

   B. Web virus filter

   C. Packet filter firewall

   D. IDS

16. Users are complaining about name resolution problems suddenly occurring that were never an issue before. You suspect that an intruder has compromised the integrity of the DNS server on your network. What is one of the primary ways in which an attacker uses DNS?

   A. Network footprinting

   B. Network sniffing

   C. Database server lookup

   D. Registration counterfeiting

17. LDAP is an example of which of the following?

    A. Directory access protocol

    B. IDS

    C. Tiered model application development environment

    D. File server

18. Your company is growing at a tremendous rate, and the need to hire specialists in various areas of IT is becoming apparent. You're helping to write the newspaper ads that will be used to recruit new employees, and you want to make certain that applicants possess the skills you need. One knowledge area in which your organization is weak is database intelligence. What is the primary type of database used in applications today that you can mention in the ads?

    A. Hierarchical

    B. Relational

    C. Network

    D. Archival

19. The flexibility of relational databases in use today is a result of which of the following?

    A. SQL

    B. Hard-coded queries

    C. Forward projection

    D. Mixed model access

20. You're redesigning your network in preparation for putting the company up for sale. The network, like all aspects of the company, needs to perform the best that it possibly can in order to be an asset to the sale. Which model is used to provide an intermediary server between the end user and the database?

    A. One-tiered

    B. Two-tiered

    C. Three-tiered

    D. Relational database

Answers to Review Questions

1. A.   Baselining is the process of establishing a standard for security.

2. B.   Hardening is the process of improving the security of an operating system or application. One of the primary methods of hardening an OS is to eliminate unneeded protocols.

3. C.   Binding is the process of associating one protocol with another protocol or to a network card.

4. C.   NetBIOS shouldn't be bound to TCP/IP if at all possible. NetBIOS is a well-established target of attackers.

5. A.   Bitlocker provides drive encryption and is available with Windows Vista.

6. C.   The open-source movement makes system source code available to developers and programmers. Linux is the operating system at the forefront of the open-source movement.

7. C.   FAT technology offers limited security options.

8. A.   NSS is Novell's newest filesystem. It's a proprietary environment for servers.

9. D.   Network File System (NFS) is the Unix standard for remote filesystems.

10. A.   A service pack is one or more repairs to system problems bundled into a single process or function.

11. B.   Never share the root directory of a disk if at all possible. Doing so opens the entire disk to potential exploitation.

12. C.   A hotfix is done while a system is operating. This reduces the necessity of taking a system out of service to fix a problem.

13. C.   A patch is a temporary workaround of a bug or problem in code that is applied manually. Complete programs usually replace patches at a later date.

14. A.   Access control lists allow individual and highly controllable access to resources in a network. An ACL can also be used to exclude a particular system, IP address, or user.

15. A.   SMTP is the primary protocol used in e-mail. An SMTP virus filter checks all incoming and outgoing e-mails for suspicious code. If a file is potentially infected, the scanner notifies the originator and quarantines the file.

16. A.   DNS records in a DNS server provide insights into the nature and structure of a network. DNS records should be kept to a minimum in public DNS servers. Network footprinting involves the attacker collecting data about the network to devise methods of intrusion.

17. A.   Lightweight Directory Access Protocol (LDAP) is a directory access protocol used to publish information about users. This is the computer equivalent of a phone book.

18. B.   Relational database systems are the most frequently installed database environments in use today.

19. A.   SQL is a powerful database access language used by most relational database systems.

20. C.   A three-tiered model puts a server between the client and the database.

Chapter

6

Securing the Network and Environment

THE FOLLOWING COMPTIA SECURITY+ EXAM OBJECTIVES ARE COVERED IN THIS CHAPTER:

✓ **3.1 Identify and apply industry best practices for access control methods.**

- Implicit deny
- Least privilege
- Separation of duties
- Job rotation

✓ **3.9 Explain and apply physical access security methods.**

- Physical access logs/lists
- Hardware locks
- Physical access control—ID badges
- Door access systems
- Man-trap
- Physical tokens
- Video surveillance—camera types and positioning

✓ **4.1 Conduct risk assessments and implement risk mitigation.**

✓ **6.4 Identify and explain applicable legislation and organizational policies.**

- User education and awareness training

✓ **6.5 Explain the importance of environmental controls.**

- Fire suppression
- HVAC
- Shielding

✓ **6.6 Explain the concept of and how to reduce the risks of social engineering.**

- Shoulder surfing
- User education and awareness training

Several years back, *InformationWeek* conducted a survey in partnership with Accenture. As part of the survey, the question, "What are the biggest security challenges facing your company?" was asked. Multiple responses were allowed, and 58 percent of the respondents stated that managing the complexity of security was one of their biggest challenges. As evident by this survey, security is a major concern for many organizations. Keeping computers and networks secure involves more than just the technical aspects of the systems and networks. You must address the physical environment and the business as it exists. Doing so involves evaluating physical security, social engineering issues, and environmental issues; some of these topics were introduced in earlier chapters, but they're tied together cohesively here. All of these issues require a balanced response from both a technical perspective and a business perspective.

This chapter will help you understand the importance of physical security measures such as access controls, physical barriers, and biometric systems. It also covers social engineering and the environment your systems need in order to be safe and operational. This chapter also discusses securing the network and looks at security zones and partitioning. Finally, this chapter addresses business issues, including planning, policies, standards, guidelines, security standards, and information classification.

Understanding Physical and Network Security

Physical security measures prevent your systems from being accessed in unauthorized ways, primarily by preventing an unauthorized user from physically touching a system or device. Most networked systems have developed high levels of sophistication and security from outside intruders. However, these systems are generally vulnerable to internal attacks, sabotage, and misuse. If an intruder has physical access to your systems, you should never consider them to be secure.

The following sections discuss the aspects of physical security that affect your environment, including access controls, social engineering, and the environment.

Implementing Access Control

Access control is a critical part of physical security. Systems must operate in controlled environments in order to be secure. These environments must be, as much as possible, safe from intrusion. Computer system consoles can be a vital point of vulnerability because many administrative functions can be accomplished from the system console. These consoles, as well as the systems themselves, must be protected from physical access. Two areas that help make a system secure are physical barriers and biometrics, both of which are discussed in the following sections.

Physical Barriers

A key aspect of access control involves *physical barriers*. The objective of a physical barrier is to prevent access to computers and network systems. The most effective physical barrier implementations require that more than one physical barrier be crossed to gain access. This type of approach is called a *multiple barrier system*.

Ideally, your systems should have a minimum of three physical barriers. The first barrier is the external entrance to the building, referred to as a *perimeter*, which is protected by burglar alarms, external walls, surveillance, and so on. The second barrier is the entrance to the computer center, which is behind a locked door, and could rely upon such items as *ID badges*, fobs, or keys to gain access. The third barrier is the entrance to the computer room itself. Each of these entrances can be individually secured, monitored, and protected with alarm systems. Figure 6.1 illustrates this concept.

FIGURE 6.1 The three-layer security model

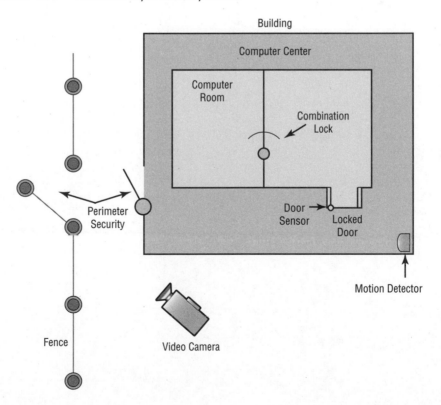

Although these three barriers won't always stop intruders, they will potentially slow them down enough that law enforcement can respond before an intrusion is fully developed. Once inside, a truly secure site should be dependent upon a *physical token* for access to the actual network resources.

Physical tokens are anything that a user must have on them to access network resources and are often associated with devices that enable the user to generate a one-time password authenticating their identity. SecurID, from RSA, is one of the best known examples of a physical token, and information on it can be found at http://www.rsa.com/node.aspx?id=1156.

No matter how secure you think your system is, you'll never be able to stop everyone. But your goal is to stop those who are less than fanatic and slow down the ones who are. As an analogy, the front door of your home may contain a lock and a deadbolt. This minimal security is enough to convince most burglars to try somewhere less secure. A fanatic who is bent on entering your home, however, could always take a chain saw or similar tool to the door.

High-security installations use a type of intermediate access-control mechanism called a *mantrap* (also occasionally written as *man-trap*). Mantraps require visual identification, as well as authentication, to gain access. A mantrap makes it difficult for a facility to be accessed in number because it allows only one or two people into the facility at a time. It's usually designed to physically contain an unauthorized, potentially hostile person until authorities arrive. Figure 6.2 illustrates a mantrap. Notice in this case that the visual verification is accomplished using a security guard. A properly developed mantrap includes bulletproof glass, high-strength doors, and locks. In high-security and military environments, an armed guard, as well as video surveillance, would be placed at the mantrap. After you're inside the facility, additional security and authentication may be required for further entrance.

FIGURE 6.2 A mantrap in action

Some mantraps even include scales to weigh the person. While the weight can be used to help identify a person, often the scales are used to make certain no one is sneaking in. If the weight of the scale appears too high, an officer can check to make sure two people haven't crowded in and are attempting to quickly bypass security.

The following sections discuss perimeter security, the establishment of security zones, and partitioning.

Perimeter Security

Perimeter security, whether physical or technological, is the first line of defense in your security model. In the case of a physical security issue, the intent is to prevent unauthorized access to resources inside a building or facility.

The network equivalent of physical perimeter security is intended to accomplish for a network what perimeter security does for a building. How do you keep unauthorized intruders from gaining access to systems and information in the network through the network?

In the physical environment, perimeter security is accomplished using locks, doors, surveillance systems, and alarm systems. This isn't functionally any different from a network, which uses border routers, intrusion detection systems, and firewalls to prevent unauthorized access. Figure 6.3 illustrates the systems used to prevent network intrusion.

Few security systems can be implemented that don't have weaknesses or vulnerabilities. A determined intruder can, with patience, overcome most security systems. The task may not be easy, and it may require careful planning and study; however, a determined adversary can usually figure out a way.

FIGURE 6.3   Network perimeter defense

If you want to deter intruders from breaking into your building, you can install improved door locks, coded alarm systems, and magnetic contacts on doors and windows. Remember that you can't always keep an intruder out of your building; however, you can make an intrusion riskier and more likely to be discovered if it happens.

> Don't overlook the obvious. Adding a security guard to the front door will go a long way toward keeping an intruder out.

Real World Scenario

Circumventing Security

Recently, a small business noticed that the level of network traffic seemed to be very high in the late evening and early morning. The business couldn't find a network-related reason why this was happening. Upon investigation, the security consultant found that a part-time employee had established a multiuser game server in his office. The game server was set to turn on after 10:00 p.m. and turn off at 5:30 a.m. This server was hidden under a desk, and it supported around 30 local game players. The part-time employee didn't have a key to the building, so an investigation was conducted to determine how he gained access to the building after hours. The building had electronic locks on its outside entrances, and a pass card was needed to open the doors. However, the door locks were designed to automatically unlock when someone was leaving the building.

The investigation discovered that the employee and a friend had figured out a way to slide a piece of cardboard under one of the external doors, which activated the door mechanisms and unlocked the doors. The intruders took advantage of this weakness in the doors to gain access after hours without using a passcard and then used the server to play games in his office.

Security Zones

A *security zone* is an area in a building where access is individually monitored and controlled. A large network, such as a large physical plant, can have many areas that require restricted access. In a building, floors, sections of floors, and even offices can be broken down into smaller areas. These smaller zones are referred to as security zones. In the physical environment, each floor is broken into separate zones. An alarm system that identifies a zone of intrusion can inform security personnel about an intruder's location in the building; zone notification tells them where to begin looking when they enter the premises.

The concept of security zones is as old as security itself. Most burglar alarms allow the creation of individual zones within a building or residence; these zones are treated separately. When you go to bed, for example, the alarm shouldn't monitor the bedroom for movement because it's perfectly acceptable there.

Real World Scenario

Security Zones in the Physical Environment

As a security administrator, you'll need to evaluate your workplace and think of physical zones that should exist in terms of different types of individuals who might be present. If your workplace is already divided into zones, forget that this has been done and start from scratch. Answer the following questions:

1. What areas represent the physical dimension of your workplace (buildings, floors, offices, and so on)?

2. Which areas are accessible by everyone from administrators to visitors? Can a visitor ever leave the reception area without an escort, and if so, to go where (bathroom, break room, and so forth)?

3. In what areas are users allowed to move about freely? Are you certain that no visitors or guests could enter those areas?

4. What areas are administrators allowed to enter that users can't? Server room? Wiring closets? How do you keep users out and verify that only administrators enter?

5. Do other areas need to be secured for entities beyond the user/administrator distinction (such as groups)?

You should evaluate your environment routinely to make certain the zones that exist within your security plan are still relevant. Always start from scratch and pretend that no zones exist; then verify that the zones that do exist are the same as those you've created from this exercise.

The networking equivalent of a security zone is a network security zone. They perform the same function. If you divide a network into smaller sections, each zone can have its own security considerations and measures—just like a physical security zone. Figure 6.4 illustrates a larger network being broken down into three smaller zones. Notice that the first zone also contains a smaller zone where high-security information is stored. This arrangement allows layers of security to be built around sensitive information. The division of the network is accomplished by implementing virtual LANs (VLANs) and instituting demilitarized zones (DMZs), both of which are discussed in Chapter 1, "General Security Concepts."

Partitioning

Partitioning a network is functionally the same as partitioning a building. In a building, walls exist to direct pedestrian flow, provide access control, and separate functional areas. This process allows information and property to be kept under physical lock and key.

FIGURE 6.4 Network security zones

 Partitions can be either temporary or permanent structures.

Hallways in an office building are usually built differently from internal office space. Hallways are usually more flame resistant, and they're referred to as *fire corridors.* These corridors allow people in the building to escape in the event of a fire. Fire corridor walls go from the floor to the ceiling, whereas internal walls can stop before they reach the ceiling (most office buildings have a false ceiling in them to hold lighting, wiring, and plumbing).

Network partitioning accomplishes the same function for a network as physical partitioning does for a building. Buildings have physical walls, whereas network partitioning involves the creation of private networks within larger networks. Partitions can be isolated from each other using routers and firewalls.

Therefore, while the network systems are all connected using wire, the functional view is that of many smaller networks. Figure 6.5 shows a partitioned network. It's important to realize that unless a physical device (such as a router) separates these partitioned networks, all the signals are shared across the wire. This device accomplishes the same function as a hallway or locked door—from a purely physical perspective.

 Partitioning and security zones are essentially interchangeable. Typically, partitioning is more narrowly focused than zones, but this need not always be the case. In a typical installation, a zone would encompass one floor, while a partition would include one room.

FIGURE 6.5   Network partitioning separating networks from each other in a larger network

 Real World Scenario

Evaluating Your Security System

You've been asked to evaluate your building's security system. The president chose you because you understand computers, and after all, these new alarm systems are computerized.

In evaluating the environment, you notice that there is a single control panel for the whole building. A few motion detectors are located in the main hallway. Beyond that, no additional security components are installed.

This situation is fairly normal in a small building. You could recommend enhancing the system by adding motion detectors in each major hallway. You could also install video surveillance cameras, such as closed-circuit television (CCTV), at all the entrances. You should also consider upgrading your perimeter security by adding contact sensors on all the doors and ground-floor windows.

Evaluate the building from a multi-tiered approach. Incorporate perimeter security, security zones, and surveillance where needed.

Biometrics

Biometric systems use some kind of unique biological trait to identify a person, such as fingerprints, patterns on the retina, and handprints. Some of the devices that are used are hand scanners, retinal scanners, and, potentially, DNA scanners, which can be used as part of the access control mechanisms. These devices should be coupled into security-oriented computer systems that record all access attempts. They should also be under surveillance in order to prevent individuals from bypassing them.

These technologies are becoming more reliable, and they will become widely used over the next few years. Many laptops sold now have a fingerprint reader built in. The costs associated with these technologies have fallen drastically in recent years.

 Real World Scenario

Installing Biometric Devices

You've been asked to solve the problem of people forgetting the smart cards that give them access to the computer center. Hardly a day goes by that a company employee doesn't forget to bring their card. This can cause a great deal of disruption in the work-place because someone has to constantly reissue smart cards. The company has tried everything it can think of short of firing people who forget their cards. What could you recommend to the company?

Investigate whether biometric devices (such as hand scanners) or number access locks can be used in lieu of smart cards for access. These devices will allow people who forget their smart cards to enter areas that they should be able to access.

Understanding Social Engineering

Social engineering is the process by which intruders gain access to your facilities, your network, and even to your employees by exploiting the generally trusting nature of people. A social engineering attack may come from someone posing as a vendor or as e-mail from a (supposedly) traveling executive who indicates that they have forgotten how to log on to the network or how to get into the building over the weekend. It's often difficult to determine whether the individual is legitimate or has nefarious intentions.

 Occasionally, social engineering is also referred to as *wetware*. This term is used because it is a form of hacking that does not require software or hardware but rather the gray matter of the brain.

Social engineering attacks can develop subtly. They're also hard to detect. Let's look at some classic social engineering attacks:

- Someone enters your building wearing a white lab jacket with a logo on it. He also has a toolkit. He approaches the receptionist and identifies himself as a copier repairman from a major local copier company. He indicates that he's here to do preventive service on your copier. In most cases, the receptionist will let him pass and tell him where the copier is. Once the "technician" is out of sight, the receptionist probably won't give him a second thought. Your organization has just been the victim of a social engineering attack. The attacker has now penetrated your first and possibly even your second layer of security. In many offices, including security-oriented offices, this individual would have access to the entire organization and would be able to pass freely anywhere he wanted. This attack didn't take any particular talent or skill other than the ability to look like a copier repairman. Impersonation can go a long way in allowing access to a building or network.

- The next example is a true situation; it happened at a high-security government installation. Access to the facility required passing through a series of manned checkpoints. Professionally trained and competent security personnel manned these checkpoints. An employee decided to play a joke on the security department: He took an old employee badge, cut his picture out of it, and pasted in a picture of Mickey Mouse. He was able to gain access to the facility for two weeks before he was caught.

Social engineering attacks like these are easy to accomplish in most organizations. Even if your organization uses biometric devices, magnetic card strips, or other electronic measures, social engineering attacks are still relatively simple. A favorite method of gaining entry to electronically locked systems is to follow someone through the door they just unlocked, a process known as *tailgating*. Many people don't think twice about this event—it happens all the time.

 Famed hacker Kevin Mitnick wrote a book called *The Art of Deception: Controlling the Human Element of Security* (Wiley Publishing, Inc., 2002), in which 14 of the 16 chapters are devoted to social engineering scenarios that have been played out. If nothing else, the fact that one of the most notorious hackers known—who could write on any security subject he wants—chose to write a book on social engineering should emphasize the importance of the topic to you.

As an administrator, one of your responsibilities is to educate users on how to avoid falling prey to social engineering attacks. They should know the security procedures that are in place and follow them to a tee. You should also have a high level of confidence that the correct procedures are in place, and one of the best ways to obtain that confidence is to check your users on occasion.

Preventing social engineering attacks involves more than just training on how to detect and prevent them. It also involves making sure people stay alert. One form of social engineering is known as *shoulder surfing* and involves nothing more than watching someone when they enter their sensitive data. They can see you entering a password, typing in a credit card number, or entering any other pertinent information. The best defense against this type of attack is simply to survey your environment before entering personal data.

Social engineering is easy to do, even with all of today's technology at our disposal. Education is the one key that can help.

Don't overlook the most common personal motivator of all: greed. It may surprise you, but people can be bribed to give away information. If someone gives out the keys, you won't necessarily know it has occurred. Those keys can be literal—as in the keys to the back door—or figurative—the keys to decrypt messages.

The movie and book *The Falcon and the Snowman* detailed the accounts of two young men, Christopher Boyce and Daulton Lee, who sold sensitive United States codes to the Russians for several years. The damage they did to U.S. security efforts was incalculable. In another case, U.S. Navy Petty Officer John Walker sold electronic key sets to the Russians that gave them access to communications between the U.S. Navy and the nuclear submarine fleet in the Atlantic. Later, he sold information and keys on ground forces in Vietnam. His actions cost the U.S. Army countless lives. During the height of his activities, he recruited family members and others to gather this information for him. In each of these cases, money was the motivating factor that led them to commit these crimes.

It is often a comforting thought to think that we cannot be bought. We look to our morals and standards and think that we are above being bribed. The truth of the matter, though, is that almost everyone has a price. Your price may be so high that for all practical purposes you don't have a price that anyone in the market would pay, but can the same be said for the other administrators in your company?

Social engineering can have a hugely damaging effect on a security system, as the previous note illustrates. Always remember that a social engineering attack can occur over the phone, by e-mail, or by a visit. The intent is to acquire access information, such as user IDs and passwords.

Scanning the Environment

The environment in which your business operates is bigger than the mere physical facility that houses your computers and employees. It also includes wireless cells, physical locations, shielding, and fire suppression. The following sections discuss these four areas to help you prepare for the exam.

Wireless Cells

The advent of wireless technology has created a wealth of solutions and problems for security professionals. The ability to use small, low-powered devices, such as cell phones, makes this technology attractive for mobile workers. Manufacturers now make smart phones that can also act as PDAs. Adapters are available for most PC systems that allow them connection to cell phones. New cell sites are being added internationally, and the coverage area of cell phones is increasing exponentially.

The technology is based upon small, low-powered transmitters located strategically throughout a coverage area. A cell provider is given approximately 800 separate frequencies to use in a coverage area. The frequencies are then broken down into roughly 56 channels in a single cell. Figure 6.6 shows this coverage scheme.

FIGURE 6.6   A cell system in a metropolitan area

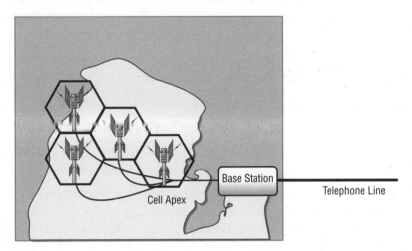

The individual cells have a high level of computer intelligence, and they hand off conversations to each other automatically. Cell phones in the United States operate in the 824MHz to 894MHz range. The Federal Communications Commission (FCC) requires police scanners to bypass these frequencies in the United States; most other countries don't require this frequency blocking in communications equipment.

For additional information on frequencies, beyond what you need to know for the exam, visit `http://electronics.howstuffworks.com/cell-phone10.htm`.

It's a federal crime to monitor or eavesdrop on cell phone frequencies, though there are exceptions, as with the Patriot Act.

Cell phones use analog as well as digital transmission capabilities. The analog cell systems allow approximately 60 simultaneous conversations to occur in a single cell. Digital technology expands that to about 180 simultaneous conversations. New applications, which will allow for cell-based banking and other transactions, are being added to cell technology.

Global System for Mobile Communications (GSM), the newest standard for cell systems, offers encryption. GSM works in conjunction with a *Subscriber Identification Module (SIM),* allowing users to change phones. The SIM is a removable card that can be moved from one phone to another. Unfortunately, U.S. and European cell standards aren't interchangeable, although many manufacturers are now selling dual-mode phones.

Many people believe that cell phones are untraceable and that you can't determine the location of a cellular user. This isn't the case. When a cell phone is turned on, it immediately identifies itself to the cell that is closest to it. The cell systems can triangulate a cell user to within a few feet. This can be done even if the phone isn't in use but is merely turned on. The point of origin can be determined in only a few moments because the process is largely computerized.

 Real World Scenario

Securing Your Wireless Devices

You've become increasingly concerned about secure access to your network using wireless devices. Many managers and other employees use wireless personal digital assistants (PDAs) to communicate when they're away from the office. What can you do to secure these devices?

You may want to implement a wireless security protocol (such as Wireless Transport Layer Security [WTLS] or Elliptic Curve Cryptography [ECC]) in these devices and in your network. Doing so would allow communications to occur between wireless users and your network.

Physical Location

The location of your computer facility is critical to its security. Computer facilities must be placed in a location that is physically possible to secure. Additionally, the location must have the proper capabilities to manage temperature, humidity, and other environmental factors necessary to the health of your computer systems. The following sections look at environmental and power systems.

Environmental Systems

Many computer systems require temperature and humidity control for reliable service. The larger servers, communications equipment, and drive arrays generate considerable amounts of heat; this is especially true of mainframe and older minicomputers. An environmental system for this type of equipment is a significant expense beyond the actual computer system costs. Fortunately, newer systems operate in a wider temperature range. Most new systems are designed to operate in an office environment.

If the computer systems you're responsible for require special environmental considerations, you'll need to establish cooling and humidity control. Ideally, systems are located in the middle of the building, and they're ducted separately from the rest of the HVAC system. It's a common practice for modern buildings to use a zone-based air conditioning environment, which allows the environmental plant to be turned off when the building isn't occupied. A computer room will typically require full-time environmental control.

Environmental systems should be monitored to prevent the computer center's humidity level from dropping below 50 percent. Electrostatic damage is likely to occur when humidity levels get too low.

Humidity control prevents the buildup of static electricity in the environment. If the humidity drops much below 50 percent, electronic components are extremely vulnerable to damage from electrostatic shock. Most environmental systems also regulate humidity; however, a malfunctioning system can cause the humidity to be almost entirely extracted from a room. Make sure that environmental systems are regularly serviced.

Environmental concerns also include considerations about water and flood damage as well as fire suppression. Computer rooms should have fire and moisture detectors. Most office buildings have water pipes and other moisture-carrying systems in the ceiling. If a water pipe bursts (which is common in minor earthquakes), the computer room could become flooded. Water and electricity don't mix. Moisture monitors would automatically kill power in a computer room if moisture were detected.

Fire, no matter how small, can cause damage to computer systems. Apart from the high heat, which can melt or warp plastics and metals, the smoke from the fire can permeate the computers. Smoke particles are large enough to lodge under the read/write head of a hard disk, thereby causing data loss. In addition, the fire-suppression systems in most buildings consist of water under pressure, and the water damage from putting out even a small fire could wipe out an entire data center.

The three critical components of any fire are heat, fuel, and oxygen. If any component of this trilogy is removed, a fire isn't possible. Most fire-suppression systems work on this concept.

Fire suppression is discussed further in this chapter in the section by the same name, "Fire Suppression."

Power Systems

Computer systems are susceptible to power and interference problems. A computer requires a steady input of AC power to produce reliable DC voltage for its electronic systems. *Power systems* are designed to operate in a wide band of power characteristics; they help keep the electrical service constant, and they ensure smooth operations.

Real World Scenario

Simple Things Can Have Huge Consequences

Water can come from anywhere, and you need to be prepared when it does. Several years ago, a business had a state-of-the-art server room on the top floor of its building. The room was climate controlled and a true thing of beauty. Directly above the server room was the roof, and on the roof was the bank of air conditioners for the six-floor building. Over the course of one extremely hot weekend, the drain lines for the condensation from the air conditioners clogged. The lines filled with water and then burst, and the water came through the roof into the attic. Once in the attic, all the water worked its way to the lowest spot and created a hole in the ceiling—directly above the servers. Everything was fried in a short period of time.

As simple as it sounds, such things happen all the time. When they do, you need to be ready with backups—backup tapes, backup servers, backup monitors, and so on.

Major fluctuations in AC power can contribute to a condition known as *chip creep*. With creep, unsoldered chips slowly work their way loose and out of a socket over time.

The following products solve most electrical line problems:

Surge protectors   *Surge protectors* protect electrical components from momentary or instantaneous increases (called *spikes*) in a power line. Most surge protectors shunt a voltage spike to ground through the use of small devices called *metal oxide varistors (MOVs)*. Large-scale surge protectors are usually found in building power supplies or at power-feed points in the building. Portable surge protectors can be purchased as part of an extension cord or power strip. If subsequent surges occur, the surge protector may not prevent them from being passed through the line to the computer system. Surge protectors are passive devices, and they accomplish no purpose until a surge occurs.

Power conditioners   *Power conditioners* are active devices that effectively isolate and regulate voltage in a building. They monitor the power in the building and clean it up. Power conditioners usually include filters, surge suppressors, and temporary voltage regulation. They can also activate backup power supplies. Power conditioners can be part of the overall building power scheme; it's also common to see them dedicated strictly to computer rooms.

Backup power   *Backup power* is generally used in situations where continuous power is needed in the event of a power loss. These types of systems are usually designed for either short-term, as in the case of a battery backup system, or long-term uses, as in an *uninterruptible power supply (UPS)*. UPS systems generally use batteries to provide short-term power. Longer-term backup power comes from power generators that frequently have their own power-loss-sensing circuitry. Power generators kick in if a power loss is detected, and they provide power until disabled. The generators require a short amount of time to start providing power, and the battery backup systems provide time for the generators to come online. Most generator systems don't automatically turn off when power is restored to a building—they're turned off manually. This is necessary because it's common for several false starts to occur before power is restored from the power grid.

Most power generators are either gas or diesel operated, and they require preventive maintenance on a regular basis. These systems aren't much use if they don't start when needed or they fail because no oil is in the motor. Newer systems are becoming available that are based on fuel cell technology; they will probably be very reliable and require less maintenance.

Shielding

Shielding refers to the process of preventing electronic emissions from your computer systems from being used to gather intelligence and to preventing outside electronic emissions from disrupting your information processing abilities. In a fixed facility, such as a computer center, surrounding the computer room with a *Faraday cage* can provide electronic shielding. A Faraday cage usually consists of an electrically conductive wire mesh or other conductor woven into a "cage" that surrounds a room. The conductor is then grounded. Because of this cage, few electromagnetic signals can either enter or leave the room, thereby reducing the ability to eavesdrop on a computer conversation. In order to verify the functionality of the cage, radio frequency (RF) emissions from the room are tested with special measuring devices.

The following section discusses the problems of electromagnetic and radio frequency interference.

Electromagnetic Interference and Radio Frequency Interference

Electromagnetic interference (EMI) and *radio frequency interference (RFI)* are two additional environmental considerations. Motors, lights, and other types of electromechanical objects cause EMI, which can cause circuit overload, spikes, or electrical component failure. Making sure that all signal lines are properly shielded and grounded can minimize EMI. Devices that generate EMI should be as physically distant from cabling as is feasible because this type of energy tends to dissipate quickly with distance.

Figure 6.7 shows a motor generating EMI. In this example, the data cable next to the motor is picking up the EMI. This causes the signal to deteriorate, and it might eventually cause the line to be unusable. The gray area in the illustration is representative of the interference generated by the motor.

RFI is the by product of electrical processes, similar to EMI. The major difference is that RFI is usually projected across a radio spectrum. Motors with defective brushes can generate RFI, as can a number of other devices. If RF levels become too high, it can cause the receivers in wireless units to become deaf. This process is called *desensitizing,* and it occurs because of the volume of RF energy present. This can occur even if the signals are on different frequencies.

Figure 6.8 demonstrates the desensitizing process occurring with a wireless access portal (WAP). The only solutions in this situation would be to move the devices farther apart or to turn off the RFI generator.

FIGURE 6.7   Electromagnetic interference (EMI) pickup in a data cable

FIGURE 6.8   RF desensitization occurring as a result of cellular phone interference

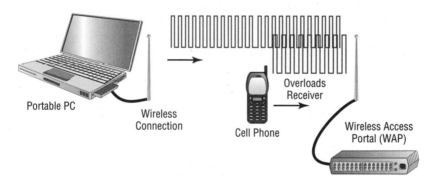

Project TEMPEST

TEMPEST is the name of a project commenced by the U.S. government in the late 1950s. TEMPEST was concerned with reducing electronic noise from devices that would divulge intelligence about systems and information. This program has become a standard for computer systems certification. *TEMPEST shielding protection* means that a computer system doesn't emit any significant amounts of EMI or RFI. For a device to be approved as a TEMPEST, it must undergo extensive testing, done to exacting standards that the U.S. government dictates. Today, control zones and white noise are used to accomplish the shielding. TEMPEST-certified equipment frequently costs twice as much as non-TEMPEST equipment.

Fire Suppression

Fire suppression is a key consideration in computer-center design. Fire suppression is the act of actually extinguishing a fire versus preventing one. Two primary types of fire-suppression systems are in use: fire extinguishers and fixed systems.

Fire Extinguishers

Fire extinguishers are portable systems. The selection and use of fire extinguishers is critical. Four primary types of fire extinguishers are available, classified by the types of fires they put out: A, B, C, and D. Table 6.1 describes the four types of fires and the capabilities of various extinguishers.

TABLE 6.1 Fire Extinguisher Ratings

Type	Use	Retardant Composition
A	Wood and paper	Largely water or chemical
B	Flammable liquids	Fire-retardant chemicals
C	Electrical	Nonconductive chemicals
D	Flammable metals	Varies, type specific

Several multipurpose types of extinguishers combine extinguisher capabilities in a single bottle. The more common multipurpose extinguishers are A-B, B-C, and ABC.

The recommended procedure for using a fire extinguisher is called the *PASS method*: Pull, Aim, Squeeze, and Sweep. Fire extinguishers usually operate for only a few seconds—if you use one, make sure you don't fixate on a single spot. Most fire extinguishers have a limited effective range of from three to eight feet.

A major concern with electrical fires is that they can reoccur quickly if the voltage isn't removed. Make sure you remove voltage from systems when a fire occurs.

Most fire extinguishers require an annual inspection. This is a favorite area of citation by fire inspectors. You can contract with services to do this on a regular basis: They will inspect or replace your fire extinguishers according to a scheduled agreement.

Fixed Systems

Fixed systems are usually part of the building systems. The most common fixed systems combine fire detectors with fire-suppression systems, where the detectors usually trigger either because of a rapid temperature change or because of excessive smoke. The fire-suppression system uses either water sprinklers or fire-suppressing gas. Water systems work with overhead nozzles, as illustrated in Figure 6.9. These systems are the most common method in modern buildings. Water systems are reliable and relatively inexpensive and require little maintenance.

FIGURE 6.9   Water-based fire-suppression system

The one drawback to water-based systems is that they cause extreme damage to energized electrical equipment such as computers. These systems can be tied into relays that terminate power to computer systems before they release water into the building.

Gas-based systems were originally designed to use carbon dioxide and later Halon gas. Halon gas isn't used anymore because it damages the ozone layer; environmentally acceptable substitutes are now available. The principle of a gas system is that it displaces the oxygen in the room, thereby removing this necessary component of a fire.

Evacuate the room immediately in the event of a fire. Gas-based systems work by removing oxygen from the fire, and this can suffocate anyone in the room as well.

The major drawback to gas-based systems is that they require sealed environments to operate. Special ventilation systems are usually installed in gas systems to limit air circulation when the gas is released. Gas systems are also expensive, and they're usually only implemented in computer rooms or other areas where water would cause damage to technology or other intellectual property.

Understanding Business Continuity Planning

Business Continuity Planning (BCP) is the process of implementing policies, controls, and procedures to counteract the effects of losses, outages, or failures of critical business processes. BCP is primarily a management tool that ensures that *critical business functions (CBF)* can be performed when normal business operations are disrupted.

Critical business functions refer to those processes or systems that must be made operational immediately when an outage occurs. The business can't function without them, and many are information intensive and require access to both technology and data.

Two of the key components of *BCP* are *Business Impact Analysis (BIA)* and *risk assessment*. BIA is concerned with evaluating the processes, and risk assessment is concerned with evaluating the risk or likelihood of a loss. Evaluating all the processes in an organization or enterprise is necessary in order for BCP to be effective.

You need only a passing knowledge of business continuity issues for the Security+ exam. If you plan on taking the Project+ exam, also from CompTIA, you will need a more thorough knowledge of the topics.

Undertaking Business Impact Analysis

Business Impact Analysis (BIA) is the process of evaluating all the critical systems in an organization to determine impact and recovery plans. The BIA isn't concerned with external threats or vulnerabilities; this analysis focuses on the impact a loss would have on the organization.

The key components of a BIA include the following:

Identifying critical functions   To identify critical functions, a company must ask itself, "What functions are necessary to continue operations until full service can be restored?" This identification process will help you establish which systems must be returned to operation in order for the business to continue. In performing this identification, you may find that a small or overlooked application in a department may be critical for operations. Many organizations have overlooked seemingly insignificant process steps or systems that have prevented BCP from being effective. Every department should be evaluated to ensure that no critical processes are overlooked.

Prioritizing critical business functions   When business is continued after an event, operations must be prioritized as to essential and nonessential functions. If the organization makes resources available to the recovery process, these resources may be limited. Further, in a widespread outage, full operation may not be possible for some time. What would happen, for example, if your data communications services went down? You can usually establish temporary services, but you probably won't be able to restore full network capability. You should be clear about which applications or systems have priority for the resources available. Your company may find itself choosing to restore e-mail before it restores its website.

Calculating a time frame for critical systems loss   How long can the organization survive without a critical function? Some functions in an organization don't require immediate action; others do. Which functions must be reestablished, and in what time frame? If your business is entirely dependent on its web presence and is e-commerce oriented, how long can the website stay inoperable? Your organization may need to evaluate and attempt to identify the maximum time that a particular function can be unavailable. This dictates the contingencies that must be made to minimize losses from exceeding the allowable period.

Estimating the tangible and intangible impact on the organization   Your organization will suffer losses in an outage. These losses will be of a tangible nature, such as lost production and lost sales. Intangible losses will also be a factor. For example, will customers lose faith in your service? Your discovery of these effects can greatly increase the company's realization of how much a loss of service will truly cost.

A thorough BIA will accomplish several things for your organization. First, the true impact and damage that an outage will cause will be visible. Second, like insurance, understanding the true loss potential may help you in your fight for a budget. Third, and perhaps most important, the process will document what business processes are being used, the impact they have on the organization, and how to restore them quickly.

The BIA will have some power in the organization as the costs of an outage become known. People buy insurance not because they intend to have an accident, but in case they do. A BIA can help identify what insurance is needed in order for the organization to feel safe.

Assessing Risk

Risk assessment (also referred to as a *risk analysis*) primarily deals with the threats, vulnerabilities, and impacts of a loss of information-processing capabilities or information. Each risk that can be identified should be outlined, described, and evaluated for the likelihood of it occurring. The key is to think out of the box. Conventional threats/risks are often too limited when considering risk assessment.

The key components of a risk-assessment process are outlined here:

Risks to which the organization is exposed   This component allows you to develop scenarios that can help you evaluate how to deal with these risks should they occur. An operating system, server, or application may have known risks in certain environments. How will your organization deal with these risks, and what is the best way to respond?

Risks that need addressing   The risk-assessment component also allows the organization to provide a reality check on which risks are real and which aren't likely. This process helps the organization focus its resources on the risks that are most likely to occur. For example, industrial espionage and theft are likely, but the risk of a pack of wild dogs stealing the entire contents of the payroll file is very low. Therefore, resources should be allocated to prevent espionage or theft as opposed to the latter possibility.

Coordination with BIA   The risk-assessment component, in conjunction with the BIA, provides the organization with an accurate picture of the situation facing it. It allows the organization to make intelligent decisions about how to respond to various scenarios.

Risk assessment can be either qualitative or quantitative, depending upon whether you are focusing on dollar amounts or not. The formulas for single loss expectancy (SLE), annual loss expectancy (ALE), and annualized rate of occurrence (ARO) are all based on doing assessments that lead to dollar amounts.

 Real World Scenario

Conducting a Risk Assessment

You've been asked to do a quick assessment of the risks your company faces from a security perspective. What steps might you take to develop an overview of your company's problems?

You should interview the department heads and the owners to determine what information they feel needs additional security and what the existing vulnerabilities are from their perspectives. You should also evaluate the servers to determine their known vulnerabilities and how you might counter them. Additionally, you should make sure you do a physical assessment of the facility to evaluate what physical risks you must counter. Armed with this information, you have a place to start, and you can determine which measures may be appropriate for the company from a risk perspective.

When you're doing a risk assessment, one of the most important things to do is to prioritize. Not everything should be weighed evenly because some events have a greater likelihood of happening; in addition, a company can live with some risks, whereas others would be catastrophic. One method of measurement to consider is *annualized rate of occurrence (ARO)*. This is the likelihood, often drawn from historical data, of an event occurring within a year. This measure can be used in conjunction with a monetary value assigned to data to compute *single loss expectancy (SLE)* and *annual loss expectancy (ALE)* values.

When you're computing risk assessment, remember this formula:

```
SLE x ARO = ALE
```

Thus, if you can reasonably expect that every SLE will be equivalent to $1,000 and that there will be seven occurrences a year (ARO), then the ALE is $7,000. Conversely, if there is only a 10 percent chance of an event occurring in a year (ARO = .1), then the ALE drops to $100.

 Real World Scenario

Risk-Assessment Computations

As a security professional, you should know how to compute SLE, ALE, and ARO. Given any two of the numbers, it's possible to calculate the third. For this exercise, compute the missing values:

1. You're the administrator of a web server that generates $25,000 per hour in revenue. The probability of the web server failing is estimated to be 25 percent, and a failure would lead to three hours of downtime and cost $5,000 in components to correct. What is the ALE?

    The SLE is $80,000 ($25,000 x 3 hours + $5,000), and the ARO is .25. Therefore the ALE is $20,000 ($80,000 x .25).

2. You're the administrator for a research firm that works on only one project at a time and collects data through the Web to a single server. The value of each research project is approximately $100,000. At any given time, an intruder could commandeer no more than 90 percent of the data. The industry average for ARO is .33. What is the ALE?

    The SLE equals $90,000 ($100,000 x .9), and the ARO is .33. Therefore, the ALE is $29,700 ($90,000 x .33).

3. You work at the help desk for a small company. One of the most common requests you must respond to is to help retrieve a file that has been accidentally deleted by a user. On average, this happens once a week. If the user creates the file and then deletes it on the server (about 60 percent of the incidents), then it can be restored in moments from the shadow copy, and there is rarely any data lost. If the user creates the file on their workstation and then deletes it (about 40 percent of the incidents), and if it can't be recovered and it takes the user an average of two hours to re-create it at $12 an hour, what is the ALE?

    The SLE is $24 ($12 x 2), and the ARO is 20.8 (52 weeks x .4). Therefore the ALE equals $499.20 ($24 x 20.8).

Developing Policies, Standards, and Guidelines

The process of implementing and maintaining a secure network must first be addressed from a policies, standards, and guidelines perspective. This sets the tone, provides authority, and gives your efforts the teeth they need to be effective. Policies and guidelines set a standard of expectation in an organization. The process of developing these policies will help everyone in an organization become involved and invested in making security efforts successful. You can think of policies as providing the big picture on issues. Standards tell people what is expected, and guidelines provide specific advice on how to accomplish a given task or activity.

The next sections discuss the policies, standards, and guidelines you need to establish in order for your security efforts to be successful.

Implementing Policies

Policies provide the people in an organization with guidance about their expected behavior. Well-written policies are clear and concise, and they outline consequences when they aren't followed. A good policy contains several key areas besides the policy:

Scope statement   A good policy has a scope statement that outlines what the policy intends to accomplish and what documents, laws, and practices the policy addresses. The scope statement provides background to help readers understand what the policy is about and how it applies to them.

> The scope statement is always brief—usually not more than a single sentence in length.

Policy overview statement   Policy overview statements provide the goal of the policy, why it's important, and how to comply with it. Ideally, a single paragraph is all you need to provide readers with a sense of the policy.

Policy statements   Once the policy's readers understand its importance, they should be informed of what the policy is. Policy statements should be as clear and unambiguous as possible. The policy may be presented in paragraph form, as bulleted lists, or as checklists.

The presentation will depend on the policy's target audience as well as its nature. If the policy is intended to help people determine how to lock up the building at the end of the business day, it might be helpful to provide a specific checklist of the steps that should be taken.

Accountability statement   The policy should address who is responsible for ensuring that it is enforced. This statement provides additional information to the reader about who to contact if a problem is discovered. It should also indicate the consequences of not complying with the policy.

> The accountability statement should be written in words the reader will understand. If the accountability statement is to be read by the users, then it must be written in such a way as to leave no room for misinterpretation.

Exception statement   Sometimes, even the best policy doesn't foresee every eventuality. The exception statement provides specific guidance about the procedure or process that must be followed in order to deviate from the policy. This may include an escalation contact, in the event that the person dealing with a situation needs to know whom to contact.

The policy development process is sometimes time consuming. The advantage of this process, though, is that the decisions can be made in advance and can be sent to all involved parties so the policy doesn't have to be restated over and over again. In fact, formally developing policies saves time and provides structure: Instead of using valuable time trying to figure out what to do, employees will know what to do.

Incorporating Standards

A *standard* deals with specific issues or aspects of the business. Standards are derived from policies. A standard should provide enough detail that an audit can be performed to determine if the standard is being met. Standards, like policies, have certain structural aspects in common.

The following five points are the key aspects of standards documents:

Scope and purpose   The standards document should explain or describe the intention. If a standard is developed for a technical implementation, the scope might include software, updates, add-ins, and any other relevant information that helps the implementer carry out the task.

Roles and responsibilities   This section of the standards document outlines who is responsible for implementing, monitoring, and maintaining the standard. In a system configuration, this section would outline what the customer is supposed to accomplish and what the installer is supposed to accomplish. This doesn't mean that one or the other can't exceed those roles; it means that in the event of confusion, it's clear who is responsible for accomplishing which tasks.

Reference documents   This section of the standards document explains how the standard relates to the organization's different policies, thereby connecting the standard to the underlying policies that have been put in place. In the event of confusion or uncertainty, it also allows people to go back to the source and figure out what the standard means. You'll encounter many situations throughout your career where you're given a standard that doesn't make sense. Frequently, by referring back to the policies, you can figure out why the standard was written the way it was. Doing so may help you carry out the standard or inform the people responsible for the standard of a change or problem.

Performance criteria   This part of the standards document outlines what or how to accomplish the task. It should include relevant baseline and technology standards. Baselines provide a minimum or starting point for the standard. Technology standards provide information about the platforms and technologies. Baseline standards spell out high-level requirements for the standard or technology.

 An important aspect of performance criteria is benchmarking. You need to define what will be measured and the metrics that will be used to do so.

If you're responsible for installing a server in a remote location, the standards spell out what type of computer will be used, what operating system will be installed, and any other relevant specifications.

Maintenance and administrative requirements   These standards outline what is required to manage and administer the systems or networks. In the case of a physical security requirement, the frequency with which locks or combinations are changed would be addressed.

As you can see, the standards documents provide a mechanism for both new and existing standards to be evaluated for compliance. The process of evaluation is called an *audit*. Increasingly, organizations are being required to conduct regular audits of their standards and policies.

Following Guidelines

Guidelines are slightly different from either policies or standards. Guidelines help an organization implement or maintain standards by providing information on how to accomplish the policies and maintain the standards.

Guidelines can be less formal than policies or standards because their nature is to help users comply with policies and standards. An example might be an explanation of how to install a service pack and what steps should be taken before doing so.

Guidelines aren't hard-and-fast rules. They may, however, provide a step-by-step process to accomplish a task. Guidelines, like standards and policies, should contain background information to help a user perform the task.

The following four items are the minimum contents of a good guidelines document:

Scope and purpose   The scope and purpose provide an overview and statement of the guideline's intent.

Roles and responsibilities   This section of the guidelines identifies which individuals or departments are responsible for accomplishing specific tasks. This may include implementation, support, and administration of a system or service. In a large organization, it's likely that the individuals involved in the process will have different levels of training and expertise. From a security perspective, it could be disastrous if an unqualified technician installed a system without guidelines.

Guideline statements   These statements provide the step-by-step instructions on how to accomplish a specific task in a specific manner. Again, these are guidelines—they may not be hard-and-fast rules.

Operational considerations   A guideline's operational considerations specify and identify what duties are required and at what intervals. This list might include daily, weekly, and monthly tasks. Guidelines for systems backup might provide specific guidance as to what files and directories must be backed up and how frequently.

Guidelines help an organization in several different ways. First, if a process or set of steps isn't performed routinely, experienced support and security staff will forget how to do them; guidelines will help refresh their memory. Second, when you're trying to train someone to do something new, written guidelines can improve the new person's learning curve. Third, when a crisis or high-stress situation occurs, guidelines can keep you from coming unglued.

Working with Security Standards and ISO 17799

Many companies are adopting comprehensive security standards for their organizations. If your organization is involved in government-related work, a standard is probably already in place and you'll be expected to follow it. The consequences can be dire if a policy violation occurs.

Increasingly, the need for security standards is being recognized worldwide. One of the security standards that is gaining acceptance is ISO 17799. This section briefly discusses this standard.

The International Organization for Standardization (ISO) published the *ISO 17799* standard, which is referred to as the Code of Practice for Information Security Management. The most recent version of the standard was published in June 2005. ISO 17799 identifies the major steps necessary to secure the IT environment.

 This material is provided only for background. You won't be tested on the ISO 17799 standard. Information about ISO 17799 is available in written form and online. A good place to get more information is http://csrc.nist .gov/publications/PubsSPs.html (the Code of Practice can be found at http://www.iso.org/iso/support/faqs/faqs_widely_used_standards/widely_ used_standards_other/information_security.htm).

The standard document outlines 11 areas of focus. An organization that successfully completes the work necessary to address these 11 areas can apply for certification. Auditors are brought in to verify that the areas are covered; this audit is comprehensive, and it requires advanced preparation.

Here are the 11 areas:

Security policy   The security policy includes the process for evaluating expectations, and it demonstrates management's support for and commitment to security.

Organization of information security   The organization area provides a structure to show who is responsible for security. This includes security coordinators, appropriate management delegation, and incident response processes.

Asset management   This area deals with assessment and inventory of the organization's information infrastructure and assets to determine whether an appropriate level of security is in place.

Human resources security   This area evaluates the human resources aspects of the business operation. Clear outlines of security expectations, screening processes, and confidentiality agreements are evaluated. This section also deals with how incident reporting occurs and who is responsible for dealing with incidents.

Physical and environmental security   This area deals with the policies and methods used to protect the IT infrastructure, physical plant, and employees. Aspects of backup power, routine maintenance, and onsite security are covered in this section.

Communications and operations management   Preventive measures (such as antivirus protection, monitoring system logs, remote communications security, and incident response procedures) are evaluated in this section.

Access control   This area evaluates mechanisms that protect an organization from internal and external intrusions. Issues such as password management, authentication systems, and event logging are part of this section.

Information systems acquisition, development, and maintenance   This area evaluates the measures that are taken in system development and software maintenance activities, including network deployment and expansion.

Information security incident management   This area deals with how the organization responds to an incident and the escalation procedures.

Business continuity management (BCM)   This area evaluates the organization's plans for dealing with man-made and natural disasters. The focus here is on how recovery will occur should an interruption occur.

Compliance   This area evaluates how well the organization complies with regulatory and legal requirements. It also evaluates compliance with internal privacy policies.

When the ISO 17799 standard was introduced in 1995, it didn't gain initial acceptance; many in the industry didn't feel that it was thorough enough to be a serious standard. Critics of the standard felt that the certification was oriented more toward giving advice than to providing a comprehensive certification process. This issue has been largely addressed in later revisions of the standard.

Classifying Information

Information classification is a key aspect of a secure network. Again, the process of developing a classification scheme is both a technical and a human issue. The technologies you use must be able to support your organization's privacy requirements. People and processes must be in place and working effectively to prevent unauthorized disclosure of sensitive information.

If you think about all the information your organization keeps, you'll probably find that it breaks down into three primary categories: public use, internal use, and restricted use. Figure 6.10 shows the typical ratios of how this information is broken down. Notice that 80 percent of the information in your organization is primarily for internal or private use. This information would include memos, working papers, financial data, and information records, among other things.

FIGURE 6.10   Information categories

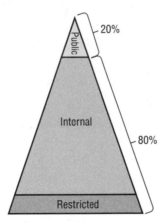

In the following sections, I'll discuss the various information classification systems, roles in the security process, and information access controls.

 You won't be tested on the information in the following sections. However, from a practical, real-world perspective, you should be familiar with these areas.

Public Information

Public information is primarily information that is made available either to the larger public or to specific individuals who need it. Financial statements of a privately held organization might be information that is available publicly, but only to individuals or organizations that have a legitimate need for it.

The important thing to keep in mind is that an organization needs to develop policies about what information is available and for what purposes it will be disseminated. It's also helpful to make sure that members of the organization know who has authorization to make these kinds of disclosures. There are organizations that gather competitive data for a fee; they often use social engineering approaches to gain information about a business. Good policies help prevent accidents from occurring with sensitive information.

The following sections discuss the difference between limited and full distribution.

Limited Distribution

Limited distribution information isn't intended for release to the public. This category of information isn't secret, but it's private. If a company is seeking to obtain a line of credit, the information provided to a bank is of a private nature. This information, if disclosed to competitors, might give them insight into the organization's plans or financial health. If disclosed to customers, it might scare them and cause them to switch to a competitor.

 Some End User License Agreements (EULAs) now limit the information that users can disclose about problems with their software. These new statements have not yet been challenged in court. Try to avoid being the test case for this new and alarming element of some software licenses; read the EULA before you agree to it.

These types of disclosures are usually held in confidence by banks and financial institutions. These institutions will typically have privacy and confidentiality regulations as well as policies that must be followed by all employees of the institution.

Software manufacturers typically release early versions of their products to customers who are willing to help evaluate functionality. Early versions of software may not always work properly, and they often have features that aren't included in the final version. This version of the software is a *beta test*. Before beta testers are allowed to use the software, they're required to sign a nondisclosure agreement (NDA). The NDA tells the tester what privacy requirements exist for the product. The product being developed will change, and any problems with the beta version probably won't be a great secret. However, the NDA reminds the testers of their confidentiality responsibilities.

 NDAs are common in the technology arena. Make sure you read any NDA thoroughly before you sign it. You don't have to sign an NDA to be bound by it: If you agree that you'll treat the information as private and then receive the information, you have in essence agreed to an NDA. In most cases, this form of verbal NDA is valid for only one year.

Statements indicating privacy or confidentiality are common on limited-access documents. They should indicate that disclosure of the information without permission is a breach of confidentiality. This may help someone remember that the information isn't for public dissemination.

Full Distribution

Marketing materials are examples of information that should be available for *full distribution*. Annual reports to stockholders and other information of a public-relations nature are also examples of full-distribution materials.

The key element of the full-distribution classification involves decision-making responsibility. Who makes the decision about full disclosure? Larger organizations have a corporate communications department that is responsible for managing this process. If you aren't sure, it's a good idea to ask about dissemination of information. Don't assume that you know: This is the purpose of an information classification policy.

Private Information

Private information is intended only for use internally in the organization. This type of information could potentially embarrass the company, disclose trade secrets, or adversely affect personnel. Private information may also be referred to as *working documents* or *work product*. It's important that private information not be disclosed because it can potentially involve litigation if the disclosure is improper.

You'll learn about the difference between internal and restricted information in the following sections.

Internal Information

Internal information includes personnel records, financial working documents, ledgers, customer lists, and virtually any other information that is needed to run a business. This information is valuable and must be protected.

In the case of personnel and medical records, disclosure to unauthorized personnel creates liability issues. Many organizations are unwilling to do anything more than verify employment because of the fear of unauthorized disclosure.

A school views student information as internal. Schools can't release information about students without specific permission from the student.

Restricted Information

Restricted information could seriously damage the organization if disclosed. It includes proprietary processes, trade secrets, strategic information, and marketing plans. This information should never be disclosed to an outside party unless senior management gives specific authorization. In many cases, this type of information is also placed on a *need-to-know basis*—unless you need to know, you won't be informed.

Government and Military Classifications

The U.S. government and the military have a slightly different set of concerns relating to information classification. Governmental agencies are concerned about privacy and national security. Because of this, a unique system of classification and access controls has been implemented to protect information.

Following is a list of some of the types of government classifications:

Unclassified   This classification is used to indicate that the information poses no risk of potential loss due to disclosure. Anybody can gain access to this category of information. Many training manuals and regulations are unclassified.

Sensitive but Unclassified   This classification is used for low-level security. It indicates that disclosure of this information might cause harm but wouldn't harm national defense efforts. The amount of toilet paper a military base uses may be considered sensitive because this information might help an intelligence agency guess at the number of personnel on the base.

Confidential   This classification is used to identify low-level secrets; it's generally the lowest level of classification used by the military. It's used extensively to prevent access to sensitive information. Information that is lower than Confidential is generally considered Unclassified. The Confidential classification, however, allows information to be restricted for access under the Freedom of Information Act. The maintenance requirements for a machine gun may be classified as Confidential; this information would include drawings, procedures, and specifications that disclose how the weapon works.

Secret   Secret information, if disclosed, could cause serious and irreparable damage to defense efforts. Information that is classified as Secret requires special handling, training, and storage. This information is considered a closely guarded secret of the military or government. Troop movements, deployments, capabilities, and other plans would be minimally classified as Secret. The military views the unauthorized disclosure of Secret information as criminal and potentially treasonous.

Top Secret   The Top Secret classification is the highest classification level. There are rumored to be higher levels of classification, but the names of those classifications are themselves classified Top Secret. Releasing information that is classified as Top Secret poses a grave threat to national security, and therefore it must not be compromised. Information such as intelligence activities, nuclear war plans, and weapons systems development would normally be classified as Top Secret.

The government has also developed a process to formally review and downgrade classification levels on a regular basis. This process generally downgrades information based on age, sensitivity, and usefulness. There are methods of overriding this downgrade process to prevent certain information from being declassified; some secrets are best left secret.

The military also uses an additional method of classifying information and access, which has the effect of compartmentalizing information. For example, if you were a weapons developer, it isn't likely that you would need access to information from spy satellites. You would be given special access to information necessary for the specific project you were working on. When the project was finished, access to this special information would be revoked. This process allows information to be protected and access limited to a need-to-know basis.

The process of obtaining a security clearance either for the military or for a government contractor can be quite involved. The normal process involves investigating you, your family, and potentially anybody else who could put you in a compromised position. The process can take months, and it includes agents doing fieldwork to complete, or augment, the investigation.

Roles in the Security Process

Effective security management requires the establishment of a clear set of roles and responsibilities for everyone involved in the process. You're learning to fill some of these roles as part of your Security+ certification:

Owner   The *owner* of data is primarily responsible for establishing its protection and use. The owner, in most situations, is a senior manager or other decision maker within an organization. The owner is responsible for making sure everyone follows all relevant and appropriate laws and regulations. Ultimately, the owner usually delegates some or all of the roles associated with the data to other individuals in the organization.

Custodian   The *custodian* of data is responsible for maintaining and protecting it. In a computer environment, the custodian is usually the IT department. Network administrators, backup operators, and others perform custodial functions on the data. The security policies, standards, and guidelines should lay out these responsibilities and provide mechanisms to perform them.

User   The *user* is the person or department that uses data. Users of data may perform input, output, editing, and other functions allowed by the role they have in the process.

Two additional roles warrant discussion, and you may find yourself doing one or both of them:

Security professional   *Security professionals* are concerned with one or more aspects of the process. They may be investigators, implementers, testers, or policy developers. Investigators become involved in the process when a security problem has been identified. Testers, on the other hand, may be called to look for exploits or to test security processes for weaknesses. Policy developers help management develop and implement policies for the organization.

Security professionals frequently encounter information they normally wouldn't need to know. Discretion is a critical skill for a security professional. For example, you may be asked to deny the existence of certain information in an organization. This implicit trust relationship shouldn't be taken lightly.

Auditor   *Auditors* are involved in the process of ensuring that practices, policies, mechanisms, and guidelines are followed within an organization. This function may involve reviewing documentation, reviewing activity logs, conducting interviews, and performing any number of other tasks necessary to ensure that organizational security policies are followed. The role of the auditor isn't that of a police officer but rather a consultant. An auditor can help an organization identify and correct deficiencies in security.

Each of these roles presents a special challenge and exposes you to information and processes that most individuals wouldn't encounter in an organization. It's important that you take these responsibilities seriously; you shouldn't divulge the information or processes you uncover to any unauthorized individuals. You must hold yourself to a higher standard than those around you.

Information Access Controls

Access control defines the methods used to ensure that users of your network can access only what they're authorized to access. The process of access control should be spelled out in the organization's security policies and standards. Several models exist to accomplish this. Regardless of the model you use, a few concepts carry over among them:

- Implicit denies are those wherein you specifically lock certain users out. In Unix, and Linux, for example, you can choose who can use the `at` service by configuring either an `at.allow` or `at.deny` file. If you configure the `at.allow` file, then only those users specifically named can use the service and all others cannot. Conversely, if you configure the `at.deny` file, then only the users named in that file cannot use the service (you are implicitly denying them) and all others can.

- Least privilege is the model you should use when assigning permissions. Give users only the permissions they need to do their work and no more.

- Rotate jobs on a frequent enough basis that you are not putting yourself—and your data—at the mercy of any one administrator. Just as you want redundancy in hardware, you want redundancy in abilities.

The following sections will briefly explain these models:

- Bell La-Padula model
- Biba model
- Clark-Wilson model
- Information Flow model
- Noninterference model

Noninterference Bell La-Padula Model

The *Bell La-Padula model* was designed for the military to address the storage and protection of classified information. The model is specifically designed to prevent unauthorized access to classified information. The model prevents the user from accessing information that has a higher security rating than they're authorized to access. The model also prevents information from being written to a lower level of security.

For example, if you're authorized to access Secret information, you aren't allowed to access Top Secret information, nor are you allowed to write to the system at a level lower than the Secret level. This creates upper and lower bounds for information storage. This process is illustrated in Figure 6.11. Notice in the illustration that you can't *read up* or *write down*. This means that a user can't read information at a higher level than they're authorized to access. A person writing a file can't *write down* to a lower level than the security level they're authorized to access.

FIGURE 6.11   The Bell La-Padula model

The process of preventing a *write down* keeps a user from accidentally breaching security by writing Secret information to the next lower level, Confidential. In our example, you can read Confidential information, but because you're approved at the Secret level, you can't write to the Confidential level. This model doesn't deal with integrity, only confidentiality. A user of Secret information can potentially modify other documents at the same level they possess.

To see how this model works, think about corporate financial information. The chief financial officer (CFO) might have financial information about the company that needs to be protected. The Bell La-Padula model would keep them from inadvertently posting information at an access level lower than their access level (writing down), thus preventing unauthorized or accidental disclosure of sensitive information. Lower-level employees wouldn't be able to access this information because they couldn't read up to the level of the CFO.

The main thing to remember about the Bell La-Padula model is that it interacts with every access—allowing it or disallowing it.

The Biba Model

The *Biba model* was designed after the Bell La-Padula model. The Biba model is similar in concept to the Bell La-Padula model, but it's more concerned with information integrity, an area that the Bell La-Padula model doesn't address. In this model, there is no write up or read down. In short, if you're assigned access to Top Secret information, you can't read Secret information or write to any level higher than the level to which you're authorized. This keeps higher-level information pure by preventing less reliable information from being intermixed with it. Figure 6.12 illustrates this concept in more detail. The Biba model was developed primarily for industrial uses, where confidentiality is usually less important than integrity.

FIGURE 6.12   The Biba model

Think about the data that is generated by a researcher for a scientific project. The researcher is responsible for managing the results of research from a lower-level project and incorporating it into his research data. If bad data were to get into his research, the whole research project would be ruined. With the Biba model, this accident couldn't happen. The researcher wouldn't have access to the information from lower levels: That information would have to be promoted to the level of the researcher. This system would keep the researcher's data intact and prevent accidental contamination.

The Biba model differs from Bell La-Padula in the implementation of a lattice of integrity levels that allows information to flow downward but not upward.

The Clark-Wilson Model

The *Clark-Wilson model* was developed after the Biba model. The approach is a little different from either the Biba or the Bell La-Padula method. In this model, data can't be accessed directly: It must be accessed through applications that have predefined capabilities. This process prevents unauthorized modification, errors, and fraud from occurring. If a user needs access to information at a certain level of security, a specific program is used. This program may only allow read access to the information. If a user needs to modify data, another application would need to be used. This allows a *separation of duties* in that individuals are granted access only to the tools they need. All transactions have associated audit files and mechanisms to report modifications. Figure 6.13 illustrates this process. Access to information is gained by using a program that specializes in access management; this can be either a single program that controls all access or a set of programs that control access. Many software-management programs work by using this method of security.

FIGURE 6.13 The Clark-Wilson model

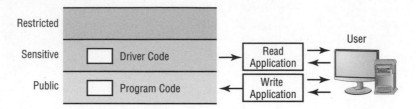

Let's say you were working on a software product as part of a team. You might need to access certain code to include in your programs. You aren't authorized to modify this code; you're merely authorized to use it. You would use a checkout program to get the code from the source library. Any attempt to put modified code back would be prevented. The developers of the code in the source library would be authorized to make changes. This process would ensure that only people authorized to change the code could accomplish the task.

The Clark-Wilson model focuses on business applications and consistency.

Information Flow Model

The *Information Flow model* is concerned with the properties of information flow, not only the direction of the flow. Both the Bell La-Padula and Biba models are concerned with information flow in predefined manners; they're considered Information Flow models. However, this particular Information Flow model is concerned with all information flow, not just up or down. This model requires that each piece of information have unique properties, including operation capabilities. If an attempt were made to write lower-level information to a higher level, the model would evaluate the properties of the information and determine if the operation were legal. If the operation were illegal, the model would prevent it from occurring. Figure 6.14 illustrates this concept.

FIGURE 6.14 The Information Flow model

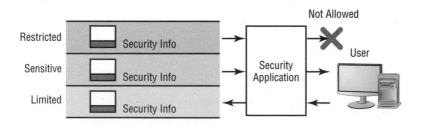

Let's use the previous software project as an example. A developer might be working with a version of the software to improve functionality. When the programmer had made improvements to the code, she would want to put that code back into the library. If the attempt to write the code were successful, the code would replace the existing code. If a subsequent bug were found in the new code, the old code would have been changed. The solution would be to create a new version of the code that incorporated both the new code and the old code. Each subsequent change to the code would require a new version to be created. While this process might consume more disk space, it would prevent things from getting lost, and it would provide a mechanism to use or evaluate an older version of the code.

Noninterference Model

The *Noninterference model* is intended to ensure that higher-level security functions don't interfere with lower-level functions. In essence, if a higher-level user were changing information, the lower-level user wouldn't know or be affected by the changes. This approach prevents the lower-level user from being able to deduce what changes are being made to the system. Figure 6.15 illustrates this concept. Notice that the lower-level user isn't aware that any changes have occurred above them.

FIGURE 6.15   The Noninterference model

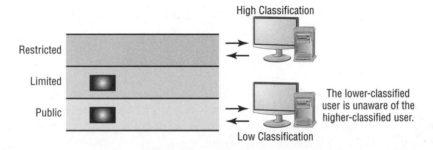

Let's take one last look at the software project with which we've been working. If a system developer were making changes to the library that was being used by a lower-level programmer, changes could be made to the library without the lower-level programmer being aware of them. This would allow the higher-level developer to work on prototypes without affecting the development effort of the lower-level programmer. When the developer finished the code, he could publish it to lower-level programmers. At this point, all users would have access to the changes, and they could use them in their programs.

Summary

In this chapter, I covered the key elements of physical security, social engineering, and the environment. This chapter also showed you how business continuity, information security, and access models work.

Physical security measures include access controls, physical barriers, and environmental systems. Environmental considerations include electrical, fire-suppression, and interference issues.

Wireless cell technology is growing at a rapid rate worldwide. The newest technology (GSM) allows interchangeable modules called SIMs to be used for international access. United States and European standards aren't interchangeable at this time. Many cell phone manufacturers are building cell phones that can operate in either environment equally well.

Security models must be concerned with physical security, security zones, partitioning, and the communications infrastructure. You should take a multilayered approach when you implement a security model.

Business continuity planning is the process of making decisions about how losses, outages, and failures are handled within an organization. The following are key aspects of BCP:

- Business impact analysis (BIA)

- Risk assessment

BIA includes evaluating the critical functions of the organization. This information is used to make informed decisions about how to deal with outages should they occur. Risk assessment is the process of evaluating and cataloging the threats, vulnerabilities, and weaknesses that exist in the systems being used. The risk assessment should tie in with BCP to ensure that all bases are covered.

Security models begin with an understanding of the business issues an organization is facing. The following business issues must be evaluated:

- Policies

- Standards

- Guidelines

A good policy design includes scope statements, overview statements, accountability expectations, and exceptions. Each of these aspects of a well-crafted policy helps set the expectation for everyone in a company. For a policy to be effective, it needs the unequivocal support of the senior management or decision makers in an organization.

A number of standards are being developed to implement security standards in organizations. One of the newest standards gaining support worldwide is ISO 17799; this standard identifies the 11 key areas that a security policy or model must include. Certification using this standard is obtained through an auditing function performed by an outside party or accrediting agency.

Information classification is the process of determining what information is accessible to what parties and for what purposes. Classifications in industry are usually based on cataloging information as *public* or *private*. Public information can be classified as either limited distribution or full distribution. Private information is usually classified for internal use or restricted.

The primary roles in a security process include owner, custodian, and user. The owner of the data is responsible for determining access rights and uses. The custodian is responsible for maintaining and protecting data. The user is the person using the data to accomplish work.

Support roles in information classification include the security professional and the auditor. A security professional is a person who has access to the information and processes to ensure protection. An auditor is primarily concerned that processes and procedures are followed to protect information.

Access control models exist to categorize the usage of sensitive information. Three of the more common models are the Bell La-Padula model, the Biba model, and the Clark-Wilson model. Less common models include the Information Flow and Noninterference models.

The Bell La-Padula model works on the philosophy that you can't read up beyond your level of classification or write down to a lower classification. This model is primarily concerned with information security.

The Biba model is designed to prevent a user from writing up or reading down. This means that a user can't write information up to a higher level or read information down at a lower level than they're authorized to access. The Biba model is designed to provide data integrity as opposed to information security.

The Clark-Wilson model requires that all data access occur through controlled access programs. The programs dictate what information can be used and how it can be accessed. This is a common model in software development systems.

The Information Flow model is concerned with the properties of information flow, not only the direction of the flow. This model is concerned with all information flow, not just up or down. It requires that each piece of information have unique properties, including operation capabilities.

The Noninterference model is intended to ensure that higher-level security functions don't interfere with lower-level functions. In essence, if a higher-level user were changing information, the lower-level user wouldn't know or be affected by the changes. This approach prevents the lower-level user from being able to deduce what changes are being made to the system.

Exam Essentials

Know the various aspects of physical security.   Physical security involves mechanisms to provide access control, physical barriers, and authentication systems such as biometric systems.

Be able to describe the types of access control methods used in physical security.   The primary methods of access control include perimeter security, security zones, physical barriers, and identification systems. These systems, when implemented in layers, make it harder for an intruder to gain access. Physical access methods should also include intrusion detection systems such as video surveillance in order to monitor the activities when they occur. This helps security professionals manage the threat and make changes when necessary.

Be able to describe the process of social engineering.   Social engineering occurs when an unauthorized individual uses human or nontechnical methods to gain information or access to security information. Individuals in an organization should be trained to watch for these types of attempts, and they should report them to security professionals when they occur.

Be able to discuss the various aspects of environmental systems and functions.   Environmental systems include heating, air conditioning, humidity control, fire suppression, and power systems. All of these functions are critical to a well-designed physical plant.

Know the purposes of shielding in the environment.   Shielding primarily prevents interference from EMI and RFI sources. Most shielding is attached to an effective ground, thereby neutralizing or reducing interference susceptibility.

Be able to describe the types of fire-suppression systems in use today.   Fire-suppression systems can be either fixed or portable. Portable systems usually are fire extinguishers. Fixed systems are part of the building, and they're generally water based or gas based. Gas-based systems are usually found only in computer rooms or other locations where water-based systems would cause more damage than is warranted. Gas systems work only in environments where airflow can be limited; they remove oxygen from the fire, causing the fire to go out. Water systems usually remove heat from a fire, causing the fire to go out.

Hands-On Lab

The lab in this chapter is as follows:

Lab 6.1: Test Social Engineering

Lab 6.1: Test Social Engineering

In this lab, you'll test your users to determine the likelihood of a social engineering attack. The following are suggestions for tests; you might need to modify them slightly to be appropriate at your workplace. Before doing any of them, make certain your manager knows that you're conducting such a test and approves of it:

1. Call the receptionist from an outside line. Tell them that you're a new salesperson and that you didn't write down the username and password the sales manager gave you last week. Tell them that you need to get a file from the e-mail system for a presentation tomorrow. Do they direct you to the appropriate person?

2. Call the human resources department from an outside line. Don't give your real name, but instead say that you're a vendor who has been working with this company for years. You'd like a copy of the employee phone list to be e-mailed to you, if possible. Do they agree to send you the list, which would contain information that could be used to try to guess usernames and passwords?

3. Pick a user at random. Call them and identify yourself as someone who does work with the company. Tell them that you're supposed to have some new software ready for them by next week and that you need to know their password in order to finish configuring it. Do they do the right thing?

The best defense against any social engineering attack is education. Make certain the employees of your company know how to react to the requests like these.

Review Questions

1. Which component of physical security addresses outer-level access control?

   A. Perimeter security

   B. Mantraps

   C. Security zones

   D. Locked doors

2. You've been drafted for the safety committee. One of your first tasks is to inventory all the fire extinguishers and make certain the correct types are in the correct locations throughout the building. Which of the following categories of fire extinguisher is intended for use on electrical fires?

   A. Type A

   B. Type B

   C. Type C

   D. Type D

3. Which of the following won't reduce EMI?

   A. Physical shielding

   B. Humidity control

   C. Physical location

   D. Overhauling worn motors

4. You're the administrator for MTS. You're creating a team that will report to you, and you're attempting to divide the responsibilities for security among individual members. Similarly, which of the following access methods breaks a large area into smaller areas that can be monitored individually?

   A. Zone

   B. Partition

   C. Perimeter

   D. Floor

5. Which of the following is equivalent to building walls in an office building from a network perspective?

   A. Perimeter security

   B. Partitioning

   C. Security zones

   D. IDS systems

6. After a number of minor incidents at your company, physical security has suddenly increased in priority. No unauthorized personnel should be allowed access to the servers or workstations. The process of preventing access to computer systems in a building is called what?

   A. Perimeter security

   B. Access control

   C. Security zones

   D. IDS systems

7. Which of the following is an example of perimeter security?

   A. Chain link fence

   B. Video camera

   C. Elevator

   D. Locked computer room

8. You're the leader of the security committee at ACME. After a move to a new facility, you're installing a new security monitoring system throughout. Which of the following best describes a motion detector mounted in the corner of a hallway?

   A. Perimeter security

   B. Partitioning

   C. Security zone

   D. IDS system

9. Which technology uses a physical characteristic to establish identity?

   A. Biometrics

   B. Surveillance

   C. Smart card

   D. CHAP authenticator

10. As part of your training program, you're trying to educate users on the importance of security. You explain to them that not every attack depends on implementing advanced technological methods. Some attacks, you explain, take advantage of human shortcomings to gain access that should otherwise be denied. What term do you use to describe attacks of this type?

    A. Social engineering

    B. IDS system

    C. Perimeter security

    D. Biometrics

11. Wireless cells have which of the following characteristics?

    A. Line-of-site communications

    B. Automatic position location

    C. High-power portable devices

    D. High levels of security

12. You're attempting to sell upper management on the concept of adopting GSM technology. It promises to provide encryption as well as international usability, and it's an example of which technology?

   A. Perimeter security

   B. Surveillance system

   C. Security zones

   D. Cell technology

13. The process of reducing or eliminating susceptibility to outside interference is called what?

   A. Shielding

   B. EMI

   C. TEMPEST

   D. Desensitization

14. You work for an electronics company that has just created a device that emits less RF than any competitor's product. Given the enormous importance of this invention and of the marketing benefits it could offer, you want to have the product certified. Which certification is used to indicate minimal electronic emissions?

   A. EMI

   B. RFI

   C. CC EAL 4

   D. TEMPEST

15. Which term defines the process of a WAP losing sensitivity due to RFI?

   A. RFI desensitization

   B. EMI pickup

   C. Access control

   D. TEMPEST

16. Due to growth beyond current capacity, a new server room is being built. As a manager, you want to make certain that all the necessary safety elements exist in the room when it's finished. Which fire-suppression system works best when used in an enclosed area by displacing the air around a fire?

   A. Gas based

   B. Water based

   C. Fixed system

   D. Overhead sprinklers

17. The CBF identifies which aspects of a business?

   A. Access control

   B. Critical access points

   C. Essential business functions

   D. BIA

18. You're the chief security contact for MTS. One of your primary tasks is to document everything related to security and create a manual that can be used to manage the company in your absence. Which documents should be referenced in your manual as the ones that identify the methods used to accomplish a given task?

   A. Policies

   B. Standards

   C. Guidelines

   D. BIA

19. Which classification of information designates that information can be released on a restricted basis to outside organizations?

   A. Private information

   B. Full distribution

   C. Restricted information

   D. Limited distribution

20. You've recently been hired by ACME to do a security audit. The managers of this company feel that their current security measures are inadequate. Which information access control prevents users from writing information down to a lower level of security and prevents users from reading above their level of security?

   A. Bell La-Padula model

   B. Biba model

   C. Clark-Wilson model

   D. Noninterference model

Answers to Review Questions

1. **A.** The first layer of access control is perimeter security. Perimeter security is intended to delay or deter entrance into a facility.

2. **C.** Type C fire extinguishers are intended for use in electrical fires.

3. **B.** Electrical devices, such as motors, that generate magnetic fields cause EMI. Humidity control won't address EMI.

4. **A.** A security zone is a smaller part of a larger area. Security zones can be monitored individually if needed. Answers B, C, and D are examples of security zones.

5. **B.** Partitioning is the process of breaking a network into smaller components that can each be individually protected. This is analogous to building walls in an office building.

6. **B.** Access control is the primary process of preventing access to physical systems.

7. **A.** Perimeter security involves creating a perimeter or outer boundary for a physical space. Video surveillance systems wouldn't be considered a part of perimeter security, but they can be used to enhance physical security monitoring.

8. **C.** A security zone is an area that is a smaller component of the entire facility. Security zones allow intrusions to be detected in specific parts of the building.

9. **A.** Biometrics is a technology that uses personal characteristics, such as a retinal pattern or fingerprint, to establish identity.

10. **A.** Social engineering uses the inherent trust in the human species, as opposed to technology, to gain access to your environment.

11. **A.** Wireless cell systems are primarily line-of-site communication systems. These systems use the microwave band for communications.

12. **D.** Global System for Mobile Communications (GSM) is the newest standard for cellular communications. GSM promises to provide encryption as well as international usability.

13. **A.** Shielding keeps external electronic signals from disrupting operations.

14. **D.** TEMPEST is the certification given to electronic devices that emit minimal RF. The TEMPEST certification is difficult to acquire, and it significantly increases the cost of systems.

15. **A.** Receivers tend to become desensitized when they're exposed to strong RF signals. This makes the receiver in the WAP seemingly go deaf to normal-strength signals.

16. **A.** Gas-based systems work by displacing the air around a fire. This eliminates one of the three necessary components of a fire: oxygen.

17. **C.** The critical business functions are those functions that must be established as soon as possible for a business to succeed after a catastrophic event.

18. C.   Guidelines help clarify processes to maintain standards. Guidelines tend to be less formal than policies or standards.

19. D.   Limited distribution information can be released to select individuals and organizations, such as financial institutions, governmental agencies, and creditors.

20. A.   The Bell La-Padula model is intended to protect confidentiality of information. This is accomplished by prohibiting users from reading above their security level and preventing them from writing below their security level.

Chapter

7

Cryptography Basics, Methods, and Standards

THE FOLLOWING COMPTIA SECURITY+ EXAM OBJECTIVES ARE COVERED IN THIS CHAPTER:

✓ **5.1 Explain general cryptography concepts.**

- Key management
- Steganography
- Symmetric key
- Asymmetric key
- Confidentiality
- Integrity and availability
- Non-repudiation
- Comparative strength of algorithms
- Digital signatures
- Trusted Platform Module (TPM)
- Single vs. Dual sided certificates
- Use of proven technologies

✓ **5.2 Explain basic hashing concepts and map various algorithms to appropriate applications.**

- SHA
- MD5
- LANMAN
- NTLM

✓ **5.3 Explain basic encryption concepts and map various algorithms to appropriate applications.**

- DES
- 3DES
- RSA

- PGP
- Elliptic curve
- AES
- AES256
- One time pad
- Transmission encryption (WEP TKIP, etc.)

✓ 5.4 Explain and implement protocols.

- SSL/TLS
- S/MIME
- PPTP
- HTTP vs. HTTPS vs. SHTTP
- L2TP
- IPSEC
- SSH

✓ 5.5 Explain core concepts of public key cryptography.

- Public Key Infrastructure (PKI)
- Recovery Agent
- Public key
- Private keys
- Certificate Authority (CA)
- Registration
- Key escrow
- Certificate Revocation List (CRL)
- Trust Models

✓ 5.6 Implement PKI and certificate management.

- Public Key Infrastructure (PKI)
- Recovery Agent
- Public key
- Private keys
- Certificate Authority (CA)
- Registration
- Key escrow
- Certificate Revocation List (CRL)

Cryptography is the art of concealing information. As data becomes more valuable, and more important, it is an area of high interest to governments, to businesses, and increasingly to individuals. People want privacy when it comes to their personal and other sensitive information. Corporations want—and need—to protect financial records, trade secrets, customer lists, and employee information. The government uses cryptography to help ensure the safety and well-being of its citizens. Entire governmental agencies have been created to help ensure secrecy, and millions of dollars have been spent trying to protect national secrets and attempting to learn the secrets of other countries.

Individuals who specialize in the development and making of codes are referred to as *cryptographers*. Individuals who specialize in breaking codes are called *cryptanalysts*. Many of these professionals are geniuses with strong backgrounds in math and computer science.

This chapter discusses the various forms of cryptography and how they are used in the computer field, and examines cryptography standards. Your private information must be protected from unauthorized access and exploitation. Your data must be protected. The primary method of protecting your data from prying eyes is cryptography.

In addition to a brief overview of cryptography, this chapter discusses some of the more common algorithms used, how encryption is used today, Public Key Infrastructure (PKI), and some of the attacks to which cryptographic systems are vulnerable. It also discusses standards, key management, and the key life cycle.

An Overview of Cryptography

Cryptography is a field almost as old as humankind. The first recorded cryptographic efforts occurred 4,000 years ago. These early efforts included translating messages from one language into another or substituting characters.

 You won't be tested on the history of cryptography in the Security+ exam; this information is included primarily for background purposes.

The following sections briefly discuss three categories of cryptography—physical, mathematical, and quantum—as well as code breaking. Quantum cryptography is extremely classified and is relatively new. The other methods discussed are well known and commonly used.

Understanding Physical Cryptography

Physical cryptography includes several different approaches. The more common methods involve transposition or substitution of characters or words. Physical methods also include a method of encryption called *steganography*, which is the science of hiding information within other information, such as within a picture.

> In general, physical cryptography refers to any method that doesn't alter a value using a mathematical process.

A *cipher* is a method used to encode characters to hide their value. *Ciphering* is the process of using a cipher to encode a message. The three primary types of cryptography, or ciphering methods—substitution, transposition, and steganography—are discussed in the following sections. The hybrid model, which is also discussed, uses one or more methods to accomplish encryption.

> It's important to know that cryptography is always changing in an effort to make algorithms that are more difficult to crack. Not that long ago, single-digit bit encryption was good enough; now triple digits are almost a minimum requirement.

Substitution Ciphers

A *substitution cipher* is a type of coding or ciphering system that changes one character or symbol into another. Character substitution can be a relatively easy method of encrypting information. You may see this method used in a childhood toy such as a decoder ring. For example, let's say you had the following message:

> You can do this easily if you put your mind to it.

And here is how the encrypted message read:

> You can do qhis zasily if you puq your mind to iq.

Notice in the encrypted example that every instance of *z* is a substitute for *e* and that every instance of *q* is a substitute for *t*. This code, while simple, may prevent someone from understanding the message for a very short period of time.

This type of coding creates two potential problems. Obviously, the system isn't highly secure. In addition, how do you know the *q* isn't really a *q*? Nevertheless, this method has been used in simple codes since time immemorial.

Real World Scenario

Working with rot13

One of the oldest known encoding algorithms is rot13—said by some to have been used in the days of Caesar. This simple algorithm rotates every letter 13 places in the alphabet. Thus an *A* becomes an *N*, a *B* becomes an *O*, and so forth. The same rotation of 13 letters that is used to encrypt the message is also used to decrypt the message. Many newsgroups offer a rot13 option that allows you to encrypt/decrypt postings.

See if you can solve these encryptions:

1. Neg snve qrohgf urer Fngheqnl.

2. Gevcyr pbhcbaf ng Xebtre!

3. Gel lbhe unaq ng chmmyrf

One of the easiest ways to solve rot13 text messages is to take a sheet of paper and write the letters from *A to M* in one column and from *N to Z* in a second. To decipher, replace the letter in the encrypted message with the one that appears beside it in the other column.

Here are the answers:

1. Art fair debuts here Saturday.

2. Triple coupons at Kroger!

3. Try your hand at puzzles.

Transposition Ciphers

A *transposition cipher* (also referred to as a *transposition code*) involves transposing or scrambling the letters in a certain manner. Typically, a message is broken into blocks of equal size, and each block is then scrambled. In the simple example shown in Figure 7.1, the characters are transposed by changing the order of the group. In this case, the letters are rotated three places in the message. You could change the way Block 1 is transposed from Block 2 and make it a little more difficult, but it would still be relatively easy to decrypt.

FIGURE 7.1   A simple transposition code in action

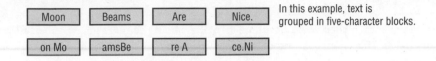

Moon beams are nice.

| Moon | Beams | Are | Nice. |

In this example, text is grouped in five-character blocks.

| on Mo | amsBe | re A | ce.Ni |

In this example, each character (including the spaces) is moved to the right three positions.

Steganography

Steganography is the process of hiding one message in another. In theory, doing this prevents analysts from detecting the real message. You could encode your message in another file or message and use that file to hide your message. This type of encryption can be somewhat harder to detect, but it's still breakable. Consider the following message:

"Meet the mini me that ate later."

The real message is every third word:

"Meet me later."

Steganography is also called *electronic watermarking*. Mapmakers and artists have used watermarking for years to protect copyrights. If an image contains a watermark placed there by the original artist, proving that a copyright infringement has occurred in a copy is relatively easy.

Hybrid Systems

By combining two or more of these methods of physical cryptography, you can make a pretty good cipher system. These types of systems are widely used, and they're difficult to break using manual methods. Many systems, such as the Enigma machine used during World War II to encode messages between the German command and their U-boats, used a combination of substitution and transposition to make a very sophisticated system.

Understanding Mathematical Cryptography

Mathematical cryptography deals with using mathematical processes on characters or messages. The most common is a function called *hashing*. Hashing refers to performing a calculation on a message and converting it into a numeric hash value. The *hash value* of the example in Figure 7.2 is computed by multiplying each character by 2, adding those results together, and then dividing the sum by 10.

FIGURE 7.2   A simple hashing process

> **Message:** this
>
> **ASCII Values:** 116 104 105 115
>
> **Calculated Values:** 232 208 210 230
>
> **Hash Value Calculation:** (232+208+210+230)/10
>
> **Hash Value:** 88

Hashing is discussed in detail in the section "The Science of Hashing" later in this chapter.

As you can see, this hash value is a single number. The hash value can't be used to derive the meaning of the message. The number is transmitted with the message to the receiver, and the receiving end uses the same hash function to determine that the message is authentic. If the hash value is different, the message has been altered in some way. This process is also known as performing a *checksum*.

This type of hashing is called a *one-way process*. There is no way to reverse the hash and turn the number back into the original message. This method of hashing is used to verify message authenticity, and it may be used in conjunction with one of the other encryption methods previously defined. It's important to note that a one-way hash can't be used to decrypt a message that is used primarily for authenticity verification. Nevertheless, it's considered an encryption process, used primarily to verify the integrity of the message.

As you can imagine, calculating all the numbers in a larger, more complicated message by hand would be cumbersome and time consuming. Computers make hashing a very fast process.

Hashing is used extensively in computer programming. Many early random access file methods used hashing to locate records in a data file.

A *Trusted Platform Module (TPM)* can be used to assist with hash key generation. A TPM is the name assigned to a chip that can store cryptographic keys, passwords, or certificates. The TPM can be used to generate values used with whole disk encryption (discussed in Chapter 5) as well as protect cell phones and devices other than PCs. More information on TPM can be found at the Trusted Computing Group's website: https://www.trustedcomputinggroup.org/home.

Working with Passwords

Many password-generation systems are based on a one-way hashing approach. You can't take the hash value and reverse it to guess the password. In theory, this makes it harder to guess or decrypt a password.

Passwords should be as long and as complicated as possible. Most security experts believe a password of 10 characters is the minimum that should be used if security is a real concern. If you use only the lowercase letters of the alphabet, you have 26 characters with which to work. If you add the numeric values 0 through 9, you'll get another 10 characters. If you go one step further and add the uppercase letters, you'll then have an additional 26 characters, giving you a total of 62 characters with which to construct a password.

Most vendors recommend that you use nonalphabetic characters such as #, $, and % in your password, and some go so far as to require it.

If you used a 4-character password, this would be $62 \times 62 \times 62 \times 62$, or approximately 14 million password possibilities. If you used 5 characters in your password, this would give you 62 to the fifth power, or approximately 920 million password possibilities. If you used a 10-character password, this would give you 62 to the tenth power, or 8.4×10^{17} (a very big number) possibilities. As you can see, these numbers increase exponentially with each position added to the password. The 4-digit password could probably be broken in a fraction of a day, while the 10-digit password would take considerably longer and much more processing power.

If your password used only the 26 lowercase letters from the alphabet, the 4-digit password would have 26 to the fourth power, or 456,000 password combinations. A 5-character password would have 26 to the fifth power, or over 11 million, and a 10-character password would have 26 to the tenth power, or 1.4×10^{14}. This is still a big number, but it would take considerably less time to break it.

To see tables on how quickly passwords can be surmised, visit http://www.lockdown.co.uk/?pg=combi&s=articles.

Mathematical methods of encryption are primarily used in conjunction with other encryption methods as part of authenticity verification. The message and the hashed value of the message can be encrypted using other processes. In this way, you know that the message is secure and hasn't been altered.

As a security administrator, you should know how to work with hashing within your operating system.

Understanding Quantum Cryptography

Quantum cryptography is a relatively new method of encryption. Prior to 2002, its application was limited to laboratory work and possibly to secret governmental applications.

This method is based on the characteristics of the smallest particles known. It may now be possible to create unbreakable ciphers using quantum methods.

 You won't be tested on quantum cryptography on the Security+ exam. It's included here for real-world knowledge.

The process depends on a scientific model called the *Heisenberg Uncertainty Principle* for security. Part of the Heisenberg Uncertainty Principle basically states that in the process of measuring the results, the results are changed. Werner Heisenberg's early works were published in 1926, and they have been greatly debated by physicists ever since.

Imagine you have a bowl of water and you want to measure the temperature of the water. When you put a thermometer into the water, you change the temperature of the water: The presence of the thermometer makes the temperature of the water rise or drop slightly. In short, the act of measuring the water temperature changes the water temperature, making it impossible to know the true temperature of the water before you measured it.

In quantum cryptography, a message is sent using a series of photons. If the receiver knows the sequence and polarity of the photons, they can decode the message. Otherwise, the photons look like random noise. If someone intercepts the photons, some of the photon positions will change polarity and the message will be altered. This will inform the receiver that someone is listening in on the message. The sender, when informed, can change the pattern and resend the message with a new photon position key. Intercepting the data alters the data and ruins the message.

Figure 7.3 demonstrates this concept. In this example, each photon is polarized in one of several directions. The process of intercepting these photons alters the polarity of some of the photons and makes the message unreadable. This alerts the receiver that an interception activity is occurring. As you can see in this example, the message has been altered as a result of the interception. Each bar in the message is part of the message: The interception changes the polarity of some of the photons (represented by the bars), making the message unreadable.

Quantum cryptography has become a solution available for private users, although it's very expensive and has a limited range. It will be interesting to see what the future holds for this technology.

 Quantum cryptography is currently only implemented using fiber-optic technology. This technology, when further developed, may make many of the systems now in use obsolete.

Uncovering the Myth of Unbreakable Codes

If time has taught us anything, it is that people frequently do things that other people thought were impossible. Every time a new code or process is invented that is thought to be invincible, someone comes up with a method of breaking it.

FIGURE 7.3 Quantum cryptography being used to encrypt a message

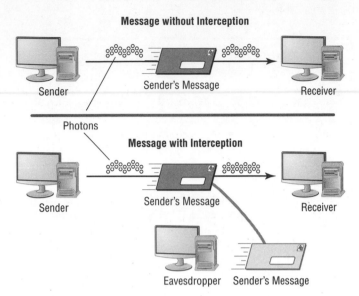

The following list includes some common code-breaking techniques:

Frequency analysis *Frequency analysis* involves looking at blocks of an encrypted message to determine if any common patterns exist. Initially, the analyst doesn't try to break the code but looks at the patterns in the message. In the English language, the letters *e* and *t* and words like *the*, *and*, *that*, *it*, and *is* are very common. Single letters that stand alone in a sentence are usually limited to *a* and *I*.

A determined cryptanalyst looks for these types of patterns and, over time, may be able to deduce the method used to encrypt the data. This process can sometimes be simple, or it may take a lot of effort.

Algorithm errors An *algorithm* is a method or set of instructions used to perform a task or instruction. In computers, algorithms are implemented in programs to perform repetitive operations. Sometimes complex algorithms produce unpredictable results; when discovered, the results can cause the entire encryption algorithm to be compromised. Cryptographic systems may have fundamental flaws in the way they're designed. An error or flaw in either the design or the implementation of the steps can create a weakness in the entire coding system. This weakness may leave a coding system open to decryption regardless of the complexity of the algorithm or steps used to process the codes.

Brute-force attacks *Brute-force attacks* can be accomplished by applying every possible combination of characters that could be the key. For example, if you know that the key is three characters long, then you know that there is a finite number of possibilities that the key could be. Although it may take a long time to find the key, the key can be found.

TIP Although it could take a long time to succeed with a brute-force attack, hackers use programs that run thousands of brute-force trial-and-error attempts in a short period of time.

Human error   Human error is one of the major causes of encryption vulnerabilities. If an e-mail is sent using an encryption scheme, someone else may send it *in the clear* (unencrypted). If a cryptanalyst gets hold of both messages, the process of decoding future messages will be considerably easier. A code key might wind up in the wrong hands, giving insights into what the key consists of. Many systems have been broken as a result of these types of accidents.

A classic example involved the transmission of a sensitive military-related message using an encryption system. Most messages have a preamble that informs the receiver who the message is for, who sent it, how many characters are in the message, the date and time it was sent, and other pertinent information. In this case, the preamble was sent in clear text and this information was also encrypted and put into the message. As a result, the cryptanalysts gained a key insight into the message contents. They were given approximately 50 characters that were repeated in the message in code. This error caused a relatively secure system to be compromised.

Understanding Cryptographic Algorithms

Cryptographic algorithms are used to encode a message from its unencrypted or clear-text state into an encrypted message. The three primary methods of encoding messages are hashing, using symmetric algorithms, and using asymmetric algorithms. The following sections discuss these methods and some of the standards in which they're used.

The Science of Hashing

As we mentioned earlier, *hashing* is the process of converting a message, or data, into a numeric value. The numeric value that a hashing process creates is referred to as a *hash total* or *value*. Hashing functions are considered either one way or two way.

A one-way hash doesn't allow a message to be decoded back to the original value. A two-way hash allows a message to be reconstructed from the hash. Most hashing functions are one way. Two primary standards exist that use the hashing process for encryption:

Secure Hash Algorithm   The *Secure Hash Algorithm (SHA)* was designed to ensure the integrity of a message. The SHA is a one-way hash that provides a hash value that can be used with an encryption protocol. This algorithm produces a 160-bit hash value. SHA has been updated; the new standard is SHA-1.

Real World Scenario

Watch for the Weakest Link

A courier who was responsible for carrying weekly encryption keys took commercial flights that caused him to arrive at his destination on Friday evenings. The courier was obligated to follow certain security methods including hand-carrying these encryption key units and getting a signature from an authorized signatory at the remote facility. Unfortunately, his flight frequently arrived late at its destination. When this happened, the courier was forced to spend the night in the remote location. On Saturday morning, the courier would go to the facility and hand the key units to the appropriate person.

This process had been going on for several years. The courier often kept the key units in the trunk of his rental car overnight. Unfortunately, one night his car was stolen from the hotel parking lot, and the key units were in the trunk. Luckily, the car was recovered later in the morning, and the trunk had not been opened. This security breach caused the courier to lose his job, and the entire cryptographic system had to have new keys issued worldwide.

As you can see, even if you're extra cautious, sometimes even the safest code isn't safe. Murphy's Law says human error will creep into the most secure security systems.

Message Digest Algorithm   The *Message Digest Algorithm (MD)* also creates a hash value and uses a one-way hash. The hash value is used to help maintain integrity. There are several versions of MD; the most common are MD5, MD4, and MD2.

 Message digests are discussed in detail later in this chapter. The primary thing to know about a message digest is that it's nothing more than text expressed as a single string of digits.

MD5 is the newest version of the algorithm. It produces a 128-bit hash, but the algorithm is more complex than its predecessors and offers greater security.

 Both SHA-1 and MD5 are good hashing algorithms. The primary difference between the two is speed; MD5 is faster to process than SHA.

LANMAN   Prior to the release of Windows NT, Microsoft's operating systems used the LANMAN protocol for authentication. While functioning only as an authentication protocol, LANMAN used LM Hash and two DES keys. It was replaced by the NT LAN Manager (NTLM) with the release of Windows NT.

NTLM   Microsoft replaced the LANMAN protocol with NTLM (NT LAN Manager) with the release of Windows NT. NTLM uses MD4/MD5 hashing algorithms. Several versions of this protocol exist (NTLMv1, NTLMv2), and it is still in widespread use despite the fact that Microsoft has pointed to Kerberos as being its preferred authentication protocol. While LANMAN and NTLM both employ hashing, they are/were used primarily for the purpose of authentication.

Working with Symmetric Algorithms

Symmetric algorithms require both ends of an encrypted message to have the same key and processing algorithms. Symmetric algorithms generate a secret key that must be protected. A *symmetric key*—sometimes referred to as a secret key or private key—is a key that isn't disclosed to people who aren't authorized to use the encryption system. The disclosure of a private key breaches the security of the encryption system. If a key is lost or stolen, the entire process is breached. These types of systems are common, but the keys require special handling. Figure 7.4 illustrates a symmetric encryption system; in this example, the keys are the same on each end.

FIGURE 7.4   Symmetric encryption system

Encrypts Using Key

Decrypts Using Key

Message

Typically, a new key isn't sent across the encrypted channel (if the current key has been compromised, the new key may also be compromised). Keys are sent using an *out-of-band method*: by letter, by courier, or by some other method. This approach may be cumbersome, and it may leave the key subject to human error or social engineering exploitation.

The other disadvantage of a symmetric algorithm is that each person who uses the encryption algorithm must have the key. If you want 50 people to access the same messages, all 50 people must have the key. As you can imagine, it's difficult for 50 people to keep a secret. On the other hand, if you want to communicate with 50 different people in private, you need to know who uses which key. This information can be hard to keep straight—you might spend all your time trying to remember who uses which key.

Encryption methods usually use either a block or stream cipher. As the name implies, with a *block cipher* the algorithm works on chunks of data—encrypting one and then moving to the next. With a *stream cipher*, the data is encrypted a bit, or byte, at a time.

Several successful encryption systems use symmetric algorithms. A strong algorithm can be difficult to break. Here are some of the common standards that use symmetric algorithms:

Data Encryption Standard   The *Data Encryption Standard (DES)* has been used since the mid-1970s. It was the primary standard used in government and industry until it was replaced by AES. It's a strong and efficient algorithm based on a 56-bit key. (*Strong* refers to the fact that it's hard to break.) A recent study showed that a very powerful system could break the algorithm in about two days. DES has several modes that offer security and integrity. However, it has become a little dated as a result of advances in computer technology, and it's being replaced. For its time, it was one of the best standards available.

Advanced Encryption Standard   *Advanced Encryption Standard (AES)* has replaced DES as the current standard, and it uses the Rijndael algorithm. It was developed by Joan Daemen and Vincent Rijmen. AES is now the current product used by U.S. governmental agencies. It supports key sizes of 128, 192, and 256 bits, with 128 bits being the default.

For more information about Rijndael (AES), see its website at `http://csrc .nist.gov/encryption/aes/rijndael/`.

AES256   *AES256* (also often written as AES-256) uses 256 bits instead of 128. This qualifies for U.S. government classification as Top Secret.

Triple-DES   *Triple-DES (3DES)* is a technological upgrade of DES. 3DES is still used, even though AES is the preferred choice for government applications. 3DES is considerably harder to break than many other systems, and it's more secure than DES.

CAST   *CAST* is an algorithm developed by Carlisle Adams and Stafford Tavares (hence the name). It's used in some products offered by Microsoft and IBM. CAST uses a 40-bit to 128-bit key, and it's very fast and efficient.

Rivest's Cipher   *RC* is an encryption family produced by RSA laboratories. RC stands for *Rivest's Cipher* or *Ron's Code*. (Ron Rivest is the author of this algorithm.) The current levels are RC5 and RC6. RC5 uses a key size of up to 2,048 bits. It's considered to be a strong system.

Blowfish   *Blowfish* is an encryption system produced by Counterpane Systems that performs a 64-bit block cipher at very fast speeds. It is a symmetric block cipher than can use variable-length keys. The original author was Bruce Schneier; he next created Twofish, which performs a similar function on 128-bit blocks.

International Data Encryption Algorithm   *International Data Encryption Algorithm (IDEA)* was developed by a Swiss consortium. It's an algorithm that uses a 128-bit key. This product is similar in speed and capability to DES, but it's more secure. IDEA is used in Pretty Good Privacy (PGP), a public domain encryption system used by many for e-mail. Currently, ASCOM AG holds the right to market IDEA.

Working with Asymmetric Algorithms

Asymmetric algorithms use two keys to encrypt and decrypt data. These *asymmetric keys* are referred to as the *public key* and the *private key*. The public key can be used by the sender to encrypt a message, and the private key can be used by the receiver to decrypt the message. As you may recall, symmetrical systems require the key to be private between the two parties. With asymmetric systems, each circuit has one key.

The public key may be truly public or it may be a secret between the two parties. The private key is kept private and is known only by the owner (receiver). If someone wants to send you an encrypted message, they can use your public key to encrypt the message and then send you the message. You can use your private key to decrypt the message. One of the keys is always kept private. If both keys become available to a third party, the encryption system won't protect the privacy of the message.

Perhaps the best way to think about this system is that it's similar to a safe deposit box. Two keys are needed: The box owner keeps the public key, and the bank retains the second, or private, key. In order to open the box, both keys must be used simultaneously. Figure 7.5 illustrates the two-key method. Notice that in the encryption process, Key 1 is used to encrypt the message and Key 2 is used to decrypt it. In this way, it's harder to break the code unless both the public and private keys are known.

FIGURE 7.5   A two-key system in use

Encrypts Using Public Key   Decrypts Using Private Key

Message   Message

Two-key systems are referred to as *Public Key Cryptography (PKC)*. Don't confuse this with Public Key Infrastructure (PKI), which uses PKC as a part of the process.

The algorithms used in this two-key process are complicated, and several volumes would be needed to explain them thoroughly. In this book, I'll focus primarily on how the two-key process is used. It's implemented in systems such as Public Key Infrastructure (PKI), which is discussed in more detail later in this chapter.

Four popular asymmetric systems are in use today:

RSA   *RSA* is named after its inventors Ron Rivest, Adi Shamir, and Leonard Adleman. The RSA algorithm is an early public-key encryption system that uses large integer numbers as the basis of the process. It's widely implemented, and it has become a de facto standard. RSA works for both encryption and digital signatures, which are discussed later in the chapter. RSA is used in many environments, including Secure Sockets Layer (SSL).

Diffie-Hellman   Dr. W. Diffie and Dr. M. E. Hellman conceptualized the *Diffie-Hellman key exchange*. They are considered the founders of the public/private key concept; their original work envisioned splitting the key into two parts. This algorithm is used primarily to send keys across public networks. The process isn't used to encrypt or decrypt messages; it's used merely for the transmission of keys in a secure manner.

Elliptic Curve Cryptography   *Elliptic Curve Cryptography (ECC)* provides similar functionality to RSA. ECC is being implemented in smaller, less-intelligent devices such as cell phones and wireless devices. It's smaller than RSA and requires less computing power. ECC encryption systems are based on the idea of using points on a curve to define the public/private key pair. This process is less mathematically intensive than processes such as RSA.

Palm, Motorola, Cisco, and others have implemented, or are implementing, the ECC system for security. Palm handhelds can now form secure connections to applications running on other systems using wireless or other means. Motorola recently released its new development system for the next generation of cellular phones; this system implements ECC and other protocols as an integral part of the toolkit. You can expect that ECC will be commonly implemented in cellular devices in the near future.

El Gamal   *El Gamal* is an algorithm used for transmitting digital signatures and key exchanges. The method is based on calculating logarithms. The process used is similar to the Diffie-Hellman key exchange and is based on the characteristics of logarithmic numbers and calculations. The El Gamal algorithm was first published in 1985. The Digital Signature Algorithm (DSA) is based on El Gamal.

Using Cryptographic Systems

A cryptographic system is a system, method, or process that is used to provide encryption and decryption. It may be a hardware, software, or manually performed process. Cryptographic systems exist for the same reasons that security exists: to provide confidentiality, integrity, authentication, nonrepudiation, and access control. The following sections discuss these issues within the framework of cryptographic systems.

Confidentiality

One of the major reasons to implement a cryptographic system is to ensure the confidentiality of the information being used. Confidentiality may be intended to prevent the unauthorized disclosure of information in a local network or to prevent the unauthorized disclosure of information across a network. A cryptographic system must do this effectively in order to be of value.

The need to keep records secure from internal disclosure may be just as great as the need to keep records secure from outside attacks. The effectiveness of a cryptographic system in preventing unauthorized decryption is referred to as its *strength*: A strong cryptographic system is difficult to crack. Strength is also referred to as the algorithm's *work factor*: The work factor describes an estimate of the amount of time and effort that would be needed to break a system.

The system may be considered weak if it allows weak keys, has defects in its design, or is easily decrypted. Many systems available today are more than adequate for business and personal use, but they are inadequate for sensitive military or governmental applications.

Integrity

The second major reason for implementing a cryptographic system involves providing assurance that a message wasn't modified during transmission. Modification may render a message unintelligible or, even worse, inaccurate. Imagine the consequences if record alterations weren't discovered in medical records involving drug prescriptions. If a message is tampered with, the encryption system should have a mechanism to indicate that the message has been corrupted or altered.

Integrity can be accomplished by adding information such as checksums or redundant data that can be used as part of the decryption process. Figure 7.6 gives a simple example of how integrity can be validated in a message. Notice that data about the message length and the number of vowels in the message are included in the message.

FIGURE 7.6   A simple integrity-checking process for an encrypted message

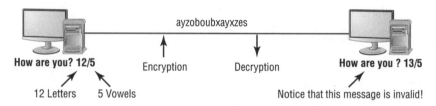

These two additions to the message provide a two-way check on the integrity of the message. In this case, the message has somehow become corrupted or invalidated. The original message had 12 characters; the decrypted message has 13 characters. Of course, the processes used in a real system are much more complicated. The addition of this information could be considered a signature of a sort.

A common method of verifying integrity involves adding a *message authentication code (MAC)* to the message. The MAC is derived from the message and a key. In Figure 7.6, the MAC is derived from the message, and the originator provides an additional piece of information. This process ensures the integrity of the message. The MAC would be encrypted with the message, adding another layer of integrity checking. From the MAC, you would know that the message came from the originator and that the contents haven't been altered. Figure 7.7 illustrates the MAC value being calculated from the message and included with the message. The receiver also calculates the MAC value and compares it to the value sent in the message. If the values are equal, the message can be assumed to be intact and genuine.

The MAC value is a key, usually derived using a hashing algorithm. The key is normally symmetrical in that the process is accomplished using the same function on both ends of the transmission.

Integrity is also provided using digital signatures that verify that the originator is who they say they are. The next section discusses digital signatures.

FIGURE 7.7   The MAC value is calculated by the sender and receiver using the same algorithm.

If the MAC values are equal, the message is valid.

Digital Signatures

A *digital signature* is similar in function to a standard signature on a document. It validates the integrity of the message and the sender. The message is encrypted using the encryption system, and a second piece of information, the digital signature, is added to the message. Figure 7.8 illustrates this concept.

FIGURE 7.8   Digital signature processing steps

Let's say that the sender in Figure 7.8 wants to send a message to the receiver. It's important that this message not be altered. The sender uses the receiver's public key to create a hash value that is stored in the message digest. The sender then sends the message to the receiver. The receiver can use their private key and compare the value of the message digest. If the message value from the private key is the same as the message digest sent with the message, the receiver knows the message is authentic.

The digital signature is derived from a hash process known only by the originator. The receiver uses a key provided by the sender or a key that will provide the same result. The receiver compares the signature area referred to as a *message digest* in the message with the calculated value. If the values match, the message hasn't been tampered with and the originator is verified as the person they claim to be. This process provides both message integrity and authentication.

Authentication

Authentication is the process of verifying that the sender is who they say they are. This is critical in many applications. A valid message from an invalid source isn't authentic.

One of the common methods of verifying authenticity is the addition of a digital signature. Authenticity can also be established using secret words that have been mutually agreed on in advance. The military has used a series of *one-time pads* that each radio or communications operator could use to verify the authenticity of the sender. Figure 7.9 illustrates this method. The operator receiving the message challenged the sender using the prescribed pattern. The sender could also challenge the receiver using the same method. In this way, both parties knew they were talking to the right person. These pads were changed either daily or weekly depending on the circumstances. Although it wasn't foolproof, the system was effective and easy to use.

FIGURE 7.9   A one-time pad used for authentication

The authentication letter is obtained below the two-letter pair.

One-Time Pad

1. Authenticate A S ➤ I authenticate: C

Second operator challenges back to first.

2. Authenticate T Y ➤ I authenticate: R

Both operators checked the card to verify correct response.

A simple process of providing authentication to an organization is the use of code words or key words. For example, you could have a set of code words that instantly identify the person on the other end of a phone conversation.

Fraternal organizations have used secret handshakes, special symbols, and other methods to authenticate an unknown member. If you were part of a fraternal organization, once you had been initiated, you would be taught the secret handshake, which would instantly identify you to other members of the organization. In this way, you would know who was a member and who was an impostor. Some fraternal organizations have extremely complicated membership handshakes that identify the level you've achieved within the organization.

Nonrepudiation

Nonrepudiation prevents one party from denying actions they carried out. To use an analogy, imagine coming home to find your house's picture window broken. All three of your kids say they didn't do it, and the babysitter says it must have been broken when she arrived. All the parties who could be guilty are "repudiating" the fact that they did it, and it's their word against common sense. Now, imagine that you had a nanny-cam running and were able to review the tape and see who actually broke it. The tape cancels out their saying they knew nothing about the broken window and offers "nonrepudiation" of the facts.

In the electronic world, a similar type of proof can be achieved in a two-key system. The problem is that anyone can claim to be the legitimate receiver, and if they have access to this type of system, they can send you a public key. So although the user would have received the message, you would have no way to verify that the user is really who they say they are and that they're a valid user; you need nonrepudiation to verify that someone is whom they report to be.

Third-party organizations called *certificate authorities (CAs)* manage public keys and issue certificates verifying the validity of the sender's message. The verifying aspect serves as nonrepudiation; a respected third party vouches for the individual. The goal of any effective cryptography system must include nonrepudiation. However, the implementation is a little more difficult than the concept.

    The CA process is covered in the section "Using Public Key Infrastructure."

Access Control

Access control refers to the methods, processes, and mechanisms of preventing unauthorized access to the systems that do the cryptography. Keys are vulnerable to theft, loss, and human security failings. A key component of access control involves both physical and operational security of these resources.

Real World Scenario

Nonrepudiation and eBay

Recently, a young man gained access to his parents' key information on eBay. He managed to successfully win several auctions, and he racked up over a million dollars in charges to his parents' account. The parents (naturally) disputed the bill. eBay invalidated the bids when the deception was discovered. The situation caused a great deal of personal embarrassment for the parents and potentially opened them up to litigation.

The term *access control* is used in many different settings, such as access control lists, access lists, and so on. The important thing to consider is that those techniques are collectively intended to limit access to information.

Key management presents a major challenge with large encryption systems. Keeping the keys in secured areas with limited access by unauthorized personnel is important. If the keys become compromised, the entire system breaks down, no matter how good it is.

Make sure the keys are kept in the highest security areas available to you. Physical keys, such as smart cards, should be immediately erased when they are retired; these keys should also be kept in a secured area for storage. One of the big problems that credit card companies are encountering is the ease with which the encoding on a credit card's magnetic strip can be counterfeited. If you can gain access to an active credit card, the magnetic strip can be duplicated onto a blank card. Make sure all your security devices are kept under tight physical control when they aren't in use.

Using Public Key Infrastructure

The *Public Key Infrastructure (PKI)* is a first attempt to provide all the aspects of security to messages and transactions that have been previously discussed. The need for universal systems to support e-commerce, secure transactions, and information privacy is one aspect of the issues being addressed with PKI.

PKI is a two-key—asymmetric—system with four key components: Certificate Authority (CA), Registration Authority (RA), RSA, and digital certificates. Messages are encrypted with a public key and decrypted with a private key. As an example, take the following scenario:

1. You want to send an encrypted message to Jordan, so you request his public key.

2. Jordan responds by sending you that key.

3. You use the public key he sends you to encrypt the message.

4. You send the message to him.

5. Jordan uses his private key to decrypt the message.

The main goal of PKI is to define an infrastructure that should work across multiple vendors, systems, and networks. It's important to emphasize that PKI is a framework and not a specific technology. Implementations of PKI are dependent on the perspective of the software manufacturers that implement it. This has been one of the major difficulties with PKI: Each vendor can interpret the documents about this infrastructure and implement it however they choose. Many of the existing PKI implementations aren't compatible with each other; however, this situation should change over the next few years because customers expect compatibility.

Most organizations have a PKI policy document that describes the uses for the electronic signing technology. Associated documents that fall under this category often include a confidentiality certificate policy document and a digital signature certificate policy document.

The following sections explain the major functions and components of the PKI infrastructure and how they work in relationship to the entire model.

Under no circumstances should you ever divulge or send your private key. Doing so jeopardizes your guarantee that only you can work with the data and can irreparably damage your security.

Using a Certificate Authority

A *certificate authority (CA)* is an organization that is responsible for issuing, revoking, and distributing *certificates*. A certificate is nothing more than a mechanism that associates the public key with an individual. It contains a great deal of information about the user. Each user of a PKI system has a certificate that can be used to verify their authenticity.

For instance, if Mike wants to send Jeff a private message, there should be a mechanism to verify to Jeff that the message received from Mike is really from Mike. If a third party vouches for Mike and Jeff trusts that third party, Jeff can assume that the message is authentic because the third party says so. Figure 7.10 shows this process happening in a communication between Mike and Jeff; the arrows in this figure show the path between the CA and the person using the CA for verification purposes.

CAs can be either private or public. Many operating system providers allow their systems to be configured as CA systems. These CA systems can be used to generate internal certificates that are used within a business or in large external settings.

The process of providing certificates to users, although effective in helping to ensure security, requires a server. Over time, the server can become overloaded and need assistance. An additional component, the registration authority (RA), is available to help offload work from the CA. Registration authorities are discussed in the next section.

FIGURE 7.10   The certificate authority process

Jeff can verify that the
message with the
certificate from Mike is
valid if he trusts the CA.

Working with Registration Authorities and Local Registration Authorities

A *registration authority (RA)* offloads some of the work from a CA. An RA system operates as a middleman in the process: It can distribute keys, accept registrations for the CA, and validate identities. The RA doesn't issue certificates; that responsibility remains with the CA. Figure 7.11 shows an RA operating in San Francisco, while the CA is located in Washington, D.C. The Seattle user obtains authorization for the session from the RA in San Francisco. The Seattle user can also use the San Francisco RA to validate the authenticity of a certificate from the Miami user. The arrows between the Seattle user and the RA server represent the certificate request from the remote user. The RA has a communications link with the CA in Washington, D.C. Because the CA in Washington, D.C., is closer, the Miami user will use it to verify the certificate.

A *local registration authority (LRA)* takes the process one step further. It can be used to identify or establish the identity of an individual for certificate issuance. If the user in Seattle needs a new certificate, it would be impractical to fly back to Washington, D.C., to get another one. An LRA can be used to verify and certify the identity of the individual on behalf of the CA. The LRA can then forward authentication documents to the CA to issue the certificate.

The primary difference between an RA and LRA is that the latter can be used to identify or establish the identity of an individual.

FIGURE 7.11 An RA offloading work from a CA

Figure 7.12 shows this process occurring between an LRA and a CA. The LRA would involve an individual or process to verify the identity of the person needing a certificate. The arrows in Figure 7.12 show the path from the user who requested the certificate (via the LRA) to the CA that issues the certificate; the arrows indicate the path from the CA sending the new certificate back to the user.

FIGURE 7.12 The LRA verifying identity for the CA

 The LRA involves the physical identification of the person requesting a certificate.

The next sections provide more detail about certificates and their uses, including validating users, systems, and devices. A certificate also has certain characteristics that will be briefly explained.

Implementing Certificates

Certificates, as you may recall, provide the primary method of identifying that a given user is valid. Certificates can also be used to store authorization information. Another important factor is verifying or certifying that a system is using the correct software and processes to communicate. What good would a certificate be to help ensure authenticity if the system uses an older cryptography system that has a security problem?

The next few sections describe the X.509 certificate structure and some of the more common usages of certification.

X.509

The most popular certificate used is the X.509 version 3. *X.509* is a standard certificate format supported by the International Telecommunications Union (ITU) and many other standards organizations. Adopting a standard certificate format is important for systems to be assured interoperability in a certificate-oriented environment.

The format and contents of a sample certificate are shown in Figure 7.13.

FIGURE 7.13   A certificate illustrating some of the information stored

Version	V3
Serial Number	1234 D123 4567 …
Signature Algorithm	Md2RSA
Issuer	Sample Certificate
Valid from:	Thursday, September 8, 2005
Valid to:	Thursday, September 15, 2005
Subject	Mr. Your Name Here, Myco
Public Key	Encrypted Value of Key
Extensions	Subject Type = End Entity
Signature Algorithm Signature	sha1 Encrypted Data

Digital Signature Area

Fields of a Simple X.509 Certificate

Notice that the certificate contains identifiers of two different algorithms used in the process. In this case, the signature algorithm is Md2RSA, and the digital signature algorithm is sha1. This certificate also has a unique serial number issued by the CA.

An X.509 certificate has more fields than are illustrated; this example is intended only to give you an overview of what a certificate looks like.

Always remember that the purpose of the certificate is to basically bind the public key to the user's identity. When authenticating, certificates can be used to authenticate only the client (*single sided*) or both parties (*dual sided*), the client and server. Aside from the Security+ objectives, no one uses the term *dual-sided certificates*.

Certificate Policies

Certificate policies define what certificates do. A CA can potentially issue a number of different types of certificates: say, one for e-mail, one for e-commerce, and one for financial transactions. The policy might indicate that it isn't to be used for signing contracts or for purchasing equipment. Certificate policies affect how a certificate is issued and how it's used. A CA would have policies regarding the interoperability or certification of another CA site; the process of requiring interoperability is called *cross certification*. The organizations using the certificates also have the right to decide which types of certificates are used and for what purposes. This is a voluntary process in that each organization involved can decide what and how to approve certificate use.

The receiving organization can use this policy to determine whether the certificate has come from a legitimate source. Think about it this way: A PKI certificate can be generated any number of ways using any number of servers. The policy indicates which certificates will be accepted in a given application.

Certificate Practice Statements

A *Certificate Practice Statement (CPS)* is a detailed statement the CA uses to issue certificates and implement its policies of the CA.

The CA provides the CPS to users of its services. These statements should discuss how certificates are issued, what measures are taken to protect certificates, and the rules CA users must follow in order to maintain their certificate eligibility. The policies should be readily available to CA users.

If a CA is unwilling to provide this information to a user, the CA itself may be untrustworthy, and the trustworthiness of that CA's users should be questioned.

 Remember that a CPS is a detailed document used to enforce policy at the CA; a certificate policy doesn't pertain to the CA but to the certificate itself.

Understanding Certificate Revocation

Certificate revocation is the process of revoking a certificate before it expires. A certificate may need to be revoked because it was stolen, an employee moved to a new company, or someone has had their access revoked. A certificate revocation is handled either through a *Certificate Revocation List (CRL)* or by using the *Online Certificate Status Protocol (OCSP)*. A *repository* is simply a database or database server where the certificates are stored.

The process of revoking a certificate begins when the CA is notified that a particular certificate needs to be revoked. This must be done whenever the private key becomes known. The owner of a certificate can request it be revoked at any time, or the request can be made by the administrator.

The CA marks the certificate as revoked. This information is published in the CRL and becomes available using the OCSP. The revocation process is usually very quick; time is based on the publication interval for the CRL. Disseminating the revocation information to users may take longer. Once the certificate has been revoked, it can never be used—or trusted—again.

The CA publishes the CRL on a regular basis, usually either hourly or daily. The CA sends or publishes this list to organizations that have chosen to receive it; the publishing process occurs automatically in the case of PKI. The time between when the CRL is issued and when it reaches users may be too long for some applications. This time gap is referred to as *latency*. OCSP solves the latency problem: If the recipient or relying party uses OCSP for verification, the answer is available immediately. Currently, this process is under evaluation and may be replaced at some time in the future.

When a key is compromised, a revocation request should be made to the CA immediately. It may take a day or longer for the CRL to be disseminated to everyone using that CA.

Implementing Trust Models

For PKI to work, the capabilities of CAs must be readily available to users. The model that has been shown to this point is the simple trust model. However, the simple trust model may not work as PKI implementations get bigger. Conceptually, every computer user in the world would have a certificate. However, accomplishing this would be extremely complex and would create enormous scaling or growth issues.

Four main types of trust models are used with PKI:

- Hierarchical
- Bridge
- Mesh
- Hybrid

PKI was designed to allow all of these trust models to be created. They can be fairly granular from a control perspective. *Granularity* refers to the ability to manage individual resources in the CA network.

In the following sections, I'll examine each of these models. I'll detail how each model works and discuss its advantages and disadvantages.

Hierarchical Trust Models

In a *hierarchical trust model*—also known as a *tree*—a root CA at the top provides all the information. The intermediate CAs are next in the hierarchy, and they only trust information provided by the root CA. The root CA also trusts intermediate CAs that are in their level in the hierarchy and none that aren't. This arrangement allows a high level of control at all levels of the hierarchical tree.

This might be the most common implementation in a large organization that wants to extend its certificate-processing capabilities. Hierarchical models allow tight control over certificate-based activities.

Figure 7.14 illustrates the hierarchical trust structure. In this situation, the intermediate CAs trust only the CAs directly above them or below them.

FIGURE 7.14   A hierarchical trust structure

Root CA systems can have trusts between them, and there can be trusts between intermediate and leaf CAs. A *leaf CA* is any CA that is at the end of a CA network or chain. This structure allows you to be creative and efficient when you create hybrid systems.

Bridge Trust Models

In a *bridge trust model,* a peer-to-peer relationship exists between the root CAs. The root CAs can communicate with each other, allowing cross certification. This arrangement allows a certification process to be established between organizations or departments. Each intermediate CA trusts only the CAs above and below it, but the CA structure can be expanded without creating additional layers of CAs.

Additional flexibility and interoperability between organizations are the primary advantages of a bridge model. Lack of trustworthiness of the root CAs can be a major disadvantage. If one of the root CAs doesn't maintain tight internal security around its certificates, a security problem can be created: An illegitimate certificate could become available to all the users in the bridge structure and its subordinate or intermediate CAs.

This model may be useful if you're dealing with a large, geographically dispersed organization or you have two organizations that are working together. A large, geographically dispersed organization could maintain a root CA at each remote location; the root CAs would have their own internal hierarchy, and users would be able to access certificates from any place in the CA structure. Figure 7.15 illustrates a bridged structure. In this example, the intermediate CAs communicate only with their respective root CA. All cross certification is handled between the two root CA systems.

FIGURE 7.15   A bridge trust structure

Mesh Trust Models

The *mesh trust model* expands the concepts of the bridge model by supporting multiple paths and multiple root CAs. Each of the root CAs shown in Figure 7.16 can cross-certify with the other root CAs in the mesh. This arrangement is also referred to as a *web structure*. Although not shown in the illustration, each of the root CAs can also communicate with the intermediate CAs in their respective hierarchies.

This structure may be useful in a situation where several organizations must cross-certify certificates. The advantage is that you have more flexibility when you configure the CA structures. The major disadvantage of a mesh is that each root CA must be trustworthy in order to maintain security.

FIGURE 7.16 A mesh trust structure

Mesh Model

Hybrid Trust Model

A *Hybrid Trust Model* can use the capabilities of any or all of the structures discussed in the previous sections. You can be extremely flexible when you build a hybrid trust structure.

The flexibility of this model also allows you to create hybrid environments. Figure 7.17 illustrates such a structure. Notice that in this structure, the single intermediate CA server on the right side of the illustration is the only server that is known by the CA below it. The subordinates of the middle-left CA are linked to the two CAs on its sides. These two CAs don't know about the other CAs, because they are linked only to the CA that provides them a connection. The two intermediate servers in the middle of the illustration and their subordinates trust each other; they don't trust others that aren't in the link.

 Real World Scenario

Designing a CA Structure for Your Organization

You've been assigned to implement a CA structure for your organization. Your organization has several large national factories and small remote facilities throughout the country. Some of these facilities have high-speed networks; others have low-speed dial-up capabilities. Your management reports that network traffic is very high, and they don't want to overburden the network with CA traffic. How would you go about implementing this structure?

You should probably install CA systems at each of the major facilities throughout the country. Additionally, you may want to install CAs in key geographic locations where certificate access is needed. You need to establish a procedure to allow certificates to be issued in remote locations, and you also need to implement an RA process in your larger locations. Remote users could receive certificates either by e-mail or by out-of-band methods if network access was limited.

FIGURE 7.17   A hybrid model

The major difficulty with hybrid models is that they can become complicated and confusing. A user can unintentionally acquire trusts that they shouldn't have obtained. In our example, a user could accidentally be assigned to one of the CAs in the middle circle. As a member of that circle, the user could access certificate information that should be available only from their root CA. In addition, relationships between CAs can continue long past their usefulness; unless someone is aware of them, these relationships can exist even after the parent organizations have terminated their relationships.

Preparing for Cryptographic Attacks

The ultimate objective of an attack on a cryptographic system is to either decipher the messages or disrupt the network. Cryptographic systems can be susceptible to denial of service (DoS) attacks, which were explained in Chapter 2, "Identifying Potential Risks."

Specific attacks on cryptographic systems can be divided into three types:

Attacking the key   Key attacks are typically launched to discover the value of a key by attacking the key directly. The keys can be passwords, encrypted messages, or other key-based encryption information. An attacker might try to apply a series of words, commonly used passwords, and other randomly selected combinations to crack a password. A key attack involves trying to crack a key by repeatedly guessing the key value. Most operating system manufacturers provide programming interfaces that allow access to password and encryption subsystems. An attacker can use this access and information to break a password. Remember that passwords are typically generated with a one-way hashing function. The anticipated amount of time it takes to break a password depends on the length of the password and the characters used in the password. Making keys longer and more complicated tends to make key attacks more difficult.

Attacking the algorithm   The programming instructions and algorithms used to encrypt information are as much at risk as the keys. If an error isn't discovered and corrected by a program's developers, an algorithm might not be able to secure the program. Many algorithms have well-publicized back doors. If a weakness in the programming or model used to develop an algorithm is discovered, a significant security exposure may exist.

 Real World Scenario

WEP (In)Security

A paper was submitted to the Internet community that discussed a theoretical weakness in the algorithm used as the basis for the Wired Equivalent Privacy (WEP) security system. WEP supporters publicly discounted the weakness to the computer community: They indicated that the vulnerability was theoretical and couldn't happen in the real world. Within seven days of their brash statements, they received over a dozen different examples of how to break the WEP system.

Intercepting the transmission   The process of intercepting a transmission may, over time, allow attackers to inadvertently gain information about the encryption systems used by an organization. The more data attackers can gain, the more likely they are to be able to use frequency analysis to break an algorithm. Human error is also a problem in security situations, and it's likely that someone will unintentionally release information that can be used to undermine a security system.

You should also be aware of the following three types of attacks:

Birthday attack   A *birthday attack* is an example of an attack targeted at the key. It isn't an attack on the algorithm itself, just on the results. A birthday attack is built on a simple premise. If 25 people are in a room, there is some probability that two of those people will have the same birthday. The probability increases as additional people enter the room. It's important to remember that probability doesn't mean that something will occur, only that it's more likely to occur.

Although two people may not share a birthday in every gathering, the likelihood is fairly high. A birthday attack works on the same premise: If your key is hashed, the possibility is that given enough time, another value can be created that will give the same hash value.

An easy way to think of a birthday attack is to look at the hashing process in Figure 7.2. The result of the operation is a value of 88. If the letters *siis* were hashed, they would give the same result even though they differ from the message originally used.

Weak key attack   *Weak key attacks* are based on the premise that many common passwords are used by lots of people. If the key length is short, the resulting hash value will be easier to guess. Make sure your users use passwords and encryption keys that are hard to guess. You may even want to consider a random-password generating system. The longer and more complicated a password is, the more difficult it is to successfully launch a weak key attack against it.

A security audit performed by the U.S. Air Force uncovered a startling problem with passwords. It discovered that one of the most popular passwords used in several locations was *WWJD*. Upon investigation, they discovered that this was an abbreviation for "What Would Jesus Do." Although the air force wasn't trying to suppress religious expression, it sent out a list of unacceptable passwords and, not surprisingly, this was one of them.

Mathematical attack   *Mathematical attacks* can be focused on the encryption algorithm itself, the key mechanism, or any potential area of weakness in the algorithm. These attacks use mathematical modeling and statistical analysis to determine how the system operates. These types of attacks depend on intercepting large amounts of data and methodically attempting to decrypt the messages using one of the methods previously described.

Understanding Cryptography Standards and Protocols

Numerous standards are available to establish secure services. Some of the standards that will be presented in the following sections have already been discussed in greater detail in earlier chapters. Here I will quickly remind you of them and introduce you to a few more standards.

The movement from proprietary governmental standards toward more unified and global standards is a growing trend that has both positive and negative implications. Higher interoperability between disparate systems will also mean that these standards will be widely utilized. The more the standards are used, the more miscreants will focus on them as they try to break them.

As a security administrator, you have to weigh the pros and cons of the different standards and evaluate them against your organization's needs. The following sections introduce you to the major standards, discuss their focus, and describe how they were developed.

The Origins of Encryption Standards

As mentioned in the beginning of the chapter, early cryptography standards were primarily designed to secure communications for the government and military. Many different standards groups exist today, and they often provide standards that are incompatible with the standards of other groups. These standards are intended to address the specific environments in which these groups work.

The following sections describe key U.S. government agencies, a few well-known industry associations, and public-domain cryptography standards.

The Role of Governmental Agencies

Several U.S. government agencies are involved in the creation of standards for secure systems. They either directly control specific sectors of government or provide validation, approval, and support to government agencies. We'll look at each of these agencies in the following sections.

National Security Agency

The *National Security Agency (NSA)* is responsible for creating codes, breaking codes, and coding systems for the U.S. government. The NSA was chartered in 1952. It tries to keep a low profile; for many years, the government didn't publicly acknowledge its existence.

The NSA is responsible for obtaining foreign intelligence and supplying it to the various U.S. government agencies that need it. It's said to be the world's largest employer of mathematicians. The NSA's missions are extremely classified, but its finger is in everything involving cryptography and cryptographic systems for the U.S. government, government contractors, and the military.

The NSA's website is http://www.nsa.gov.

National Security Agency/Central Security Service

The *National Security Agency/Central Security Service (NSA/CSS)* is an independently functioning part of the NSA. It was created in the early 1970s to help standardize and support Department of Defense (DoD) activities. The NSA/CSS supports all branches of the military. Each branch of the military used to have its own intelligence activities. Frequently, these branches didn't coordinate their activities well. NSA/CSS was created to help coordinate their efforts.

National Institute of Standards and Technology

The *National Institute of Standards and Technology (NIST)*, which was formerly known as the National Bureau of Standards (NBS), has been involved in developing and supporting standards for the U.S. government for over 100 years. NIST has become very involved in cryptography standards, systems, and technology in a variety of areas. It's primarily concerned with governmental systems, and it exercises a great deal of influence on them. NIST shares many of its findings with the security community because business needs are similar to government needs.

NIST publishes information about known vulnerabilities in operating systems and applications. You'll find NIST very helpful in your battle to secure your systems.

You can find NIST on the Web at http://www.nist.gov.

Industry Associations and the Developmental Process

The need for security in specific industries, such as the banking industry, has driven the development of standards. Standards frequently begin as voluntary or proprietary efforts.

The *Request for Comments (RFC)*, originated in 1969, is the mechanism used to propose a standard. It's a document-creation process with a set of practices. An RFC is categorized as standard (draft or standard), best practice, informational, experimental, or historic.

Draft documents are processed through a designated RFC editor who makes sure the document meets publication standards. Editors play a key role in the RFC process; they are responsible for making sure proposals are documented properly, and they manage the discussion. The RFC is then thrown open to the computer-user community for comments and critique. This process ensures that all interested parties have the opportunity to comment on an RFC.

The RFC process allows open communications about the Internet and other proposed standards. Virtually all standards relating to the Internet that are adopted go through this process.

Several industrial associations have assumed roles that allow them to address specific environments. The following sections briefly discuss some of the major associations and the specific environments they address.

American Bankers Association

The *American Bankers Association (ABA)* has been very involved in the security issues facing the banking and financial industries. Banks need to communicate with each other in a secure manner. The ABA sponsors and supports several key initiatives regarding financial transactions.

You can find more information on the ABA at http://www.aba.com/default.htm.

Internet Engineering Task Force

The *Internet Engineering Task Force (IETF)* is an international community of computer professionals that includes network engineers, vendors, administrators, and researchers.

The IETF is mainly interested in improving the Internet; it's also very interested in computer security issues. The IETF uses working groups to develop and propose standards.

IETF membership is open to anyone. Members communicate primarily through Internet list servers and public conferences.

 You can find additional information about the IETF on its website at `http://www.ietf.org`.

Internet Society

The *Internet Society (ISOC)* is a professional group whose membership consists primarily of Internet experts. The ISOC oversees a number of committees and groups, including the IETF.

 You can find a history of ISOC and IETF at `http://www.isoc.org/internet/history/ietfhis.shtml`.

World Wide Web Consortium

The *World Wide Web Consortium (W3C)* is an association concerned with the interoperability, growth, and standardization of the World Wide Web (WWW). It's the primary sponsor of XML and other web-enabled technologies. Although not directly involved in cryptography, the W3C recently published a proposed standard for encryption in XML.

 The W3C's website is located at `http://www.w3.org`.

International Telecommunications Union

The *International Telecommunications Union (ITU)* is responsible for virtually all aspects of telecommunications and radio communications standards worldwide. The ITU is broken into three main groups that are targeted at specific areas of concern: ITU-R is concerned with radio communication and spectrum management, ITU-T is concerned with telecommunications standards, and ITU-D is concerned with expanding telecommunications throughout undeveloped countries. The ITU is headquartered in Switzerland, and it operates as a sponsored agency of the United Nations.

 For more information on the ITU, visit `http://www.itu.int/`.

Comité Consultatif International Téléphonique et Télégraphique

The *Comité Consultatif International Téléphonique et Télégraphique (CCITT)* standards committee has been involved in developing telecommunications and data communications standards for many years. The functions performed by the CCITT have been taken over by the ITU, and the ITU-T committee now manages CCITT standards. Existing CCITT standards (such as X.400 and X.500) are still referred to as CCITT standards, but soon they will be reclassified and referred to as ITU-T standards.

Institute of Electrical and Electronics Engineers

The *Institute of Electrical and Electronics Engineers (IEEE)* is an international organization focused on technology and related standards. Pronounced "I Triple-E," the IEEE is organized into several working groups and standards committees. IEEE is actively involved in the development of PKC, wireless, and networking protocol standards.

You can find information on the IEEE at `http://www.ieee.org`.

Public Domain Cryptography

Public domain cryptography refers to the standards and protocols that emerge from individual or corporate efforts and are released to the general public for use. Public domain structures are developed for many reasons: Developers may merely have a passing interest in something, or they may want to test a new theory.

PGP and RSA are two common public cryptographic initiatives:

Pretty Good Privacy   One of the most successful involves a system called *Pretty Good Privacy (PGP)*. It was developed by Phil Zimmerman, who developed this encryption system for humanitarian reasons. In 1991, he published the encryption system on the Internet. His stated objective was to preserve privacy and protect citizens from oppressive governments. Since its release, PGP has become a de facto standard for e-mail encryption. PGP uses both symmetrical and asymmetrical encryption.

The U.S. government prosecuted Zimmerman for three years because he released PGP. The government claimed he violated U.S. laws prohibiting the exportation of sensitive technology. The government claimed the encryption method supported terrorism and oppression instead of reducing it. The case was finally dropped. PGP has continued to grow in popularity worldwide.

RSA   RSA provides cryptographic systems to both private businesses and the government. The name RSA comes from the initials of its three founders (Rivest, Shamir, and Adleman). RSA has been very involved in developing Public-Key Cryptography Standards (PKCS), and it maintains a list of standards for PKCS.

Public-Key Infrastructure X.509/Public-Key Cryptography Standards

The *Public-Key Infrastructure X.509 (PKIX)* is the working group formed by the IETF to develop standards and models for the PKI environment. The PKIX working group is responsible for the X.509 standard, which is discussed in the next section.

The *Public-Key Cryptography Standards (PKCS)* is a set of voluntary standards created by RSA and security leaders. Early members of this group included Apple, Microsoft, DEC (now HP), Lotus, Sun, and MIT.

Currently, there are 15 published PKCS standards:

- PKCS #1: RSA Cryptography Standard
- PKCS #2: Incorporated in PKCS #1
- PKCS #3: Diffie-Hellman Key Agreement Standard
- PKCS #4: Incorporated in PKCS #1
- PKCS #5: Password-Based Cryptography Standard
- PKCS #6: Extended-Certificate Syntax Standard
- PKCS #7: Cryptographic Message Syntax Standard
- PKCS #8: Private-Key Information Syntax Standard
- PKCS #9: Selected Attribute Types
- PKCS #10: Certification Request Syntax Standard
- PKCS #11: Cryptographic Token Interface Standard
- PKCS #12: Personal Information Exchange Syntax Standard
- PKCS #13: Elliptic Curve Cryptography Standard
- PKCS #14: Pseudorandom Number Generators
- PKCS #15: Cryptographic Token Information Format Standard

These standards are coordinated through RSA; however, experts worldwide are welcome to participate in the development process.

X.509

The X.509 standard defines the certificate formats and fields for public keys. It also defines the procedures that should be used to distribute public keys. The X.509 version 2 certificate is still used as the primary method of issuing Certificate Revocation List (CRL) certificates. The current version of X.509 certificates is version 3, and it comes in two basic types:

- The most common is the *end-entity certificate*, which is issued by a certificate authority (CA) to an end entity. An *end entity* is a system that doesn't issue certificates but merely uses them.
- The CA certificate is issued by one CA to another CA. The second CA can, in turn, issue certificates to an end entity.

For the exam, remember X.509 v2 for CRL and v3 for certificate.

All X.509 certificates have the following:

- Signature, which is the primary purpose for the certificate
- Version
- Serial number
- Signature algorithm ID
- Issuer name
- Validity period
- Subject name
- Subject public key information
- Issuer unique identifier (relevant for versions 2 and 3 only)
- Subject unique identifier (relevant for versions 2 and 3 only)
- Extensions (in version 3 only)

SSL and TLS

Secure Sockets Layer (SSL) is used to establish a secure communication connection between two TCP-based machines. This protocol uses the handshake method of establishing a session. The number of steps in the handshake depends on whether steps are combined and/or mutual authentication is included. The number of steps is always between four and nine, inclusive, based on who is doing the documentation.

Netscape originally developed the SSL method, which has gained wide acceptance throughout the industry. SSL establishes a session using asymmetric encryption and maintains the session using symmetric encryption.

You can find details on how the SSL process works at http://support.microsoft.com:80/ support/kb/articles/Q257/5/91.ASP.

Regardless of which vendor's implementation is being discussed, the steps can be summarized as illustrated in Figure 7.18. When a connection request is made to the server, the server sends a message back to the client indicating that a secure connection is needed. The client sends the server a certificate indicating the capabilities of the client. The server then evaluates the certificate and responds with a session key and an encrypted key. The session is secure at the end of this process.

FIGURE 7.18 The SSL connection process

This session will stay open until one end or the other issues a command to close it. The command is typically issued when a browser is closed or another URL is requested.

As a security administrator, you will occasionally need to know how to configure SSL settings for a website running on your operating system. You should also know that in order for SSL to work properly, the clients must be able to accept the level of encryption that you apply. Internet Explorer 5.5 and later, as well as Netscape 4.72 and later, can work with 128-bit encrypted sessions/certificates. Earlier browsers often needed to use 40- or 56-bit SSL encryption. As an administrator, you should push for the latest browsers on all clients.

VeriSign used a clever advertising strategy that makes this point readily comprehensible: It mailed flyers in a clear bag with the lines, "Sending sensitive information over the Web without the strongest encryption is like sending a letter in a clear envelope. Anyone can see it." This effectively illustrates the need for the strongest SSL possible.

Transport Layer Security (TLS) is a security protocol that expands upon SSL. Many industry analysts predict that TLS will replace SSL in the near future. Figure 7.19 illustrates the connection process in the TLS network.

FIGURE 7.19 The TLS connection process

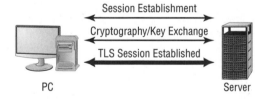

The TLS protocol is also referred to as *SSL 3.1*, but despite its name, it doesn't interoperate with SSL. The TLS standard is supported by the IETF.

 Think of TLS as an updated version of SSL. TLS is based on SSL and is intended to supersede it.

Certificate Management Protocols

Certificate Management Protocol (CMP) is a messaging protocol used between PKI entities. This protocol isn't yet widely used, but you may encounter it in some PKI environments.

XML Key Management Specification (XKMS) is designed to allow XML-based programs access to PKI services. XKMS is being developed and enhanced as a cooperative standard of the World Wide Web Consortium (W3C). XKMS is a standard that is built upon CMP and uses it as a model.

CMP is expected to be an area of high growth as PKI usage grows.

Secure Multipurpose Internet Mail Extensions

Secure Multipurpose Internet Mail Extensions (S/MIME) is a standard used for encrypting e-mail. S/MIME contains signature data. It uses the PKCS #7 standard (Cryptographic Message Syntax Standard) and is the most widely supported standard used to secure e-mail communications.

MIME is the de facto standard for e-mail messages. S/MIME, which is a secure version of MIME, was originally published to the Internet as a standard by RSA. It provides encryption, integrity, and authentication when used in conjunction with PKI. S/MIME version 3, the current version, is supported by IETF.

S/MIME is defined by RFC 2633. For the exam, know that it's a secure version of MIME used for encrypting e-mail. Know, as well, that it uses asymmetric encryption algorithms for confidentiality and digital certificates for authentication.

Secure Electronic Transaction

Secure Electronic Transaction (SET) provides encryption for credit card numbers that can be transmitted over the Internet. It was developed by Visa and MasterCard and is becoming an accepted standard by many companies.

SET is most suited for transmitting small amounts of data.

SET works in conjunction with an electronic wallet that must be set up in advance of the transaction. An *electronic wallet* is a device that identifies you electronically in the same way as the cards you carry in your wallet.

Figure 7.20 illustrates the process used in an SET transaction. The consumer must establish an electronic wallet that is issued by the consumer/issuing bank. When the consumer wants to make a purchase, they communicate with the merchant. The wallet is accessed to provide credit/payment information. The merchant then contacts the credit processor to complete the transaction. The credit processor interfaces with the existing credit network. In this situation, the transactions between the issuing bank, the consumer, the merchant, and the credit processor all use SET.

FIGURE 7.20   The SET transaction in process

Secure Shell

Secure Shell (SSH) is a tunneling protocol originally used on Unix systems. It's now available for both Unix and Windows environments. The handshake process between the client and server is similar to the process described in SSL. SSH is primarily intended for interactive terminal sessions.

SSH can be used in place of the older Remote Shell (RSH) utility that used to be a standard in the Unix world. It can also be used in place of rlogin and Telnet.

Figure 7.21 illustrates the SSH connection process. Notice that SSH connections are established in two phases: The first phase is a secure channel to negotiate the channel connection, and the second phase is a secure channel used to establish the connection.

Working with Credit Card Information Online

You've been asked to participate in a project that involves the transmission of credit card information between a group of retail stores and a credit card processing center. The security of this information is very important. Store employees will be using direct dial-in connections to the credit card processing center or the Internet. What should you evaluate?

You have several ways to go in this situation. Your dial-up and Internet connections present different concerns. Because you're dealing with credit card information, the volume of information to be transmitted is relatively small. The information will include a card number, name, and the amount of the sale, as well as the expiration date. The processing center will probably send back a coded message and approval. Compared to a lot of interactions, this is a fairly small amount of data.

Your direct dial-in connections to the credit card center may not need to be encrypted. It's difficult to tap a telephone line, and public access is hard to create. If your organization feels this is necessary, you'll want to use a relatively quick encryption system, such as SET. Your Internet connections could use SET, SSL, TLS, or one of the other secure protocols discussed in this chapter.

FIGURE 7.21   The SSH connection-establishment process

Phase 1: Secure Channel Negotiation

E-mail client   SSH Server

Phase 2: Session Establishment

E-mail client   SSH Tunnel   SSH Server   E-mail Server

An open-source, Telnet/SSH client gaining popularity on the Win32 platform is PuTTY (putty.exe). The download page for this utility can be found at http://www.chiark.greenend.org.uk/~sgtatham/putty/download.html.

 Real World Scenario

Securing Unix Interactive Users

You've been asked to examine your existing Unix systems and evaluate them for potential security weaknesses. Several remote users need to access Telnet and FTP capabilities in your network. Telnet and FTP connections send the logon and password information in the clear. How could you minimize security risks for Telnet and FTP connections?

You should consider using a VPN connection between these remote connections and your corporate systems. One workable solution might be to provide SSH to your clients and install it on your Unix servers. Doing so would allow FTP and Telnet connectivity in a secure environment.

Pretty Good Privacy

Pretty Good Privacy (PGP) is a freeware e-mail encryption system. As mentioned earlier in the chapter, PGP was introduced in the early 1990s, and it's considered to be a very good system. It's widely used for e-mail security.

PGP uses both symmetrical and asymmetrical systems as a part of its process. Figure 7.22 provides an overview of how the various components of a PGP process work together to provide security. During the encryption process, the document is encrypted with the public key and also a session key, which is a one-use random number, to create the ciphertext. The session key is encrypted into the public key and sent with the ciphertext.

On the receiving end, the private key is used to weed out the session key. The session key and the private key are then used to decrypt the ciphertext back into the original document.

HTTP Secure

Hypertext Transport Protocol Secure (HTTPS) is the secure version of HTTP, the language of the World Wide Web. HTTPS uses SSL to secure the channel between the client and server. Many e-business systems use HTTPS for secure transactions. An HTTPS session is identified by the https in the URL and by a key that is displayed on the web browser.

HTTPS uses port 443 by default.

FIGURE 7.22   The PGP encryption system

Secure HTTP

Secure Hypertext Transport Protocol (S-HTTP) is HTTP with message security (added by using RSA or a digital certificate). Whereas HTTPS creates a secure channel, S-HTTP creates a secure message. S-HTTP can use multiple protocols and mechanisms to protect the message. It also provides data integrity and authentication.

S-HTTP also uses port 443 by default.

IP Security

IP Security (IPSec) is a security protocol that provides authentication and encryption across the Internet. IPSec is becoming a standard for encrypting virtual private network (VPN) channels. It's available on most network platforms, and it's considered to be highly secure.

One of the primary uses of IPSec is to create VPNs. IPSec, in conjunction with Layer 2 Tunneling Protocol (L2TP) or Layer 2 Forwarding (L2F), creates packets that are difficult to read if intercepted by a third party. IPSec works at layer 3 of the OSI model.

As a security administrator, it's important to know the operations under way on your servers. As an administrator, you need to be able to evaluate operations and performance at all times and be able to establish a baseline of current operations.

The two primary protocols used by IPSec at the bottom layer are *Authentication Header (AH)* and *Encapsulating Security Payload (ESP)*. Both can operate in either the transport or tunnel mode. Protocol 50 is used for ESP, while protocol 51 is used for AH.

You can find the best overview of IPSec and AH/ESP in "An Illustrated Guide to IPSec" by Steve Friedl at http://www.unixwiz.net/techtips/iguide-ipsec.html.

Tunneling Protocols

Tunneling protocols add a capability to the network: the capability to create tunnels between networks that can be more secure, support additional protocols, and provide virtual paths between systems. The best way to think of tunneling is to imagine sensitive data being encapsulated in other packets that are sent across the public network. After they're received at the other end, the sensitive data is stripped from the other packets and recompiled into its original form.

The most common protocols used for tunneling are as follows:

Point-to-Point Tunneling Protocol   *Point-to-Point Tunneling Protocol (PPTP)* supports encapsulation in a single point-to-point environment. PPTP encapsulates and encrypts *Point-to-Point Protocol (PPP)* packets. This makes PPTP a favorite low-end protocol for networks. The negotiation between the two ends of a PPTP connection is done in the clear. Once the negotiation is performed, the channel is encrypted. This is one of the major weaknesses of the PPTP protocol. A *packet-capture device*, such as a sniffer, that captures the negotiation process can potentially use that information to determine the connection type and information about how the tunnel works. Microsoft developed PPTP and supports it on most of the company's products. PPTP uses port 1723 and TCP for connections.

Layer 2 Forwarding   *Layer 2 Forwarding (L2F)* was created by Cisco as a method of creating tunnels primarily for dial-up connections. It's similar in capability to PPP and shouldn't be used over WANs. L2F provides authentication, but it doesn't provide encryption. L2F uses port 1701 and TCP for connections.

Layer 2 Tunneling Protocol   Relatively recently, Microsoft and Cisco agreed to combine their respective tunneling protocols into one protocol: *Layer 2 Tunneling Protocol (L2TP)*. L2TP is a hybrid of PPTP and L2F. It's primarily a point-to-point protocol. L2TP supports multiple network protocols and can be used in networks besides TCP/IP. L2TP works over IPX, SNA, and IP, so it can be used as a bridge across many types of systems. The major problem with L2TP is that it doesn't provide data security: The information isn't encrypted. Security can be provided by protocols such as IPSec. L2TP uses port 1701 and UDP for connections.

Federal Information Processing Standard

The *Federal Information Processing Standard (FIPS)* is a set of guidelines for the United States federal government information systems. FIPS is used when an existing commercial or government system doesn't meet federal security requirements. FIPS is issued by NIST.

Common Criteria

Common Criteria (CC) is an internationally agreed-upon set of standards to evaluate IT security. The growing market and the need for standardized security-system ratings have created the need for a common set of definitions. CC is a combination of European, U.S., and Canadian standards compiled into a single document. Using CC, security evaluations can be consistently applied across technologies.

Wireless Transport Layer Security

Wireless Transport Layer Security (WTLS) provides an encrypted and authenticated connection between a wireless client and a server. WTLS is similar in function to TLS, but it uses a lower bandwidth and less processing power. It's used to support wireless devices, which don't yet have extremely powerful processors.

Wired Equivalent Privacy

Wired Equivalent Privacy (WEP) is a wireless protocol designed to provide privacy equivalent to that of a wired network. WEP is implemented in a number of wireless devices, including PDAs and cell phones. To make the encryption stronger, *Temporal Key Integrity Protocol (TKIP)* can also be employed. This places a 128-bit wrapper around the WEP encryption with a key that is based on such things as the MAC address of your machine and the serial number of the packet. Without the use of TKIP, WEP—as mentioned earlier in this chapter—is considered weak.

The *Wi-Fi Protected Access (WPA)* and *Wi-Fi Protected Access 2 (WPA2)* technologies were designed to address the core problems with WEP. These technologies implement the 802.11i standard. The difference between WPA and WPA2 is that the former implements most—but not all—of 802.11i in order to be able to communicate with older wireless cards (which may still need an update through their firmware in order to be compliant), while WPA2 implements the full standard and is not compatible with older cards.

Extensible Authentication Protocol (EAP) provides a framework for authentication that is often used with wireless networks. Among the five EAP types adopted by the WPA/WPA2 standard are EAP-TLS and EAP-MD5.

ISO 17799

ISO 17799 is a 10-part security audit designed to audit virtually all aspects of your IT department. It is a comprehensive and in-depth audit/review.

 ISO 17799 was discussed in detail in Chapter 6, "Securing the Network and Environment."

Understanding Key Management and the Key Life Cycle

Key management refers to the process of working with keys from the time they are created until the time they are retired or destroyed. Key management includes the following stages/areas:

- Centralized versus decentralized key generation

- Key storage and distribution

- Key escrow

- Key expiration

- Key revocation

- Key suspension

- Key recovery and archival

- Key renewal

- Key destruction

- Key usage

 Throughout this discussion, the terms *certificate* and *key* will be used interchangeably. Certificates contain keys that provide security. The process used is the same in either situation.

The term *key life cycle* describes the stages a key goes through during its entire life. You can think of this as a cradle-to-grave situation. By expressing these relationships in the terms of a life cycle, evaluating each phase of a key's use from its creation to its destruction becomes easier. If any aspect of a key's life isn't handled properly, the entire security system may become nonfunctional or compromised.

Key management is one of the key aspects of an effective cryptographic system. Keys, as you may remember, are the unique passwords or passcodes used to encrypt or decrypt messages. You can think of a key as one of the primary components of certificates; this is why these terms are used together. Certificates are used to transport keys between systems.

The following sections compare and contrast centralized and decentralized key generation as well as key storage and distribution. The other aspects of key management are also covered.

Comparing Centralized and Decentralized Key Generation

Key generation (the creation of the key) is an important first step in the process of working with keys and certificates. Using certificates is one of the primary methods for delivering keys to end entities. Key length and the method used to create the key also affect the security of the system in use. The security of a key is measured by how difficult it is to break the key. The longer it takes to break the key, the more secure the key is considered to be.

According to RSA, it would take 3 million years and a $10 million budget to break a key with a key length of 1,024 bits. The amount of time it would take to break a 2,048-bit key is virtually incalculable. Of course, these numbers are based on the assumption that the algorithm is secure and no other methods of attack would work to break the algorithm or the key.

A common method used to generate keys creates very large prime numbers. Computing prime numbers is a laborious process. Most systems use a sophisticated approximation method to calculate prime numbers as opposed to calculating them directly. If the calculation method is flawed, the numbers may not be prime and, consequently, may be easier to determine.

One main thing to consider is where to create the keys. Should they be generated on a central machine or in a decentralized environment? A third method used to generate keys is called the *split generation system*, which is a combination of a centralized and decentralized process.

Centralized Key Generation

Centralized key generation allows the key-generating process to take advantage of large-scale system resources. Key-generating algorithms tend to be extremely processor intensive. Using a centralized server, this process can be managed with a large single system. However, problems arise when the key is distributed. How can it be transported to end users without compromising security?

Figure 7.23 shows a centralized generation process. In this example, all the physical resources are in a single location, under centralized management control.

Centralized generation has the advantage of allowing additional management functions to be centralized. A major disadvantage is that the key archival and storage process may be vulnerable to an attack against a single point instead of a network. Reliability, security, and archiving can be addressed if the proper systems, procedures, and policies are put into place and followed.

FIGURE 7.23 A centralized key-generating facility

Decentralized Key Generation

Decentralized key generation allows the key-generating process to be pushed out into the organization or environment. The advantage of this method is that it allows work to be decentralized and any risks to be spread. This system isn't vulnerable to a single-point failure or attack. Decentralized generation addresses the distribution issue, but it creates a storage and management issue.

Figure 7.24 demonstrates a decentralized system. In this situation, the loss of any single key-generating system doesn't disrupt the entire network. The RA in the figure refers to a registration authority, and the CA refers to a certificate authority.

FIGURE 7.24 A distributed key-generating system

Split-System Key Generation

Many systems, including the PKI system, require the use of a split system. In a split system, the central server generates encryption keys. Digital signature keys are created at the client or in a smart card.

Storing and Distributing Keys

Where and how keys are stored affects how they are distributed. Distributing keys is usually accomplished using a *Key Distribution Center (KDC)*, as used in Kerberos, or by using a *Key Exchange Algorithm (KEA)*, as in the case of PKI.

> In order for Kerberos to function properly, time synchronization must be working correctly. If clocks drift from the correct time, problems can occur with trying to compare time stamps and authenticate.

A KDC is a single service or server that stores, distributes, and maintains cryptographic session keys. When a system wants to access a service that uses Kerberos, a request is made via the KDC. The KDC generates a session key and facilitates the process of connecting these two systems. The advantage of this process is that once it's implemented, it's automatic and requires no further intervention. The major disadvantage of this process is that the KDC is a single point of failure; if it's attacked, the entire security system could be compromised. Figure 7.25 illustrates the KDC creating a session between two systems.

FIGURE 7.25   The KDC process in a Kerberos environment

KDC   Client   Applications Server

KDC provides the key.   The key is used by the client
                           to connect to the server.

The KEA process is slightly different from the KDC process. The KEA negotiates a secret key between the two parties; the secret key is a short-term, single-use key intended strictly for key distribution. The KEA process should not be used to transmit both the public and private keys. Figure 7.26 illustrates the KEA process. The KEA session terminates once the key has been successfully transmitted.

Protecting keys from unauthorized access while making them available for use by authorized personnel is important. The process can utilize physical security measures such as locked cabinets and safes, and it can involve software such as Kerberos and PKI.

FIGURE 7.26 The KEA process

1. Key exchange

2. KEA session finishes

Client

3. Secure session

Server

> Physical protection methods include physical storage devices that place a key under lock and key. Storage devices include, but aren't limited to, filing cabinets and safes.

Keys can be either hardware devices or software devices. An example of a hardware device would be a smart card. Software keys may be generated by CA-oriented systems such as PKI. Whether they're hardware or software, protecting keys is essential for a security system to operate effectively.

Protecting keys is a difficult process. Public keys don't require full protection; they require only integrity protection. Private keys, on the other hand, require full protection. The unknowing disclosure of a private key in a symmetrical or public/private key system potentially compromises the system. Armed with a private key, an attacker could read all the communications in the system and also sign information and impersonate the real owner. This fraudulent signature could be difficult to repudiate. The following section briefly discusses private key protection and key server protection, which are both essential for good security.

Physically, private keys should be kept under close supervision. If possible, multiple keys should be required to open the storage facility, and the two keys should never be stored together. If two different people are responsible for storing the keys, both of them must consent and be present for the storage facility to be opened.

Key servers also pose potential security problems, both from an access control perspective and from a physical access perspective. If a fault is introduced into the system, a resulting *core dump* (also known as a *memory dump*) may leave the key information in a core dump file. A sophisticated attacker could use the core dump to get key information.

Most private-key security failures can be traced back to physical security or human errors. Make sure that private keys are well guarded and secure.

> Under no circumstances should you ever divulge or send your private key. Doing so jeopardizes your guarantee that only you are able to work with the data and may irreparably damage your security.

Using Key Escrow

A *key escrow* system stores keys for the purpose of law enforcement access. If a criminal investigation is under way, law enforcement agents with a search warrant have the right to access and search records within the scope of the warrant. In general, the key archival system will provide the access needed. Key escrow is listed separately because the usage is important to a law enforcement investigation.

> *Key escrow* refers to both a process and an organization or system that stores keys for access at a later date.

One of the proposed methods of dealing with key escrow involves the storage of key information with a third party, referred to as a *key escrow agency*. This agency would provide key information only when ordered by a court. In general, key escrow is handled by the key archival system.

> In an early encryption system offered by the NSA for civilian use, the NSA would have acted as the key escrow agency. The system was called *Clipper*, and it wasn't widely accepted by industry. The key escrow controversy was one of the chief reasons cited for its lack of acceptance.

Key escrow systems can also be a part of the key recovery process. Several government agencies are attempting to implement regulations requiring mandated key escrow. Mandated key escrow would allow law enforcement agencies to investigate a key escrow user without their knowledge. Many individuals and organizations view this as an invasion of their privacy, and they're fighting the use of mandated key escrow on the basis that it violates personal freedom. The key escrow process is covered in more detail in the section "Recovering and Archiving Keys" later in this chapter.

> The FBI and other national agencies are rumored to use keystroke logging software—often delivered as a Trojan Horse—for bypassing encryption. One of the most well known of these programs is Magic Lantern.

Identifying Key Expiration

A key expiration date identifies when a key is no longer valid. Normally, a key is date stamped; this means that it becomes unusable after a specified date. A new key or certificate is normally issued before the expiration date.

Keys with expiration dates work similarly to credit cards that expire. Usually, the card issuer sends another card to the cardholder before the expiration date.

Most applications that are key enabled or certificate enabled check the expiration date on a key and report to the user if the key has expired. PKI gives the user the opportunity to accept and use the key.

Revoking Keys

Keys are revoked when they are compromised, the authentication process has malfunctioned, people are transferred, or other security risks occur. Revoking a key keeps it from being misused. A revoked key must be assumed to be invalid or possibly compromised.

The credit card analogy is applicable here too. Consider a credit card that was stolen from a customer. This card, for all intents and purposes, is a certificate. A retailer could take its chances and accept the card, or it could verify that the card is accurate by running the card through a card verification machine to check its status. If the card has been reported stolen, the credit card authorization process will decline the charge.

Systems such as PKI use a CRL to perform a check on the status of revoked keys. Revocations are permanent. Once a certificate is revoked, it can't be used again; a new key must be generated and issued.

Suspending Keys

A *key suspension* is a temporary situation. If an employee were to take a leave of absence, the employee's key could be suspended until they came back to work. This temporary suspension would ensure that the key wouldn't be usable during their absence. A suspension might also occur if a high number of failed authentications or other unusual activities were occurring. The temporary suspension would give administrators or managers time to sort out what is happening.

Checking the status of suspended keys is accomplished by checking with the certificate server or by using other mechanisms. In a PKI system, a CRL would be checked to determine the status of a certificate. This process can occur automatically or manually. Most key or certificate management systems provide a mechanism to report the status of a key or certificate.

 Key management systems use the same general process when checking the status of keys. The Security+ exam distinguishes between status checking for suspension and revocation. The major difference is that a revoked key can't be used again, whereas the status of a suspended key can be changed to allow the key to be used again. Once a key is revoked, a new key is required.

Recovering and Archiving Keys

One of the problems with a key-based system is that older information, unless processed with a new key, may become inaccessible. For example, if you have a two-year-old file on your system and it's still encrypted, will you remember which key was used to encrypt it two years ago? If you're like most people, you won't. If you can't decrypt the data, it's useless.

To deal with this problem, archiving old keys is essential: Any time a user or key generator creates and issues a key, the key must also be sent to the key archive system. This is most easily done on a server that offers secure storage. Older keys can be stored and retrieved when necessary. Figure 7.27 illustrates this relationship with a CA. This server requires strong physical security and at least the same security as the key-generating system.

FIGURE 7.27   The key archival system

Key recovery is an important part of an encryption system. Information that is stored using older keys will be inaccessible using a new key. Key recovery allows you to access information that is encrypted with older keys. For example, key recovery could be used to retrieve information from an ex-employee. Three different factors must be considered when implementing a key archival system:

Current keys   *Current keys* are the keys in use at the present time. They haven't been revoked. In the event that a current key becomes lost, destroyed, or damaged, you need a way to recover the key so that data loss doesn't occur. A smart card can also become damaged, and a method must be established to reload the card with key information.

If the current key isn't recoverable, all information that was encrypted using it will be unavailable. This type of data loss could be expensive. Some newer systems allow the creation of "virtual" smart cards that can be used temporarily to initialize a new card. This card would generally be good only for a short period of time, such as during a work shift.

This process should be relatively easy for administrators to manage because people do forget to bring their authentication devices to work from time to time.

Previous Keys   *Previous keys* have recently expired and are no longer current. An employee who comes to work today may not know that a key rollover has occurred until they try to open yesterday's e-mail. Depending on what's in the e-mail, this could be a disaster. Many newer systems keep copies of recent keys in a key store on the system; this key store may contain the last two or three keys. If a local key store isn't provided, a key restoration process will be required from the archive system. Again, this may involve manual intervention by administrators.

Archived keys   Archived keys were discussed earlier. You should expect that older messages will be needed from time to time. This is especially true in a situation where litigation is involved; during the discovery phase of litigation, all records, correspondence, and memoranda must be presented to attorneys when subpoenaed. Failure to comply will result in sanctions from the court. Imagine that you had to access all the e-mails and files from a particular department for the last five years; it would be a very labor-intensive undertaking if you didn't have an archive system.

Many recovery and archive systems use the *M of N Control* method of access. This method, simply stated, says that in order to access the key server if *n* number of administrators have the ability to perform a process, *m* number of those administrators must authenticate for access to occur. This may require the administrators' physical presence.

A typical M of N Control method may stipulate that six people have access to the archive server and at least three of them must be present to accomplish access. In this situation, $m = 3$ and $n = 6$. This would ensure that no one person could compromise the security system.

 It's important to remember that your key archival system contains the complete history of all the keys that have been issued by your system. This information might also include all the current keys in use. Access to this server would be the equivalent of discovering the Rosetta stone of your organization. An attacker with this information would have full and unrestricted access to every bit of information in your network.

Renewing Keys

Key renewal defines the process of enabling a key for use after its scheduled expiration date. A key would be reissued for a certain time in this situation. This process is called a *key rollover*. In most cases, the rollover of keys occurs for a given time frame. What would happen, however, if an organization found itself in a situation where a key rollover must not occur? Many systems include means to prevent rolling keys over.

In general, key rollovers are a bad practice and should not be performed except in the direst of situations. The longer a key is used, the more likely it is to be compromised. It is always better to renew keys than to do a key rollover.

If an earthquake occurred in your area and your building was inaccessible for two weeks, you would want to allow the existing keys to be used until higher-priority matters could be resolved when you went back to your building. In a natural disaster, a key rollover could add an inordinate amount of stress to an already very stressful situation.

Destroying Keys

Key destruction is the process of destroying keys that have become invalid. For example, an electronic key can be erased from a smart card. In older mechanical key systems, keys were physically destroyed using hammers.

Many symmetrically based encryption systems use a dedicated device to carry the key for the encryption. This key would be physically delivered to the site using the encryption system. Old keys would be recovered and destroyed.

 Always remember that symmetric encryption uses the same key to encrypt and decrypt the data (a primary weakness being that you have to share the key with others). Asymmetric encryption uses two keys: one to encrypt and another to decrypt the data.

Whether you're using physical keys or software-oriented key systems, old keys must be destroyed in a manner that ensures they don't fall into unauthorized hands.

Identifying Key Usage

During the time when the key is not being revoked, suspended, renewed, or destroyed, it is being used. *Key usage* is simply the use (and management) of public and private keys for encryption. While the topic appears as an objective on the exam, there is nothing additional to know here that is not addressed elsewhere in this chapter.

🌐 Real World Scenario

Selling the Company's Old Computers

You've been asked to verify that the computers your company has liquidated are ready to be sold. What steps should you take to verify that unauthorized access to information doesn't occur?

You need to be concerned about two issues in this case. First, you need to make sure all corporate records, software, and other sensitive information are removed from the system. Second, you need to make sure any special access devices or encryption systems have been removed. Encryption systems that use key-based models may store keys in hidden areas of the disks. As a general practice, the disks on systems that are sold as surplus should be completely zeroed out; doing so prevents any sensitive information from being released inadvertently.

Summary

This chapter focused on the basic elements of cryptography and the PKI implementation. There are three primary methods of encryption:

- Symmetric
- Asymmetric
- Hashing

Symmetric systems require that each end of the connection have the same key. Asymmetric systems use a two-key system. In public key cryptography, the receiver has a private key known only to them; a public key corresponds to it, which they make known to others. The public key can be sent to all other parties; the private key is never divulged. Hashing refers to performing a calculation on a message and converting it into a numeric hash value.

There are five main considerations in implementing a cryptography system:

- Confidentiality
- Integrity
- Authentication
- Nonrepudiation
- Access control

Confidentiality means that the message retains its privacy. *Integrity* means the message can't be altered without detection. *Authentication* is used to verify that the person who sent the message is actually who they say they are. *Nonrepudiation* prevents either the sender or receiver from denying that the message was sent or received. *Access control* is the methods, processes, and mechanisms of preventing unauthorized access to the systems that do the cryptography.

PKI is a system that has been widely implemented to provide encryption and data security in computer networks. It's being implemented globally by both governmental agencies and businesses. The major components of a PKI system include the certificate authority, the registration authority (which could be local), and certificates. The most common certificate implemented in PKI is X.509 v3.

CA systems can establish trusting relationships based on a hierarchical, bridge, mesh, or hybrid structure. This relationship can be defined based upon the needs of the organization.

The three cryptographic attacks covered in this chapter were mathematical, weak key, and birthday attacks. In mathematical attacks, mathematical methods are used to find ways to break an algorithm and decrypt a message. The birthday attack is based on the probability that patterns and common events become more likely as collections get larger. The weak key attack exploits either poorly chosen passwords or flaws in the password encryption algorithm.

In this chapter, you also learned about the standards, agencies, and associations that are interested in cryptography. You learned about the standards associated with cryptographic systems and the key-management life cycle.

Several government agencies have been specifically charged with overseeing security and encryption. The NSA and NIST are both concerned with government encryption standards. NIST is primarily concerned with nonmilitary standards; NSA/CSS is concerned with military applications.

The IETF, ISOC, ITU, and the IEEE are industrial associations concerned with different aspects of security. They aren't required to coordinate their activities, but as a general rule, they do. The IEEE publishes many standards and guidelines that are adhered to by most manufacturers.

The series of stages during the process of managing a key or a certificate is called a key/certificate life cycle. A life cycle encompasses all the major aspects of the life of a key or a certificate from the time it's generated until the time it's retired. There are 10 areas/stages of a key's life cycle:

- Key generation
- Key storage and distribution
- Key escrow
- Key expiration
- Key revocation
- Key suspension
- Key recovery and archival
- Key renewal
- Key destruction
- Key usage

You need to consider each of these stages when you implement a key or certificate within your organization. If you fail to properly address these issues, you can compromise the process or make more work for yourself. If the process isn't followed, the entire system is vulnerable.

You must decide whether to use a centralized or a decentralized process to generate keys. Centralized key generation can potentially create a bottleneck or a single point of failure. Decentralized key generation can create administrative and security problems. Most modern implementations support both centralized and decentralized key generation.

Appropriate key storage is critical to maintaining a secure environment. Keys should be stored on hardened systems under close physical control. Keys can be stored in physical cabinets or on servers. Security storage failures are usually the result of human error. Distributing keys and transporting keys can present security challenges. Private keys should never be sent through the communications network; out-of-band transmission should be used to transport or distribute them. If an existing key has been compromised, the new key will be just as compromised. Public keys are intended for circulation; however, steps must be taken to protect their integrity.

Key escrow is the process where keys are made available to law enforcement or other authorized agencies to utilize them to conduct an investigation. Key escrow agents store these keys, and they release them to authorized authorities.

A key expires when it reaches the end of its life cycle. Typically, this is a date-driven event. An expired key may be reissued using a rollover process, but generally this is considered a bad practice. The longer a key is used, the more likely it is to be broken.

When a key or certificate has been identified as corrupt, compromised, or lost, it can be revoked. A CRL informs all of the end users and CAs that the certificate has been revoked. Once a key is revoked, it can no longer be used.

Keys are suspended to disable them for a period of time. Suspension may occur because the key holder has become ill or has taken time off. A key can be unsuspended and reused.

Key recovery is the ability to recover a lost key or to use a previously active key. Three types of keys must be considered in this process: current keys, previous keys, and archived keys. An organization can use a key archival system to recover information that has been encrypted using older keys. Key archival systems usually utilize some type of access control such as the M of N Control method, which stipulates that a certain number of people must be present to access key archives. A key archival system usually works in conjunction with a key-generating system to provide complete archiving.

Key destruction is the process of rendering a key unusable. Physical keys must be physically destroyed. Software keys and smart card keys should have their key files erased to prevent them from being used.

Exam Essentials

Be able to describe the process of a hashing algorithm.   Hashing algorithms are used to mathematically derive a key from a message. The most common hashing standards for cryptographic applications are the SHA and MD algorithms.

Know the principles of a symmetric algorithm. A symmetric algorithm requires that receivers of the message use the same *private key*. Symmetric algorithms can be extremely secure. This method is widely implemented in governmental applications. The private key is changed using out-of-band transmission.

Be able to describe the process of asymmetric algorithms. Asymmetric algorithms use a two-key method of encryption. The message is encrypted using the public key and decrypted using a second key or private key. The key is derived from the same algorithm.

Know the primary objectives for using cryptographic systems. The main objectives for these systems are confidentiality, integrity, authentication, and nonrepudiation. Digital signatures can be used to verify the integrity and provide nonrepudiation of a message.

Understand the process used in PKI. PKI is an encryption system that utilizes a variety of technologies to provide confidentiality, integrity, authentication, and nonrepudiation. PKI uses certificates issued from a CA to provide this capability as well as encryption. PKI is being widely implemented in organizations worldwide.

Be able to describe the revocation process in PKI. PKI issues a CRL from a CA when a revocation request is made. The CRL can take anywhere from a few hours to several days to propagate through a community.

Know the trust models used in PKI. PKI provides the ability to use hierarchical, bridged, meshed, and hybrid models for trust. A CA hierarchy, or tree, is broken into subcomponents. The subcomponents are called root authorities, intermediate CAs, and leaf CAs.

Know the primary attack methods used against cryptographic systems. The primary attacks against cryptographic systems are birthday attacks, mathematical attacks, and weak key attacks.

Identify the common technologies and methods used in encryption. Although this chapter introduced many different protocols and standards, you need to be familiar with PKIX/PKCS, X.509, SSL/TLS, S/MIME, SSH, PGP, HTTPS, IPS, WTLS, WEP, and IPSec. Each of these standards provides specific capabilities.

Identify the stages in a key/certificate life cycle. A life cycle involves the generation, distribution, protection, archiving, recovery, and revocation of a key or certificate. Each of these aspects of key management must be considered to provide an effective and maintainable security process.

Identify the relative advantages and disadvantages of centralized versus decentralized key management. Centralized key management uses centralized computers to generate keys. Key generation is a very computer-intensive process. When centralized processes are used, the processes are open to single-point failure and key transmission problems. Decentralized key generation allows work to be spread over an entire organization. The disadvantage is that spreading out the process makes securing the keys more difficult. Most systems use a split method. Private keys should be transmitted using an out-of-band method.

Be able to describe the storage methods used for keys. Physical protection methods include physical storage devices that place a key under lock and key. Storage devices include, but aren't limited to, filing cabinets and safes. Software storage refers to hardened servers or other computer systems that are used to store keys. Most keys are compromised as a result of human error.

Know the purpose of key escrow.   Key escrow allows law enforcement or other authorized governmental officials to access keys to conduct investigations. A key escrow agency or agent is a third party that is trusted to provide this service. A key archival system would normally be able to accomplish this task.

Be able to describe the purpose of key expiration.   Keys are usually stamped with an expiration date. The longer a key stays in use, the more likely it is to be compromised. The more a key is used, the more often it will need to be changed.

Understand the difference between a key revocation and a suspension.   A key revocation is performed when a key has potentially become compromised or lost. Key revocation is usually accomplished using some form of key revocation list. A certificate is revoked using a CRL process. A key is suspended when it needs to be made temporarily inactive. A suspension can be undone; a revocation can't.

Be able to describe the purpose of key recovery   Key recovery allows information to be accessed that is encrypted with older keys. For example, key recovery could be used to retrieve information from an ex-employee.

Be able to describe the M of N Control method.   The M of N Control method basically states that of n number of people, m number must be present to perform the process of key recovery. For example, if six people are authorized to use a system, three of the six must be present to recover a key. In this example, $m = 3$ and $n = 6$. This control method prevents any one person from compromising the key archival system.

Explain the purpose of key renewal.   Key renewal isn't a recommended practice. However, sometimes it may be necessary to renew a key in order to continue to use a system for a short time. The longer keys or certificates are used, the more vulnerable they are to decryption.

Know the purpose of key destruction.   Key destruction is an important part of physical control. When a physical key is retired, it should be physically destroyed. When a software key is retired, it should be erased and zeroed out to prevent inadvertent disclosure.

Hands-On Labs

The labs in this chapter are as follows:

Lab 7.1: Hash Rules in Windows Server 2003

Lab 7.2: SSL Settings in Windows Server 2003

Lab 7.3: Encrypting a File System in Linux

Lab 7.4: Look for Errors in IPSec Performance Statistics

Lab 7.1: Hash Rules in Windows Server 2003

This lab requires a test machine (nonproduction) running Windows Server 2003.

> **NOTE** On a generic 2003 Server with Active Directory, you must access the local security policy slightly differently. Launch an MMC, then choose to add the GPO Editor, and select Local Computer. Everything else will then work the same.

To create a new hash rule, follow these steps:

1. Choose Start ➢ Administrative Tools ➢ Local Security Policy.
2. Expand Software Restriction Policies.
3. Right-click Additional Rules and choose New Hash Rule from the context menu.
4. Click the Browse button and choose the file `hisecws.inf` from the Templates folder (this is under `\Winnt\Security\Templates`).
5. Notice the file hash that appears and the file information. Click OK.
6. Notice that the new hash rule is added to the right pane along with the default path rules that appear there.

Lab 7.2: SSL Settings in Windows Server 2003

This lab requires a test machine (nonproduction) running Windows Server 2003. To configure the SSL port setting, follow these steps:

1. Open the Internet Information Services Manager by choosing Start ➢ Administrative Tools ➢ Internet Information Services (IIS) Manager.
2. Expand the left pane entries until your website becomes an option. Right-click the website and choose Properties from the context menu.
3. Select the Web Site tab. Check whether the port number for SSL is filled in. If it isn't, enter a number here.
4. Click OK and exit the Internet Information Services Manager.

Notice that the SSL port field is blank by default, and any port number can be entered here—this differs from the way some previous versions of IIS worked. The default SSL port is 443; if you enter a number other than that in this field, then clients must know and request that port in advance in order to connect.

Lab 7.3: Encrypting a File System in Linux

This lab requires access to a server running SuSE Linux Enterprise Server 9. To encrypt a filesystem, follow these steps:

1. Log in as root and start YaST.

2. Choose System, then Partitioner.

3. Answer Yes to the prompt that appears. Select a filesystem and click Edit.

4. Select the Encrypt File System check box and click OK.

Lab 7.4: Look for Errors in IPSec Performance Statistics

This lab requires access to a server running Windows Server 2003. To configure IPSec monitoring, follow these steps:

1. Open the System Monitor by choosing Start ➢ Administrative Tools ➢ Performance ➢ System Monitor.

2. Click the + icon to add counters.

3. For an object, select IPSec v4 IKE.

4. Choose each counter that appears in the list, and click the Explain button to learn what it is able to show you.

5. Add the following counters: Total Authentication Failures and Total Negotiation Failures.

6. Click Close.

You're now monitoring the failures as they occur. On a properly functioning system, this graph should show no activity. Any activity that appears is indicative of problems since IPSec was last started and should be carefully examined.

Review Questions

1. What is the process of deriving an encrypted value from a mathematical process called?

    A. Hashing

    B. Asymmetric

    C. Symmetric

    D. Social engineering

2. During a training session, you want to impress upon users how serious security and, in particular, cryptography is. To accomplish this, you want to give them as much of an overview about the topic as possible. Which government agency should you mention is primarily responsible for establishing government standards involving cryptography for general-purpose government use?

    A. NSA

    B. NIST

    C. IEEE

    D. ITU

3. Assuming asymmetric encryption, if data is encoded with a value of 5, what would be used to decode it?

    A. 5

    B. 1

    C. 1/5

    D. 0

4. You're a member of a consortium wanting to create a new standard that will effectively end all spam. After years of meeting, the group has finally come across a solution and now wants to propose it. The process of proposing a new standard or method on the Internet is referred to by which acronym?

    A. WBS

    B. X.509

    C. RFC

    D. IEEE

5. Mary claims that she didn't make a phone call from her office to a competitor and tell them about developments her company is working on. Telephone logs, however, show that such a call was placed from her phone, and time clock records show she was the only person working at the time. What do these records provide?

    A. Integrity

    B. Confidentiality

    C. Authentication

    D. Nonrepudiation

6. Mercury Technical Solutions has been using SSL in a business-to-business environment for a number of years. Despite the fact that there have been no compromises in security, the new IT manager wants to use stronger security than SSL can offer. Which of the following protocols is similar to SSL but offers the ability to use additional security protocols?

   A. TLS

   B. SSH

   C. RSH

   D. X.509

7. MAC is an acronym for what as it relates to cryptography?

   A. Media access control

   B. Mandatory access control

   C. Message authentication code

   D. Multiple advisory committees

8. You've been brought in as a security consultant for a small bicycle manufacturing firm. Immediately you notice that it's using a centralized key-generating process, and you make a note to dissuade them from that without delay. What problem is created by using a centralized key-generating process?

   A. Network security

   B. Key transmission

   C. Certificate revocation

   D. Private key security

9. Which of the following terms refers to the prevention of unauthorized disclosure of keys?

   A. Authentication

   B. Integrity

   C. Access control

   D. Nonrepudiation

10. As the head of IT for MTS, you're explaining some security concerns to a junior administrator who has just been hired. You're trying to emphasize the need to know what is important and what isn't. Which of the following is *not* a consideration in key storage?

    A. Environmental controls

    B. Physical security

    C. Hardened servers

    D. Administrative controls

11. What is the primary organization for maintaining certificates called?

    A. CA

    B. RA

    C. LRA

    D. CRL

12. Due to a breach, a certificate must be permanently revoked, and you don't want it to ever be used again. What is often used to revoke a certificate?

    A. CRA

    B. CYA

    C. CRL

    D. PKI

13. Which organization can be used to identify an individual for certificate issue in a PKI environment?

    A. RA

    B. LRA

    C. PKE

    D. SHA

14. Kristin, from Payroll, has left the office on maternity leave and won't return for at least six weeks. You've been instructed to suspend her key. Which of the following statements is true?

    A. In order to be used, suspended keys must be revoked.

    B. Suspended keys don't expire.

    C. Suspended keys can be reactivated.

    D. Suspending keys is a bad practice.

15. What document describes how a CA issues certificates and what they are used for?

    A. Certificate policies

    B. Certificate practices

    C. Revocation authority

    D. CRL

16. After returning from a conference in Jamaica, your manager informs you that he has learned that law enforcement has the right, under subpoena, to conduct investigations using keys. He wants you to implement measures to make such an event run smoothly should it ever happen. What is the process of storing keys for use by law enforcement called?

    A. Key escrow

    B. Key archival

    C. Key renewal

    D. Certificate rollover

17. The CRL takes time to be fully disseminated. Which protocol allows a certificate's authenticity to be immediately verified?

    A. CA

    B. CP

    C. CRC

    D. OCSP

18. Which set of specifications is designed to allow XML-based programs access to PKI services?

    A. XKMS

    B. XMLS

    C. PKXMS

    D. PKIXMLS

19. An attack that is based on the statistical probability of a match in a key base is referred to as what?

    A. Birthday attack

    B. DoS attack

    C. Weak key attack

    D. Smurf attack

20. A brainstorming session has been called. The moderator tells you to pull out a sheet of paper and write down your security concerns based on the technologies that your company uses. If your company uses public keys, what should you write as the primary security concern?

    A. Privacy

    B. Authenticity

    C. Access control

    D. Integrity

Answers to Review Questions

1. A.   Hashing algorithms are used to derive an encrypted value from a message or word.

2. B.   NIST is responsible for establishing the standards for general-purpose government encryption. NIST is also becoming involved in private-sector cryptography.

3. C.   With asymmetric encryption, two keys are used—one to encode and the other to decode. The two keys are mathematical reciprocals of each other.

4. C.   The Request for Comments (RFC) process allows all users and interested parties to comment on proposed standards for the Internet. The RFC editor manages the RFC process. The editor is responsible for cataloging, updating, and tracking RFCs through the process.

5. D.   Nonrepudiation offers undisputable proof that a party was involved in an action.

6. A.   TLS is a security protocol that uses SSL, and it allows the use of other security protocols.

7. C.   A MAC as it relates to cryptography is a method of verifying the integrity of an encrypted message. The MAC is derived from the message and the key.

8. B.   Key transmission is the largest problem from among the choices given. Transmitting private keys is a major concern. Private keys are typically transported using out-of-band methods to ensure security.

9. C.   Access control refers to the process of ensuring that sensitive keys aren't divulged to unauthorized personnel.

10. A.   Proper key storage requires that the keys be physically stored in a secure environment. This may include using locked cabinets, hardened servers, and effective physical and administrative controls.

11. A.   A certificate authority (CA) is responsible for maintaining certificates in the PKI environment.

12. C.   A Certificate Revocation List (CRL) is created and distributed to all CAs to revoke a certificate or key.

13. B.   A local registration authority (LRA) can establish an applicant's identity and verify that the applicant for a certificate is valid. The LRA sends verification to the CA that issues the certificate.

14. C.   Suspending keys is a good practice: It disables a key, making it unusable for a certain period of time. This can prevent the key from being used while someone is gone. The key can be reactivated when that person returns.

15. A.   The certificate policies document defines what certificates can be used for.

16. A.   Key escrow is the process of storing keys or certificates for use by law enforcement. Law enforcement has the right, under subpoena, to conduct investigations using these keys.

17. D.   Online Certificate Status Protocol (OCSP) can be used to immediately verify a certificate's authenticity.

18. A.   XML Key Management Specification (XKMS) is designed to allow XML-based programs access to PKI services.

19. A.   Birthday attacks are based on the statistical likelihood of a match. As the key length grows, the probability of a match decreases.

20. D.   Public keys are created to be distributed to a wide audience. The biggest security concern regarding their use is ensuring that the public keys maintain their integrity. This can be accomplished by using a thumbprint or a second encryption scheme in the certificate or key.

Chapter

8

Security Policies and Procedures

THE FOLLOWING COMPTIA SECURITY+ EXAM OBJECTIVES ARE COVERED IN THIS CHAPTER:

✓ **3.2 Explain common access control models and the differences between each.**

- MAC
- DAC
- Role and Rule based access control

✓ **3.6 Summarize the various authentication models and identify the components of each.**

- One, two, and three-factor authentication
- Single sign-on

✓ **4.6 Execute proper logging procedures and evaluate the results.**

- Security application
- DNS
- Firewall
- Antivirus

✓ **4.7 Conduct periodic audits of system security settings.**

- User access and rights review
- Storage and retention policies

✓ **6.1 Explain redundancy planning and its components.**

- Hot site
- Cold site
- Warm Site
- Backup generator

- Single point of failure
- RAID
- Spare parts
- Redundant servers
- Redundant ISP
- UPS
- Redundant connections

✓ **6.2 Implement disaster recovery procedures.**

- Planning
- Disaster recovery exercises
- Backup techniques and practices—storage
- Schemes
- Restoration

✓ **6.4 Identify and explain applicable legislation and organizational policies.**

- Secure disposal of computers
- Acceptable use policies
- Password complexity
- Change management
- Classification of information
- Mandatory vacations
- Personally Identifiable Information (PII)
- Due care
- Due diligence
- Due process
- SLA
- Security-related HR policy
- User education and awareness training

While this chapter focuses on the topic of policies, it is far from the first time the subject has appeared in this book. As a security professional, you must strive not only to prevent losses, but also to make contingency plans for recovering from any losses that do occur. Plans are the building blocks on which your company is built, and policies are the tools used to implement those plans.

This chapter deals with the crucial aspects of business continuity, vendor support, security policies and procedures, and privilege management from an operations perspective. A solid grasp of these concepts will help you prepare for the exam because they appear in multiple objectives. It will also help you become a more proficient and professional security team member. The process of working with, helping to design, and maintaining security in your organization is a tough job. It requires dedication, vigilance, and a sense of duty to your organization.

Understanding Business Continuity

One of the oldest phrases still in use today is "the show must go on." Nowhere is that more true than in the world of business, where downtime means the loss of significant revenue with each passing minute. Business continuity is primarily concerned with the processes, policies, and methods that an organization follows to minimize the impact of a system failure, network failure, or the failure of any key component needed for operation—essentially, whatever it takes to ensure that the business continues, that the show does indeed go on.

Contingency and disaster-recovery planning make up a significant part of business continuity. The plans that you formulate for dealing with disasters are known as *schemes* and scheming is a key part of maintaining the infrastructure of a secure network. Utilities, high-availability environments, and disaster recovery are all parts of business continuity. In the following sections, we'll look at them and examine the roles that they play.

Utilities

Basic utilities such as electricity, water, and natural gas are key aspects of business continuity. In the vast majority of cases, electricity and water are restored—at least on an emergency basis—fairly rapidly. The damage created by blizzards, tornadoes, and other natural disasters is managed and repaired by utility companies and government agencies. Other disasters, such as a major earthquake or hurricane, can overwhelm these agencies, and services may be interrupted for quite a while. When these types of events occur, critical infrastructure may be unavailable for days, weeks, or even months.

 Real World Scenario

The Importance of Utilities

When the earthquake of 1989 occurred in San Francisco, California, portions of the city were without electricity, natural gas, and water for several months. Entire buildings were left unoccupied, not because of the earthquake, but because the infrastructure was badly damaged. This damage prevented many businesses whose information systems departments were located in those buildings from returning to operation for several weeks. Most of the larger organizations were able to shift the processing loads to other companies or divisions.

When you evaluate your business's sustainability, realize that disasters do indeed happen. If possible, build infrastructures that don't have single points of failure or connection. After the September 11, 2001, terrorist attack on the World Trade Center (WTC), several ISPs and other companies became nonfunctional because the WTC housed centralized communications systems and computer departments.

Consider the impact of weather on your contingency plans. What if you needed to relocate your facility to another region of the country? How would you get personnel there? What personnel would be relocated? How would they be housed and fed during the time of the crisis? You should consider these possibilities in advance. Although the likelihood that a crippling disaster will occur is relatively small, you still need to evaluate the risk.

 The year 2005 was the year of the natural disaster. Starting with the tsunami that hit parts of Asia a few days before the start of the year and continuing through Hurricane Katrina that hit Louisiana and other parts of the South, it seemed as if there was a nonstop juggernaut of adversity underfoot. Many a business will never be able to recover from those catastrophes, while many paused for a short period of time, then were back up and running again.

As an administrator, you should always be aware of problems that can occur and have an idea of how you'll approach them. It's impossible to prepare for every emergency, but you can plan for those that could conceivably happen.

High Availability

High availability refers to the process of keeping services and systems operational during an outage. In short, the goal is to provide all services to all users, where they need them and when they need them. With high availability, the goal is to have key services available 99.999 percent of the time (also known as *five nines availability*).

 Real World Scenario

Formulating Business Continuity Plans

As a security administrator, you'll need to think through a way to maintain business continuity should a crisis occur. Imagine your company is in each of the following three scenarios:

Scenario 1   Your company is in the business of monitoring criminal offenders who are under electronic house arrest nationwide. Every offender wears an anklet that wirelessly communicates with a device in their home. The home device communicates to your site in real time over phone lines by calling a toll-free number to report if the offender is in or out of the home; you alert local authorities immediately if someone isn't in compliance. The number of offenders, and the number of home devices that call your center, is in the tens of thousands. How could business be maintained if the trunk line for the toll-free phone carrier were disrupted in the middle of the night? How could you verify offender compliance if the problem took hours to correct?

Scenario 2   You're the administrator for a small educational company that delivers certification exams locally. The exams are downloaded the night before and delivered throughout the day as students—who have registered over the Internet—arrive. You show up at 8:00 a.m. on Friday, knowing that there are more than 20 exams to be administered that were downloaded Thursday night. What you find, however, is that someone has broken into the testing room and trashed all the workstations and monitors. Some of those coming to take the exams are driving from far away. How will you approach the situation?

Scenario 3   You're the database administrator for a large grocery chain. When you leave on Wednesday, there are no problems. When you arrive on Thursday—the day a new sale starts—you learn that the DSL lines are down. They went down before the local stores could download the new prices. All scanned goods will ring up at the price they were last week (either sale or regular) and not at current prices. The provider says it's working on the DSL problem but can't estimate how long repairs will take. How do you approach the problem?

Just like in the real world, there are no right or wrong answers for these scenarios. However, they all represent situations that have happened and that administrators planned for ahead of time.

There are several ways to accomplish this, including implementing redundant technology, fault-tolerant systems, and backup communications channels. A truly redundant system won't utilize just one of these methods but rather some aspect of all of them. The following sections address these topics in more detail.

Redundancy

Redundancy refers to systems that are either duplicated or that *fail over* to other systems in the event of a malfunction. *Fail-over* refers to the process of reconstructing a system or switching over to other systems when a failure is detected. In the case of a server, the server switches to a redundant server when a fault is detected. This allows service to continue uninterrupted until the primary server can be restored. In the case of a network, processing switches to another network path in the event of a network failure in the primary path.

> Fail-over systems can be very expensive to implement. In a large corporate network or e-commerce environment, a fail-over might entail switching all processing to a remote location until your primary facility is operational. The primary site and the remote site would synchronize data to ensure that information is as up-to-date as possible.

Many newer operating systems, such as Linux, Windows Server 2008, and Novell Open Enterprise Server, are capable of *clustering* to provide fail-over capabilities. Clustering involves multiple systems connected together cooperatively and networked in such a way that if any of the systems fail, the other systems take up the slack and continue to operate. The overall capability of the server cluster may decrease, but the network or service will remain operational.

> To appreciate the beauty of clustering, contemplate the fact that it is this technology upon which Google is built. Clustering not only allows the company to have redundancy, it also offers it the ability to scale as demand increases.

Figure 8.1 shows the clustering process in a network. In this cluster, each system has its own data storage and data-processing capabilities. The system that is connected to the network has the additional task of managing communication between the cluster and its users. Many clustering systems allow all the systems in the cluster to share a single disk system. In either case, reliability is improved when clustering technologies are incorporated in key systems.

Most ISPs and network providers have extensive internal fail-over capability to provide high availability to clients. Business clients and employees who are unable to access information or services tend to lose confidence. The trade-off for reliability and trustworthiness, of course, is cost: Fail-over systems can become prohibitively expensive. You'll need to carefully study your needs to determine whether your system requires this capability.

For example, if your environment requires a high level of availability, your servers should be clustered. This will allow the other servers in this network to take up the load if one of the servers in the cluster fails.

FIGURE 8.1 Server clustering in a networked environment

Fault Tolerance

Fault tolerance is primarily the ability of a system to sustain operations in the event of a component failure. Fault-tolerant systems can continue operation even though a critical component, such as a disk drive, has failed. This capability involves over-engineering systems by adding redundant components and subsystems.

Fault tolerance can be built into a server by adding a second power supply, a second CPU, and other key components. Several manufacturers (such as HP, Unisys, and IBM) offer fault-tolerant servers; these servers typically have multiple processors that automatically fail over if a malfunction occurs.

 In addition to fault-tolerant servers, you can have fault-tolerant implementations such as Tandem, Stratus, and HP. In these settings, multiple computers are used to provide the 100 percent availability of a single server.

There are two key components of fault tolerance you should never overlook: spare parts and electrical power. *Spare parts* should always be readily available to repair any system-critical component if it should fail. The redundancy strategy N+1 means that you have the number of components you need, plus one to plug into any system should it be needed. For example, a small company with five standalone servers that are all the same model should have a power supply in a box nearby to install in any one of the servers should there be a failure. (The redundancy strategy 1+1 has one spare part for every component in use.)

Since computer systems cannot operate in the absence of electrical power, it is imperative that fault tolerance be built into your electrical infrastructure as well. At a bare minimum, an *uninterruptible power supply (UPS)*—with surge protection—should accompany every server and workstation. That UPS should be rated for the load it is expected to carry in the event of a power failure (factoring in the computer, monitor, and any other device connected to it) and be checked periodically as part of your preventative maintenance routine to make sure the battery is operational. You will need to replace the battery every few years to keep the UPS operational.

A UPS will allow you to continue to function in the absence of power for only a short duration. For fault tolerance in situations of longer duration, you will need a *backup generator.* Backup generators run off of gasoline or diesel and generate the electricity needed to provide steady power. While some backup generators can come on instantly in the event of a power outage, most take a short time to warm up before they can provide consistent power, and thus you will find that you still need to implement UPSs within your organization.

Redundant Array of Independent Disks

Redundant Array of Independent Disks (RAID) is a technology that uses multiple disks to provide fault tolerance. There are several designations for RAID levels.

RAID stands for not only *Redundant Array of Independent Disks,* but also *Redundant Array of Inexpensive Disks.* While the latter term has lost its popularity, you might still encounter it in some texts.

The most commonly implemented RAID levels are as follows:

RAID level 0   RAID 0 is *disk striping.* It uses multiple drives and maps them together as a single physical drive. This is done primarily for performance, not for fault tolerance. If any drive in a RAID 0 array fails, the entire logical drive becomes unusable.

RAID level 1   RAID 1 is *disk mirroring.* Disk mirroring provides 100 percent redundancy because everything is stored on two disks. If one disk fails, another disk continues to operate. The failed disk can be replaced, and the RAID 1 array can be regenerated. This system offers the advantage of 100 percent data redundancy at the expense of doubling the storage requirements. Each drive keeps an exact copy of all information, which reduces the effective storage capability to 50 percent of the overall storage. Some implementations of disk mirroring are called *disk duplexing* (*duplexing* is a less commonly used term). The only difference between mirroring and duplexing is one more controller card. With mirroring, one controller card writes sequentially to each disk. With duplexing, the same data is written to both disks simultaneously. Disk duplexing has much faster write performance than disk mirroring. Many hardware implementations of RAID 1 are actually duplexing but they are still generally referred to as mirrors.

The data is intact in a RAID 1 array if either one of the two drives fails. After the failed drive is replaced with a new drive, you remirror the data from the good drive to the new drive to re-create the array.

RAID level 3   RAID 3 is *disk striping with a parity disk.* RAID 3 arrays implement fault tolerance by using striping (RAID 0) in conjunction with a separate disk that stores parity information. *Parity information* is a value based on the value of the data stored in each disk location. This system ensures that the data can be recovered in the event of a failure. The process of generating parity information uses the arithmetic value of the data binary. This process allows any single disk in the array to fail while the system continues to operate. The failed disk is removed, a new disk is installed, and the new drive is then regenerated using the parity information. RAID 3 is common in older systems, and it's supported by most Unix systems.

RAID level 5   RAID 5 is *disk striping with parity* and is one of the most common forms of RAID in use today. It operates similarly to disk striping, as in RAID 0. The parity information is spread across all the disks in the array instead of being limited to a single disk, as in RAID 3. Most implementations require a minimum of three disks and support a maximum of 32.

These four types of RAID drives, or arrays, are illustrated in Figure 8.2.

FIGURE 8.2   The four primary RAID technologies used in systems

A RAID 5 array can survive the failure of any one drive and still be able to function. It can't survive the failure of multiple drives.

You aren't required to know the current RAID capabilities for the Security+ exam. They are presented here primarily for your knowledge. They are commonly used in highly reliable systems.

RAID levels 0, 1, 3, and 5 are the most commonly implemented in servers today. RAID 5 has largely replaced RAID 3 in newer systems.

RAID levels are implemented either in software on the host computer or in the disk controller hardware. A RAID hardware-device implementation will generally run faster than a software-oriented RAID implementation because the software implementation uses the system CPU and system resources. Hardware RAID devices generally have their own processors, and they appear to the operating system as a single device.

 Real World Scenario

How Many Disks Does RAID Need?

As a security administrator, you must determine how many RAID disks you'll need. Compute how many disks will be needed for each scenario or the amount of storage capacity you'll end up with (answers appear at the end of each scenario).

Scenario 1   Your company has standardized on 500GB disks. A new server will go online next month to hold the data files for a new division; the server will be disk-duplexed and needs to be able to store 800GB of data. How many drives should you order?

Disk duplexing is the same as disk mirroring except there is also a second controller. Fifty percent of the overall storage capacity must be used for RAID, so you must purchase four 500GB drives. This will give you excess data capacity of 200GB.

Scenario 2   Your primary server is currently running four 300GB disks in a RAID 5 array. Storage space is at a premium, and a purchase order has just been approved for four 500GB disks. Still utilizing a RAID 5 array, what is the maximum data storage space this server will be able to host?

The solution that will generate the most data storage capacity is to install all eight drives (the four current ones and the four new ones) into the server. The array must use the same size storage on each drive, thus all eight drives will appear as if they are 300GB drives. Under this scenario, 2100GB can be used for data storage and 300GB will be used for parity.

Scenario 3   Access speed is of the utmost importance on the web server. You want to purchase some fast 300GB hard drives and install them in a RAID 0 array. How many drives will you need to purchase to host 900GB of data?

RAID 0 doesn't perform any fault tolerance and doesn't require any extra disk space. You can obtain 900GB of data by using three disks.

You must do a fair amount of planning before you implement RAID. Within the realm of planning, you must be able to compute the number of disks needed for the desired implementation.

Disaster Recovery

Disaster recovery is the ability to recover system operations after a disaster. A key aspect of disaster-recovery planning is designing a comprehensive backup plan that includes backup storage, procedures, and maintenance. Many options are available to implement disaster recovery. The following sections discuss backups and the disaster-recovery plan.

It's important to recognize that during a recovery, it may not always be necessary to immediately bring all systems and services back up. Critical systems should be the priority; extraneous services (such as an informational website for the public) can often be of lesser priority and attended to after everything else is up and running.

Depending on Backups

Backups are duplicate copies of key information, ideally stored in a location other than the one where the information is currently stored. Backups include both paper and computer records. Computer records are usually backed up using a backup program, backup systems, and backup procedures.

The primary starting point for disaster recovery involves keeping current backup copies of key data files, databases, applications, and paper records available for use. Your organization must develop a solid set of procedures to manage this process and ensure that all key information is protected. A security professional can do several things in conjunction with system administrators and business managers to protect this information. It's important to think of this problem as an issue that is larger than a single department. The following are examples of key paper records that should be archived:

- Board minutes
- Board resolutions
- Corporate papers
- Critical contracts
- Financial statements
- Incorporation documents
- Loan documents
- Personnel information
- Tax records

This list, while not comprehensive, gives you a place to start when you evaluate your archival requirements. Most of these documents can be easily converted into electronic form. However, keeping paper copies is strongly recommended because some government agencies don't accept electronic documentation as an alternative to paper documentation.

Computer files and applications should also be backed up on a regular basis. Here are some example of critical files that should be backed up:

- Applications
- Appointment files
- Audit files
- Customer lists
- Database files
- E-mail correspondence
- Financial data
- Operating systems
- Prospect lists
- Transaction files
- User files
- User information
- Utilities

Again, this list isn't all-inclusive, but it provides a place to start.

In most environments, the volume of information that needs to be stored is growing at a tremendous pace. Simply tracking this massive growth can create significant problems.

 An unscrupulous attacker can glean as much critical information from copies as they can from the original files. Make sure your storage facilities are secure, and it is a good idea to add security to the backup media as well.

You might need to restore information from backup copies for any number of reasons. Some of the more common reasons are listed here:

- Accidental deletion
- Applications errors
- Natural disasters
- Physical attacks
- Server failure
- Virus infection
- Workstation failure

The information you back up must be immediately available for use when needed. If a user loses a critical file, they won't want to wait several days while data files are sent from a remote storage facility. Several types of storage mechanisms are available for data storage:

Working copies *Working copy* backups—sometimes referred to as *shadow copies*—are partial or full backups that are kept at the computer center for immediate recovery purposes. Working copies are frequently the most recent backups that have been made.

Typically, working copies are intended for immediate use. They are usually updated on a frequent basis.

Working copies aren't usually intended to serve as long-term copies. In a busy environment, they may be created every few hours.

Many file systems used on servers include *journaling*. A journaled file system (JFS) includes a log file of all changes and transactions that have occurred within a set period of time (such as the last few hours). If a crash occurs, the operating system can check the log files to see what transactions have been committed and which ones have not.

This technology works well and allows unsaved data to be written after the recovery, and the system is usually successfully restored to its precrash condition.

Onsite storage *Onsite storage* usually refers to a location on the site of the computer center that is used to store information locally. Onsite storage containers are available that allow computer cartridges, tapes, and other backup media to be stored in a reasonably protected environment in the building.

As time goes on, tape is losing its popularity as a medium for backups to other technologies. The Security+ exam, however, is a bit dated and still considers tape the ideal medium.

Onsite storage containers are designed and rated for fire, moisture, and pressure resistance. These containers aren't *fireproof* in most situations, but they are *fire rated*: A fireproof container should be guaranteed to withstand damage regardless of the type of fire or temperature, whereas fire ratings specify that a container can protect the contents for a specific amount of time in a given situation.

If you choose to depend entirely on onsite storage, make sure the containers you acquire can withstand the worst-case environmental catastrophes that could happen at your location. Make sure, as well, that they are in locations where you can easily find them after the disaster and access them (near exterior walls, on the ground floor, and so forth).

General-purpose storage safes aren't usually suitable for storing electronic media. The fire ratings used for safes generally refer to paper contents. Because paper does not catch fire until 451° Fahrenheit, electronic media is typically ruined well before paper documents are destroyed in a fire.

Offsite storage   *Offsite storage* refers to a location away from the computer center where paper copies and backup media are kept. Offsite storage can involve something as simple as keeping a copy of backup media at a remote office, or it can be as complicated as a nuclear-hardened high-security storage facility. The storage facility should be bonded, insured, and inspected on a regular basis to ensure that all storage procedures are being followed.

Determining which storage mechanism to use should be based on the needs of the organization, the availability of storage facilities, and the budget available. Most offsite storage facilities charge based on the amount of space you require and the frequency of access you need to the stored information.

Crafting a Disaster-Recovery Plan

A *disaster-recovery plan*, or *scheme*, helps an organization respond effectively when a disaster occurs. Disasters may include system failure, network failure, infrastructure failure, and natural disaster. The primary emphasis of such a plan is reestablishing services and minimizing losses.

In a smaller organization, a disaster-recovery plan may be relatively simple and straightforward. In a larger organization, it may involve multiple facilities, corporate strategic plans, and entire departments. In either case, the purpose is to develop the means and methods to restore services as quickly as possible and to protect the organization from unacceptable losses in the event of a disaster.

A major component of a disaster-recovery plan involves the access and storage of information. Your backup plan for data is an integral part of this process. The following sections address backup plan issues and backup types. They also discuss developing a backup plan, recovering a system, and using alternative sites. These are key components of a disaster-recovery plan: They form the heart of how an organization will respond when a critical failure or disaster occurs.

Understanding Backup Plan Issues

When an organization develops a *backup plan* for information, it must be clear about the value of the information. A backup plan identifies which information is to be stored, how it will be stored, and for what duration it will be stored. You must look at the relative value of the information you retain. To some extent, the types of systems you use and the applications you support dictate the structure of your plan.

Let's look at those different systems and applications:

Database systems   Most modern database systems provide the ability to globally back up data or certain sections of the database without difficulty. Larger-scale database systems also provide transaction auditing and data-recovery capabilities.

For example, you can configure your database to record in a separate file each addition, update, deletion, or change of information that occurs. These transaction or audit files can be stored directly on archival media, such as magnetic tape cartridges. In the event of a system outage or data loss, the audit file can be used to roll back the database and update it to the last transactions made.

Figure 8.3 illustrates the auditing process in further detail. In this situation, the audit file is directly written to a DAT tape that is used to store a record of changes. If an outage occurs, the audit or transaction files can be rolled forward to bring the database back to its most current state. This recovery process brings the database current to within the last few transactions. Although it doesn't ensure that all the transactions that were in process will be recovered, it will reduce potential losses to the few that were in process when the system failed.

FIGURE 8.3 Database transaction auditing process

Most database systems contain large files that have only a relatively few records updated in relation to the number of records stored. A large customer database may store millions of records—however, only a few hundred may be undergoing modification at any given time.

User files Word-processing documents, spreadsheets, and other user files are extremely valuable to an organization. Fortunately, although the number of files that people retain is usually large, the number of files that change after initial creation is relatively small. By doing a regular backup on user systems, you can protect these documents and ensure that they're recoverable in the event of a loss. In a large organization, backing up user files can be an enormous task. Fortunately, most operating systems date-stamp files when they're modified. If backups that store only the changed files are created, keeping user files safe becomes a relatively less-painful process for an organization.

Many organizations have taken the position that backing up user files is the user's responsibility. Although this policy decision saves administrative time and media, it isn't a good idea. Most users don't back up their files on a regular basis—if at all. With the cost of media being relatively cheap, including the user files in a backup every so often is highly recommended.

Applications   Applications such as word processors, transaction systems, and other programs usually don't change on a frequent basis. When a change or upgrade to an application is made, it's usually accomplished across an entire organization. You wouldn't necessarily need to keep a copy of the word-processing application for each user, but you should keep a single up-to-date version that is available for download and reinstallation.

Some commercial applications require each copy of the software to be registered with a centralized license server. This may present a problem if you attempt to use a centralized recovery procedure for applications. Each machine may require its own copy of the applications for a recovery to be successful.

Knowing the Backup Types

Three methods exist to back up information on most systems:

Full backup   A *full backup* is a complete, comprehensive backup of all files on a disk or server. The full backup is current only at the time it's performed. Once a full backup is made, you have a complete archive of the system at that point in time. A system shouldn't be in use while it undergoes a full backup because some files may not get backed up. Once the system goes back into operation, the backup is no longer current. A full backup can be a time-consuming process on a large system.

During a full backup, every single file on the system is copied over, and the archive bit on each file is turned off.

Incremental backup   An *incremental backup* is a partial backup that stores only the information that has been changed since the last full or the last incremental backup. If a full backup were performed on a Sunday night, an incremental backup done on Monday night would contain only the information that changed since Sunday night. Such a backup is typically considerably smaller than a full backup. Each incremental backup must be retained until a full backup can be performed. Incremental backups are usually the fastest backups to perform on most systems, and each incremental backup tape is relatively small.

An incremental backup backs up only files that have the archive bit turned on. That is how it can identify which files have changed or been created. At the conclusion of the backup, the archive bit is turned off for all the files that were included in the backup.

Differential backup   A *differential backup* is similar in function to an incremental backup, but it backs up any files that have been altered since the last full backup; it makes duplicate copies of files that haven't changed since the last differential backup. If a full backup were performed on Sunday night, a differential backup performed on Monday night would capture the information that was changed on Monday. A differential backup completed on Tuesday night would record the changes in any files from Monday and any changes in files on Tuesday. As you can see, during the week each differential backup would become larger; by Friday or Saturday night, it might be nearly as large as a full backup. This means the backups in the earliest part of the weekly cycle will be very fast, and each successive one will be slower.

A differential backup backs up only files that have the archive bit turned on. At the conclusion of the backup, the archive bit is left on for those files so they are then included again in the next backup.

When these backup methods are used in conjunction with each other, the risk of loss can be greatly reduced, but you can never combine incremental and differential backups in the same set. One of the major factors in determining which combination of these three methods to use is time—ideally, a full backup would be performed every day. Several commercial backup programs support these three backup methods. You must evaluate your organizational needs when choosing which tools to use to accomplish backups.

Almost every stable operating system contains a utility for creating a copy of configuration settings necessary to reach the present state after a disaster. In Windows Vista, for example, this is accomplished with an Automated System Recovery (ASR) disk. Make certain you know how to do an equivalent operation for the operating system you are running.

As an administrator, you must know how to do backups and be familiar with all the options available to you.

Developing a Backup Plan

Several common models are used in designing backup plans. Each has its own advantages and disadvantages. Numerous methods have been developed to deal with archival backup; most of them are evolutions of the three models discussed here:

Grandfather, Father, Son method   The *Grandfather, Father, Son method* is based on the philosophy that a full backup should occur at regular intervals, such as monthly or weekly. This method assumes that the most recent backup after the full backup is the son. As newer backups are made, the son becomes the father, and the father, in turn, becomes the grandfather. At the end of each month, a full backup is performed on all systems. This backup is stored in an offsite facility for a period of one year. Each monthly backup replaces the monthly backup from the previous year. Weekly or daily incremental backups are performed and stored until the next full backup occurs. This full backup is then stored offsite and the weekly or daily backup tapes are reused (the January 1 incremental backup is used on February 1, and so on).

This method ensures that in the event of a loss, the full backup from the end of the last month and the daily backups can be used to restore information to the last day. Figure 8.4 illustrates this concept: The annual backup is referred to as the grandfather, the monthly backup is the father, and the weekly backup is the son. The last backup of the month becomes the archived backup for that month. The last backup of the year becomes the annual backup for the year. Annual backups are usually archived; this allows an organization to have backups available for several years and minimizes the likelihood of data loss. It's a common practice for an organization to keep a minimum of seven years in archives.

FIGURE 8.4   Grandfather, Father, Son backup method

The last full backup of the year is permanently retained. This ensures that previous years' information can be recovered if it's needed for some reason.

The major difficulty with this process is that a large number of tapes are constantly flowing between the storage facility and the computer center. In addition, cataloging daily and weekly backups can be complicated. It can become difficult to determine which files have been backed up and where they're stored.

Full Archival method   The *Full Archival method* works on the assumption that any information created on any system is stored forever. All backups are kept indefinitely using some form of backup media. In short, all full backups, all incremental backups, and any other backups are permanently kept somewhere.

This method effectively eliminates the potential for loss of data. Everything that is created on any computer is backed up forever. Figure 8.5 illustrates this method. As you can see, the number of copies of the backup media can quickly overwhelm your storage capabilities. Some organizations that have tried to do this have needed entire warehouses to contain their archival backups.

FIGURE 8.5   Full Archival backup method

Server

Think about the number of files your organization has: How much storage media would be required to accomplish full archiving? The other major problem involves keeping records of what information has been archived. For these reasons, many larger companies don't find this to be an acceptable method of keeping backups.

Backup Server method   The costs of disk storage and servers have fallen tremendously over the past few years. Lower prices have made it easier for organizations to use dedicated servers for backup. The *Backup Server method* establishes a server with large amounts of disk space whose sole purpose is to back up data. With the right software, a dedicated server can examine and copy all the files that have been altered every day.

Figure 8.6 illustrates the use of backup servers. In this instance, the files on the backup server contain copies of all the information and data on the APPS, ACCTG, and DB servers. The files on the three servers are copied to the backup server on a regular basis; over time, this server's storage requirements can become enormous. The advantage of this method is that all backed-up data is available online for immediate access.

This server can be backed up on a regular basis, and the backups can be kept for a specified period. If a system or server malfunctions, the backup server can be accessed to restore information from the last backups performed on that system.

Backup servers don't need overly large processors; however, they must have large disk and other long-term storage media capabilities. Several software manufacturers take backup servers one additional step and create hierarchies of files: Over time, if a file isn't accessed, it's moved to slower media and may eventually be stored offline. This helps reduce the disk storage requirements, yet it still keeps the files that are most likely to be needed for recovery readily available

FIGURE 8.6   A backup server archiving server files

APPS Server

ACCTG Server

DB Server

Backup Server

Backup Files

Many organizations utilize two or more of these methods to back up systems. The issue becomes one of storage requirements and retention requirements. In establishing a backup plan, you must ask users and managers how much backup (in terms of frequency, size of files, and so forth) is really needed and how long it will be needed.

NOTE   Make sure you obtain input from all who are dealing with governmental or regulatory agencies. Each agency may have different archival requirements, and compliance violations can be expensive. Both HIPAA and Sarbanes-Oxley are affecting—and driving—archival and disposal policies around the nation.

Recovering a System

When a system fails, you'll be unable to reestablish operation without regenerating all of the system's components. This process includes making sure hardware is functioning, restoring or installing the operating systems, restoring or installing applications, and restoring data files. It can take several days on a large system. With a little forethought, you may be able to simplify the process and make it easily manageable.

When you install a new system, make a full backup of it before any data files are created. If stored onsite, this backup will be readily available for use. If you've standardized your systems, you may need just one copy of a base system that contains all the common applications you use. The base system can usually be quickly restored, which allows for reconnection to the network for restoration of other software. Many newer operating systems now provide this capability, and system restores are very fast.

Figure 8.7 demonstrates this process further. Notice that the installation CDs are being used for the base OS and applications.

FIGURE 8.7 System regeneration process for a workstation or server

Data CD

APPS CD

Base O/S CD

When the base system has been restored, data files and any other needed files can be restored from the last full backup and any incremental or differential backups that have been performed. The last full backup should contain most of the data on the system; the incremental backup or differential backups contain the data that has changed since the full backup.

Many newer operating systems, such as Windows Server 2008, allow you to create a model user system as a disk image on a server; the disk image is downloaded and installed when a failure occurs. This method makes it easier for administrators to restore a system than it would be to do it manually. It's all well and good to know how to make backups and the importance of doing so. There will come a time, however, when a recovery—the whole reason for disaster planning—will be necessary. As an administrator, you must be ready for this event and know how to handle it.

An important recovery issue is to know the order in which to progress. If a server is completely destroyed and must be re-created, ascertain which applications are the most important and should be restored before the others. Likewise, which services are most important to the users from a business standpoint and need to be available? Conversely, which are nice but not necessary to keep the business running? The answers will differ for every organization, and you must know them for yours.

Planning for Alternate Sites

Another key aspect of a disaster-recovery plan is to provide for the restoration of business functions in the event of a large-scale loss of service. You can lease or purchase a facility that is available on short notice for the purpose of restoring network or systems operations. These are referred to as *alternate* or *backup sites*.

Another term for *alternate site* is *alternative site;* the terms are often used interchangeably.

If the power in your local area were disrupted for several days, how would you reestablish service at an alternate site until primary services were restored? Several options exist to do this; I'll briefly present them here. None of these solutions are ideal, but they are always considered to be significantly less costly—in terms of time—to implement than the estimated time of bringing your original site back up to speed. They are used to allow you to get your organization back on its feet until permanent service is available. An alternative site can be a hot site, a warm site, or a cold site:

Hot site   A *hot site* is a location that can provide operations within hours of a failure. This type of site would have servers, networks, and telecommunications equipment in place to reestablish service in a short time. Hot sites provide network connectivity, systems, and preconfigured software to meet the needs of an organization. Databases can be kept up-to-date using network connections. These types of facilities are expensive, and they're primarily suitable for short-term situations. A hot site may also double as an offsite storage facility, providing immediate access to archives and backup media.

 A hot site is also referred to as an *active backup model.*

Many hot sites also provide office facilities and other services so that a business can relocate a small number of employees to sustain operations.

 Given the choice, every organization would choose to have a hot site. Doing so is often not practical, however, on the basis of cost.

Warm site   A *warm site* provides some of the capabilities of a hot site, but it requires the customer to do more work to become operational. Warm sites provide computer systems and compatible media capabilities. If a warm site is used, administrators and other staff will need to install and configure systems to resume operations. For most organizations, a warm site could be a remote office, a leased facility, or another organization with which yours has a reciprocal agreement.

 Another term for a warm site/reciprocal site is *active/active model.*

Warm sites may be for your exclusive use, but they don't have to be. A warm site requires more advanced planning, testing, and access to media for system recovery. Warm sites represent a compromise between a hot site, which is very expensive, and a cold site, which isn't preconfigured.

 An agreement between two companies to provide services in the event of an emergency is called a *reciprocal agreement.* Usually, these agreements are made on a best-effort basis: There is no guarantee that services will be available if the site is needed. Make sure your agreement is with an organization that is outside your geographic area. If both sites are affected by the same disaster, the agreement is worthless.

Cold site   A *cold site* is a facility that isn't immediately ready to use. The organization using it must bring along its equipment and network. A cold site may provide network capability, but this isn't usually the case; the site provides a place for operations to resume, but it doesn't provide the infrastructure to support those operations. Cold sites work well when an extended outage is anticipated. The major challenge is that the customer must provide all the capabilities and do all the work to get back into operation. Cold sites are usually the least expensive to put into place, but they require the most advanced planning, testing, and resources to become operational—occasionally taking up to a month to make operational.

Almost anywhere can be a cold site; if necessary, users could work out of your garage for a short time. Although this may be a practical solution, it also opens up risks that you must consider. For example, while you're operating from your garage, will the servers be secure should someone break in?

Herein lies the problem. The likelihood that you'll need any of these facilities is low—most organizations will never need to use these types of facilities. The costs are usually based on subscription or other contracted relationships, and it's difficult for most organizations to justify the expense. In addition, planning, testing, and maintaining these facilities is difficult; it does little good to pay for any of these services if they don't work and aren't available when you need them.

One of the most important aspects of using alternative sites is documentation. To create an effective site, you must have solid documentation of what you have, what you're using, and what you need in order to get by.

Management must view the disaster-recovery plan as an integral part of its business continuity planning (BCP). Management must also provide the resources needed to implement and maintain an alternative site after the decision has been made to contract for the facilities.

 Real World Scenario

Some Protection Is Better than None—Or Is It?

You've been tasked with the responsibility of developing a recovery plan for your company to have in place in a critical infrastructure failure. Your CEO is concerned about the budget and doesn't want to invest many resources in a full-blown hot site.

Several options are available to you in this situation. You need to evaluate the feasibility of a warm site, a cold site, or a reciprocal agreement with another company. The warm site and cold site options will cost less than a hot site, but they will require a great deal of work in the event of a failure. A reciprocal site may be a good alternative to both, if a suitable partner organization can be found. You may want to discuss this possibility with some of your larger vendors or other companies that may have excess computer capacity. No matter which direction you recommend, you should test and develop procedures to manage the transition from your primary site to an offsite facility.

Reinforcing Vendor Support

Software vendors and hardware vendors are necessary elements in the process of building systems and applications. The costs associated with buying preconfigured software, hardware, and services are usually less than building them yourself. Unfortunately, this makes you dependent on a vendor's ability to stay in business.

The following sections discuss service-level agreements and code escrow. These agreements help you protect yourself in the event that a software vendor goes out of business or you have a dispute with a maintenance provider for your systems.

Service-Level Agreements

A *service-level agreement (SLA)* is an agreement between you or your company and a service provider, typically a technical support provider. SLAs are also usually part of network availability and other agreements. They stipulate the performance you can expect or demand by outlining the expectations a vendor has agreed to meet. They define what is possible to deliver and provide the contract, if you will, to make sure what is delivered is what was promised.

 Some SLAs may put you in a vendor-dependent position that can potentially open up your data to eyes that should not see it. Consider a medical practice that must grant an application vendor full access to all patient records in the spirit of being able to maintain the application. Just as with any other contract, you must carefully scrutinize the SLA and make certain you are not unintentionally opening your organization to harm.

Quite often, SLAs exist even within a company. They serve the same purpose within departments of a company as they do between a vendor and a supplier.

 SLAs are also known as *maintenance contracts* when referring to hardware or software.

If a vendor promises to provide you with a response time of four hours, this means it will have someone involved and dedicated to resolving any difficulties you encounter—either a service technician in the field or a remote diagnostic process occurring on your system. In either case, the customer has specific remedies that it can demand from the vendor if the terms of an SLA aren't met.

Most computer manufacturers offer a variety of SLA levels. Some can guarantee support in hours, whereas others may require days. Different levels of coverage and different response times usually have different costs associated with them. A 4-hour service agreement will typically cost much more than a 24-hour or 48-hour agreement. An SLA should also stipulate how long the repair will take once the support process has been activated: Having a service technician on site in four hours won't do much good if it takes two weeks to get a replacement for a defective part.

Make sure that you understand the scope and terms of your SLAs; periodically review them to verify that the performance criteria match your performance needs. Doing so can help prevent frustration and unanticipated disruptions from crippling your organization. The following are key measures in SLAs:

Mean time between failure　The *mean time between failure (MTBF)* is the measure of the anticipated incidence of failure for a system or component. This measurement determines the component's anticipated lifetime. If the MTBF of a cooling system is one year, you can anticipate that the system will last for a one-year period; this means you should be prepared to replace or rebuild the system once a year. If the system lasts longer than the MTBF, your organization has received a bonus. MTBF is helpful in evaluating a system's reliability and life expectancy.

Mean time to repair　The *mean time to repair (MTTR)* is the measurement of how long it takes to repair a system or component once a failure occurs. In the case of a computer system, if the MTTR is 24 hours, this tells you it will typically take 24 hours to repair it when it breaks.

While MTTR is considered a common measure of maintainability, be careful when evaluating it because it doesn't typically include the time needed to acquire a component and have it shipped to your location. I once worked with a national vendor that thought MTTR meant mean time to response. A technician would show up on site within the time the contract called for but would only begin to look at the problem and make a list of any needed supplies as well as get coffee. Make sure the contract agreements spell out exactly what you want.

Most SLAs stipulate the definitions of these terms and how they apply to the agreement. Make sure you understand how these terms are used and what they mean to the vendor.

 Real World Scenario

Should I Buy the Computer Store's SLA for My New Laptop?

You just purchased that new laptop you've been eyeing at the computer store. The store you bought it from is a large, national computer and software retailer. When you purchased the laptop, the salesperson worked hard to sell you an extended warranty agreement. Was it a good deal?

You should evaluate the SLA offered by the computer store and compare it to the manufacturer's warranty and service options. Many retail computer stores can't repair laptops in house, and they send most of them to the manufacturer for all but the simplest service. On the other hand, most laptop manufacturers offer a variety of service options including 24-hour delivery of replacement systems. You should verify the length of time it will take to have the store repair your laptop before you purchase an SLA. In some situations, a store's repair program is more expensive and slower than a manufacturer's repair program.

Code Escrow Agreements

Code escrow refers to the storage and conditions of release of source code provided by a vendor. For example, a code escrow agreement would stipulate how source code would be made available to customers in the event of a vendor's bankruptcy.

If you contract with a software developer to perform a customized programming effort, your contract may not give you the right to access and view the source code this vendor creates. If you want changes made to the program's functionality, you will be required to contract with the developer or integrator that installed it to perform those changes. This practice is common in applications software projects, such as setting up accounting systems.

 In recent years, a number of software companies have been forced to close their doors due to trying economic times. In many cases, the software they sold has become *orphanware*—existing without support of any type. As a purchaser who must rely on applications for a number of years, you should try as hard as possible to avoid falling into situations like this.

If the vendor ceases operations, you won't be able to obtain the source code to make further changes unless your agreement stipulates a code escrow clause. Unfortunately, this situation effectively makes your investment a dead-end street. Make sure your agreements provide you with either the source code for projects you've had done or a code escrow clause to acquire the software if the company goes out of business.

Generating Policies and Procedures

The policies and procedures your organization uses have a huge impact on your ability to manage a secure environment. Although your primary role isn't that of policy maker, you need to understand four critical areas to succeed. The following sections discuss human resource policies and business, certificate, and incident-response policies.

Human Resource Policies

Human resource policies help the organization set standards and enforce behaviors. From a security perspective, this is critical. As a security administrator, you won't generally be making policy decisions, but you have an impact on how policies are developed and enforced.

Human resource policies that consider security requirements will make your job easier. If the people the company hires are trustworthy, internal security problems will diminish. This will free up resources to address other aspects of the business that need attention. In the following sections, we'll look at each type of personnel security policy.

Hiring Policies

Hiring policies define how individuals are brought into an organization. They also establish the process used to screen prospective employees for openings. Your organizational hiring policies should establish expectations for both the interviewer and the prospective employee.

Most organizations that work with the government have mandatory drug-testing requirements. Experience and studies have shown that drug users have a tendency to perform inconsistently, have higher incidents of theft, and are vulnerable to social engineering or compromises such as blackmail.

Your organization should also investigate references, college degrees, certifications, and any other information that is provided as part of the screening process. Security professionals should be screened more thoroughly than many other employees. A special trust is being imparted to security professionals, and this trust should be given only to people who are worthy of it.

Policies should exist to define how users are added to a company's network when hired. Those policies should dictate who can add a new account as well as who can formally request one. They should also define who approves access to the system and the levels of access granted to initial accounts.

Termination Policies

Termination policies involve more than simply firing a person. Your organization needs to have a clear process for informing affected departments about voluntary and involuntary terminations. When an employee leaves a company, their computer access should be discontinued immediately.

If an involuntary termination occurs, you should back up the system they use as well as any files on servers before the termination occurs. Terminations are emotional times; if information is archived before the termination, there is less chance that critical records will be lost if the employee does something irrational. Most people won't do anything unusual, but you're better safe than sorry.

> In many cases, ex-employees find themselves with time on their hands. That time could be spent trying to hurt the company that hurt them—through social engineering or other means. Your job is to make certain they can't use that time to find weaknesses in your system and cause harm.

Make sure your termination policies mandate that the appropriate staff is notified when a termination is about to occur so that accounts can be disabled, systems backed up, and any other measures taken that are deemed appropriate. Other accounts may be arguable, but you must always disable a privileged user account in the event of that user's termination.

> Many times, a termination policy includes the clause that, upon termination, a former employee must be escorted at all times while performing post-termination activities (cleaning out their desk, hauling items to their car, and so on).

While it is easy to think of hiring and termination when it comes to HR issues, don't forget to consider what lays between the two. It is important that as an organization draft their policies, they include one for *mandatory vacations* (requiring users to take time away from work). Studies have shown that without a respite, employees can become myopic. Time away from work, even when forced, can not only be relaxing, but also advantageous.

Ethics Policies

Ethics is perhaps best described as the personnel or organizational rules about how interactions, relationships, and dealings occur. Ethics affect business practices, are the basis of laws, and are highly subjective. An *ethics policy* is the written policy governing accepted organizational ethics.

Many organizations define ethical behavior and the consequences of not behaving in an ethical manner. Most professional organizations have adopted codes of ethics or conduct for their members; in many cases, a violation of these ethics laws will result in suspension, expulsion, or censure by the organization.

One organization, the Computer Professionals for Social Responsibility (CPSR), has created the "Ten Commandments of Computer Ethics" in conjunction with the Computer Ethics Institute (CEI). These commandments (as found on the website www.cpsr.org) are listed here:

- Thou shalt not use a computer to harm other people.

- Thou shalt not interfere with other people's computer work.

- Thou shalt not snoop around in other people's computer files.

- Thou shalt not use a computer to steal.

- Thou shalt not use a computer to bear false witness.

- Thou shalt not copy or use proprietary software for which you have not paid.

- Thou shalt not use other people's computer resources without authorization or proper compensation.

- Thou shalt not appropriate other people's intellectual output.

- Thou shalt think about the social consequences of the program you are writing or the system you are designing.

- Thou shalt always use a computer in ways that ensure consideration and respect for your fellow humans.

This list, as you can see, outlines computer usage and ethical behavior for computer professionals. The commandments establish a code of behavior and trust that is important for security and computer-security professionals. This list is a good place to start in the development of both a personnel ethics code and an organizational ethics code.

Acceptable-Use Policies

Acceptable-use policies (AUP) deal primarily with computers and information provided by the company. Your policy should clearly stipulate what activities are allowed and what activities aren't allowed. This policy can be as simple as a blanket statement such as "Computers provided by the company are for company business use only."

From a security perspective, you should make sure the people using your systems and accessing your information aren't using them in ways inconsistent with the policy. This usually includes some type of monitoring package or log file examination.

Many companies have developed comprehensive policies concerning Web access, e-mail usage, and private usage. Acceptable-use policies should also include rules regarding telephone-system usage, information usage, and other related issues. Having an acceptable-use policy in place eliminates any uncertainty regarding what is and what isn't allowed in your organization. After these policies are put into place, enforcing them is critical. If an employee is using your corporate computer systems for an unacceptable purpose such as downloading pornography, you must consistently enforce company policy to stop the behavior and discourage future abuses. If your organization fails to enforce its policies consistently, it's opening itself to potential lawsuits because inconsistent enforcement could be perceived to be linked to discriminatory practices.

Privacy and Compartmentalized Information Policies

Privacy policies for corporate information are essential. You must clearly state what information can and can't be disclosed. Privacy policies must also specify who is entitled to ask for information within the organization and what types of information are provided to employees.

The process of establishing boundaries for information sharing is called *compartmentalization*. It's a standard method of protecting information.

Your policies must clearly state that employees should have no expectations of privacy. Employers are allowed to search desks, computers, files, and any other items brought into the building. Your policy should also state that e-mails and telephone communications can be monitored and that monitoring can occur without the employee's permission or knowledge. Many employees wrongly assume they have a right to privacy when in fact they don't. By explicitly stating your policies, you can avoid misunderstandings and potentially prevent employees from embarrassing themselves.

Need-to-Know Policies

Need-to-know policies allow people in an organization to withhold the release of classified or sensitive information from others in the company. The more people have access to sensitive information, the more likely it is that this information will be disclosed to unauthorized personnel. A need-to-know policy isn't intended to prohibit people from accessing information they need; it's meant to minimize unauthorized access.

Many naturally curious individuals like to gain sensitive information just for the fun of it. No doubt you've known someone who is a gossip—they will tell everybody the secrets they know. This can prove embarrassing to the organization or the people in the organization.

 The need-to-know section of most policies usually contains a statement to the effect of "Data containing any confidential information shall be readily identified and treated as confidential."

Conducting Background Investigations

Background investigations potentially involve more than checking references. A good background investigation should include credit history and criminal-record checks as well as information about work experience and education. These checks must be done with the permission of the employee or prospective employee. Refusing to agree to this type of investigation doesn't mean that the individual has a problem in their background; it may mean they value their privacy.

It's a good idea for employees who deal with sensitive information, such as security professionals, to have a thorough background investigation. This ensures that employees are who they say they are and have the education they say they do. A background check should weed out individuals who have misrepresented their background and experiences.

Business Policies

Business policies also affect the security of an organization. They address organizational and departmental business issues as opposed to corporate-wide personnel issues. When developing your business policy, you must consider these three primary areas of concern:

- Separation of duties
- Physical access control
- Document destruction

The following sections discuss these three areas.

Separation-of-Duties Policies

Separation-of-duties policies are designed to reduce the risk of fraud and prevent other losses in an organization. A good policy will require more than one person to accomplish key processes. This may mean that the person who processes an order from a customer isn't the same person who generates the invoice or deals with the billing.

Separation of duties helps prevent an individual from embezzling money from a company. To successfully embezzle funds, an individual would need to recruit others to commit an act of *collusion* (an agreement between two or more parties established for the purpose of committing deception or fraud). Collusion, when part of a crime, is also a criminal act in and of itself.

In addition, separation-of-duties policies can help prevent accidents from occurring in an organization. Let's say you're managing a software development project. You want someone to perform a quality assurance test on a new piece of code before it's put into production. Establishing a clear separation of duties prevents development code from entering production status until quality testing is accomplished.

Many banks and financial institutions require multiple steps and approvals to transfer money. This helps reduce errors and minimizes the likelihood of fraud.

Due Care Policies

Due care policies identify the level of care used to maintain the confidentiality of private information. These policies specify how information is to be handled. The objectives of due care policies are to protect and safeguard customer and/or client records. The unauthorized disclosure of this information creates a strong potential for liability and lawsuits. Everyone in an organization must be aware of and held to a standard of due care with confidential records.

It's easy to say that everyone else should adhere to policies and then overlook the importance of doing so yourself. As an administrator, you have access to a great deal of personal information, and you need to be as careful with it, if not more so, than anyone else in the organization. In many cases, something as simple as a printed list of user information sitting in plain view on your desk can violate rules of disclosure.

One of the leading ways to handle due care policies is to implement *best practices*. Best practices are based on what is known in the industry and how others would respond to similar situations.

Physical Access Control Policies

Physical access control policies refer to the authorization of individuals to access facilities or systems that contain information. Implementing a physical access control policy helps prevent theft and unauthorized disclosure of information and keeps other problems from cropping up. Many organizations limit office hours of employees to prevent them from accessing computer systems during odd hours. (This may not be appropriate for some positions, but it may be essential in others.) What would happen in your company if a payroll clerk decided to give himself a raise? In all probability, he wouldn't do this under the supervision of the payroll manager—he would do it when no one was around. By limiting access to the physical premises and computer systems, you reduce the likelihood that an individual will be tempted to commit a crime.

Document Disposal and Destruction Policies

Document disposal and destruction policies define how information that is no longer needed is handled. You should ensure that financial, customer, and other sensitive information is disposed of properly when it's no longer needed. Most organizations use mountains of paper, and much of it needs to be shredded or burned to prevent unauthorized access to sensitive information. Investigate the process that your organization uses to dispose of business records; it may need to be reevaluated.

Many large cities have businesses that do nothing but destroy paper for banks and other institutions. Using a truck that resembles a mobile shredder on wheels, they will come to your site and guarantee that the paper is destroyed. If your organization works with data of a sensitive nature, you should investigate the possibility of using such a service.

Certificate Policies

The advent of e-commerce has created a grave concern about trust. How does a customer know that they're working with a legitimate supplier? How does a retailer know they're dealing with a legitimate customer? One of the major problems facing e-commerce providers, as well as other businesses, is fraud. Fraud, theft, and other illegal transactions cost businesses billions of dollars a year.

Certificate policies aren't part of the Security+ exam. They are, however, an important aspect of an overall security program and are presented here for your consideration. All you need to know about certificates for the Security+ exam can be found in Chapter 7, "Cryptography Basics, Methods, and Standards."

There are ways to minimize if not eliminate the losses that organizations and individuals face. One method entails the use of digital certificates and certificate policies.

Certificates allow e-mails, files, and other transactions to be signed by the originator. This digital signing process usually carries close to the same weight as a hand signature. Using digital signatures allows business transactions to occur in a manner that provides a level of trust between the parties involved.

One of the most common certificates in use today is the X.509 certificate. It includes encryption, authentication, and a reasonable level of validity. A certificate issued by a valid certificate authority is valid in almost all cases; exceptions are few and far between. Most e-commerce providers accept the X.509 certificate or equivalent technologies.

Certificate policies refer to organizational policies regarding the issuing and use of certificates. These policies have a huge impact on how an organization processes and works with certificates.

A certificate policy needs to identify which certificate authorities (CAs) are acceptable, how certificates are used, and how they're issued. An organization must also determine whether to use third-party CAs, such as VeriSign, or create its own CA systems. In either case, the policies have implications about trust and trusted transactions.

A *trusted transaction* occurs under the security policy administered by a trusted security domain. Your organization may decide that it can serve as its own trusted security domain and that it can use third-party CAs, thus allowing for additional flexibility. Third-party CAs are usually accredited. However, the process of having an internal CA accredited is difficult and requires compliance with the policies and guidelines of the accrediting organization.

Transactions require the involvement of a minimum of two parties. In the CA environment, the two primary parties are identified as the *subscriber* and the *relying party*. The subscriber is the individual who is attempting to present the certificate that proves authenticity. The relying party is the person receiving the certificate. The relying party is dependent on the certificate as the primary authentication mechanism. If this certificate comes from a CA, the CA is known as the *third party*. The third party is responsible for providing assurance to the relying party that the subscriber is genuine. Figure 8.8 illustrates these relationships between the parties.

FIGURE 8.8   Parties in a certificate-based transaction

If a dispute occurs, these terms will be used to identify all the parties in the transaction. Your certificate policies should clearly outline who the valid subscribers and third parties are in any transactions. These policies provide your organization with a framework to identify parties, and they provide the rules detailing how to conduct transactions using e-commerce, e-mail, and other electronic media.

The practices or policies that an organization adopts for the certificate process are as important as the process that uses them. Your organization needs to develop practices and methods for dealing with certificate validity, expiration, and management. These policies tend to become extremely complicated. Most CAs require a *Certificate Practice Statement (CPS)*, which defines certificate issue processes, record keeping, and subscribers' legal acceptance of the terms of the CPS.

The CA should also identify certificate expiration and revocation processes. The CA must clearly explain the certificate revocation list (CRL) and CRL dissemination policies.

Incident-Response Policies

Incident-response policies define how an organization will respond to an incident. These policies may involve third parties, and they need to be comprehensive. The term *incident* is somewhat nebulous in scope; for our purposes, an incident is any attempt to violate a security policy, a successful penetration, a compromise of a system, or any unauthorized access to information. This includes systems failures and disruption of services in the organization.

It's important that an incident-response policy establish at least the following items:

- Outside agencies that should be contacted or notified in case of an incident
- Resources used to deal with an incident
- Procedures to gather and secure evidence
- List of information that should be collected about an incident
- Outside experts who can be used to address issues if needed
- Policies and guidelines regarding how to handle an incident

According to CERT, a *Computer Security Incident Response Team (CSIRT)* can be a formalized or ad hoc team. While you can toss a team together to respond to an incident after it arises, investing time in the development process can make an incident more manageable. Many decisions about dealing with an incident will have been considered in advance. Incidents are high-stress situations; therefore, it's better to simplify the process by considering important aspects in advance. If civil or criminal actions are part of the process, evidence must be gathered and safeguarded properly.

Let's say you've just discovered a situation where a fraud has been perpetrated internally using a corporate computer. You're part of the investigating team. Your incident-response policy lists the specialists you need to contact for an investigation. Ideally, you've already met the investigator or investigating firm, you've developed an understanding of how to protect the scene, and you know how to properly deal with the media (if they become involved).

Your policies must also clearly outline who needs to be informed in the company, what they need to be told, and how to respond to the situation. Incidents should not only include intrusions, but also attempts.

Enforcing Privilege Management

Privilege management involves making decisions about what information is accessed, how it's accessed, and who is authorized to access it. Unlike hardware access control, these concerns deal with policy and implementation issues. Additionally, the issue of auditing is a key factor: You should ensure that your organization doesn't provide more access or privileges than individuals need to do their work.

The following sections cover user and group roles, privilege escalation, single sign-on initiatives, auditing, and access control. Each of these considerations can be used to form an effective and coherent privilege management process. These processes allow users to gain access to the information they need, to be denied access to information they don't need, and to effectively gain access to system resources.

While single sign-on is not the opposite of multi-factor authentication, they are often mistakenly thought of that way. One-, two-, and three-factor authentication merely refers to the number of items a user must supply to authenticate. Authentication can be based on something they have (a smart card), something they know (a password), something unique (biometric), and so forth. After factor authentication is done, then single sign-on can still apply throughout the user's session.

User and Group Role Management

The process of user, group, and role management involves recognizing how work is accomplished in an organization. Most organizations have a high level of standardized tasks that can be accomplished without a great deal of privileged information. Some departments may routinely work with sensitive information about the organization or its customers. A clear set of rules specifying and limiting access can make the job of managing the process much simpler.

Let's take the example of a small business. Company XYZ has departments that are involved in sales, finance, manufacturing, vendor relations, and customer relations. Each of these departments has different information needs.

The sales department may not need to access all of the company's financial information. However, someone in manufacturing might need that information. The job of establishing the various privilege levels in a company can become complicated. Some individuals may need to view certain information but should be prohibited from changing it, whereas other individuals may need to update that same information.

In a company of several dozen employees, establishing access control can be difficult, but in a company of thousands, establishing access control at an individual level can be overwhelming. If each individual needs different access capabilities, thousands of access rules are required.

Most operating systems allow you to organize users into groups with similar access needs so that you can more easily manage an otherwise cumbersome access puzzle. Individuals, and even other groups, can then be embedded into top-layer groups known as *security groups*.

A *security group* can have predefined access capabilities associated with it. In this way, you can develop a comprehensive security model that addresses the accessibility needs of everyone in an organization. Figure 8.9 illustrates the group process. In this example, most individuals are placed into one of two departmental groups. The top user in the picture only has access to accounting applications on the ACCTG server, the middle user has access to both, and the bottom user only has access to the APPS server. Departmental groups access information based on established needs and predefined access.

FIGURE 8.9   Security grouping

Each department may have different access capabilities. In some cases, different roles within a department have different needs. Although you may want a supervisor to have access to information about a department's performance, you may not want a clerical worker to have that same access. It comes down to an issue of trust, experience, and need.

Privilege Escalation

Privilege escalation is the process of increasing permissions. Often this is done temporarily and innocently, but it can also be accomplished by exploiting local vulnerabilities.

For example, many utilities in the Unix/Linux environment require permissions beyond those given to a user, but a user must run them to accomplish their task. An example is the password utility that allows users to change their passwords. Because the passwords are stored in files that aren't normally accessible by users, during the time that the user is making the change, the utility elevates their privilege to that of a higher (root) user. After the change is made, the utility ends its run and the user ends up with the same permissions/ privileges they had before.

Now suppose the utility crashed in the middle of its operation. Theoretically, this could create a situation where the user was left with the elevated privileges and could do things on the system that they otherwise could not. A privilege escalation attack looks for vulnerabilities on the system that could create this situation and then takes advantage of them.

Single Sign-On Initiatives

One of the big problems that larger systems must deal with is the need for users to access multiple systems or applications. This may require a user to remember multiple accounts and passwords. The purpose of a *single sign-on (SSO)* is to give users access to all the applications and systems they need when they log on. This is becoming a reality in many environments, including Kerberos, Microsoft Active Directory, Novell eDirectory, and some certificate model implementations.

 Single sign-on is both a blessing and a curse. It's a blessing in that once the user is authenticated, they can access all the resources on the network and browse multiple directories. It's a curse in that it removes the doors that otherwise exist between the user and various resources.

In the case of Kerberos, a single token allows any "Kerberized" applications to accept a user as valid. The important thing to remember in this process is that each application that wants to use SSO must be able to accept and process the token presented by Kerberos.

Active Directory (AD) works off a slightly different method. A server that runs AD retains information about all access rights for all users and groups in the network. When a user logs on to the system, AD issues the user a globally unique identifier (GUID). Applications that support AD can use this GUID to provide access control.

Figure 8.10 illustrates this process in more detail. In this instance, the database application, e-mail client, and printers all authenticate with the same logon. Like Kerberos, this process requires all the applications that want to take advantage of AD to accept AD controls and directives.

FIGURE 8.10   AD validating a user

In this way, the user doesn't have to have separate sign-on, e-mail, and application passwords. Using AD simplifies the sign-on process for users and lowers the support requirements for administrators. Access can be established through groups, and it can be enforced through group memberships.

On a decentralized network, SSO passwords are stored on each server and can represent a security risk. It's important to enforce password changes and make certain passwords are updated throughout the organization on a frequent basis.

Privilege Decision Making

The process of making decisions about privilege is important. It must be clear and unambiguous to be effective. In the case of a highly centralized environment, a single department or person is responsible for making decisions about access that affect the entire organization. In a decentralized environment, decision making is spread throughout the organization.

The people who are the most aware of the security needs should conduct the decision-making process. This process can involve everyone in the organization.

If someone is unable to accomplish the work they need to do, then the security system isn't working. On the other hand, it's important that personnel receive access only to the information they really need. Establishing a standardized policy or set of policies is important; these policies, and their effects, must be well documented and enforced.

 Many operating systems automatically replicate or send changes in access throughout an organization. A single change in a user's access may inadvertently give them access to sensitive information. Careful study of privileges is needed for an effective security policy.

From time to time, individuals may need special access to information that they wouldn't normally be given. For example, an office or clerical person might need to gather information for a special report. Specialized access should be granted only for the period of time during which they need the access. A separate account with these special privileges is usually the best way to manage these types of situations. When the special project is finished, the account can be disabled or deleted. This ensures that privileges don't become associated permanently with a user or a department. Security professionals who ensure that only authorized access occurs can monitor special accounts to reduce the potential for a security violation to occur.

Systems administrators are also subject to privilege issues. If an organization has multiple servers, it may not want administrators to have access to all the servers for administrative purposes. In larger organizations, company-wide access could create a serious security risk. As a rule, you should grant administrative access only to specific systems and possibly grant it only at specific times. Again, doing so limits a company's exposure to security violations.

Auditing

Auditing is the process of ensuring that policies, procedures, and regulations are carried out in a manner consistent with organizational standards. A periodic security audit of *user access and rights review* can help determine whether privilege-granting processes are appropriate and whether computer usage and escalation processes are in place and working. Think of an auditor as a consultant charged with helping to ensure that procedures are followed.

An auditor who is doing a good job should pull no punches and should offer concrete suggestions on how to improve. These suggestions may pertain to areas of improvement in contingency planning, to security and access problems, or to physical control issues. The information an auditor provides is extremely valuable; acting on it can save your organization time and aggravation. You may not like the results of the audit, but they can be used as a valuable tool to help improve the organization.

Many will argue over the correct steps to go through when performing an audit. The specifics may differ, but the following general steps should always be undertaken: Plan for the audit, conduct the audit, evaluate the results, communicate the results and needed changes, and follow up.

The following sections discuss the need to verify that users are given appropriate permissions to accomplish the work they're assigned.

Privilege Auditing

Privilege audits verify that accounts, groups, and roles are correctly assigned and that policies are being followed. An audit should verify that access is established correctly, security is in place, and policies are effective. A privilege audit might entail a complete review of all accounts and groups to ensure that they're correctly implemented and up-to-date.

The problems associated with the transfer of an individual in an organization are common. When a personnel transfer occurs, the transferred user needs to be removed from old groups. Failing to do so can result in *privilege creep*, which occurs when an individual accidentally gains a higher level of access than they would normally be entitled to or need.

Usage Auditing

Usage auditing verifies that systems and software are used appropriately and consistently with organizational policies. A usage audit may entail physically inspecting systems, verifying software configurations, and conducting other activities intended to prove that resources are being used appropriately.

A major concern (although not primarily a security concern) is the issue of installed software and licensing. Illegal use of unlicensed software can carry stiff penalties. Examining systems on a periodic basis verifies that only the software an organization is licensed to use is installed.

From a security perspective, some software is more vulnerable to exploitation than other software. If vulnerable software is installed, it may create a back door or other unauthorized usage problem. Periodically inspecting systems to ensure that software updates are current and that only approved software is installed is a good idea.

Usage audits also examine network usage. Is your network being used for illicit purposes? Is pornography present in your environment? Any number of other problems may also be discovered. By performing audits, you can help deter potentially embarrassing or even illegal activities from occurring in your environment.

Escalation Auditing

Escalation audits help ensure that procedures and communications methods are working properly in the event of a problem or issue. Escalation is primarily focused around the issue of gaining access to decision makers in a time of crisis. These types of audits test your organization to ensure that it has the appropriate procedures, policies, and tools to deal with any problems in the event of an emergency, catastrophe, or other need for management intervention.

Disaster recovery plans, business continuity plans, and other plans are tested and verified for accuracy. These types of plans require constant care or they become dated and ineffective. An audit can help ensure that all bases are covered and that your plans have a high likelihood of success when needed.

A good way to determine if your escalation audits are working is to test them. Many organizations develop scenarios to verify that mechanisms are in place to deal with certain situations. If the president of the organization is out of town or unavailable, who has the authority to make a decision about transitioning to an alternative site? If such issues can be worked out in advance, they're much less difficult to deal with in emergencies.

 Real World Scenario

Performing a Usage Audit

Your company has undergone its umpteenth reorganization. Many people have been moved to new positions within the new organizational chart. You've been asked to verify that users can access the information they need to perform their jobs. You also need to make sure that any inappropriate access is removed.

To successfully complete your assignment, you'll need to inspect every user account and group to verify which user accounts belong to which groups. You also need to verify that each group has the appropriate access to the servers and other resources needed to accomplish their assignments.

In many newer systems, you can accomplish this by inspecting the access groups that users belong to and by adding or deleting user accounts as appropriate. If you're using a network that doesn't support security groups, you'll need to modify the access rights of each account individually.

Administrative Auditing

One of the most overlooked components of an audit involves administrative elements. It is important to document the procedures undertaken during the *classification of information* (classifying information was discussed in Chapter 6), and who is involved in this process. You must also document who is involved in investigations, when it is suspected that something is awry, and the procedures they follow—known as *due diligence*.

This section of the audit should also address *change management*—the structured approach that is followed to secure the company's assets. Details here should include the controls that are in place to prevent unauthorized access to, and changes of, all IT assets. Among the assets you must be able to demonstrate appropriate controls on are all those related to *Personally Identifiable Information (PII)*. PII exists within your databases for all users, customers, vendors, and contacts and includes such things as their phone number, address, credit card number, employee status, and so on. In general, any attribute of any person is considered PII and is thus subject to privacy protection—and liability—issues.

Auditing and Log Files

One operation you will need to perform when working with log files if you are going to evaluate entries from security applications is carefully monitoring their size. In some operating systems, the files are allowed to grow indefinitely (until the drive runs out of space), while in others the size is fixed and older entries are overwritten by new ones. Most Windows server-based operating systems, for example, set the security log to a maximum size and overwrite the file as needed.

If you are running Windows 2003/2008, it is recommended that you start Event Viewer and right-click on the Security Log object. Choose Properties from the popup menu and change the Maximum Log Size entry to as large as you can afford and select Do Not Overwrite Events. Each time you audit the log entries (at least weekly is recommended), choose to manually clear the file once you are certain there are no alarms you should respond to.

The log files created by crucial network services such as DNS need to be routinely examined regularly. The DNS service, when running on Windows Server 2003/2008 for example, writes entries to the log file that can be examined using Event Viewer. Just as the size and overwrite options were set for the Security Log object, it is recommended those same actions be taken for the DNS Server logs as well.

A firewall, whether software or hardware, often creates log files the same as most other services when enabled. Given the importance of the firewall and its purpose, the entries written to those logs should be held in high esteem and evaluated regularly. These log files can be created anywhere a firewall is running, from a workstation to an appliance.

In Windows XP, for example, the firewall log and its settings can be accessed by opening Windows Firewall in the Control Panel and then choosing the Advanced tab. Beneath Security Logging, choose Settings and you can set such attributes as the size of the log file, and its name. To view the file, choose Save As, then find the file in the dialog box that opens, right-click on it and choose Open.

Most antivirus programs also create log files when they run that should be regularly checked. Not only do you want to verify that the program is running, but that the definition file(s) being used is current. Pay attention to the viruses that are found and deleted/quarantined, as well as any files that are being skipped.

Log files should be regularly checked from every antivirus program running, from the workstation to the server and you can educate users on how to routinely examine their own log files. With Sophos Anti-Virus, for example, users right-click on the icon that appears in their taskbar, and choose Open Sophos Anti-Virus from the popup menu. Next, they click

Configure Sophos Anti-Virus and choose View log. Changes to the default logging settings are made by choosing Configure log and tweaking the settings that appear in the dialog box shown in Figure 8.11.

FIGURE 8.11 Configuring logging with Sophos Anti-virus

Reporting to Management

An audit should always conclude with a report to management. This report should outline any organizational strengths and weaknesses as they existed at the time of the audit. The audit should also explain any violations of policy, recommendations for improvement, and recommendations for the organization overall. This report is a vital part of the process, and it provides a mechanism that can be used to develop corrective action plans and updated policies.

There must always be one person who can gain access when things go awry. In the summer of 2008, a rogue network administrator in San Francisco was charged with resetting the passwords on all the city's fiber switches and routers making them inaccessible to administrators. With all other administrators lacking the permission needed to change the passwords, the city was unable to control the backbone.

Access Control

The three primary methods of access control are Mandatory (MAC), Discretionary (DAC), and Role-Based (RBAC). A fourth method, Rule-Based Access Control (which also uses the RBAC acronym) is gaining in popularity. Each of these methods has advantages and disadvantages to the organization from a security perspective.

The method you choose will be greatly affected by your organization's beliefs about how information needs to be shared. In a high-security environment, the tendency would be to implement either a MAC or RBAC method. In a traditional business environment or school, the tendency would be to implement a DAC method. You should do some consulting within the organization to understand how a particular department and how the entire organization wants to implement access control models. Doing so will allow you to gather input from all concerned parties regarding how access guidelines should be established and how security should be implemented.

In the following sections, we'll look at each of these methods from a business perspective. You learned about the technical aspects in earlier chapters.

Mandatory Access Control

Mandatory Access Control (MAC) is clearly an inflexible method for how information access is allowed. In a MAC environment, all access capabilities are predefined. Users can't share information unless their rights to share it were established by administrators; administrators must make any changes that need to be made. This process enforces a rigid model of security

For a MAC model to work effectively, administrators and network designers must think relationships through carefully. The advantage of this model is that security access is well established and defined, making security breaches easier to investigate and correct. A well-designed MAC model can make the job of information control easier and can essentially lock down a network. The major disadvantages of this model are the lack of flexibility and the fact that its needs change over time. The inability of administrative staff to address these changes can sometimes make the model hard to keep up.

Discretionary Access Control

In a *Discretionary Access Control (DAC)* model, network users have some flexibility regarding how information is accessed. This model allows users to dynamically share information with other users. The method allows a more flexible environment, but it increases the risk of unauthorized disclosure of information. Administrators have a more difficult time ensuring that information access is controlled and that only appropriate access is given out.

Role-Based Access Control

Role-Based Access Control (RBAC) models approach the problem of access control based on established roles in an organization. RBAC models implement access by job function or by responsibility. Each employee has one or more roles that allow access to specific information. If a person moves from one role to another, the access for the previous role will no longer be available. RBAC models provide more flexibility than a MAC model and less flexibility than the DAC model. They do, however, have the advantage of being strictly based on job function as opposed to individual needs.

Rule-Based Access Control

Rule-Based Access Control (RBAC) uses the settings in pre-configured security policies to make all decisions. These rules can be to deny all but those who specifically appear in a list (an allow list), or deny only those who specifically appear in the list (a true deny list). Entries in the list may be actual usernames, IP addresses, hostnames, or even domains. Rule-Based models are often being used in conjunction with Role-Based to add greater flexibility.

Summary

In this chapter, you learned about the many aspects involved in the operations of a secure environment. You studied business continuity, vendor support, security policies, security procedures, and privilege management. Each of these areas must be addressed and considered before you can be assured of a reasonable level of safety.

The issue of reliable service from utility companies, such as electricity and water, should be evaluated as part of your disaster recovery process. Addressing potential problems as part of your business decision making can prevent unanticipated surprises.

High-availability systems usually provide fail-over capabilities. These systems can use redundant components or fault-tolerant technologies. *Clustering* is a method of using multiple systems to ensure continuous operations in the event of server failure. One of the most common methods of improving fault tolerance is to utilize RAID devices for disk storage.

Disaster recovery is the process of helping your organization prepare for recovery in the event of an unplanned situation, and it's a part of your organization's business continuity plans.

Vendors can provide support and services to an organization. SLAs set a benchmark for expected performance when needed. Service performance and reliability are measured by MTBF and MTTR. Vendors that provide software or programming support should have code escrow agreements to ensure that software can be maintained if the vendor ceases business.

Human resource policies define all the key relationships between the employee, the organization, and the information they use. These policies dictate the expectations between all the parties involved. They should be comprehensive, and they should have a huge impact on security expectations.

Business policies drive security efforts and confidentiality issues. They should address physical access, due care, separation of duties, document destruction, and certificate usage.

Understanding how *certificate policies* affect certificate usage requires a clear understanding of the parties involved in a transaction. The subscriber is the presenter of a certificate. The relying party depends on the subscriber or a third party to verify authenticity. A CA should have a clear set of practices (a CPS) to define how business activities are conducted.

The process of dealing with a security problem is called *incident response*. An incident-response policy should clearly outline what resources, individuals, and procedures are to be involved in the event of an incident.

Privilege management involves making decisions regarding user and group roles, sign-on procedures, how information is accessed and used, auditing, and access control methods. Privilege management is one of the key components of an effective security policy.

Exam Essentials

Understand the aspects of disaster recovery. Disaster recovery is concerned with the recovery of critical systems in the event of a loss. One of the primary issues is the effectiveness of backup policies and procedures. Offsite storage is one of the more secure methods of protecting information from loss.

Know the types of backups that are typically performed in an organization. The three backup methods are full, incremental, and differential. A full backup involves the total archival of all information on a system. An incremental backup involves archiving only information that has changed since the last backup. Differential backups save all information that has changed since the last full backup.

Be able to discuss the process of recovering a system in the event of a failure. A system recovery usually involves restoring the base operating systems, applications, and data files. The operating systems and applications are usually either restored from the original distribution media or from a server that contains images of the system. Data is typically recovered from backups or archives.

Be able to discuss the types of alternative sites available for disaster recovery. The three types of sites available for disaster recovery are hot sites, warm sites, and cold sites. Hot sites typically provide high levels of capability, including networking. Warm sites may provide some capabilities, but they're generally less prepared than a hot site. A cold site requires the organization to replicate critical systems and all services to restore operations.

Define the elements of a security policy. The security policy sets the internal expectations of how situations, information, and personnel are handled. These policies cover a broad range of the organization. Most policies in an organization affect the security policies.

Define the various types of policies that affect security efforts in an organization. The major policies that affect security are human resources, business, security, certificate, and incident-response policies. Human resource policies describe expected behavior and other policies concerning employees. Business policies drive all other policies, set expectations of how the organization will do business, and protect information.

Be able to describe the needed components of an incident-response policy. The incident-response policy explains how incidents will be handled, including notification, resources, and escalation. This policy drives the incident-response process, and it provides advance planning to the incident-response team.

Know the aspects of privilege management. Privilege-management decision making involves evaluating the roles of individuals and departments in an organization. This includes centralized versus decentralized decision making, sign-on procedures, auditing, and role control.

Be able to describe the purpose of an audit. An audit is the process of testing and verifying the effectiveness of policies and procedures in an organization. A security audit may include evaluating privileges, systems usage, and escalation. The final product of an audit is the report to management, which outlines the results of the audit and pinpoints areas that need improvement.

Be able to describe the three roles of access control.   The three roles are MAC, DAC, and RBAC. Mandatory Access Control (MAC) establishes rigid access control methods in the organization. Discretionary Access Control (DAC) allows for flexibility in access control. Role-Based Access Control (RBAC) is based on the role the individual or department has in the organization.

Hands-On Labs

The labs in this chapter are as follows:

Lab 8.1: Use Automated System Recovery in Windows Server 2003

Lab 8.2: Create a Rescue Disk in Linux

Lab 8.3: Create a Backup with SuSE Linux

Lab 8.1: Use Automated System Recovery in Windows Server 2003

In this lab, you'll use the backup utility included with Windows Server 2003 to create an ASR backup:

1. Start the backup utility by choosing Start ➢ All Programs ➢ Accessories ➢ System Tools ➢ Backup.

2. Choose the Automatic System Recovery Wizard.

3. Walk through the wizard and answer the questions appropriately. When you finish, you'll create the backup set first and a floppy second. The floppy contains files necessary to restore system settings after a disaster.

Lab 8.2: Create a Rescue Disk in Linux

This lab assumes the use of either SuSE Linux or Novell Desktop Linux. To create a disk, follow these steps:

1. Open YaST and choose System.

2. Beneath System, select Create A Boot, Rescue, Or Module Floppy. Seven choices appear here:

    - Standard Boot Floppy 1
    - Standard Boot Floppy 2
    - Standard Boot Floppy 3
    - Rescue Floppy
    - Module Floppies
    - Custom Floppy
    - Download Floppy Image

3. Choose Rescue Floppy, and the disk image will be copied to the media.

Lab 8.3: Create a Backup with SuSE Linux

This lab assumes the use of SuSE Linux Enterprise Server 9. To create a backup, follow these steps:

1. Log in as root and start YaST.

2. Choose System and System Backup.

3. Click Profile Management and choose Add, then enter a name for the new profile, such as **fullsystemback**.

4. Click OK.

5. Enter a backup name (using an absolute path such as /home/mybackup.tar), and make certain the archive type is set to a tar variety. Then click Next.

6. At the File Selection window, leave the default options and click Next.

7. Leave the Search Constraints at the defaults and click OK.

8. At the main YaST System Backup dialog box, click Start Backup. After several minutes of reading packages, the backup will begin.

Review Questions

1. Which plan or policy helps an organization determine how to relocate to an emergency site?

   A. Disaster-recovery plan

   B. Backup site plan

   C. Privilege management policy

   D. Privacy plan

2. Although you're talking to her on the phone, the sound of the administrative assistant's screams of despair can be heard down the hallway. She has inadvertently deleted a file that the boss desperately needs. Which type of backup is used for the immediate recovery of a lost file?

   A. Onsite storage

   B. Working copies

   C. Incremental backup

   D. Differential backup

3. Which system frequently has audit files/transaction logs that can be used for recovery?

   A. Database system

   B. Application server

   C. Backup server

   D. User system

4. You're trying to rearrange your backup procedures to reduce the amount of time they take each evening. You want the backups to finish as quickly as possible during the week. Which backup system backs up only the files that have changed since the last backup?

   A. Full backup

   B. Incremental backup

   C. Differential backup

   D. Backup server

5. Which backup system backs up all the files that have changed since the last full backup?

   A. Full backup

   B. Incremental backup

   C. Differential backup

   D. Archival backup

6. You're a consultant brought in to advise MTS on its backup procedures. One of the first problems you notice is that the company doesn't utilize a good tape-rotation scheme. Which backup method uses a rotating schedule of backup media to ensure long-term information storage?

   A. Grandfather, Father, Son method

   B. Full Archival method

   C. Backup Server method

   D. Differential Backup method

7. Which site best provides limited capabilities for the restoration of services in a disaster?

   A. Hot site

   B. Warm site

   C. Cold site

   D. Backup site

8. You're the head of information technology for MTS and have a brother in a similar position for ABC. Both companies are approximately the same size and are located several hundred miles apart. As a benefit to both companies, you want to implement an agreement that would allow either company to use resources at the other site should a disaster make a building unusable. What type of agreement between two organizations provides mutual use of their sites in the event of an emergency?

   A. Backup-site agreement

   B. Warm-site agreement

   C. Hot-site agreement

   D. Reciprocal agreement

9. The process of automatically switching from a malfunctioning system to another system is called what?

   A. Fail safe

   B. Redundancy

   C. Fail-over

   D. Hot site

10. You've been brought in as a temporary for FRS, Inc. The head of IT assigns you the task of evaluating all servers and their disks and making a list of any data not stored redundantly. Which disk technology isn't fault tolerant?

   A. RAID 0

   B. RAID 1

   C. RAID 3

   D. RAID 5

11. Which agreement outlines performance requirements for a vendor?

    A. MTBF

    B. MTTR

    C. SLA

    D. BCP

12. Your company is about to invest heavily in an application written by a new startup. Because it is such a sizable investment, you express your concerns about the longevity of the new company and the risk this organization is taking. You propose that the new company agree to store its source code for use by customers in the event that it ceases business. What is this model called?

    A. Code escrow

    B. SLA

    C. BCP

    D. CA

13. Which policy describes how computer systems may be used within an organization?

    A. Due care policy

    B. Acceptable-use policy

    C. Need-to-know policy

    D. Privacy policy

14. You're the administrator for STM and have been summoned to an unannounced audit. The auditor states that he is unable to find anything in writing regarding confidentiality of customer records. Which policy should you produce?

    A. Separation-of-duties policy

    B. Due care policy

    C. Physical access policy

    D. Document destruction policy

15. Which policy dictates how an organization manages certificates and certificate acceptance?

    A. Certificate policy

    B. Certificate access list

    C. CA accreditation

    D. CRL rule

16. You're giving hypothetical examples during a required security training session when the subject of certificates comes up. A member of the audience wants to know how a party is verified as genuine. Which party in a transaction is responsible for verifying the identity of a certificate holder?

    A. Subscriber

    B. Relying party

    C. Third party

    D. Omni registrar

17. Which of the following would normally *not* be part of an incident-response policy?

    A. Outside agencies (that require status)

    B. Outside experts (to resolve the incident)

    C. Contingency plans

    D. Evidence collection procedures

18. MTS is in the process of increasing all security for all resources. No longer will the legacy method of assigning rights to users as they're needed be accepted. From now on, all rights must be obtained for the network or system through group membership. Which of the following groups is used to manage access in a network?

    A. Security group

    B. Single sign-on group

    C. Resource sharing group

    D. AD group

19. Which process inspects procedures and verifies that they're working?

    A. Audit

    B. Business continuity plan

    C. Security review

    D. Group privilege management

20. The present method of requiring access to be strictly defined on every object is proving too cumbersome for your environment. The edict has come down from upper management that access requirements should be reduced slightly. Which access model allows users some flexibility for information-sharing purposes?

    A. DAC

    B. MAC

    C. RBAC

    D. MLAC

Answers to Review Questions

1. **A.** The disaster-recovery plan deals with site relocation in the event of an emergency, natural disaster, or service outage.

2. **B.** Working copies are backups that are usually kept in the computer room for immediate use in recovering a system or lost file.

3. **A.** Large-scale database systems usually provide an audit file process that allows transactions to be recovered in the event of a data loss.

4. **B.** An incremental backup backs up files that have changed since the last full or partial backup.

5. **C.** A differential backup backs up all the files that have changed since the last full backup.

6. **A.** The Grandfather, Father, Son backup method is designed to provide a rotating schedule of backup processes. It allows for a minimum usage of backup media, and it still allows for long-term archiving.

7. **B.** Warm sites provide some capabilities in the event of a recovery. The organization that wants to use a warm site will need to install, configure, and reestablish operations on systems that may already exist at the warm site.

8. **D.** A reciprocal agreement is between two organizations and allows one to use the other's site in an emergency.

9. **C.** Fail-over occurs when a system that is developing a malfunction automatically switches processes to another system to continue operations.

10. **A.** RAID 0 is a method of spreading data from a single disk over a number of disk drives. It's used primarily for performance purposes.

11. **C.** A service-level agreement (SLA) specifies performance requirements for a vendor. This agreement may use MTBF and MTTR as performance measures in the SLA.

12. **A.** Code escrow allows customers to access the source code of installed systems under specific conditions, such as the bankruptcy of a vendor.

13. **B.** The acceptable-use policy dictates how computers can be used within an organization. This policy should also outline the consequences of misuse.

14. **B.** Due-care policies dictate the expected precautions to be used to safeguard client records.

15. **A.** A certificate policy dictates how an organization uses, manages, and validates certificates.

16. **C.** The third party is responsible for assuring the relying party that the subscriber is genuine.

17. C.   A contingency plan wouldn't normally be part of an incident-response policy. It would be part of a disaster-recovery plan.

18. A.   A security group is used to manage user access to a network or system.

19. A.   An audit is used to inspect and test procedures within an organization to verify that those procedures are working and up-to-date. The result of an audit is a report to management.

20. A.   DAC allows some flexibility in information-sharing capabilities within the network.

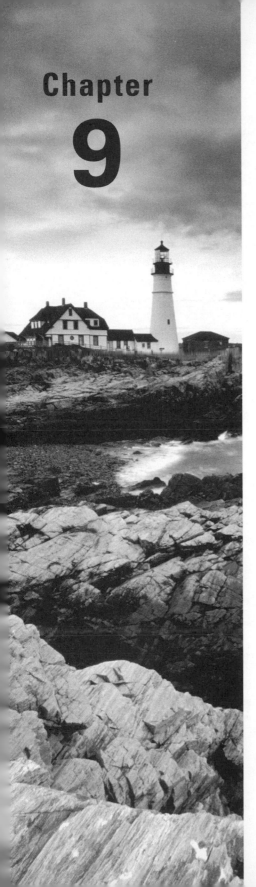

Chapter

9

Security Administration

THE FOLLOWING COMPTIA SECURITY+ EXAM OBJECTIVES ARE COVERED IN THIS CHAPTER:

✓ **1.2 Explain the security risks pertaining to system hardware and peripherals.**

- BIOS
- USB devices
- Cell phones

✓ **3.3 Organize users and computers into appropriate security groups and roles while distinguishing between appropriate rights and privileges.**

✓ **3.4 Apply appropriate security controls to file and print resources.**

✓ **3.5 Compare and implement logical access control methods.**

- ACL
- Group policies
- Password policy
- Domain password policy
- User names and passwords
- Time of day restrictions
- Account expiration
- Logical tokens

The title of administrator implies management—management of resources, computers, users, and so on. Most important, from your perspective, is the management of security. While you must oversee it, security management is the responsibility of everyone. The job requires the cooperation of every department and every individual in an organization. However, many people don't understand or know how to improve security. Your job is to help educate those people in your organization, to assist in policy development, to act as a consultant, and to be part of the security process. This means that you must become knowledgeable about best practices, computer privacy and security laws, and incident response. In short, you have to be knowledgeable in many different areas and constantly (as well as cautiously) keep on top of new developments.

This chapter discusses the key elements of implementing, supporting, and maintaining security efforts in an organization. You're faced with the task of keeping current in an environment that is changing constantly. Not only are the technologies shifting rapidly, but the laws that govern how we must protect our stakeholders are also constantly changing.

Understanding Security Management

The process of *security management* is all encompassing. The process includes managing strategic policies, departmental policies, technology issues, and personnel issues. You need to address each of these areas as part of an effective security system. One of the more difficult aspects of managing security is that change is a constant part of the process, and change is difficult in the best of circumstances. Your job includes understanding the best practices of security management and change documentation, and you must ensure that people are informed when changes need to be made.

Drafting Best Practices and Documentation

The term *best practices* refers to a set of recommendations about a practice or process. The recommendations, in this case, will help provide an appropriate level of security for an organization. The following sections provide an overview of the best practices involved in a security program and the components you must consider when evaluating your current security practices.

Using Policies and Procedures

Organizational security policies help describe what activities, processes, and steps are necessary to continue your security program. They provide the glue that holds the security program together. Policies and procedures also set expectation levels within the organization to help keep things moving forward. Your organization should minimally have policies and procedures that define information and storage, information destruction, security, use of company resources, backups, configuration management, logs and inventories, system architecture, change documentation, and user management.

Information Classification and Notification Policies

Information classification policies define how information is classified. The most common types of classification involve an evaluation of whether information is internal or external and whether it can be used for public dissemination or controlled distribution. These policies help everyone in an organization understand the requirements of information usage and confidentiality.

Notification policies define who is notified when information classifications need to be evaluated, changes are made, and information is updated.

Many organizations have mountains of information that needs to be classified. Many have implemented automatic downgrading policies for information; these policies may indicate a length of time that information must be retained or reviewed. The review can determine whether the information must be retained or can be disposed of. This process can significantly reduce the amount of information that requires special storage in an organization.

The U.S. government implemented an automatic declassification system several years ago, and it has saved the government billions of dollars in storage and security costs.

Information Retention and Storage Policies

Information retention and *storage policies* deal with how information is stored, how long it's retained, and any other significant considerations. These policies should identify who owns certain types of information.

One of the biggest problems facing larger facilities is the amount of data that is backed up and stored. Information organization, data library capabilities, and good operational procedures can help make this task manageable.

Schools and similar organizations are required to keep certain information, such as transcripts, forever. The information retention problems associated with these types of situations can be overwhelming for some organizations. The University of Washington in Seattle had to convert a large underground parking garage into a storage facility for student records. The university has the transcript of every student who has attended since it opened over 100 years ago.

Information Destruction Policies

Information destruction policies define how information is destroyed when it has reached the end of its useful life. The elimination of unneeded paper and other confidential files is a big job for many organizations.

 Paper documents containing sensitive information should be shredded or incinerated when they're no longer needed. Doing so reduces the likelihood that this information will wind up in the wrong hands.

When computer systems are retired, the disk drives should be zeroed out and all magnetic media should be *degaussed*. Degaussing involves applying a strong magnetic field to initialize the media (this is also referred to as *disk wiping*). Erasing files on a computer system doesn't guarantee that the information isn't still on the disk; a low-level format can be performed on the system, or a utility can be used to completely wipe the disk clean. This process helps ensure that information doesn't fall into the wrong hands.

The low-level format returns a disk drive or other magnetic media back to the state it was in when it was brand new. The process physically rewrites every location on the disk back to its original state. Windows and DOS systems can use a program called FISK to perform this task. Most disk manufacturers either provide utilities to accomplish this or can recommend what tools to use. You should verify the procedures and settings for a low-level format from the disk manufacturer because incorrect settings can cause a disk drive to work unreliably or become extremely slow.

 Real World Scenario

Selling Your Old Computers

Recently, a company decided that it needed to close its doors and go out of business. It had an extensive inventory of computer equipment and licensed software, so it decided to hold a "going out of business sale" on the computer equipment. The company merely deleted sensitive information from the systems it sold; it left the operating systems installed. When the sale was announced, the company received a nasty letter from one of the large software manufacturers saying that it was in violation of the End User License Agreement (EULA). It had to remove the operating systems from all the computers in order to comply. The company could sell the computers, and it could sell the operating systems media separately, but it could not sell them together.

Within a computer—be it a workstation or server—there exists on the motherboard a *basic input/output system (BIOS)* chip. This special memory chip contains software that tells the processor how to interact with the rest of the hardware in the computer. One of the things that falls beneath the BIOS control is the *complimentary metal oxide semiconductor (CMOS)* that holds settings such as the date, time, hard drive configuration, memory, and any passwords that you want to assign at this base level.

Don't think that a BIOS-based password will keep your data safe when you're throwing away old equipment. Most data within the BIOS can be overwritten (it is flash based) and maintained by a battery. By removing and reinstalling the battery, it is often possible to wipe BIOS settings and get prompted for new values at boot. Doing so can allow someone with one of your old computers to access the data that you thought was secure when you tossed the workstation in the trash.

Security Policy

A *security policy* defines what controls are required to implement and maintain the security of systems, users, and networks. This policy should be used as a guide in system implementations and evaluations. Security policies have been extensively discussed throughout the book, and you should be aware of their key aspects at this point.

Use Policy

Use policies describe how the employees in an organization can use company systems and resources: both software and hardware. This policy should also outline the consequences for misuse. In addition, the policy (also known as an *acceptable use policy*) should address installation of personal software on company computers and the use of personal hardware such as USB devices.

Even secure workstations that contain no traditional media devices (CD, DVD, floppy, and so forth) usually contain USB ports. Unless those ports are disabled, a user can easily connect a flash drive and copy files to and from it. Not only should you make every attempt to limit USB ports, but you should also have the use of such devices spelled out in the acceptable use policy to circumvent the "I didn't know" defense.

A few years ago, an employee in a large company was using corporate computer systems to run a small accounting firm he had started. He was using the computers on his own time. When this situation was discovered, he was immediately fired for the misuse of corporate resources. He sued the company for wrongful discharge and won the case. The company was forced to hire him back and pay his back wages, and he was even awarded damages. The primary reason the company lost the case was that its acceptable use policy didn't say he couldn't use the company computers for personal work, only that he couldn't use them for personal work during work hours. The company wasn't able to prove that he did the personal work during work hours.

Every acceptable use policy today should include a section on cell phone usage (and even presence) within the workplace. While a cell phone can be convenient for employees (they can now more easily take personal calls at work), it can be a headache for the security administrator. Most cell phones can store files the same as any USB device and can be used to copy files to and from the workstation. Additionally, the camera feature of most phones make it possible for a user to take pictures of such things as documents, your servers, your physical security implementation, and many others things you probably don't want to share. For this reason, most secure facilities have stringent restrictions on the presence of cell phones within the vicinity.

Make sure your acceptable use policies provide you with adequate coverage regarding all acceptable uses of corporate resources.

Backup Policy

An organization's *backup policy* dictates what information should be backed up and how it should be backed up. Ideally, a backup plan is written in conjunction with the business continuity plan.

Backup policies also need to set guidelines for information archiving. Many managers and users don't understand the difference between a backup and an archive. A *backup* is a restorable copy of any set of data that is needed on the system; an *archive* is any collection of data that is removed from the system because it's no longer needed on a regular basis.

Configuration Management Policies

Configuration management refers to the types of steps that are needed to make changes in either hardware or software systems. These procedures help define the process for upgrades as well as system retirement procedures. In a large organization, configuration management is a difficult job. Most organizations have multiple generations of hardware and software.

Many older or legacy systems have applications on them that have been installed for years. In some organizations, these systems have little if any documentation about configuration or usage. If a legacy system has mission-critical data stored on it, provisions must be made to archive the information or upgrade it to a newer system.

Logs and Inventories

Logs and inventories help an organization know what is happening to organizational systems and assets. Keeping track of system events and asset inventories is an important aspect of security. *System logs* tell you what is happening with the systems in the network. Periodically review and clear these logs (they tend to fill up and become hard to work with). It's a good practice to review system logs on a weekly basis to look for unusual errors, activities, or events. Establish logging levels to focus logging on certain types of events, such as failed logon attempts; this information can help you discover if attackers are trying to break in to your system before they succeed.

Inventories refer to both the physical assets and the software assets that your company owns. Software assets, in many situations, exceed the value of the hardware assets of companies. Inventory installed software periodically to make sure it's current, licensed, and authorized for use in your network. Products such as Microsoft's Systems Management Server and CA Unicenter can assist with asset management and inventory. In addition, software needs to be secured when it isn't needed.

⊕ **Real World Scenario**

Always Think of the Obvious

A large manufacturer once lost $1,000,000 worth of computer equipment—the equipment couldn't be found when an audit was performed. This loss caused a major panic for the organization because the equipment was part of a government project and the government wanted to know where it was.

It turned out that the equipment had been moved and put into storage. Unfortunately, the equipment move hadn't been entered in the inventory, and the equipment had somehow become misplaced. This company had to search all of its extensive warehouse space in order to find it. Finally, the company located it, and a major confrontation with the U.S. government was averted. Had the company not been able to locate this equipment, it would potentially have had to pay to replace it.

System Architecture

The *system architecture* of many organizations includes an infrastructure made up of both software and hardware. Good drawings and documentation of your system architecture are immensely valuable when you're troubleshooting or considering making changes. These documents provide you with the blueprint of your organization's infrastructure. Keep these documents up-to-date because it's hard to troubleshoot a network with out-of-date information.

Change Documentation

Change documentation involves keeping records about how your network or organization changes over time. As with system architecture information, it's extremely helpful to have changes in your network well documented.

Change documentation accomplishes several things during the change process. It helps keep track of what changes have occurred, and it also helps implementers remember what was accomplished and why. In a large implementation, hundreds or even thousands of changes might be occurring across a network. These changes can become confusing if a crisis develops in the middle of the process—it might become hard to remember which systems have been changed, which systems have not, and which systems developed difficulties.

By documenting changes, you help establish a history and share knowledge about the difficulties and experiences in the change process. Documentation doesn't have to be any more complicated than keeping records about systems, implementations, and experiences. Many smaller companies use a three-ring binder that contains notes about changes that are made to the system. The binders are usually kept with system logs for fast review.

Many older systems have little if any documentation about what was done to them and why. A system review is a great time to investigate these systems and bring documentation up-to-date.

Large change processes may involve formalized documentation methods, databases, and other technologies to help track changes. It's usually best to enter these changes into whatever system is used immediately after you complete a step. You'll have to do the paperwork eventually, so why not do it while the facts are fresh in your mind? In any case, follow the procedures established by your organization for documenting changes; doing so will save you hours of research later.

User Management

Procedures for *user management* identify authorization, access, and methods used to monitor access of organizational computer systems. These procedures may involve multiple systems, multiple platforms, and organizational issues.

User management procedures need to address hiring, termination, and reclassification of employee access. Reporting, notification procedures, and responsibility are also key components of these procedures.

Allocating Resources

Resource allocation refers to the staffing, technology, and budget needed to implement an effective security environment. Your organization will frequently have to deal with the issues of balancing risk management and preventive measures. History has shown that a well-developed, properly implemented plan costs more to design than a plan that is thrown together and hastily implemented. However, although the costs are usually initially higher, such plans tend to be a sound investment over the long run. This planning process requires staff, time, and budget.

Budgetary issues can be contentious when you're considering security options. Security initiatives are sometimes hard to quantify, and it is difficult to provide real numbers to justify them. This is in part because security is as much a process-oriented environment as it is a product-oriented environment.

Process-oriented issues involve research, planning, architecture, audits, and policy development. They tend to become complicated, and they should be considered before any action is taken. Funds must be allocated for the planning process: While someone is planning, other work isn't being accomplished. If an organization isn't willing to allocate a budget for planning processes, the likelihood of a successful implementation decreases dramatically.

Budget is always an issue for security processes. The major problem lies in the fact that security isn't often viewed as adding value to an organization. In addition, security efforts are often implemented on a piecemeal basis. If you're trying to establish the need for security, you should involve the whole organization. When possible, make sure department heads, managers, and other key people become involved in the process; most successful security efforts have been implemented as enterprise-wide solutions. Security affects everyone—a breach of security can embarrass and potentially cause financial risks to the organization. These issues can be discovered if everyone is involved in figuring out the true costs of security problems from both a customer and organizational perspective.

 The negative attention that data breaches generate can be sufficient to financially ruin a company. For a chronology of data breaches, visit http://www.privacyrights.org/ar/ChronDataBreaches.htm.

Defining Responsibility

Clear areas of responsibility must be implemented for a security initiative to be successful. This includes implementation, management, and ongoing maintenance. Effective security requires effective management; this responsibility may reside at an executive level, as part of a management committee, or as a separate department within an organization.

Members of the security team, as well as other members of the organization, must be clear about reporting paths and authority. Your training and security knowledge make you the ideal candidate to be the champion of security efforts in your organization.

Minimizing Mistakes

A big component of the security effort revolves around prevention. Accidents happen, incidents occur, and humans make mistakes. Mistakes can be minimized if strong preventive measures are considered as part of the process. Such measures include training, awareness, and careful reviews of processes and policies. The old saying "An ounce of prevention is worth a pound of cure" is always the truth in any security effort.

Make sure managers and employees are aware of the types of activities that occur in the field and that they know how to implement and continue to support security efforts. These tasks are key aspects of prevention.

IT staff, including network administrators, must be kept up-to-date on industry trends, measures, exploits, and countermeasures to deal with threats. You can be a big asset to the IT staff if you help them remain current. Virtually all network administrators want to have secure environments; unfortunately, just keeping a large network functioning can be overwhelming.

Enforcing the Policies and Procedures

When an incident or a security violation happens, swift and decisive action must be taken. This might include additional training, disciplinary action, or other measures. It's human nature to neglect policies and procedures when they aren't enforced. You should make sure everyone involved in information processing is aware of the organization's policies and procedures. In addition, when a problem is discovered, the specifics must be clear to management.

Before you take corrective action involving employees, it's a good idea to understand the knowledge level of the employees involved; it does no good to punish someone who doesn't know better. The intention here isn't to turn you into security police, but to remind people that policies matter, that there are consequences for not following them, and that someone is watching activity. In many cases, this is enough of a deterrent to prevent dishonest acts, and it's a reminder that people can't let their guard down about security.

🌐 Real World Scenario

The World of Monitoring

You've been monitoring the activities of users in your company. You unintentionally intercepted an e-mail on the system indicating that a key employee has a drug problem and is in a treatment program. What should you do with this information?

This is a tough situation to be in, and you'll find yourself in similar circumstances more often than you want. This information was gained by accident, and it's potentially embarrassing and sensitive in nature. Both ethical and legal issues are involved. You would probably be best served by not disclosing this information to anyone. If you're uncertain, you should discuss the general situation with your human resources department; avoid specifics until you know how the company wants to handle it. You should never discuss such a situation with anybody without first consulting HR, and you should certainly never discuss it with anybody but authorized personnel.

Simplifying Security Administration

As an administrator, one of your goals should be to always simplify your security implementation as much as possible. The simpler you can make it, the easier it is to enforce.

Allow me to share a straightforward analogy. When my son was small, I had a simple policy, and it was easy to enforce: Never touch matches. When he was much older and had become a Boy Scout, I had another simple policy that was easy to enforce: Use your best judgment when it comes to fire. Problems never occurred at either end of the spectrum, but there were many years in between when the prevailing policy didn't work and incidents had to be addressed.

The problems first began when he was a Webelos scout and was encouraged by his leaders to have a fire starting kit. This caused me to change the no matches policy to exclude the fire starting kit—that is until he thought it alright to demonstrate his expertise with the kit to neighborhood boys in his room.

I could tell story after story of how problems occurred when I made exceptions to the rule—as long as the rule was absolute (one way or the other), problems stayed away. As soon as I deviated from the absolute, however ("it is now okay to have matches..."), the problems appeared. The same is true when you administer a network.

The easiest way to simplify network security is to organize users into groups and computers into roles. Rather than managing each user individually, you manage each group collectively. The group(s) the user is placed into should always be based upon the roles they need to perform their jobs with the minimum set of rights and privileges.

The rights and privileges available for assigning will differ in name based upon the operating system(s) you run (Chapter 5, "Implementing and Maintaining a Secure Network," discusses different operating systems), but all employ similar concepts. The most important thing is to make certain that you assign users to a group only when they need the rights and privileges that group offers, and that you regularly monitor group ownership and remove users from groups when they no longer need those rights and privileges.

 Real World Scenario

The Wide World of Groups

One of the system administrators in your office is going on paternity leave. Normally, he is the only one authorized to access certain files and run key reports. One of the accountants has graciously offered to run these reports while he is gone. How should you assign the needed permissions to the accountant?

There are two approaches to this scenario: one you should avoid, and one you should take. The first approach is to assign the necessary permissions specifically to the accountant—both to the data files and to the executables needed to run the report. This approach is not recommended because the number of files could be substantial and there is always a risk that you will overlook one when adding (or, worse yet, later removing) permissions.

The second approach—and the one that is recommended—is to add the accountant to a Reports group, which contains only the bare minimum permissions needed to run reports, and remove him from there when the administrator returns. If such a group does not exist, you should immediately create one.

Based upon the operating system(s) that you are using, a number of logical access control methods should factor into your implementation. Many of these have been discussed throughout this book, and Table 9.1 summarizes some factors to consider.

TABLE 9.1   Common Logical Access Control Methods/Topics

Security Topics	Notes
Access control lists (ACLs)	These hold permissions for users and groups, and each entry in an ACL can specify what type of access is given—such as Read-Only, Change, or Full Control.
Account Expiration	Every account should be configured to expire. As the account continues to be used, the expiration should be deferred, but any account not being used should be allowed to expire.

TABLE 9.1   Common Logical Access Control Methods/Topics *(continued)*

Security Topics	Notes
Domain Password Policy	The domain password policy gives permission to reset the password of a user object, and thus the policy should restrict this privilege/power to only administrators.
Group Policies	One of the easiest ways to restrict access to operating system components and resources is through the use of group policies. The settings defined within a policy are automatically applied.
Logical Tokens	Similar to certificates, tokens contain the rights and access privileges of the token bearer.
Password Policy	The password policy needs to define what you are willing to accept as password values: minimum number of characters, required use of nonalphabetic characters, unique values, and so forth.
Time-of-day restrictions	Most users need to access the system only during working hours, and by restricting their access to these times, you increase security by decreasing the likelihood that a miscreant can access the system using a hijacked account after hours.
Usernames and passwords	Consistency is crucial when defining policies related to usernames and passwords. The more standardization you can apply, the more secure the system can become.

Assigning appropriate controls does not apply only to users and groups, it is equally important for those items they access, such as file and print resources. Make certain the permissions assigned to those resources are the minimum necessary to use the resources properly.

Understanding Security Awareness and Education

Security awareness and education are critical to the success of a security effort. They include explaining policies, procedures, and current threats to both users and management.

A security-awareness and education program can do much to assist in your efforts to improve and maintain security. Such efforts need to be ongoing, and they should be part of the organization's normal communications to be effective. The following sections discuss some of the things you can do as a security professional to address the business issues associated with training the people in your organization to operate in a manner that is consistent with organizational security goals.

Using Communication and Awareness

Communication and awareness help ensure that information is conveyed to the appropriate people in a timely manner. Most users aren't aware of current security threats. If you set a process in place to concisely and clearly explain what is happening and what is being done to correct current threats, you'll probably find acceptance of your efforts to be much higher.

Communication methods that have proven to be effective for disseminating information include internal security websites, news servers, and e-mails. You might want to consider a regular notification process to convey information about security issues and changes. In general, the more you communicate about this in a routine manner, the more likely people will internalize the fact that security is everybody's responsibility.

Providing Education

Your efforts in education must help users clearly understand prevention, enforcement, and threats. The security department will also probably be responsible for a security-awareness program. Your training and educational programs need to be tailored for at least three different audiences:

- The organization as a whole
- Management
- Technical staff

These three organizational roles have different considerations and concerns. For example, with organization-wide training, everyone understands the policies, procedures, and resources available to deal with security problems; it helps ensure that all employees are on the same page. The following list identifies the types of issues that members of an organization should be aware of and understand.

Organization   Ideally, a security-awareness training program should cover the following areas:

- Importance of security
- Responsibilities of people in the organization
- Policies and procedures
- Usage policies
- Account and password-selection criteria
- Social engineering prevention

You can accomplish this training either by using internal staff or by hiring outside trainers. I recommend doing much of this training during new-employee orientation and staff meetings.

Management   Managers are concerned with larger issues in the organization, including enforcing security policies and procedures. Managers will want to know the whys of a security program, as well as how it works. They should receive additional training or exposure that explains the issues, threats, and methods of dealing with threats. Management will also be concerned about productivity impacts, enforcement, and how the various departments are affected by security policies.

Technical staff   The technical staff needs special knowledge about the methods, implementations, and capabilities of the systems used to manage security. Network administrators will want to evaluate how to manage the network, best practices, and configuration issues associated with the technologies they support. Developers and implementers will want to evaluate the impact these measures have on existing systems and new development projects. The training that both administrators and developers need will be vendor specific; vendors have their own methods of implementing security.

Microsoft, Novell, and Cisco each offer certification programs to train administrators on their environments. All of these manufacturers have specific courseware on security implementations, and some offer security certification. You should implement security systems consistent with the manufacturer's suggestions and guidance. Implementing security in a non-standard way may leave your system unsecure.

One of the most important aspects of education is that it needs to reach an appropriate audience. Spending an hour preaching on back-end database security will likely be an hour wasted if the only members of the audience are data-entry personnel who get paid by the keystroke to make weekly changes as quickly as possible.

 Real World Scenario

Applying Education Appropriately

As a security administrator, you need to know the level of knowledge that is appropriate for the audience you're addressing and be able to understand the importance of speaking to them at that level. Imagine that you find yourself in each of the following situations, and think through your response.

Scenario 1   You've been assigned the task of giving a one-hour briefing on the topic of security to management during their weekly luncheon (no other subtopics or specifics were given). Most of those in attendance will be upper management who know little about computers and tend to focus on financial sheets. What topics will you discuss and at what depth?

Scenario 2   You've been told to meet with the developers of a new application that will soon be rolled out to all branch offices. The application will hold all human resource records as well as a small amount of patient information. Your boss tells you that after the meeting, you're to sign off on the application as being okay to deploy. What type of security questions will you focus on?

Scenario 3   The annual company meeting is next month. Representatives, including those in IT, from all remote offices will arrive at headquarters for a three-day visit. You've been asked to speak about the importance of strong passwords throughout the organization. What will you say, and how will you make your one-hour presentation stay with them after they return to their offices?

It's important to give the right message to the right people. When giving any presentation, you should always tailor it for the audience and be able to make your discussion relevant to them.

A recommendation for scenario 1 would be to keep the talk at the overview level and focus only on the basics of security: why it's needed, how valuable data is, how to use good passwords, and so on.

For scenario 2, you should push to test the application in a test environment first (nonproduction). You want to make certain that no back doors have been left in by the developers and that no negative interactions will occur between the new application and what is already running on your systems.

In scenario 3, you must bear in mind that you're talking to an IT audience: The level of the presentation should be appropriate for them. To make the presentation stay with them, make it relevant. Talk about why this subject is important and how it affects their job.

Staying on Top of Security

The landscape of security is changing at a fast pace. You, as a security professional, are primarily responsible for keeping current on the threats and changes that are occurring, as well as staying on top of new developments in the field. At times, it can seem as if new buzzwords and acronyms (such as SPIM for Spam over Instant Messaging) are added daily. You're also responsible for ensuring that systems are kept current and up-to-date. The following list briefly summarizes the areas you must be concerned about:

Operating systems updates   Make sure all scheduled maintenance, updates, and service packs are installed on all the systems in your environment. Many manufacturers are releasing security updates on their products to deal with newly discovered vulnerabilities. For example, Novell, Microsoft, and Linux manufacturers offer updates on their websites. In some cases, you can have the operating system automatically notify you when an update becomes available; this notification helps busy administrators remember to keep their systems current.

As a security administrator, you understand the importance of applying all patches and updates to keep systems current and to close found weaknesses.

> Most vendors offer sites specifically devoted to security. For example, Red Hat has http://www.redhat.com/security, Ubuntu has https://help.ubuntu.com/community/Security, Microsoft has http://www.microsoft.com/security, and so on.

Application updates   Make sure all applications are kept to the most current levels. Older software might contain vulnerabilities that weren't detected until after the software was released. New software may have recently discovered vulnerabilities as well as yet-to-be-discovered ones. Apply updates to your application software when they are released to help minimize the impact of attacks on your systems.

One of the biggest exploitations that occurs today involves applications such as e-mail clients and word-processing software. The manufacturers of these products regularly release updates to attempt to make them more secure. Check for updates regularly and apply them the same as you would for operating systems.

Network device updates   Most newer network devices can provide high levels of security, or they can be configured to block certain types of traffic and IP addresses. Make sure logs are reviewed and, where necessary, access control lists (ACLs) are updated to prevent attackers from disrupting your systems. These network devices are also frequently updated to counter new vulnerabilities and threats. Network devices should have their BIOS updated when the updates become available; doing so allows for an ever-increasing level of security in your environment.

Cisco, 3Com, and other network manufacturers regularly offer network updates. These can frequently be applied online or by web-enabled systems. These devices are your front line of defense; you want to make sure they are kept up-to-date.

Policies and procedures   A policy that is out-of-date might be worse than no policy. Be aware of any changes in your organization and in the industry that make existing policies out-of-date. Many organizations set a review date as part of their policy-creation procedures. Periodically review your documentation to verify that your policies are still effective and current.

Personal development   Remember that you're one of your organization's most precious commodities. Like any precious commodity, you need to keep yourself current. Stay abreast of current trends in the industry, new threats, and other issues that might affect your business; doing so will ensure that your skills are always honed. You'll feel more confident about your ability to deal with situations—and so will your company. Attend seminars, subscribe to relevant periodicals, and continue to grow in your knowledge and skills. This is your best bet to ensure career growth. Professional societies and associations are invaluable for gaining knowledge about an industry and its trends. Networking will also help you build a list of people whom you can call for advice or assistance when you encounter an unusual problem or situation. It's likely that someone has already experienced what you're encountering; you can learn from their experiences, and you won't have to repeat their mistakes. Take your career seriously.

In addition to focusing on these areas, you must stay current on security trends, threats, and tools available to help you provide security. The volume of threats is increasing, as are the measures, methods, and procedures being used to counter them. The following sections will help you find places to keep current. Some of these resources are governmental; many other informational sources are available through corporations, schools, and associations concerned with security-related issues. A great deal of information also exists on the Internet and is available through the Web or newsgroup mailing lists. The lists that follow aren't intended to be comprehensive; many of these sources contain links to other sources of information.

You must keep abreast of what is happening in the field and stay informed of the current best practices of the systems and applications you support. You're basically going to be functioning as a clearinghouse and data repository for your company's security. Make it a point to become a walking encyclopedia on security issues: Doing so will improve your credibility and demonstrate your expertise. Both of these aspects enhance your career opportunities and equip you to be a leader in the field.

Websites

Several websites actively track security issues. This list provides you with the major providers of security information on the Web. Many of these organizations also provide newsletters and mailings to announce changes or security threats:

Center for Education and Research in Information Assurance and Security   Center for Education and Research in Information Assurance and Security (CERIAS) is an industry-sponsored center at Purdue University that is focused on technology and related issues. CERIAS provides news and information on technology threats. The website is `http://www.cerias.purdue.edu`.

CERT Coordination Center   The CERT/CC is a federally sponsored partnership in conjunction with Carnegie Mellon University that provides Internet security expertise. CERT offers a wide variety of information about current threats and best practices in security. The website is `http://www.cert.org`. One of the most interesting pages you can find there details the steps to take to recover after your computer has been compromised; this is located at `http://www.cert.org/tech_tips/win-UNIX-system_compromise.html`.

Computer Security Institute   Computer Security Institute (CSI) is a professional organization that offers national conferences, membership publications, and information on computer security issues. CSI is one of the oldest societies in this area. The website is `http://www.gocsi.com`.

European Institute for Computer Anti-Virus Research   European Institute for Computer Anti-Virus Research (EICAR) is an association of European corporations, schools, and educators that are concerned with information security issues. The website is `http://www.eicar.org`.

LinuxSecurity   The latest news and articles related to Linux security issues can be found here. The website is `http://www.linuxsecurity.com`.

McAfee Corporation   McAfee is a leading provider of antivirus software. The company's site provides information and updates for its software. The website is `http://www.mcafee.com`.

National Institute of Standards and Technology   National Institute of Standards and Technology (NIST) is the governmental agency involved in the creation and use of standards. These standards are generally adopted by governmental agencies, and they are used as the basis for other standards. NIST has an organization specifically addressed to computer issues: the Computer Security Response Center (CSRC). The CSRC/NIST maintains a database of current vulnerabilities and other useful information. The website is `http://www.csrc.nist.gov`.

National Security Institute   The National Security Institute (NSI) is a clearinghouse of information relating to security. This site offers a wealth of information on many aspects of physical and information security, including a free e-newsletter. The website is `http://www.nsi.org`.

SANS Institute   The SysAdmin, Audit, Network, Security (SANS) Institute is a research and educational organization. SANS offers seminars, research, and other information relating to the security field. The website is `http://www.sans.org`.

Security Focus   General news and information on security topics of all sorts are archived here. There is also a weekly newsletter that you can subscribe to. The website is `http://www.securityfocus.com`.

Symantec Corporation   Symantec is a leading provider of antivirus software. Its website lists current threats, provides research abilities, and gives information about information security. The website is `http://www.symantec.com`.

Trade Publications

Numerous trade publications exist that address issues relating to security at different levels of difficulty. Some of these publications are good sources of overview information and case studies; others go into the theoretical aspects of security. Trade publications are good places to start in furthering your education. Remember that one of the most valuable jobs you perform is to consult for your organization on current issues in the field. Following is a brief list of trade publications you might find useful in your quest for knowledge and websites where you can subscribe:

2600: The Hacker Quarterly   This interesting little magazine provides tips and information on computer security issues. Don't let the name fool you—there is a wealth of information on current issues about security in this magazine. The website is `http://www.2600.com`.

CertCities   *CertCities* is an online magazine that covers the broad field of certification. It also does features on the pros and cons of various certifications, and it contains articles related to the computer profession. The website is `http://www.certcities.com`.

CIO   *CIO* is a monthly publication that specializes in IT management issues and periodically offers security-related articles that tend to be high level. The website is `http://www.cio.com`.

CSO Magazine　　*CSO* is a monthly magazine that focuses on issues of interest to security executives. The website is `http://www.csoonline.com`.

Hackin9　　*Hackin9* is a bimonthly publication aimed at those with an interest in "hard core IT security". The website is `http://www.en.hakin9.org/`.

Information Security Magazine　　*Information Security Magazine* is a monthly publication that focuses on computer security issues. The website is `http://informationsecurity.techtarget.com`.

InformationWeek　　*InformationWeek* addresses management and other IT issues. This magazine provides updates in the field of technology. The website is `http://www.informationweek.com`.

InfoWorld　　*InfoWorld* deals with PC issues from an IT management perspective. This magazine offers regular articles on security and related topics. The website is `http://www.infoworld.com`.

 Real World Scenario

Security-Awareness Program

You've just been appointed to the security department of your IT organization. The organization needs to implement a new set of plans and standards for computer security. You've been asked to create a way to communicate this information to the organization. What could you recommend to accomplish this?

You might consider creating a security-awareness seminar for everyone in the organization. This seminar would ideally address the following areas:

- Importance of security

- Responsibilities of people in the organization

- Policies and procedures

- Usage policies

- Account and password-selection criteria

- Social engineering prevention

If a seminar is not possible, training can also be done using an intranet site that is updated regularly. The site should require employees to log in to document that they have reviewed the latest security information. Disseminating the information this way gives the employee more latitude but still gets the job done in the absence of a seminar.

Additionally, you would want to develop training programs for management to address the needs of the department heads and managers. Your organization may need to determine if additional training is needed for network administrators and development personnel.

Regulating Privacy and Security

An organization's security management policies don't exist in a vacuum. Regulatory and governmental agencies are key components of a security management policy. These agencies have made large improvements over the last several years to ensure the privacy of information; several laws have been passed to help ensure that information isn't disclosed to unauthorized parties. The following sections provide a brief overview of a few of these regulations. As a security professional, you must stay current with these laws because you're one of the primary agents to ensure compliance.

 In addition to the federal laws, most states have laws on computer crime as well. Check http://nsi.org/Library/Compsec/computerlaw/statelaws.html for information on your state.

The Health Insurance Portability and Accountability Act

The *Health Insurance Portability and Accountability Act (HIPAA)* is a relatively new regulation that mandates national standards and procedures for the storage, use, and transmission of personal medical information. Passed into law in 1996, HIPAA has caused a great deal of change in healthcare record keeping.

HIPAA covers three areas—confidentiality, privacy, and security of patient records—and it's being implemented in phases to make the transition easier. Confidentiality and privacy of patient records had to be implemented by a set date, followed by security of patient records. Standards for transaction codes in medical record transmissions had to be completed by a given date as well. Deadlines through 2008 are currently being implemented.

The penalties for HIPAA violations are very stiff: They can be as high as $250,000 based on the circumstances. Medical practices are required to appoint a security officer. All related parties, such as billing agencies and medical records storage facilities, are required to comply with these regulations.

 For more information on HIPAA, you can visit http://www.cms.hhs.gov/HIPAAGenInfo/.

The Gramm-Leach-Bliley Act of 1999

The *Gramm-Leach-Bliley Act*, also know as the *Financial Modernization Act*, requires financial institutions to develop privacy notices and to notify customers that they are entitled to privacy. The act prohibits banks from releasing information to nonaffiliated third parties without permission. Many consumer groups have criticized the implementation of this act by financial institutions.

Employees need to be trained on information security issues, and security measures must be put into place and tested to verify information privacy. The act includes a number of other provisions that allow banks and financial institutions to align and form partnerships.

The act requires banks to explain to individual consumers information-sharing policies. Customers have the ability to "opt out" of sharing agreements.

The act prohibits institutions from sharing account information for marketing purposes. It also prohibits the gathering of information about customers using false or fraudulent methods.

The law went into effect in July 2001. Financial officers and the board of directors can be held criminally liable for violations.

 For more information on the Gramm-Leach-Bliley Act, visit http://www.ftc
.gov/privacy/privacyinitiatives/glbact.html.

The Computer Fraud and Abuse Act

The *Computer Fraud and Abuse Act* was introduced into law in 1986. The original law was introduced to address issues of fraud and abuse that weren't well covered under existing statutes. The law was updated in 1994, in 1996, and again in 2001.

This act gives federal authorities, primarily the FBI, the ability to prosecute hackers, spammers, and others as terrorists. The law is primarily intended to protect government and financial computer systems from intrusion. Technically, if a governmental system, such as an Internet server, were used in the commission of the crime, virtually any computer user who could be shown to have any knowledge or part in the crime could be prosecuted.

The law is comprehensive and allows for stiff penalties, fines, and imprisonment of up to 10 years for convictions under this statute.

 For more information on the Computer Fraud and Abuse Act, visit http://
cio.doe.gov/Documents/CFA.HTM.

The Family Educational Rights and Privacy Act

The *Family Educational Rights and Privacy Act (FERPA)* dictates that educational institutions may not release information to unauthorized parties without the express permission of the student or, in the case of a minor, the parents of the student. This act also requires that educational institutions must disclose any records kept on a student when demanded by that student. This law has had a huge impact on privacy requirements of student records. It jeopardizes the federal funding of schools by government agencies if any violations occur.

For more information on FERPA, visit http://www.ed.gov/policy/gen/guid/ fpco/ferpa/index.html. To view a database of losses involving personally identifiable information, visit http://attrition.org/dataloss/.

The Computer Security Act of 1987

The *Computer Security Act* requires federal agencies to identify and protect computer systems that contain sensitive information. This law requires agencies that keep sensitive information to conduct regular training and audits, and to implement procedures to protect privacy. All federal agencies must comply with this act.

For more information on the Computer Security Act, visit http://epic.org/ crypto/csa/.

The Cyberspace Electronic Security Act

The *Cyberspace Electronic Security Act (CESA)* gives law enforcement the right to gain access to encryption keys and cryptography methods. The initial version of this act allowed federal law enforcement agencies to secretly use monitoring, electronic capturing equipment, and other technologies to access and obtain information. These provisions were later stricken from the act, although federal law enforcement agencies were given a large amount of latitude to conduct investigations relating to electronic information. This act is generating a lot of discussion about what capabilities should be allowed to law enforcement in the detection of criminal activity.

For more information on CESA, visit http://www.cdt.org/crypto/CESA/.

The Cyber Security Enhancement Act

The *Cyber Security Enhancement Act* of 2002 allows federal agencies relatively easy access to ISPs and other data-transmission facilities to monitor communications of individuals suspected of committing computer crimes using the Internet. The act is also known as *Section 225 of the Homeland Security Act* of 2002.

For more information on the Cyber Security Enhancement Act, visit http:// www.usdoj.gov/criminal/cybercrime/homeland_CSEA.htm.

The Patriot Act

The *Uniting and Strengthening America by Providing Appropriate Tools Required to Intercept and Obstruct Terrorism (USA PATRIOT)* Act of 2001 was passed partially because of the World Trade Center attack on September 11, 2001. This law gives the U.S. government extreme latitude in pursuing criminals who commit terrorist acts. The definition of a terrorist act is broad.

The law provides for relief to victims of terrorism as well as the ability to conduct virtually any type of surveillance of a suspected terrorist. This act is currently under revision, and it will probably be expanded.

For more information on the Patriot Act and the current budget, visit http://www.cbo.gov/showdoc.cfm?index=3180&sequence=0&from=6. A transcript of the act can be found at http://www.fincen.gov/hr3162.pdf.

Familiarizing Yourself with International Efforts

Many governments are now evaluating their current laws regarding cyberterrorism, cybercrime, and privacy. Among the agencies that are currently evaluating cyber laws are the European Union (EU) and the G8.

The EU, which is a common governance agency that includes many member nations, is soon expected to enact tough legislation regarding computer use. In the next few years, the EU is likely to be formidable in its ability to pursue and prosecute cyber criminals.

The EU is adopting the strategy of looking at all EU member nations as a large "Information Society," and it will be passing laws and regulations regarding computer security and privacy among all members. It's also working on laws to protect computer systems and prevent cybercrime. The most all-encompassing law under consideration is the Cybercrime Treaty, which would make all hacking illegal in Europe. It's generating concern about legitimate research among security researchers in Europe.

International agencies (such as Interpol and the G8) are evaluating guidelines and laws about cybercrime. Asian and Pacific nations appear to be dealing with cybercrime issues on an individual basis.

Summary

In this chapter, you learned the key elements of security management, best practices, and privacy regulations.

Security management is an ongoing process that requires the use of best practices and documentation. The processes help you to document and classify the policies, procedures, and guidelines you need to implement an effective security policy.

The best practices of computer security include information classification, retention, storage, and destruction policies. Best practices also include the security policy, usage policies, backups, configuration management, inventories, change policies, and user management.

To carry out an effective security management process, an organization must allocate sufficient resources; identify responsibilities; and implement prevention, enforcement, and educational opportunities. It's unrealistic to expect that an effective security policy can be implemented and maintained unless users, managers, and technical staff are equipped to deal with the changes.

Your job as a security professional includes keeping yourself up-to-date on current issues as well as informing affected parties of changes occurring in the industry and new threats. Numerous trade publications and websites are available to help you and to educate decision makers in your organization.

The process of raising sensitivity about security is part of a security-awareness program. This program should include communications about the nature of the issues, education about policies and procedures, and clear support from management.

For an organization to stay on top of security issues, it must keep operating systems, applications, and network devices up-to-date. Policies must be kept current as the environment changes, and personal development initiatives of individuals must be considered. This helps the organization stay current and provides a growing base of knowledge.

Numerous security and privacy regulations affect security management and your environment. These laws or acts govern privacy, security, and the use of information systems and resources. Become aware of them and the impact they have on your organization.

Exam Essentials

Be able to explain the process used to educate an organization about security issues.   The four major aspects of a security management policy are communications, user awareness, education, and online resources. Communication should be ongoing and help the organization make decisions about security requirements and threats. A user-awareness program helps individuals in an organization understand how to implement policies, procedures, and technologies to ensure effective security. A wealth of online information is available to help you learn about current trends in the field. One of your primary responsibilities should be staying current on threats and trends.

Understand the elements of documentation needed to maintain an effective security management program.   The documentation that an organization needs to develop for an effective security management process includes numerous policies. The collection of these policies is based on the best practices in the industry; they provide a comprehensive guide for developing an effective security program.

Hands-On Labs

The labs in this chapter are as follows:

Lab 9.1: Configure Windows Automatic Updates

Lab 9.2: Run the Microsoft Baseline Security Analyzer

Lab 9.1: Configure Windows Automatic Updates

One of the most important things you can do to keep your systems secure is to keep them up-to-date. In this lab, you'll turn on Automatic Updates for a Windows XP Professional workstation:

1. Start the System applet by choosing Start ➢ Control Panel ➢ System.

2. Click the Automatic Updates tab.

3. Check the Keep My Computer Up To Date option (with some service packs, this becomes simply an Automatic radio button).

4. In the Settings section, choose the Download the Updates Automatically and Notify Me When They Are Ready to Be Installed radio button (based upon the version of service pack you have installed, this option may not be present).

5. Click OK, and exit the System applet.

This option allows the operating system to download and install updates as they become available. Some updates—such as service packs—usually require a reboot in order to be active after the installation.

Lab 9.2: Run the Microsoft Baseline Security Analyzer

The Microsoft Baseline Security Analyzer (MBSA) currently works with Microsoft Windows Sever 2003/2008, as well as Windows Vista, Windows XP, and Windows 2000. It allows you to scan a system and identify weaknesses and misconfigurations. To run MBSA, follow these steps:

1. Log in with administrator privileges and download the latest version of MBSA from http://technet.microsoft.com/en-us/security/cc184924.aspx.

2. When prompted, choose to install the application. After the installation is complete, run MBSA.

3. Choose the option Scan a computer.

4. The default computer to scan will be the one you are sitting at, but you can change this to another on the network by specifying either the computer's name or IP address.

5. Click Start Scan.

6. View the report that is given when the scan finishes. The report will include information on missing security updates, and service packs for the operating system as well as Microsoft applications. It will also identify any user accounts that have blank or simple passwords, firewall status, the number of local administrators configured, unnecessary services.

Review Questions

1. Which policy includes all aspects of an organization's security?

    A. Security management policy

    B. Information security policy

    C. Physical security policy

    D. Information classification policy

2. You're assisting with a policy review to make certain your company has in place all the policies it should. One of your fellow administrators mentions that he has never seen anything detailing information sensitivity and usage. Which policy would cover this topic?

    A. Security policy

    B. Information classification policy

    C. Use policy

    D. Configuration management policy

3. Which policy identifies the software and hardware components that can be used in an organization?

    A. Backup policy

    B. Configuration management policy

    C. Inventory policy

    D. Use policy

4. Which of the following involves keeping records about how your network or organization changes over time?

    A. Change documentation

    B. Use policy

    C. Systems architecture

    D. BIA

5. The process of ensuring that all policies, procedures, and standards are met is a function of which process?

    A. Education

    B. Enforcement

    C. Responsibility

    D. Change management

6. Mercury Technical Services is formulating a set of guidelines that outline the components of effective security management. After these have been tried and tested at the Anderson branch, they will be rolled out to all other divisions. What is this set of guidelines called?

    A. Best practices

    B. Forensics

    C. Chain of evidence

    D. Use policy

7. Which policy identifies the files and data that must be archived?

    A. Information classification policy

    B. Use policy

    C. Logs and inventories policy

    D. Information retention policy

8. Which policy defines upgrade and systems requirements?

    A. Configuration management policy

    B. Use policy

    C. Logs and inventory policy

    D. Backup policy

9. A policy review is under way. The new head of HR wants to show that a formal policy exists for every aspect of IT. You've been assigned the role of producing whatever information he asks for. Which policy dictates the processes used to create archival copies of records?

    A. Backup policy

    B. Security policy

    C. Use policy

    D. User management policy

10. Which topic would not normally be covered in a user-oriented security-awareness program?

    A. Security management policy

    B. Use policy

    C. Network technology and administration

    D. Account and password criteria

11. You're a new hire at SMT. One of your job responsibilities is to provide monthly training sessions on security topics over lunch. You want to prioritize the presentations and first give those that are the most important. Which group would most benefit from an overall briefing on security threats and issues?

    A. Management

    B. Users

    C. Developers

    D. Network administrators

12. Thanks to the awarding of a grant, you'll now be able to replace all the outdated work-stations with newer models. Many of those workstations will be coming from the business office. Which of the following should occur when a computer system becomes surplus?

    A. All files should be erased.

    B. Disk drives should be initialized.

    C. Disk drives should be formatted.

    D. Computer screens should be degaussed.

13. BIOS-based passwords are typically lost when what occurs on a workstation?

    A. Electrical power is removed.

    B. The cover is removed.

    C. The computer's battery is removed and replaced.

    D. The hard drive is changed.

14. Which type of policy should define the use of USB devices?

    A. Information retention policy

    B. Configuration management policy

    C. Change documentation

    D. Acceptable use policy

15. You are interested in simplifying security management at your site. The simplest way to manage users is by assigning them to which of the following entities?

    A. Groups

    B. Pools

    C. Units

    D. Categories

16. Which of the following hold permissions for users and groups, such as Read-Only, Full Control, or Change?

    A. Group policies

    B. Access control lists

    C. SIDs

    D. DNS

17. If you want to carefully govern who can reset the password of a user object, which of the following permissions should you focus on?

    A. Logical token

    B. Landlord

    C. Domain password

    D. Change

18. Which of the following are most similar in content to certificates?

    A. Password policies

    B. Device access policies

    C. Datagrams

    D. Logical tokens

19. Which of the following allow you to automatically implement restrictions on operating system components?

    A. Group policies

    B. Access control lists

    C. SIDs

    D. DNS

20. Which type of policy should define the use of cell phones within an organization?

    A. Information retention policy

    B. Configuration management policy

    C. Change documentation

    D. Acceptable use policy

Answers to Review Questions

1. **A.** All aspects of security in the organization are included in the security management policy, including the policies in options B, C, and D.

2. **B.** The information classification policy discusses information sensitivity and access to information.

3. **B.** The configuration management policy is concerned with how systems are configured and what software can be installed on systems.

4. **A.** Change documentation involves keeping records about how your network or organization changes over time.

5. **B.** Enforcement of policies, procedures, and standards is essential for effective sustainability of security efforts. The saying "Inspect what you expect" is relevant in this situation.

6. **A.** The term *best practices* refers to the essential elements of an effective security management effort.

7. **D.** Information retention policies dictate what information must be archived and how long those archives must be kept.

8. **A.** Configuration management policy dictates the configurations and upgrades of systems in an organization.

9. **A.** The backup policy identifies the methods used to archive electronic and paper file systems. This policy works in conjunction with the information retention and storage policies.

10. **C.** Network technology and administration would not be covered in a user security-awareness program. Issues of policy, responsibilities, and importance of security would be key aspects of this program.

11. **A** .Managers would derive the most benefit from a high-level explanation of security threats and issues. Users need to know how to follow the policies and why they are important. Developers and network administrators need specific and focused information on how to better secure networks and applications.

12. **B.** The only way to guarantee that data and applications on a disk drive are unreadable is to perform a low-level initialization of the storage media, thereby setting every storage location into a newly initialized state. This process is also referred to as disk wiping.

13. **C.** The removal and replacement of the computer battery will often cause the loss of values stored in the BIOS.

14. **D.** The acceptable use policy should clearly define the use of USB devices within an organization.

15. **A.** Users should be placed in groups and managed by membership in those groups.

16. B.   Access control lists (ACLs) hold permissions for users and groups.

17. C.   The domain password permission identifies who can reset the password of a user object.

18. D.   Logical tokens are similar in content to certificates. They contain the rights and access privileges of the token bearer.

19. A.   Group policies allow you to automatically implement restrictions on operating system components.

20. D.   The acceptable use policy should clearly define the use of cell phones within an organization.

Appendix A

Security Administrator's Troubleshooting Guide

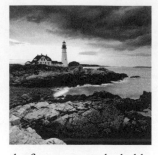

CompTIA's Security+ certification is often seen as the first step on the ladder toward becoming the ultimate security professional. While most people would not necessarily label Security+ the first rung on the ladder, the next step up the ladder is often a big one. Whether the act of achieving Security+ certification proves to be a significant challenge or a minor hurdle, the most important part of achieving this (or any) certification is putting what you learn into practice. Unless you can soundly demonstrate the skills and expertise that a certification implies, you should not boast of it on your resume or elsewhere. Furthermore, by putting your obtained knowledge into practice, you will be assisting yourself in expanding your abilities to the next level of achievement.

While it is not possible to offer a troubleshooting guide that fits every operating system and every implementation, you'll find that the administrative information that this appendix provides will be helpful for troubleshooting most environments. You should also relish the fact that Security+ is a vendor-neutral certification and does not require you to know how to troubleshoot every operating system.

The arena of security certifications is fairly delineated into foundational certifications and high-level certifications. While a handful of moderate-level certifications do exist, they don't seem to have gained serious footing (such as recognition) in the IT industry. So, in order to move on from Security+ certification to high-level certifications such as CISSP, CEH, Cisco Security, and Microsoft Security, you need to know more than just concepts and theories of security. You need to be able to apply what you know and troubleshoot problems as they arise. This appendix to the *CompTIA Security+ Study Guide Deluxe Edition* was written to assist you in integrating your new Security+ knowledge directly into your daily life at work and at home.

Before you embark on the recommendations presented here, you should take several precautionary steps:

1. Discuss your actions with your supervisor and/or the security administrator.

2. Thoroughly read and understand all of the policies you are required to adhere to as an employee.

3. Obtain and maintain copies of these policies so you can review them and double-check yourself often.

WARNING　　If there are any written policies or direct instructions that preclude your participation in any of the activities discussed here, *do not attempt them.*

Failing to take these precautionary steps could result in performing actions that are against company policy, that violate your assigned privileges, or that may actually be criminal activities. You are responsible for the results of your own actions.

 Think of this appendix and Appendix B as complements. The administrative issues addressed here will be put into practice in the labs in the next appendix.

Getting Started

The Security+ certification contains mainly concepts and theories; the actual implementation of these will vary greatly from one organization to another. You will need to learn how these concepts and theories are put into practice in your company. There is significantly more information about security than any single book or certification exam can contain. So you'll need to do the reading and research to learn about the technologies, software, hardware, and procedures you encounter. This is an important step because without a complete understanding of implemented solutions, you won't know how to adapt and apply these generic recommendations.

Knowing how to do something doesn't mean you should do it. You have been assigned a certain job description that entails a specific set of work tasks and related privileges and permissions. You should not attempt to exceed your assigned authority. If it is not your job, then *it is not your job*. You can learn anything you want, but without authorization, you cannot do anything you want—at least, not at work.

If you want to be able to experiment and implement anything, you should create your own personal lab environment at home. Your lab could consist of a small network of physical machines or a single high-end machine running a virtual operating system (OS) emulator system, such as VMware or Microsoft's Virtual Server. Then, when you can't implement something at work, you can do it at home. Unless you are the security administrator for your employer, it is doubtful you'll be able to implement many of the security recommendations covered in this appendix. Although you should submit requests and suggestions to the appropriate personnel, if you want to gain hands-on experience, you'll need to find another avenue to explore and develop your new security skills. A home lab is the best place to start. Even if your home lab is just one underpowered system with a dial-up modem to an ISP, it is enough to start the learning process.

 VMware Player allows you to work in multiple environments on one system (http://www.vmware.com/products/player/).

In some cases, the actions you take, although motivated by good intentions and dictated by sound security concepts, can be perceived as unethical, abnormal, suspicious, antisocial, a breach of security, and even criminal. Think before you act. Consider the effects your actions will produce. Ponder how others will perceive you if they notice your actions. If you are seen peeking around a corner, you might be perceived as spying or trying to hide something. If you are caught looking at network traffic, you can be perceived as a hacker. If you are caught in an area where you are not assigned to work, you can be perceived as a thief or trespasser. Remember, even when doing good, without proper permission and authority your actions can be perceived as unethical and criminal.

If your job is important, then keep communication open with your superiors and the security administration. Often they will be supportive of your desire to learn and improve yourself, which is especially the case when your new skills will benefit the organization directly. However, pushing too far, overstepping your limits, or encroaching on another person's boundaries or areas of responsibility can have negative consequences. These can range from minor verbal warnings to job termination or even criminal prosecution. When in doubt, don't. Instead, be proactive and ask for help and guidance from those in your organization with the authority and the know-how.

 Not only should you always seek permission, it is highly recommended that you get permission in writing.

There is at least one dark secret that everyone in the IT industry has been keeping from you: No operating system—not Windows, not Unix, not Novell, not Sun, not Linux, not Macintosh—can be fully and completely secured. Therefore, given enough time and resources, every network, every system, and every file can be compromised. While it is true that some solutions and systems offer more security than others, each product, hardware, or software has its own share of problems and issues. Every technological security mechanism has a fault, flaw, oversight, weakness, workaround, or maximum strength that can be overcome. Therefore, picking the "right" OS is not the whole solution—especially because anyone can be an attacker. Modern-day attack tools are powerful, and they don't necessarily require a high level of sophistication from the attacker (hence the terms *script kiddie* and *ankle biter*).

Security breaches can arise from a myriad of vectors, including external intruders, internal attackers, misguided insiders, contractors, malicious code, accidents, and oversights. A complete security solution does not stop all attacks, but it reduces the possibility that attacks will be successful and strives to detect any attempts.

This solution requires that you take the following steps:

- Create, maintain, and use a written security policy.
- Make informed technology choices.
- Make your best effort to secure your OS using IT technology.
- Deploy multiple overlapping layers of defense.

- Consider protection for confidentiality, integrity, and availability.

- Implement stronger authentication to support realistic accountability.

- Secure your personnel through training.

- Secure the physical environment.

- Watch for the inevitable security breach attempt.

- Be prepared to respond to incidents.

- Maintain that security is a never-ending process.

- Keep in mind that protections should prevent, then deter, then deny, then detect, then delay.

In the sections that follow, these and many other security concepts are explored and their application discussed.

Access Control Issues

Access control is the scheme or mechanism used to control who is granted access to what within the environment as a whole. You should recall that there are three primary options for this: Discretionary Access Control (DAC), Mandatory Access Control (MAC), and Role-Based Access Control (RBAC). What is the access control scheme used in your work environment?

If you don't already know what scheme is used at your office, think about it before asking your network administrator (NA) or security administrator (SA). First, does the office use standard, off-the-shelf operating systems for both client and servers, such as Microsoft, Linux, and Apple? If so, then it is more likely you work in a DAC environment. Second, do you work in an environment where clearances and classifications are used? If so, that is a direct indication of MAC. If you are a private sector company, then the answer is probably DAC. If you are a government agency or even a government contractor, then the answer is probably MAC.

You might discover that few, if any, environments are completely RBAC based. When RBAC is used at all, it is for those areas of the organization that have a high rate and frequency of staff changes.

If you think you've figured it out, take the time to verify your conclusion. Then discuss with the NA or SA why that specific scheme is used. You might learn some unique perspectives on your organization or discover how the company's decision-making process works.

Accountability Concerns

Accountability is the process of holding individuals responsible for their actions. In the IT world, we want to hold employees accountable for the actions of their user accounts.

In order to do this, the entire accountability process must be supportable in a court of law. The ultimate test of how well your security works is if you are able to criminally prosecute someone because of your organization's strong accountability infrastructure. That infrastructure must be able to be explained and proven to a jury so that there remains no reasonable doubt about its reliability. If a defense attorney can reveal a weakness in your accountability infrastructure, then the evidence of a user account performing illegal actions may not be sufficient to prove that a specific human was controlling that user account at that time.

There are five steps of accountability:

1. Identification
2. Authentication
3. Authorization
4. Auditing
5. Accountability

Among the items in this list, authorization stands out as appearing repeatedly throughout this appendix because so many mechanisms and methodologies exist that govern the processes granting and restricting access to resources.

Auditing

An excellent security principle for you to follow to protect your assets is to lock everything down and then watch them as if they were not locked down. If you secure every asset to the best of your abilities, using your available technologies and your available budget, and then watch for the inevitable breach or attempt to breach, you make your deployed security even better. Locking down an asset and then walking away doesn't mean it won't be attacked; it just means you won't know when it is attacked. And you won't know an attack was successful until you return and notice damage or loss.

You should consider auditing, monitoring, logging, and watching all forms of security. They actually prevent many attacks from being attempted in the first place, and they detect any attempt that is made to breach security. Most forms of auditing should be announced to all entities trying to gain entry into your secured environment, the computer network as well as the physical building. You should notify anyone trying to enter your environment that only authorized personnel are allowed to enter, that all actions are recorded and monitored, and that any violation of security policy or law will be prosecuted. This type of sign or banner should be clearly visible at every entry point of your building and at every logon or access point on your public and private IT systems.

Auditing prevents casual attacks and detects intentional attacks. But auditing by itself is not enough. Your audit logs need to be protected against tampering and loss. This protection is required while the log is open and active as well as when it is closed and stored on backup media. Your best choice for storage media for auditing is a write once, read many

(WORM) device. WORM devices are designed so that once data is written to them, it cannot be altered by any means short of physical destruction of the storage device itself. If you want your audit logs to be 100 percent accurate, to have perfect integrity, and to be supportable in court, WORM devices are your *only* choice. Other forms of storage devices allow written data to be altered. If that is even possible, a good defense attorney can cast doubt on the reliability and integrity of the audit details. Your WORM devices should be of sufficient capacity to collect audit logs for a reasonable amount of time. You must protect your WORM devices from theft and physical damage.

You should review your audit logs regularly both by automated means (such as a security auditor or an IDS tool) and by human means. Look for abnormalities or specific violations of security policy. Each incident should be investigated. As you discover issues or weaknesses, take action to prevent reoccurrence or future exploitation.

Audit logs should be backed up and retained—not just for a few months or years, but indefinitely. You never know how far back malicious events reach until they are discovered and investigated. If your retention policy allows for backups to be destroyed after only six months, you could easily be destroying essential evidence against internal and external attackers. This might require a separate backup system for audit logs so that the amount of physical space required to maintain all audit logs does not become too significant of a burden.

Authentication Schemes

No matter which access control scheme you use (DAC, MAC, and so forth), the basic two-step process to log onto the network is always required. Every authorized user has (or should have) their own user account. To use the IT system, the user must first log on. The two-step logon process is to claim an identity (identification) and then prove that you are responsible for that identity (authentication). There are at least three important aspects to this two-step process that require investigation.

- Number and type of factors
- Client, server, or mutual authentication
- Mechanism of authentication protection

Authentication Factors

The number and type of factors reflect the strength of the authentication process. Remember that there are three basic types of authentication factors:

- Type 1 (something you know)
- Type 2 (something you have)
- Type 3 (something you are)

Only a single factor is needed for identification because you only need to claim a single identity. But when it comes to authentication, more and different is always better (and here better means stronger).

All Type 1 (something you know) examples are the same no matter what they are called. They are just long or short strings of characters typed onto a keyboard from memory. No matter how many passwords are used, multiple passwords are ultimately no stronger than any single password by itself. This is due to the nature of the password-cracking attack. The same attack can crack (or, more specifically, discover) any password of any type of any length. Yes, longer and more complex passwords will take more time and more processing power, but this does not change the fact that the same attack tool and methodology works against every single example of a Type 1 factor.

Type 2 (something you have) factors start to offer a greater level of variety even within this single-factor concept. A smart card is different from a token device. At the least, they are different enough that two different attack tools and methodologies must be used to successfully break them.

Type 3 (something you are) factors, commonly known as biometrics, are even more varied than Type 2 factors. A fingerprint scanner is different from a palm scanner, which is different from a retina scanner, which is different from a voice recognition system, and so on. Just about every biometric characteristic (each using a different body part) is practically a factor type in and of itself. Thus, multiple Type 3 factors of different body parts are much stronger than dozens or hundreds of passwords. Each and every biometric reader works differently and thus requires a unique attack tool and methodology.

The higher the number and the more varied the form of authentication factors, the stronger the resulting authentication becomes. The ultimate purpose of authentication is to prevent unauthorized people from logging on to another person's user account. This prevention must be so strong that it will hold up in court. A single password is not supportable because of its numerous weaknesses. Using just a password as your authentication mechanism is as secure as locking a screen door on a submarine. However, a long complex password combined with a smart card and a fingerprint scan may be supportable in court.

If you are not already using at least two-factor authentication, then seek it out. For your company as a whole, migrating up to two or more factors will be a significant expense. But you might be allowed to add multifactor authentication to your user account at your desktop or notebook without forcing it company wide. The simplest two-factor system is to use a long and complex password as one factor and a fingerprint scanner as the second factor. USB fingerprint scanners can be obtained for less than $100. Your administrator can add them to any system with an open USB port. USB smart card readers are another option if you employ public certificate authority (CA) certificates rather than attempting to deploy your own private internal CA trust structure.

If you are not allowed to include additional factors, then take full advantage of the password length and complexity supported by your environment. We provide some stronger password recommendations in the section "Making Stronger Passwords" later in this appendix.

Mutual Authentication

Even with strong multifactor authentication, it is important to know just who is authenticating to whom. Most logons are client authentications. This means that the client (or, more specifically, the user) proves their identity to the system or environment they want to gain entry or access to. Unfortunately, this one-sided authentication process leaves open significant opportunities for spoofing and misdirection.

Logon spoofing has become a serious problem, especially over the Internet. If you are unable to verify the system you are connecting to, then it is possible that it is not who it claims to be. Numerous spoofing attacks have taken place in the last few years in which attackers create real-looking but fake websites of banks, auction sites, e-commerce sites, and even charity sites. These fake sites then fool visitors into "logging on" when all that is really happening is the user's logon credentials are being recorded (stolen) so that the attackers can log on as victims on the actual sites. This action has been called identity theft, impersonation, masquerading, and phishing. No matter what it is labeled, it is avoidable simply by requiring that all logons be mutual.

A mutual authentication is where both the client and the server must adequately prove their identity to each other before a logon session is started. You need to actively seek out mutual authentication solutions whenever possible. Within your company's private network, mutual authentication may not be necessary. But for any communication occurring outside of your company-controlled LAN, mutual authentication should be considered a requirement.

Another form of authentication is server authentication—when a server proves its identity to the client but does not require the client to return the favor. Many Internet sites and even some ISPs (broadband and wireless) use server authentication.

The best recommendation is to employ mutual authentication whenever it is available. This provides protection for both partners in a communication and will help reduce identity theft, impersonation, masquerading, and phishing attacks.

Authentication Protection

When it comes to authentication, consider the protection of the logon credentials as they travel from the client to the authentication server. This notion is called *authentication protection* or *authentication encryption*. It is simply a mechanism that serves as a transport and as a security barrier for the identification and authentication factors.

There are many forms of authentication protection. Some, such as PAP and CHAP, are used mainly on remote access connections. Others, like Kerberos or NTLM, are used on private network connections. Still others, such as certificates, are suited for larger or more distributed environments.

In every case, authentication systems and clients are designed to negotiate the highest level of common authentication security between them. However, some forms of network attacks can subvert this process, causing the systems to use a lower security mechanism that can be easily broken by an eavesdropper. Whenever possible, disable all of the lower forms of authentication protection on a system that are not used or required. Obviously, you'll need to test such changes thoroughly. Many legacy applications or systems might still exist on large networks that are unable to use more modern and secure methods of authentication.

Backup Management

If there is something you can take from real estate success and apply to security success, it is this: *location, location, location*. Now, you might want to change that to *backup, backup, backup*, but even keeping the original still stresses an important point. Backups are your only insurance against data loss. Without a backup, it is impossible to restore data. However, even the best backups are worthless if you do not protect them against damage or loss in the event of an intrusion, incident, or disaster. Thus, offsite storage of backups is essential. A backup site should be far enough away from the main site that it is not affected by the same disaster. You need to understand your organization's backup strategy and do your best to support it; ensure that every bit of data that is important to the company is ultimately stored on a server that is included in the regular backup system of the network. It is not enough to make your own local backup; you need to let the company backup system protect the company data. If you make local backups for personal data or in-progress projects, that should be seen as a supplement protection, not as a primary protection.

Baselining Security

Using security baselines is an administrative tool to ensure that all systems within your environment have the same basic security elements. Think of security baselines as the absolute minimum security that a system must be in compliance with in order to connect to and communicate with the LAN. Any system falling below the baseline threshold should be removed from production until it can be properly resecured.

A security baseline is a subjective thing between one organization and another. Baseline parameters need to be defined as part of your security policy. The baseline can be a written policy document, it can be implemented via a configuration tool, or it can be imposed via an installation/deployment system (such as image clones of a secured original).

Your best effort for establishing or defining a baseline lies in a full understanding of your operating system, business goals, and the vulnerabilities, threats, and risks of your environment. To get started on creating a security baseline, seek out existing public baseline recommendations. Use these as a seed to generate your own customized version. Every OS vendor provides "how to secure this OS" documents, numerous security product vendors provide them, and many third-party security watch groups (grassroots, commercial, and governmental) provide them as well. A few Internet searches should produce more than sufficient results. Some great keywords to search with include the name of your selected OS along with *security policy, system hardening, how to secure, security baselines*, and *security recommendations*.

The SANS policy site is a good first stop for information on using security baselines (http://www.sans.org/resources/policies).

As previously mentioned, no one operating system is significantly better or worse than any other. So pick the one you are most familiar with and have the most knowledge and experience with. The more you already know about an OS, the less you have to learn. As all of the lockdown or hardening guides will tell you, keeping the system updated and imposing the principle of least privilege are your two best efforts.

After a security baseline is established, you will need to regularly reassess the security state of every system. Time and change can result in the lowering of security. To prevent such a diminishment, you need to be proactive in testing the security of each and every system on a periodic basis. Any system failing to meet baseline requirements should be taken offline, corrected, and verified before being returned to the operating environment.

It should also be a point of procedure that after every security incident, no matter how minor, every system involved should be reassessed. If any system cannot be given a clean bill of health (i.e. returned to baseline security levels or better), it should be reconstituted. Any system that has experienced a full-blown intrusion, rootkit deposit, Trojan horse attack, or malware infection should be reconstituted.

Reconstitution is the act of completely purging hardware of all software elements and then reinstalling the entire system from original media or from trusted backups. The purpose of reconstitution is to reestablish the trustworthiness of a compromised system. If a serious compromise occurs, there is no way to fully verify that all aspects of the compromise are removed or thwarted. Thus, reconstitution removes all traces of possible corruption and rebuilds a new trustable system.

Certificate Management

Certificates are currently the top-shelf method of proving identity. However, it is important to stress that identity proof (such as authentication) is the *only* purpose of certificates. Certificates in no way provide proof of reliability, trustworthiness, compatibility, or benevolence of an entity. The only proof provided by a certificate is the identity of that entity. It is a separate and distinct choice to trust in an entity once you know who they are. Certificates are used as the primary means of identity proof on the Internet for e-commerce and resource download sites. However, too many people associate having a certificate with some type of proof of goodness. This is an absolutely incorrect assumption.

A simple understanding of what a certificate is and how they are created can easily dispel this misguided notion. Certificates are issued by CAs after they prove the identity of the requesting subject. The identity is proven through various means, which could be as simple as sending an e-mail to a given e-mail address or checking with public records that a business exists at a specific address and is able to be contacted via a specific phone number. That's it; the CA verifies the identity details of a subject and nothing else.

Further proof: Have you ever downloaded an update from a well-known vendor who proved their identity with a digital certificate only to have that update crash your system? Enough said.

To gain the most from certificate security troubleshooting, follow these guidelines:

- Stop assuming certificates prove trustworthiness.

- Consider why you would want to trust each specific entity whose identity is proven by a CA.

- Consider why you trust the CAs that you do (review the trusted roots list in your web browser to see which CAs you are trusting already).

- Only choose to make the same selection for this certificate in the future when you are denying acceptance or trust of an entity.

- When asked to retrust an entity, reconsider.

- If any utility questions any aspect of a certificate, such as the common name (CN) on the certificate not matching the claimed name of a site, *deny acceptance of the certificate.*

- Obtain your own certificate from a reputable CA, such as VeriSign. But don't settle for a free or e-mail-only certificate; obtain a certificate that validates more than just a working e-mail inbox.

- Require mutual certificate-based authentication from all Internet sites whenever available.

- Make sure your client tools update their Certificate Revocation Lists (CRLs) before each check of a received certificate.

Certificates themselves cannot currently be spoofed or stolen after use. However, this security does not mean that fake certificates don't exist or that abuse doesn't occur. You need to be vigilant at inspecting certificates and assume the worst even when accepting the identity from a trusted CA.

Communications Security

Communications security is an ever-expanding branch of IT security and one that is often not given the respect and attention it truly deserves. Communications security encompasses all the means by which data can enter or leave your otherwise private LAN. Even with a strongly secured LAN, weak communications security can bring it all crashing down. Each pathway by which data can move is yet another route through which malware can gain entry and intrusions can take place. In the realm of remote access, several areas fall in this category and demand specific attention: dial-up, remote control/remote shell, and VPN.

Remote access is the broad collection of mechanisms that allow external entities to interact with an internal closed environment. These can vary greatly in regard to speed and breadth of access. But even a trickle of data can be used to infiltrate an apparent fortress.

Consider how the Grand Canyon was carved through solid rock by just running water. You need to be aware of every flow of data that penetrates the boundaries of your private LAN and fully control each and every bit of data moving across such a gateway.

One of the most important steps in securing your LAN against malicious events performed over remote access links is to erect a first-stage defense. A first-stage remote access defense is a separate authentication system for remote access that preauthenticates all connections before they are allowed to interact with the LAN itself. These preauthentication systems serve as domain controllers for remote access connections. Thus, if the remote access user fails to properly authenticate to the first-stage defense barrier, they cannot even approach the internal domain controllers or servers on the LAN.

These preauthentication systems make full network attacks from remote links much more difficult. Without them, a remote access attack can directly affect any aspect of the internal LAN. Thus, a successful remote-access-based attack can affect all users. However, with a preauthentication system, most attacks, even initially successful ones, are prevented from gaining access to the private LAN. If the preauthentication system is disabled, then no communication is allowed from any remote access link. The preauthentication system serves as a dead-man switch for all remote access links. It protects the core private LAN. Keep in mind that it is better to lose remote access capabilities than it is to lose the entire private LAN.

You can use preauthentication systems for any form of remote access that connects into a private LAN. These systems include dial-up, broadband, VPN, wireless, satellite, remote control, and remote shell. You need to know what forms of remote access are needed and how to deploy a preauthentication system to provide that additional layer of protection for the rest of your LAN.

Preauthentication systems can sometimes offer connection filtering. Connection filtering allows for restrictions to be placed on remote access links. These can include the type of OS used, the protocols supported, the user accounts involved, the time of day, the logical addressing of the client, the LAN systems the remote client is allowed to communicate with, and even the content of the communication. The use of connection filtering can reduce an otherwise full-network-access remote link to a limited-functionality, single-purpose link. This filtering greatly reduces the potential for exploitation.

Another important aspect of remote access to consider is that even with the best security on the remote access link itself, if the remote client is compromised, it could lead to the compromise of the LAN. Remote clients can be compromised by malware, theft, or physical intrusion of their storage location. In most cases, the locations where remote access clients reside is much less secure than the physical location of the LAN. Remote access clients also typically use the same system for personal activities and Internet access. These are risky behaviors that can lead to security breaches. You should use a remote access client only to connect securely to the LAN. You should not use a remote access client for any other purpose—especially not for personal Internet access.

Dial-Up

Any form of remote access can serve as a means to bypass the network's security policies and filtering devices, but dial-up links are the most notorious for this. This notoriety is due to their ease of use and their existence on nearly every computer. Modems are rarely used for business purposes in today's broadband, high-speed-access world. But from time to time, your organization might need to interact with a legacy service that still supports only telephone line modem dial-up connections.

If possible, modems should be barred from your private LAN except on those systems that absolutely require them. If the modem cannot be removed from the computer, then create a hardware profile that disables the modem when the computer is connected to the LAN. You might also consider disabling it through the computer's CMOS or BIOS.

All unused phone connection ports should be disabled. If a Private Branch Exchange (PBX) system is used, configure it to detect and block all computer communication calls. Regularly inspect every device in the building for improper cabling, especially telephone lines connected to modems that should not even be present anyway.

Impose callback security and caller ID verification whenever possible on inbound calls. Don't use phone numbers for dial-in modems that are in the same prefix range as your company's voice numbers as it makes discovery of your dial-in modem lines too easy. A single war dialer could discover them in minutes.

Remote Control/Remote Shell

Remote control is the ability to manipulate a remote computer system without having to be physically present at its keyboard. This allows your local keyboard, monitor, and mouse to be used as the interface I/O devices for the remotely controlled system. This mechanism greatly eases administration because numerous systems can be managed from a single workstation. However, it also generally reduces security. Your ability to control a system remotely means that a hijacker or intruder can do so as well.

Remote shell tools are similar to remote control tools except that they are limited to command-line or text-only interaction. Common examples of this include Telnet and Secure Shell (SSH). Telnet should be avoided completely because it offers no security or encryption. Telnet can be deployed securely within a Secure Sockets Layer (SSL) tunnel, but doing so is often too involved for most situations, especially since SSH can be easily installed and offers greater protection than Telnet via SSL. SSH provides encryption for both authentication and data communications.

If you will be using remote control/remote shells tools, enable and require any and all security features available for the product employed. Limit the use of remote control tools over the Internet. Limit who can use these tools, and monitor when and why they are used.

Virtual Private Networks

Using virtual private networks (VPNs) is usually a more secure option for remote access than dial-up connections. However, to support VPNs you need an Internet connection on your LAN. If the Internet connection is controlled so that it is only used for VPN links, most of the security issues with Internet connectivity are eliminated. However, if both VPN and general Internet communications are to be supported, a more extensive security solution is required.

VPN security is usually a factor of solution selection and configuration. There are three widely used VPN protocols: Point-to-Point Tunneling Protocol (PPTP), Layer 2 Tunneling Protocol (L2TP), and Internet Protocol Security (IPSec). PPTP is often considered a default to use if you are communicating with systems that don't support L2TP or IPSec. If you don't need it for this purpose, PPTP should be avoided due to the vulnerabilities and weak encryption it employs. You should use L2TP alone (without IPSec) when a dial-up link is involved in the VPN, which usually means the remote client is connecting to an ISP via dial-up, and then establish the VPN link across the resultant pathway. IPSec should be employed if broadband connections are present throughout the pathway between the LAN VPN server and the remote client.

Always enable only the strongest authentication and data encryption supported; avoid pre-shared keys and relying on unique session keys and certificates. While the client is connected to the VPN, prevent any other form of communication from occurring over the Internet link. Force periodic reauthentication during the VPN session to check for and prevent hijacking.

Directory Services Protection

As a network user, there is not much you can do to improve or change the security of the directory services deployed. However, you *can* ensure that you don't become a tool for an attacker bent on compromising your organization's security:

- Ensure that your client is using the most secure form of authentication encryption supported by both your client and the authentication servers.

- Use encrypted software and protocols whenever possible, even for internal communications.

- Change your password according to the company's password policy.

- Use a 16+ character password that is unique for each account.

- Never write your password down, or if you do, divide it up into several pieces and store each in a different secure location (such as a home safe, a gun cabinet, a chemical supply locker, or safety deposit box).

- Never share your password or your logon session with another person; this includes your friends, spouse, and children.

- Verify that your client always interacts with an authentication server during the network logon process and does not use cached credentials.

- Every single time, just before you log on to the network, double-check that a hardware keystroke catcher has not been surreptitiously installed (see the KeyKatcher at www.thinkgeek.com).

- Allow all approved updates and patches to be installed onto your client.
- Ensure that all company data is copied back to a central file server before disconnecting from a logon session.
- Back up any personal data onto verified removable media.
- Never walk away from a logged-on workstation.
- Employ a password-protected screensaver.
- Don't use auto-logon features.
- Be aware of who is around you (and may be watching you) when you log on and when you work with valuable data.
- Never leave a company notebook, cell phone, or PDA in a position where it can be stolen or compromised while you are away from the office. Cable locks should be used to keep notebooks securely in place whenever you are off site.

The protection of a directory service is based on the initial selection of network operating system and its deployment infrastructure. After these foundational decisions are made, you need to fully understand the technologies employed by your selected directory services system and learn how to make the most functional, yet secure, environment possible. This will usually require the addition of third-party security devices, applications, services, and solutions.

Disaster Planning

Disaster recovery planning and business continuity planning are also an important part of a complete security solution. As an employee, you might not have any involvement in these plans whatsoever. If that's the case, realize that keeping the details of these plans from the general population of employees is in and of itself a security precaution. The disaster recovery plan and business continuity plan can be used for malicious purposes if they get into the wrong hands. It is common practice to give only relevant portions of the plans to just those specific individuals who are responsible for carrying out sections of the larger plan when an emergency actually occurs.

If you happen to be a person with responsibilities within one of these plans, be sure you keep this information confidential. Always work from the latest and most up-to-date version of the plan. Also, be sure you are fully versed in the steps of the plan long before an emergency occurs. You want to be able to respond by instinct when the pressure is on—don't wait until an actual event to read all the fine print.

Regardless of whether you have a part in the recovery or continuity plans, you do have a responsibility to yourself and your fellow employees in the event of emergencies. Your responsibility is to assist with anything that will reduce harm and loss of life. This includes knowing how to perform CPR and the Heimlich maneuver, knowing how to use a fire extinguisher, being familiar with multiple escape routes, and more. Your first priority in a disaster is to get everyone to safety. Then you can consider how to minimize losses to the organization.

Documenting Your Environment

When it comes to troubleshooting, documentation might sound mundane and superfluous, but it is a vital aspect of a complete, functioning, and successful security endeavor. With good exhaustive documentation, everything about an environment, from good to bad, will be recorded for future inspection. So, as a budding security expert, you need to document everything. You should document your actions, your discoveries, and your results. Get every instruction, request, or order in writing. Always get "official authority" to perform some action in writing, especially if the action without that authority would be a security breach or a crime. Always document your communications as well as changes to hardware and software. If it is related to security in any way, it needs to be documented.

E-Mail Issues

If malware is one of your biggest security concerns (as it should be), then you need to consider e-mail. It's the most common delivery mechanism used to deposit malware into your secured environment. E-mail is also often the bearer of hoaxes, spam, phishing, and social engineering attacks. Unfortunately, Internet-based e-mail will always be subject to attack (as well as a means to wage attacks). Internet e-mail delivery is performed in clear text with few means to prevent eavesdropping, alterations, delay, interceptions, and so forth. Currently, the only option is to use a client-side encryption scheme, such as PGP and S/MIME. But they offer security only for messages between other users of the same tool. Thus, most messages are still sent in the clear without any form of protection.

E-mail security is a product of reducing its functionality and user behavior modification. As for functionality, secure e-mail is e-mail that does not execute mobile code, nor does it interpret and display HTML. Consider not allowing attachments to reach your clients; strip them off at the firewall. However, this will greatly reduce the ease of data exchange many rely on daily. Spam filtering services should be added to your e-mail delivery system, if they are not already part of your antivirus solution and your ISP's e-mail services. All inbound e-mail should be quarantined until scanned. E-mail servers should be deployed as separate systems from all other services on the LAN. As for user behavior modification, teach your users the following rules:

- Don't open any attachments from unknown entities.
- If you receive an attachment from a known entity, contact them to verify that they intended to send it.
- Don't send any attachments to anyone; use a true file exchange system instead, such as Secure FTP (SFTP), yousendit.com, or hushmail.com.
- If attachments are needed, set up a separate account for sending and receiving them (Gmail is a great tool for that).

- Never click on links sent via e-mail.
- Never believe what you read in an e-mail message without confirming it with a third-party source.
- Set up one e-mail address for business communications, a second for personal communications, and a third for all other forms of communication.
- Use only your third e-mail address when registering with a website or handing out your contact information to others. Only after they prove trustworthy should you hand out one of your two primary e-mail addresses.
- Don't blindly follow any instructions included in an e-mail; hoaxes are common.
- Report all suspicious activities or messages to the security administrator.
- Don't attempt to unsubscribe from spam; it's just a ruse to get you to verify that the e-mail address used is valid, and it will encourage more spam.
- Learn to use client-side black lists and white lists.
- Never reveal personal data to anyone via e-mail because phishing attacks are prevalent and con artists are trying to steal your identity.
- Don't forward malicious e-mails to others.
- Report fraud, abuse, spoofing, and spam to the proper authorities (such as spoof@ebay.com and spoof@paypal.com).

As you can see, most of the security benefits with e-mail communication arise from user behavior modification. User behavior modification is often an important part of the overall security infrastructure. However, it cannot operate alone; actual technical security mechanisms and physical access controls must be used to enforce security policy. User behavior modification combines awareness, training, and education. Your goal with user behavior modification is to encourage people to "buy into" the company's security stance. The more people understand and believe in a security mechanism, the more likely they will uphold it and work within its confines. Without it, people will find ways to get around, subvert, or disable the security mechanism. This concept of user behavior modification applies to every aspect of security, not just e-mail communication security.

File-Sharing Basics

Many work tasks require exchanging files regularly. Unfortunately, the most convenient method of exchange is to attach them to e-mails, which is a problematic issue (see the discussion in the preceding section). So, if security is important and file exchange essential for productivity, a secure method of exchanging files is needed. There are several secure file-exchange solutions available that either add security to the standard FTP solution or are built on more proprietary technology.

When deploying a file-sharing system, here are some important security ideas to keep in mind:

- Don't use plain FTP.
- Use a file transfer client that employs both authentication and data transfer encryption.
- Don't allow anonymous access for both reading and writing; allow it for only one or the other.
- Use a separate system for writing from anonymous Internet users.
- Monitor file size and usage quota limits.
- Don't allow users to employ the same logon credentials as their domain logons.
- Regularly scan all files on the sharing system for malware.
- Don't enable execution privileges for file-sharing visitors.
- Don't store confidential, private, proprietary, or other forms of highly valuable data on the server that allows remote or anonymous users to exchange files.
- Regularly back up all files stored in the file-sharing server.
- Periodically check that your file-sharing server has not become an underground illegal file exchange repository.
- Consider setting a maximum file size of 10MB (or whatever is reasonably appropriate for the types of files shared).
- Consider requiring that all files be uploaded in an archived state (via a ZIP, RAR, or ARJ compression/archiving tool).
- Consider requiring that all files be password locked.
- Consider requiring that all files be encrypted.

A file-sharing system can be a method to prevent e-mail being used as a malware carrier. However, file sharing itself is not a 100 percent secure option either. Taking the proper precautions will help reduce the likelihood of abuse.

Working with IDSs and Honey Pots

Intrusion detection systems (IDSs) can be outstanding security assets, but it is important not to rely too heavily on them. There are numerous drawbacks to IDS solutions that are often downplayed to the detriment of those implementing them. An IDS is only as good as its programming and detection mechanism. Also, like an antivirus solution, an IDS needs to have its signature database regularly updated and its engine patched. An IDS will not detect all attacks (not detecting an attack is known as a false negative). Nor will all IDS alerts be for actual malicious events (this is known as a false positive). It might be necessary to have a staff member monitor the IDS and investigate every alert produced.

The following warnings and suggestions will help you get the most out of an IDS:

- IDS systems can be hindered by switched networks if not deployed properly. This includes either deploying the IDS off the mirror or audit port of the switch or deploying remote sensors in every disparate network segment.

- An IDS or a sensor should be located in every subnet and in every security zone, including the subnet on the other side of your most external firewall (such as on the Internet link itself).

- A network IDS should be deployed as a separate stand-alone system to give it full access to the processing and storage capabilities of the host.

- IDS systems should not be configured to retaliate against intrusions or attacks; at most, a malicious session should be disconnected.

Often the use of an IDS will warrant the discussion of what to do about a discovered intruder. Initially there are two options: disconnect or watch and learn. Disconnect stops the attack from continuing. Watching and learning often involves a honey pot or padded cell environment. Such environments raise the issue of enticement versus entrapment. Discuss this issue with your legal department as the specifics and ramifications are complex.

Incident Handling

Incident handling often means a criminal investigation. Whenever a criminal activity is suspected, back away from the environment, leave it as is, and contact law enforcement. Unless you are instructed by law enforcement to perform actions to gather evidence, do not do anything. Your actions in looking for, collecting, or analyzing evidence can be easily thrown out of court. This inadmissibility is due to your lack of official training in forensic investigations, your conflict of interest, and the likelihood that you will violate the rules of evidence and/or the chain of custody.

Internet Common Sense

In light of the security recommendations discussed so far, you should already have a good grasp of the obvious when it comes to Internet communications. But just so you don't forget anything, here is a rundown of the guidelines that you should instruct your users to adhere to:

- Never share personal data with a website.

- Be careful what you reveal about yourself in chat rooms, via messaging, on discussion boards, to surveys, and so forth.

- Be suspicious of whom you interact with over the Internet until you have absolute proof of their identity and trustworthiness.

- Only make e-commerce purchases from trusted sites (such as sites with a reputation of protecting its users/visitors).

- Use temporary credit card numbers to make online purchases.

- Keep an eye on the domain name in the URL you visit; if it turns into an IP address, a large decimal number, or a strange two-letter country code site, you may have been redirected.

- Use encrypted communications whenever possible.

- Make sure Transport Layer Security (TLS) is enabled on your browser (it's the even more secure replacement for SSL).

- If the URL prefix is not `https`, then it is not a secure connection.

- Encrypted does not mean you cannot be attacked—it just means the attack will come to you over the encrypted link.

- Don't allow unknown sites to download mobile code to your system.

- Don't allow unsigned code to download or execute.

- Only allow signed code from well-trusted sites to execute.

- Don't allow third-party cookies.

- Limit the use of first-party cookies to trusted sites and then only to those sites that actually require them (for example, Amazon.com doesn't require cookies to purchase but Buy.com does).

- Keep your client utilities updated and patched.

- Don't download data from unknown sites.

- Use only downloaded data from trusted sites after verifying the integrity of the download.

- Remember that you are probably being watched by an unknown malicious entity while you surf the Internet.

- Don't leave Internet connections open and active when you are not actively using your computer.

- Social engineering, spoofing, phishing, and hoaxes can all take place via computer communications such as e-mail and chat and on the Web—watch out!

The Internet should be thought of as a necessary evil that must be controlled in order to get beneficial tasks accomplished. It is like electricity, which provides uncountable benefits to our lives, but if we lose control of it, the results can include electrocution and property damage through fire. The Internet is a powerful tool that can cause serious harm to your organization and your personal lives if not managed properly. So don't use the Internet without proper protection and awareness.

Key Management Conventions

When working with any form of cryptography, using reasonable key management techniques helps maximize security and minimize potential breaches. Ultimately, key management depends on the deployed cryptosystem product. Thus, know what you are buying and exactly what it does and does not offer.

Based on that, here are some tips to make the most out of what you have (at least in terms of encryption):

- If a PKI system is used, have one public/private key pair set to use for session management and encryption and a second set for identity proof.

- Always use a new and unique public/private key pair set when requesting a new certificate.

- Attempt to renew certificates before they expire in order to maintain existing trust relationships.

- If you are concerned that existing trust relationships might be problematic, allow your current certificate to expire or ask the CA to revoke it.

- Store symmetric and asymmetric keys separately.

- Use a password or biometrics-locked removable storage media to store and transport your keys (for example, USB drive or smart card).

- When available, use key escrow database systems for keys involved in stored data encryption.

- Never store keys for identity proof in a key escrow database.

- Be aware of the length of assigned lifetime to keys and certificates.

- Be prepared to renew or reissue keys and certificates after they expire.

- Regularly purge your software to remove copies or caches of both current and expired keys—your current keys should only be stored on a removable media.

- Don't leave active keys or certificates on portable systems.

- Never store the removable media used for key storage in the same luggage or carryall as the device for which it is used.

- Purge all keys that have expired.

- Always check the revocation status of keys and certificates before acceptance or use.

- When a key or certificate will be unused or dormant for seven days or more, request a key/certificate suspension to temporarily "disable" them.

- Ensure that some form of M of N Control is employed on key recovery as well as key/certificate generation and issuance.

- Use session keys only once.

- Generate new session keys at the beginning of each session.

- When available, use a one-time pad form of encryption for highly valuable transmissions.

- Try to make the work function/work factor of a key just barely exceed the length of time the protected data will be valuable.

- Each time a key is reused, consider its useful lifetime or work function/factor reduced by a factor of 2.

- Whenever a compromise of the trust structure, secured server, secured client, or storage media is suspected, destroy all keys and certificates and obtain new ones.

- Never share your keys or certificates with anyone.

- Never encrypt and transmit data as is that is received or extracted from an outside source.

- Never rely on static keys or certificates for protection on truly valuable assets.

As you can see, for the most part, improving your key management tactics is a matter of common sense and a healthy dose of paranoia.

Preventing Common Malicious Events

If you don't know what you are up against, then you don't know how to prepare. "Know your enemy" is an admonishment from Sun Tzu that all security administrators should heed. If you are fully versed in the tools and techniques of your opponents, then you can be well prepared to stave off their attacks. We're sure you've heard the phrase *ethical hacking*. It is a flashing marketing phrase for security assessment or penetration testing. Ultimately, it refers to using cracker/attacker techniques and tools to test the security of your environment. But before you can perform ethical hacking, you must have two things:

- Thorough knowledge and skill in cracker/attacker techniques and tools

- Written approval from the owner/manager/administrator of the target network

Study is the best way to obtain knowledge and skill in cracker/attacker techniques and tools. You have four options to accomplish this:

- Learn what you can as you stumble upon relevant materials at work or on the Internet.

- Read relevant books, study guides, and self-paced courses.

- Attend online or computer-based training (CBT) classes.

- Attend instructor-led training.

The first of these options is the cheapest, but it's the least effective. The last option is the most expensive, but it is the most direct route to accomplishing the goal of being well versed in cracker/attacker techniques and tools. If you are serious about learning more about ethical hacking, several official certifications are available, such as Certified Ethical Hacker (CEH) from the EC Council (www.eccouncil.org) or the SysAdmin, Audit, Network, Security (SANS) and Global Information Assurance Certification (GIAC) (www.sans.org and www.giac.org) line of security certification pathways.

After you have a basic foundation of cracker/attacker techniques and tools, you then have to perform self-imposed continuing education, which involves the following:

- Setting up a lab where you can perform attack/defend activities safely. I recommend the book *Build Your Own Security Lab* by Michael Gregg (Wiley, 2008).

- Finding a partner to learn and experiment with. You could turn the attack/defend activities into a competition.

- Watching security topic mailing lists and discussion groups.

- Watching major OS, software, and hardware vendor websites.

- Reading about any new vulnerability, exploit, or attack that appears in technical news.

- Endeavoring to learn how and why attacks and exploits function.

- Investigating the vulnerabilities and weaknesses addressed in newly released patches and updates.

Ethical security experts all agree: Never perform any attack activity against any system without written authorization from the owner of that system. Approval is your get-out-of-jail-free card. It is your protection from prosecution and job loss. If you want to experiment with an attack or exploit, do it only in your private lab. Never perform attack or exploit testing over the Internet. If you don't own and control the system, you don't have the legal authority to do what you want on that system. So obtain approval.

After you recognize the vulnerabilities and threats a system faces, you can begin to construct your lines of defense. In a corporate environment, the basics of defense should already be in place. If not, you need to make some strong recommendations to those with the authority to make network security decisions.

Of the basic prevention mechanisms available, here are the items deemed essential for every system:

- Firewall

- Antivirus

- Antispyware

- Anti-adware

- E-mail filtering

A few of the latest editions of antivirus solutions have combined capabilities that encompass all of these features in a single product (or at least a single suite of products from the same company). Every client and every server in a network should have these security mechanisms installed, configured, and maintained. Depending on the size of your network and available security budget, you should also consider an intrusion detection system (IDS) to watch for the things these five foundational filtering/scanning tools might miss.

If you have systems that do not have these basic security tools present, then obtain permission to get them installed. But your security protections can't stop there. As you'll see in a moment, there are many forms of attacks and threats that require your focused attention.

Denial-of-service (DoS) attacks come in two major forms: flaw exploitation and traffic generation. You can protect against flaw-exploitation DoS attacks by applying vendor-supplied patches and updates as well as by installing firewalls and other traffic-filtering tools. Traffic-generation DoS attacks are not as easy to stop. They require detection and network traffic filtering. It is usually possible to block such attacks from entering your network, but you'll have to convince an upstream network (such as an ISP) to filter out the malicious traffic as well. Otherwise, your communication pipeline might be consumed with the bogus attack traffic and thus be unable to support your legitimate communications.

Back doors are popular because they allow easy access into a computer or network device without having to deal with the authentication systems protecting them. Some back doors are left in accidentally by the vendor but are usually patched quickly by a vendor update. If the back door is a known user account and/or admin or configuration password, then you need to make sure that the accounts are renamed and a strong password defined. Other back doors are deposited by hackers or various forms of malicious code, such as Trojan horses. If your security perimeter is working properly and you are actively watching for attacks, depositing back doors or other malicious code is made significantly more difficult.

Spoofing, as described earlier, is faking information. Common spoofing attacks use e-mail source addresses, packet source addresses, and system MAC addresses. While it is not possible to stop all spoofing attacks, you can eliminate a great number with a few simple actions. Your network traffic filters and e-mail filters should be configured to check for source spoofing in network packets and e-mails, respectively. If a packet or message is leaving your private LAN, then it cannot have a valid source address from the Internet. Conversely, if a packet or message is entering your private LAN from the Internet, then it cannot have a valid source address from the LAN. These types of filters are known as egress (exiting) and ingress (entering) filters. They need to be configured on every border system.

Using reverse lookups and white/black lists also allows you to limit spoofing attacks. Reverse lookups check to see if a source MAC address, IP address, or e-mail address is real, currently in use, and from the expected location before allowing traffic to enter or leave. White lists and black lists are filters that have lists of addresses that are known to be either legitimate and trustworthy or illegitimate and malicious. All addresses on a white list are trusted and are allowed to pass with little interference, whereas all addresses on a black list are either blocked outright or subject to greater levels of inspection before being allowed to pass. Black lists can result in a form of DoS if benign addresses are placed on the black list accidentally. This threat is something to watch for, and be prepared to verify and rectify list entries when necessary.

Man-in-the-middle, replay, and session hijacking attacks are thwarted by several means: complex packet sequencing rules, time stamps in session packets, periodic mid-session reauthentication, mutual authentication, the use of encrypted communication protocols, and spoof-proof authentication mechanisms (such as certificates). Whenever possible, use only modern OSs that are fully updated. Also, attempt to limit your out-of-LAN communications to encrypted sessions verified with certificates.

Antivirus Protection

The appearance of malicious code is at an all-time high, and it will only get worse. As more and more countries, cities, and population groups move into the Internet age, many people are learning how to program. Inevitably, human nature leads some of these new programmers to the dark side, and they become the authors of malicious code. Your job is to erect sufficient barriers to the malware threat to prevent any and all breaches.

The best initial protection against malicious code is antivirus software. However, these packages are not perfect. Even properly managed and fully updated antivirus scanners can still overlook 4 percent of known viruses. This oversight means that you cannot rely on a single scan to provide realistic protection; you need to scan everywhere. It is highly recommended that you employ at least three different antivirus vendors' scanning solutions in your environment. However, *never install two antivirus products on the same computer!* Install one product on all clients, a second product on all internal servers, and a third product on all border systems. In this manner, every bit of data entering or leaving your environment is scanned at least twice, if not three times, thus reducing the likelihood of missing a known virus from 4 percent to .16 percent (4 percent of 4 percent) or 0.0064 percent (4 percent of 4 percent of 4 percent).

Every antivirus product should scan data as it enters the computer, as it leaves the computer, as data is written to the hard drive, as data is read from the hard drive, and as data is used in memory. Plus, on a weekly or biweekly basis, scan every file on every drive. Yes, this will affect your system's performance, but in most cases a small reduction in performance is worth the trade-off for greatly improved malware protection.

Automate the downloading of virus signature databases, but restrict and control the deployment of engine updates. Virus signature database updates have rarely been the cause of problems, but delaying the deployment of the signature database can result in undetected infections. Most modern antivirus solutions offer a staged deployment controller for updates. A single server should poll the public website for antivirus updates two to four times a day. Then, that server should be the host that provides the updates to all other internal systems. This deployment controller usually allows you to make signature database updates immediately available while quarantining all other forms of updates. After updates are tested and verified, you can release the ones that you want deployed.

Users should be trained to avoid malware and risky behavior. You should issue the following warnings to users:

- Don't download anything from the Internet.
- Never install any unapproved software.
- Don't bring in storage media from outside.
- Don't leave removable media in drives.
- Don't boot with removable media connected to a computer.
- Stay away from private or noncommercial sites.
- Always type links into a browser; never click on them from e-mails or documents.

- Don't accept certificates from unknown CAs.
- Never trust an entity just because you know the CA that issued their certificate.

Consider deploying a sheep-dip system for precleaning removable media before use on your LAN. A sheep-dip system is a stand-alone machine that is used solely to scan portable storage devices for malware before they are used on secured LANs. The sheep-dip system needs to be manually updated several times a day with signature database updates because it is air-gapped from the rest of the network. Every device that can store data must be checked by the sheep-dip system before it is connected to the LAN. This scrutiny needs to include cell phones, PDAs, audio/video players, digital cameras, USB drives, floppies, and CD/DVDs.

Each time a vendor releases a new version of its product, upgrade to it. Well, don't rush and do this immediately in a knee-jerk fashion. Give the new version a few months of "public" testing before making the migration. This testing lets others discover and experience the growing pains of new solutions. You can learn and benefit from earlier adaptors. Plus, always thoroughly test new software before deployment. This testing applies to any code, including new versions of software, engine patches, function upgrades, and even signature and pattern database updates. The newer the technology, the more likely it will provide reliable protection against newer malware attacks.

Making Stronger Passwords

Passwords are the most common form of authentication; at the same time, they are the weakest form of authentication. Password attacks have become ubiquitous. Reliance solely on passwords is not true security. At least four attack methods are used to steal or crack passwords. All of them involve *reverse hash matching*. This is the process of stealing the hash of a password directly from an authentication server's account database or plucking out of network traffic, then reverse-engineering the original password. Reverse-engineering, in this case, is done by taking potential passwords, hashing them, and then comparing the stolen hash with the potential password hash. If a match is found, then the potential password is probably the actual password. (By the way, even if the potential password is not the actual password, if it happens to produce the same hash, it will be accepted by the authentication system as the valid password.)

There are four password-cracking or -guessing attacks:

Dictionary These attacks generate hashes to compare by using prebuilt lists of potential passwords. Often these lists are related to a person's interests, hobbies, education, work environment, and so forth. Dictionary attacks are remarkably successful against non-security professionals.

Brute force Brute-force attacks generate hashes based on generated passwords. A brute-force attack tries every valid combination for a password, starting with single characters and adding characters as it churns through the process. Brute-force attacks are always successful, given enough time. Fortunately, brute-force attacks against strong passwords eight characters long can take up to three years.

Hybrid   These attacks take the base dictionary list attack and perform various single-character and then multiple-character manipulations on the base passwords. This includes adding numbers or replacing letters with numbers or symbols. Hybrid attacks are often successful against even security professionals who think they are being smart by changing *a* to @ and *o* to *0* and adding the number 12 to the end of the name of their favorite movie character.

Rainbow tables   The really worrisome tool for password attacks is called a rainbow table. Traditionally, password crackers hashed each potential password and then performed an Exclusive Or (XOR) comparison to check it against the stolen hash. The hashing process is much slower than the XOR process, so 99.99 percent of the time spent cracking passwords was actually spent generating hashes. So, a new form of password cracking was developed to remove the hashing time from the cracking time. Massive databases of hashes are created for every potential password, from single characters on up, using all keyboard characters (or even all ASCII 255 characters). Currently, a rainbow table for cracking Windows OS passwords is available that contains all the hashes for passwords that contain from 1 to 14 characters using any keyboard character. That database is 64GB in size, but it can be used in an attack to crack a password in less than three hours—meaning that all Windows OS passwords of 14 characters or fewer are worthless.

To protect yourself from this threat, change all of your Windows OS and network passwords to a minimum of 16 characters. Or, if you get approval from your security administrator, start using one or more higher-order ASCII characters in a password of at least 8 characters. You can't just use the higher-order ASCII characters because many legacy systems (for example, those written prior to 2000) do not support them. If every system you interact with does not support higher-order ASCII characters, then you can't use them.

 One of the smartest—and most secure—things you can do is turn off LANMAN passwords.

Another protection is the addition of a salt to the password before it is hashed. Windows 2003/8, Windows XP Professional (SP1+), SE Linux variants, and many other modern and secure OSs employ salts. The purpose of a salt is to thwart easy hash cracking and prebuilt hash databases. Often the salt is the SID of the user account, thus a 40-character (or so) phrase is added to a, say, 12-character password to create a 52-character entity that is then hashed. An attacker may be able to learn the salt value, especially if it is the SID, but it still stops all of the easy attack methods. The use of salts forces a true real-time brute force approach to cracking hashes, thus allowing OSs to once again provide real protection for passwords (assuming the password is complex and long to begin with).

Use as many different types of characters as possible, including lowercase letters, uppercase letters, numbers, and symbols. Change your password frequently, at least every 45 days if not more often. Never reuse a previous password, and never use the same password for more than one account. Don't use password-storage tools, whether software or hardware. However, if you have to juggle so many passwords that a management tool is essential, then make sure the passwords are stored with strong encryption and the lock on the tool is stronger than the best password it is storing.

Managing Personnel

Personnel management is a security concept that focuses on minimizing the vulnerabilities, threats, and risks that people themselves bring to an organization. Ultimately, people are the last line of defense for your company's assets. There are many mechanisms imposed to help improve personnel security, such as separation of duties, the principle of least privilege, acceptable use policies, job reviews, mandatory vacations, and even exit interviews.

You need to be aware of these controls and learn how to do your job within the boundaries that they dictate. Here are some important recommendations for management:

- Know exactly which privileges you are assigned.

- Don't attempt to exceed your assigned authority.

- Know which actions require multiple people to work together, and then attempt them only with the correct number of admins.

- If you discover that you have a privilege or capability that you should not have, report it.

- Never perform any activity that is unethical or illegal, even if not doing so will cost you the petty respect of your peers and/or your job.

- Watch out for conflicts of interest and make them known to the security administrator when they occur.

- The person who configures a system should not be the auditor.

- The person who designs a system should not be the tester.

- Only log on with your admin account when you actually need that level of access.

- Log on as a normal user account for your daily activities.

- Limit the use of admin accounts over the network; try to use them directly at the console/terminal to reduce the risk of eavesdropping.

Be aware of all of the policies that govern your behavior. Knowing what you are responsible for makes it much easier to comply. Ignorance is never a valid excuse when a violation occurs.

Keeping Physical Security Meaningful

It is difficult to overstress the importance of physical security. Physical security is controlling who can and cannot gain physical proximity to assets. It is a form of access control: defining who has access where and who doesn't. Without physical access control, there is no security. Every technological security control can be overcome with the right tools or enough time. Even cryptography will fail eventually. Brute-force attacks are always successful, given enough time. But time itself is becoming an ever smaller relative value with the onset of massive parallel distributed processing. For example, with the services of `distributed.net` or its competitors, 10,000 computing hours can be harnessed in an hour of real time.

Two of the scariest issues today in terms of physical security are bootable portable OSs and hardware-based keystroke loggers. A bootable portable OS on a CD, a DVD, or a USB drive can fully bypass any OS-enforced security because they don't allow the host OS to load! Without the host OS, no security is actually being enforced. In fact, the only security remaining is file- or drive-based encryption. Thus, an attacker can make copies of encrypted files and then take them elsewhere to break the encryption at their leisure.

Hardware-based keystroke loggers are another security nightmare. As mentioned earlier, these gadgets are available for under $100 and are designed to be unobtrusive to even the most observant of users. A few seconds to plant, a few seconds to extract days later, and presto! The attacker now has possession of your password-based logon credentials and anything else you might have. Your only protections are multifactor authentication and strong physical security.

To prevent the compromise of technological security, you must use good physical security. As an employee of any organization, it is part of your job to be aware and be suspicious.

To assist with the physical security of the company's facilities, here are some suggestions:

- Make sure that every time you unlock and open a door, you then close and relock it before you walk away.

- If you discover an unlocked door that should be locked, report it immediately.

- If you discover that a door's locking mechanism has been damaged or tampered with, report it immediately.

- If you discover a door propped open when it should be closed and locked, report it immediately.

- Regularly take notice of whether windows are closed and locked; report any changes.

- Regularly look at the security cameras in the area, and report any changes to their direction, whether they become obstructed, or if they become damaged.

- Get to know the faces of as many of your fellow employees as possible so you can spot outsiders or intruders.

- If you see any suspicious activity, especially by personnel you do not recognize, report it.

- Don't hold open locked doors that require each person to self-authenticate.

- Never allow anyone into a secured environment who does not have their authentication credentials, even if you think you know them.

- Keep your keys, smart cards, and other access devices under your complete control at all times, especially when away from work.

- Never grant access to a secured area to anyone who is not specifically authorized to be in that area, including your family and friends.

- Don't help strangers if it involves violating company security procedures; it could be a social engineering attack attempt.

- Regularly check the inspection tags on fire extinguishers, detectors, and sprinkler systems, and report any expired tags.

- Never install equipment or computer hardware, especially wireless devices, without specific written authorization.

- Watch for roof leaks, window leaks, or bathroom overflows and report them.

- Avoid touching computer equipment or electronic devices until you have grounded yourself; static electricity can build up in any low-humidity environment, not just during the winter.

- Don't run any device that might overheat and start a fire.

- Never store or place combustible materials near electronic equipment, especially near electrical distribution points or heat exhaust fans.

Reporting actual malicious activity will be rewarded and encouraged. However, if you become the squeaky wheel and most of your reports turn out to be false positives, you may get a reprimand or a strong encouragement to mind your own business. So, be sure that what you are reporting is worth reporting and that you're not just being a nosy neighbor.

Securing the Infrastructure

Defense in depth should always be the guiding principle when designing the security of an entire LAN. Start with the location of your most important, valuable, and essential assets. From that location, design multiple overlapping layers of security. Each layer should provide some aspect of deterrence, denial, detection, and delay as appropriate for the value of the assets being protected.

Here are some good ideas for developing and deploying a solid and secure network infrastructure:

- Every inbound or outbound communication stream should be monitored and filtered by a firewall.

- Firewalls should be deployed between different departments, security levels, and geographically distant subnets.

- Firewalls should be configured with a basic deny by default and allow by explicit necessary exception.

- When possible, deploy firewalls with packet filtering, application filtering, session filtering, and stateful inspection filtering capabilities.

- Firewalls should be deployed as stand-alone network appliances.

- Software firewalls should be deployed on all internal systems, clients, and servers.

- All internal user interaction with the Internet should be controlled through a proxy server.

- All internal clients should be assigned an RFC 1918 IP address and their access to the Internet supported through a NAT system.

- The proxy server should automatically block known malicious sites.

- The proxy server should cache often-accessed sites to improve performance.
- Routers should be configured to prevent unauthorized modifications to routing tables.
- All network devices should be stored/located in locked rooms or cabinets to prevent nonauthorized physical interaction.
- Hubs should be replaced with switches.
- Switches should be configured to watch for ARP and MAC flooding attacks.
- Switches should be used to block sniffing attacks.
- Switch configuration should be protected.
- Wireless networks should be avoided.
- Infrared and Bluetooth should be avoided; wires are always more secure and more reliable, and they have greater throughput.
- Modem-based remote access should be avoided.
- Remote access should be properly secured (see the discussion in the section "Communications Security" earlier in this chapter).
- Standard telephone systems should be replaced with a securable PBX or Voice over IP (VoIP) system.
- Audit phone usage.
- VPN usage should be limited.
- VPNs should always have the strongest authentication and data encryption available.
- Network IDSs should be deployed throughout the environment.
- Host-based IDSs should be deployed on mission-critical systems or identified common attack targets.
- Regularly monitor the health and performance of the network.
- Watch for traffic direction, load, and performance trends.
- Build in sufficient growth capacity in every important area of IT productivity. Monitor the consumption of this extra capacity.
- Realize that the compromise of a workstation can result in the compromise of the entire LAN.
- Provide clients with reasonable security that supports the security of servers.
- Avoid the use of mobile devices that interact with the LAN.
- Restrict the type of data that can be stored on mobile devices.
- Treat mobile devices as an attack and malware entry point.
- Always run cables in shielding conduits.
- If multiple copper cables are run through the same conduit, use cables with significantly different twists per inch and use STP instead of UTP.
- Don't run communication cables and power cables in the same conduit.

- Avoid running any type of cable near an EMI or RFI source.

- Use higher-grade cables than what is currently needed for your networking performance levels.

- Use fiber-optic cables if possible.

- Regularly inspect every cable run for tampering or damage.

- Replace any cable that shows wear or damage.

- Use the shortest cable runs possible.

- Use power conditioners for every network device.

Proper infrastructure planning is essential to long-term success of company security policy. Security should be designed from the beginning rather than being imposed after the fact. However, most of us don't get to make the choice of when security is considered, so we must do the best we can with what we are given. Even if it's late in the game to impose security, take the time to plan out the security strategy before starting the implementation.

Working with Security Zones

Even in a purely discretionary access control environment, security zones are important. Security zones are a form of classification. Basically, it is a designation of what portions of the company-controlled IT are accessible to which types of users. You will have at least three user types to deal with: employees, nonemployee business contacts, and external users. These easily lend themselves to the three standard security zones of intranet, extranet, and DMZ, respectively.

In addition to the basic ideas covered in the Security+ content, here are a few considerations:

- Never place the only copy of data or other resources into the DMZ or extranet.

- Regularly back up all data present in the DMZ and extranet.

- Never grant access to external entities into the intranet.

- Audit and monitor all activities in all security zones.

- Erect strong security barriers between each security zone.

- Public and anonymous access in a DMZ does not mean anything goes—detect and block attacks in every zone.

- Whenever possible, deploy the DMZ so that it has *no* connection whatsoever with your intranet or extranet.

- Consider co-location or site hosting at an ISP for your DMZ.

Understanding and respecting these three groups is important for a strong security endeavor. Different forms of security, different levels of access, and different types of data are present in each security zone. Making a mistake and placing the wrong element into a zone can have disastrous consequences. In the company security policy and in the deployed infrastructure, it's essential to set clear definitions of what each security zone will entail.

Social Engineering Risks

Social engineering is quickly becoming a predominant attack method against technically savvy security environments. While no technology is foolproof, some forms of IT protection, such as encryption, are becoming so difficult to penetrate that it is in the interest of the assailant to find a weaker point of attack. The weakest point of any secured environment is the people who work and interact with that environment. Often, if an attacker can compromise someone on the inside, they can get around the protections that prevented a direct external attack. *Rubber hose attack* is the nickname for going directly to people to convince them to give you access to what is otherwise too secured to break into.

While rubber hose attacks are sensationalized on television and in the movies, most often they are more benign in nature and less noticeable. In fact, most victims of successful attacks are unaware that they were ever considered a target. This form of attack is called *social engineering*. Social engineering involves a con artist running a scam on unsuspecting people to gain access or privilege the attacker would otherwise be unable to obtain. Social engineering attacks exploit human nature and thus everyone is vulnerable.

Unfortunately, there are no technical security controls that will directly affect, prevent, block, or deter social engineering attacks. Understanding that you are a potential target for social engineering attacks is the best defense against such attacks. Watching out for abnormal, strange, or slightly confusing events, communications, or interactions will often reveal elements of social engineering. Social engineering can take place face-to-face, over the phone, via e-mail, or via a website. Never take anything for granted—verify, verify, verify.

A sure sign of a social engineering attack is when someone asks you to perform an action that is a violation of security policy or that seems unethical or questionable. Never reveal private, confidential, proprietary, or valuable data to anyone via phone, e-mail, the Web, or even face-to-face without absolutely verifying their identity. In most cases, asking for proof of identity will scare away the social engineering attacker. When anything that is slightly odd occurs, report it to your security administrator immediately.

System Hardening Basics

No computer is ever without vulnerabilities. It is not possible to make a fully secured, impenetrable system. However, it is possible to make a system so secure that most attacks will fail and those that don't will be noticed before significant damage is done. Fully hardening a system is beyond the scope of this appendix, but the foundations of system hardening are well within your grasp.

System hardening has many facets, but one core and overriding principle to follow is this: If you don't need it, get rid of it. By eliminating all but the bare essentials needed to accomplish your work tasks, you remove numerous vulnerabilities and avenues of attack. Any active process that is not actually being used is simply increasing the complexity of the environment and expanding your attack surface.

The attack surface is the conceptual idea of the area exposed to potential attackers. A nonhardened system is said to have a larger attack surface than a hardened one because more exposed vulnerabilities exist for the attacker to target. Your job is to understand your systems thoroughly enough to know what is essential and what is extraneous.

One obvious place to start removing the chaff from a computer system is to examine its services. After you think you know which services are extraneous, you need to test them one by one. Here is the basic process:

1. Perform a systemwide backup (an image-level backup is preferred for complete recovery ability).

2. Disable a single service.

3. Reboot the system.

4. Verify that the service is not functioning.

5. Test all required features, functions, and capabilities, both locally and on the network.

6. If all is working as needed, leave this service disabled and repeat the process, starting with step 2, for another service.

7. If all is not working as needed, reenable this service, reboot, and start again with step 2 for another service.

Obviously, this process will take considerable time because there are often dozens of services on basic systems to consider. However, as you learn more about the services themselves and the system you are managing, this process can be truncated greatly. You'll soon recognize which services can be disabled without negative consequences and thus you won't need to test every service change.

This "keep it only if you need it" mentality should be applied to every aspect of your computer, from hardware to software. Don't install or keep installed any hardware device that is not used on a regular basis, especially if it is an internal device. Keep external devices, such as USB devices or other automatically installable connection devices, disconnected and powered off until they are actually needed.

As for software, be careful about installing anything new, especially if it is from the Internet. Go out of your way to verify the source identity and reliability before downloading. Then check the file for authenticity and integrity before you launch it. This action often requires you to check the filename, time/date stamps, exact file size, hash value, and certificate/digital signature.

Only install software you actually need and will regularly use. If you find yourself often "test-driving" new software and then removing it later, consider creating a test-drive system, which can be a completely separate physical computer or just a virtual computer in a VMware or Virtual Server environment. A test-drive system provides you with two security improvements. First, it greatly reduces the risk of installing malicious code onto your primary system. Second, it prevents you from cluttering your primary system with unneeded, useless software. Even if you elect to uninstall software, it often leaves traces of itself in the form of Registry entries, data folders, configuration files, and shortcuts. These orphaned items clutter the system, can eventually cause performance and storage problems, and might be increasing your attack surface. Each time you test-drive new software, just delete the virtual machine file and create a new one for the next program down the road.

Review all of the software utilities and add-ons that come with the OS. If you don't need them, remove them or prevent them from loading. Disable all unneeded protocols.

When you've completed the hardware/software weight-loss program, take a complete inventory of the resultant system and create an image-level backup. This image-level backup will serve as your road map should you ever need to reconstitute the computer in the event of a major catastrophe. Securing new systems is always a long and involved process. But through detailed documentation and good backup solutions, rebuilding, duplicating, or improving a secured system is much simpler the next time.

Once you know what you are left with, you need to perform more research to learn about the strengths and weaknesses of every aspect of the OS, active services, employed protocols, and installed software. After you know the vulnerabilities, methods, and tools of attacks, along with the resultant risks, you can take steps to reduce the risks by implementing safeguards and countermeasures.

Securing the Wireless Environment

Wireless networking is a hot feature of many networks. Unfortunately, too many organizations rushed in and deployed wireless networks without realizing the security implications. Wireless networking as defined in IEEE 802.11 does not actually provide for realistic security, in spite of its claim. 802.11 defines a form of authentication and data encryption named Wired Equivalent Privacy (WEP). WEP never did—and wireless in general never will—provide the same level of privacy (aka security) as a wire. A wire can be run inside an insulating and difficult-to-penetrate conduit, making eavesdropping, hijacking, and even interruption nearly impossible. Wireless networking is actually radio wave networking. It will always be possible to capture, hijack, and interrupt radio waves. As new communication encryption protocols are deployed over wireless networks, it becomes harder to extract the transmitted data or use a wireless connection without authorization, but it doesn't make packet capturing and jamming any less difficult.

The wireless network is not and never will be secure. Use wireless only when absolutely necessary or when attempting to attract customers. But even customers probably won't have to access your secured private company LAN. If you must deploy a wireless network, here are some tips to make some improvements to wireless security:

- Change the default SSID.
- Disable SSID broadcasts.

- Disable DHCP or use reservations.

- Use MAC filtering.

- Use IP filtering.

- Use the strongest security available on the wireless access point: WEP, Wi-Fi Protected Access (WPA), Wi-Fi Protected Access 2 (WPA2), and so on.

- Change the static security keys on a two- to four-week basis.

- When new wireless protection schemes become available (and reasonably priced), consider migrating to them.

- Limit the user accounts that can use wireless connectivity.

- Use a preauthentication system, such as RADIUS.

- Use remote access filters against client type, protocols used, time, date, user account, content, and so forth.

- Use IPSec tunnels over the wireless links.

- Turn down the signal strength to the minimum needed to support connectivity.

- Seriously consider removing wireless from your LAN.

Wireless discussions sometimes include mobile devices, which are not 802.11 wireless networking devices themselves but instead are specialized services providing limited Internet connectivity to cell phones, PDAs, and pocket PCs. These devices often use WAP or an equivalent communication protocol suite. Unfortunately, providers are required by the Communications Assistance for Law Enforcement Act of 1994 (CALEA) to make wiretaps possible on all forms of communications offered regardless of the technologies employed (requiring a search warrant for actual use, of course)—lovingly referred to as "the gap in WAP." Therefore, if you want security over a wireless mobile device, your handheld device and the server you ultimately communicate with must have their own encryption scheme rather than relying on that provided by the provider's service.

You should be aware that malicious entities could be actively seeking to eavesdrop on all of your communications. In addition to personally imposed encryption for handheld devices, be careful of what is actually discussed or communicated over your mobile devices. Even if someone can't grab the information while in transit, it is possible they can look over your shoulder at your screen or be within earshot of your voice. There are many ways to collect data; in order to be secure, you need to be aware of all of them and provide protection against all of them.

Appendix

B

Workbook Exercises

This appendix consists of 50 lab exercises that you can perform to become more familiar with security features available in popular operating systems and utilities. It is recommended that you perform these exercises on lab machines and never in a production environment. As was discussed in Appendix A, using production machines and failing to take precautionary steps could result in performing actions that are against company policy, that violate your assigned privileges, or that may actually be criminal activity. You are responsible for the results of your own actions. In other words, perform these exercises on your own machine(s) in a lab of your own.

The recommended setup for these exercises is as follows:

- Two workstations running Windows XP Professional with network and Internet access. You should have administrator privileges on both and the Internet Explorer or Firefox browser installed.

- One workstation running the latest version of openSUSE with network and Internet access. You should have root privileges and the Firefox browser installed.

None of the labs intermingle openSUSE with Windows XP, so it is possible to have openSUSE installed on one of the workstations that also has Windows XP. The workstation can be configured in a dual-boot scenario, or you can have virtualization software such as VMware Player installed.

If you are comfortable with a Linux distribution other than openSUSE, you can use that instead and substitute any lab instruction referencing YaST for the configuration utility present in that distribution.

Most Linux distributions—including openSUSE—give you the ability to download a bootable CD (see http://en.opensuse.org/Download). The bootable CD (often called a *live CD)* allows you to experiment hands-on with the operating system and perform all the tasks in this appendix without needing to actually install the operating system.

The labs in this chapter are as follows:

Lab B.1: Change to WPA Security in Windows XP

Lab B.2: Turn on the Firewall in Windows XP: Method One

Lab B.3: Turn on the Firewall in Windows XP: Method Two

Lab B.4: Create a Baseline for Internet Access

Lab B.5: Turn on a Screensaver Password for Windows XP

Lab B.6: Look for Security Events within Windows XP

Lab B.7: Identify User Accounts with Administrator Access in Windows XP

Lab B.8: Turn on a Screensaver Password for openSUSE

Lab B.9: Change a Password in Linux

Lab B.10: Find SUID and SGID Files in Linux

Lab B.11 Change ACLs on All Files in a Linux Directory

Lab B.12: Change Permissions on All Files in a Linux Directory

Lab B.13: Change the Default Permissions for All Newly Created Files in Linux

Lab B.14: View all Linux Logins

Lab B.15: Change the Group Associated with Files

Lab B.16: View Failed Login Attempts

Lab B.17: Hide a Linux File

Lab B.18: Hide and Access a Windows Share

Lab B.19: Encrypt a Windows File

Lab B.20: Count the Number of Running Linux Processes

Lab B.21: Display the Security Tab in Windows XP

Lab B.22: View Effective Permissions in Windows XP

Lab B.23: Turn the Guest Account Off

Lab B.24: View Internet Explorer Security Settings

Lab B.25: Change Internet Explorer Pop-up Blocker Settings

Lab B.26: Prevent a Folder from Being Shared

Lab B.27: Enable openSUSE Firewall

Lab B.28: Configure openSUSE Local Security

Lab B.29: Set the Defaults for New Users

Lab B.30: View Logged Warnings in openSUSE

Lab B.31: Configure AppArmor

Lab B.32: View AppArmor Reports

Lab B.33: Configure openSUSE as a Kerberos Client

Lab B.34: Configure openSUSE as an LDAP Client

Lab B.35: Turn Off IPv6 in openSUSE

Lab B.36: Turn On Folder Encryption with cipher

Lab B.37: Change the Minimum Password Age

Lab B.38: Compare Your System to a Security Template

Lab B.39: Clear Private Data in Internet Explorer

Lab B.40: Clear Private Data in Firefox

Lab B.41: Configure SELinux in Fedora

Lab B.42: Limit Cookies to First Party

Lab B.43: Configure the Phishing Filter

Lab B.44: Add a Legal Notice

Lab B.45: Configure Windows XP Startup

Lab B.46: Run a Remote Desktop

Lab B.47: Secure the Account Database

Lab B.48: Create a Restore Point

Lab B.49: Return to a Restore Point

Lab B.50: Boot to a Good Configuration

Lab B.1: Change to WPA Security in Windows XP

This lab requires a Windows XP workstation with a wireless connection.

To change the wireless connection to Wi-Fi Protected Access (WPA) from any other security setting, follow these steps:

1. Right-click the wireless connection icon in the notification area at the right of the Taskbar.

2. Choose View Available Wireless Networks.

3. On the left side of the dialog box, click Change Order of Preferred Networks.

4. Select the Wireless Networks tab and click on the network you want to change beneath the Preferred Networks section. When it is highlighted, click Properties.

5. On the Association tab (shown in Figure B.1), choose either WPA or WPA-PSK (the latter incorporates Pre Shared Key and is recommended if you don't have a central authentication server) for Network Authentication.

FIGURE B.1   The Association tab allows you to configure encryption.

6. From the Data Encryption drop-down menu, choose either TKIP (Temporal Key Integrity Protocol) or AES (Advanced Encryption Standard) and enter the network key (your wireless password). Confirm the network key by reentering it in the next box.

7. Click OK to exit this dialog box and OK to exit the earlier dialog boxes.

Lab B.2: Turn on the Firewall in Windows XP: Method One

This lab requires a Windows XP workstation with a wireless connection.

To turn on the firewall, follow these steps:

1. Right-click the wireless connection icon in the notification area at the right of the Taskbar.

2. Choose View Available Wireless Networks.

3. On the left side of the dialog box, click Change Order of Preferred Networks.

4. Select the Advanced tab, and beneath Windows Firewall, click Settings. The dialog box that appears is shown in Figure B.2.

5. Click the On button to enable the firewall, then choose the Exceptions tab and configure any exceptions that you want to allow.

6. Click OK to exit this dialog box and OK to exit the earlier dialog boxes.

FIGURE B.2 The Windows Firewall configuration dialog box

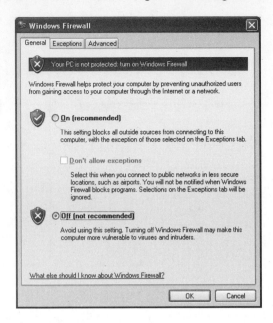

Lab B.3: Turn on the Firewall in Windows XP: Method Two

This lab requires a Windows XP workstation.

To turn on the firewall, follow these steps:

1. Choose Start ≻ Control Panel ≻ Security Center. The dialog box shown in Figure B.3 appears.

 Instead of choosing Security Center in Control Panel, you could choose Windows Firewall and immediately access the Firewall Configuration dialog box. The advantage of choosing Security Center is that you see the other options that are also available.

2. Toggle the setting for the firewall from Off to On.

3. Exit the Security Center.

4. Exit Control Panel.

Note that from this location, you can toggle the status of the firewall. If the firewall is already turned on, you can follow these same steps to turn it off should you need to.

FIGURE B.3   Firewall configuration appears first in the Security Center dialog box.

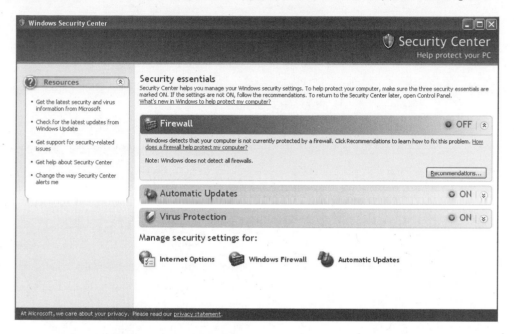

Lab B.4: Create a Baseline for Internet Access

This lab works with any workstation.

Creating a baseline involves gathering information about normal operations and then looking for deviations. A good baseline is constructed from collecting data on several variables. To collect information about Internet access speed from a workstation, follow these steps:

1. Open the workstation's browser.

2. Set the URL to http://bandwidthplace.com/speedtest/.

3. Click the button to begin the test. The speed is returned to you within seconds.

4. Test the workstation from this site over the course of a few days, varying the time of day you do so in order to build a good baseline.

Lab B.5: Turn on a Screensaver Password for Windows XP

This lab requires a Windows XP workstation.

All workstations should require authentication after a time of nonuse. One of the easiest ways to accomplish this protection is to use a screensaver that requires a password to exit:

1. Choose Start ➢ Control Panel ➢ Display.

2. Click the Screensaver tab and choose a screensaver.

3. Set the wait duration to 30 minutes, or whatever is appropriate for your firm.

4. Check the box labeled On Resume, Password Protect. Click OK to exit the Display applet.

5. Exit Control Panel.

Lab B.6: Look for Security Events within Windows XP

This lab requires a Windows XP workstation.

Logging is automatically enabled for many items on a workstation, but the log entries are only meaningful if examined. To view the security events logged on a workstation, follow these steps:

1. Choose Start ➢ Control Panel ➢ Administrative Tools.

2. Choose Event Viewer and open it.

3. Within the left frame, click Security. All logged security events appear.

4. To gather more information on any logged entry, double-click it.

5. Exit the Event Viewer.

6. Exit Control Panel.

Lab B.7: Identify User Accounts with Administrator Access in Windows XP

This lab requires a Windows XP workstation.

User management is simplified by adding users to groups. To see which users are members of the Administrators group, follow these steps:

1. Choose Start ➢ Control Panel ➢ Administrative Tools.

2. Choose Computer Management and open it.

3. Within the left frame, expand Local Users and Groups and then expand Groups, as shown in Figure B.4.

FIGURE B.4   Expand the Groups folder to see the local groups.

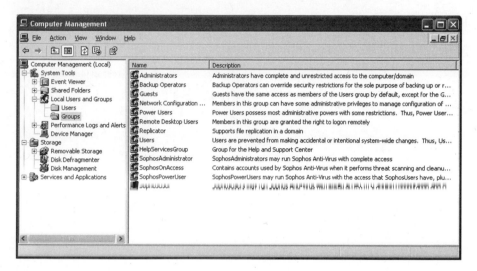

4. Double-click Administrators and a list of users appears. You can use the Add or Remove button to place users in this group or take them from it, respectively.

5. Exit the Computer Management console.

6. Exit Control Panel.

Lab B.8: Turn on a Screensaver Password for openSUSE

This lab requires a SUSE (or openSUSE) workstation.

All workstations should require authentication after a time of nonuse. One of the easiest ways to protect a workstation is to use a screensaver that requires a password to exit:

1. From the desktop, choose System ➤ Personal Settings ➤ Shortcuts.

2. Click the action titled Lock Screen.

3. Enter the keyboard combination for this action (the default is Alt+F12).

4. Click Close.

5. Exit the Settings dialog box and verify that the screensaver works when you press the key combination.

Lab B.9: Change a Password in Linux

This lab requires a Linux workstation.

A user can change their password at any time (unless you have locked this ability) and should be encouraged to do so if they feel their password might have become compromised. Here are the steps a user would follow to change their own password:

1. From the desktop, choose Programs ➤ Accessories ➤ Terminal.

 Your menu choices might differ slightly based upon the Linux distribution you are using.

2. At the prompt, type **passwd**.
3. Enter the old password at the prompt.
4. Enter what you want the password to now be at the next prompt. If the value given does not meet the requirements configured for the system (password length, mix of alphanumeric characters, and so forth), it will not be accepted.
5. At the next prompt, enter the new value again. This value must match what was typed in before or the password will not be changed.
6. When the message appears stating that the password has been changed, exit the terminal window.

Lab B.10: Find SUID and SGID Files in Linux

This lab requires a Linux workstation.

In addition to standard permissions, Linux contains two special permissions that can pose security risks. The first permission, SUID, makes anyone running the file the user that created the file, so if root created the file, the user running it becomes root during its execution. The second permission, SGID, makes anyone running the file a temporary member of the group associated with the file.

Because these permissions are so powerful, you need to routinely monitor the files in which they are set. To file all SUID and SGID files on the system, follow these steps:

1. From the desktop, choose Programs ➤ Accessories ➤ Terminal.

 Your menu choices might differ slightly based upon the Linux distribution you are using.

2. At the prompt, type **su** to become the root user (you can also use **sudo**). Enter the appropriate password at the prompt.

3. Type the command `find / -perm -2000 -print | more`.

4. Study the list and make certain you can explain every file that appears as being a system file or other special utility.

5. When you are finished, exit the terminal window.

Lab B.11: Change ACLs on All Files in a Linux Directory

This lab requires a Linux workstation.

Two utilities exist in Linux to allow you to work directly with the access control lists (ACLs) for files: `getfacl`, which shows the ACL information, and `setfacl`, which allows you to set the ACL information.

Using these two together, you can take the ACLs from one file and make them apply to others. In this lab, you'll take the ACLs from the `.fonts.cache-1` file (beneath `/root`) and make it apply to all files in the `/tmp` directory. To do so, follow these steps:

1. From the desktop, choose Programs ➢ Accessories ➢ Terminal.

> **NOTE**   Your menu choices might differ slightly based upon the Linux distribution you are using.

2. At the prompt, type **su** to become the root user. Enter the appropriate password at the prompt.

3. Type the command `cd /tmp`.

4. Type the command `getfacl /root/fonts.cache-1 | setfacl –set-file=- *`.

5. When you are finished, exit the terminal window.

Lab B.12: Change Permissions on All Files in a Linux Directory

This lab requires a Linux workstation.

You can use the `chmod` utility to change the permissions on one or many files. This exercise changes the permissions on all files beneath the `/tmp` directory to readonly for everyone (r--r--r--).

To accomplish this change, follow these steps:

1. From the desktop, choose Programs ➢ Accessories ➢ Terminal.

 Your menu choices might differ slightly based upon the Linux distribution you are using.

2. Type the command **cd /tmp**.

3. Type the command **chmod 444 ***.

4. When you are finished, exit the terminal window.

Lab B.13: Change the Default Permissions for all Newly Created Files in Linux

This lab requires a Linux workstation.

The umask utility/value is used to determine the default permissions on newly created files. On most systems, the umask default is 022, meaning that newly created files have permissions of 644 (rw-r--r--).

In this exercise, the value will be changed to 026, meaning that newly created files will have permissions of 640 (rw-r-----). To accomplish this change, follow these steps:

1. From the desktop, choose Programs ➢ Accessories ➢ Terminal.

 Your menu choices might differ slightly based upon the Linux distribution you are using.

2. Type the command: **umask 026**.

3. This setting makes the value temporary. To make it permanent, type the command **cd /etc**.

4. Use any editor (such as Vi) to open the profile file and change the default entry in it from umask 022 to umask 026. Save your change and exit the editor.

5. When you are finished, exit the terminal window.

Lab B.14: View all Linux Logins

This lab requires a Linux workstation.

The `lastlog` utility can be used to generate a list of every user account and the last time they logged in to the system. Unfortunately, it lists the account even if the user associated with it has never logged in.

In this exercise, you'll get a list of user accounts and then remove all the entries that have never logged in so that you are left with only accounts that have actually accessed the workstation:

1.   As root, from the desktop, choose Programs ➢ Accessories ➢ Terminal.

Your menu choices might differ slightly based upon the Linux distribution you are using.

2.   Type the command `lastlog | grep -vi "never"`.

3.   Make a list of the usernames and verify that each is a legitimate account that should be accessing your system.

4.   To see each login of a particular account (providing the wtmp file has not been parsed), use that account with the last command. For example, to see the logins for the user christine, type the command `last christine`.

5.   When you are finished, exit the terminal window.

Lab B.15: Change the Group Associated with Files

This lab requires a Linux workstation.

The root user has the ability to do anything on the system, from deleting the entire operating system to changing miniscule settings. Between those two ends of the spectrum resides the ability to change the owner or group associated with files.

In this exercise, you change the group associated with all files beneath a directory to root. This action can be useful if a user quits and you need to give access permissions to others. This exercise uses the user account staley, but it should be changed to one that exists on your system:

1.   As root, from the desktop, choose Programs ➢ Accessories ➢ Terminal.

Your menu choices might differ slightly based upon the Linux distribution that you are using.

2.   Type the command `cd /home/staley`.

3. Type the command `chgrp root *.*`.

4. When you are finished, exit the terminal window.

You could similarly change the owner by using `chown` in place of `chgrp`.

Lab B.16: View Failed Login Attempts

This lab requires a Linux workstation.

One of the signs that an attacker might be attempting to break into a system will be failed login attempts. The `/var/log/faillog` file keeps track of failed authentication attempts. Follow these steps to view this information on a workstation:

1. As root, from the desktop, choose Programs ➤ Accessories ➤ Terminal.

 NOTE Your menu choices might differ slightly based upon the Linux distribution that you are using.

2. Type the command `faillog`. The list that appears, if any, will show accounts that have not had a successful login since the last failure.

3. Type the command `faillog -a`. The list that appears will show all failed login attempts, including those that have since had a successful authentication.

4. When you are finished, exit the terminal window.

Lab B.17: Hide a Linux File

This lab requires a Linux workstation.

If an attacker is truly looking for something on your system, they will find it. A great many problems, however, occur from users who are acting out of maliciousness, spite, or similar motives, and it is much easier to keep files safe from them because they often don't have the same tools or knowledge as outside attackers.

One simple method for "protecting" a file is to hide it. To hide a file in Linux, you use the period character (.) as the first character of its name. It will then no longer appear in listings unless you use the –a option (such as `ls  -a`). Here are the steps for the user sven to hide the text file `pageup` within his home directory:

1. From the desktop, choose Programs ➤ Accessories ➤ Terminal.

2. Type the command `cd /home/sven`.

3. Type the command `mv pageup .pageup`. The file is now considered "hidden."

4. When you are finished, exit the terminal window.

Lab B.18: Hide and Access a Windows Share

This lab requires two Windows workstations.

A simple method for "protecting" shares is to make them hidden. To hide a share in Windows, you use the dollar sign character ($) as the last character of its name. It will then no longer appear in listings and will need to be referred to specifically to be accessed. Follow these steps:

1. On Computer1, choose to share the `C:\WINDOWS` directory, and name the share DATA$.

2. On Computer2, look for the share. Use My Network Places (or Network Neighborhood on older Windows operating systems) to look for the share. You should not be able to see the share because the name ends with $.

3. Right-click My Network Places and choose Map Network Drive.

4. In the Path box, type `\\Computer1\DATA$`.

5. Click OK. You should now be able to access the share.

Lab B.19: Encrypt a Windows File

This lab requires a Windows workstation.

Windows operating systems since Windows 2000 have included the ability to encrypt files. Follow these steps:

1. Within Windows Explorer or the Desktop, right-click an individual file and choose Properties.

2. On the General tab, click the Advanced button that appears underneath Attributes.

3. Check the Encrypt box contents to secure data. Notice that you cannot choose to both encrypt the data and compress it.

4. Click OK to exit. Click OK again at the Properties dialog box.

5. A warning box appears asking if you want to encrypt only the file or the entire directory (the parent folder). Choose to only encrypt the one file and click OK again.

Lab B.20: Count the Number of Running Linux Processes

This lab requires a Linux workstation.

To view only a count of the number of processes running on a Linux workstation, follow these steps:

1. As root, from the desktop, choose Programs ➤ Accessories ➤ Terminal.

2. Type the command **ps -ef | grep -c $**. This number can be used to generate a simple baseline as you rerun the command occasionally and look for massive fluctuations.

3. When you are finished, exit the terminal window.

Lab B.21: Display the Security Tab in Windows XP

This lab requires a Windows XP workstation.

By default, Windows XP does not display the Security tab for files and folders. To turn this feature on, follow these steps:

1. Choose Start ➤ Control Panel ➤ Folder Options.

2. Click the View tab.

3. Scroll to the bottom of the Advanced Settings (shown in Figure B.5) and uncheck the Use Simple File Sharing [Recommended] box.

4. Click OK to exit. Close Control Panel.

FIGURE B.5   Simple file sharing prevents the Security tab from being displayed for files and folders.

Lab B.22: View Effective Permissions in Windows XP

This lab requires a Windows XP workstation.

Permissions can be assigned at multiple levels—to folders, files, and so on. Additionally, sometimes what is granted to one group may be denied to another, and when a user is a member of more than one group, permissions can become confusing.

To view effective permissions for a file in Windows XP, follow these steps:

1. Within Windows Explorer or the Desktop, right-click an individual file and choose Properties.

2. Click the Security tab (if this tab does not appear, see Exercise B.21).

3. Click the Advanced button.

4. Click the Effective Permissions tab.

5. Click the Select button and type in a username; then press Enter. The permissions that appear are now those that would apply for that user on that resource.

6. Click OK to exit. Click OK again at the Properties dialog box.

Lab B.23: Turn the Guest Account Off

This lab requires a Windows XP workstation.

The Guest account is used when someone must access a system but lacks a user account on that system. The Guest account leaves a security risk at the workstation and should be disabled.

To turn the Guest account off, follow these steps:

1. Choose Start ➢ Control Panel ➢ User Accounts.

2. Click Guest. The dialog box shown in Figure B.6 appears.

FIGURE B.6 The options for the Guest account

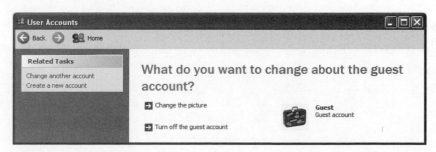

3. Click Turn Off the Guest Account.

4. Exit the User Accounts dialog box.

5. Exit Control Panel.

Lab B.24: View Internet Explorer Security Settings

This lab requires a workstation running Internet Explorer.

A great many security threats come through the Internet, and the browser is the interface most commonly used to reach the Internet, making the security settings for the browser critically important. To view the security settings for Internet Explorer, follow these steps:

1. Within Internet Explorer, click Tools ➤ Internet Options.

2. Choose the Security tab.

3. Chose the Internet icon, and then click the Custom level button.

4. Choose to enable or disable any settings, then click OK to exit.

5. Click OK to exit the Internet Options dialog box.

Lab B.25: Change Internet Explorer Pop-up Blocker Settings

This lab requires a workstation running Internet Explorer.

To view and change the pop-up blocker settings for Internet Explorer, follow these steps:

1. Within Internet Explorer, click Tools ➤ Internet Options.

2. Choose the Privacy tab.

3. Make certain the box is checked to turn on pop-up blocking.

4. Click Settings. The dialog box shown in Figure B.7 appears.

5. Type in the address of a site from which you want to allow pop-ups, and then click Add.

6. When you are finished adding sites, click Close.

7. Click OK to exit the Internet Options dialog box.

FIGURE B.7 Configure sites to allow pop-ups from within the Pop-up Blocker Settings dialog box.

Lab B.26: Prevent a Folder from Being Shared

This lab requires a workstation running a current Windows-based operating system.

Folders can be marked as Private to prevent them from being shared or accessed by anyone but you locally. To mark folders as Private, follow these steps:

1. Within Windows Explorer, right-click a folder and choose Properties from the pop-up menu.

2. Choose the Sharing tab.

3. Check the Make This Folder Private box.

4. Click OK.

5. When you are finished, close Windows Explorer.

Lab B.27: Enable openSUSE Firewall

This lab requires a workstation running openSUSE and KDE.

You can start and configure the firewall in openSUSE by following these steps:

1. Click the launcher on the desktop and choose Applications.
2. Choose System.
3. Choose Administrator Settings. This choice starts YaST2.
4. Choose Security and Users.
5. Choose Firewall. The Firewall Configuration dialog box appears.
6. Choose Enable Firewall Automatic Starting. If the firewall is not currently running, click Start Firewall Now (if the firewall is running, this option will be grayed out and you will not be able to click it).
7. Click Next to see the summary screen.
8. Click Finish to exit the firewall configuration.
9. Exit YaST2.

Lab B.28: Configure openSUSE Local Security

This lab requires a workstation running openSUSE and KDE.
   To configure local security in openSUSE, follow these steps:

1. Click the launcher on the desktop and choose Applications.
2. Choose System.
3. Choose Administrator Settings. This choice starts YaST2.
4. Choose Security and Users.
5. Choose Local Security. With Custom Settings chosen, click Next.
6. Change the Minimum Acceptable Password Length value from the default of 5 characters to 7.
7. Click Next.
8. Click Next through the following screens, then click Finish to exit Local Security Configuration.
9. Exit YaST2.

Lab B.29: Set the Defaults for New Users

This lab requires a workstation running openSUSE and KDE.

To change the default settings for new users in openSUSE, follow these steps:

1. Click the launcher on the desktop and choose Applications.
2. Choose System.
3. Choose Administrator Settings. This choice starts YaST2.
4. Choose Security and Users.
5. Choose User and Group Management. Click the Defaults for New Users tab.
6. Change the Days after Password Expiration Login Is Usable from its default of -1 to 0.
7. Click Finish to exit the configuration.
8. Exit YaST2.

Lab B.30: View Logged Warnings in openSUSE

This lab requires a workstation running openSUSE and KDE.

To view logged warnings in openSUSE, follow these steps:

1. Click the launcher on the desktop and choose Applications.
2. Choose System.
3. Choose Administrator Settings. This choice starts YaST2.
4. Choose Miscellaneous.
5. Choose Start-up Log. The dialog box that appears displays the contents of /var/log/boot.msg and starts the display at the bottom of the log file (the most recent entries).
6. Change the drop-down box to /var/log/warn. The warning entries now display. Take note of overflow and buffer errors.
7. Click OK.
8. Exit YaST2.

Lab B.31: Configure AppArmor

This lab requires a workstation running openSUSE and KDE.

To configure AppArmor, follow these steps:

1. Click the launcher on the desktop and choose Applications.
2. Choose System.
3. Choose Administrator Settings. This choice starts YaST2.

4. Choose Novell AppArmor.

5. Choose AppArmor Control Panel. This option starts the AppArmor Configuration dialog box. Make certain Enable AppArmor is checked; then click Configure beneath Configure Profile Modes.

6. By default, only active profiles are shown. Click the Show All Profiles button.

7. Highlight the entry for usr.sbin.inetd and click Toggle Mode. This action changes the mode from enforce to complain.

8. Click Done.

9. Click Done again.

10. Exit YaST2.

Lab B.32: View AppArmor Reports

This lab requires a workstation running openSUSE and KDE.

After AppArmor is configured (Lab B.31), follow these steps to view reports:

1. Click the launcher on the desktop and choose Applications.

2. Choose System.

3. Choose Administrator Settings. This choice starts YaST2.

4. Choose Novell AppArmor.

5. Choose AppArmor Reports. By default, Executive.Security.Summary is highlighted (you can change it if you want to run another report type). Click Run Now.

6. A summary report appears, but it's not as helpful as you might like. Click Back, change the report type to Applications.Audit, and click Run Now. This report shows the program, PID, and type of entry logged.

7. Click Done.

8. Exit YaST2.

Lab B.33: Configure openSUSE as a Kerberos Client

This lab requires a workstation running openSUSE and KDE.

To configure a Kerberos client in openSUSE, follow these steps:

1. Click the launcher on the desktop and choose Applications.

2. Choose System.

3. Choose Administrator Settings. This choice starts YaST2.

4. Choose Network Services.

5. Choose Kerberos Client. The Kerberos Client Configuration dialog box appears.

6. Click the Use Kerberos button and enter the KDC server address.

7. Click Finish.

8. Exit YaST2.

Lab B.34: Configure openSUSE as an LDAP Client

This lab requires a workstation running openSUSE and KDE.

To configure an LDAP client in openSUSE, follow these steps:

1. Click the launcher on the desktop and choose Applications.

2. Choose System.

3. Choose Administrator Settings. This choice starts YaST2.

4. Choose Network Services.

5. Choose LDAP Client. The LDAP Client Configuration dialog box appears.

6. Beneath User Authentication, click the Use LDAP button.

7. Click Finish.

8. Exit YaST2.

Lab B.35: Turn Off IPv6 in openSUSE

This lab requires a workstation running openSUSE and KDE.

If you are not using Internet Protocol version 6 (IPv6) in your network, support for it can be disabled on the workstation. To turn off IPv6 in openSUSE, follow these steps:

1. Click the launcher on the desktop and choose Applications.

2. Choose System.

3. Choose Administrator Settings. This choice starts YaST2.

4. Choose Network Devices.

5. Choose Network Settings. The Network Settings dialog box appears and defaults to the Overview tab. Click the Global Options tab.

6. Beneath IPv6 Protocol Settings, uncheck the Enable IPv6 box.

7. A warning appears that tells you that a reboot is needed to apply this change. Click OK.

8. Click Finish.

9. Exit YaST2.

10. Reboot the workstation.

Lab B.36: Turn On Folder Encryption with cipher

This lab requires a Windows XP workstation.

Folders can be encrypted from the command line in Windows XP using the `cipher` command.

 Earlier versions of `cipher` allowed you to work with individual files as well as folders. Starting with Windows XP, `cipher` now works at the folder level only.

To use `cipher` to turn on folder encryption, follow these steps:

1. Choose Start ➢ Run.

2. Type **cmd** and press Enter. This action opens a command window.

3. Type **cipher /e directory**, where *directory* is replaced by the name of a directory/folder on your system. Press Enter.

4. A message appears that the directory is now encrypted. To see the status of the directory, type **cipher *directory***. A message appears stating that all new files added to this directory will be encrypted.

5. Create a file within that directory (creating a file is easily accomplished by typing **echo hello > test.txt**, which creates a text file with only the word *hello* in it).

6. Within that directory, type **cipher**. In the list of files that appears, you'll see a *U* to the left of all files that were initially there and an *E* to the left of the newly created file, which indicates that it is encrypted.

7. Type **exit** to close the command window.

Lab B.37: Change the Minimum Password Age

This lab requires a Windows XP workstation.

Security Templates can give you access to system settings and allow you to make policy changes. The Minimum Password Age setting defines how long a user must have a password before they can change it. The default is usually 2 days, but there can be little reason for a user needing to change their password every 2 days. This exercise walks you through the steps of changing the minimum password age to 10 days:

 You must be logged in as a member of the Administrators group (or as Administrator) to be able to make this change.

1. Choose Start ➢ Run.
2. Type **mmc** and press Enter. This action opens a console window.
3. Choose File and then Add/Remove Snap-In. Beneath Add/Remove Snap-In, click Add, and a list of available add-ins appears.
4. Choose Security Templates and click Add.
5. Click Close.
6. Click OK.
7. Expand Security Templates.
8. Expand hisecws (high security workstation).
9. Click Password Policy and the available policies/settings appear on the right.
10. Double-click Minimum Password Age and change the 2 to 10.
11. Click OK.
12. Click File and then Save.
13. Close the console. A prompt appears that asks if you want to save your change to the hisecws.inf file. Click Yes.

Lab B.38: Compare Your System to a Security Template

This lab requires a Windows XP workstation.

After you finish Lab B.37, you can compare the security settings actually employed on your system against those you specified.

 You must be logged in as a member of the Administrators group (or as Administrator) to be able to make this change.

To do so, follow these steps:

1. Choose Start ➢ Run.

2. Type **mmc** and press Enter. This command opens a console window.

3. Choose File and then Add/Remove Snap-In. Beneath Add/Remove Snap-In, click Add, and a list of available add-ins appears.

4. Choose Security Configuration and Analysis and click Add.

5. Click Close.

6. Click OK.

7. Right-click Security Configuration and Analysis and choose Open Database.

8. Type in the name of a database you want to create (such as **test**) and click Open.

9. At the prompt to import a template, select hisecws and click Open.

10. Right-click Security Configuration and Analysis and choose Analyze Computer Now.

11. At the prompt for an error log file path, click OK to keep the default.

12. Expand Security Configuration and Analysis and then Password Policy. A red circle should appear beside Minimum Password Age (and likely others), showing that the computer is not configured as the template is.

13. To make all settings in the template apply, right-click Security Configuration and Analysis and choose Configure Computer Now.

14. Repeat the analysis step, and all settings should now equal those in the template.

Lab B.39: Clear Private Data in Internet Explorer

This lab requires a workstation running Internet Explorer.

Private data for a web user includes such items as the cache, cookies, sessions, and any temporary files. To delete this information in Internet Explorer, follow these steps:

1. Within Internet Explorer, click Tools ➢ Delete Browsing History.

2. If you only want to clear one item (such as Cookies), click that button. Otherwise, click Delete All.

   Alternatively, if you want to be more secure, you can open Internet Options, choose the Advanced tab, and click the Reset button beneath Reset Internet Explorer Settings.

In addition to clearing the collected data from sites, this action will reset the web browser settings to their default. Be sure to read the warning carefully before you continue.

3. Click OK to exit Internet Options. You will need to restart Internet Explorer for the changes to take effect.

Lab B.40: Clear Private Data in Firefox

This lab requires a workstation running Firefox.

Private data for a web user includes such items as the cache, cookies, sessions, and any temporary files. To delete this information in Firefox, follow these steps:

1. Within Firefox, click Tools ➤ Clear Private Data.

2. At the dialog box that appears, check the box beside those items you want to clear: Browsing History, Cache, Cookies, and so on.

3. Click the Clear Private Data Now button.

Lab B.41: Configure SELinux in Fedora

This lab requires a Linux workstation running Fedora.

Security Enhanced Linux (SELinux) adds several security features to Linux that are not otherwise there in many distributions. To check the status of and configure SELinux in Fedora, follow these steps:

1. From the desktop, choose System ➤ Administration ➤ SELinux Management.

2. Beneath Status, set System Default Enforcing Mode to Enforcing.

3. Set Current Enforcing Mode to Enforcing.

4. Exit the dialog box.

Lab B.42: Limit Cookies to First Party

This lab requires a workstation running Internet Explorer.

When cookies come from the site for which they are associated, they are known as first-party cookies. When cookies come from advertisers on a site, they are known as third-party cookies. Within Internet Explorer, it is possible to limit cookies so that only first-party are accepted (the default is to accept both). To do so, follow these steps:

1. Within Internet Explorer, click Tools ➤ Internet Options and choose the Privacy tab.
2. Click the Advanced button.
3. Check the Override Automatic Cookie Handling box.
4. Choose Accept for First-party Cookies.
5. Choose Block for Third-party Cookies.
6. Check the Always Allow Session Cookies box.
7. Click OK.
8. Click OK to exit Internet Options.

Lab B.43: Configure the Phishing Filter

This lab requires a workstation running Internet Explorer.

The checking component of the phishing filter in Internet Explorer can be turned on or off, or the entire filter can be disabled. To turn on automatic website checking, follow these steps:

1. Within Internet Explorer, click Tools ➤ Internet Options and choose the Advanced tab.
2. Scroll down beneath Settings to Phishing Filter.
3. Click Turn On Automatic Website Checking.
4. Click OK.
5. A message appears telling you that website addresses will be sent to Microsoft and checked against a database of reported phishing websites. Click OK.
6. Exit the Internet Options.

Lab B.44: Add a Legal Notice

This lab requires a Windows XP workstation.

 This lab requires editing the Windows Registry. Do not perform this lab unless you are comfortable doing so because improperly changing Registry settings can crash the system.

The Registry can be thought of as a database holding most of the configuration settings in current Windows-based operating systems. In this lab, you create a legal notice prompt that will appear before a user gives their username and password. That banner tells the user that they are expected to follow the acceptable use policy as defined by your firm:

1. Choose Start ➢ Run.

2. Type **regedit** and press Enter.

3. Expand HKEY_LOCAL_MACHINE.

4. Expand SOFTWARE.

5. Expand Microsoft.

6. Expand Windows.

7. Expand CurrentVersion.

8. Expand Policies.

9. Click on System. A list of values appears on the right.

10. Within the right frame, double-click legalnoticecaption. At the prompt, type **Attention!** and click OK.

11. Within the right frame, double-click legalnoticetext. At the prompt, type **All users are expected to adhere to the Acceptable Use Policy. There is zero tolerance for violations.** Click OK.

12. Exit the Registry Editor.

13. Log off and back on to the workstation. The legal notice should appear and require you to click OK before you are allowed access to the login prompt.

Lab B.45: Configure Windows XP Startup

This lab requires a Windows XP workstation.

Initial settings for the operating system are contained in the Windows Registry and a handful of other files. Microsoft XP includes a utility that provides quick access to the system startup files. To access that utility, follow these steps:

1. Choose Start ➢ Run.

2. Type **msconfig** and press Enter. The dialog box shown in Figure B.8 appears.

3. Click the BOOT.INI tab.

4. Check the box labeled /SOS. This setting displays each driver as it is loaded during the boot process.

5. Click OK.

6. A dialog box appears that states that you must restart your computer before the changes you made will take effect. Click Restart.

FIGURE B.8   To start the System Configuration Utility, type `msconfig`.

Lab B.46: Run a Remote Desktop

This lab requires two Windows XP workstations networked together.

The purpose of a remote desktop session is to allow an administrator who might not be in close proximity to a workstation to help a user. Unfortunately, allowing remote access/control can always open vulnerabilities.

This lab illustrates the correct way to run a session between two workstations—one is the user's, and the other is the administrator's:

1. On the User's workstation, choose Start ≻ Control Panel ≻ System.

2. Click the Remote tab and check the box labeled Allow Users to Connect Remotely to This Computer.

3. Click the Select Remote Users button. The Remote Desktop Users dialog box appears.

4. Enter the user account you want to use to access the system. All members of the Administrators group can access the system even if they are not listed.

5. Click OK.

6. Click OK to exit System Properties.

7. Close out of Control Panel.

8. On the administrator's workstation, choose Start ≻ All Programs ≻ Accessories ≻ Remote Desktop Connection.

The location of the Remote Desktop Connection option can vary based upon the service pack installed. If you do not see it under Accessories, look beneath Communications.

9. Type in the name of the user's computer and click Connect.

10. At the prompt, enter the username and password to use.

11. Warnings appear on both systems stating that the remote desktop connection is proceeding. Agree to all of them.

12. The remote desktop now appears on the administrator's workstation, and the person sitting there can access the remote system as if they were a local user. At the top of the screen, a box allows you to minimize the session or exit it. When you are finished, exit the session (a warning will state that you are about to disconnect the session. Click OK).

Lab B.47: Secure the Account Database

This lab requires a Windows XP workstation.

The Windows XP account database can be secured through encryption to prevent it from being compromised. To perform this action, follow these steps:

1. Choose Start ➤ Run.

2. Type **syskey** and press Enter. The dialog box shown in Figure B.9 appears.

FIGURE B.9   Use encryption to secure the Windows XP account database.

   Note the warning—once encryption is enabled, it cannot be disabled.

3. Click Update. The dialog box shown in Figure B.10 appears.

4. Choose Password Startup.

5. Enter a password that you want to require during startup.

6. Enter the same password in the Confirm box.

7. Click OK.

FIGURE B.10 By default, the startup key is stored locally.

8. Click OK to the dialog box telling you that the account database startup key was changed.

9. Restart the system. You must now provide a password for Windows XP startup to complete.

Lab B.48: Create a Restore Point

This lab requires a Windows XP workstation.

When workstations are functioning as they should, you should routinely create restore points. A restore point is a configuration you can return to if the workstation's operating system suddenly becomes corrupted.

This lab illustrates the correct way to manually create a restore point:

1. Choose Start ➤ Control Panel ➤ System.

2. Click the System Restore tab and verify that the box labeled Turn Off System Restore is not checked (if it is checked, clear it).

3. Click OK.

4. Choose Start ➤ All Programs ➤ Accessories ➤ System Tools ➤ System Restore.

5. Choose Create a Restore Point and click Next.

6. At the prompt, type in a descriptive name, such as a name that describes the reason you are creating it (for example, right_before_service_pack_update).

7. Click Create.

8. A message appears that informs you that the restore point has been created. Click Close.

Lab B.49: Return to a Restore Point

This lab requires a Windows XP workstation and the successful completion of Lab B.48.

The best thing about restore points is that you can actually revert to them when the operating system goes awry. This lab illustrates the correct way to manually revert to a restore point:

1. Choose Start ➤ All Programs ➤ Accessories ➤ System Tools ➤ System Restore.

2. Choose Restore My Computer to an Earlier Time (the default selection) and click Next.

3. On the calendar presented, choose the date the restore point was made and a name from the list (this list includes automatic restore points created and the manual one created in Lab B.48). Choose the restore point created in the preceding lab.

4. Click Next.

5. A confirmation screen appears asking if you are sure you want to perform this action. Click Next. The system will restore and reboot.

Lab B.50: Boot to a Good Configuration

This lab requires a Windows XP workstation.

Occasionally, the operating system settings on a workstation become so corrupted that the system does not properly boot. When this happens with Windows XP settings, you can choose to boot into the last known good configuration. In Microsoft-speak, this is equal to the settings that were in existence the last time a user was able to successfully log into the system (in other words, before the degradation occurred).

This lab walks through the steps of booting into the last known good configuration:

1. Allow the system to restart and watch for the BIOS settings to appear. As soon as they clear, press F8.

2. A menu of operating system choices appears. If there is only one operating system on the workstation (the most common scenario), it will be the only item on the menu. Press F8 again.

3. The Windows Advanced Options Menu appears. Use the arrow keys to move down the list to the Last Known Good Configuration option.

4. Press Enter. You might need to press Enter again if the system reverts back to the operating system list menu.

5. The system now boots using the configuration settings from the previous good configuration.

Appendix
C

Security+
Acronym List

For its Security+ certification exam, CompTIA expects you to be familiar with many common industry acronyms. Table C.1 contains a list of the acronyms that you should know (more information on each can be found in the glossary as well as throughout the book).

TABLE C.1 Security+ Acronyms

Acronym	Definition
3DES	Triple Digital Encryption Standard
ACL	access control list
AES	Advanced Encryption Standard
AES256	Advanced Encryption Standard 256 bit
AH	Authentication Header
ALE	Annual or annualized loss expectancy
ARO	annualized rate of occurrence
ARP	Address Resolution Protocol
AUP	acceptable use policy
BIOS	basic input/output system
BOTS	network robots
CA	certificate authority
CAN	Controller Area Network
CCTV	closed-circuit television
CHAP	Challenge Handshake Authentication Protocol
CRL	Certification Revocation List

TABLE C.1   Security+ Acronyms *(continued)*

Acronym	Definition
DAC	Discretionary Access Control
DDoS	distributed denial of service
DES	Digital Encryption Standard
DHCP	Dynamic Host Configuration Protocol
DLL	Dynamic Link Library
DMZ	demilitarized zone
DNS	Domain Name Service (Server)
DoS	denial of service
EAP	Extensible Authentication Protocol
ECC	Elliptic Curve Cryptography
FTP	File Transfer Protocol
GRE	Generic Routing Encapsulation
H-IDS	host-based intrusion detection system
H-IPS	host-based intrusion prevention system
HTTP	Hypertext Transfer Protocol
HTTPS	Hypertext Transfer Protocol (Hypertext Transfer Protocol over SSL)
HVAC	heating, ventilation, and air conditioning
ICMP	Internet Control Message Protocol
ID	Identification, or Intrusion Detection
IM	instant messaging
IMAP4	Internet Message Access Protocol v4
IP	Internet Protocol
IPSec	Internet Protocol Security

TABLE C.1   Security+ Acronyms *(continued)*

Acronym	Definition
IRC	Internet Relay Chat
ISP	Internet service provider
KDC	Key Distribution Center
L2TP	Layer 2 Tunneling Protocol
LANMAN	Local Area Network Manager
LDAP	Lightweight Directory Access Protocol
MAC	Mandatory Access Control
MAC	Media Access Control
MAC	message authentication code
MAN	metropolitan area network
MD5	Message Digest 5
MSCHAP	Microsoft Challenge Handshake Authentication Protocol
MTU	Maximum Transmission Unit
NAC	network access control
NAT	Network Address Translation
N-IDS	network-based intrusion detection system
N-IPS	network-based intrusion prevention system
NOS	network operating system
NTFS	New Technology File System
NTLM	New Technology LANMAN or New Technology LAN Manager
NTP	Network Time Protocol
OS	operating system

TABLE C.1   Security+ Acronyms *(continued)*

Acronym	Definition
OVAL	Open Vulnerability and Assessment Language
PAP	Password Authentication Protocol
PAT	Port Address Translation
PBX	Private Branch Exchange
PGP	Pretty Good Privacy
PII	Personally Identifiable Information
PKI	Public Key Infrastructure
PPP	Point-to-Point Protocol
PPTP	Point-to-Point Tunneling Protocol
RAD	Rapid Application Development
RADIUS	Remote Authentication Dial-In User Service
RAID	Redundant Array of Inexpensive Disks also Redundant Array of Independent Disks
RAS	Remote Access Server
RBAC	Role-Based Access Control
RBAC	Rule-Based Access Control
RSA	Rivest, Shamir, and Adleman
S/MIME	Secure Multipurpose Internet Mail Extensions
SCSI	Small Computer System Interface
SHA	Secure Hashing Algorithm or Secure Hash Algorithm
SHTTP	Secure Hypertext Transfer Protocol
SLA	service-level agreement
SLE	single loss expectancy

TABLE C.1   Security+ Acronyms *(continued)*

Acronym	Definition
SMTP	Simple Mail Transfer Protocol
SNMP	Simple Network Management Protocol
SPIM	Spam over Internet Messaging
SSH	Secure Shell
SSL	Secure Sockets Layer
SSO	single sign-on
STP	Shielded Twisted Pair
TACACS	Terminal Access Controller Access Control System
TCP/IP	Transmission Control Protocol/Internet Protocol
TKIP	Temporal Key Integrity Protocol
TKIP	Temporal Key Interchange Protocol
TLS	Transport Layer Security
TPM	Trusted Platform Module
UPS	uninterruptable power supply
URL	Universal Resource Locator or Uniform Resource Locator
USB	Universal Serial Bus
UTP	Unshielded Twisted Pair
VLAN	virtual local area network
VoIP	Voice over IP
VPN	virtual private network
WEP	Wired Equivalent Privacy
WPA	Wi-Fi Protected Access

Appendix

D

About the Companion CD

IN THIS APPENDIX:

✓ What You'll Find on the CD

✓ System Requirements

✓ Using the CD

✓ Troubleshooting

What You'll Find on the CD

The following sections are arranged by category and summarize the software and other goodies you'll find on the CD. If you need help with installing the items provided on the CD, refer to the installation instructions in the section "Using the CD" later in this appendix.

Some programs on the CD might fall into one of these categories:

Shareware programs are fully functional, free, trial versions of copyrighted programs. If you like particular programs, register with their authors for a nominal fee and receive licenses, enhanced versions, and technical support.

Freeware programs are free, copyrighted games, applications, and utilities. You can copy them to as many computers as you like—for free—but they offer no technical support.

GNU software is governed by its own license, which is included inside the folder of the GNU software. There are no restrictions on distribution of GNU software. See the GNU license at the root of the CD for more details.

Trial, *demo*, or *evaluation* versions of software are usually limited either by time or by functionality (such as not letting you save a project after you create it).

Sybex Test Engine

For Windows

The CD contains the Sybex test engine, which includes the assessment test and all of the chapter review questions in electronic format, as well as four bonus exams located only on the CD.

PDF of the Book

For Windows

We have included an electronic version of the text in PDF format. You can view the electronic version of the book with Adobe Reader.

Adobe Reader

For Windows

We've also included a copy of Adobe Reader so you can view PDF files that accompany the book's content. For more information on Adobe Reader or to check for a newer version, visit Adobe's website at www.adobe.com/products/reader/.

Electronic Flashcards

For PC, Pocket PC, and Palm

These handy electronic flashcards are just what they sound like. One side contains a question, and the other side shows the answer.

System Requirements

Make sure your computer meets the minimum system requirements shown in the following list. If your computer doesn't match up to most of these requirements, you may have problems using the software and files on the companion CD. For the latest and greatest information, please refer to the ReadMe file located at the root of the CD-ROM.

- A PC running Microsoft Windows 98, Windows 2000, Windows NT4 (with SP4 or later), Windows Me, Windows XP, or Windows Vista
- An Internet connection
- A CD-ROM drive

Using the CD

To install the items from the CD to your hard drive, follow these steps:

1. Insert the CD into your computer's CD-ROM drive. The license agreement appears.

> *Windows users:* The interface won't launch if you have autorun disabled. In that case, click Start ➤ Run (for Windows Vista, Start ➤ All Programs ➤ Accessories ➤ Run). In the dialog box that appears, type **D:\Start.exe**. (Replace *D* with the proper letter if your CD drive uses a different letter. If you don't know the letter, see how your CD drive is listed under My Computer.) Click OK.

2. Read the license agreement, and then click the Accept button if you want to use the CD.

The CD interface appears. The interface allows you to access the content with just one or two clicks.

Troubleshooting

Wiley has attempted to provide programs that work on most computers with the minimum system requirements. Alas, your computer may differ, and some programs may not work properly for some reason.

The two likeliest problems are that you don't have enough memory (RAM) for the programs you want to use and you have other programs running that are affecting the installation of a program or how it runs. If you get an error message such as "Not enough memory" or "Setup cannot continue," try one or more of the following suggestions and then try using the software again:

Turn off any antivirus software running on your computer. Installation programs sometimes mimic virus activity and may make your computer incorrectly believe that it's being infected by a virus.

Close all running programs. The more programs you have running, the less memory is available to other programs. Installation programs typically update files and programs, so if you keep other programs running, installation may not work properly.

Have your local computer store add more RAM to your computer. This is, admittedly, a drastic and somewhat expensive step. However, adding more memory can really help the speed of your computer and allow more programs to run at the same time.

Customer Care

If you have trouble with the book's companion CD-ROM, please call the Wiley Product Technical Support phone number at (800) 762-2974. Outside the United States, call +1 (317) 572-3994. You can also contact Wiley Product Technical Support at http://sybex.custhelp.com. John Wiley & Sons will provide technical support only for installation and other general quality-control items. For technical support on the applications themselves, consult the program's vendor or author.

To place additional orders or to request information about other Wiley products, please call (877) 762-2974.

Glossary

3DES   Also known as Triple Digital Encryption Standard (DES). A block cipher algorithm used for encryption.

802.11   *See* IEEE 802.11 Wireless LAN.

802.11a   The standard that provides for bandwidths of up to 54Mbps in the 5GHz frequency spectrum.

802.11b   The standard that provides for bandwidths of up to 11Mbps in the 2.4GHz frequency spectrum. This standard is also called Wireless Fidelity (Wi-Fi) or 802.11 high rate.

802.11g   The standard that provides for bandwidths of 20Mbps in the 2.4GHz frequency spectrum.

802.11n   A proposed amendment to the 802.11 standard that provides for bandwidths of 74Mbps in the 2.4GHz and 5GHz frequency spectrums. The standard is expected to be released in 2009.

A

acceptable use policy   Agreed-upon principles set forth by a company to govern how the employees of that company may use resources such as computers and Internet access.

access attack   An attack aimed at gaining access to resources.

access control   The means of giving or restricting user access to network resources. Access control is usually accomplished through the use of an access control list (ACL).

access control list (ACL)   A table or data file that specifies whether a user or group has access to a specific resource on a computer or network.

access point (AP)   The point at which access to a network is accomplished. This term is often used in relation to a wireless access point (WAP).

accountability   Being responsible for an item. The administrator is often accountable for the network and the resources on it.

accounting   The act of keeping track of activity. Most often, this term is used to refer to tracking users' interactions with network resources via log files that are routinely scanned and checked.

ACK   *See* acknowledgment (ACK).

acknowledgment (ACK)   A message confirming that a data packet was received. Acknowledgment occurs at the Transport layer of the Open Systems Interconnection (OSI) and TCP/IP models.

ACL   *See* access control list (ACL).

Active Directory   The replacement for NT Directory Service (NTDS) that is included with Windows 2000/2003. It acts similarly to Novell Directory Services (NDS), which is now known as eDirectory in NetWare 6.x/OES because it's a true X.500-based directory service.

active response   A response generated in real time.

active sniffing   Involves an attacker gaining access to a host in the network through a switch and logically disconnecting it from the network.

ActiveX   A Microsoft technology that allows customized controls, icons, and other features to increase the usability of web-enabled systems.

activity   Any action a user undertakes.

ad hoc radio frequency network   A network created when two RF-capable devices are brought within transmission range of each other. (RF stands for radio frequency.)

Address Resolution Protocol (ARP)   Protocol used to map known IP addresses to unknown physical addresses.

AD-IDS   Anomaly-detection intrusion detection system. An AD-IDS works by looking for deviations from a pattern of normal network traffic.

administrative policies   A set of rules that govern administrative usage of a system.

administrator   The user who is accountable and responsible for the network.

Advanced Encryption Standard (AES)   A FIPS publication that specifies a cryptographic algorithm for use by the U.S. government. *See also* Federal Information Processing Standard (FIPS).

adware   Software that gathers information to pass on to marketers or intercepts personal data such as credit card numbers and makes them available to third parties.

AES   *See* Advanced Encryption Standard (AES).

AES256   An implementation of Advanced Encryption Standard (AES) that uses 256-bit encryption.

ALE   *See* annual loss expectancy (ALE).

alert   A notification that an unusual condition exists and should be investigated.

algorithm   The series of steps/formulas/processes that is followed to arrive at a result.

analyzer   The component or process that analyzes the data collected by the sensor.

annual loss expectancy (ALE)   A calculation that is used to identify risks and calculate the expected loss each year.

annualized rate of occurrence (ARO)   A calculation of how often a threat will occur. For example, a threat that occurs once every five years has an annualized rate of occurrence of 1/5, or 0.2.

anomaly detection   The act of looking for variations from normal operations (anomalies) and reacting to them.

anonymous authentication   Authentication that doesn't require a user to provide a user-name, password, or any other identification before accessing resources.

antivirus   A category of software that uses various methods to prevent and eliminate viruses in a computer. It typically also protects against future infection. *See also* virus.

antivirus engine   The core program that runs the virus-scanning process.

antivirus software   Software that identifies the presence of a virus and is capable of removing or quarantining the virus.

API   *See* application programming interface (API).

AppleTalk   A networking capability included with all Macintosh computers.

appliance   A freestanding device that operates in a largely self-contained manner.

Application layer   The seventh layer of the Open Systems Interconnection (OSI) model. This layer deals with how applications access the network and describes application func-tionality, such as file transfer, messaging, and so on.

application programming interface (API)   An abstract interface to the services and proto-cols provided by an operating system.

armored virus   A virus that is protected in a way that makes disassembling it difficult. The difficulty makes it "armored" against antivirus programs that have trouble getting to, and understanding, its code.

ARO   *See* annualized rate of occurrence (ARO).

ARP   *See* Address Resolution Protocol (ARP).

ARP table   The table that the Address Resolution Protocol uses. Contains a list of known TCP/IP addresses and their associated physical addresses. The table is cached in memory so that ARP lookups don't have to be performed for frequently accessed addresses. *See also* Media Access Control (MAC).

asset   Any resource of value that you want to secure and protect.

asymmetric algorithm   An algorithm that utilizes two keys.

asymmetric encryption   Encryption in which two keys must be used. One key is used to encrypt data, and the other is needed to decrypt the data. Asymmetric encryption is the opposite of symmetric encryption, where a single key serves both purposes.

attack   Any unauthorized intrusion into the normal operations of a computer or computer network. The attack can be carried out to gain access to the system or any of its resources.

audit files   Files that hold information about a resource's access by users.

auditing   The act of tracking resource usage by users.

auditors   Individuals involved in auditing log and security files.

authenticating the evidence   Verifying that the logs and other resources collected are legitimate. This technique can be useful in verifying that an attack has occurred.

authentication   The means of verifying that someone is who they say they are.

Authentication Header (AH)   A header used to provide connectionless integrity and data origin authentication for IP datagrams and to provide protection against replays.

availability   The ability of a resource to be accessed, often expressed as a time period. Many networks limit users' ability to access network resources to working hours, as a security precaution.

B

back door (backdoor)   An opening left in a program application (usually by the developer) that allows additional access to data. Typically, these are created for debugging purposes and aren't documented. Before the product ships, the back doors are closed; when they aren't closed, security loopholes exist.

Back Orifice   Originally created as a support tool, it is now well known as an illicit server program that can be used to gain access to Windows NT/2000 servers and take control.

backup   A usable copy of data made to media. Ideally, the backup is made to removable media and stored for recovery should anything happen to the original data.

backup plan   A documented plan governing backup situations.

backup policy   A written policy detailing the frequency of backups and the location of storage media.

Bell La-Padula model   A model designed for the military to address the storage and protection of classified information. This model is specifically designed to prevent unauthorized access to classified information. The model prevents the user from accessing information that has a higher security rating than they are authorized to access. It also prevents information from being written to a lower level of security.

best practices   A set of rules governing basic operations.

BGP   *See* Border Gateway Protocol (BGP).

BIA   *See* Business Impact Analysis (BIA).

Biba model   A model similar in concept to the Bell La-Padula model but more concerned with information integrity (an area the Bell La-Padula model doesn't address). In this model, there is no write up or read down. If you're assigned access to top-secret information, you can't read secret information or write to any level higher than the level to which you're authorized. This model keeps higher-level information pure by preventing less-reliable information from being intermixed with it.

biometric device   A device that can authenticate an individual based on a physical characteristic.

biometrics   The science of identifying a person by using one or more of their features. The feature can be a thumbprint, a retinal scan, or any other biological trait.

BIOS   The basic input/output system for an IBM-based PC. It is the firmware that allows the computer to boot.

birthday attack   A probability method of finding collision in hash functions.

Blowfish   A type of symmetric block cipher created by Bruce Schneier.

boot sector   Also known as the Master Boot Record (MBR). The first sector of the hard disk, where the program that boots the operating system resides. It's a popular target for viruses.

Border Gateway Protocol (BGP)   An ISP protocol that allows routers to share information about routes with each other.

border router   A router used to translate from LAN framing to WAN framing.

bot   An automated software program that collects information on the Web. For example, the Googlebot collects website information for the Google index. Bots can be used for malicious purposes as well.

brute force attack   A type of attack that relies purely on trial and error.

buffer overflow attack   A type of denial of service (DoS) attack that occurs when more data is put into a buffer than it can hold, thereby overflowing it (as the name implies).

Business Continuity Planning (BCP)   A contingency plan that allows a business to keep running in the event of a disruption to vital resources.

Business Impact Analysis (BIA)   A study of the possible impact if a disruption to a business's vital resources were to occur.

C

CA   *See* certificate authority (CA).

Carlisle Adams Stafford Tavares (CAST)   A type of symmetric block cipher defined by RFC 2144.

CAST   *See* Carlisle Adams Stafford Tavares (CAST).

CC   *See* Common Criteria (CC).

CCRA   *See* Common Criteria Recognition Agreement (CCRA).

central office   The primary office from which most resources extend.

certificate   A digital entity that establishes who you are and is often used with e-commerce. It contains your name and other identifying data.

certificate authority (CA)   An issuer of digital certificates (which are then used for digital signatures or key pairs).

certificate policies   Policies governing the use of certificates.

Certificate Practice Statement (CPS)   The principles and procedures employed in the issuing and managing of certificates.

certificate revocation   The act of making a certificate invalid.

Certificate Revocation List (CRL)   A list of digital certificate revocations that must be regularly downloaded to stay current.

chain of custody   The log of the history of evidence that has been collected.

Challenge Handshake Authentication Protocol (CHAP)   A protocol that challenges a system to verify identity. CHAP is an improvement over Password Authentication Protocol (PAP) in which one-way hashing is incorporated into a three-way handshake. RFC 1334 applies to both PAP and CHAP.

change documentation   Documentation required to make a change in the scope of any particular item. In the realm of project management, a change document is a formal document requiring many signatures before key elements of the project can be modified.

CHAP   *See* Challenge Handshake Authentication Protocol (CHAP).

checkpoint   A certain action or moment in time that is used to perform a check. It allows a restart to begin at the last point the data was saved as opposed to from the beginning.

checksum   A hexadecimal value computed from transmitted data that is used in error-checking routines.

cipher   *See* cryptographic algorithm.

circuit switching   A switching method where a dedicated connection between the sender and receiver is maintained throughout the conversation.

Clark-Wilson model   An integrity model for creating a secure architecture.

clear text   Unencrypted text that can be read with any editor.

client   The part of a client/server network where the computing is usually done. In a typical setting, a client uses the server for remote storage, backups, or security (such as a firewall).

client/server network   A server-centric network in which all resources are stored on a file server and processing power is distributed among workstations and the file server.

clipper chip   An early encryption system from the NSA for civilian use; it was a hardware implementation of the skipjack encryption algorithm.

clustering   A method of balancing loads and providing fault tolerance.

coax   A type of cabling used in computer networks.

code escrow   The storage and conditions for release of source code provided by a vendor, partner, or other party.

cold site   A physical site that has all the resources necessary to enable an organization to use it if the main site is inaccessible (destroyed). Commonly, plans call for turning to a cold site within a certain number of hours after the loss of the main site.

collection of evidence   The means and orderly fashion by which evidence is collected, identified, and marked.

collusion   An agreement between individuals to commit fraud or deceit.

Common Criteria (CC)   A document of specifications detailing security evaluation methods for IT products and systems.

Common Criteria Recognition Agreement (CCRA)   A set of standards, formerly known as the Mutual Recognition Agreement (MRA), that defines Evaluation Assurance Levels (EALs).

Common Gateway Interface (CGI)   An older form of scripting that was used extensively in early web systems.

companion virus   A virus that creates a new program that runs in place of an expected program of the same name.

compartmentalization   Standards that support a nonhierarchical security classification.

confidentiality   Assurance that data remains private and no one sees it except for those expected to see it.

configuration management   The administration of setup and changes to configurations.

connectionless   Type of communications between two hosts that have no previous session established for synchronizing sent data. The data isn't acknowledged at the receiving end. This method can allow data loss. Within the TCP/IP suite, User Datagram Protocol (UDP) is used for connectionless communication.

connection-oriented   Type of communications between two hosts that have a previous session established for synchronizing sent data. The receiving PC acknowledges the data. This method allows for guaranteed delivery of data between PCs. Within the TCP/IP suite, TCP is used for connection-oriented communications.

cookie   A plain-text file stored on your machine that contains information about you (and your preferences) and is used by a database server.

CPS   *See* Certificate Practice Statement (CPS).

cracker   *See* hacker.

CRC   *See* cyclical redundancy check (CRC).

critical business functions   Functions on which the livelihood of the company depends.

CRL   *See* Certificate Revocation List (CRL).

cryptanalysis   The study and practice of finding weaknesses in ciphers.

cryptanalyst   A person who does cryptanalysis.

cryptographer   A person who participates in the study of cryptographic algorithms.

cryptographic algorithm   A symmetric algorithm, also known as a cipher, used to encrypt and decrypt data.

cryptography   The field of mathematics focused on encrypting and decrypting data.

custodian   An individual responsible for maintaining the data, and the integrity of it, within their area.

cyclical redundancy check (CRC)   An error-checking method in data communications that runs a formula against data before transmission. The sending station then appends the resultant value (called a checksum) to the data and sends it. The receiving station uses the same formula on the data. If the receiving station doesn't get the same checksum result for the calculation, it considers the transmission invalid, rejects the frame, and asks for retransmission.

D

DAC   *See* Discretionary Access Control (DAC).

data integrity   A quality that provides a level of confidence that data won't be jeopardized and will be kept secret.

Data Link layer   The second layer of the Open Systems Interconnection (OSI) model. It describes the physical topology of a network.

data packet   A unit of data sent over a network. A packet includes a header, addressing information, and the data itself.

data repository   A centralized storage location for data, such as a database.

data source   Where data originates.

datagram   A Layer 3, User Datagram Protocol (UDP) packet descriptor.

DDoS attack   *See* distributed denial of service (DDoS) attack.

decryption   The process of converting encrypted data back into its original form.

default gateway   The router to which all packets are sent when the workstation doesn't know where the destination station is or when it can't find the destination station on the local segment.

demilitarized zone (DMZ)   An area for placing web and other servers that serve the general public outside the firewall, therefore, isolating them from internal network access.

denial of service (DoS) attack   A type of attack that prevents any users—even legitimate ones—from using a system.

destination port number   A portion of a complete address of a PC to which data is being sent from a sending PC. The port portion allows for the demultiplexing of data to be sent to a specific application.

detection   The act of noticing an irregularity as it occurs.

DHCP   *See* Dynamic Host Configuration Protocol (DHCP).

dictionary attack   The act of attempting to crack passwords by testing them against a list of dictionary words. With today's powerful computers, an attacker can combine one of many available automated password-cracking utilities with several large dictionaries or "wordlists" and crack huge numbers of passwords in a matter of minutes. Any password based on any dictionary word is vulnerable to such an attack.

differential backup   A type of backup that includes only new files or files that have changed since the last full backup. Differential backups differ from incremental backups in that they don't clear the archive bit upon their completion.

Diffie-Hellman   An asymmetric standard for exchanging keys. This cryptographic algorithm is used primarily to send secret keys across public networks. The process isn't used to encrypt or decrypt messages; it's used merely for the transmission of keys in a secure manner.

digital signature   An asymmetrically encrypted signature whose sole purpose is to authenticate the sender.

directory   A network database that contains a listing of all network resources, such as users, printers, groups, and so on.

directory service   A network service that provides access to a central database of information, which contains detailed information about the resources available on a network.

direct-sequence (DS)   A method of communication between wireless receivers.

direct-sequence spread spectrum (DSSS)   A communications technology that is used to communicate in the 802.11 standard.

disaster recovery   The act of recovering data following a disaster that has destroyed it.

disaster recovery plan   A plan outlining the procedure by which data is recovered after a disaster.

Discretionary Access Control (DAC)   A method of restricting access to objects based on the identity of the subjects or the groups to which they belong.

disk mirroring   Technology that keeps identical copies of data on two disks to prevent the loss of data if one disk faults.

disk striping   Technology that enables writing data to multiple disks simultaneously in small portions called stripes. These stripes maximize use by having all the read/write heads working constantly. Different data is stored on each disk and isn't automatically duplicated (this means disk striping in and of itself doesn't provide fault tolerance).

disk striping with parity   A fault-tolerance solution of writing data across a number of disks and recording the parity on another. In the event any one disk fails, the data on it can be re-created by looking at the remaining data and computing parity to figure out the missing data.

distributed denial of service (DDoS) attack   A derivative of a DoS attack in which multiple hosts in multiple locations all focus on one target to reduce its availability to the public. *See* denial of service (DoS) attack.

DMZ   *See* demilitarized zone (DMZ).

DNS   *See* Domain Name Service (DNS).

DNS server   Any server that performs address resolution from a DNS fully qualified domain name (FQDN) to an IP address. *See also* Domain Name Service (DNS), Internet Protocol (IP).

DNS zone   An area in the DNS hierarchy that is managed as a single unit. *See also* Domain Name Service (DNS).

DoD Networking Model   A four-layer conceptual model describing how communications should take place between computer systems. The four layers are Process/Application, Host-to-Host, Internet, and Network Access.

domain   Within the Internet, a group of computers with shared traits and a common IP address set. A domain can also be a group of networked Windows computers that share a single SAM database. *See also* Security Accounts Manager (SAM).

Domain Name Service (DNS)   The network service used in TCP/IP networks that translates hostnames to IP addresses. *See also* Transmission Control Protocol/Internet Protocol (TCP/IP).

DoS attack   *See* denial of service (DoS) attack.

DS   *See* direct-sequence (DS).

dual-homed host   A host that resides on more than one network and possesses more than one physical network card.

dumb terminal   A keyboard and monitor that send keystrokes to a central processing computer (typically a mainframe or minicomputer) that returns screen displays to the monitor. The unit has no processing power of its own, hence the moniker "dumb."

Dumpster diving   Looking through trash for clues—often in the form of paper scraps—to find users' passwords and other pertinent information.

duplexed hard drives   Two hard drives to which identical information is written simultaneously. A dedicated controller card controls each drive. Used for fault tolerance.

duplicate servers   Two servers that are identical, for use in clustering.

Dynamic Host Configuration Protocol (DHCP)   A protocol used on a TCP/IP network to send client configuration data, including IP address, default gateway, subnet mask, and DNS configuration, to clients. DHCP uses a four-step process: Discover, Offer, Request, and Acknowledgement. *See also* default gateway, Domain Name Service (DNS), Transmission Control Protocol/Internet Protocol (TCP/IP).

dynamic packet filtering   A type of firewall used to accept or reject packets based on their contents.

dynamic routing   The use of route-discovery protocols to talk to other routers and find out what networks they are attached to. Routers that use dynamic routing send out special packets to request updates from the other routers on the network as well as to send their own updates.

dynamically allocated port   A TCP/IP port that is not constantly used but accessed by an application when needed.

E

EAL   *See* Evaluation Assurance Level (EAL).

eavesdropping   Any type of passive attack that intercepts data in an unauthorized manner—usually in order to find passwords. Cable sniffing, wiretapping, and man-in-the-middle attacks are eavesdropping attacks.

ECC   *See* Elliptic Curve Cryptosystem (ECC).

EF   *See* exposure factor (EF).

electromagnetic interference (EMI)   The interference that can occur during transmissions over copper cable because of electromagnetic energy outside the cable. The result is degradation of the signal.

Elliptic Curve Cryptosystem (ECC)   A type of public key cryptosystem that requires a shorter key length than many other cryptosystems (including the de facto industry standard, RSA).

EMI   *See* electromagnetic interference (EMI).

Encapsulating Security Payload (ESP)   A header used to provide a mix of security services in IPv4 and IPv6. ESP can be used alone or in combination with the IP Authentication Header (AH).

encoding   The process of translating data into signals that can be transmitted on a transmission medium.

encryption   The process of converting data into a form that makes it less likely to be usable to anyone intercepting it if they can't decrypt it.

encryption key   A string of alphanumeric characters used to decrypt encrypted data.

enticement   The process of luring someone.

entrapment   The process of encouraging an attacker to perform an act, even if they don't want to do it.

enumeration   An attempt to gain information about a network by specifically targeting network resources, users and groups, and applications running on the system.

escalation   The act of moving something up in priority. Often, when an incident is escalated, it's brought to the attention of the next highest supervisor. *See also* privilege escalation.

Ethernet   A shared-media network architecture. It operates at the Physical and Data Link layers of the Open Systems Interconnection (OSI) model. As the media access method, it uses baseband signaling over either a bus or a star topology. The cabling used in Ethernet networks can be coax, twisted-pair, wireless, or fiber-optic.

Ethernet address   *See* MAC address.

Evaluation Assurance Level (EAL)   A level of assurance, expressed as a numeric value, based on standards set by the Common Criteria Recognition Agreement (CCRA).

event   Any noticeable action or occurrence.

exposure factor (EF)   A calculation of how much data (or other assets) could be lost from a single occurrence. If all the data on the network could be jeopardized by a single attack, the exposure factor is 100 percent.

external threat   A threat that originates from outside the company.

extranet   Web (or similar) services set up in a private network to be accessed internally and by select external entities, such as vendors and suppliers.

extrusion   Examining data leaving a network for signs of malicious traffic.

F

fail-over/failover   The process of reconstructing a system or switching over to other systems when a failure is detected.

fail-over device   A device that comes online when another fails.

fail-over server   A hot-site backup system in which the fail-over server is connected to the primary server. A heartbeat is sent from the primary server to the backup server. If the heartbeat stops, the fail-over system starts and takes over. Thus, the system doesn't go down even if the primary server isn't running.

false positive   A flagged event that isn't really an event and has been falsely triggered.

Faraday cage   An electrically conductive wire mesh or other conductor woven into a "cage" that surrounds a room and prevents electromagnetic signals from entering or leaving the room through the walls.

fault-resistant network   A network that is up and running at least 99 percent of the time or that is down less than 8 hours a year.

fault tolerance   The ability to withstand a fault (failure) without losing data.

fault-tolerant network   A network that can recover from minor errors.

Federal Information Processing Standard (FIPS)   An agreed-upon standard published under the Information Technology Management Reform Act. The secretary of commerce approves the standards after they're developed by the National Institute of Standards and Technology (NIST) for federal computer systems.

File Transfer Protocol (FTP)   TCP/IP and software that permit transferring files between computer systems and utilize clear-text passwords. Because FTP has been implemented on numerous types of computer systems, files can be transferred between disparate computer systems (for example, a personal computer and a minicomputer). *See also* Transmission Control Protocol/Internet Protocol (TCP/IP).

FIPS   *See* Federal Information Processing Standard (FIPS).

fire suppression   The act of stopping a fire and preventing it from spreading.

firewall   A combination of hardware and software that protects a network from attack by hackers who could gain access through public networks, including the Internet.

footprinting   The process of systematically identifying the network and its security posture.

forensics   In terms of security, the act of looking at all the data at your disposal to try to figure out who gained unauthorized access and the extent of that access.

frequency-hopping spread spectrum (FHSS)   A communications technology used to communicate in the 802.11 standard. FHSS accomplishes communication by hopping the transmission over a range of predefined frequencies.

FTP   *See* File Transfer Protocol (FTP).

FTP proxy   A server that uploads and downloads files from another server on behalf of a workstation.

full backup   A backup that copies all data to the archive medium.

full distribution   An information classification stating that the data so classified is available to anyone.

G

Gramm-Leach-Bliley Act   A government act containing rules on privacy of consumer finance information.

Grandfather, Father, Son   One of the most popular methods of backup tape rotation. Three sets of tapes are rotated in this method. The most recent backup after the full backup is the Son. As newer backups are made, the Son becomes the Father and the Father, in turn, becomes the Grandfather. At the end of each month, a full backup is performed on all systems. This backup is stored in an off-site facility for a period of one year. Each monthly backup replaces the monthly backup from the previous year. Weekly or daily incremental backups are performed and stored until the next full backup occurs. This full backup is then stored off site, and the weekly or daily backup tapes are reused.

H

hacker   Generally used to refer to someone who gains access to a system, software, or hardware without permission. Also can be called a cracker.

handshake   The process of agreeing to communicate and share data. TCP uses a three-way handshake to establish connections, and part of this process can be exploited by certain types of attacks.

hardening   The process of making an entity, usually an operating system, more secure by closing known holes and addressing known security issues.

hash/hashing   The process of transforming characters into other characters that represent (but are not) the originals. Traditionally, the results are smaller and more secure than the original.

hash value   A single number used to represent an original piece of data.

Health Insurance Portability and Accountability Act (HIPAA)   An act that addresses security and privacy of health-related data.

H-IDS   *See* host-based IDS (H-IDS).

high availability   A clustering solution to provide resource reliability and availability.

hijacking (TCP/IP hijacking)   *See* man-in-the-middle attack.

HIPAA   *See* Health Insurance Portability and Accountability Act (HIPAA).

HIPS   *See* host-based IPS (H-IPS).

hoax   Typically an e-mail message warning of something that isn't true, such as the outbreak of a new virus. The hoax can send users into a panic and cause more harm than the virus.

honeypot (also known as Honey pot)   A bogus system set up to attract and slow down a hacker. A honeypot can also be used to learn of the hacking techniques and methods that hackers employ.

host   Any network device with a TCP/IP network address.

host-based IDS (H-IDS)   An intrusion detection system that is host based. The alternative is network based.

host-based IPS (H-IPS)   An intrusion prevention system that is host based. To prevent the intrusion, it must first detect it (thus making it a superset of H-IDS) and then act accordingly.

hostile code   Any code that behaves in a way other than in the best interest of the user and the security of data.

host-to-host   Describes communication that occurs between hosts.

hot fix/hotfix   Another word for a patch. When Microsoft rolls a bunch of hotfixes together, they become known as a service pack.

hot site   A location that can provide operations within hours of a failure.

HTML   *See* Hypertext Markup Language (HTML).

HTTP   *See* Hypertext Transfer Protocol (HTTP).

HTTPS   *See* Hypertext Transfer Protocol (Secure).

HVAC   A common acronym used for *heating, ventilation,* and *air conditioning.*

Hypertext Markup Language (HTML)   A set of codes used to format text and graphics that will be displayed in a browser. The codes define how data will be displayed.

Hypertext Transfer Protocol (HTTP)   The protocol used for communication between a web server and a web browser.

Hypertext Transfer Protocol (Secure)   Also known as HTTPS. A combination of HTTP with Secure Sockets Layer (SSL) to make for a secure connection. It uses port 443 by default.

I

IAB   *See* Internet Architecture Board (IAB).

IANA   *See* Internet Assigned Numbers Authority (IANA).

ICMP   *See* Internet Control Message Protocol (ICMP).

ICMP attack   An attack that occurs by triggering a response from the Internet Control Message Protocol (ICMP) when it responds to a seemingly legitimate maintenance request. *See also* Internet Control Message Protocol (ICMP).

identification and authentication (I&A)   A two-step process of identifying a person (usually when they log on) and authenticating them by challenging their claim to access a resource.

IDS   *See* intrusion detection system (IDS).

IEEE   *See* Institute of Electrical and Electronics Engineers, Inc. (IEEE).

IEEE 802.10 LAN/MAN Security   A series of guidelines dealing with various aspects of network security.

IEEE 802.11   A family of protocols that provides for wireless communications using radio-frequency transmissions.

IEEE 802.11 Wireless LAN   Defines the standards for implementing wireless technologies such as infrared and spread-spectrum radio.

IETF   *See* Internet Engineering Task Force (IETF).

IGMP   *See* Internet Group Management Protocol (IGMP).

illicit server   An application/program that shouldn't be there but is operating on the network, and one that is commonly used to gain unauthorized control by allowing someone to bypass normal authentication. NetBus is one of the best-known examples of an illicit server.

IM   *See* instant messaging (IM).

IMAP   *See* Internet Message Access Protocol (IMAP).

incident   An attempt to violate a security policy, a successful penetration, a compromise of a system, or unauthorized access to information.

incident response   How an organization responds to an incident.

incident response plan (IRP)   A policy that defines how an organization will respond to an incident.

incident response team (IRT)   Also known as a Computer Security Incident Response Team (CSIRT). The group of individuals responsible for responding when a security breach has occurred.

incremental backup   A type of backup in which only new files or files that have changed since the last full backup or the last incremental backup are included. Incremental backups clear the archive bit on files upon their completion.

information classification   The process of determining what information is accessible to what parties and for what purposes.

information classification policies   Written policies detailing dissemination of information.

information destruction policies   Policies that define how information is destroyed when it has reached the end of its useful life.

Information Flow model   A model concerned with all the properties of information flow, not just the direction of the flow.

information policies   Policies governing the various aspects of information security. Information policies include access, classifications, marking and storage, and the transmission and destruction of sensitive information. The development of information policies is critical to security.

information retention   A designation of how long data is retained and any other significant considerations about information.

information security   Security practices applied to information.

infrastructure   The hardware and software necessary to run your network.

infrastructure security   Security on the hardware and software necessary to run your network.

instant messaging (IM)   Immediate communication that can be sent back and forth between users who are currently logged on. From a security standpoint, there are risks associated with giving out information via IM that can be used in social engineering attacks; in addition, attachments sent can contain viruses.

Institute of Electrical and Electronics Engineers, Inc. (IEEE)   An international organization that sets standards for various electrical and electronics issues.

Integrated Services Digital Network (ISDN)   A telecommunications standard that is used to digitally send voice, data, and video signals over the same lines.

integrity   *See* data integrity.

interception   The process of covertly obtaining information not meant for you. Interception can be an active or passive process.

internal information   Information intended to remain within an organization.

internal threat   A threat that arises from within an organization.

International Data Encryption Algorithm (IDEA)   An algorithm that uses a 128-bit key. This product is similar in speed and capability to Digital Encryption Standard (DES), but it's more secure. IDEA is used in Pretty Good Privacy (PGP).

International Organization for Standardization (ISO)   The standards organization that developed the Open Systems Interconnection (OSI) model. This model provides a guideline for how communications occur between computers.

International Telecommunications Union (ITU)   Organization responsible for communications standards, spectrum management, and the development of communications infrastructures in underdeveloped nations.

Internet   A global network made up of a large number of individual networks that are interconnected and use TCP/IP. *See also* Transmission Control Protocol/Internet Protocol (TCP/IP).

Internet Architecture Board (IAB)   The committee that oversees management of the Internet. It's made up of two subcommittees: the Internet Engineering Task Force (IETF) and the Internet Research Task Force (IRTF). *See also* Internet Engineering Task Force (IETF) and Internet Research Task Force (IRTF).

Internet Assigned Numbers Authority (IANA)   The organization responsible for governing IP addresses.

Internet Control Message Protocol (ICMP)   A message and management protocol for TCP/IP. The Ping utility uses ICMP. *See also* Ping, Transmission Control Protocol/Internet Protocol (TCP/IP).

Internet Engineering Task Force (IETF)   An international organization that works under the Internet Architecture Board to establish standards and protocols relating to the Internet. *See also* Internet Architecture Board (IAB).

Internet Group Management Protocol (IGMP)   A protocol used for multicasting operations across the Internet.

Internet layer   The network layer responsible for routing, IP addressing, and packaging.

Internet Message Access Protocol (IMAP)   A protocol with a store-and-forward capability. It can also allow messages to be stored on an e-mail server instead of downloaded to the client.

Internet Protocol (IP)   The protocol in the TCP/IP suite responsible for network addressing. *See also* Transmission Control Protocol/Internet Protocol (TCP/IP).

Internet Research Task Force (IRTF)   An international organization that works under the Internet Architecture Board to research new Internet technologies. *See also* Internet Architecture Board (IAB).

Internet service provider (ISP)   A company that provides direct access to the Internet for home and business computer users.

Internet Society (ISOC)   A professional membership group composed primarily of Internet experts. It oversees a number of committees and groups, including the Internet Engineering Task Force (IETF).

Internetwork Packet Exchange (IPX)   A connectionless, routable network protocol based on the Xerox XNS architecture. It's the default protocol for versions of NetWare before NetWare 5. It operates at the Network layer of the Open Systems Interconnection (OSI) model and is responsible for addressing and routing packets to workstations or servers on other networks.

intranet   Web (or similar) services set up in a private network to be accessed internally only.

intrusion   The act of entering a system without authorization to do so.

intrusion detection system (IDS)   Tools that identify and respond to attacks using defined rules or logic. An IDS can be network based or host based.

intrusion detector   The item/application performing intrusion detection. *See also* intrusion detection system (IDS).

IP proxy   A server that acts as a go-between for clients accessing the Internet. All communications look as if they originated from a proxy server because the IP address of the user making a request is hidden. Also known as Network Address Translation (NAT).

IP Security (IPSec)   A set of protocols that enable encryption, authentication, and integrity over IP. IPSec is commonly used with virtual private networks (VPNs) and operates at Layer 3.

IP spoofing   An attack during which a hacker tries to gain access to a network by pretending their interface has the same network address as the internal network.

IPSec   *See* IP Security (IPSec).

IPX   *See* Internetwork Packet Exchange (IPX).

ISO 17799   A 10-part plan designed to provide a generic security audit on the best practices of security for virtually all aspects of your IT department.

ISP   *See* Internet service provider (ISP).

J

JavaScript   A programming language that allows access to system resources of the system running the script. These scripts can interface with all aspects of an operating system just like programming languages, such as the C language.

journaling   The ability of a filesystem to use a log file of all changes and transactions that have occurred within a set period of time (for example, the last few hours). If a crash occurs, the operating system can look at the log files to see what transactions have been committed and which ones have not.

K

KDC   *See* Key Distribution Center (KDC).

KEA   *See* Key Exchange Algorithm (KEA).

Kerberos   An authentication scheme that uses tickets (unique keys) embedded within messages. Named after the three-headed guard dog who stood at the gates of Hades in Greek mythology.

key/certificate life cycle   The time during which the processes of a key or certificate take place.

Key Distribution Center (KDC)   An organization/facility that generates keys for users.

key escrow agency   An agency that stores keys for the purpose of law-enforcement access.

Key Exchange Algorithm (KEA)   A method of offering mutual authentication and establishing data encryption keys.

key generation   The act of creating keys for use by users.

key suspension   The temporary deferment of a key for a period of time (such as for a leave of absence).

Keyed-Hash Message Authentication Code (HMAC)   "A mechanism for message authentication using cryptographic hash functions" per the draft of the Federal Information Processing Standard (FIPS) publication. Addressed in RFC 2104.

L

L2F   *See* Layer 2 Forwarding (L2F).

L2TP   *See* Layer 2 Tunneling Protocol (L2TP).

LAN   *See* local area network (LAN).

LANMAN   An old authentication method used with early Windows-based systems.

latency   The wait time between the call for an action or activity and the actual execution of that action.

lattice   The concept that access differs at different levels. Often used in discussion with the Biba and Bell La-Padula models as well as with cryptography to differentiate between security levels based upon user/group labels.

Layer 2 Forwarding (L2F)   A tunneling protocol often used with virtual private networks (VPNs). L2F was developed by Cisco.

Layer 2 Tunneling Protocol (L2TP) A tunneling protocol that adds functionality to Point-to-Point Protocol (PPP). This protocol was created by Microsoft and Cisco and is often used with virtual private networks (VPNs).

LCP *See* Link Control Protocol (LCP).

LDAP *See* Lightweight Directory Access Protocol (LDAP).

Lightweight Directory Access Protocol (LDAP) A set of protocols that was derived from X.500 and operates at port 389.

limited distribution Describes information that isn't intended for release to the public. This category of information isn't secret, but it's private.

Link Control Protocol (LCP) The protocol used to establish, configure, and test the link between a client and PPP host. *See also* Point-to-Point Protocol (PPP).

local area network (LAN) A network that is restricted to a single building, group of buildings, or even a single room. A LAN can have one or more servers.

local registration authority (LRA) An authority used to identify or establish the identity of an individual for certificate issuance.

logic bomb Any code that is hidden within an application and causes something unexpected to happen based on some criteria being met. For example, a programmer could create a program that always makes sure his name appears on the payroll roster; if it doesn't, then key files begin to be erased.

logs and inventories Tools used to help an organization know what is happening to its systems and assets. System logs tell what is happening with the systems in the network. Inventories refer to both the physical assets and the software assets a company owns.

M

M of N Control method A rule stating that in order to access the key server if *n* number of administrators have the ability to perform a process, *m* number of those administrators must authenticate for access to occur. M of N Control may involve physical presence.

MAC *See* Media Access Control (MAC), Mandatory Access Control (MAC), and message authentication code (MAC).

MAC address The address that is either assigned to a network card or burned into the network interface card (NIC). PCs use MAC addresses to keep track of one another and keep each other separate.

macro virus A software exploitation virus that works by using the macro feature included in many applications.

malicious code Any code that is meant to do harm.

Mandatory Access Control (MAC)   A security policy wherein labels are used to identify the sensitivity of objects. When a user attempts to access an object, the label is checked to see if access should be allowed (that is, whether the user is operating at the same sensitivity level). This policy is "mandatory," because labels are automatically applied to all data (and can be changed only by administrative action), as opposed to "discretionary" policies that leave it up to the user to decide whether to apply a label.

man-in-the-middle attack   An attack that occurs when someone/-thing that is trusted intercepts packets and retransmits them to another party. Man-in-the-middle attacks have also been called TCP/IP hijacking in the past.

mantrap   A device, such as a small room, that limits access to one or a few individuals. Mantraps typically use electronic locks and other methods to control access.

mathematical attack   An attack focused on the encryption algorithm itself, the key mechanism, or any potential area of weakness in the algorithm.

mean time between failure (MTBF)   The measure of the anticipated incidence of failure of a system or component.

mean time to repair (MTTR)   The measurement of how long it takes to repair a system or component once a failure occurs.

media   Any storage medium.

Media Access Control (MAC)   A sublayer of the Data Link layer of the Open Systems Interconnection (OSI) model that controls the way multiple devices use the same media channel. It controls which devices can transmit and when they can transmit.

message authentication code (MAC)   A common method of verifying integrity. The MAC is derived from the message and a secret key.

message digest   The signature area within a message.

Message Digest Algorithm (MDA)   An algorithm that creates a hash value. The hash value is also used to help maintain integrity. There are several versions of MD; the most common are MD5, MD4, and MD2.

Microsoft Challenge Handshake Authentication Protocol (MSCHAP)   An implementation of the Challenge Handshake Authentication Protocol (CHAP) common in Microsoft's Windows-based operating systems. The latest version, and the only one supported in Windows Vista, is MSCHAPv2.

misuse-detection IDS (MD-IDS)   A method of evaluating attacks based on attack signatures and audit trails.

modem   A communications device that converts digital computer signals into analog tones for transmission over the Public Switched Telephone Network (PSTN) and converts them back to digital upon reception. The word *modem* is an acronym for *modulator/demodulator*.

modification attack   An attack that modifies information on your system.

MSCHAP   *See* Microsoft Challenge Handshake Authentication Protocol (MSCHAP).

multicasting   Sending data to more than one address.

multi-factor   The term employed anytime more than one factor must be considered.

multipartite virus   A virus that attacks a system in more than one way.

N

NAC   *See* network access control (NAC).

NAT   Network Address Translation. *See* IP proxy.

National Computing Security Center (NCSC)   The agency that developed the Trusted Computer System Evaluation Criteria (TCSEC) and the Trusted Network Interpretation Environmental Guideline (TNIEG).

National Institute of Standards and Technology (NIST)   An agency (formerly known as the National Bureau of Standards [NBS]) that has been involved in developing and support-ing standards for the U.S. government for over 100 years. NIST has become involved in cryptography standards, systems, and technology in a variety of areas. It's primarily con-cerned with governmental systems, where it exercises a great deal of influence.

National Security Agency (NSA)   The U.S. government agency responsible for protecting U.S. communications and producing foreign intelligence information. It was established by presidential directive in 1952 as a separately organized agency within the Department of Defense (DoD).

NCP   *See* Network Control Protocol (NCP).

NCSC   *See* National Computing Security Center (NCSC).

NDPS   *See* Novell Distributed Print Services (NDPS).

NDS   *See* NetWare Directory Services (NDS).

need-to-know   A method of information dissemination based on passing information only to those who need to know it.

NetBIOS Extended User Interface (NetBEUI)   A protocol used to transport Network Basic Input Output System (NetBIOS) traffic in a LAN.

NetWare Core Protocol (NCP)   The upper-layer NetWare protocol that functions on top of IPX and provides NetWare resource access to workstations. *See also* Internetwork Packet Exchange (IPX).

NetWare Directory Services (NDS)   A directory management service used to manage all of the resources in a network. In later versions, the acronym was changed to Novell Directory Services, and the service is now known as eDirectory. NDS provides a database of all of the network objects or resources.

NetWare Link State Protocol (NLSP)   A protocol that gathers routing information based on the link-state routing method. Its precursor is the Routing Information Protocol (RIP). NLSP is a more efficient routing protocol than RIP.

NetWare Loadable Module (NLM)   A component used to provide a NetWare server with additional services and functionality. Unneeded services can be unloaded, thereby conserving memory.

network   A group of devices connected by some means for the purpose of sharing information or resources.

network access control (NAC)   The set of standards defined by the network for clients attempting to access it. Usually, NAC requires that clients be virus free and adhere to specified policies before allowing them on the network.

Network Address Translation (NAT)   *See* IP proxy.

network attached storage   Storage, such as hard drives, attached to a network for the purpose of storing data for clients on the network. Network attached storage is commonly used for backing up data.

network-based IPS (N-IPS)   An intrusion prevention system that is network based. To prevent the intrusion, it must first detect it (thus making it a superset of IDS), and then act accordingly.

Network Basic Input Output System (NetBIOS)   The native protocol of Windows PCs. It provides a 15-character naming convention for resources on the network. NetBIOS is a broadcast-oriented network protocol in that all traffic is available to all devices in a LAN. The protocol can be transported over NetBIOS Extended User Interface (NetBEUI), TCP/IP, or Internetwork Packet Exchange/Sequenced Packet Exchange (IPX/SPX).

Network Control Protocol (NCP)   The protocol Point-to-Point Protocol (PPP) employs for encapsulating network traffic.

Network File System (NFS)   A protocol that enables users to access files on remote computers as if the files were local.

network interface card (NIC)   A physical device that connects computers and other network equipment to the transmission medium.

Network Interface layer   The lowest level of the TCP/IP suite; it is responsible for placing and removing packets on the physical network.

Network layer   The third layer of the OSI model, it is responsible for logical addressing and translating logical names into physical addresses. This layer also controls the routing of data from source to destination as well as the building and dismantling of packets. *See also* Open Systems Interconnection (OSI) model.

Network Operations Center (NOC)   A single, centralized area for network monitoring and administrative control of systems.

network operating system (NOS)   The software enabling networking; NOS can be on a LAN or WAN.

network sniffer   A device that has access to the signaling on the network cable.

network-based IDS (N-IDS)   An approach to an intrusion detection system (IDS), it attaches the system to a point in the network where it can monitor and report on all network traffic.

network-based IPS (N-IPS)   *See* host-based IPS (H-IPS).

New Technology LAN Manager (NTLM)   The protocol that Microsoft Windows–based operating systems use for authentication with remote access protocols.

NFS   *See* Network File System (NFS).

NIC   *See* network interface card (NIC).

nonessential service   A service that isn't necessary to keep the server operating at the expected level in its expected role.

Noninterference model   A model intended to ensure that higher-level security functions don't interfere with lower-level functions.

nonrepudiation   Verifying (by whatever means) that data was seen by an intended party. It makes sure they received the data and can't repudiate (dispute) that it arrived.

notification   The act of being alerted to an event.

notification policies   A set of rules about what triggers notification.

Novell Distributed Print Services (NDPS)   A Novell-designed printing system that uses NetWare Directory Services (NDS), known as eDirectory in NetWare 6, to install and manage printers. NDPS supports automatic network printer installation, automatic distribution of client printer drivers, and centralized printer management without the use of print queues.

NSA   *See* National Security Agency (NSA).

O

offsite storage   Storing data off site, usually in a secure location.

one-tier model   A model in which the database and applications exist on the same system.

one-time pad   Words added to values during authentication. The message to be encrypted is added to this random text before hashing.

onsite storage   Storing backup data at the same site as the servers on which the original data resides.

Open Shortest Path First (OSPF)   A link-state routing protocol used in IP networks.

Open Systems Interconnection (OSI) model   A model defined by the ISO to categorize the process of communication between computers in terms of seven layers. The seven layers are Application, Presentation, Session, Transport, Network, Data Link, and Physical. *See also* International Organization for Standardization (ISO).

operational security   Security as it relates to how an organization does things (operates).

operator   The person primarily responsible for the intrusion detection system (IDS).

OS hardening   The process of applying all security patches and fixes to an operating system to make it as secure as possible.

OSI model   *See* Open Systems Interconnection (OSI) model.

OSPF   *See* Open Shortest Path First (OSPF).

out-of-band method   A way to transmit the encryption key by using a method other than the one used to transmit the data. The key value is sent by letter, by courier, or by some other separate means.

OVAL   An acronym for Open Vulnerability and Assessment Language, it is a community standard for system analysis that focuses on testing, analyzing, and reporting.

owner   The person responsible for the current existence of a resource.

P

packet filtering   A firewall technology that accepts or rejects packets based on their content.

packet switching   The process of breaking messages into packets at the sending router for easier transmission over a WAN.

pad   A number of characters often added to data before an operation such as hashing takes place. Most often unique values, known as one-time pads, are added to make the resulting hash unique.

PAP   *See* Password Authentication Protocol (PAP).

partitioning   The process of breaking a network into smaller components that can be individually protected.

passive detection   A type of intruder detection that logs all network events to a file for an administrator to view later.

passive response   A nonactive response, such as logging. Passive response is the most common type of response to many intrusions. In general, passive responses are the easiest to develop and implement.

Password Authentication Protocol (PAP)   One of the simplest forms of authentication. Authentication is accomplished by sending the username and password to the server and having them verified. Passwords are sent as clear text and, therefore, can be easily seen if intercepted.

password guessing   Attempting to enter a password by guessing its value.

password history   A list of passwords that have already been used.

PAT   *See* Port Address Translation (PAT).

patch   A fix for a known software problem.

penetration   The act of gaining access.

perimeter security   Security set up on the outside of the network or server to protect it.

PGP   *See* Pretty Good Privacy (PGP).

phage virus   A virus that modifies and alters other programs and databases.

phishing   A form of social engineering in which you simply ask someone for a piece of information that you are missing by making it look as if it is a legitimate request. Commonly sent via e-mail.

phreaker   Someone who abuses phone systems, as opposed to data systems.

physical access control   Control access measures used to restrict physical access to the server(s).

physical barrier   An object, such as a locked door, used to restrict physical access to network components.

Physical layer   The first layer of the OSI model; controls the functional interface. *See also* Open Systems Interconnection (OSI) model.

physical port   On a computer, an interface where you can connect a device.

physical security   Security that guards the physical aspects of the network.

Ping   A TCP/IP utility used to test whether another host is reachable. An Internet Control Message Protocol (ICMP) request is sent to the host, which responds with a reply if it's reachable. The request times out if the host isn't reachable.

ping of death   A large Internet Control Message Protocol (ICMP) packet sent to overflow the remote host's buffer. A ping of death usually causes the remote host to reboot or hang.

Plain Old Telephone Service (POTS)   Standard telephone service, as opposed to other connection technologies like Digital Subscriber Line (DSL).

point-to-point   Network communication in which two devices have exclusive access to a network medium. For example, a printer connected to only one workstation is using a point-to-point connection.

Point-to-Point Protocol (PPP)   A full-duplex line protocol that supersedes Serial Line Internet Protocol (SLIP). It's part of the standard TCP/IP suite and is often used in dial-up connections.

Point-to-Point Tunneling Protocol (PPTP)   An extension to Point-to-Point Protocol (PPP) that is used in virtual private networks (VPNs). An alternative to PPTP is L2TP.

policies   Rules or standards governing usage.

polymorphic   An attribute of some viruses that allows them to mutate and appear differently each time they crop up. The mutations make it harder for virus scanners to detect (and react) to the viruses.

POP   *See* Post Office Protocol (POP).

POP3   *See* Post Office Protocol Version 3 (POP3).

port   Some kind of opening that allows network data to pass through.

Port Address Translation (PAT)   A means of translating between ports on a public and private network. Similar to Network Address Translation (NAT), which translates addresses between public and private.

port scanner   The item (physical or software) that scans a server for open ports that can be taken advantage of. Port scanning is the process of sending messages to ports to see which ones are available and which ones aren't.

postmortem   Anything that occurs "after the fact," such as an audit or review.

Post Office Protocol (POP)   An e-mail access program that can be used to retrieve e-mail from an e-mail server.

Post Office Protocol Version 3 (POP3)   The protocol used to download e-mail from an SMTP e-mail server to a network client. *See also* Simple Mail Transfer Protocol (SMTP).

POTS   *See* Plain Old Telephone Service (POTS).

power conditioner   A device that "conditions" the electrical supply to take out spikes and surges.

power system   A device that provides electrical power.

PPP   *See* Point-to-Point Protocol (PPP).

PPTP   *See* Point-to-Point Tunneling Protocol (PPTP).

Presentation layer   The sixth layer of the OSI model; responsible for formatting data exchange, such as graphic commands, and converting character sets. This layer is also responsible for data compression, data encryption, and data stream redirection. *See also* Open Systems Interconnection (OSI) model.

preservation of evidence   The process of controlling access to evidence within chain-of-custody measures, often by placing it in a controlled-access area with a single custodian responsible for all access.

Pretty Good Privacy (PGP)   An implementation of RSA encryption. *See also* RSA.

privacy   A state of security in which information isn't seen by unauthorized parties without the express permission of the party involved.

Private Branch Exchange (PBX)   A system that allows users to connect voice, data, pagers, networks, and almost any other application into a single telecommunications system. A PBX system allows an organization to be its own phone company.

private information   Information that isn't for public knowledge.

private key   An asymmetric encryption technology in which both the sender and the receiver have different keys. A public key is used to encrypt messages and the private key is used to decrypt them. *See also* public key.

private network   The part of a network that lies behind a firewall and isn't "seen" on the Internet. *See also* firewall.

privilege audit   An audit performed to verify that no user is accessing information, or able to access information, beyond the security level at which they should be operating.

privilege escalation   The result when a user obtains access to a resource they wouldn't normally be able to access. Privilege escalation can be done inadvertently, by running a program with Set User ID (SUID) or Set Group ID (SGID) permissions or by temporarily becoming another user (via su or sudo in Unix/Linux or RunAs in Windows 2000/2003).

process list   The list of processes currently running on a system. In Windows NT/2000, it can be seen with Task Manager; the ps command shows it in Unix/Linux. Viewing a process list is one of the first steps to take to look for rogue processes running on a server.

promiscuous mode   A mode wherein a network interface card (NIC) intercepts all traffic crossing the network wire and not just the traffic intended for it.

protocol analyzer   A software and hardware troubleshooting tool that is used to decode protocol information to try to determine the source of a network problem and to establish baselines.

protocols   Standards or rules.

proxy   A type of firewall that prevents direct communication between a client and a host by acting as an intermediary. *See also* firewall.

proxy cache server   An implementation of a web proxy. The server receives an HTTP request from a web browser and makes the request on behalf of the sending workstation. When the response comes, the proxy cache server caches a copy of the response locally. The next time someone makes a request for the same web page or Internet information, the proxy cache server can fulfill the request out of the cache instead of having to retrieve the resource from the Web.

proxy firewall   A proxy server that also acts as a firewall, blocking network access from external networks.

proxy server   A type of server that makes a single Internet connection and services requests on behalf of many users.

public information   Information that is publicly made available to all.

public key   A technology that uses two keys—a public key and a private key—to facilitate communication. The public key is used to encrypt a message to a receiver. *See also* private key.

Public Key Cryptography Standards (PKCS)   A set of voluntary standards created by RSA security and industry security leaders.

Public Key Infrastructure (PKI)   A two-key encryption system wherein messages are encrypted with a private key and decrypted with a public key.

Public Key Infrastructure X.509 (PKIX)   The Internet Engineering Task Force (IETF) working group developing standards and models for the Public Key Infrastructure (PKI) environment.

public network   The part of a network outside a firewall that is exposed to the public. *See also* firewall.

public key system   An encryption system employing a key that is known to users beyond the recipient.

Q

quantum cryptography   Cryptography based on changing the polarity of a photon. Quantum cryptography makes the process of interception difficult because any attempt to intercept the message changes the value of the message.

R

radio frequency (RF)   The part of the radio spectrum that a device uses.

radio frequency interference (RFI)   The byproduct of electrical processes, similar to electromagnetic interference. The major difference is that RFI is usually projected across a radio spectrum.

RADIUS   *See* Remote Authentication Dial-In User Service (RADIUS).

RAID   *See* Redundant Array of Independent (or Inexpensive) Disks (RAID).

RAID levels   The different types of RAID, such as RAID-0, RAID-1, and so on.

RAS   *See* Remote Access Server (RAS).

RBAC   *See* Role-Based Access Control (RBAC).

RC5   *See* Rivest Cipher 5 (RC5).

Redundant Array of Independent (or Inexpensive) Disks (RAID)   A configuration of multiple hard disks used to provide fault tolerance, should a disk fail, or gains in efficiency. Different levels of RAID exist.

registration authority (RA)   An organization that offloads some of the work from a certificate authority (CA). An RA system operates as a middleman in the process. The RA can distribute keys, accept registrations for the CA, and validate identities. The RA doesn't issue certificates; that responsibility remains with the CA.

relying party   The person receiving a certificate.

remote access protocol   Any networking protocol that is used to gain access to a network over public communication links.

remote access server (RAS)   A computer that has one or more modems installed to enable remote connections to the network.

Remote Authentication Dial-In User Service (RADIUS)   A mechanism that allows authentication of dial-in and other network connections. RADIUS is commonly used by Internet service providers (ISPs) and in the implementation of virtual private networks (VPNs).

replay attack   Any attack where the data is retransmitted repeatedly (often fraudulently or maliciously). In one such possibility, a user can replay a web session and visit sites intended only for the original user.

replication   The process of copying directory information to other servers to keep them all synchronized.

repository   A database or database server where the certificates are stored.

repudiation attack   An attack in which the intruder modifies information in a system.

Request for Comments (RFC)   A document creation process and a set of practices that originated in 1969 and is used for proposed changes to Internet standards.

response   How you react to an event.

restricted information   Information that isn't made available to all and to which access is granted based on some criteria.

retrovirus   A virus that attacks or bypasses the antivirus software installed on a computer.

reverse DNS   Using an IP address to find a domain name rather than using a domain name to find an IP address (normal DNS). Pointer (PTR) records are used for the reverse lookup, and often reverse DNS is used to authenticate incoming connections.

reverse engineering   The process of re-creating the functionality of an item by first deciding what the result is and then creating something from scratch that serves the same purpose.

revocation   The process of canceling credentials that have been lost or stolen (or are no longer valid). With certificates, revocation is accomplished with a Certificate Revocation List (CRL).

RIP   *See* Routing Information Protocol (RIP).

risk analysis   An evaluation of each risk that can be identified. Each risk should be outlined, described, and evaluated on the likelihood of it occurring.

risk assessment   An evaluation of how much risk you and your organization are willing to take. An assessment must be performed before any other actions—such as how much to spend on security in terms of dollars and manpower—can be decided.

Rivest Cipher 5 (RC5)   A cipher algorithm created by Ronald Rivest (for RSA) and known for its speed. It works through blocks of variable sizes using three phases: key expansion, encryption, and decryption.

roaming profile   A profile downloaded from a server at each logon. When a user logs out at the end of the session, changes are made and remembered for the next time the user logs on.

rogue server   An active Dynamic Host Configuration Protocol (DHCP) server that has been added to the network and is now leasing addresses to users instead of them obtaining an address from your server.

Role-Based Access Control (RBAC)   A type of control wherein the levels of security closely follow the structure of an organization. The role the person plays in the organization (accountant, salesman, and so on) corresponds to the level of security access they have to data.

rootkit   Software program that has the ability to obtain root-level access and hide certain things from the operating system.

route   The path to get to the destination from a source.

route cost   The number of router hops between the source and the destination in an internetwork.

router   A device that connects two or more networks and allows packets to be transmitted and received between them. A router determines the best path for data packets from source to destination.

routing   A function of the Network layer that involves moving data throughout a network. Data passes through several network subnetworks using routers that can select the path the data takes. *See also* router.

Routing Information Protocol (RIP)   A distance-vector route discovery protocol used by Internetwork Packet Exchange (IPX) and Internet Protocol (IP). IPX uses hops and ticks to determine the cost for a particular route. *See also* Internetwork Packet Exchange (IPX).

routing table   A table that contains information about the locations of other routers on the network and their distance from the current router.

RSA   One of the providers of cryptography systems to industry and government. RSA stands for the initials of the three founders of RSA Security Inc.: Rivest, Shamir, and Adleman. RSA maintains a list of standards for Public Key Cryptography Standards (PKCS).

RSA   A commercial company that produces encryption software. RSA stands for Rivest, Shamir, and Adleman, the founders of the company.

RSBAC   *See* Rule Set-Based Access Control (RSBAC).

Rule Set-Based Access Control (RSBAC)   An open-source access control framework for the Linux kernel that uses access control modules to implement Mandatory Access Control (MAC).

S

SAM   *See* Security Accounts Manager (SAM).

sandbox   A set of rules used when creating a Java applet that prevents certain functions when the applet is sent as part of a web page.

scanning   The process that attackers use to gather information about how a network is configured.

screened host   A router that is in front of a server on the private network. Typically, this server does packet filtering before reaching the firewall/proxy server that services the internal network.

secret key   *See* private key.

Secure Electronic Transaction (SET)   A protocol developed by Visa and MasterCard for secure credit card transactions. The protocol is becoming an accepted standard by many companies. SET provides encrypted credit card numbers over the Internet, and it's most suited to small amounts of data transmission.

Secure Hash Algorithm (SHA)   A one-way hash algorithm designed to ensure the integrity of a message.

Secure Hypertext Transfer Protocol (S-HTTP)   A protocol used for secure communications between a web server and a web browser.

Secure Shell (SSH)   A replacement for rlogin in UNIX that includes security. rlogin allowed one host to establish a connection with another with no real security being employed; SSH replaces it with slogin and digital certificates.

Secure Sockets Layer (SSL)   A protocol that secures messages by operating between the Application layer (HTTP) and the Transport layer.

Secure WLAN Protocol (SWP)   A method of securing wireless networks that is beginning to gain momentum and acceptance.

Security Accounts Manager (SAM)   A database within Windows NT–based operating systems that contains information about all users and groups and their associated rights and settings within a domain.

security audit   An audit of the system (host, network, and so on) for security vulnerabilities and holes.

security log   A log file used in Windows NT to keep track of security events specified by the domain's audit policy.

security policies   Rules set in place by a company to ensure the security of a network. These may include how often a password must be changed or how many characters a password should be.

security professionals   Individuals who make their living working with computer security.

security token   A piece of data that contains the rights and access privileges of the token bearer as part of the token.

security zone   A method of isolating a system from other systems or networks.

segment   A unit of data transmission found at the Transport layer of the Open Systems Interconnection (OSI) model and used by TCP.

sensor A device that collects data from the data source and passes it on to the analyzer.

separation of duties A set of policies designed to reduce the risk of fraud and prevent other losses in an organization.

sequence number A number used to determine the order in which parts of a packet are to be reassembled after the packet has been split into sections.

Sequenced Packet Exchange (SPX) A connection-oriented protocol that is part of the Internetwork Packet Exchange (IPX) protocol suite. It operates at the Transport layer of the OSI model. It initiates the connection between the sender and receiver, transmits the data, and then terminates the connection. *See also* Internetwork Packet Exchange (IPX), Open Systems Interconnection (OSI) model.

Serial Line Internet Protocol (SLIP) An older protocol that was used in early remote-access environments. SLIP was originally designed to connect Unix systems together in a dial-up environment, and it supports only serial communications.

server A computer that provides resources to the clients on the network.

server and client configuration A network in which the resources are located on a server and accessed by clients.

server authentication A process that requires the workstation to authenticate against the server.

service An item that adds functionality to a network by providing resources or doing tasks for other computers. In Windows-based operating systems, services include file and printer sharing for Microsoft or Novell networks.

service account An account created on a server for a user to perform special services, such as a backup operator, an account operator, and a server operator.

service-level agreement (SLA) An agreement that specifies performance requirements for a vendor. This agreement may use mean time before failure (MTBF) and mean time to repair (MTTR) as performance measures in the SLA.

service pack Operating system updates from Microsoft.

session key The agreed-upon (during connection) key used between a client and a server during a session. This key is generated by encrypting the server's digital ID (after validity has been established). The asymmetric key pair is then used to encrypt and verify the session key that is passed back and forth between client and server during the length of the connection.

Session layer The fifth layer of the OSI model. It determines how two computers establish, use, and end a session. Security authentication and network naming functions required for applications occur here. The Session layer establishes, maintains, and breaks dialogs between two stations. *See also* Open Systems Interconnection (OSI) model.

SHA   *See* Secure Hash Algorithm (SHA).

share-level security   A network security method that assigns passwords to individual files or other network resources (such as printers) instead of assigning rights to network resources to users. The passwords are then given to all users that need access to these resources. All resources are visible from anywhere in the network, and any user who knows the password for a particular network resource can make changes to it.

Shielded Twisted Pair (STP)   Network cabling media that has a shield, similar to coax, wrapped over the wires.

shoulder surfing   Watching someone when they enter their username/password/ sensitive data.

S-HTTP   *See* Secure Hypertext Transfer Protocol (S-HTTP).

signal   Transmission from one PC to another. A signal could be a notification to start a session or end a session.

signal encoding   The process whereby a protocol at the Physical layer receives information from the upper layers and translates all the data into signals that can be transmitted on a transmission medium.

signaling method   The process of transmitting data across the medium. Two types of signaling are digital and analog.

signed applet   An applet that doesn't run in the Java sandbox and has higher system access capabilities. Signed applets aren't usually downloaded from the Internet but are provided by in-house or custom programming efforts.

Simple Mail Transfer Protocol (SMTP)   A protocol for sending e-mail between SMTP servers.

Simple Network Management Protocol (SNMP)   The management protocol created for sending information about the health of the network-to-network management consoles.

single loss expectancy (SLE)   The cost of a single loss when it occurs. This loss can be a critical failure, or it can be the result of an attack.

single sign-on (SSO)   A relationship between the client and the network wherein the client is allowed to log on one time, and all resource access is based on that logon (as opposed to needing to log on to each individual server to access the resources there).

site survey   A generic site survey involves listening in on an existing wireless network using commercially available technologies. A wireless site survey, or wireless survey, is the process of planning and designing a wireless network, in particular an 802.11.

SLIP   *See* Serial Line Internet Protocol (SLIP).

SMTP *See* Simple Mail Transfer Protocol (SMTP).

SMTP relay A feature designed into many e-mail servers that allows them to forward e-mail to other e-mail servers. While the ability to act as a relay exists to allow networks to grow, the possibility exists for rogue servers to also participate.

smurf attack An attack in which large volumes of ICMP echo requests (pings) are broadcast to all other machines on the network and in which the source address of the broadcast system has been spoofed to appear as though it came from the target computer. When all the machines that received the broadcast respond, they flood the target with more data than it can handle.

snapshot backup A method of performing backups that creates a compressed file of a database as it exists at the moment, without taking the users offline. A snapshot backup can take the place of other backups. It's often run on mirrored servers, but the snapshot captures only the most recent version of files.

sniffer A physical device that listens in (sniffs) on network traffic and looks for items it can make sense of. There is a legitimate purpose for these devices: Administrators use them to analyze traffic. However, when they're used by sources other than the administrator, they become security risks.

sniffing Analyzing data to look for passwords and anything else of value. Sniffing is also known as wiretapping, eavesdropping, and a number of other terms (packet sniffing, network sniffing, and so on).

SNMP *See* Simple Network Management Protocol (SNMP).

snooping Looking through files in hopes of finding something interesting.

social engineering An attack that uses others by deceiving them.

socket The primary method used to communicate with services and applications such as the Web and Telnet. The socket is a programming construct that enables communication by mapping between ports and addresses.

software exploitation An attack launched against applications and higher-level services.

spam Unwanted, unsolicited e-mail sent in bulk.

spike A momentary or instantaneous increase in power over a power line.

spoofing attack An attempt by someone or something to masquerade as someone else.

SPX *See* Sequenced Packet Exchange (SPX).

spyware Software programs that work—often actively—on behalf of a third party.

SSH *See* Secure Shell (SSH).

SSL   *See* Secure Sockets Layer (SSL).

state table   A firewall security method that monitors the status of all the connections through the firewall.

stateful packet filtering   Inspections that occur at all levels of the network and provide additional security using a state table that tracks every communications channel.

static Address Resolution Protocol (ARP) table entry
An entry in the Address Resolution Protocol (ARP) table that a user adds manually when a PC will be accessed often.

static routing   A method of routing packets where the router's routing table is updated manually by the network administrator instead of automatically by a route discovery protocol.

stealth port   A port that is open but might not be obvious (invisible to those who don't know it exists). Trojan horses often exploit them.

stealth virus   A virus that attempts to avoid detection by masking itself from applications.

steganography   The science of hiding information within other information, such as a picture.

strength   The effectiveness of a cryptographic system in preventing unauthorized decryption.

subscriber   An individual who is attempting to present a certificate proving authenticity.

surge protector   A device that protects electrical components from momentary or instantaneous increases (called spikes) in a power line.

switched   A network that has multiple routes to get from a source to a destination. Switching allows for higher speeds.

SWP   *See* Secure WLAN Protocol (SWP).

symmetrical keys   The keys used when the same key encrypts and decrypts data.

SYN flood   A denial of service attack in which the hacker sends a barrage of spoofed SYN packets. The receiving station tries to respond to each SYN request for a connection, thereby tying up all the resources. All incoming connections are rejected until all current connections can be established.

system architecture   Documents that provide you with the blueprint of your organization's software and hardware infrastructure.

T

tap   A type of connection that directly attaches to a cable.

TCP   *See* Transmission Control Protocol (TCP).

TCP ACK attack   An attack that begins as a normal TCP connection and whose purpose is to deny service. It's also known as a TCP SYN flood.

TCP sequence attack   An attack wherein the attacker intercepts and then responds with a sequence number similar to the one used in the original session. The attack can either disrupt a session or hijack a valid session.

TCP SYN flood   *See* TCP ACK attack.

TCP wrapper   A low-level logging package designed for Unix systems.

TCP/IP   *See* Transmission Control Protocol/Internet Protocol (TCP/IP).

TCP/IP hijacking   An attack in which the attacker commandeers a TCP session from a legitimate user after the legitimate user has achieved authentication, thereby removing the need for the attacker to authenticate himself.

teardrop attack   A DoS attack that uses large packets and odd offset values to confuse the receiver and help facilitate a crash.

Telnet   A protocol that functions at the Application layer of the OSI model, providing terminal emulation capabilities. *See also* Open Systems Interconnection (OSI) model.

Temporal Key Interchange/Integrity Protocol (TKIP)   A wrapper that works with wireless encryption to strengthen WEP implementations.

Terminal Access Controller Access Control System (TACACS)   An authentication system that allows credentials to be accepted from multiple methods, including Kerberos. The TACACS client/server process occurs in the same manner as the Remote Authentication Dial-In User Service (RADIUS) process.

terminal emulator   A program that enables a PC to act as a terminal for a mainframe or a Unix system.

termination policy   A clear process of informing affected departments of a voluntary or involuntary termination.

test account   An administrator-created account for confirming the basic functionality of a newly installed application, for example. The test account has equal rights to accounts that will use the new functionality. It's important to use test accounts instead of administrator accounts to test new functionality. If an administrator account is used, problems related to user rights might not manifest themselves because administrator accounts typically have full rights to all network resources.

TFTP   *See* Trivial File Transfer Protocol (TFTP).

thin client   Systems that don't provide any disk storage or removable media on their workstations.

third party   A party responsible for providing assurance to the relying party that a subscriber is genuine.

threat   Any perceivable risk.

three-tier model   A system that effectively isolates the end user from the database by introducing a middle-tier server.

time to live (TTL)   A field in an IP packet that indicates how many routers the packet can cross (hops it can make) and how long it takes before it's discarded. TTL is also used in Address Resolution Protocol (ARP) tables to indicate how long an entry should remain in the table.

TLS   *See* Transport Layer Security (TLS).

token   A piece of data holding information about the user. This information can contain group IDs, user IDs, privilege level, and so on.

Traceroute   *See* Tracert.

Tracert   The command-line utility that shows the user every router interface a packet passes through on its way to a destination.

trailer   A section of a data packet that contains error-checking information.

transceiver   A device that allows the network interface card (NIC) to connect to the network.

transmission   Sending packets from the PC to the server. The transmission can occur over a network cable, wireless connection, or other medium.

Transmission Control Protocol (TCP)   The protocol found at the Host-to-Host layer of the Department of Defense (DoD) model. This protocol breaks data packets into segments, numbers them, and sends them in order. The receiving computer reassembles the data so that the information is readable for the user. In the process, the sender and the receiver confirm that all data has been received; if not, it's resent. TCP is a connection-oriented protocol. *See also* connection-oriented.

Transmission Control Protocol/Internet Protocol (TCP/IP)   The protocol suite developed by the Department of Defense (DoD) in conjunction with the Internet. It was designed as an internetworking protocol suite that could route information around network failures. Today it's the de facto standard for communications on the Internet.

transmission media   Physical cables and/or wireless technology across which computers are able to communicate.

Transport layer   The fourth layer of the OSI model. It's responsible for checking that the data packet created in the Session layer was received. If necessary, it also changes the length of messages for transport up or down the remaining layers. *See also* Open Systems Interconnection (OSI) model.

Transport Layer Security (TLS)   A protocol whose purpose is to verify that secure communications between a server and a client remain secure. Defined in RFC 2246.

Triple-DES (3DES)   A symmetric block cipher algorithm used for encryption.

Trivial File Transfer Protocol (TFTP)   A UDP-based protocol similar to FTP that doesn't provide the security or error-checking features of FTP. *See also* File Transfer Protocol (FTP).

Trojan horse   Any application that masquerades as one thing in order to get past scrutiny and then does something malicious. One of the major differences between Trojan horses and viruses is that Trojan horses tend not to replicate themselves.

Trust List   A list of objects signed by a trusted entity. Also known as a Certificate Trust List (CTL).

Trusted Platform Module (TPM)   A method of utilizing encryption and storing the passwords on a chip. The hardware holding the chip is then needed to unencrypt the data and make it readable.

TTL   *See* time to live (TTL).

tunneling   The act of sending data across a public network by encapsulating it into other packets.

two-factor authentication   Using two access methods as a part of the authentication process.

two-tier model   A model in which the client PC or system runs an application that communicates with a database that is running on a different server.

U

UDP   *See* User Datagram Protocol (UDP).

Uniform Resource Locator (URL)   A way of identifying a document on the Internet. It consists of the protocol used to access the document and the domain name or IP address of the host that holds the document; for example, http://www.sybex.com.

uninterruptible power supply (UPS)   A device that can provide short-term power, usually by using batteries.

Unshielded Twisted Pair (UTP)   The most common networking cable currently in use; Unshielded Twisted Pair (UTP) is 8-wire cabling used with Ethernet.

uptime   The amount of time a particular computer or network component has been functional.

URL   *See* Uniform Resource Locator (URL).

usage policies   Defined policies governing computer usage.

user   The person who is using a computer or network or a resource.

User Datagram Protocol (UDP)   The protocol at the Host-to-Host layer of the TCP/IP Department of Defense (DoD) model, which corresponds to the Transport layer of the OSI model. Packets are divided into datagrams, given numbers, sent, and put back together at the receiving end. UDP is a connectionless protocol. *See also* connectionless, Open Systems Interconnection (OSI) model.

user-level security   A type of network security in which user accounts can read, write, change, and take ownership of files. Rights are assigned to user accounts, and each user knows only their own username and password—which makes this the preferred method for securing files.

user management policies   Defined policies that detail user management.

V

virtual LAN (VLAN)   Local area network (LAN) that allows users on different switch ports to participate in their own network separate from, but still connected to, the other stations on the same or a connected switch.

virtual link   A link created by using a switch to limit network traffic.

virtual private network (VPN)   System that uses the public Internet as a backbone for a private interconnection (network) between locations.

virus   A program intended to damage a computer system. Sophisticated viruses are encrypted and hide in a computer, and might not appear until the user performs a certain action or until a certain date. *See also* antivirus.

volume   The loudness of a sound, or the portion of a hard disk that functions as if it were a separate hard disk.

VPN   *See* virtual private network (VPN).

W

WAN   *See* wide area network (WAN).

war driving   Driving around with a laptop looking for open wireless access points with which to communicate.

warm site   A site that provides some capabilities in the event of a disaster. The organization that wants to use a warm site will need to install, configure, and reestablish operations on systems that might already exist in the warm site.

weak key   A cipher hole that can be exploited.

weak key attack   An attack that looks for cipher holes.

web proxy   A type of proxy that is used to act on behalf of a web client or web server.

web server   A server that holds and delivers web pages and other web content using HTTP. *See also* Hypertext Transfer Protocol (HTTP).

WEP   *See* Wired Equivalent Privacy (WEP).

wide area network (WAN)   A network that crosses local, regional, and/or international boundaries.

Wi-Fi   *See* Wireless Fidelity (Wi-Fi).

Windows Internet Naming Service (WINS)   A Network Basic Input Output System (NetBIOS) name resolution service employed in Windows networks. Windows Internet Naming Service (WINS) translates hostnames into network addresses.

Windows NT service   A type of Windows program (a file with either an .exe or a .dll filename extension) that is loaded automatically by the server or manually by the administrator.

Windows socket   A Microsoft API used to interact with TCP/IP.

WinNuke   A Windows-based attack that affects only computers running Windows NT 3.51 or 4. It's caused by the way the Windows NT TCP/IP stack handles bad data in the TCP header. Instead of returning an error code or rejecting the bad data, it sends NT to the Blue Screen of Death (BSOD). Figuratively speaking, the attack "nukes" the computer.

Wired Equivalent Privacy (WEP)   A security protocol for 802.11b (wireless) networks that attempts to establish the same security for them as would be present in a wired network.

wireless access point   A wireless bridge used in a multipoint radio frequency (RF) network.

wireless bridge   A bridge that performs all the functions of a regular bridge but uses RF instead of cables to transmit signals.

Wireless Fidelity (Wi-Fi)   An 802.11b or 802.11g wireless network operating in the 2.4Ghz or 5Hhz frequency range.

wireless local area network (WLAN)   A local area network that employs wireless access points (WAPs) and clients using the 802.11 standards.

wireless portal   The primary method of connecting a wireless device to a network.

wireless technologies   Technologies employing wireless communications.

Wireless Transport Layer Security (WTLS)   The security layer of the Wireless Applications Protocol (WAP). WTLS provides authentication, encryption, and data integrity for wireless devices.

WLAN   *See* wireless local area network (WLAN).

work factor   An estimate of the amount of time and effort that would be needed to break a system.

workgroup   A specific group of users or network devices, organized by job function or proximity to shared resources.

working copy   The copy of the data currently in use on a network.

workstation   A computer that isn't a server but is on a network. Generally, a workstation is used to do work, whereas a server is used to store data or perform a network function.

World Wide Web Consortium (W3C)   An association concerned with interoperability, growth, and standardization of the World Wide Web (WWW). This group is the primary sponsor of XML and other web-enabled technologies.

worm   A program similar to a virus. Worms, however, propagate themselves over a network. *See also* virus.

X

X.500   The International Telecommunications Union (ITU) standard for directory services in the late 1980s. The standard was the basis for later models of directory structure, such as Lightweight Directory Access Protocol (LDAP).

Z

zombie   Any system taking directions from a master control computer. Zombies are often utilized in distributed denial of service (DDoS) attacks.

zone   An area in a building where access is individually monitored and controlled.

Index

Note to the reader: Throughout this index **boldfaced** page numbers indicate primary discussions of a topic. *Italicized* page numbers indicate illustrations.

Symbols and Numbers

$ (dollar sign), for hidden shares, lab, 519
3DES (Triple-DES), 324
8.3 file naming, **204–205**
802.11 protocol, 135
802.16 standard, 135
2600: The Hacker Quarterly, 452

A

ABA (American Bankers Association), 345
acceptable use policy, **409**, 433, 439, 465, 466
access control, **262–270**, 379, 415
    common methods, 445–446
    in cryptographic systems, **330–331**
    implementation, **14–15**
    for information, **295–299**
    location of computers, **274–277**
    partitioning, 267–268, 269
    perimeter security, 265, **265–266**
    physical barriers, **263–268**
    security zones, 266–267
    three-layer security model, *263*
    troubleshooting, **471**
access control list (ACL), 14, 240, 259, 445, 466
    changing on all files in Linux directory, lab, 515
    to control spam, 242
access control models
    Bell La-Padula model, *296*, **296**
    Biba model, **297**, *297*
    Clark-Wilson model, **297–298**, *298*
    Information Flow model, 298, **298–299**
    Noninterference model, *299*, **299**
account database in Windows XP, encryption, lab, **535–536**
accountability, 49
    as topology design goal, **24–25**

accountability statement, in policy, 285–286
accounts
    changing default names, 129
    expiration, 445
ACL. *See* access control list (ACL)
active/active model, 402
active backup model, 402
Active Directory (AD), 231, 248, 417, *417*
active sniffing, 76
ActiveX, vulnerabilities of, **141**
activity, 101
AD. *See* Active Directory (AD)
Adams, Carlisle, 324
AdAware, 80
Address Resolution Protocol (ARP), 67, 72
Adleman, Leonard, 325
administrative auditing, **420–421**
administrative policies, **9**
administrative requirements, in standards, 287
administrative shares, in Windows systems, 236
administrator, 181
    user accounts with access as, lab, 512–513
Adobe Reader, 547
Advanced Encryption Standard (AES), 324
adware, 80
AES (Advanced Encryption Standard), 324
AES256, 324
AFS (Apple File Sharing), 236
AH (Authentication Header), 356
alarm systems, 5
ALE (annual loss expectancy), 283
alert, 181
algorithms
    attacking, 342
    errors, for code breaking, 320
American Bankers Association (ABA), 345
analyzer, 181
annual loss expectancy (ALE), 283
annualized rate of occurrence (ARO), 283
anomaly-detection IDS, 183–184, *184*

anonymity, on Internet, 26
anonymous authentication, in WAP, 130
anonymous logon, to FTP site, 145, 243
anti-antiviruses, 104
antiquated protocols, 67
antivirus software, **13–14**, 83, **89–90**, 196, 490
    definition database files for, 90
    log files, 421–422
    retrovirus attack of, 85
    troubleshooting, **492–493**
APIPA (Automatic Private IP Addressing), 247
AppArmor
    configuring in openSUSE, lab, *525–526*
    viewing reports, lab, *526*
Apple File Sharing (AFS), 236
Apple Macintosh, hardening, **233–234**
Apple protocol, **178**
AppleTalk, 178, 236
appliances, 113
    firewalls as, 239
Application layer, **66–67**
application-level proxy functions, 117
Application Programming Interface (API), 72
applications
    backup plan for, 396
    design requirements, **10–11**
    exploitation, **78–80**
    hardening, **240–250**
        DHCP services, **246**
        DNS servers, **243–244**
        e-mail servers, **241–242**
        file and print servers, **245–246**
        FTP servers, **242–243**
        NNTP servers, **244–245**
        web servers, **240–241**
    removing unneeded, 501–502
    types, 546
    updates, 450
    upgrades to new versions, timing of, 493
    users installing unauthorized, 130
apropos utility, 180
archive, 440
archive bit, 397
archiving
    keys, *365*, **365–366**
    media for, 170
armored virus, 83, 104

ARO (annualized rate of occurrence), 283
*Art of Deception: Controlling the Human
    Element of Security* (Mitnick), 271
assets identification, **34**, 49
asymmetric algorithms, **324–326**, *325*, 379
at service, 295
AT&T Wireless, Network Operations Center
    (NOC), 112
attachments to e-mail, 484
    common file extensions, 80–81
attack strategies, **53–58**
    access attacks, **54–55**
    exam essentials, **95–97**
    modification attacks, **55–56**
    recognizing, **58–63**
        backdoor attacks, **59**, *59*, 63, 104, 491
        man-in-the-middle attacks, **60–62**, *61*,
            104, 202, 491
        password-guessing attacks, **62–63**, 105
        privilege escalation, **63**, **416**
        replay attacks, *62*, **62**, 104, 491
        spoofing attacks, **60**, *61*, 491
    repudiation attacks, *56*
    responding to, 64
    review questions, 100–105
attacks, 470
    frequency of, 222
    through NetBIOS services, 245
attributes, for Unix file or directory, 235
audit, 287, 434
audit files, 93
    for database transactions, *395*, 395
audit logs, 473
auditing, 414, **418–422**
    administrative auditing, **420–421**
    escalation auditing, **420**
    and log files, **421–422**
    privilege auditing, **419**
    processes, **93–94**
    reporting to management, **422**
    usage auditing, **419**
auditors, 295
authentication, **15–20**, 48
    biometrics, **15**, 48, 270, 308, 474
    certificates, *16*, **16**. *See also* certificates
    Challenge Handshake Authentication
        Protocol (CHAP), **16**, *17*, 132

in cryptographic systems, **329–330**
issues, **21–22**
Kerberos, **17**, *18*, 48
   SSO and, 417
   time synchronization for, 361
multi-factor, **17**, *18*, 22, 48, 415
mutual, **19**
Password Authentication Protocol (PAP), **19**
for remote user, 132
security tokens, **19**, *19*
smart cards, **20**, *20*, **159**, 170, 474
   individuals forgetting, 367
   for keys, 362
username/password, **20**, *21*
in WAP, 130
authentication factors, **473–474**
Authentication Header (AH), 356
authentication protection, **475–476**
Automated System Recovery, in Windows
   Server 2003, lab, 427
Automatic Private IP Addressing
   (APIPA), 247
availability, as topology design goal, **24**

B

Back Orifice, 59
backdoor attacks, *59*, **59**, 63, 104, 491
background investigations, **410**
BackTrack, 207
backup plan, **394–396**
   developing, **397–400**
backup policy, 465
   drafting and documentation, 440
backup power, 276
Backup Server method, 399, *400*
backups
   for disaster recovery, **391–394**
   media, 170
   recovery, **400–401**, *401*
   security for, *55*, 392
   in SuSE Linux, lab, 428
   troubleshooting management, **476**
   types, **396–397**
baseband signaling
   vs. broadband, *150*
   coaxial cable support for, 149

baselines, 259
   for Internet access, lab, 511
   for security, **222–224**
      troubleshooting, **476–477**
   standards, 287
basic input/output (BIOS) chip, 438
.bat file extension, 80, 204
BCP. *See* Business Continuity Planning (BCP)
behavior-based baseline for IDS, 183
Bell La-Padula model of information access,
   296, *296*, 309
benchmarking, 287
best practices, 411, 465
   defining responsibility, **443**
   drafting and documentation, **436–443**
      backup policy, **440**
      change documentation, **441–442**
      configuration management policies, **440**
      information classification policies, 437
      information destruction policies,
         438–439
      information retention and storage
         policies, 437
      logs and inventories, **440**
      notification policies, 437
      security policies, 439
      system architecture, **441**
      use policies, **439–440**
      user management, 442
   minimizing mistakes, **443**
   policy and procedure enforcement, **443**
   resource allocation, **442–443**
beta test software, 291
BIA (Business Impact Analysis), **281–282**
Biba model of information access, **297**, *297*
bindery services, in NetWare, 175
binding, **225–226**, *226*, 259
biometrics, **15**, 48, **270**, 308, 474
BIOS (basic input/output) chip, 438
birthday attack, **342–343**, 380
Bitlocker, 228, 259
black lists, 491
blind/anonymous FTP, **145**
block cipher, 323
Blowfish encryption system, 324
blue jacking, 202
bluesnarfing, 202
Bluetooth, 202

BNC connectors, *149*
bootable CD, 506
bootable portable operating system, 496
booting to good Windows configuration,
    lab, 537
botnet, 57
bounced e-mails, log report of, 195
bridge trust models for PKI, **339–340**, *340*
bridges, 73
broadband signaling
    vs. baseband, *150*
    coaxial cable support for, 149
broadcasts, 118, 147
    in IM systems, 203
brute-force attack, 63, 493
    for code breaking, 320–321
budget, for security, 442
buffer overflow, 57, 204
    vulnerabilities of, **141**
Business Continuity Planning (BCP), 281–284,
    383–403
    disaster recovery plans (DRPs), 9,
        391–403, 433
        backups, 391–394
        creating, 394–403
        planning for alternate sites, 401–403
        testing, 420
        troubleshooting, **482**
    high availability, 385–386
        fault tolerance, 387–388
        formulating, 385
        RAID, 388–391
        redundancy, 386
    testing, 420
    troubleshooting, **482**
    utilities, **384**
    vendor support reinforcement, **404–406**
        code escrow agreements, **406**
        service-level agreement (SLA), **404–405**
Business Impact Analysis (BIA), 281–282
business partner, creating corporate connection
    to, 34
business policies, 410–412
    document disposal and destruction policies,
        411–412
    due care policies, 411
    physical access control policies, 411
    separation of duties, 410–411

C

CA. *See* certificate authorities (CA)
cabling
    coaxial, *148*, **148–150**
    fiber-optic technology, **152–153**
    unshielded (UTP) and shielded twisted pair
        (STP), **150–152**, *151*
cache in web browser, clearing, lab, 530–531
CALEA (Communications Assistance for Law
    Enforcement Act of 1994), 503
callback security, 480
caller ID verification, 480
Canonical Name (CN), 248
carrier, victim system as, 86
CAST algorithm, 324
Category 5 cable standard, 152
CC (Common Criteria), 222–224, 357
CCITT (Comité Consultatif International
    Téléphonique et Télégraphique), 347
CD-R/DVD-R, **157**
CD-RW, 157
CEH (Certified Ethical Hacker), 489
cell phones, *155*, *156*, 272–274, *273*
    acceptable use policies on, 439–440
Center for Education and Research in
    Information Assurance and Security
    (CERIAS), 451
centralization, of network monitoring, 112
centralized key generation, **359**, *360*
CERIAS (Center for Education and Research in
    Information Assurance and Security), 451
CERT/CC Current Activity web page, 87
CERT Coordination Center (CERT/CC),
    221–222, 451
CERT organization, 87
CertCities, 452
certificate authorities (CA), 16, 330, 379
    designing, 340
    in hierarchical trust model, 337, 338
Certificate Management Protocol (CMP), 351
certificate policies, **412–413**, 433
Certificate Practice Statement (CPS), 16, 413
Certificate Revocation List (CRL), 16,
    336–337
certificates, *16*, **16**
    implementing, **335–336**
    management, troubleshooting, **477–478**

certification programs, 448
Certified Ethical Hacker (CEH), 489
CGI (Common Gateway Interface), 241
   vulnerabilities of, **141–142**
chain of custody, 37, 193
Challenge Handshake Authentication Protocol
   (CHAP), **16**, *17*, 48, 132
change documentation, 465
   drafting and documentation, **441–442**
change management, 421
checksums, 190, 317
chgrp command, 518
chip creep, 276
chmod utility, lab, *515–516*
CIO, 452
cipher, 314
cipher command, lab, *528*
ciphering, 314
circuit-level proxy, 117
Cisco
   IP Telephony Security in Dept white
      paper, 39
   Switched Port Analyzer (SPAN), 185
Cisco Certified Internetwork Expert (CCIE)
   certification, 239
Clark-Wilson model of information access,
   297–298, *298*
classified information model, 296
classifying information
   classifying, *290*, **290–299**
   full distribution information, **292**
   government and military, **293–294**
   internal information, **292**
   limited distribution information, **291–292**
   private information, **292**
   public information, **290 291**
   restricted information, **292**
client, 71
Clipper, 363
clustering, for fail-over capabilities, 386, *387*
CMOS (complimentary metal oxide
   semiconductor), 438
CMP (Certificate Management Protocol), 351
CN (Canonical Name), 248
code escrow agreements, **406**, 433
Code Red attack, *57*
code words, 330
cold site, 402–403

collusion, 410
.com file extension, 80, 204
Comité Consultatif International Téléphonique
   et Télégraphique (CCITT), 347
Common Criteria (CC) standards,
   222–224, *357*
Common Gateway Interface (CGI), 241
   vulnerabilities of, **141–142**
communications
   of security issues, **447**
   troubleshooting security, **478–481**
Communications Assistance for Law
   Enforcement Act of 1994 (CALEA), 503
companion CD, **546–548**
   system requirements, **547**
   troubleshooting, **548**
   using, **547**
companion virus, 84
compartmentalization, 409
complimentary metal oxide semiconductor
   (CMOS), 438
CompTIA Security+ certification, 468
computer battery, 465
computer crime, state laws on, 454
Computer Fraud and Abuse Act, **455**
Computer Management console, *513*
Computer Professionals for Social
   Responsibility (CPSR), 408
Computer Security Act of 1987, **456**
Computer Security Incident Response Team
   (CSIRT), 414
Computer Security Institute, 451
computer startup in Windows XP
   adding legal notice, lab, *532–533*
   configuration, lab, *533*, *534*
confidential data classification, 10
confidentiality
   in cryptographic systems, **326–327**
   of information, 293, 411
   as topology design goal, 23
configuration settings
   group policies to lock, 129
   management policies, 465
      drafting and documentation, **440**
connection
   filtering for remote access, 479
   Initial Sequence Number (ISN) for, 71

contingency plan, 434. *See also* Business
  Continuity Planning (BCP)
Control Panel (Vista), Security applet, 228
cookies
  limiting to first party, lab, 531–532
  vulnerabilities of, **142**
  in web browser, clearing, lab, 530–531
core dump, to obtain key, 362
Counterpane Systems, 324
counters, in System Monitor, 229
CPS (Certificate Practice Statement), 413
CPSR (Computer Professionals for Social
  Responsibility), 408
cracking systems, 37
credit card numbers
  encryption for, 351–352, *352*
  transmission of information, 353
criminal investigation, 486
critical business functions (CBF), 281, 308
  identifying and prioritizing, 281–282
CRL (Certificate Revocation List), 16, 336–337
cross certification, 336, 338
cross-site scripting (XSS), vulnerabilities
  of, **142**
cryptanalysts, 313
cryptographers, 313
cryptographic algorithms, **321–326**
cryptographic systems
  access control, 330–331
  attacks, **341–343**
  authentication, 329–330
  confidentiality, 326–327
  digital signature, *328*, **328–329**
  integrity, 327, *327*
  nonrepudiation, 330
cryptography, **313–321**
  exam essentials, 370–372
  mathematical, 316–317
  myth of unbreakable codes, 319–321
  physical, 314–316
    hybrid systems, 316
    steganography, 316
    substitution ciphers, **314**
    transposition ciphers, 315, *316*
  public domain, **347**
  quantum, 318–319, *320*
  review questions, 374–380

SSL (Secure Sockets Layer), **349–350**, *350*
standards, **343–358**
  origins, **344–347**
CSIRT (Computer Security Incident Response
  Team), 414
CSO Magazine, 453
current keys, in archiving system, 365
custodian of data, 294
customer care from Wiley, 548
Cyber Security Enhancement Act, **456**
Cybercrime Treaty, 457
Cyberspace Electronic Security Act
  (CESA), **456**

D

DAC (Discretionary Access Control) method,
  14–15, **423**, 434
Daemen, Joan, 324
data assets, assigning value to, 35
data breaches, chronology of, 443
data classification matrix, 10
data depositories, **246–249**
data emanation, radio frequency signals
  for, 201
Data Encryption Standard (DES), 323–324
data source, 181
data storage. *See* removable media
database transactions, audit files for,
  395, 395
databases, **249–250**
  exploitation, 78–79
date-stamp, and user file backup, 395
DDoS (distributed denial-of-service) attacks,
  57, *58*
decentralized key generation, **360**, *360*
default account names, changing, 129
default password, changing, 113
default permissions, for new files in Linux,
  lab, 516
definition database files, for antivirus
  software, 90
degaussing, 438
deleting files, 438
demilitarized zones (DMZ), **28**, **29**, 49
demo versions of software, *546*

denial-of-service (DoS) attacks, **56–57**, 104,
146, 203, 243, 491
and NetWare, 233
DES (Data Encryption Standard), 323–324
desensitizing, 277
destination port, 137
destroying keys, 367
detection, as information security goal, 13
DHCP (Dynamic Host Configuration
Protocol), 246
troubleshooting, 247
dial-up, troubleshooting security, 480
dictionary attack, 63, 493
differential backup, 397, 433
Diffie-Hellman key exchange, 325–326
digital signature, 412
in cryptographic systems, 328, 328–329
direct-sequence spread spectrum (DSSS),
199–200
directory services, **246–248**, *247*
troubleshooting, **481–482**
disaster recovery plans (DRPs), **9,**
391–403, 433
backups, 391–394
creating, **394–403**
planning for alternate sites, **401–403**
testing, 420
troubleshooting, **482**
Discretionary Access Control (DAC) model,
14–15, 423, 434
disk duplexing, 388
disk mirroring, 388
disk striping, 388, *389*
disk striping with parity, 389, *389*
disk striping with parity disk, 388
disk wiping, 438, 465
diskettes, **157**
Distinguished Name (DN), 248
distributed denial-of-service (DDoS) attacks,
57, *58*
distributing keys, **361–362**
DMZ (demilitarized zones), 28, *29*, 49
DN (Distinguished Name), 248
DNA scanners, 15
DNS (Domain Name Service), 66, 259, 421
hardening servers, **243–244**
DNS poisoning, 60

DNS spoofing, 60
.doc file extension, 80
documentation. *See also* best practices,
drafting and documentation
for alternative sites, 403
disposal and destruction policies, **411–412**
troubleshooting, **483**
dollar sign ($), for hidden shares, lab, 519
Domain Name Kiting, 60
Domain Name Service (DNS). *See* DNS
(Domain Name Service)
domain password policy, 446, 466
DoS (denial-of-service) attacks, **56–57**, 104,
146, 203, 243, 491
and NetWare, 233
draft documents, 345
DSSS (direct-sequence spread spectrum),
199–200
dual-homed firewall, 116, *116*, 117
dual sided certificates, 336
due care policies, **411**, 433
due diligence, 420
dumpster diving, 54
duplexing, 388
DVD-R, **157**
Dynamic Host Configuration Protocol
(DHCP), 246
troubleshooting, 247

E

e-mail incident, 195
e-mail servers, hardening, **241–242**
e-mails
attachments, 184
common extensions for, 80–81
encrypting, 351
exploitation, 79
troubleshooting, **483–484**
and virus spread, 83, *84*
viruses in, 38
EALs (Evaluation Assurance Levels), 223
EAP (Extensible Authentication Protocol), 357
eavesdropping, 54
eBay, nonrepudiation and, 331
EC Council, 489

ECC (Elliptic Curve Cryptography), 274, 326
EDGAR (business research website), 206
eDirectory, 176, 233, 249
education
    to prevent virus spread, 90
    on security issues, **447–448**
    against social engineering, 92, 272
El Gamal algorithm, 326
electromagnetic interference (EMI), **277**,
    278, 308
electronic flashcards, 547
electronic wallet, 351
electronic watermarking, 316
Elliptic Curve Cryptography (ECC), 274, 326
EMI (electromagnetic interference), **277**,
    278, 308
employees. *See also* users
    knowledge of security policies, 8–9
    and privacy expectations, 409
    transfers and access rights, 11
Encapsulating Security Payload (ESP), 356
encapsulation, **68**, *69*
encryption, 93. *See also* cryptography
    asymmetric algorithms, **324–326**, *325*
    authentication, 475
    of folders with cipher, lab, 528
    in Linux, lab, 373–374
    origins of standards, **344–347**
    symmetric algorithms, **323–324**
    weakest link, 322
    of Windows account database, lab, 535–536
    of Windows file, lab, 519
end-entity certificate, 348
End User License Agreements (EULAs), 291
    and selling old computers, 438
enticement, 192
entrapment, 192, 217
environment, scanning, **272–280**
erasing files, on computer system, 438
escalation, 194
escalation auditing, 420
ESP (Encapsulating Security Payload), 356
ethical hacking, 489
ethics policies, **408**
EULAs (End User License Agreements), 291
    and selling old computers, 438
European Institute for Computer Anti-Virus
    Research, 451

European Union (EU), cyber laws, 457
Evaluation Assurance Levels (EALs), 223
evaluation versions of software, *546*
Event Viewer, 231, *231*
    Security Log object, 421
events, 181
    as incident, 193
    locating in Windows XP, lab, 512
exam essentials
    attack strategies, **95–97**
    cryptography, **370–372**
    hardening, **252**
    information security, **40–42**
    infrastructure, **162–163**
    intrusion detection systems (IDSs), **208–209**
    physical security, **301–302**
    policies and procedures, **425–426**
    security management, **458**
exception statement, in policy, 286
.exe file extension, 80, 204
expiration of key, **363–364**
extended warranty agreement, 405
Extensible Authentication Protocol (EAP), 357
Extensible Markup Language (XML), 81, 140
external security threats, 36, *36*, 37
extranets, *28*, **28**
extrusion, 26

F

fail-over, 386, 433
failed login attempts, viewing in Linux,
    lab, 518
faillog utility, 191, 518
false positives, 194, 497
    from IDSs, 194
Family Education Rights and Privacy Act,
    455–456
Faraday cage, 277
FAT (File Allocation Table), 234, *259*
fault tolerance, **387–388**
Federal Information Processing Standard
    (FIPS), 357
Fedora, SELinux configuration in, lab, 531
FHSS (frequency-hopping spread spectrum),
    199, 200

fiber-optic technology, **152–153**
    networks, 170
fiber splitter, *153*
File Allocation Table (FAT), 234, *259*
file exchange systems, 483
file extensions, 204
    and attacks, 80
    hiding, 205
    making visible in Windows XP, lab, 211
file names, 8.3 convention, **204–205**
file servers, hardening, **245–246**
file sharing
    in FTP, 145
    troubleshooting, **484–485**
file structure, in Unix, 232
File Transfer Protocol (FTP), 66, **144–146**, 230
    hardening servers, **242–243**
    ports, 115
    security risks, 354
files, disappearance of, 82
files in Linux
    changing access control list, lab, *515*
    changing group, lab, *517–518*
    changing permissions, lab, *515–516*
    default permissions for new, lab, *516*
    hiding, lab, *518–519*
files in Windows
    displaying Security tab for, lab, *520*
    encryption, lab, *519*
    viewing effective permissions, lab, *521*
filesystems, hardening, **234–236**
filters, to limit web traffic, 241
Financial Modernization Act, 454
fingerprint reader, 270, 474
FIPS (Federal Information Processing
    Standard), 357
fire corridors, 268
fire detectors, 275
fire extinguishers, **279**, 308
fire-rated storage, 393–394
fire suppression, **279–280**
Firefox, 225
    clearing private data, lab, *531*
firewalls, 93, **113–117**, *114*, 180
    configuring, **239–240**
    for DMZ, 28
    and IDS, *128*, 128

IDS location based on, 184
log files, 421
NAT as, 32
packet filter, **114–115**
proxy, *116*, **116–117**
stateful inspection, **117–118**
    in Windows XP, lab, *509–511*, *510*, *511*
firmware, 113
first-party cookies, lab, *531–532*
first responders, 194
FISK program, 438
five nines availability, 385
fixed systems for fire suppression, **279–280**
Flash, 140
flash cards, **158**
flaw-exploitation DoS attacks, 491
flood attack, IDS active response to, *187*, 187
flooding channel, 203
floppy disks, 157
Folder Options dialog box (Windows), View
    tab, *520*, 520
folders
    encryption with cipher, lab, *528*
    preventing sharing, lab, *523*
footprinting, **206**, 217, 243–244
forensics, 192
fraud, 412
freeware, 546
frequencies, 272
frequency analysis, for code breaking, 320
frequency-hopping spread spectrum (FHSS),
    199, 200
FTP (File Transfer Protocol), 66,
    144–146, 230
    hardening servers, **242–243**
    ports, 115
    security risks, 354
Full Archival backup method, 398–399, *399*
full backup, 396
full distribution information, **292**

G

gap in the WAP, 198, 200, 503
gas-based fire-suppression systems, 280, 308
GET command (FTP), 145

Global Information Assurance Certification
(GIAC), 489
Global System for Mobile Communications
(GSM), 274, 308
GNU software, *546*
goals, of information security, **12–13**
Good Time virus, 87
Googlebot, *57*
government
    agencies role in cryptography standards,
       344–345
    archival requirements, 400
    classification of information, **293–294**
Gramm-Leach-Bliley Act of 1999, **454–455**
Grandfather-Father-Son backup method, 397–
    398, *398*, 433
grep, 191
group policies, 229, 446, 466
    to lock configuration settings, 129
groups, **444–445**
    changing association for file, lab, *517–518*
GroupWise, 176
GSM (Global System for Mobile
    Communications), 274, 308
Guest account, turning off in Windows XP,
    lab, *521*, 521–522
guidelines, **287–288**, 309

H

Hacken9, 453
hacking, international laws in, *457*
hand scanners, 15
hard drives, **158**
hardening, 221, 259
    Apple Macintosh, **233–234**
    applications, **240–250**
        DHCP services, **246**
        DNS servers, **243–244**
        e-mail servers, **241–242**
        file and print servers, **245–246**
        FTP servers, **242–243**
        NNTP servers, **244–245**
        web servers, **240–241**
    exam essentials, **252**
    filesystems, **234–236**

network devices, **238–240**
Novell NetWare, **232–233**
operating systems, **224–238**
review questions, 255–260
troubleshooting, **500–502**
Unix/Linux, **231–232**
Windows 2000, **230–231**
Windows Server 2003, **229–230**
Windows Vista, **227–228**
Windows XP, **228–229**
hardware-based keystroke loggers, 496
hash total, 321
hash value, 316–317, 321
    creating rule, lab, 373
hashing, 316–317, *317*
    science of, **321–323**
hashing algorithm, 379
Health Insurance Portability and
    Accountability Act (HIPAA), **454**
Heisenberg, Werner, 319
Heisenberg Uncertainty Principle, 319
hiding
    files in Linux, lab, *518–519*
    IP addresses, 116
    Windows shares, lab, *519*
hierarchical trust models for PKI, 337–338, *338*
high availability, **385–386**
    fault tolerance, **387–388**
    formulating, 385
    RAID, **388–391**
    redundancy, 386
HIPAA (Health Insurance Portability and
    Accountability Act), **454**
hiring policies, **407**
.hlp file extension, 80
hoaxes, identifying, **87–88**
Homeland Security Act of 2002, Section
    225, 456
honeyd, 191
Honeynet Project, 191–192
honeypot, *188*, **191–192**, 217
    troubleshooting, **485–486**
host, *65*
host-based intrusion detection systems
    (HIDSs), **189–190**, *190*, 217
Host-to-Host (Transport) layer, **67**
hostnames, resolving to IP addresses, 243

hot site, 9, 402
hotfixes, **237**, *259*
HTML (Hypertext Markup Language), 139
HTTP (Hypertext Transfer Protocol), 66
    port, 115
HTTPS (Hypertext Transport Protocol Secure),
    140, **354**
    port, 115
hubs, 118
    attaching N-IDS to network, 185, *185*
human error, and encryption vulnerabilities,
    321, 322
human resource policies, **406–410**
    acceptable use policy, **409**
    background investigations, **410**
    ethics policies, **408**
    hiring policies, 407
    need-to-know policies, **409–410**
    privacy policies, **409**
    termination policies, **407**
human vulnerabilities, 3
humidity control, 274–275
hushmail.com, 483
hybrid attacks, 494
hybrid physical cryptography systems, **316**
hybrid trust models for PKI, **340–341**, *341*
Hypertext Markup Language (HTML), 139
Hypertext Transfer Protocol (HTTP), 66
    port, 115
Hypertext Transport Protocol Secure
    (HTTPS), **354**
    port, 115

I

IANA (Internet Assigned Numbers
    Authority), 70
ICMP (Internet Control Message Protocol), 68,
    72, 117, 146, 169
    disabling traffic, 147
    packets, *57*
    tunneling, 78
IDEA (International Data Encryption
    Algorithm), 324
identification and authentication (I & A), 15
identity proofing, 21

identity theft, 475
IDPS, 190
IDSs (intrusion detection systems), 127, **128**,
    128, 169, **179–198**
    active response, **187–189**
    components, *182*
    exam essentials, **208–209**
    host-based, **189–190**, *190*
    network-based, **184–189**, *185*
    passive response, **186**
    review questions, 213–218
    troubleshooting, **485–486**
IEEE (Institute of Electrical and Electronics
    Engineers), 347
    802.1x protocols, 135
    802.11x wireless protocols, **199–200**
IETF (Internet Engineering Task Force),
    345–346
IGMP (Internet Group Management Protocol),
    67, 147, 169
IIS. *See* Internet Information Services (IIS)
IIS (Internet Information Services), 230, 240
    default mail system in early versions, 130
    security patches, 73–74
IM (instant messaging), **202–204**, *203*, 217
    attacks by, 91
    privacy, 204
    vulnerabilities, **203**
IMAP (Internet Message Access Protocol),
    138, 169
    port, 115
impersonation, 475
    to gain access, 271
implicit denies, *295*
incident response, **192–198**, 217
    adjusting procedures, **198**
    cycle, *193*
    damage repair, **196**
    documenting and reporting, **196–197**
    identification, **193–194**
    investigation, **194**
    plan functioning, 197
    troubleshooting, **486**
incident response plan (IRP), 192
incident response policies, **413–414**
incidents, 12
    detection, 13

incremental backup, 396–397, 433
inductive pickup, 150
industry associations, 345–347
info utility, 180
information
    access control, **295–299**
    classifying, *290*, **290–299**
        full distribution information, **292**
        government and military, **293–294**
        internal information, **292**
        limited distribution information,
          291–292
        private information, **292**
        public information, **290–291**
        restricted information, **292**
    social engineering to obtain, 91
information classification policies, 465
    drafting and documentation, 437
information destruction policies, drafting and
    documentation, **438–439**
Information Flow model of information access,
    298, **298–299**
information integrity, 23
    Biba model and, 297
information policies, **10**
information retention and storage policies, 465
    drafting and documentation, 437
information security, **3–12**
    exam essentials, **40–42**
    goals of, **12–13**
    review questions, 44–49
Information Security Magazine, 453
InformationWeek, 453
InfoWorld, 453
infrared (IR), **154**
infrastructure
    compiling list, 111
    exam essentials, **162–163**
    network devices, **113–127**
        firewalls, **113–117**, *114. See*
          also firewalls
        hubs, 118, 185, *185*
        modems, **118–119**, 480
        Remote Access Services (RAS), **119–120**
        routers, *120*, **120–121**. *See also* routers
        switches, 73, **122**, *122*, 169
        telecom/PBX systems, **122–124**, *123*

virtual private networks (VPNs), *124*,
    124–125. *See also* virtual private
    networks (VPNs)
    wireless access points, **125**, *126*, **127**
    review questions, 165–170
infrastructure security, **109–112**
    hardware components, *110*, **110–111**
    software components, **112**
    troubleshooting, **497–499**
Initial Sequence Number (ISN), for
    connection, 71
inline BNC connector, *149*
input validation, vulnerabilities of, **142**
installing
    biometric devices, 270
    software, preventing, 130
instant messaging (IM), **202–204**, *203*, 217
    attacks by, 91
    privacy, 204
    vulnerabilities, **203**
Institute of Electrical and Electronics Engineers
    (IEEE), 347
    802.1x protocols, 135
    802.11x wireless protocols, **199–200**
integrity
    in cryptographic systems, *327*, **327**
    as topology design goal, **23**
interception, *54*
intermediate CA, 337
internal data classification, 10
internal information, **292**
internal security threats, 36, 36–37
International Data Encryption Algorithm
    (IDEA), 324
international efforts, in privacy
    regulation, **457**
International Organization for Standardization
    (ISO), Code of Practice for Information
    Security Management, 288–289
International Telecommunications Union
    (ITU), 346
    X.500 standard, 248
    X.509 certificate structure, 335
Internet, **26**, 27
Internet Assigned Numbers Authority
    (IANA), 70
Internet Connection Sharing, 32

Internet connections, 111
    baselines for, lab, 511
    common sense, troubleshooting and,
        486–487
    security, **136–146**
        for e-mail, **137–138**, *138*
        port and sockets, **136–137**
        for Web, *139*, **139–140**
Internet content filter, 228
Internet Control Message Protocol (ICMP), 68,
    72, 117, 146, 169
    disabling traffic, 147
    packets, 57
    tunneling, 78
Internet Engineering Task Force (IETF),
    345–346
Internet Explorer
    clearing private data, lab, 530–531
    limiting cookies to first party, lab, 531–532
    phishing filter configuration, lab, 532
    popup blocker settings, lab, 522, *523*
    susceptibility to exploitation, 225
    viewing security settings, lab, 522
Internet Group Management Protocol (IGMP),
    68, 147, 169
Internet Information Services (IIS), 230, 240
    default mail system in early versions, 130
    security patches, 73–74
Internet layer, **67–68**
Internet Message Access Protocol (IMAP),
    138, 169
    port, 115
Internet Packet Exchange/Sequence Packet
    Exchange (IPX/SPX), 225
    vulnerability, **227**
Internet Protocol (IP), 67, 72
Internet Protocol Security (IPSec), 134, 169,
    355–356, 481
    errors in performance statistics, lab, 374
Internet Protocol v6 (IPv6), turning off in
    openSUSE, lab, 527–528
Internet service provider (ISP), 26
Internet Storm Center, 222
Internetwork Packet Exchange (IPX), 175
intranets, *27*, **27**
intrusion, 180. *See also* social engineering
    immediate response to current, 195

intrusion detection systems (IDSs), 127, **128**,
    128, 169, **179–198**
    active response, **187–189**
    components, *182*
    exam essentials, **208–209**
    host-based, **189–190**, *190*
    network-based, **184–189**, *185*
    passive response, **186**
    review questions, 213–218
    troubleshooting, **485–486**
inventories, drafting and documentation,
    440–441
involuntary termination, 407
IP (Internet Protocol), 137
IP addresses
    hiding, 116
    origination, 247
    resolving hostnames to, 243
IP forwarding, 117
IP spoofing, 60
IP Telephony Security in Dept white paper
    (Cisco), 39
IPSec (Internet Protocol Security), 134, 169,
    355–356, 481
    errors in performance statistics, lab, 374
IPX (Internetwork Packet Exchange), 175
IPX/SPX (Internet Packet Exchange/Sequence
    Packet Exchange), 225
    vulnerability, **227**
Irina virus, 87
IRP (incident response plan), 192
ISN (Initial Sequence Number), for
    connection, 71
ISO 17799 security standard, **288–289**, *358*
ISOC (Internet Society), 346
ISP (Internet service provider), 26
ITU (International Telecommunications
    Union), 346
    X.500 standard, 248
    X.509 certificate structure, 335
IUSR_*computername* account, 241, 243

J

jamming, 203, 218
Java, 140
    applet vulnerabilities, **143**

JavaScript, vulnerabilities, **143**
journaled file system (JFS), 393
journaling, 393
.js file extension, 204

K

KDC (Key Distribution Center), *361*, 361
KEA (Key Exchange Algorithm), 361, *362*
Kerberos, 17, *18*, 48
   openSUSE as client, lab, 526–527
   SSO and, 417
   time synchronization for, 361
key attacks, 341
Key Distribution Center (KDC), 17, 48,
      361, *361*
key escrow, **363**, 379
Key Exchange Algorithm (KEA), 361, *362*
key life cycle, 358
key management, 358–367. *See also* private
      key; public key infrastructure (PKI)
   centralized vs. decentralized generation,
      358–361
   destruction, **367**
   expiration, **363–364**
   key escrow, **363**
   recovery and archiving, **365–366**
   renewal, **366**
   revocation, **364**
   storage and distribution, **361–362**
   suspension, **364**
   troubleshooting, **488–489**
   usage, **367**
keystroke loggers, hardware-based, 496
Klez32 virus, 90

L

L2F (Layer 2 Forwarding), 134, *355*, 356
L2TP (Layer 2 Tunneling Protocol), 33, 134,
      355, 356, 481
LANMAN protocol, 322
   passwords, 494
last command, 191
last known good configuration, booting to,
   lab, 537

lastlog utility, 191
   lab, 517
latency, 337
law enforcement
   key escrow for, **363**
   rules of evidence, 193
Layer 2 Forwarding (L2F), 134, *355*, 356
Layer 2 Tunneling Protocol (L2TP), 33, 134,
      355, *356*, 481
LCP (Link Control Protocol), 133
LDAP (Lightweight Directory Access Protocol),
      248, 259
   openSUSE as client, lab, 527
   port, 115
leaf CA, 338
leaf objects in NetWare, 175
least privilege, 295
legal notice, adding to computer startup, lab,
      532–533
license server, 396
Lightweight Directory Access Protocol (LDAP),
      248, 259
   openSUSE as client, lab, 527
   port, 115
limited distribution information, **291–292**, 309
Link Control Protocol (LCP), 133
Linux. *See also* Unix/Linux
   changing ACL on all files in directory,
      lab, 515
   changing password, lab, 514
   changing permissions on all files in
      directory, lab, 515–516
   counting number of running processes,
      lab, 520
   default permissions for new files, lab, 516
   encryption in, lab, 373–374
   help for utilities, 180
   hiding file, lab, 518–519
   identifying running processes, lab, 98–99
   installing snort, lab, 211
   log files in, **191**
   network traffic monitoring, lab, 211–212
   Novell product conversion to, 176
   rescue disk in, lab, 427
   resources in, 180
   routing table, lab, 164
   setup for lab exercises, 506
   updating system, lab, 43

viewing failed login attempts, lab, 518
viewing logins, lab, *516–517*
LinuxSecurity, 452
Local Area Connection Properties dialog box,
    General tab, *226*
local policies, 230
local registration authority (LRA), 333–334,
    334, 379
locking down desktop, 130
locks, 496
logged warnings, viewing in openSUSE,
    lab, *525*
logging
    in IDS, 186
    in Linux, 232
logic bombs, 88–89, *89*, 94, 104
logical tokens, 446, 466
login prompt, message display prior to
    accessing, lab, 532–533
logins
    viewing failed attempts in Linux, lab, 518
    viewing in Linux, lab, *516–517*
logon process, 20, *21*
    spoofing attacks as part of, 60
logon spoofing, 475
logs
    and auditing, **421–422**
    drafting and documentation, **440**
    Event Viewer for reviewing, 231, *231*
    in Linux, **191**
    reviewing, 421
low-level format, 438, 465
LRA (local registration authority), 333–334,
    334, 379

M

M of N Control method of access, 366
MAC, various meanings of acronym, 68
MAC (Mandatory Access Control) model, **14**,
    48, **423**
MAC (Media Access Control) address, 67
MAC (message authentication code), 379
    for verifying integrity, 327, *328*
macro virus, 79, **84**
Magic Lantern, 363
maintenance contracts, 404

maintenance requirements, in standards, 287
malicious code, surviving, **81–90**
malicious events, preventing, **489–494**
malware, 483
    training users to avoid, 492–493
man-in-the-middle attacks, **60–62**, *61*, 104,
    202, 491
man tool, 180
Managed Security Service Provider
    (MSSP), 112
management, **7–11**
    education on security issues, 448
manager, 181, 217
Mandatory Access Control (MAC) model, **14**,
    48, **423**
mandatory vacations, 408
mantrap, *264*, 264–265
masquerading, 475
mathematical attacks, 343
mathematical cryptography, **316–317**
McAfee Corporation, 452
MD (Message Digest Algorithm), 322
mean time between failure (MTBF), 405
mean time to repair (MTTR), 405
media, 109
Media Access Control (MAC) address, 67
Media Access layer, 14
Melissa virus, 81, 89
memory dump, to obtain key, 362
memory sticks, 158
mesh trust models for PKI, **339**, *340*
message authentication code (MAC), 379
    for verifying integrity, 327, *328*
Message Digest Algorithm (MD), 322
metal oxide varistors (MOVs), 276
Microsoft
    AntiSpyware, 80
    Baseline Security Analyzer, lab, *459–460*
    Internet Information Services (IIS),
        230, 240
        default mail system in early versions, 130
        security patches, 73–74
    Office, susceptibility to exploitation, 225
    protocols, **176–178**
    SQL Server, 249
    Systems Management Server (SMS)
        package, 73
    TechNet website, 230

website on security, 450
Windows Group Policy FAQ, 230
microwave systems, **154–155**, 170
middletier server, 250
military classification of information, **293–294**
MIME, 351
minimum age of passwords, changing in
Windows XP, lab, *528–529*
misuse-detection IDS, 183
Mitnick, Kevin, *Art of Deception: Controlling
the Human Element of Security*, 271
mobile devices, **130–132**, *131*
modems, **118–119**, 480
MOVs (metal oxide varistors), 276
msconfig command, lab, *533*
MSSP (Managed Security Service
Provider), 112
MTBF (mean time between failure), 405
MTTR (mean time to repair), 405
multi-factor authentication, **17**, *18*, 22, 48, 415
multicasting, 118, 147
multihomed system, 117
multipartite virus, **85**, *85*
multiple barrier system, 263
mutation of virus, 85
mutual authentication, **19**, **475**
myth of unbreakable codes, **319–321**

N

NAC (network access control), 5
NAT (Network Address Translation), **30–32**,
32, 48
National Institute of Standards and Technology
(NIST), 344–345, 379, 452
National Security Agency/Central Security
Service (NSA/CSS), 344
National Security Agency (NSA), 232, 344
National Security Institute (NSI), 452
natural disaster, impact on utilities, 384
NCP (Network Control Protocol), 133
NDS (NetWare Directory Services), 175
tree structure, *175*
NDS (Novell Directory Services), 175, 233
need-to-know policies, 292, **409–410**
Nessus, 94, 222

NetBIOS (Network Basic Input Output
System), 176, *259*
attacks through services, 245
NetBIOS Extended User Interface
(NetBEUI), 225
vulnerability, **227**
NetBIOS Session service, port, 115
NetBus, *59*
NetMeeting, 139
Netscape, 349
susceptibility to exploitation, 225
NetWare, 174
hardening, **232–233**
NetWare Directory Services (NDS), 175
tree structure, *175*
NetWare File System (NFS), 235, *259*
NetWare Loadable Modules (NLMs), 233
network access control (NAC), *5*
Network Address Translation (NAT), **30–32**,
32, 48
network attached storage, **158**
network audit files, **186**
network-based IDS, **184–189**, *185*
Network Basic Input Output System
(NetBIOS), 176, *259*
attacks through services, 245
Network Control Protocol (NCP), 133
network devices
hardening, **238–240**
updates, 450
updating, **238–239**
Network File System (NFS), 236
Network File System Protocol (NFS), *178*, **178**
network interface cards (NICs)
Media Access Control (MAC) address
for, 67
promiscuous mode for, 73
for proxy firewall, 116
Network Interface layer, **68**
Network Intrusion Prevention Systems
(NIPSs), **190**
network mapping, 74, 207
Network Monitor, lab, 210–211
network monitoring, **127–128**, 173–179
Network News Transfer Protocol (NNTP)
hardening servers, **244–245**
port, 115

network operating systems, hardening,
    224–238
Network Operations Center (NOC), 112
network protocols. *See* protocols
network security zone, 267, *268*
network share, connection, *245*
network sniffer, 73, 217
    T-connector attached to, 149
network threats, overview, **221–222**
network traffic
    monitoring in Linux, lab, 211–212
    recognizing types, **174–178**
        Apple protocol, **178**
        Microsoft protocols, **176–178**
        Network File System Protocol (NFS),
           178, *178*
        Novell protocols, **174–176**
        TCP/IP, **174**
networks, virus transmission in, **86**
New Technology File System (NTFS), 234–235
NFS (NetWare File System), 235, 259
NFS (Network File System), *178*, **178**, 236
NICs (network interface cards)
    Media Access Control (MAC) address
        for, 67
    promiscuous mode for, 73
    for proxy firewall, 116
NIDS, 217
NIPSs (Network Intrusion Prevention
    Systems), **190**
NIST (National Institute of Standards and
    Technology), 344–345, 379, 452
NLMs (NetWare Loadable Modules), 233
nmap, 74, 207
NMAP port scanner, 222
NNTP (Network News Transfer Protocol)
    hardening servers, **244–245**
    port, 115
nondisclosure agreement (NDA), 291
Noninterference model of information access,
    299, **299**
nonrepudiation, *56*, 379
    in cryptographic systems, **330**
    and eBay, 331
notification, 182
    in IDS, 186
notification policies, drafting and
    documentation, 437

Novell. *See also* Netware
    product conversion to Linux, 176
    protocols, **174–176**
Novell Directory Services (NDS), 175, 233
Novell NetWare Storage Services, 235
NSA/CSS (National Security Agency/Central
    Security Service), 344
NSA (National Security Agency), 232, 344
NSI (National Security Institute), 452
NT LAN Manager (NTLM), 322
NTFS (New Technology File System), 234–235
null session attack, 57

O

OCSP (Online Certificate Status Protocol),
    336–337, 380
OES (Open Enterprise Server), 176
OFDM (orthogonal frequency division
    multiplexing), 199, 200
Office, susceptibility to exploitation, 225
offsite storage, 394
old computers, selling, 368
    and operating systems, 438
one-tier model for database, 250
one-time pad, 329, *329*
one-way hash, 321
one-way process, 317
Online Certificate Status Protocol (OCSP),
    336–337, 380
onsite storage, 393
    for backups, 393
Open Enterprise Server (OES), 176
open relay, 144
open source movement, 259
open-systems philosophy, 231
Open Vulnerability and Assessment Language
    (OVAL), 81
OpenLDAP, installing on SuSE server, lab, 253
openSUSE, 506
    AppArmor configuration, lab, 525–526
    AppArmor reports, lab, 526
    configuring local security, lab, 524
    defaults for new users, lab, 524–525
    firewalls, lab, 523–524
    as Kerberos client, lab, 526–527
    as LDAP client, lab, 527

screensaver password for, lab, 513
turning off IPv6, lab, 527–528
view logged warnings, lab, 525
operating systems
   bootable portable, 496
   hardening, 129
   security limitations, 470, 477
   updates, **237–238**, 449–450
operational considerations, in guidelines
      document, 288
operational environment, survey of, 8
operational security, **5–7**
   issues, 7
operator, 182
orphanware, 406
orthogonal frequency division multiplexing
      (OFDM), 199, 200
OS X, 234, 236
out-of-band method to send key, 323
Outlook, and virus spread, 90, 195
Outlook Express, and virus spread, 90, 195
OVAL (Open Vulnerability and Assessment
      Language), 81
overload, from manual network
      monitoring, 194
overview statement, in policy, 285
owner of data, 294

P

packet-capture device, 133, 356
packet filter firewalls, **114–115**, 169
packet sniffing, 205
parental controls, applying to accounts, 228
parity information, 388
partitioning network, 267–268, *269*, 308
Password Authentication Protocol (PAP), **19**
password crackers, 62
password expiration policy, 6–7
password-guessing attacks, **62–63**, 105
password utility, 416
passwords, 93, **318**, 474. *See also*
      username/password
   access to, 55
   BIOS-based, 439
   changing default, 113

changing minimum age in Windows XP,
      lab, 528–529
encryption for Macintosh, 233
external requirements for, 91
for FTP, 145
in Linux, lab, 514
policies, 446
for smart cards, 159
on sticky notes, 94
troubleshooting, **493–494**
U.S. Air Force security audit on, 343
for Windows XP screensaver, lab, 512
PAT (Port Address Translation), 32
patches, **238**, 259
   to close backdoors, 59
   for Linux, lab, 43
   in Unix/Linux, 232
PATRIOT act, **457**
PBX (Private Branch Exchange) system, 169
   attack, 39
.pdf file extension, 80
PDF file of book, 546
peer-to-peer connection, 145
penetration
   detection, 5
   testing, 222
performance
   criteria in standards statement, 287
   virus impact, 82
performance baseline, 222
Performance Monitor, 231
   lab, 253–254
perimeter security, 173, *265*, **265–266**, 308
permissions
   changing on all files in Linux directory, lab,
      515–516
   viewing effective in Windows XP, lab, 521
personal development, 450–451
personal lab environment, 469
Personally Identifiable Information (PII), 421
personnel management, **495**
PGP (Pretty Good Privacy), 324, 347, **354**, *355*
phage virus, **85**
phishing, 92, 475
   configuring filter in Internet Explorer,
      lab, 532
physical access control policies, **411**

physical barriers, **263–268**
physical cryptography
    hybrid systems, **316**
    steganography, **316**
    substitution ciphers, **314**
    transposition ciphers, **315**, *316*
physical environment, survey of, 6
physical security, **4–5, 48, 262–280**
    access control, **262–270**
        location of computers, **274–277**
        partitioning, **267–268**, *269*
        perimeter security, *265*, **265–266**
        physical barriers, **263–268**
        security zones, **266–267**
        three-layer security model, *263*
    biometrics, **15, 48, 270, 309, 474**
    exam essentials, **301–302**
    review questions, 304–309
    troubleshooting, **495–497**
physical token, for access, 264
.pif file extension, 81
PII (Personally Identifiable Information), 421
PIN, for smart cards, 159
ping, 146, 206
ping of death, 57
PKC (Public Key Cryptography), 325
PKCS (Public-Key Cryptography
    Standards), 348
PKI. *See* Public Key Infrastructure (PKI)
Plain Old Telephone Service (POTS), 119
platform hardening, 129
plumbing, 148
Point-to-Point Protocol (PPP), 169
    remote access with, **132–133**, *133*
Point-to-Point Tunneling Protocol (PPTP), 133,
    356, 481
policies and procedures, **7–11, 406–414**. *See
    also* best practices; security policies
    administrative, **9**
    assembling and examining, **11–12**
    business policies, **410–412**
        document disposal and destruction
            policies, **411–412**
        due care policies, **411**
        physical access control policies, **411**
        separation of duties, **410–411**
    certificate policies, **412–413**

enforcement, **443**
exam essentials, **425–426**
human resource policies, **406–410**
    acceptable use policy, **409**
    background investigations, **410**
    ethics policies, **408**
    hiring policies, **407**
    need-to-know policies, **409–410**
    privacy policies, **409**
    termination policies, **407**
implementing, **285–286**
incident response policies, **413–414**
information, **10**
review questions, 429–434
updates, 450
usage, **11**
user management, **11**
polymorphic virus, 85, *86*
POP (Post Office Protocol), 66, 138
    port, 115
popunders, 143
popup blocker, Internet Explorer settings, lab,
    522, *523*
popup blockers, 143
popups, vulnerabilities of, **143**
Port Address Translation (PAT), 32
port mirroring, 185
port scan, 73–74, 185, 206
    to reveal Trojan horse, 88
ports, **136–137**
    checking available on system, 74
    packet filtering based on, 114
    security with hubs, 118
    viewing active, lab, 210
    and vulnerability, 139
    well-known, **69–71**
Post Office Protocol (POP), 66, 138
    port, 115
postmortem, 198
POTS (Plain Old Telephone Service), 119
power conditioners, 276
power generators, 277
power systems, **275–277**
PPP (Point-to-Point Protocol), 169
    remote access with, **132–133**, *133*
PPTP (Point-to-Point Tunneling Protocol), 133,
    356, 481

preauthentication systems, for remote
access, 479
Pretty Good Privacy (PGP), 324, 347, **354**, *355*
prevention, as information security goal, 12–13
previous keys, 365–366
prime numbers, and key generation, 359
principle, for Key Distribution Center, 17
print servers, hardening, **245–246**
privacy
for IM systems, 204
information obtained through
monitoring, 444
policies, 409
privacy regulation, 454–457
Computer Fraud and Abuse Act, **455**
Computer Security Act of 1987, **456**
Cyber Security Enhancement Act, **456**
Cyberspace Electronic Security Act
(CESA), **456**
Family Education Rights and Privacy Act,
455–456
Gramm-Leach-Bliley Act of 1999, **454–455**
Health Insurance Portability and
Accountability Act (HIPAA), **454**
international efforts, 457
PATRIOT act, 457
Private Branch Exchange (PBX) system, 169
attack, 39
private information, **292**
clearing from Firefox, lab, 531
clearing from Internet Explorer, lab,
530–531
data classification, 10
private IP addresses, 48
NAT assignment to internal hosts, 32
private key, 324–325
protection, 362
privilege auditing, **419**
privilege creep, 11, 419
privilege management, **414–424**
access control, **422–424**
auditing, 418–422
administrative auditing, **420–421**
escalation auditing, **420**
and log files, **421–422**
privilege auditing, **419**
reporting to management, **422**
usage auditing, **419**

decision making, **418**
privilege escalation, **63, 416**
user and group role management, **415–416**
procedures. *See* best practices; policies
and procedures
processes
counting number running in Linux, lab, 520
identifying running, lab, 98–99
terminating, 187
programs. *See* applications
promiscuous mode, for NIC, 73
protocol analyzers, 205
protocols, **146–147**
antiquated, 67
checking available on system, 74
configuring, **225–227**
enabling and disabling, 240
well-known ports, **69–71**
working with, **69–72**
proxy, NAT as, 32
proxy firewalls, *116*, **116–117**
ps utility (Linux), lab, 99
public data classification, 10
public domain cryptography, **347**
public information, **290–291**
public key, 324, 380
distribution procedure, 348
Public Key Cryptography (PKC), 325
Public-Key Cryptography Standards
(PKCS), 348
Public Key Infrastructure (PKI), 10,
331–341
certificate authorities (CA), **332**, *333*
certificate implementation, **335–336**
certificate policies, 336
certificate revocation, **336–337**
trust models, **337–341**
bridge, **339–340**, *340*
hierarchical, **337–338**, *338*
hybrid, **340–341**, *341*
mesh, **339**, *340*
X.509 standard, **348**
purpose statement
in guidelines document, 287
in standards statement, 286
PUT command (FTP), 145
PuTTY, 354

Q

quantum cryptography, **318–319**, *320*
queries in SQL, 249

R

radio frequency interference (RFI), **277**, *278*
radio frequency (RF) communications,
    154, *155*
RADIUS (Remote Authentication Dial-In User
    Service), *135*, **135–136**, 479
RAID (Redundant Array of Independent
    Disks), **388–391**, 433
rainbow tables, 63, 494
RDN (Relative Distinguished Name), 248
real time detection, 218
reciprocal agreement, 402, 403, 433
reconstitution, 477
recovering keys, *365*, **365–366**
recovery, 5. *See also* disaster recovery
    plans (DRPs)
    from backups, **400–401**, *401*
Red Hat, website on security, 450
redundancy, **386**
Redundant Array of Independent Disks
    (RAID), **388–389**, 433
reference documents, for standards, 286
registrar, 243
registration authority (RA), 332, 333
Registry
    editing to display message at login, 532–533
    virus change to, 84
relational database, 249
Relative Distinguished Name (RDN), 248
releases, to repair multiple problems, 238
relying party, in transaction, 413
remote access, **132–136**
    network connections for, 134
    with Point-to-Point Protocol, **132–133**, *133*
    troubleshooting, 478–479
    with tunneling protocols, **133–134**
    with wireless protocols, **135**
Remote Access Services (RAS), **119–120**
remote authentication, 132

Remote Authentication Dial-In User Service
    (RADIUS), *135*, **135–136**, 479
remote clients, compromise of, 479
remote control/remote shell, troubleshooting
    security, **480**
remote desktop, running, lab, *534–535*
Remote Procedure Call (RPC), 245
removable media, **156–161**
    CD-R/DVD-R, **157**
    diskettes, **157**
    flash cards, **158**
    hard drives, **158**
    network attached storage, **158**
    smart cards, **159**
    tape, **159–160**
    USB drives, **161**, 439, 465
    and virus spread, 82, *83*
renewing keys, **366**
replay attacks, **62**, *62*, 104, 491
reporting audit to management, **422**
repudiation attacks, 56
Requests for Comments (RFCs), 345, 379
    1466 on subnetting, 32
    1918 on subnetting, 32
rescue disk, in Linux, lab, 427
resources, in Linux, 180
response, as information security goal, 13
responsibilities
    accountability and, 471
    defining, **443**
    in guidelines document, 287
    in standards statement, 286
restore point in Windows XP, lab, *536–537*
restricted information, **292**
retinal scanners, 15
retrovirus, **85**
reverse hash matching, 493
reverse lookups, 491
review questions
    attack strategies, 100–105
    cryptography, 374–380
    hardening, 255–260
    information security, 44–49
    infrastructure, 165–170
    intrusion detection systems (IDSs),
        213–218
    physical security, 304–309

policies and procedures, 429–434
security management, 461–466
revoking keys, **364**
RF collar, 150
RF (radio frequency) communications,
154, *155*
RFCs. *See* Requests for Comments (RFCs)
RFI (radio frequency interference), **277**, *278*
Rijmen, Vincent, 324
Rijndael algorithm, 324
RIP (Routing Information Protocol), 66
risk analysis, 282
risk assessment, 35, 281, **282–284**
computations, 284
conducting, 283
Rivest, Ron, 325
Rivest, Shamir, and Adleman (RSA) algorithm,
325, 347
Rivest's Cipher, 324
rogue access points, 202
rogue servers, 247
Role-Based Access Control (RBAC) model, **15**,
48, **423**
roles
in guidelines document, 287
in security process, **294–295**
in standards statement, 286
root CA, 337
root directories, 236
rootkits, 80
rot13 encoding algorithm, 315
rotation schemes for tape, 160
routers, *120*, **120–121**, 169
and block for external attacks, 72
configuring, **239–240**
as defense against external attacks,
238–239
and security zones, 26
Routing and Remote Access Services
(RRAS), 119
Routing Information Protocol (RIP), 66
routing table, lab, 164
RPC (Remote Procedure Call), 245
RSA (Rivest, Shamir, and Adleman) algorithm,
325, 347
rubber hose attack, 500
Rule-Based Access Control (RBAC), **423–424**

S

S-HTTP (Secure HTTP), 140, **355**
S/MIME (Secure Multipurpose Internet Mail
Extensions), 351
salt, 494
sandbox, for Java applets, 143
SANS Institute, 452
policy website, 477
scanner, 73
scanning, **206–207**, 217
environment, 272–280
scanning ports, 73–74
schemes, 383
Schneier, Bruce, 324
scope statement
in guidelines document, 287
in policy, 285
in standards statement, 286
.scr file extension, 80, 81
screensaver password
for openSUSE, lab, 513
for Windows XP, lab, 512
scripts
Common Gateway Interface (CGI), 241
disabling, 142
to turn off unneeded Unix service, 232
secret handshake, 330
secret information, 293
Secure Electronic Transaction (SET),
351–352, *352*
Secure File Transfer Protocol (SFTP), 145,
243, 483
Secure Hash Algorithm (SHA), 321
Secure HTTP (S-HTTP), 140, **355**
Secure Multipurpose Internet Mail Extensions
(S/MIME), 351
Secure Shell (SSH), 134, 145, **352**, *353*, 480
Secure Sockets Layer (SSL), 140, **349–350**, *350*
in Windows Server 2003, lab, 373
SecureLogix, voice firewall, 39
SecurID, 264
security, 2
analogy, 92–93
baselines for, **222–224**
troubleshooting, **476–477**
circumventing, 266

evaluating, 269
standards, 288–289
from Windows Server 2003 administrator's
view, 224
of wireless connection, 202
Security Center dialog box, *511*
Security+ certificate, 2
Security Enhanced Linux (SELinux), 232
configuring in Fedora, lab, 531
security events, locating in Windows XP,
lab, 512
Security Focus, 452
security groups, 415–416, *416*, 434
security guard, 266
security logs, 93
security management, 436, 465. *See also*
best practices
exam essentials, **458**
privacy regulation, 454–457
Computer Fraud and Abuse Act, **455**
Computer Security Act of 1987, **456**
Cyber Security Enhancement Act, **456**
Cyberspace Electronic Security Act
(CESA), **456**
Family Education Rights and Privacy
Act, 455–456
Gramm-Leach-Bliley Act of 1999,
454–455
Health Insurance Portability and
Accountability Act (HIPAA), **454**
international efforts, **457**
PATRIOT act, **457**
review questions, 461–466
security awareness and education program,
446–448
simplifying, 444–446
staying current, 449–453
trade publications, 452–453
websites tracking issues, **451**–452
security policies, 10
drafting and documentation, 439
personnel knowledge of, 8–9
security process, 13–20
access control implementation, 14–15
antivirus software, 13–14
authentication, 15–20, 48
biometrics, 15, 48, 270, 308, 474
certificates, 16, *16. See also* certificates
Challenge Handshake Authentication
Protocol (CHAP), **16**, *17*, 132
in cryptographic systems, 329–330
issues, 21–22
Kerberos, 17, *18*, 48, 361, 417
multi-factor, 17, *18*, 22, 48, 415
mutual, 19
Password Authentication Protocol
(PAP), **19**
for remote user, 132
security tokens, **19**, *19*
smart cards, **20**, *20*, **159**, 170, 362,
367, 474
username/password, **20**, *21*
in WAP, 130
security professional, 294–295
security templates, 229
comparing system to, lab, 529–530
security tokens, 19, *19*
security topologies, 22–39
business concerns, 33–38
assets identification, **34**
risk assessment, **35**
threat identification, 35–37
design goals, 23–25
security zones, 26–29
demilitarized zones (DMZ), **28**, *29*
extranets, *28*, **28**
Internet, **26**, *27*
intranets, *27*, **27**
technologies, 29–33
Network Address Translation (NAT),
30–32, *32*
tunneling, **33**
virtual local area networks (VLAN),
30, *31*
virtualization, 29–30
telephony issues, 38–39
vulnerabilities, **38**
security triad, *4*
security zones, 266–267, 308
troubleshooting, 499–500
SEI (Software Engineering Institute), 221
SELinux (Security Enhanced Linux), 232
configuring in Fedora, lab, 531
selling old computers, 368
and operating systems, 438
sender, authenticating, 329

sensitive but unclassified information, 293
sensor, 182
separation of duties, 297, **410–411**
Sequenced Packet Exchange (SPX), *175*
Serial Line Internet Protocol (SLIP), 132
servers
    authentication, 475
        in WAP, 130
    as e-mail relay, 144
    hardening, 131
    implementing secure environment, 223
    security for, **129–130**
service-level agreement (SLA), **404–405**, 433
service packs (Microsoft), 233, **237**, 259
services
    enabling and disabling, 240
    removing unneeded, 501
session hijacking attacks, 491
sessions in web browser, clearing, lab, 530–531
sessions, terminating, 187
SET (Secure Electronic Transaction),
        351–352, *352*
SFTP (Secure File Transfer Protocol), 145,
        243, 483
SGID files, finding in Linux, lab, 514–515
SHA (Secure Hash Algorithm), 321
shadow copies, 393
Shamir, Adi, 325
shared folders, preventing, lab, 523
shared resources, and security risk, 36
shareware software, 546
sheep-dip system, 493
shielded twisted pair (STP), **150–152**, *151*
    common cable specifications, 152
shielding, **277–278**, 308
shoulder surfing, 271–272
SHTTP (Secure HTTP), 140, **355**
shunning, in IDS, 186
signal analysis, **205–207**
signal intelligence, **205–207**
signature-based-detection IDS, *183*, 183
signed applets, vulnerabilities of, **143–144**
SIM (Subscriber Identification Module), 274
Simple Mail Transfer Protocol (SMTP), 66,
        138, 259
    port, 115
    relay vulnerabilities, **144**
    virus, 195

Simple Network Management Protocol
        (SNMP), 66, 72, 146
single loss expectancy (SLE), 283
single sided certificates, 336
single sign-on (SSO), 415, **416–418**
single-tier environment, 250
site surveys, 201, 217
SLA (service-level agreement), **404–405**, 433
Slammer attack, 57
Slapper attack, 57
SLE (single loss expectancy), 283
SLIP (Serial Line Internet Protocol), 132
smart cards, *20*, **20**, *159*, 170, 474
    individuals forgetting, 367
    for keys, 362
SMTP (Simple Mail Transfer Protocol), 66,
        138, 259
    port, 115
    virus, 195
    vulnerabilities of relay, **144**
smurf attack, 104, 147
sniffers, 127–128, 169, 205
    10Base-T network with, *153*
SNMP (Simple Network Management
        Protocol), 66, 72, 146
snooping, 54
snort, 205
    lab, 211
social engineering, **91–93**, 104, **270–272**, 308
    testing, lab, 303
    troubleshooting, **500**
sockets, **136–137**, 169
software. *See* applications
Software Engineering Institute (SEI), 221
software exploitation attack, 105
Sophos Anti-Virus, 421–422, *422*
source code, conditions of release, 406
source port, 137
spam, 87–88
    ACL to control, 242
spare parts, 387
sPing, 57
split generation system, 359
split-system key generation, 361
spoofing attacks, **60**, *61*, 491
SPX (Sequenced Packet Exchange), 175
Spybot, 80
spyware, 79–80, 88

Spyware Doctor, 80
SQL (Structured Query Language), 249, 259
SQL Server (Microsoft), 249
SSH (Secure Shell), 134, 145, **352**, *353*, 480
SSID broadcast, 201
SSL (Secure Sockets Layer), 140, **349–350**, *350*
    in Windows Server 2003, lab, 373
SSO (single sign-on), 415, **416–418**
standards, **286–287**
state laws on computer crime, 454
stateful inspection firewalls, **117–118**
stateful packet filtering, 117
static electricity, 497
    preventing, 275
stealth virus, **86**, *86*, 104
steganography, 314, **316**
storage. *See* removable media
storing keys, 361–362
STP (shielded twisted pair), **150–152**, *151*
    common cable specifications, 152
stream cipher, 323
Structured Query Language (SQL), 249, 259
Subscriber Identification Module (SIM), 274
subscriber, in transaction, 413
substitution ciphers, **314**
SUID files, finding in Linux, lab, 514–515
support packs (Novell), 233, **237**
surge protectors, 276
surveillance systems, 5
survey
    of operational environment, 8
    of physical environment, 6
    of surroundings, 55
SuSE Linux
    backups in, lab, 428
    installing OpenLDAP, lab, 253
suspending keys, **364**, 379
switches, 73, *122*, **122**, 169
Sybex test engine, 546
Symantec Corporation, 87, 452
symmetric algorithms, **323–324**
symmetric key, 323
SysAdmin, Audit, Network, Security (SANS)
    certification, 489
system architecture, drafting and
    documentation, **441**

System Configuration Utility (Windows),
    lab, *534*
system files, clearing infection from, 196
system logs, 49, 440
    reviewing, 173
system vulnerabilities, 3
Systems Monitor, 228–229

T

T-connector (BNC), *149*, 150, *151*
TACACS (Terminal Access Controller Access
    Control System), **136**, 479
    port, 115
TACACS/+, 136
tailgating, 271
tap, *179*, *179*
tape, **159–160**
    for backups, 393
tar pit, 192
Tavares, Stafford, 324
TCP (Transmission Control Protocol), 67, 72
    attacks, **74–76**
    three-way handshake, **71–72**
    well-known ports, 70
TCP ACK flood attack, 74–75, 104
TCP/IP (Transmission Control Protocol/
    Internet Protocol), **174**, 225
    NetBIOS binding to, *226*
    vulnerability, **227**
TCP/IP hijacking, 62, **76**, *76*, 104, 105
TCP/IP (Transmission Control Protocol/
    Internet Protocol), 38
    architectural layers, *65*, **65–68**
        Application layer, **66–67**
        encapsulation, **68**, *69*
        Host-to-Host (Transport) layer, **67**
        Internet layer, **67–68**
        Network Interface layer, **68**
    common ports, 115
    recognizing attacks, **72–78**
    security concerns, **64–78**
    susceptibility to attacks, 79
TCP packet, *137*
TCP ports, viewing active, lab, 210
TCP sequence number attack, **75–76**, *76*

TCP SYN flood attack, 74–75, *75*
TCP wrappers, 232
technical staff, education on security
   issues, 448
technology standards, 287
telecom/PBX systems, **122–124**, *123*
telephony issues, **38–39**
Telnet, 66, 480
   for attacks, 74
   port, 115
   security risks, 354
temperature, 274–275
TEMPEST project, 278, 308
Temporal Key Integrity Protocol (TKIP), 357
temporary files in web browser, clearing, lab,
   530–531
"Ten Commandments of Computer
   Ethics", 408
Terminal Access Controller Access Control
   System (TACACS), **136**, 479
terminated employees, as threat, 11
terminating processes or sessions, 187
termination policies, **407**
termination process, in coax network, 149
testing environment, 501–502
   setup for lab exercises, 506
TFTP (Trivial File Transfer Protocol), 145
theft, detection, 5
thin clients, 159
third party, 433
   in transaction, 413
third-party cookies, lab, 531–532
thp, 191
threat
   assessment, 49
   identification, 35–37
   terminated employees as, 11
three-layer security model, *263*
three-tier model for database, 250, 259
thumb drives, **161**
tickets, for Kerberos, 17
time-of-day restrictions, 446
time synchronization, for Kerberos, 361
TKIP (Temporal Key Integrity Protocol), 357
TLS (Transport Layer Security), 140, 350,
   350, 379
tokens, 49

Top Secret information, 293
TPM (Trusted Platform Module), 317
Traceroute, 146, 206
trade publications, on security, **452–453**
traffic generation DoS attacks, 491
training, importance of, 25
Transmission Control Protocol. *See* TCP
   (Transmission Control Protocol)
Transmission Control Protocol/Internet
   Protocol (TCP/IP). *See* TCP/IP
   (Transmission Control Protocol/Internet
   Protocol)
transmission in network, intercepting, 342
Transport Layer Security (TLS), 140, *350*,
   350, 379
transposition ciphers, 315, *316*
trash, access to, 55
tree structure, in hierarchical trust model, 337
trial versions of software, *546*
Triple-DES (3DES), 324
Trivial File Transfer Protocol (TFTP), **145**
Trojan horse, *59*, 88, 104, 491
troubleshooting, companion CD, **548**
troubleshooting guide, **468–503**
   access control issues, **471**
   accountability concerns, **471–472**
   antivirus software, **492–493**
   auditing, **472–473**
   authentication schemes, **473–476**
   backup management, **476**
   baselining security, **476–477**
   certificate management, **477–478**
   communications security, **478–481**
   directory services, **481–482**
   disaster planning, **482**
   documentation, **483**
   e-mail issues, **483–484**
   file sharing, **484–485**
   getting started, **469–471**
   hardening, **500–502**
   honeypot, **485–486**
   incident response, **486**
   infrastructure security, **497–499**
   Internet common sense and, **486–487**
   intrusion detection systems (IDSs), **485–486**
   key management, **488–489**
   passwords, **493–494**

personnel management, **495**
physical security, **495–497**
preventing malicious events, **489–494**
security zones, **499–500**
social engineering, 500
wireless network security, **502–503**
trust, and e-commerce, 412
trust models for PKI, **337–341**
   bridge, **339–340**, *340*
   hierarchical, **337–338**, *338*
   hybrid, **340–341**, *341*
   mesh, **339**, *340*
Trusted Computer System Evaluation Criteria
   (TCSEC), 223
Trusted Computing Group, 317
Trusted Platform Module (TPM), 317
trusted transaction, 412–413
tunneling, 33, 48
tunneling protocols, **133–134**, 356
two-factor authentication system, 17, *18*
two-tier model for database, 250
two-way (client and server) authentication, in
   WAP, 130
two-way hash, 321
Twofish, 324
.txt file extension, 80

U

Ubuntu, website on security, 450
UDP ports, viewing active, lab, 210
umask utility, lab, *516*
unclassified information, 293
undeliverable e-mails, log report of, 195
unicasts, 118, 147
uninterruptible power supply (UPS), 276,
   387–388
United States
   automatic declassification system, 437
   federal laws on privacy and security,
      454–457
      Computer Fraud and Abuse Act, **455**
      Computer Security Act of 1987, **456**
      Cyber Security Enhancement Act, **456**
      Cyberspace Electronic Security Act
         (CESA), **456**

      Family Education Rights and Privacy
         Act, **455–456**
      Gramm-Leach-Bliley Act of 1999,
         454–455
      Health Insurance Portability and
         Accountability Act (HIPAA), **454**
      PATRIOT act, 457
U. S. Air Force, security audit on
   password, 343
Uniting and Strengthening America by
   Providing Appropriate Tools Required to
   Intercept and Obstruct Terrorism (USA
   PATRIOT) Act of 2001, 457
University of Maryland, A. James School of
   Engineering, 74
Unix Filesystem, 235, *235*
Unix/Linux. *See also* Linux
   file structure in, 232
   hardening, **231–232**
   Network File System (NFS), 236
      as default file-sharing protocol, 178
   networking, lab, 254
   securing for interactive users, 354
unshielded twisted pair (UTP), **150–152**,
   151, 170
   common cable specifications, 152
updates
   network devices, **238–239**
   operating systems, **237–238**
   in Unix/Linux, 232
upgrades, policies on, 9
UPN (User Principal Name), 248
UPS (uninterruptible power supply), 276,
   387–388
uptime, 24
usage auditing, **419**
usage policies, **11**
USB flash drives, 161
   policies on use, 439, 465
use policies, drafting and documentation,
   439–440
user access and rights review, 418
user accounts, identifying those with
   administrator access in Windows XP, lab,
   512–513
user behavior modification, 484
User Datagram Protocol (UDP), 67, 72, 117
   well-known ports, 71

user files, 395–396
user management policies, **11**
    drafting and documentation, 442
user of data, 294
User Principal Name (UPN), 248
username/password
    authentication, **20**, *21*
    policies, 446
users
    defaults for new, in open SUSE, lab,
        524–525
    education
        to prevent virus spread, 90
        on security issues, **447–448**
        against social engineering, 92, 272
utilities
    for Linux, help for, 180
    natural disaster impact, 384
UTP (unshielded twisted pair), **150–152**,
    151, 170
    common cable specifications, 152

V

vacations, mandatory, 408
validation of input, vulnerabilities of, 142
vampire tap, 149–150, *151*
/var/log/faillog file, 191, 518
/var/log/lastlog file, 191
/var/log/messages file, 191
/var/log/wtmp file, 191
.vbs file extension, 204
vendor support reinforcement, **404–406**
    code escrow agreements, **406**
    service-level agreement (SLA), **404–405**
VeriSign, 350
VeriSign/InterNic, 206
virtual local area networks (VLAN), **30**, *31*
Virtual Network Computing (VNC), 119
virtual private networks (VPNs), 48, *124*,
    124–125, 354
    IPSec for, 355
    troubleshooting security, **480–481**
    tunnels as, 33
virtualization, 29–30
virus scanner, on e-mail servers, 241, *242*

viruses, 13, 81–86
    with CD-R, 157
    how they work, **82–83**, *83*
    losses due to, 82
    present activity, 87
    in removable media, 156
    symptoms of infection, 82
    transmission in network, **86**
    types, **83–86**
VLAN (virtual local area networks), **30**, *31*
VMware Player, 469
VNC (Virtual Network Computing), 119
Voice over IP (VoIP), 39
VPN. *See* virtual private networks (VPNs)
vulnerabilities, 3, **38**
    scans, 74, 94, 207
    testing, 222

W

W3C (World Wide Web Consortium), 346
W32/Klez.mm virus, 90
WAP (Wireless Application Protocol), 198,
    200, 217
    security levels, 130
war driving, 201–202
warm site, 402, 433
warranties, 405
warscan, 207
water, 276
    damage from, 275
    in fire-suppression system, **280**
watermarking, electronic, 316
WDP (Wireless Datagram Protocol), 132
weak key attack, 343
Web connections
    security, *139*, 139–140
    vulnerabilities of add-ins, **141–144**
        ActiveX, **141**
        buffer overflow, **141**
        Common Gateway Interface (CGI),
            141–142
        cookies, **142**
        cross-site scripting (XSS), **142**
        input validation, **142**
        Java applets, **143**

JavaScript, **143**
popups, **143**
signed applets, **143–144**
SMTP relay, **144**
web request, TCP connection process for, 71
web servers, hardening, **240–241**
web structure, 339
websites, 139
for tracking security issues, **451–452**
well-known ports, **69–71**
WEP (Wired Equivalent Privacy), 61, 127,
200–201, *201*, 342, **357**, 502
wetware, 270
whatis utility, 180
whereis utility, 180
white lists, 491
whole disk encryption, 228
Wi-Fi, 199
Wi-Fi Alliance, 127
Wi-Fi Protected Access (WPA), 127,
201, 357
changing to, lab, 508–509
Wi-Fi Protected Access 2 (WPA2), 201,
217, 357
Wiley Tech Support, 548
Windows
file encryption, lab, 519
identifying running processes, lab, 98
password cracking, 494
preventing shared folders, lab, 523
routing table, lab, 164
Windows 2000, hardening, **230–231**
Windows Media Center, 228
Windows Registry, lab, 532–533
Windows Server 2003
Automated System Recovery, lab, 427
hardening, **229–230**
hash rules, lab, 373
security from administrator's view, 224
SSL in, lab, 373
updating system, lab, 43
Windows Server 2008, updating system,
lab, 43
Windows shares, hiding and accessing,
lab, 519
Windows Socket (WinSock), 72, 72
Windows Vista, hardening, **227–228**

Windows XP
account database encryption, lab,
535–536
adding legal notice to computer startup, lab,
532–533
Automatic Updates, lab, *459*
booting to good configuration, lab, 537
changing password minimum age, lab,
528–529
changing to Wi-Fi-Protected Access (WPA),
lab, 508–509
displaying Security tab for files and folders,
lab, 520
firewall in, lab, *509–511*, *510*, *511*
firewall log, 421
folder encryption with cipher, lab, 528
hardening, **228–229**
identifying user accounts with administrator
access, lab, 512–513
locating security events, lab, 512
making file extensions visible, lab, 211
network binding in, *226*
restore point, lab, 536–537
screensaver password, lab, 512
startup configuration, lab, 533, *534*
turning off Guest account, lab, *521*,
521–522
viewing effective permissions, lab, 521
Windows XP Home edition, 228
Windows XP Professional, 228
WinSock (Windows Socket), 72, 72
Wired Equivalent Privacy (WEP), 61, 127,
200–201, *201*, 342, **357**, 502
wireless access points, **125**, *126*, **127**
Wireless Application Protocol (WAP), 198,
200, 217
security levels, 130
wireless cells, **272–274**, *273*, 308
security for, 274
Wireless Datagram Protocol (WDP), 132
Wireless Markup Language (WML), 200
wireless networks, 155, **198–202**
troubleshooting security, **502–503**
vulnerabilities, **201–202**
wireless protocols, **135**
Wireless Session Protocol (WSP), 132
Wireless Transaction Protocol (WTP), 132

Wireless Transport Layer Security (WTLS),
132, **198**, *199*, 274, 357
Wireshark, 73
wiring
coaxial, *148*, **148–150**
fiber-optic technology, **152–153**
unshielded twisted pair (UTP) and shielded
twisted pair (STP), **150–152**, *151*
WML (Wireless Markup Language), 200
WMLScript, 200
work factor, of cryptography algorithm, 326
working copy backups, 393, 433
working documents, 292
workstations, security for, **129–130**
World Wide Web Consortium (W3C), 346
WORM (write once, read many) device,
472–473
worms, **89**, 104, 196
WPA (Wi-Fi Protected Access), 127, 201, 357
WPA2 (Wi-Fi Protected Access 2), 201, 217, 357
write down, preventing, 296
write-protected tape, and backup, 25
WSP (Wireless Session Protocol), 132
WTLS (Wireless Transport Layer Security),
132, **198**, *199*, 274, 357
WTP (Wireless Transaction Protocol), 132

X

X.509 standard, **348–349**, 412
certificate structure, *335*, **335–336**
XKMS (XML Key Management Specification),
351, 380
.xls file extension, 80
XML (Extensible Markup Language),
81, 140
XML Key Management Specification (XKMS),
351, 380

Y

YaST, *506*
yousendit.com, 483

Z

ZENworks, 176
Zimmerman, Phil, 347
.zip file extension, 81
zombies, 57

The Absolute Best Security+ Book/CD Package on the Market!

Get Ready for CompTIA's Security+ Exam with the most comprehensive and challenging sample tests anywhere!

The Sybex Test Engine features:

- All the review questions, as covered in each chapter of the book.
- Challenging questions representative of those you'll find on the real exam.
- Bonus exam(s) available only on the CD.

Use then Electronic Flashcards for PCs or Palm Devices to jog your memory and prep last-minute for the exam!

- Reinforce your understanding of key concepts with these hardcore flashcard-style questions.
- Download the Flashcards to your Palm device and go on the road. Now you can study for the Security+ exam any time, anywhere.

Search through the complete book in PDF!

- Access the entire *CompTIA Security+ Deluxe Study Guide* complete with figures and tables, in electronic format.
- Search the *CompTIA Security+ Deluxe Study Guide* chapters to find information on any topic in seconds.